Empire of the Periphery

Also by Boris Kagarlitsky and published by Pluto Press

New Realism, New Barbarism (1999)

Russia Under Yeltsin and Putin (2002)

Globalization and its Discontents
(edited with Roger Burbach and Orlando Nuñez, 1996)

The Politics of Empire
(edited with Alan Freeman, 2004)

Empire of the Periphery

Russia and the World System

Boris Kagarlitsky

Translated by Renfrey Clarke

PLUTO **PRESS**

First published 2008 by Pluto Press
345 Archway Road, London N6 5AA
and 839 Greene Street, Ann Arbor, MI 48106

www.plutobooks.com

British Library Cataloguing in Publication Data
A catalogue record for this book is available from the British Library

ISBN-13   978 0 7453 2682 5
ISBN-10   0 7453 2682 X

Library of Congress Cataloging in Publication Data applied for

10 9 8 7 6 5 4 3 2 1

Designed and produced for Pluto Press by
Chase Publishing Services Ltd, Sidmouth, EX10 9QG, England
Typeset from disk by Stanford DTP Services, Northampton, England

Contents

Introduction: Topic and Method

For us, experience of the times does not exist. For us, generations and centuries have passed fruitlessly. To look at us, you might say that the universal law of humanity has been reduced to nothingness. Alone in the world, we have given the world nothing, and have taken nothing from it. To the mass of human ideas, we have added not a single thought. We have not contributed to the advance of human reason in any way, and everything of this advance that we have come by, we have mutilated.

This was the bitter observation of the outstanding nineteenth-century Russian thinker Pyotr Chaadaev.[1] His pessimism did not prevent Chaadaev from later declaring:

I consider our generation fortunate, if we can only recognise this. I think our great advantage is that we can survey the whole world from the heights of thought, free from the unrestrained passions and wretched self-interest which in other places obscure people's vision and distort their judgment. Moreover, I am profoundly convinced that we are fated to resolve many of the problems of the social order, to perfect many of the ideas that have arisen in older societies, and to answer the most important questions that preoccupy humanity. I have often said and emphatically repeat that we are, so to speak, destined in the very nature of things to act as the true moral court judging the many suits that are brought before the great tribunal of the human spirit and human society.[2]

HISTORY AS POLITICS

In the early 1990s Russia once again astonished the world with a deluge of rapid and unexpected changes. The collapse of the Soviet Union, the instantaneous transformation of distinguished Communist Party figures into fervent liberals, the stunningly quick and easy switch of slogans by the ruling elites, who recast their whole set of political ideas from 'the rebirth of socialism' and 'the law-governed state' to a strong executive authority and Russian national revival – all within a single decade!

In 'quiet' periods people start to feel that the past has no bearing on them. It is something to be studied from textbooks and monographs. A sharpening of political struggle forces everyone, at times against their will, to 'live within history', and to 'create history'. In such times we unexpectedly discover that our hopes and illusions, our errors and successes, are also part of history; that we are accountable to the past as well as to the future. We are compelled to understand the meaning that accumulated experience has for the present day, for the simple reason that if we do not, we risk understanding nothing about our own actions. An important element in being a Marxist is to be aware of the continuity of history. When the anticommunist forces gained the upper hand in Moscow in August and September 1991, they immediately set about demolishing monuments and renaming streets, trying to banish the spectres of the communist past from the Russian capital and to repopulate the city with new spectres, this time pre-communist ones. But to no avail; ghosts are not to be exorcised so readily. The renaming of streets and cities was self-defeating, revealing the extent to which the ideas, words and concepts that had been instilled in popular consciousness during the decades of communist rule had become an inalienable part of national culture.

Everything that happened in our country might have seemed like a bizarre and tasteless fantasy, had it not involved our own lives and fates. In Russia, political errors always exact an unbelievable price. Not from the politicians, of course, but from the country. When we look into the past, we usually find ourselves in the position of judges, if not of prosecutors. Nevertheless, searching through history to find someone to blame does nothing to elevate us above events. Quite the reverse. In history there are not and should not be categorical verdicts and final sentences with no right of appeal. Therefore, we should not judge, but seek to understand. To understand does not mean to forgive. To understand the past is to be capable of transcending it. Ultimately, what is involved is knowing how to change the present. This, properly speaking, is the purpose of history.

Unfortunately, history has always been closely bound up with politics. From ancient times, the events of the past have been used to justify the ambitions of rulers. It is enough to read the ancient chronicles, or the works of Titus Livius, to appreciate how much the description of events depends on the religious and political views of the writer. In Europe in later years various national myths, resting on historical fact, served as the basis for state ideologies. From the late eighteenth century the criticising of historical myths itself became a powerful weapon of revolutionaries. In the Marxist tradition, historicism and the critical approach to society are inseparably linked.

Nowhere in Europe do people argue so fiercely about figures from the remote past as in Russia. The views expressed on Ivan the Terrible, Peter the Great or Alexander II are inseparable from the political positions of the writer. These historical figures and symbols are still present among us. People talk about them as though they had just gone out the door. The whole country is like an immense haunted house in which ghosts move invisibly (and sometimes visibly) among the participants in modern-day events. The past is linked directly to the future, and at times seems to these participants to be more important than the present. Meanwhile, history is exceedingly ideologised and politicised. Of course, there is nothing exclusively Russian about this.

To 'hold power over the past' is to exercise a form of political control. A peculiarity of Russia, however, is the fact that the lack of developed forms of popular representation has made history crucially important for the legitimisation of the authorities. Unable to confirm their legality with an honestly obtained popular mandate, successive regimes and governments have been forced to appeal to the past, to the well-springs.

Russian historians have produced numerous volumes in the genre of the 'search for the guilty party'. From the times of Karamzin, some have laid blame on the Tatar-Mongol invasion of the thirteenth century, seeing this as having 'held back the country's development'. For others, the villain is the 1917 revolution or the Bolsheviks, who 'forced Russia off the correct path'. Slavophiles see the source of Russia's problems in Peter the Great, who sacrificed Russia's distinctive character to Western influences. It is possible to seek an explanation for the country's miseries in the decision by Vladimir Krasnoe Solnyshko (Vladimir the Sun Prince) to accept Christianity from Byzantium rather than Rome. The medieval chroniclers, it is true, mention that Prince Vladimir had other options – for example, to embrace Judaism, a thought which has 'Jewish conspiracy' theorists horrified. 'Russia is not to be understood with the mind, Nor with a common arshin will you measure it...', wrote the poet Tyutchev. Indeed, the usual 'European' schemas have generally been discredited by attempts to apply them to Russia. The trouble is that attempts to analyse Russian history from the position of national uniqueness and distinctiveness have failed just as completely.

Throughout the nineteenth century, the liberal and Slavophile schools waged a struggle over Russian history. After the collapse of the Soviet Union these schools reappeared in their original forms, as if neither the experience of the twentieth century, nor the discoveries of archaeologists, nor Western revisionist historiography had ever existed. Standing counterposed to one another, the Westernisers and Slavophiles are united in understanding Russian history as isolated and 'special', not subject to the logic that is common to other countries. The Westernisers see the country's history as a strange anomaly, the result of a number of chance circumstances; overcoming this 'abnormal' situation is the job of an enlightened ruling authority that is ready to break with the past, and if necessary to carry out a ritual outrage against the people and its culture.

By contrast, the Slavophiles believe in Russia's 'special path', and exult in the country's uniqueness. They cherish and foster everything that might serve as proof of the existence of a special 'Orthodox' or 'Eurasian' civilisation, everything that differentiates Russia from the rest of the world.

Meanwhile, there is simply no way that Russia's history can be divorced from that of Europe or of the world in general, and not only in the chronological and geographical senses. Russia's distinctiveness, even uniqueness, is merely a specific manifestation of processes general throughout the world. Often, this has been an extreme manifestation, but for precisely this reason a grasp of Russian history is indispensable for understanding what is going on in the world at large. The reverse is also true; without an understanding of world history, the Russian past becomes a series of absurd puzzles which, as the poet says, can be neither understood with the mind nor measured in terms of a common arshin. To talk of a 'common arshin' is itself a contradiction, since this measure of length has never existed except in Russia. This poetical slip of the tongue, however, reflects the complete pointlessness of the cultural and historical discussions of Russia's fate. Any number of facts can be cited to prove Russia's 'uniqueness'; this is a country where, as Peter the Great put it, the unheard-of is commonplace. The 'uniqueness' of Russia is due not to the 'mysterious Slavic soul', and not to a lag behind the 'advanced West', but to the specific position which our country has occupied in the world economic system. There is nothing 'incorrect' or mysterious in Russian history. But the history of Russia, like that of any other country, can be understood only within the context provided by the development of the world as a whole.

THE POKROVSKY SCHOOL

Fortunately, the ideas of the Slavophiles and Westernisers are far from being the only ones spawned by the Russian historical tradition. The revolution of 1917 placed in question the myths of official Russian historiography. The very concept of the Russian cultural tradition was destined for a fundamental re-evaluation. In the early years of the twentieth century, when the coming shocks were still sensed only dimly, liberal commentators wrote that a people who made a revolution were doomed to be born anew. The self-awareness of the English and French, their concept of themselves, changed radically as a result of their experience of revolution.

In the first quarter of the twentieth century, the Russian past was destined to become the object of rethinking, of Marxist historical criticism. The leading figure in this criticism, and in essence the first revisionist historian in the modern sense of the term, was Mikhail Pokrovsky. A pupil of the outstanding liberal historian Klyuchevsky, Pokrovsky concluded that the Russian past needed a radical rethinking, and that Marxist analysis provided the key to a new understanding of events. Nevertheless, the fate of the 'historical revisionism' represented in Soviet Russia by the Pokrovsky school was unenviable. During the years of revolutionary upsurge its ideas were in demand, but once the bureaucracy headed by Stalin had gained the upper hand over the revolutionary currents, the approach to history changed as well.

The rout of the Pokrovsky school began in the fateful year 1937 (Pokrovsky himself had died five years earlier), and took on the character of a serious ideological campaign. The 'Old Bolsheviks' who were in the dock during the Moscow Trials were sentenced to be shot, and Pokrovsky's theories were condemned to disappear not only from history courses, but also from the collective memory. Surviving pupils of the distinguished historian suffered repression. Their late teacher was accused of having come up with a conception 'devoid of a feeling for the homeland', while his works were said to exhibit 'disregard for the Leninist-Stalinist guidelines on questions of history'.[3] Just what these guidelines stipulated (especially on the part of the long-dead Lenin) no one, predictably, troubled to explain. The propaganda campaign, in the style of the Moscow Trials, consisted of spreading absurd accusations with no more relation to reality than the charges – of espionage on behalf of all the imperialist powers simultaneously – that had been brought against the Old Bolsheviks. Stalin's court publicist Yemelyan Yaroslavsky summarised the results of the offensive, writing in *Pravda* that the views of the now-suppressed school amounted to 'anti-Marxist distortions and vulgarisation'.[4]

The reality was that once the Pokrovsky school had been smashed, official history in the Soviet Union returned to the pre-revolutionary tradition. The 'Soviet Thermidor' needed its own myths. Lists of rulers, augmented with descriptions of the victories of the Russian state, alternated with periodic complaints of economic and cultural 'backwardness'. The Soviet era appeared as a triumphant culmination, for it signified that the victories were continuing while the backwardness was being overcome. The Communist Party represented the summation of a thousand-odd years of Russian development. History had carried out its task, and had become unnecessary.

The country now proceeded 'from congress to congress'; at each of them, the joyful populace reported its successes to the party. After the suppression of the Pokrovsky school in the 1930s, Soviet history returned in the main to the concepts that had been traditional for nineteenth-century scholars, merely embellishing them with quotations from Marx, Lenin and Stalin. After the downfall of the Soviet system, all these quotations could be removed without difficulty from the textbooks and academic monographs, changing nothing of substance. Naturally, the official historical line underwent a process of ideological correction. But only with regard to the Soviet period – from an age of great victories, this period was transformed into a succession of 'dark pages of the past'. In other words, despite the changes of political course, the approach to pre-Soviet history (and to the cultural tradition) remained unaltered. Soviet historians continued to put the line they had inherited from nineteenth-century liberal authors, while anti-communist writers, condemning everything Soviet, proclaimed a return to the liberal tradition, dispensing with the now-unnecessary quotations. The ideas that had been dominant in the late nineteenth century remained unshakeably official in the early twenty-first century as well. For the most part, social and economic history was outside the field of view of educated society. It was not that new books on these topics were failing to appear – new studies were being published, some of them brilliant – but they had very little impact on the general conception of the past that held sway in popular consciousness and even among the intelligentsia.

Pokrovsky, by contrast, had from the very first formulated his ideas in sharp opposition to the thinking then dominant in historical writing. With a high regard for the comparatively neutral Solovyev, he counterposed his views clearly to the liberal conception of Russia's past, promising to reinterpret Russian history from a materialist standpoint. Above all, Pokrovsky addressed the reader whose brain had not been 'put out of joint by school history textbooks'.[5] The official historiography paid Pokrovsky back in the same coin, effectively striking his name out of the generally accepted list of Russian historians. After the abolition of the Soviet censorship, when the works of numerous pre-revolutionary historians (including second- and third-rate ones) began to be republished in large editions, Pokrovsky's writings remained unknown to the general public. In the official school text of readings on Russian history, Pokrovsky is the only major historian to whose writings not even a line is allotted, and whose name is not even mentioned. But what, when all is said and done, is the main difference between these historians?

The Russian historical tradition is characterised by exaggeration of the role of external political factors, by undervaluation of external economic factors, and by an extremely weak understanding of the links between these two categories.

Attempts to understand the history of any country without taking into account the links with the history of humanity as a whole are doomed to failure. The attempt to analyse Russian history as an independent and isolated narrative could lead only to the rise of the competing myths of Westernisers (ascribing all of Russia's ills to insufficient Western influence) and Slavophiles (convinced that these misfortunes all flow from an excess of this influence). The question of how Russia's relations with the outside world have in fact been constructed, what the nature of these relations has been, and the reasons for their anguished quality, remains a mystical puzzle for both currents, and one which they have a superstitious reluctance even to touch.

Orthodox Marxism, as interpreted by the Russian 'legal Marxists' in the early twentieth century, did little to improve this situation. The history of each country was viewed in isolation from worldwide processes, while development was perceived as something like a race in which the runners were moving at the same time and in the same direction, but in parallel lanes. These ideas, which contradicted not only the dialectical thinking of Marx but also the experience of the Russian revolution, lay at the basis of the official Soviet Marxism of the Stalin era. Hence also the classic images of Stalinist rhetoric – 'catch up with and overtake America', 'forward on the road to communism', and so forth. Pyotr Struve and other liberal ideologues of legal Marxism would scarcely have supposed that they were laying the methodological bases for a whole school of communist propagandists and official historians, but the Marxist vaccination which they administered to the liberal-historical tradition was extraordinarily effective. Instead of applying the critical method to the achievements of nineteenth-century historical thought, Soviet official history turned its Marxism to repeating ideas which, in Marx's view, needed to be viewed with scepticism.

THE CIVILISATION SCHOOL

Restoring the traditions of the Pokrovsky school is necessary at least in the interests of intellectual honesty and historical justice. Nevertheless, a simple return to the ideas of Pokrovsky is no longer sufficient. If the dominant concepts in Russian historiography have changed little in the last hundred years, archaeology and archival studies have made notable progress. At the same time, the school of 'world-system' analysis in English-language sociological and historical literature has given us important ideas for understanding social development. Paradoxically, a rereading of Pokrovsky from this angle can easily lead one to conclude that the dominant concepts of Russian history need an even more radical rethinking than that which the Marxist scholar of the early twentieth century carried out.

Meanwhile, the actual development of social thought in post-communist Russia has followed a quite different course. The discrediting of Soviet ideology could not fail to give rise to a serious crisis in the social sciences as well. Since Marxism was ruled out of account, and endlessly repeating hundred-year-old theses was now impossible, the 'theory of civilisations' came into fashion.

Samuel F. Huntington's *The Clash of Civilizations*[6] immediately became popular, even before anyone had read it. Adherents of diametrically different political viewpoints could refer to it, in some cases while promising the return of Russia to the bosom of European civilisation (from which the country had fallen either in the eighth century or in 1917, depending on one's viewpoint), and, in others, while calling for the defence of the fundamentals of Russian or Eurasian civilisation.

The accepted founder of the 'civilisational' approach to history was Oswald Spengler. But even before Spengler wrote his famous work *The Decline of Europe*, similar ideas about history had been formulated by the conservative Russian thinker Nikolay Danilevsky. The latter's book, *Russia and Europe*, published in 1871 at a time when Russian society was gradually recovering from the shock dealt by defeat in the Crimean War, is suffused with hostility toward the 'ungrateful West', still refusing to give Russian 'generosity' its due. Danilevsky stressed in particular that it was not the governments of Western countries who were Russia's enemy, but these countries' societies and peoples. Danilevsky was convinced that during the Crimean War 'European public opinion was far more hostile to Russia than were governmental and diplomatic circles'.[7] The problem lay in the profound enmity which Western civilisation, founded on the principles of 'utility' and 'practical benefit', felt for Russian civilisation, which embodied harmony between practice and high spirituality. In the West, Danilevsky argued, there was 'no place for the law of love and self-sacrifice'.[8] By contrast, the Russian empire did everything in the most moral fashion; even its policy of conquest was aimed exclusively at benefiting the subjugated peoples. 'Never has the taking by a people of the historical realm predestined for them cost less blood and fewer tears.' Everyone abused and oppressed the Russian people, but the latter did offence to no one.

The edifice of state erected by the Russian people does not have its foundations on the bones of downtrodden nationalities. The Russian people either took possession of deserted lands, or joined to themselves through non-violent historical assimilation such tribes as the Chudi, Vesi and Meri, or the present-day Zyryane, Cheremisy and Mordvy, who have no rudiments of historical life and no desire for it; or, finally, the Russian people took under their shelter and protection tribes and peoples such as the Armenians and Georgians who, surrounded by enemies, had already lost their national independence or who could no longer preserve it. In all this, conquest played only a negligible role, as can easily be seen if we examine how Russia acquired its southern border regions, a process reputed in Europe to have consisted of conquest by an insatiably greedy Russia.[9]

At the time when Danilevsky wrote his book, half a century of war was nearing its end in the Caucasus. This conflict had been accompanied by the mass killing and 'ethnic cleansing' of Circassians, Chechens and other nationalities who did not understand the blessing represented by Orthodox civilisation. In the same way, 'the partitioning of Poland, to the extent that Russia took part in it, was a completely legal and just affair, the fulfilment of a sacred debt to Russia's own sons, in which Russia should not have been disturbed by outbursts of sentimentality or of false generosity'.[10] The uprisings by the Poles and other subject peoples is explained solely as the result of their ingratitude and ambition. If many people in Russia itself disagreed with this, it was merely because Western education had 'beaten humanitarian ravings firmly into Russian heads'.[11] In Danilevsky's view, the other calamities which had befallen the Russian people included novelties as alien to the national cultural character as the adoption of Western dress, the granting to defendants of the right to legal defence, and the freeing-up of the press that took place in the late 1860s.

Not only imperial conquests, but also the oppression of Russian peasants under serfdom failed to arouse Danilevsky's condemnation. He glorified the Orthodox Russian bureaucrat in the same way as Rudyard Kipling extolled the 'white man's mission'. Danilevsky's dim-witted conservatism, however, rested on a perfectly serious methodological basis – the theory of cultural-historical types, subject to precise laws of development. In this respect, neither Samuel Huntington nor other stars of the present-day 'civilisation' school have added anything new to the thinking of Danilevsky's time. The only difference is that these writers all offer their own lists of 'civilisations', and their own interpretation of the differences between them.

The anti-historicism of the civilisation school becomes glaring as soon as these writers come into contact with the facts. The very concept of civilisation is viewed in rigid fashion, as something fundamental and immutable. The truth is that if things seem basic and unchanging, it is because they have been retained from history. The reverse, however, is not necessarily correct; that which is fundamental is not always retained. In reality, civilisations are constantly changing, under the impact of external economic, political and historical factors.

The 'civilisation' approach has always been convenient for warring political tendencies. In the West in the early twenty-first century, this approach has served as the ideology for new 'crusades' and as a justification for neocolonialism. In the nineteenth century, Kipling glorified the 'white man's burden', bringing the achievements of industrial civilisation to the East. Now, advanced countries are supposedly grafting the values of democracy onto the 'backward world'; these values, it would seem, are completely absent from Islamic or Confucian cultures. For the purposes of this 'grafting', it is no sin to occupy one or another backward country and make use of its resources, until such time as the local population becomes ripe for democracy. Islamic fundamentalists have found in the same concepts an additional basis for their hatred of the 'godless West'. Meanwhile, Russian nationalists cite Huntington while arguing for the defence of the Orthodox faith and 'holy Russia' against the onset of 'Atlantic culture', the 'Islamic threat' and 'Chinese pressure'.

The advantage of the civilisation approach lies in its unscientific character, in the diffuseness and imprecision of its ideas, which are capable of being turned to any purpose. The discussion which is developing on this basis around the topic of whether a Eurasian or Russian civilisation exists is itself indicative. Every participant in this debate has come up with his or her own definitions, with the result that even the term 'Eurasian' is the subject of a multitude of interpretations.

Nevertheless, the main problem of the civilisation school is not the diffuseness of its definitions, but its reluctance to take account of history, and of facts in general. Here we are faced with a classic example of 'ideology' as understood by the young Marx, of false consciousness, amounting to a set of rigid stereotypes not subject to the test of practice. 'Civilisation' is perceived in this case as something that remains stable over centuries, a set of cultural principles that determine the development of peoples through the ages. From this arises the conviction that there are generalised Western or Russian types of humanity, existing outside of a specific political, social or cultural context. Cultural traditions are indeed durable, but they also evolve. Their content is shaped and altered by the influence of history, along with the development of society. They are themselves the product of this development, a means through which the results of social evolution are collectively understood and fixed. Consequently, civilisations and cultures undergo striking metamorphoses. Max Weber saw in Confucianism (unlike the 'Protestant ethic'), a cultural mechanism holding back entrepreneurship. Post-Weberian sociology sees Confucianism as the Asiatic equivalent of the Protestant ethic, ensuring the success of Japan, Korea and China in world markets.

Was Weber wrong? Not at all. In his period Confucianism functioned as a conservative and traditionalist ideology. But along with the modernisation of the countries of the Far East, the manner in which the Confucian tradition was realised changed as well. The mistake lies not in the interpretation made of one culture or another, but in the fact that the cart, in this case, is put before the horse. It is not culture that determines the success or failure of modernisation, but, on the contrary, the success or failure of modernisation that decides whether one or another variant of the development of culture will take hold. In this sense, the 'conservatism' or 'radicalism' of Islam in the second half of the twentieth century is not something inherited from the time of Mohammed. Islam became what it is through the failure of modernising initiatives in the Middle East. Modern Islam is a distinctive response to a tragic experience, a reaction to the series of failures and humiliations undergone by the Arab world.

It is not hard to establish that in an age of political and economic successes, Islamic culture was quite different. Consider European civilisation and the Islamic East in the eleventh century, at the beginning of the Crusades. The West at this time was closed off, conservative, hostile to innovations, militarised, and aggressive. The Franks (this is what all Western Europeans were called in the East) arrived in Constantinople and then in Jerusalem as a horde of barbarians, the bearers of blanket destruction. The leaders of the Crusader forces had trouble restraining their warriors from plundering the territory of their Byzantine allies. The Crusaders were illiterate and unscrupulous. They lacked even an elementary idea of how the world of their time was organised, and were cruel and superstitious. The East, by comparison, was dynamic, tolerant, open and inclined to innovation. It was precisely for this reason that it initially met with defeat. The success in battle enjoyed by the Europeans was the result of their higher level of militarisation. This success, however, did not last long, since the East, with technological superiority and a more dynamic social system, came to outplay the West in the thirteenth and fourteenth centuries.[12] The Crusades can, of course, be depicted as a clash of systems or civilisations. The situation was quite similar to that in the twenty-first century, though it was not the West that played the role of the 'open society' and the 'culture of enlightenment', but the Islamic world.

A mutual interpenetration of cultures did of course occur, but this does not explain why the West leapt ahead in the fifteenth century. The Crusades opened up Eastern knowledge and technology to the West, but still did not guarantee successful development. On the military level, the Crusades ended in failure, followed by the assault of the Ottoman empire on South-Eastern Europe. It was only in the sixteenth century that the Western countries, now entering the era of bourgeois development, halted the Turkish onslaught.The East in the sixteenth century did not become more 'conservative'; rather, it came to be perceived as conservative by comparison with the dizzying development of the West. What exactly happened in Europe around the beginning of the sixteenth century?

It might be said that at the end of the Middle Ages a sort of civilisational mutation took place. It began with the Crusades. Then, in the fifteenth and sixteenth centuries, Europe experienced the Renaissance and the Reformation; on the cultural level, the former had perhaps more impact than the latter. There is no doubt that European culture changed radically; the question is – why? 'Culturological' methods yield no clarifications, however much one might rummage about in the history of the early medieval period. Meanwhile, the answer lies right on the surface; the reason for the cultural transformation was the development of bourgeois relations. It is no accident that the breeding grounds of cultural modernisation in the Middle Ages were precisely those regions where the most dynamic development of the new market economy was evident – that is, in Italy and the Netherlands. Life was changing, people's everyday experience was changing, and their consciousness was changing as well.

WORLD-SYSTEM ANALYSIS

The Marxist view of history rests on manifest facts, in contrast to the abstractions, myths and ideological speculations of the civilisation school. Nevertheless, Marxist scholars themselves, as they have sought to understand the origins of European capitalism, have finished up divided into two currents. One group of writers has turned its attention to the technological revolution unfolding in the West in the fifteenth and sixteenth centuries, to the growth of the internal market and to the formation of the bourgeois mode of production. The growth of cities created a heightened demand for the products of the countryside, the natural economy was finally replaced by commodity exchange, and this meant that the entire organisation of the economy had to be changed as well. Eventually, agriculture too began to change, becoming more and more oriented to the demands of the market. Capitalism was growing out of the development of feudalism.

On the other hand, the suspicion has grown that this rapid growth was spurred not only and not so much by the internal dynamic of the system as by external shocks. In the fourteenth and fifteenth centuries, two developments changed the face of Europe. Both these events were perceived by contemporaries not as ushering in a new era, but as divine punishment, or at any rate as unprecedented calamities. These two events were the Black Death and the fall of Constantinople.

The Black Death, by wiping out as much as a third of the European population, created a demand for hired labour, including in the countryside. The fall of Byzantium brought about a trade crisis and the search for new sea routes, leading to the discovery of America and to voyages to India. The flood of precious metals from the New World led to the 'prices revolution', when gold and silver lost their previous buying power, provoking a sharp rise in the demand for goods. This was the first practical demonstration of the future theory of J.M. Keynes concerning inflation as a stimulus to economic growth. The colonisation of America created the transatlantic economy, in the framework of which capitalism also took shape.

The world-system analysis school, founded by Fernand Braudel, Immanuel Wallerstein, Samir Amin and Andre Gunder Frank, focuses its attention on these global processes. The question arises, however, that if there had not been first the plague and then the fall of Constantinople, would European capitalism have come to exist? Especially since bourgeois relations had clearly been ripening in Italy, Flanders, Bohemia, and several other parts of Europe long before the period of the great geographical discoveries.

History does not, of course, have a subjunctive mood. But what are we to do when we encounter two different but equally convincing explanations of one and the same process? More than likely, the internal development of the European cities and the external shocks augmented one another. In late feudal Europe, a vast creative, technological and, most importantly, social and organisational potential had accumulated. But external stimuli were needed for all these forces to suddenly burst free.

In any case, without the great turning point of the fourteenth and fifteenth centuries capitalism would not have taken on the form in which we know it in modern history. Meanwhile, these events played an important role in determining the cultural forms of the bourgeois civilisation of the West. Andre Gunder Frank, in his book *ReOrient*, sets out to explain the triumph of the West throughout the modern era as the result of a purely accidental confluence of circumstances.[13] Columbus accidentally discovered America, where, as it happened, there was a great deal of silver, and by chance this coincided with a period of economic decline in Asia, and so forth. *ReOrient* is notable precisely in the sense that it shows the limited theoretical scope of world-system analysis. Beginning with a demonstration of the limited nature of orthodox Marxist schemas which reduce economic history exclusively to the 'natural' development of productive forces and productive relations, this school at a certain stage discovered that without an understanding of the motive forces of social history, it is impossible to make sense either of the development of world trade or of geopolitics.

In reality, medieval Europe lagged far behind the East. Africans laughed when they saw the caravels of the Portuguese, since they had already seen the mighty ships of the Chinese fleet. Nevertheless, it was these little ships that transformed the entire world economy and political scene, since China, possessing an incomparable wealth of resources, achieved nothing revolutionary during that period. The East remained backward because capitalism could not take shape within the framework of the Asian mercantile civilisation. The Asian mode of production which Marx discerned in China, Egypt and India was a reality, and not a myth. The state was powerful, ensuring a degree of economic equilibrium and progressive development that was not seen in Europe. Because of this, China in ancient times outstripped the West for an entire era. The lack of equilibrium in the West, however, also concealed vast possibilities. Historical development is an uneven process, not a linear one. Even in the seventeenth century, Europe was still learning from China in the technological sphere. The East had also overtaken the West in the degree of literacy, in the productivity of labour, and in general prosperity. But the West was developing rapidly, while the East was stagnating. The reason was simple, and Marx defined it convincingly. In the West capitalism had triumphed, forcing a pitiless but exceedingly effective mobilisation of all available human and technological resources for the sake of accumulation. The East did not turn the accumulation of merchant capital into the bourgeois mode of production.

The great geographical discoveries played an enormous role in the history of capitalism. Capitalism was maturing within feudalism in natural fashion, but it was the geographical expansion of the Western world that turned the possibility of bourgeois revolution in Western Europe into a reality. The proto-bourgeois movements in fourteenth- and fifteenth-century Europe all met with defeat – until the beginning of the great geographical discoveries. The Italian Renaissance was in essence the first bourgeois revolution, above all in the area of culture and ideology, but also in the field of politics; it is not by chance that we find it summarised in theoretical terms in Machiavelli's *The Prince*. The Hussites were the earliest prototype of a bourgeois national movement – in the wealthy, developed and flourishing cities of Bohemia. The ideology of the Hussites was a direct rehearsal for the Reformation. The Hussites were isolated and defeated, but a century later the flames of the Reformation took hold throughout Europe. What had changed during that time? The external conditions. The possible became real. The dramatic expansion of the economic world opened the way for a different line of development, sharply altering the relationship of social forces in society, stimulating the appearance of new technologies and allowing bourgeois relations to grow in breadth and depth. Capitalism thus arose historically as a world system, and acquired its specific traits in the process of development of the world economy.

Bourgeois relations also existed before the great geographical discoveries. Merchant capital existed much earlier, but nowhere could it become the dominant social force. The Italy of the fourteenth and fifteenth centuries had finished up in a dead end, with no prospects for commercial expansion. It was the discoveries of the fifteenth and sixteenth centuries that established the conditions for bourgeois relations to become economically dominant. Most importantly, the great discoveries would in time make the transformation of merchant capital into industrial capital indispensable. The revolution of the fifteenth and sixteenth centuries set free the destructive and creative forces of capitalism. Capitalism, meanwhile, allowed the West to realise the unique social and cultural possibilities that had opened up on the boundary between the Middle Ages and the modern era.

Supporters of traditional Marxism have reacted suspiciously to the school of world-system analysis. As they see it, capitalism is presented in the writings of the world-system scholars not as a mode of production, but rather as a system of exchange. The world system described in the works of Wallerstein and his followers does, indeed, appear above all as hierarchically organised international trade. What is involved here, however, is not trade as such, but the international division of labour. International trade existed long before the rise of capitalism. It was only once the world division of labour had begun to take shape that trade came to play the decisive role in capital accumulation that Marx later noted. The international division of labour is inseparable from production. The division of labour of course appeared long before capitalism, but without it the bourgeois order would have been impossible. The form which the international division of labour began to assume in the course of the Middle Ages determined the socio-economic, technological and even cultural processes in a whole series of countries. Byzantium, for example, had an acute need for the raw materials that were brought to Constantinople from the northern coastal region of the Black Sea and from Kievan Rus. Byzantine demand stimulated the development in these regions of the corresponding production, then the spread of trades employing Byzantine technologies, and finally, the spread of Orthodox Christianity. This precise kind of technology transfer was impossible and pointless in Western European countries that were not linked by the division of labour with the Greek empire.

A still more striking example is provided by the enclosures in England in the sixteenth century, when thousands of peasants were driven from their lands, which were turned into sheep pastures. This was provoked not by the internal requirements of English agriculture, but by the demand for wool that resulted from the rapid development of textile production in Flanders. To paraphrase Thomas More, it could be said that sheep had begun to 'eat people' because capitalism had begun its rise in the Netherlands. In England itself, this demand also spurred the development of bourgeois relations, above all in the agrarian sector.[14] In other words, the international division of labour necessitated the rise of productive and social processes that would otherwise not have appeared at all, or that would have emerged in quite different forms, at different times, and perhaps in different countries as well.

Capitalism arose simultaneously as a world economic system and as a mode of production. The one would have been impossible without the other. Bourgeois productive relations could not have developed and become dominant had there not been an economic system that favoured this. Correspondingly, the revolutionary transformation of the world would have been impossible had new productive relations not arisen in the 'advanced' countries that became the centre of the new world system.

Orthodox Marxism stresses the importance of productive relations, while the world-system analysis school has set out to show that the decisive role in capitalist development has been played by the globalisation of economic ties which began in the late fifteenth century and allowed the countries of the 'centre' to exploit the cheap resources and labour of the 'periphery'. In each case, what is involved is the accumulation of capital. Orthodox Marxism stresses the internal sources of this accumulation, the world-system school the external ones. Accordingly, the question is posed: what exactly is capitalism – a world system, or a mode of production? The one, of course, does not exclude the other. Capitalism is a world system that is based on the bourgeois mode of production, but which is not reducible to it. The effective mobilisation of internal resources was essential for the successful exploitation of external ones. This is why the rapidly bourgeoisifying Britain and Holland triumphed, while the Spanish empire with its vast possessions and wealth – but still-feudal social order – suffered defeat. Lacking the internal conditions for the development of capitalism, Spain was unable to implant the system in the sixteenth and seventeenth centuries, despite enjoying huge geopolitical advantages.

CENTRE AND PERIPHERY

The exploitation of the periphery has taken various forms in the course of history. The specific forms of this exploitation are well-known to sociologists and economists, but the underlying mechanisms of redistribution have remained the topic of heated discussion. The division of the capitalist world system into centre and periphery has been the subject of analysis over a prolonged period, starting with the works of Rosa Luxemburg, and ending with the writings not only of Wallerstein, Amin, and so on, but also with the books of the well-known financial speculator George Soros. Statistical data collected during the nineteenth and twentieth centuries show that the relationship between the zones of the periphery and the centre has remained relatively stable, though most indicators have the gap between 'advanced' and 'backward' countries steadily widening. This gap is superbly illustrated by regional economic statistics. There is no shortage of historical and statistical data to confirm the global redistribution of resources to the advantage of the wealthy countries. Nevertheless, economists and politicians are often mystified as to why this happens; they are unable to say just what gives rise to and perpetuates the subjection of the periphery to the centre.

Why is this situation continually reproduced, even though capitalism is altering its form, and the relationships between countries are also changing? Marxists were at first inclined to explain the wretched position of the countries of the periphery as the result of their colonial dependency on the West. In the mid twentieth century this approach determined the strategy of decolonisation, which by putting an end to political control, was supposed to guarantee economic independence as well. As early as the nineteenth century, however, the experience of Latin America showed that political independence does not allow the countries of the periphery to radically change their position in the world system. In analogous fashion, tsarist Russia displayed obvious features of a peripheral society despite being not only an independent state, but also an influential European power. After freeing itself from its European conquerors, the former colonial East by the 1960s had become part of the 'Third World', merging in economic terms into a united whole with the countries of Latin America, which had won their independence in the early nineteenth century. The global hierarchy, however, did not change radically as a result. From this time on, the dominant position of the centre was explained on the basis that it was here that industrial production was concentrated, while the periphery had taken on the role in the world division of labour of the supplier of resources. In the 1960s, sociologists and economists were accustomed to speak of the dependency of poor countries on the rich West. Accordingly, liberation movements posited the task of industrialisation and modernisation, with the first Soviet Five-Year Plans serving as an inspiring example. Unfortunately, industrialisation did not solve the problems, despite many obvious successes. Technological dependency then came to take centre stage, along with the ability of the West to concentrate strategic monopolies (on high technology, weapons of mass destruction, the mass information media, and so forth) in its hands. Meanwhile, not even the developing of the Indian and Pakistani nuclear bombs or the formation of the Arab television company Al-Jazeera altered the global economic hierarchy. Moreover, after the collapse of the USSR, Russia and Ukraine, on joining the world economy, came to display all the features of peripheral development. This was despite the fact that they already possessed developed industries, and had inherited powerful armed forces and advanced science from the Soviet Union. In similar fashion, a high degree of industrialisation and urbanisation did not save Argentina and Uruguay from drastic decline in the late twentieth century.

A great deal has also been written about unequal exchange between developed and developing countries. The Western monopolies that control world markets dictate the prices for the resources pumped out of the countries of the periphery. An effort to change this situation was the setting up of a cartel of oil producers (OPEC), which in the first half of the 1970s managed to sharply alter energy prices. The result was a flood of petrodollars pouring into the Middle East and to some extent, Eastern Europe. Some countries, possessing important reserves of oil and relatively small populations, managed to grow wealthy. This was not enough, however, to make these countries part of the capitalist centre, as emerged especially clearly during the wars started by the United States in the Persian Gulf in 1991 and 2003.

After the collapse of the Soviet bloc in the years from 1989 to 1991, the former communist world finally became part of the bourgeois world system, with most of it clearly gravitating toward the countries of the Third World. By late in the twentieth century numerous countries in the periphery had become urbanised and industrialised. By contrast, many Western countries had undergone a process of deindustrialisation. Large numbers of jobs had moved from the 'developed' North to the 'backward' South. Nevertheless, the relations between North and South did not change radically as a result. Observing how international financial institutions functioned in the late twentieth century, their critics demonstrated that the exploitation of the periphery and control over it were being realised through the system of foreign debt.

Even though the global division of labour changed repeatedly in the course of history, the tendency to the accumulation, concentration and centralisation of capital that lay at the basis of the bourgeois mode of production remained unaltered. The centralisation of capital on a world scale results in the formation of several centres of accumulation, often competing among themselves. The very logic of the accumulation and concentration of capital leads to it being systematically redistributed to the advantage of world 'leaders'. Not even the dramatic growth of the peripheral economy has changed this situation radically. In certain circumstances, a rise of production in these countries can even weaken their position. The better a country functions, the greater the volume of 'free' or 'excess' capital that arises there; this capital is redistributed to the advantage of the main centres of accumulation. The concrete forms of the international division of labour are the consequence of this global process. The forms change, but the logic of accumulation remains the same.

Russia in the 1990s presented an exceptionally clear picture in this respect, since against the background of a massive crisis, the country was one of the 'donors' to the world economy. Vast sums were converted into Western currency, mainly US dollars, and taken out of the country. Significantly, the upturn from the late 1990s did not alter this trend; in the relatively prosperous years from 2000 to 2003, the direct and indirect export of capital remained considerable.

Changes in the forms of exploitation and control accompany every new stage in the evolution of capital, but the logic of the accumulation and cen-tralisation of capital remains unaltered. The 'open economy' that is imposed on the countries of the periphery means that a redistribution of capital to the advantage of the centre is inevitable. Hence it was only Japan, Stalinist Russia and a handful of strategically important and deliberately favoured countries in East and South-East Asia which at various times managed to separate themselves off from the world capital markets, and to radically change their position in the global hierarchy.

Naturally, the social processes unfolding on the periphery of the capitalist system have differed from those in the centre. In the early twentieth century Rosa Luxemburg observed that as countries were drawn into the orbit of bourgeois development, they underwent radical transformations. Their evolution, however, was in no sense a mechanical repetition of the processes that had occurred in the West. Luxemburg examined colonial and semi-colonial countries that had been drawn into capitalist development. The feudal or traditional elites had become bourgeoisified and were included in market exchange, but had not become capitalist. Free labour had triumphed in the centre, but on the periphery the slave trade developed and became a vital source of the accumulation of capital. Slave labour subsidised and stimulated the development of free labour; cheap raw materials and foodstuffs, along with additional capital, ensured rapid economic growth in the countries of the centre.

The process of globalisation, about which it became fashionable to speak in the 1990s, not only failed to alter the situation, but even deepened the social contradictions on a world scale. Around the end of the twentieth century a number of scholars argued that in future, the division of the world into poor and rich countries would turn into conflict between transnational capital and the working layers of the population on a global scale.[15] Global conflict between labour and capital, however, is nothing new; Marx and Engels wrote of it in *The Communist Manifesto*. Similarly, the world-system analysis school has never argued that contradictions exist only between countries. The social conflicts within each individual society are too obvious for anyone to ignore them. Meanwhile, the social structures and the character of the social conflicts are different in the centre and on the periphery. The main difference is that the ruling elites in the countries of the centre have much greater resources, providing them with far greater opportunities for social compromise and the forming of consensus. As a result, the political systems of the West are more stable, their democracy less erratic, their political and electoral processes 'cleaner', and so forth. It is not that the presence of a 'rich democratic tradition' ensures the durability of Western freedoms, but, on the contrary, that the inevitable economic instability of the periphery makes creating rich democratic traditions there impossible.

From this point of view, what is happening in Russia and Eastern Europe is especially important. Rosa Luxemburg examined the evolution of the colonial world; in Russia and Eastern Europe, we see societies in which bourgeois relations have begun to emerge, as they did in the West. Moreover, these countries are being actively incorporated into the new global development (unlike significant parts of southern Europe, which have not been included in the new system of world economic ties, and which therefore have stagnated). However, Russia and Eastern Europe are being integrated into the world system as its periphery. In these countries, bourgeois development is subject to a logic quite different from that which applied in the West. Economic growth and the development of the market are not leading to the emancipation of the population, but to its enslavement. The bourgeoisie is growing in numbers, but at the same time, its business culture is being degraded. The upshot is that Russia, from being a 'normal' European nation with specific peculiarities, is being turned into a 'backward' country, desperately trying to modernise itself, seeking to catch up with the West but continually falling behind.

Unlike the centre, representing a more or less pure model of bourgeois relations, the periphery creates its own model of capitalism.[16] This capitalism is characterised by a high, sometimes even hypertrophied degree of development of market links, together with a low level of development of bourgeois relations where production is directly concerned. In tsarist Russia in the mid nineteenth century, grain produced by serf farmers in the Voronezh *guberniya* (province) was sold on the world market in exactly the same way as the produce of free farmers. The Russian countryside itself, however, lived in a fashion that owed nothing to the laws of bourgeois society. There was no market in labour power. The result of this situation was the unreceptiveness of society to innovation (at times despite vast productive potential); technological backwardness and dependency on the West; a chronic shortage of capital in industry, despite an abundance of raw materials and labour; and the incapacity of the local bourgeoisie to independently convert its sometimes huge financial assets into effective investments. The business world constantly experienced an acute need of help from the state or from foreign partners.

Russia has never been a country isolated from the world. However much sixteenth-century zealots of Orthodox piety might have striven to wall the country off from foreign influences, it was precisely at this time that the ties of the Moscow tsardom with the West reached a qualitatively new level. In the pre-capitalist period, trade represented the exchange of surpluses between communities or regions. As the bourgeois market developed, trade became transformed into a means of integrating the country into the world system, while production, which earlier had served local needs, was now subject to external demand. Production for the market meant reorganising the whole system of social ties within the community, even if the community itself remained in no sense bourgeois. Trade was the means through which production that was non-capitalist in its internal organisation was subordinated to the logic of capitalist accumulation.

In Pokrovsky's historical thinking, the concept of mercantile capitalism has an important place. This early form of bourgeois entrepreneurship, which had developed in the age of the great geographical discoveries, was still restricted by the framework represented by traditional technologies. It was the industrial revolution that opened up to capitalism the prospect of mass production. Already in the sixteenth and seventeenth centuries, however, the transporting of goods required centralisation, a high degree of managerial control, and large investments. A single ship contained the production of a multitude of craft workshops or peasant households. In Western Europe manufacturing production was being set in motion, but on the periphery, which above all supplied raw materials, the situation was evolving differently. In order to exploit petty producers, mercantile capital needed an alliance with the large landowners and with the state. With the help of coercion, the petty producer was subjected to the logic of capitalist accumulation, and incorporated into the new division of labour.

It is significant that Pokrovsky himself did not fully understand why this alliance, which in one form or another had also appeared in the West, had there been a relatively short-lived phenomenon, while in Russia it persisted almost until the twentieth century. The answer to this question lies in comparing the productive tasks of the centre and the periphery, within the framework of the growing division of labour. The factory system of production immediately showed its effectiveness in manufacturing industry, while in the raw materials and agrarian sectors it was more advantageous to rely on compulsion. The result was that the integration of Russia into the world economy was accompanied not be a weakening of auctocracy, but by its strengthening, and not by a transition to capitalist agriculture, but by a strengthening of serfdom. 'Merchant capital travelled about Russia in a Monomakh cap, and the landowners and nobility were merely the agents for this capital, its administrative apparatus.'[17] This is how Pokrovsky explains the familiar examples of the powerlessness of the aristocracy and nobility before the autocracy in the eighteenth century, when the members of the privileged strata were not only packed off to war and forced to serve in government offices, but could even be whipped. There is, of course, a certain polemical sharpness in Pokrovsky's thesis. Ultimately, the nobility had its own interests, and even in the eighteenth century was well able to defend them by carrying out *coups d'état*, in the process securing freedoms for itself. Nevertheless, the significance of merchant capital and of global economic processes in Russian history is impossible to exaggerate.

It is easy to establish that each new phase in the development of the European economy, and later of the global economy as well, coincided with crucial events for Russia. There was nothing accidental about this. In the Muscovite state, the great transformations that took place in sixteenth and seventeenth century Europe were reproduced as the repressions of Ivan the Terrible and of the Time of Troubles. The economic boom of the eighteenth century became the golden age of the Russian nobility, an era of grandeur and enlightenment based on merciless exploitation of the peasants. In the 1860s and 1870s, a new revolutionary transformation of the world system was under way. In Russia, the era of reforms was beginning. The crisis of world capitalism in the years from 1914 to 1918 manifested itself not only in the First World War, but also in the Russian revolution. The Great Depression of 1929 to 1932 was accompanied by Stalin's collectivisation, and so forth.

In comparing Russia with Britain, Pokrovsky saw in the British empire a 'felicitous' combination of industrial capitalism in the metropolis and of commercial capitalism, which 'relocated itself to the colonies'.[18] This idyll was disturbed only by the revolution and the War of Independence in North America. In Russia, by contrast, endless conflicts erupted between the two types of capitalism, conflicts which as a rule were not concluded to the advantage of the industrialists. It can be seen that Pokrovsky here expounds one of the main differences between the development of capitalism in the centre and on the periphery. One of the principal advantages of the centre has always been its ability to resolve its contradictions by exporting them beyond its borders – that is, to the periphery. What Pokrovsky perceives as a peculiarity of Britain is in fact a general historical law.

The international division of labour and the development of the world system presuppose a gradual shift from trade to production. As this shift proceeds, and as Marx was able to demonstrate, merchant capital ceases to be self-sufficient; it begins servicing the accumulation of industrial capital.

It was this transformation of commercial into industrial capital, rather than plunder and violence, that formed the essence of the primitive accumulation which Marx described. It is not surprising that commercial capital moved into colonies and dependent countries, pumping out resources and establishing new markets there for the products of industry. From the periphery the centre continually demands new resources, new production of an increasingly complex character. The development of the periphery creates additional opportunities for its exploitation, including through financial mechanisms. The creation of a world market in capital requires the development of bourgeois structures in the 'backward' countries precisely because the opportunities for exploiting these countries would otherwise remain extremely restricted.

Nationalists in developing countries who proclaim the slogan of modernisation are certain that they are throwing down a challenge to the West. In fact, the modernisation of the periphery has always been a requirement of the West, among the West's most important goals. Of course, this modernisation has had to be subordinated to the worldwide logic of the the accumulation of capital. The relations between the centre and the periphery change their form with each cycle of capitalist development.

KONDRATYEV CYCLES

In the mid 1920s the great Russian economist N.D. Kondratyev, after studying statistical data beginning with the late eighteenth century, concluded that there were 'big cycles' in the development of capitalism. These cycles, or waves, were uneven in their duration, usually lasting between 40 and 60 years, but they featured one and the same dynamic. First came an upturn, with production, prices and profits steadily growing. The crises during this period were not deep, and the depressions were brief. Then came the downturn, when growth in the economy was erratic, the crises more frequent, and the depressions drawn-out.[19] The first cycle which Kondratyev studied began in the late 1780s together with the industrial revolution, and reached its height around the end of the Napoleonic Wars.

After 1817 the conjuncture in Europe worsened, with economic depression combined with political reaction. The years from 1844 to 1851 saw a turning point, accompanied by a growth of the revolutionary movement and a rash of armed conflicts. A new economic upturn finally appeared in the late 1850s, after the Crimean War and the crisis of industry that followed it. The upturn continued until the early 1870s. Then came another period of economic difficulties, continuing until the 1890s. The recovery that made its presence felt at the end of the nineteenth century proved short-lived. By 1914, signs of a new decline were clearly evident. In the early 1920s Kondratyev's data indicated the approach of a major depression which hit the world in 1929 and lasted until 1933.

Having discovered long cycles in the world economy, Kondratyev was unable to clearly explain what they were associated with. The existence of such waves of development is a statistical fact, which becomes more obvious as new data enter into scholarly circulation. But what causes periods of relative upturn to alternate with equally lengthy periods of stagnation?

Attempts to mechanically predict the onset of the next 'Kondratyev wave' on the basis of chronology have invariably had comic results. The forecasting of long waves by present-day economists is at times reminiscent of astrology.[20] The main thing in the Kondratyev cycles is not the timescales, but the phases. This is the history of the formation, development and then disintegration of successive models of capitalism. For this reason, any forecasting of cycles that is based on chronology is completely pointless. What is important is the state of the global system itself, not which millennium we are now living in.

Kondratyev himself did not try to predict anything, but merely summarised facts.

Prior to the beginning of the upturn in every big cycle, and sometimes at its very beginning, significant transformations are to be observed in the basic conditions of society's economic life. These transformations, in one combination or another, are usually expressed in profound changes to the technology of production and exchange (these changes are in turn preceded by important technical inventions and discoveries); in changes to the conditions of monetary circulation; and in the strengthened role of new countries in world economic life.[21]

In Kondratyev's view, capitalism periodically undergoes 'reconstruction'. It is not only equipment that is changed. New actors appear, and the relationship of forces between the players changes. Kondratyev ascribes such reconstructions of capitalism to the necessity to replace worn-out equipment with machines of a new generation. And indeed, each Kondratyev cycle is associated in one way or another with the renewal of technology. Often, however, several generations of equipment are replaced in the course of a single cycle, and even of one of its phases. Technological revolutions, that involve replacing not just equipment, but the entire productive model, are a different matter. Such revolutions really do accompany the beginning of each new cycle.

But what is the replacing of a technological model tied up with? In this case, what is involved is not simply the need to replace old machines with new ones, but the fact that the market potential of the old technological model is exhausted. A renewal of the bases of production, the widespread introduction of new equipment, cannot fail to affect social life as well. The efficient use of the new productive forces is impossible without changes in society itself. Therefore, the reconstructions cannot be purely technical. They affect the social order, political life, and the relations between countries.

New technologies do not merely create new products and change old ones, but often give rise to new markets as well. Marx noted that as the capitalist economy develops and its technical basis grows more complex, a tendency is observed for the average rate of profit to decline. Every new generation of machines is more expensive than the preceding one, the cost of amortising the machines is greater, they require more highly qualified workers, and competition keeps forcing prices down. The result is that the average rate of return on investment heads steadily downward. 'Although Marx did not speak directly of long cycles,' the Soviet economist Stanislav Menshikov noted, 'he laid the basis for distinguishing variations in the dynamic of capitalist development, variations that are distinct from the medium-term economic cycle, and he also pointed to a possible material basis for them.'[22] It is in fact the decline in the average rate of profit noted by the author of *Capital* that is the key to understanding long waves. Throughout the twentieth century economists argued constantly about this thesis of Marx, one of them citing empirical data to refute the author of *Capital*, and another using statistics to show that Marx was right.

Marxists have also noted that a declining rate of profit sets capitalists on the road of external expansion (the seizure of new markets, armed conflicts, and so forth). In most cases, however, the people concerned have lost sight of the fact that the tendency noted by Marx applies to an economy with a more or less stable sectoral structure.

Menshikov writes:

It could be argued that Marx lacked a highly developed theoretical model that would explain the interaction between technological progress and profit rates. That is perhaps true, but Marx at the very least suggested some of the key elements of such a theory. Kondratyev was able to make use of these in the 1920s.[23]

Once Marx's analysis is applied to a system characterised by technological change, everything falls into place. Each time a new sector of the economy appears, the rates of profit in it are spectacularly high, helping to create the illusion of rapid and stable growth. This is why technological innovations that revolutionise production fail initially to bring about social and economic transformations; their immediate effect, paradoxically, is to stabilise the existing system of rule, strengthening the position of conservative forces by showing that the economic and social order works effectively. In reality, innovations in technology and other areas are used by the ruling classes in parasitical fashion. A great many scientific discoveries and technological innovations are made in times of political and cultural reaction. Before long, however, the rates of profit start to decline in the new sectors as well, and even more rapidly than in the traditional sectors. This does not mean that technology ceases to develop, but its development no longer creates qualitatively new markets. The exhaustion of the technological model creates the effect of an overaccumulation of capital. At this point we see the onset of a crisis – economic, political and social – of the ruling order. The outcome of the crisis is a new model of society that is capable of effectively using the accumulated technological potential. As Menshikov puts it, the society 'changes its skin'.[24]

The appropriation of new markets is like the cultivating of virgin soil, when excellent harvests can be had for several years without a great deal of fertiliser or effort. At times of technological revolution, new markets also arise as previously unknown goods go on sale. At the next stage, however, the average rate of profit can be raised only by drawing new territories, new areas of life, and new masses of people into the orbit of capitalism. This is why, as Kondratyev revealed, capitalism found it vitally important to 'widen its orbit' by drawing ever-greater numbers of countries into the world market.[25] In this sense, colonialism is a natural accompaniment to capitalism. In a striking manner, colonial expansion first dies down, then renews itself. After the conquests of the sixteenth and early seventeenth centuries the West, as it were, paused for a time; then colonisation was resumed in the eighteenth century, before again dying down by the beginning of the century that followed. The late nineteenth century saw a race for conquests and the 'division of the world'. After the decolonisation of the 1950s and 1960s, it appeared that such practices had vanished forever into the past. But the period around the beginning of the twenty-first century has been a time of new colonial wars, in essence if not in name. This type of repetition, as Kondratyev showed, is not accidental. 'It is quite clear that under capitalism new territories are drawn into the system's orbit precisely during periods when the countries of old culture experience a heightened need for new export markets and sources of raw materials.'[26]

When Kondratyev speaks of the periodic reconstructions of capitalism, he notes that a precondition 'is the concentration of capital at the disposal of powerful entrepreneurial centres'.[27] On the geographical level this automatically results in a redistribution of resources between countries. Within the world system, the pressure of the centre on the periphery intensifies. When the next reconstruction is basically complete, 'an abundance of "free" capital' is observed, 'and consequently, capital is cheap'.[28] The crisis of overaccumulation is resolved by moving the excess funds to the periphery of the system, creating the illusion of successful development there. The impression arises that thanks to the free play of market forces the periphery, or at least its most advanced section, is about to catch up with the West. Unfortunately, this happiness is short-lived, since the time draws near for the next reconstruction, and capital begins to move in the opposite direction. Each major reconstruction of capitalism has turned out to be a defeat, and sometimes a catastrophe, for the periphery.

Capitalism is cyclical in principle, since in this system both production and consumption are subject to the logic of commodity exchange. The short-term, conjunctural market cycles, already studied extensively by economists back in the nineteenth century, are superimposed on far more massive and complex processes of social, economic and technological development. In the same way, medium-term cycles are also, as Kondratyev puts it, 'knitted into the waves of the big cycles'.[29]

Marx wrote that the development of the productive forces of society requires the periodic revision of productive relations. In the course of history the technological basis of capitalism has changed repeatedly. The steam engine forced the shutting down of factories based on hand labour and water mills, while electricity revolutionised industry around the end of the nineteenth century. A new technological revolution occurred in the first quarter of the twentieth century. Automobiles, conveyor-belt assembly, the telephone and commercial aviation created a new economy. The resulting model was later given the name 'Fordism'. The technological revolution of the late twentieth century was merely another stage in this process.

Meanwhile, every radical change in technology culminates in the replacing of the economic model of capitalism, and sometimes of the socio-political model as well. These changes are inevitably superimposed on the 'ordinary' market cycles. What is involved here is not just the 'long waves' of economic upturn and decline, but also the alternation of periods when capital is rapidly being internationalised and periods of 'national development'. Phases marked by the pre-eminence of financial and commercial capital give way to phases when industrial capital is dominant. Periods of the free market are replaced by periods of state intervention. Conservative political periods are often accompanied by rapid technological development, but as a rule the changes affect communications, transport and trade far more than production. At such a time financial and commercial capital predominates over industrial capital, while the global economy is more important than the national market. The phases of globalisation and localisation reflect this dynamic, with trade and finance always striving for maximum expansion. Borders merely restrain them. Production, however, is always local. Labour power has to be reproduced, and people need somewhere to live, since they cannot be constantly on the move. Meanwhile, world trade cannot expand endlessly, especially against the background of a decline in the internal market. The state comes to the rescue of the entrepreneurs, guaranteeing 'the defence of national interests' and 'social responsibility'. Despite liberal mythology, it is during these periods that economic growth is at its most stable. The free trade of pirate times was replaced by mercantilism, then by a new bacchanalia of the free market, after which inevitably followed the next bout of protectionism, and so forth.

The cycles of decline and upturn coincide with periods of revolution and reaction. Kondratyev discovered that 'the periods of rising trend in the big cycles include the greatest number of major social convulsions, in terms both of revolutions and of wars'.[30] Limiting himself to stating this 'empirical fact', the great economist did not try to explain in detail the principle he had discovered. It is clear, however, that this is not mere coincidence. The cycles which Kondratyev described are not an automatic mechanism, not a 'natural' process occurring with the same consistency and inevitability as the change in the seasons. This is why the beginning of a new stage is always so difficult to predict. For a new cycle of growth to begin, society must undergo radical changes. Revolutions and reforms create a new model, on the basis of which the economic upturn unfolds. The exhaustion of this model brings the economy into a phase of decline, from which it emerges only through a series of crises, leading to new revolutions and reforms.

All of this proceeds within the framework of capitalism. But the French revolution with its plebeian fury already showed that every such convulsion is fraught with the collapse of the entire capitalist order. For capitalism, revolution acts as a mechanism of modernisation, but also represents a mortal threat. The Paris Commune of 1870 demonstrated this even more clearly, while in Russia the year 1917 led to the first socialist experiment, even if this was unsuccessful.

THE FATE OF RUSSIA

The fact that long waves of capitalist development were first analysed in Russia was not accidental. It is enough to compare the dates of key historical events in Russian history with the cycles of the world economy to note the coincidences. This applies to the *oprichnina*[31] of Ivan the Terrible, to the Time of Troubles, to the imposing of serfdom and its abolition, to the revolution of 1917, to collectivisation, to the dismantling of the Soviet Union, and to the great privatisation of the 1990s. Russia from the seventeenth to the twentieth centuries was continually trying to catch up with the West and continually falling behind, and was overwhelmed by each new economic wave. The historical analyses of Pokrovsky and the economic researches of Kondratyev were not only spawned by the same country and age. Together, they provide a key to understanding the main dramas and tragedies of Russian history.

The long waves of world development have set the rhythm of social and political change in Russia no less than in other parts of the world. In Russia, however, everything has been even more dramatic, and at times more horrifying. The drastic turnabouts of world history have taken the form of huge shocks. 'Everything there is without limits – the sufferings and the retribution, the sacrifices and the hopes', wrote the French traveller Adolphe de Custine, who visited Russia in 1839. 'Russian passions are like those of the ancients. Everything among the Russians recalls the Old Testament – their hopes and their torments are as vast as their state.'[32] This country seemed to him to be terrifying, unhappy and great, capable of improbable achievements that would, however, be bought at the price of the people's happiness.

Everything that struck the Marquise de Custine in the nineteenth century was only a prelude to the truly enormous shocks that would begin once the following century was under way. But neither the catastrophes which Russia has experienced, nor the heroic feats accomplished here, have been the result of any special, extraordinary destiny.

The dramatic nature of Russian history stems from the fact that processes affecting all humanity have manifested themselves here in extreme and tragic form. In this sense there is not, and cannot be, any special Russian fate. Our fate is that of humanity.

1
A Land of Cities

Russia – or as it was known in early medieval times, Rus – arose later than most European countries, and made its appearance under quite distinct circumstances. It was born 'along the route from the Varyags to the Greeks'. In the Middle Ages travel by water was both quicker and safer than by land. Ships could carry greater loads than horse-drawn vehicles. The roads were in an appalling state, and in some places simply did not exist. Moreover, journeys by land were relatively perilous; storms at sea were a less serious threat than robbers in the forests, half-savage tribes, and bands of feudal retainers who were always ready to enrich themselves with the goods of others. The ancient world was centred on the Mediterranean Sea. On the periphery of the Mediterranean economy were the Black Sea and the stretch of the Atlantic that directly adjoined the Mediterranean countries. Between the seventh and tenth centuries merchant navigation spread to the Baltic. Until the time of the Crusades, the Byzantine Greeks remained dominant in the south. In the north, the rising Baltic economy was the creation of the Vikings, or as they were known in Rus, the Varyags.

Rus was the connecting link between the two world-economies. A trading ship could come up the River Dnepr from the Black Sea. The Dnepr rapids of course presented an obstacle, but relatively easy ways were found to overcome them. Further on, ships could sail down the northern rivers to the Baltic. Only a small stretch in the middle was not suited to the transit route; here, the ships had to be dragged overland.

Close by the 'route from the Varyags to the Greeks' lay the Volga trade route. Merchant fleets with Persian wares from the Caspian Sea came up the Volga, and then along its tributaries. In the Novgorodian lands, these two routes intersected. From Novgorod, Persian and Byzantine goods reached northern Europe.[1]

In the year 862, according to the chronicles, the Novgorodian aristocracy invited the Varyag Prince Ryurik and his brothers Sineus and Truvor to take the throne, stating: 'Our land is great and rich, but there is no order in it. Come and rule over us.'[2] As Karamzin says, 'The words are simple, brief and powerful!'[3] In short, the Varyags were urged to found a state in Rus. Throughout the second half of the nineteenth and the entire twentieth century Russian historians argued incessantly over the 'summoning of the Varyags'; supporters of the 'Scandinavian theory' ascribed the birth of Russian statehood to the influence of Western neighbours, while Slavophiles and, later, official Soviet historians not only rejected this influence, but also tried to prove that Ryurik never existed at all. And even if Ryurik had existed, then Sineus and Truvor were pure invention, an error of transcription, an incorrect translation of some Scandinavian saying. For all its heat, this discussion was completely meaningless. The real question did not concern the role of the Varyags, or how many of them there were, or whether they were simply mercenaries or had come to Novgorod as a military and political elite. The real question was why, in the 860s, the Novgorodian leaders suddenly and unexpectedly started wanting to impose 'order' on their territory, and how it came about that in 882 Prince Oleg, after capturing Kiev, founded a state that was given the name 'Rus'.

For centuries Slavic and Finno-Ugrian tribes had lived on what is now the Russian plain, and had somehow got by without a state. In the ninth century the situation suddenly changed dramatically, and in the space of 20 years a powerful state had come into existence on the lands from the Baltic to the Black Sea, uniting under a single authority a multitude of tribes of the most diverse origins. Moreover, this state proved astonishingly stable, maintaining itself relatively intact at least until the early twelfth century – significantly longer than, for example, the empire of Charlemagne.

The need for a state arose abruptly, but not by accident. Nor was it the result solely of the internal development of Novgorod. Something else was of decisive importance. In Europe in the ninth and tenth centuries the Dark Ages were drawing to a close. The West was entering an age of economic growth. The natural economy was beginning to yield ground, and a trading economy was developing. This was the time of the first geographic and politico-economic expansion of Christian Europe. In all, there were three such periods during the Middle Ages: in the ninth and tenth centuries, when the European world was expanding rapidly to the north-east, incorporating Scandinavia and large parts of Eastern Europe; in the twelfth and thirteenth centuries, the time of the Crusades, of the building of towns and castles, and also of the second Baltic expansion, when in the north-east the last pagan tribes – Finno-Ugrians, Slavs and Balts – were subdued and Christianised; and finally, in the fifteenth and sixteenth centuries, the time of the great geographic discoveries. Each of these periods was crucial to the history of Russia, changing the character, national composition and even geography of the Russian state.

TIME TO IMPOSE ORDER

The prominent historian S.M. Solovyev noted that it is impossible to explain the development of Old Russian trade on the basis of the economic processes occurring in the Slavic communities themselves.

Throughout the country inhabited by the Slavic tribes, the almost identical nature of the products posed a major obstacle to exchange. What could the Polyane and Severyane, Drevlyane and Dregovichi, Krivichi and Radimichi exchange with one another? Their way of life was identical; they had the same pursuits, the same needs, and the same means for satisfying them. The Drevlyane had grain, honey, wax and animal skins; so did the Polyane and the other tribes.[4]

In Solovyev's view, trade appeared only with the coming of the Varyags, and especially with the appearance of the armed retainers under the princes' command. But in reality, the retainers also depended on the natural economy. They did not buy the foodstuffs they needed, but 'fed themselves', gathering tribute or simply robbing agrarian communities, while at the same time providing them with defence against raids by other, precisely similar gangs. Even in the fourteenth and fifteenth centuries, notes M. Pokrovsky, the feudal estate was still a 'self-contained whole', with few ties to the outside world.[5] What was the situation in the ninth and tenth centuries?

Official Soviet historians often viewed Kievan Rus above all as an agrarian society, arguing that it represented 'a powerful agricultural defence stopping the nomadic hordes from penetrating unhindered from east to west'.[6] According to such writings, the Kievan state acted as a sort of boundary; beyond it was a region, like the nineteenth-century American Wild West, in which all civilisation came to an end. Even if one leaves out of account the racist flavour of such theories, they have the shortcoming of not corresponding to the facts. In the first place, it is implied that the people to the east of the Dnepr had no knowledge of agriculture. In reality, the eastern neighbours of Rus in the eighth and ninth centuries were not savage nomadic tribes, but prosperous states – the Khazar khaganate (khanate) and the Volga Bulgars. Initially, both these societies were far more developed and wealthy than the eastern Slavs or the Varyags.[7] Second, the nomads repeatedly penetrated through Rus into Europe. In the late ninth century the Hungarians rode past Kiev unopposed, going on to terrorise Western countries for 60 years until the German King Otto I defeated them near Augsburg. After this, Hungary soon adopted Catholicism and transformed itself into the 'shield of Christendom', the bulwark of the Western world. In the thirteenth century the Tatar-Mongols, after sacking Rus, reached as far as the Danube, and were stopped not by military resistance, but by political problems in their own camp.

The Soviet historians were in principle correct when they linked the development of towns with the division of labour, with the separation of handicrafts from agriculture.[8] This, however, applies to the rise of towns throughout the common history of humanity. The towns of Kievan Rus were clearly not the first in world history. Nor are their swift rise and above all, their rapid enrichment, to be explained by the internal processes unfolding in Slavic tribal communities.[9]

Following the Dark Ages, Western Europe began to awaken late in the eighth century. France experienced a cultural revival that was later termed the 'Carolingian Renaissance'. In the year 800 Charlemagne proclaimed himself emperor in Rome. His armies penetrated as far as Moravia, forcing the Avars from that region. In the ninth and tenth centuries rapid political and economic development also took place in north-eastern Europe. The year 874 saw the rise of the first West Slavic state, Great Moravia. By the end of the ninth century the Hungarians had founded their own state on the Danube, and in 906 seized part of the lands belonging to Great Moravia, but the kingdom of Bohemia continued to develop within the framework of the Holy Roman Empire. In the tenth century the kingdom of Poland appeared on the map of Europe. The Scandinavian states began taking shape during the ninth century as well. The Vikings plundered the European coastline as far as Italy, and as the stolen wealth enriched the Scandinavian notables, it stimulated the development of peaceful trade and the formation of state institutions. A trading economy began to develop. By the middle of the tenth century, Denmark had united in a single kingdom. State authority was being established in Norway and Sweden. In ninth- and tenth-century Byzantium, an important economic upturn was also taking place. Two commercial-economic zones were thus appearing in Europe simultaneously; alongside the traditional Mediterranean zone a new Baltic–North Sea zone was emerging, uniting England and Scandinavia. The rivers of the Russian plain, forming a conduit between these two zones, were becoming vitally important for trade. The route from the Varyags to the Greeks was becoming a crucial link in the new, expanding commercial economy, uniting Europe in a single whole. It was not only goods that moved from south to north along these trade routes. Spreading along them as well were civilisation, Christianity, and craft technologies.

Alongside the route from Scandinavia to the Black Sea coast, other trade routes as well passed over the huge plain that would later form the basis for the Russian state. One of these routes extended through the Caspian Sea and the Volga to the north, providing the backward Europeans with manufactured goods from the far more developed countries of the East, the Arab khalifate and Persia. Another route led overland to Western Europe. Much less is known about this latter route, but hoards that have been unearthed allow historians to draw conclusions about 'a relatively ancient trans-European trade route', whose middle section was 'the route from the central Dnestr region to the Danube lands of southern Germany'.[10] As is clear, all these routes met and intersected in the area between Novgorod and Kiev.

The rapid development of international trade spurred the quick growth of cities, and of intensive links between them. Pokrovsky observes justifiably that to a significant degree this was 'bandit trade',[11] and that the towns were at first fortified stopping places for merchant-bandits travelling between the Baltic and the Black Sea; the towns, he remarks, were 'far more closely tied to those foreign markets than to the country round about'.[12] For a product to become a commodity, it needed to be taken from its direct producer; the process involved was either the levying of tribute, or outright theft. Both the Slavs and the Scandinavians, as they expanded to the north-east, began collecting tribute from the local tribes. This tribute was paid mainly in the form of furs. Slaves were seized as well.

Both the furs and the slaves were popular items of commerce in the more developed lands of the south. Tenth-century Arab authors wrote that the Russo-Scandinavian traders of the time were, in another capacity, the leaders of well-armed bands which at times numbered hundreds of armed men. It was these small private armies which, as Scandinavian historians acknowledge, 'enabled their leaders to extort tribute from the natives and to protect what was collected'.[13] By no means all the trade was militarised, however. The Russian, Scandinavian, and later the German merchants as well were simultaneously warriors, but a substantial proportion of the trade on the great river route was conducted by Greeks, Armenians, Arabs and Jews who did not have military organisation available to them, or at least, not in the same degree as the Slavs and Scandinavians. Meanwhile, it was the foreign merchants who brought with them a considerable amount of the coinage that was in circulation.

In such circumstances the state needed, on the one hand, to ensure that foreign merchants on the rivers were safe from local desperadoes, and, on the other hand, to defend its own traders from bandits and from each other. It is not surprising that when the Novgorod notables called in the Varyags, they should have referred to perennial fallings-out among themselves. In other words, a Varyag prince from outside Novgorod was required not only as a defender, but also as an arbiter.

The combination of trade and plunder made establishing order in the state a vital necessity; without this, clashes between armed merchants could simply have paralysed trade. Armed retainers of the prince were needed not only to guard the overseas convoys, but also to act as judges to sort out conflicting claims, and as an authority capable of guaranteeing the fulfilment of judicial decisions. The expansion of the ninth and tenth centuries made Rus indispensable. There are no 'dark ages' in Russian history for the simple reason that in the Dark Ages there was not and could not have been any Russian history. The state itself arose as a consequence of the commercial expansion that began with the overcoming of barbarism in the West. The Baltic became a swiftly growing trade zone. The Varyags, who not long before had been completely savage, suddenly became potential customers for the sophisticated manufactured goods produced in Byzantium and in the East. The trade route between the Black Sea and the Baltic was becoming profitable and necessary, but it had to be supported and secured. 'Order' was required. Before the rise of the Baltic market, the navigable rivers of the south and the numerous lakes and connecting streams of the north had been of no economic or geopolitical value. The tribes living on their shores were self-sufficient. The rise of the Varyag economy, however, changed everything. Not only did links become possible and necessary between the wealthy and developed Byzantine south and the dynamically developing Varyag north. There was now a need to maintain order and safety throughout the territory of the long river route. A unified state was essential.

It was no accident that the founders of Russian statehood were the Novgorodians, who were not so much warriors as merchants. Nor was it mere chance that in the establishing of the Russian state, the Varyags played a highly active role. It was not that the Varyags subjugated the Slavs, nor that the Slavs united themselves, but that numerous Slavic, Finno-Ugrian and Scandinavian tribes and armed groups located along the rivers joined forces to make up a state. The Slavs, as the most numerous, were dominant. The Varyags provided the beginnings of a military elite. The Finno-Ugrian tribes were subdued and assimilated.

KIEV AND ITS ENEMIES

In his book *The Origin of the Family, Private Property and the State*, Friedrich Engels wrote that the state amounts to organised coercion, and arises when society becomes divided into classes. Studying the East, Marx noted another reason for the formation of a state – the need for the organising and maintenance of an irrigation system on extensive territories. This also required compulsion – labour power had to be moved about in accordance with a centralised plan – but it was possible for the class division of society to be present only in embryo. The history of Russia shows that the need for a state could also arise in just as compelling a way when it became necessary to maintain order along trade routes. In this sense, Russian statehood was originally close to the 'Asiatic model', but at the same time it developed in continual, close contact with Western Europe. The state ensured the safety of trade. It was not at all a matter of the ethnic unity of the Slavs. The new state power included Finno-Ugrians, Varyags and, later on, Greeks. It was not tribes that were being united, but territories. On the broad expanses through which the navigable rivers flowed, there needed to be a system of security and a unified authority. From a certain point, control over territory would become an end in itself for the rulers, but that would only come later. In the early period, all that was needed was order along the route followed by the merchant convoys. 'This was trade organised in regular fashion by the state authorities', wrote the historian of Byzantium, G.G. Litavrin.[14] The Novgorodian elite knew why they were inviting the Varyag warriors.

Moving south toward Kiev, the Novgorodian traders and Varyag troops united vast territories in an astonishingly brief period, and ensured an uninterrupted flow of goods and knowledge in the direction of the Baltic. Russia as a state had its genesis in a transit route. Describing the organisation of the first Russian state, V.O. Klyuchevsky remarks:

There is no mistaking the fundamental economic interest that governed this life, drawing together and uniting separate and fragmented areas of land. The tribute that came to the Kiev prince and his retainers fed the growing foreign trade of Rus. This same commercial interest also directed the foreign activity of the first Kiev princes. This activity had two main goals: 1) to obtain overseas markets; and 2) to open up and protect the trade routes that led to these markets.[15]

Of course, trade in the middle ages was by no means a peaceful pursuit. If the Dutch in the seventeenth century said that war and trade always accompanied one another, this was even more true in the ninth and tenth centuries. Mikhail Pokrovsky notes that the life of Rus at this time was typified by 'a combination of war, trade and brigandage.'[16] Klyuchevsky also observes that the Russian military campaigns against Tsargrad (Constantinople) were invariably linked to commercial conflicts, while the peace agreements that ended the wars were usually 'commercial treaties':

All the agreements between Rus and the tenth-century Greeks that have come down to us have this commercial character. Of the agreements of this period, we have two negotiated by Oleg, one by Igor and one short agreement, or the basis for an agreement, by Svyatoslav. The agreements were drawn up in Greek, and with due changes of form, were translated into a language understandable to the Russians. Reading these agreements, it is not hard to see the interests that linked Rus with Byzantium in the tenth century. In these documents, we find the conduct of the annual trade dealings between Rus and Byzantium set out with ever greater detail and precision, and also the way in which the Russians in Constantinople were to conduct their personal relations with Greeks. In this respect, the agreements are distinguished by their remarkable development of juridical norms, especially as regards international law.[17]

A fight had to be waged not only with bandits, but also with the nomads who roamed the steppes of the lower Dnepr, the 'Savage Fields'. Although the Pechenegs and later the Polovtsy mounted frequent raids on Russian towns, the more usual cause of the expeditions against them was the obstacle which the nomads posed to trade with the Greeks. The Russian forays into the Savage Fields were primarily punitive expeditions, a fact the Kievan princes did not conceal. Explaining to his troops the reason for a campaign against the Polovtsy in 1167, Prince Mstislav stated plainly that they needed to be punished, since they were interfering with trade. 'They are preventing travel on the Greek route, on the salt route and the iron route.'[18] By the 'Greek' route Mstislav meant the one from Constantinople, while the 'salt' route linked Kiev with the Greek colonies in Crimea and, in the view of Solovyev, the 'iron' route provided supplies of metalwares from Byzantium and the Near East.[19] After defeating the Pechenegs or Polovtsy, the retainers of the Kiev princes would often follow the Dnepr downstream, and wait there for merchant convoys.

At least until the end of the twelfth century, the struggle of Rus with the steppe peoples was successful. The Pechenegs were conquered, and from bandits were gradually transformed into commercial intermediaries. While not themselves merchants, they took control of what we might now call 'information brokerage' between the Greeks and Russians. From the Greeks of Cherson they received trade commissions, something like mail orders, which they forwarded to Russian merchants in Kiev before navigation began on the rivers. The Cherson commissions, the Soviet historian Litavrin writes, 'consisted of orders by assortment and quantity of particular goods from Rus, so that these would be available by the time (in spring?) when the goods ordered from the Cherson merchants arrived in Rus'.[20] With a little exaggeration, it might be said that the Greeks ordered goods via the Pechenegs in the same way as people in our time order them through the internet.

The Pechenegs gradually became assimilated with the Russians. A new threat to the trade between Russians and Greeks was the Polovtsy, but by the early thirteenth century they too had been transformed from enemies of Rus to its allies (it was to defend the Polovtsians against a new, previously unknown steppe people that a Russian army went in 1223 to the River Kalka, where it was routed by the Tatars).

Rus also waged numerous wars against the Khazars, who in the ninth and tenth centuries controlled the southern part of the route from the Varyags to the Greeks. Before the rise of Kievan Rus, the Khazars had been dominant in trade as well. The unification of the entire river route under a single power also required the removal of the Khazars. Initially, the struggle went ahead with varying degrees of success. For example, the Radimichi, who lived on the border territories, paid tribute to Kiev and the Khazars by turns. Other allies of the Khazars were the Vyatichi. It was only in the year 966 that Prince Svyatoslav finally crushed the Khazars, subduing the Vyatichi at the same time.

The attitude of the Greeks to the Russian trade was ambiguous at first. On the one hand, Constantinople needed raw materials, while, on the other, the merchant convoys were painfully reminiscent of military expeditions. Every spring some 100–200 ships set out from Kiev, not only laden with goods, but also accompanied by an impressive protective force. Without military protection, the convoys could not have passed round the Dnepr rapids, where they would have been easy prey for the nomads. When such convoys arrived at Cherson or Constantinople, they themselves posed a threat to the Greeks. The Byzantine authorities thus tried to limit access by the Russians to the Bosphorus, which in turn aroused the displeasure of the Russians and provoked conflicts.

There are records of seven Russian military campaigns against the Greeks. In the year 860 or 865 the Kievan ruler Askold mounted the first expedition against Byzantium to avenge the murder of Russian merchants there. According to the Russian chronicles, Prince Igor twice set out against Constantinople. Later, Svyatoslav waged war in Bulgaria, first as an ally of the emperor, and then in 971 as his enemy. Vladimir Krasnoe Solnyshko, before ordering the baptism of Rus in the Greek rite, first sacked the Byzantine city of Cherson in Crimea. The last such campaign was organised in 1043 by Vladimir's son Yaroslav.

Most of these campaigns were something between pillaging raids and punitive expeditions, and it was only Svyatoslav, in the Balkans, who conducted a genuine drawn-out war. Svyatoslav first waged war on the Khazars, Volga Bulgars and Vyatichi, defeating them and laying the groundwork for a Russian princedom in Tmutarakan, in the Crimean peninsula. Then, in response to a plea from the Byzantine Emperor Nikifor, he went to Bulgaria as an ally of the Greeks. The alliance was paid for with a substantial amount of Byzantine gold, with the Greeks also promising to leave Bulgaria in Svyatoslav's hands if he could conquer it. As well as everything else, the Greek ambassador Kalokir made a personal deal with Svyatoslav: if the latter could help him become emperor in place of Nikifor, the help would be rewarded with countless riches from the imperial treasury.

In the year 967 Svyatoslav's army arrived in Bulgaria. The country was conquered, with the victors taking ferocious revenge on their 'brother Slavs'. Svyatoslav remained in Pereyaslavets on the Danube, leaving Kiev without a ruler. The prince's ageing mother, the Princess Olga, could no longer cope with the tasks of administration, the Pecheneg nomads were at the gates of the capital, and discontent was rising within the city itself. The citizens of Kiev sent Svyatoslav a reproachful letter:

You, prince, seek a foreign land and watch over it, while you have renounced your own. The Pechenegs have almost captured us together with your mother and children. If you do not come and defend us, they will take us next time. Have you really no pity for your homeland, for your aged mother, or for your little children?[21]

Svyatoslav had to return. But after spending a certain time in Kiev, he divided up power between his sons and made off for the Balkans, where he encountered a new Byzantine emperor, Ionn Tsimishiy. The Bulgarians had no wish to let the Russians back into Pereyaslavets, while the Greeks were trying to force Svyatoslav out of Bulgaria. Meanwhile, the Russian prince was threatening to seize Greek towns just as he had seized Bulgarian ones. Despite the desperate courage of the Russian army, Svyatoslav had no chance of victory, since the Greeks could put significantly more troops in the field and, most importantly, Svyatoslav could not make up his losses. He was forced to leave Bulgaria. On the way back, he fell into a Pecheneg ambush and was killed. They made a cup from his skull, decorating it with gold and drinking from it.

It is not surprising that the military campaigns of Svyatoslav aroused sharp debate among nineteenth-century historians. To Karamzin, Prince Svyatoslav was the 'Alexander of our early history'. Unlike Alexander the Great, however, Prince Svyatoslav did not found a state, and ended up utterly defeated. Therefore,

Svyatoslav, the model of the great commander, is not the model of the great sovereign, since he had more regard for the glory of victories than for the good of the state. While his personality captivates the imagination of the poet, Svyatoslav merits the reproach of the historian.[22]

To Karamzin, in other words, Prince Svyatoslav was in the nature of an irresponsible military adventurer, whose bravery was in essence foolish. Historians of the second half of the nineteenth century were still more categorical, declaring that when the Kievan prince set off for the Balkans, he had in view 'nothing but plunder'.[23] Soviet authors, by contrast, set out to show that Svyatoslav's actions were aimed 'at resolving major tasks of state that required the exertion of all his strength'.[24]

Meanwhile, the interpretation of these 'tasks of state' was at times thoroughly in line with the geopolitics of the nineteenth century – to strengthen the Russian presence in the Balkans, to defend the brother Slavs from the expansion of the Byzantine empire, and so forth. At odd moments, mention is made of the need to protect trade routes; this is mainly with reference to the earlier campaigns against the Khazars.

In reality, it is impossible to detect any geopolitical logic in the actions of Svyatoslav. He first waged war on the side of the Greeks against the Bulgarians, then against the Greeks and Bulgarians simultaneously. He directed his forces to the south-east, then, without completing what he had undertaken, rushed to the south-west. Nevertheless, it is also hard to describe Svyatoslav's campaigns as bandit raids. If he had wanted plunder, he had no need to go to the Balkans, since he could have attacked the wealthy Greek cities in Crimea. Also, the military, political and diplomatic organisation that lay behind the campaigns was too complex for simple pillaging expeditions. In those times, of course, there was no such thing as war without plunder. Does this mean, however, that the prince had no goals apart from brigandage? A number of writers suspect that the Russian chronicles greatly exaggerate both the strength of Svyatoslav's forces and their success. Nevertheless, it is clear that the campaigns were painstakingly prepared, diplomatically as well as in the technical military sense. The naval actions were coordinated with those on land, the military operations were interspersed with negotiations, and so forth. A struggle of this sort presupposes a more or less developed state, in which the elite can no longer allow itself to live by simple banditry.

Svyatoslav went further than others; he tried, even if without particular success, to do what subsequent Russian rulers would also do over the centuries. The Kievan prince fought for military and political control over trade routes. The site of the main conflict with the Greeks and Bulgarians was the mouth of the Danube, which united the route from the Varyags to the Greeks with another European trade artery that was rapidly taking shape. On capturing the Bulgarian city of Pereyaslavets, Svyatoslav declared:

I do not like it in Kiev; I want to live in Pereyaslavets on the Danube. There is the middle of my lands, and goods of all sorts are brought there from all sides – from the Greeks, gold, cloth, wines, and various spices; from the Czechs and Hungarians, silver and horses; from Rus, furs, wax, honey and slaves.[25]

As S.M. Solovyev correctly notes, the conclusion can be drawn from this that Pereyaslavets was designated as the centre not in relation to its position among the territories Svyatoslav controlled, but as the 'mid-point of trade'.[26]

Unfortunately, the goal Svyatoslav had set for Rus was beyond the country's strength. The prince mistook the situation, putting his stake exclusively on the superiority of his army, and failing to understand that this war did not consist simply of battles. He did not succeed in consolidating the victories he had won in the Volga region and in the Balkans. Moreover, the defeat inflicted on the Khazars created more problems for Rus than it brought gains.

THE FATE OF THE KHAZARS

History is written by victors, and in this respect the fate of the Khazars resembles that of Carthage. We view the history of this state primarily through the prism of Russian history, just as we view Carthage through a Roman prism. The hostility with which some authors wrote of the Khazars arouses the suspicion that this is linked to the dominant religion among the Khazars – Judaism. Hence B.A. Rybakov, for example, insists that the Khazar state was 'parasitical', and hence destined to destruction.[27] The Soviet scholar M.I. Artamonov admits in straightforward fashion that the view of Khazar history held by many writers was distorted by hostility toward Jews.[28]

Meanwhile, the notion that the Khazar state was Jewish is also less than completely accurate. The subjects of the Khazar khan included Christians, Jews and Muslims. Between 851 and 863 Christianity was preached on these territories by St Cyril, the same individual who together with Methodius is famed for his missionary activity in Moravia, and who devised the Slavonic alphabet. Cyril was received at the court of the khagan, where he repeatedly argued questions of faith with the local rabbis. An Orthodox bishopric operated on the territory of the khaganate, and Islam was also widespread. The French historian René Grousset considers that Judaism, which was officially accepted by the Khazar khagans late in the eighth century, was mainly a religion of the court and of the Khazar aristocracy; 'among the people, Muslims and Christians seem to have outnumbered the Jews'.[29] In the tenth century one of the khagans converted to Islam for political reasons, and in the early eleventh century the Taman peninsula was ruled by a Khazar khagan who had accepted Orthodoxy and taken the Greek name Georgy. On a few occasions, khagans entered into conflict with the Greek and Islamic worlds over issues of faith, but for the most part they traded with both. From 695 to 705 the Greek emperor Justinian II hid from his enemies among the Khazars, marrying a sister of the khagan who became the Empress Theodora.

The Soviet historian M.I. Artamonov, in his *History of the Khazars*, writes:

The elevation of Judaism to the state religion was an act of political self-affirmation, a demonstration not only of independence, but also of the equality of the Khazar khaganate with the Byzantine empire and the Arab khalifate. It was also a reply to attempts by both to subordinate the Khazars to their interests. In foreign policy terms, this was an extremely effective act. The Khazars raised Judaism to the status of a third world religion, but were unable to consolidate this position for it, because the ancient Judaism was less suited to a feudal society than the younger religions, Christianity and Islam.[30]

The adoption of Judaism by the ruling class did not require that the subject population be converted in large numbers to this faith. The medieval Jewish tradition, unlike its Christian and Muslim counterparts, took a very restrained and at times negative attitude to attempts to convert members of other ethnic groups. In the Khazar lands, the hereditary character of the Jewish faith made it the distinctive ideology of the ruling layer, a mark differentiating this layer from other dwellers in the khanate, who professed different religions.

In ethnic terms, the population of the khaganate was not homogeneous either. The Khazars themselves were Turks, but controlled extensive territories colonised earlier by Greeks. Meanwhile, the official adoption of Judaism created the conditions for Jewish immigration from Byzantium, especially in the tenth century, when Jews there were undergoing persecution. The population of the khaganate was thus an ethnic conglomerate of Turks, Jews and Greeks, just as Kievan Rus united Slavs, Scandinavians and Finno-Ugrian tribes in the one territory. Such formations typically feature an ethnic division of labour, and here a Hellenised rural population and Jewish and Muslim merchants and tradesmen were subject to a Khazar military aristocracy.

'The Jewish religion did not displace either the old paganism, or Christianity, or Islam', writes Artamonov. 'The religious tolerance of the Khazars was an exception to the religious practice that was usual in the middle ages, but among the Khazars it was not elevated into theory, and was not a principle of the internal politics of the Khazar government.'[31] The religious pluralism of the

Khazars was thus not only the result of parallel missionary activity, but also a consequence of ethnic diversity.

Meanwhile, the rivalry of three religions in the Khazar state shows that there was nothing far-fetched about the story, related in the Russian chronicles, concerning an analogous rivalry in Kiev, when preachers of Christianity, Islam and Judaism came in turn to Prince Vladimir. The victory of the 'Kievan khagan' Svyatoslav over the Khazars did not mean the complete annihilation of their state. As Artamonov notes, once Svyatoslav had begun the war, he sought to 'take complete control of the Eastern trade, which played an extremely important role in the economy of the Russian state'.[32] The Kievan prince, however, was unable to maintain his hold on the territories he had seized.

Drawn into a difficult war on the Danube, he was forced to divert his attention from the east before he could succeed in consolidating the Russian hold on the Volga region. Rus retained control only of the Don region and of the shores of the Kerch straits, while the Volga Bulgars and Khazars, it appears, were not subject to Rus for long, and re-established their independence.[33]

After Svyatoslav's campaigns, a military and political vacuum appeared in the south-east. Rus, Khorezm and Byzantium fought with varying success over the fragments of the Khazar khaganate. The Khazar state was finally crushed only in the year 1016, by a joint expedition of Russians and Greeks in Taman and Crimea. René Grousset notes in this regard that when the Greeks and Rus joined forces to destroy the khanate, they 'badly miscalculated'.[34] It was Khazaria that had played the role of a covering force blocking the path of the nomadic tribes. These tribes had moved westward across an area of steppeland south of Kiev, an area ruled by the Khazars. The decline of the Khazars had begun with an unsuccessful attempt to hold back the movement of the Hungarians. The defeat of the Khazar armies by Svyatoslav resulted in the Pechenegs feeling themselves much more free. The consequences of this for Rus were already being felt under Svyatoslav; first the Pechenegs, no longer restrained by the Khazars, approached Kiev without hindrance, and then Svyatoslav himself died at their hands. After crushing the Khazars, Rus proved unable to establish political control over the whole vast territory that had earlier been subject to the khanate – except for the small but very wealthy princedom of Tmutarakan, where a Slavic-Varyag military aristocracy took the place of its Khazar predecessor. The rest of the territory became part of the Savage Fields, where tribes of nomads moved about unobstructed. The Pechenegs were soon replaced by the much more dangerous Polovtsy, and in the thirteenth century the Mongols came by the same route.

CHRISTIANITY AND TRADE

Svyatoslav's campaigns in the Balkans ended in total defeat, but their main result was that in the Black Sea region between Kiev and Constantinople, the spheres of influence were definitively settled. From the time of Prince Vladimir, the military and commercial expansion southward by the Kievan princes was replaced by collaboration with the Byzantines. Vladimir still carried out a pillaging expedition to Crimea, but it was he who acted as the decisive champion of Greek religious and political influence in Kiev. Rus was being stabilised, and from now on, Kiev would no longer act as a rival of Constantinople but as an ally. Conflicts arose from time to time between Kiev and Constantinople, but collaboration predominated. Russian merchants received exceptional commercial privileges in Byzantium. The Greek emperor recruited warriors for his forces in Rus. Tradesmen, priests and counsellors went from Constantinople to Kiev.

The Christianisation of Rus, begun by Princess Olga and completed by Vladimir, was the logical result of this process. In both Rus and Scandinavia, Christian merchants had preceded the missionaries. Even before the Christianising of Denmark, the building of Christian churches had been an important matter for the local kings, since it allowed them to attract traders. Now, as the chronicles note, merchants came 'readily and without any fear', and as a result 'there was an abundant supply of goods of every kind'.[35] Traders returning from Constantinople, along with their Greek colleagues, spread Christianity in Rus not only to Prince Vladimir, but also to Princess Olga. The first church, that of St Ilya, was built in Kiev in the year 940, while Princess Olga was baptised only in the 950s. It was only in 988 that Vladimir officially adopted Orthodoxy as the state religion.

Since the mid nineteenth century, liberal historians have seen the adoption of the Eastern rite of Christianity as a supreme misfortune for Russia, since it meant that in matters of religion the country put itself in opposition to the West. The truth was that in the time of Prince Vladimir the schism between the Eastern and Western churches was not yet complete or definitive. The effect of baptism, even if by the Byzantine rite, was not therefore to counterpose Rus to Western Europe, but, on the contrary, to draw it closer. Much more importantly, Byzantium in the time of Olga and Vladimir was a developed and enlightened country, while the West was still only in the process of overcoming the Dark Ages. The story in the chronicles of how Vladimir sent a diplomatic mission to various countries to compare the Islamic, Catholic and Orthodox forms of worship is usually considered to be an invention of later chroniclers. But even if this is so, the story still speaks volumes. The Russian ambassadors were struck above all by the magnificence of the Orthodox churches in Constantinople, by 'the rich vestments, the decoration of the icons, the beauty of the paintings, and the perfume of the incense', while the rites of the Catholics were 'lacking in any grandeur or beauty'.[36] By orienting themselves culturally toward Byzantium, the Kievan princes gained a huge advantage over their neighbours to the west.

OLD RUSSIAN URBANISATION

If the eastern Slavs in the eighth century had possessed neither a developed state nor large cities, 200 years later a mighty and extremely wealthy power extended from the Baltic to the Black Sea. It not only encompassed a vast territory, but astonished foreigners with the number and wealth of its cities. At the beginning of the ninth century the Byzantines still knew nothing of Rus, but in the year 860 the patriarch Fotiy was already speaking of the Russians as a people who not long before had been unknown, but who were quickly attaining 'brilliant heights and incalculable riches'.[37] Foreign travellers called Kievan Rus 'a land of cities'.[38] The wealth and development of Rus, recognised by the Greeks, was even more striking to Scandinavians. As historians note,

According to the incomplete data of the Russian chronicles, there were eighty-six cities and towns in eleventh-century Rus. In the twelfth century the chronicles mention a further one hundred and twenty urban centres, and by the time of the Mongol-Tatar invasion, that is, the early thirteenth century, the number had reached two hundred and fifty. In reality, there were significantly more, since not all cities and towns were mentioned in the chronicles.[39]

The Soviet scholar M.N. Tikhomirov counted 271 cities and towns in Rus. By comparison, Germany in the year 900 had only 30. Even taking into account the fact that Tikhomirov's data refer to a later period, the contrast is striking.[40]

Of course, and as I.N. Danilevsky notes, the urban centres involved were not always towns 'in our sense of the word'.[41] In the ninth and tenth centuries, the word for 'town' or 'city' (*gorod*) could also denote a village surrounded by a palisade, or a prince's fortress. Nevertheless, the testimonies of Arab travellers – who, unlike backward Westerners, were familiar with developed urban culture – leave no doubt that the level of urbanisation in Kievan Rus was quite remarkable. 'The Russians in general struck the Arabs as a non-agrarian people who occupied themselves solely with trade and military campaigns', modern scholars observe.[42] In the view of the Arab travellers, at least a third of the people were engaged 'exclusively in international trade'.[43] The Arab traveller Ibn-Dast encountered no villages at all in Rus; it appeared to him that the Russians all lived in towns!

If some regional centres were no more than overgrown princely estates, Kiev and Novgorod were unquestionably among the most impressive cities in Europe at that time, and not only in terms of their size, but also of their public amenities. The streets in Novgorod had wooden pavements, which distinguished the city sharply from most centres in the West. According to archaeologists, the oldest of these pavements dated from the year 953, and the latest from the mid fifteenth century.

In Western Europe in the ninth and tenth centuries, monetary circulation was still poorly developed. The Russians, by contrast, traded with the Byzantines and Arabs, who paid in silver; consequently, the economy of Rus was far more market-oriented. This is also recognised by Western historians.

Viewed from the economic and social point of view, Kievan Russia was in some ways more advanced than backward manorial Western Europe, where markets, fairs and industries were only beginning to spring up in Flanders, along the Baltic shore, and in northern Italy.[44]

In Rus it was not the natural economy that was dominant, but commodity-money relations. In the ninth and tenth centuries, Rus exported silver to Scandinavia.[45]

This silver was coming for the most part not from Byzantium, but from the countries of the East. Late in the ninth century, large deposits of silver were discovered in the territory of modern-day Afghanistan. The Samanid shahs were able to mint large numbers of coins, helping trade to flourish not only in Central Asia, but also in the Caspian region and along the Volga. The study of hoards has led historians and numismatists to conclude that 'European-Arab trade arose late in the eighth century, in the form of trade between Eastern Europe and the countries of the khalifate'.[46]

Of course, not all the coins arrived in Rus or Scandinavia as a result of trading operations. Silver could simply be stolen. Such distinctions, however, have importance only for people living according to the ideas of later times. In the age of early medieval trade, plunder and military service were interlinked.

Samanid coins began arriving in Rus around the year 910. Samanid dirhams became popular coins in Rus, and from there reached the Scandinavian countries, in turn stimulating trade in the Baltic. Kiev also minted its own coins, but in insignificant numbers. There was no need for them – money was coming in abundance from the south. The minting of coins in Kiev was evidently dictated less by economic needs than by political ones. It was necessary to show that the Kievan prince was in no way inferior to his southern neighbours. The monetary circulation in Kievan Rus reflected the peculiarities of the country, situated, as a modern-day historian has put it, 'between the Arabs and the Varyags, the West and Constantinople'. In the same way, the system of weights and measures that became established in Rus showed clear traces of 'interethnic cultural reciprocity'.[47] From Rus, wax, honey, furs, hunting falcons and slaves were sent to Byzantium, to the Arab countries and to the Khazars. The slave trade was an important source of income for the 'robber merchants', and, as Pokrovsky notes, it was not only foreign captives who were sold into slavery but also fellow tribespeople, especially young women.[48]

Later, Russian princes provided the Greeks with military help in return for money – also an example of the export of services. As early as the year 910, long before the Christianisation of Rus, Russian warriors staged a raid on the Caspian region of Persia, evidently by agreement with the Greeks. In the same year, a Russian force landed on Crete as part of a Byzantine army. When a Byzantine army disembarked in Italy in the year 935, it again included a Russian detachment, probably made up not only of Slavs but also of Varyags. In 964, according to Arab historians, Russians fought against the Saracens in Sicily 'as hirelings of the Greeks'.[49]

Subsequently, the Byzantine army always included a 'Russian corps'; in the eleventh and twelfth centuries its numbers were made up not only of Russians and Scandinavians, but also of English. Finally, and as historians note, the links between the Russian and Byzantine churches included not only religious but also commercial ties.[50]

When the Russians founded the Crimean princedom of Tmutarakan on lands formerly controlled by the Khazars, they obtained an important commercial and military outpost. Historians record that while the princes and soldiers were Russians, the population of Tmutarakan 'consisted in the main not of Slavic immigrants, but of local people', that is, Greeks or Hellenised Crimeans.[51] According to Artamonov, economic power in the city lay in the hands of 'Jewish-Khazar merchants'. This group consisted both of Khazars of Jewish faith, and of ethnic Jews who 'after the adoption by the Khazars of the Judaic religion had come to be considered Khazars'.[52]

Turks and Greeks, like the Varyags earlier, increasingly became part of Russian society. From Tmutarakan an important strategic raw material – oil – was exported to the empire. It was used in preparing the 'Greek fire' that was hurled by the imperial fleet. These supplies were so important for Byzantium that late in the tenth century, on the threshold of the Crusades, the Greeks seized Tmutarakan from the Russian princes.

THE FLOURISHING OF TRADE

Manufactured goods, jewellery, wines and bullion flowed from the East to the North. In this trade, furs also held a special place. The fact that Rus supplied furs to Arab cities might appear somewhat comic, but such was then the fashion. Solovyev writes:

The demand for furs grew in the East with the spread of wealth and luxury during the splendid reign of Harun al-Rashid. Fur coats came to be highly regarded as clothing, and were purchased for large sums. We are told that it was Zobeyda, the wife of Harun, who first created the fashion for coats lined with the fur of Russian ermines or sables. As well as furs, the Russians also brought slaves to the Volga. In exchange for these goods, the Russians could obtain from the Arabs precious stones; beads, especially of a green colour (strings of these were the favourite jewellery of Russian women, whose husbands ruined themselves by often paying a dirham, fifteen to twenty silver kopecks, for each bead); gold and silver wares; chains; other jewellery such as bracelets, rings and pins; sword-hilts; buttons; metal plates for the decoration of clothing and harnesses, and perhaps also silken, woollen and cotton cloth, herbs, spices and wine. But as can be seen, the Russians were especially anxious to exchange their goods for Arab coins, dirhams, which were of great value in any place and for any purpose. By this route, the Arab coins spread through diverse areas of the Russian provinces of the time. As rare, always valuable objects, they passed as adornments from family to family, from hand to hand. They were buried in graves along with the dead, or were buried in hoards, and in this way have come down to us.[53]

A substantial proportion of the goods were delivered to the Khazar town of Itil, and from there were resold to the Middle East by Jewish merchants. But as Pokrovsky notes, Russisan merchants also made the journey to Baghdad, and Arabs travelled about Russia. Trade flourished, and 'it was a rare monarch in Eastern countries who did not have a coat made of Russian furs'.[54]

While silver coins were brought in their hundreds of thousands from the East, manufactured items were coming from Byzantium. The movement of silver was thoroughly studied by historians in Soviet times. 'Using archaeological methods, the Byzantine and northern maritime imports have been traced along the whole extent of the "route from the Varyags to the Greeks", and to the region of Beloozero.'[55] Scandinavian sources also bear witness that from Greece, the Varyags preferred to obtain 'silk and other cloth, metal and glassware and wines, rather than cash'.[56] The Russians were also anxious to acquire manufactured goods from Constantinople. Overall, Rus had a trade deficit with Byzantium, and a surplus in its trade with Islamic countries. To Byzantium, the Russians supplied mainly raw materials for manufacturing, obtaining in return the products of Greek workshops, while to the south they sent luxury items and slaves in return for silver, which the Persians and Arabs had in abundance. 'Islamic goods were certainly imported into Russia and some reached Scandinavia', wrote P. Sawyer in *Kings and Vikings*,

but the demand in the caliphate for Russian produce appears to have been so much greater than the reciprocal demand for Islamic goods that the balance was paid in silver, which for many of those involved was acceptable and may even have been preferred. Some Islamic coins were exported from Russia to neighbouring parts of Europe and large numbers have been found in Scandinavia.[57]

As G. Litavrin observes, many Russians and Varyags also set off to Byzantium 'for wages'.[58] This was clearly a phenomenon of some scope, since it was specifically regulated by Russian-Byzantine agreements. At the same time, about a thousand Russians were to be found in Constantinople. The Varyags and Russians in the Byzantine capital were not emigrants, but traders, religious figures (intellectuals), and also, as we would now say, *Gastarbeiter* (foreign workers) – tradesmen and hired soldiers who planned, after they had accumulated money and expertise, to return to their homeland.[59]

After the Christianisation of Russia, the trade in goods was accompanied by the spread of Greek enlightenment and technology. In the Middle Ages 'technology transfer' meant, as a rule, the resettling of people. In the tenth and eleventh centuries this was occurring between Byzantium and Rus on a massive scale, with 'the migration of tradesmen and the organisation of production in new places, and the arrival of "tradesmen from Greece" for the building and decorating of churches'.[60] Master glassmakers from Constantinople settled in Kiev. It is typical that this same type of production began developing rapidly in Venice 200 years later, when the necessary technology became available in Western Europe as a result of the Crusades. Church utensils produced using Byzantine techniques were arriving in large quantities in Scandinavia, where Christianisation was occurring later than in Rus. Just as Byzantium had far outstripped the other European countries, Rus in the tenth and eleventh centuries was clearly ahead of most countries of the West in its cultural and technological development. Although Kievan Rus was not renowned for its own discoveries, its close ties to Byzantium allowed it to develop more quickly than the Western states. As military historians remark,

Where armour is concerned, chain mail was known in Rus from the tenth century, while this type of equipment appeared in Western Europe only in the eleventh and twelfth centuries. Chronicle sources also establish that Russians in the period from the tenth to the twelfth centuries were not only familiar with 'Greek fire', but also knew how to use flame-throwing weapons.[61]

In the twelfth century there are already instances of the mass production of weapons. In the view of archaeologists, the level of military production had become 'immense'.[62]

Numismatists remark on the high quality of the minting of Kievan coins compared with Western European examples from the same period.[63] In the twelfth century Rus was ahead of the countries of northern Europe in the level of its metalworking. Clear proof of this is provided both by archaeological evidence and by chronicle sources. As historians note:

The metalworking industry was using complex technical methods such as the heat-treatment of steel, various methods of cold processing, and welding. To prepare the most common products, knives, steel was welded onto the iron core of the blade. The two and three-layered knives were of especially high quality during the first stage of development of the trade in Novgorod.[64]

The development of craft production meant that by the twelfth century Rus was already exporting to Byzantium not only raw materials, but also manufactured products, including works of art.[65] Russian products have been found in Corinth, and the Byzantine poet Ioann Tsepa mentioned 'an ink-well of Russian manufacture that had been given to him'.[66] Still more manufactured goods were exported from Russia to other European countries.

To export Russian products to the East was more difficult, since here the local production was on an incomparably higher level than in the West. Nevertheless, Russians managed to export weapons and armour (which were taken as far as India), flax and linen cloth. Right up until the fourteenth century all these goods continued to be sent regularly from Rus to the east, regardless of historical upheavals. Flax was exported through Derbent, and from there reached Central Asia, Persia and India.[67] In this fashion, Russian agriculture too began gradually to be drawn into international trade. Agricultural practices as well were being improved. During this period of Russian history, geographical closeness to the Greek lands was a decisive factor even within the country. Hence in the southern regions of Rus, nearer to Byzantium, peasants used the iron ploughshare, while cultivators in the north used the wooden scratch plough.

Over a period of 200 years, Russian and Soviet historians followed the chronicles in stating the importance of the'route from the Varyags to the Greeks, but it is striking that with few exceptions they showed no particular interest in this route. After repeating in general phrases the evidence contained in the chronicles, they move on immediately to describing princely strife and military campaigns, or to polemics on the role of Scandinavian (Varyag) princes in Novgorod and Kiev. Among a great multitude of works on Kievan Rus in the catalogue of Moscow's Historical Library, you will find scarcely half a dozen books on the ties between Rus and Byzantium. On the route from the Varyags to the Greeks, there is not even one! Russian-Byzantine relations have been approached mainly from the point of view of church history, and sometimes on the level of the cultural influence of the Greeks on Rus.[68] But trading relations preceded cultural exchanges by at least a century! It could be said that the medieval Russian chroniclers showed a better understanding of the historical process than the scholars of the nineteenth and twentieth centuries.

What is the reason for the extremely limited interest in the 'Byzantine trail' in Russian history? On the one hand, no one denies the Byzantine influence, so unlike the 'Scandinavian theory', it cannot be a topic for political discussions. On the other hand, Byzantium has been on the periphery of Russian ideological consciousness. The 'Westernising' school took a hostile attitude to everything Byzantine, seeing in the Greek and Orthodox influence an obstacle to cultural integration with the West. For the champions of 'uniqueness' and those sympathetic to Byzantium, meanwhile, the Scandinavians were just as repellent. Since the Westernisers paid special attention to the Varyags, the entire polemic of the 'native soil' current was directed against the Scandinavian theory. Neither school was prepared to acknowledge that Rus arose precisely as the point of contact between Byzantines and Scandinavians.

The situation changed little in the Soviet period. Interest in economic history grew somewhat under the influence of Marxism, but Soviet historians devoted their attention mainly to local production, and also to the relations that were taking shape on the feudal estates. After the purging of the Pokrovsky school in the 1930s, trade was rarely considered to merit specific study. Such a concentration of attention on the agrarian economy was fully justified in the case of Western Europe. There the medieval economy really did grow out of the natural economy. Rus, however, knew virtually nothing of the natural economy in the Western sense of the word. More precisely, in the era of the natural economy there was neither a Russian state, nor a Russian people. In trying to understand 'whence the Russian land is come', the chroniclers immediately and quite justifiably pointed to trade.

2
The Thirteenth-Century Decline

If Russia in its early history seemed so prosperous and developed, why was the main goal of the state from the seventeenth until the late twentieth century overcoming the gap in relation to the West? What was the cause of the backwardness? From late in the eighteenth century, liberal historians sought to identify the reason in the 200 years of the 'Tatar yoke'. This view goes back to Karamzin.

The cloak of barbarism that darkened the Russian horizon hid Europe from us at the very time when beneficial knowledge and skills were increasingly multiplying there, when the people were freeing themselves from servitude, and when close bonds were being forged between cities for their mutual defence in troubled times; when the discovery of the compass had widened navigation and trade; when governments were encouraging artisans, artists and scholars; when universities were arising for the pursuit of higher learning; when minds were growing used to contemplation, to correctness of thought; when manners were becoming more mild; when wars were losing their earlier ferocity; when the well-born had grown ashamed of slaughters, and when noble heroes were famed for their mercy to the weak, for their magnanimity and honour; when urbanity, humaneness and courtesy had become known and admired.[1]

WAS THE TATAR YOKE TO BLAME?

Unfortunately, the picture which Karamzin draws of successful development in Western Europe is far from truthful. The main burden of the Tatar yoke was felt in the fourteenth century. Russian historians who lay the blame for their country's backwardness on the Tatar yoke rarely ask what was happening in the West at this time. The fourteenth century in Europe was a time of ruinous wars, of economic crisis and of plague. In the early years of the century Italy and southern France did indeed develop quickly, but this development was followed by a drawn-out economic crisis that would only be overcome completely in the following century. Finally, it is not altogether clear what is meant by the collective term 'the West'. The rates of development and the level attained were markedly different, depending on whether we are looking at Italy or at Hungary, Bohemia or Poland.

As a true representative of his time, Karamzin sees the source of the problems in a lack of enlightenment, which in turn was due to oppression. 'Russia, tormented by the Mongols, harnessed all its forces to the sole aim of surviving; enlightenment was not within our powers!'[2] Later historians sought the reasons for backwardness either in Orthodoxy, or in the 'unfortunate' unification of the Russian lands around Moscow, and not beneath the banners of Tver, Lithuania or Novgorod. In the twentieth century the two latter explanations became less popular, but references to the Tatar yoke became a common element in all the textbooks of the Soviet era. Soviet historians continually stressed that

while Kievan Rus in the tenth and eleventh centuries and the Russian princedoms in the twelfth and thirteenth centuries followed the same path as the advanced countries of Western Europe, without falling behind them, the Tatar-Mongol invasion, which lasted for more than two hundred years, disturbed the normal life of Rus for a prolonged period. It held back the development of the productive forces, of technology, of learning and of culture.[3]

Western historians, following their Russian colleagues, repeated the argument that the Tatar invasion 'had an effect of retarding the material and political progress of the country; it may also be said to have had a certain moral effect on the character of the people, by lowering national pride, and accustoming them to subjection'.[4] Even Marx shared these ideas. In his view, authoritarianism, backwardness and serfdom were the fruit of the 'terrible and abject school of Mongol slavery'.[5]

This thesis, repeated in thousands of texts and not disputed particularly by anyone, in fact begs serious questions. It is noteworthy that Karamzin, who first formulated the idea of Russian backwardness being due to the Tatar yoke, has earned the reputation of being a first-rate authority on the chronicles, but a poor analyst. His *History of the Russian State* was written right at the beginning of the nineteenth century, and scholars since then have made enormous progress in discovering the facts and studying their implications. As early as the mid nineteenth century, most of the arguments which Karamzin employed were no longer being taken seriously. For example, Karamzin saw as proof of Russian backwardness and savagery in the fourteenth and fifteenth centuries the custom according to which lawsuits were decided 'in the field' – that is, one of the contending parties could challenge the other, or even the judge, to a duel, and in this way decide the outcome. A century later, Pokrovsky cited the same example as proof that Russia on the whole was developing in a way analogous to the West, since in medieval France the same custom had existed, lasting approximately as long as in Russia.[6]

Nevertheless, and irrespective of the changed attitude to Karamzin, the thesis he had expounded became a generally accepted position of Russian history, subject neither to doubt nor to discussion, if we except a few pronouncements of Solovyev and the attempts at historical criticism mounted by Pokrovsky. After the Pokrovsky school had been officially condemned under Stalin, and many of its members repressed, discussion was definitively stifled.

It is significant that Soviet historians did not usually specify whether the cause of the decline was the Tatar invasion itself or the 200-year 'yoke' that followed. The invasion by Khan Batu in the thirteenth century was certainly a disaster for Rus, but it must be remembered that medieval societies repeatedly suffered various disasters.

THE MONGOL EMPIRE

The Mongols differed from the Polovtsy and other nomads with whom the Russians had earlier had to contend in that they knew how to capture cities. Battering down stone walls was quite beyond the powers of the Polovtsy and Pechenegs, against whom even wooden fortifications provided reliable protection. But before the Mongols came to Russia, they had already seized control of China, and consequently possessed military technology of a totally different order. Siege engines capable of smashing down stone walls were perfectly familiar to them.

This demonstrates, moreover, that the Tatar-Mongols were by no means half-savage nomads, as they have usually been depicted. They had a qualitatively higher level of military and political organisation than the Polovsty or Pechenegs, and this was one of the secrets behind their victories.

The sacking of Kiev and other cities was devastating, but in those times the plundering of captured cities by their conquerors was normal practice, and Russian rulers were no exception in this regard. In the twelfth and thirteenth centuries the soldiers of Russian princes massacred the inhabitants even of Russian cities as a matter of course, and sold captured compatriots to the Volga Bulgars as slaves. In 1169 Andrey, Prince of Vladimir, who, for his learning and piety, was known as 'the God-loving' (Bogolyubsky), took Kiev by storm, subjecting the city to appalling devastation.

The conquerors, to their shame, forgot they were Russians; for three days they plundered not only the population and the houses, but also monasteries and churches, and the splendid Sofia and Desyatinny temples. They stole valuable icons, vestments, books, and even bells....[7]

Such unconcealed pillage was new to Kiev, which had not been captured before, but other trading centres had endured such disasters repeatedly.

The destruction of particular Russian cities often led to the rise of others. Hence the decline of Kiev had aided the rise of Vladimir and Suzdal. All the Russian cities, however, suffered simultaneously from the Tatar-Mongol invasion, apart from Novgorod and Pskov, into which the Tatars did not penetrate. In this respect, the invasion differed qualitatively from the massacres which the Russian princes carried out regularly in one another's domains. The scale of the disaster is hard to exaggerate. It is important to note that the leading commercial centres of the Russian north, Novgorod and Pskov, which had managed to defend themselves from the predation of the Russian princes in the twelfth century, did not suffer from the Tatars in the thirteenth century either. The Tatars, however, not only laid waste to Rus, but also inflicted heavy losses on the country's western neighbours, Poland and Hungary. Medieval sources themselves differ on the extent of the catastrophe that Rus endured following the campaigns of Batu. For example, the papal envoy Fra Giovanni Piano Carpini reported that the destruction of Kiev was almost total: 'It was a great and populous city, and now it has been reduced almost to nothing.

Barely two hundred buildings remain.[8] Nevertheless, the materials of the same mission speak of 'two hundred prominent citizens of Kiev with whom the papal ambassador met'.[9] If the number of prominent citizens who remained was no fewer than 200, there were clearly more inhabitants in the city. Scholars also note other evidence:

The question of the real state of affairs in Kiev after its capture by the Mongols (that is, of whether life there died out or not) has to be viewed in the context of a later report by Fra Giovanni. In the ransacked city, the papal envoy met with wealthy merchants from Genoa, Venice, Pisa and Acre. The names of the merchants listed by Fra Giovanni are linked to wealthy family clans, possessing large amounts of commercial capital. One wonders what these people were doing in the devastated Kiev.[10]

The ferocity of the Mongol invasion was astonishing even by the standards of the Middle Ages. Poland and Hungary were laid waste in catastrophic fashion. In Rus the northern commercial cities avoided the slaughter, but in Hungary virtually everything was wiped out. Exterminating the populations of whole cities and even provinces down to the last person was a common practice. 'The Mongols stormed and burned Pest, while King Bela took refuge on the Adriatic', writes René Grousset.

The population was subjected to unspeakable atrocities, often followed by mass execution. The Rogerii carmen miserabile is full of stories, all alike: the Mongols treacherously encourage the fleeing inhabitants to return to their homes, with the promise of complete amnesty; having thus reassured them, they cut them down to the last man.

The slaughter of the population was deliberate and well-planned, occurring not just in the towns, but also in the countryside. 'Having compelled the peasants to harvest their crops for them, they killed them as they killed – after violating them – the women of the areas they evacuated, before going on to continue their ravages elsewhere.'[11]

Rus did not serve as a 'covering force' blocking the path of the Mongols out of Asia into Europe. After passing through Rus, Batu's hordes entered the territory of the countries to the west completely ready for battle. After laying waste to Poland and Hungary, defeating the German hussars in Silesia and devastating Bohemia, the Mongols even planned to carry on to Italy and France, where rich booty awaited them. 'Actually, Batu's forces had defeated European mounted knights at every encounter', Western historians note. 'Neither exhaustion nor geography saved Europe, but rather the sudden death of the great Khan Ugedei, which precipitated a succession crisis within the Mongol Empire.'[12]

Surviving the Mongol invasion, Hungary, Poland and Bohemia gradually recovered, and continued to develop along with the backward West. In Bohemia, the fourteenth century even became a period of economic boom, that was to culminate in the following century in the revolutionary actions of the Hussites, actions that heralded the Reformation and the bourgeois revolutions of the modern era.

THE WEST IN THE FOURTEENTH CENTURY

Karamzin's thesis of the successful development of the West in the fourteenth century simply does not correspond to reality. The Tatar yoke in Russia coincided with a period of severe setbacks for most of Western Europe. Some historians even speak of a 'fourteenth-century crisis'.[13] As the French historian Jacques Le Goff observes,

> in the late thirteenth and early fourteenth centuries the Christian world was not simply standing still, but was on a downward path. The tilling of new soil and the appropriation of new lands had ceased, and even marginal lands that had been brought into cultivation under the pressure of population growth or in the heat of expansion were being abandoned, since their yields were low. Fields and even villages began to lie deserted....The building of great cathedrals came to a halt. The demographic curve turned downward. Prices stopped rising, which fed the tendency to depression.[14]

Currencies began to be debased, throwing markets into disarray and leading to bank crashes. Italian merchant and financial companies suffered a series of bankruptcies. The rapid growth of cities was replaced by stagnation.

In no way was the fourteenth century an era of humanism and enlightenment, as described by Karamzin. The rapid economic and cultural development that had changed the face of the West in the twelfth and thirteenth centuries gave way to a series of disasters. A period of acute social conflicts and fierce wars opened up, as the rise of market relations disorganised the traditional society. Armies became more massive, and the destruction they caused, more ruinous. First urban uprisings shook France and Belgium; later, peasant revolts threatened social order in France and England. Meanwhile, the population had grown more rapidly than the productivity of agricultural labour, and the growth of the towns had heightened the demand for foodstuffs. The result was that Europe in the fourteenth century suffered periodically from hunger. The culmination of the demographic and nutritional crisis was a plague epidemic. The plague reached Europe in 1348 from Crimea, to which it had been brought by the Tatars. The Genoese from Kafa spread the Black Death about the Mediterranean, infecting first Byzantium and then Italy. As a rule the disease spread along trade routes; after passing right around Europe, it arrived in Rus from Germany, ravaging Novgorod and Pskov.

In some European countries, the plague wiped out as much as half of the population. By the early fourteenth century the population of England had reached 4 million; of these, at least 1 million died in 1349. After this, the plague returned in 1360–62, in 1369, and again in 1375. Describing the epidemic in Novgorod and Pskov, Karamzin concludes his account with the optimistic avowal that

> everywhere, once the infection had passed, the population multiplied at an extraordinary rate. So miraculous is nature, that it is always ready to make up losses in its realms with new exertions of its fruitful strength.[15]

In fact, most of the Western countries underwent a lengthy depopulation. In England, for example, the level of population that had been reached by the fourteenth century was again attained only in the seventeenth century. British historians note that 'the population steadily declined to about two and a half million or even less by the mid-fifteenth century'. The catastrophe transformed the whole appearance of the country; 'entire communities were deserted – the "lost villages of England" – and many of these were abandoned as a result of the twin afflictions of demographic crisis and prolonged war'.[16]

The economic and demographic catastrophes were accompanied by ideological and cultural shifts. 'The Black Death left men with a sense of spiritual crisis to which the church in its existing form failed adequately to respond', writes the British historian R. Strong.[17] The chronicles of those years paint a picture of devastation and despair similar to the one that Rus experienced after the invasion by Batu:

After the pestilence many buildings both great and small in all cities, towns and boroughs fell into total ruin for lack of inhabitants; similarly many small villages and hamlets became desolate and no houses were left in them, for all those who dwelt were dead, and it seemed likely that many such little villages would never again be inhabited.[18]

The combination in the West of epidemics, hunger, social conflicts and wars could not fail to lead to a drawn-out economic crisis. The only exception was in Bohemia, which was virtually untouched by the plague and remained on the sidelines of the main wars of the fourteenth century. This allowed an extraordinary flourishing of the Czech lands, and the consequent rise there of reforming movements.

In most of the countries of the West, the plague led to structural shifts in the economy that had far-reaching consequences.

For those who survived an ugly death, life may not have been as wretched in the late fourteenth and fifteenth centuries as it undoubtedly was before. For many peasants, this became an age of opportunity, ambition and affluence....[19]

By the end of the century, the decline had been replaced by rapid economic growth. The shortage of labour power had created a new relationship of forces in society. The demand for free workers had grown, and the use of hired labour had spread not only in the towns, but also in the countryside. Meanwhile, the shortage of workers encouraged technical improvements, which by the middle of the fifteenth century were making an impact on the general state of the economy. Production for exchange now held a much more important place; with labour power now in chronic short supply, and grain production lower, maintaining the 'natural economy' had simply become impossible.

Rus was not insulated from this process, though the plague dealt it less of a blow than was the case in the West. The devastation of Pskov in the spring and summer of 1352 was just as terrible as in Western cities, and Novgorod suffered as well. But judging by the sources that have come down to us, Moscow suffered less, a fact which may have been reflected in the city's subsequent development. Overall, the 'crisis of the fourteenth century' affected Russia less than other countries of Europe, and it cannot be said that in this period Rus developed more slowly than its neighbours. Similarly, there are no grounds for asserting that the country's trajectory of development was somehow different or special. Moreover, the 1340s were a time of conflict within the Golden Horde (the Tatar state). The Tatar yoke was growing lighter, the fear of raids was gradually vanishing into the past, and economic life was becoming more vigorous even in the most 'vulnerable' Russian regions.

UNDER THE POWER OF THE TATARS

It was not only Karamzin's notion of Western European prosperity in the fourteenth century that was false. Just as mystifying is his conviction that Rus was isolated by the Tatars from the rest of Europe. There are excellent reasons for asserting that an intention on the part of the Mongols to keep Russia under their power, and to collect tribute from it, saved Rus from still more terrible devastation – of the kind, for example, that was inflicted on Hungary. After founding the Golden Horde in 1242, the Tatars led an existence quite distinct from Rus, and did not try to impose either their culture or their customs on the country. They intervened in neither legal nor religious matters. In the thirteenth century all the major religions, from Christianity to Buddhism, were represented at the court of the khans. But the Tatar state, unlike Rus, had come into being on the European frontier in a period when Byzantium was already in decline; therefore the rulers of the Golden Horde, when they renounced paganism, did not accept Orthodoxy but Islam, though individual members of the Tatar elite in Crimea became Christians. In any case, it is wrong to speak of the khans as having been hostile to Christianity. The Tatar khans were not only conspicuous for their religious tolerance (or more precisely, indifference to religious questions), but also collaborated directly with the Orthodox church. Karamzin states:

One of the memorable consequences of the Tatar rule over Russia was a further rise of our clergy, with monks and church estates multiplying. While the khans oppressed the common people and the princes, they had a policy of protecting the church and its priests, displaying particular benevolence toward them. They treated the metropolitans and bishops with lenience, listened indulgently to their submissive pleas, and often, out of respect for the pastors, showed mercy instead of anger toward the flock.[20]

The collaboration of the church hierarchy with the invaders stands as one of the most shameful episodes in the history of Russian Orthodoxy, and memories of it have invariably undermined the claims of the church to be playing a special national role in Russia. Ideologues of official Orthodoxy have sought to justify themselves in hindsight by explaining that the khans and the church hierarchs had no interests in common, and that the Tatars supported Orthodoxy solely because they felt 'a superstitious fear of the unknown God of the Christians'.[21]

The reality, of course, is that the khans knew perfectly well what Christianity was – priests and missionaries had appeared at their court as early as the 1250s. Charters granted by the khans provided the church with immunity. The Orthodox hierarchs, for their part, called on their flock to pray for the khans. Pokrovsky writes:

> The alliance between the Orthodox church and the Tatar khans was at first equally advantageous to both sides. If later it proved more advantageous to the former than to the latter, this was something the Tatars did not manage to foresee, precisely because they were too much the practical politicians.[22]

The tribute levied on the Russian princes by the Tatars provided the model for an up-to-date tax system. In this respect the Mongol khans, who were familiar with the methods of the Chinese bureaucracy, were far in advance of many Western European rulers. It was thanks to the Tatars that a unified and more or less orderly system for the collecting of taxes was established on the scale of Russia as a whole. The khan's tax collector, the *baskak*, served as the prototype for the Russian bureaucrat. Pokrovsky notes that 'the Tatar method of apportioning taxes (so much per plough, the so-called "plough letter"), lasted until the middle of the seventeenth century'.[23]

As Karamzin acknowledges, the Tatar tributes in the first instance enriched Moscow, which acted as the fiscal intermediary between the Horde and the other Russian princedoms:

> The Tatar yoke enriched the treasury of the Great Princes by counting the people and instituting a poll tax, as well as through imposing various previously unknown taxes which, though ostensibly collected for the khan, were cunningly diverted by the princes to their own income. The complex accounts meant that the baskaki, initially tyrants and later the bribe-taking friends of our rulers, could easily be deceived. The people complained, but paid up....[24]

The financial services rendered to the khan of the Golden Horde by the Moscow Prince Ivan Kalita allowed Ivan not only to accumulate an extraordinary fortune, but in effect to buy up the lands of poorer rulers. It is understandable that Ivan should appear to historians as a collaborator and indeed traitor, especially since his denunciation doomed Prince Aleksandr of Tver, who tried to incite the people to revolt against the Tatars. Some writers, however, have been inclined to see Ivan Kalita as an astute tactician, who, unlike his naïve neighbour, realised that the time had not yet come for open struggle. Meanwhile, Moscow and the Horde were united by common commercial interests that extended far beyond the mere collecting of taxes.

The Tatar yoke did not by any means lead to the complete isolation of Russia from Europe. The route from Moscow to Crimea and the Mediterranean passed through the lands of the khan, and there is no evidence to show that the Tatars impeded contacts between the Russian princedoms and the West or Byzantium. Quite the reverse; the sources show that these ties were continuing, with all their previous intensity. In 1253 the ambassador of the French King Louis IX, the Franciscan monk and missionary Guillaume de Rubruck, was present in the court of Khan Batu. In Crimea, the ambassador observed a flourishing commerce in which Russian merchants played a substantial part. Soon after Batu had laid waste to Kiev, the papal envoy Piano Carpini found Genoan and Venetian merchants there who had come to Kiev from Constantinople and Acre through the lands of the Tatars; Rubruck also reported the presence of merchants from Rus who had come to Surozh (Soldaiya).[25] The Russian chronicle also mentions 'guests from Constantinople' as being in the Kursk lands, and Surozhans in Volynia, during the second half of the thirteenth century.[26] We also encounter numerous mentions from the same period of trade by 'Latin' merchants in the Russian lands. In Vladimir and Suzdal, Germans purchased goods that had come by way of the Volga from Muslim countries. An Arab traveller reported that on the Lower Volga in 1263, Russian vessels were 'constantly visible'.[27]

At the court of the khan, Rubruck found not only Nestorian Christians, but also artisans from Europe, including the Parisian jeweller Guillaume Buchier and his brother Roger, and even Knights Templar.[28] For the khan in Karakorum, Guillaume Buchier created a famous silver tree, from which there poured wine and fermented mare's milk. As is well-known, the Tatars maintained close relations with the Genoese, who were based in Crimea (at the battle of Kulikovo, Genoese infantry fought on the Tatar side). The Kremlin cathedrals and fortifications were built by Italian and English architects. The close ties between Russia and Italy are in clear contrast to what we see in northern Europe, where the Swedish kings, for example, went no further than inviting in German builders.

THE FRAGMENTATION OF RUS

The sources of 'Russian backwardness' need to be sought in events that began before the arrival of Batu in Rus.[29] The military defeats suffered by the Russians in the thirteenth century were the result of a dispersal of forces. This fragmentation, however, was itself the result of the earlier economic, social and political development. In the ninth and tenth centuries, the establishing of a unified state aided the flowering of trade and the growth of cities, and this led inevitably to the appearance of new commercial and political centres which posed a challenge to Kiev. The enmity between the increasingly powerful princedoms of north-eastern Rus, the traditional Kievan 'centre', and Novgorod led to the collapse of the unified state. Commercial rivalry was accompanied by raids and acts of plunder. Overall, the attacks which the Russian princedoms mounted against one another in the late twelfth century were quite comparable in their impact to those which the Tatars were to carry out a few decades later. The sale by Russians of captured compatriots in the slave markets of the Volga Bulgars also became commonplace. Within the growing cities social conflicts grew more acute, leading periodically to revolts and internecine warfare.

In Pokrovsky's view, the crisis and decline of the Russian cities in the twelfth and thirteenth centuries was due ultimately to the same causes as their rapid rise in the ninth and tenth centuries. The cities had grown up primarily on the basis of international trade. But in order to live and develop, they had at the same time to obtain foodstuffs and raw materials from the countryside, to which they provided very little in return. This parasitic development of the cities at the expense of the countryside, a sort of unequal exchange, has characterised many periods of Russian history right up until the twentieth century. In principle, the relations between city and countryside were not equal anywhere in Europe, but it was the orientation by Kiev, Novgorod and other major urban centres in Rus toward international trade that rendered the contradiction fatal. 'Laying waste to everything around itself with its rapacious practices, the Old Russian city fell, and nothing could slow this fall.'[30] The self-destruction of the city was especially noticeable in the Kievan lands, where the twelfth-century chronicles constantly report social conflicts and uprisings. Vladimir and Suzdal, located further from the main trade routes, were tied more closely to the internal market, and hence continued to grow even when the crisis of Kiev had become obvious. But this in turn led to a new relationship of political forces and to constant attacks by the northern princes on the wealthy but ailing south.

Overall, the picture of feudal fragmentation in Rus differs little from what could be seen in the West during the same period. The eleventh and twelfth centuries in Europe not only saw the growth of cities, but were also the period of *castellisazzione*, an Italian term that historians in the twentieth century began using to denote the widespread building of stone castles. The wooden fortifications of the early Middle Ages were rarely able to withstand a prolonged siege, and only the largest political centres had well-built stone walls. The development of the economy in the tenth century enabled improvements in the quality of construction as well. The fortified structures became more complex and reliable and, most importantly, any more or less influential *seigneur* could build them. In Wales, the widespread building of castles was undertaken by the English kings in order to keep disloyal subjects under control, while in France, Italy and Germany the feudal elite built castles to defend themselves against both the peasants and the neighbouring nobles, and also against the king.

Just as in the First World War, the means of defence were dramatically more effective than the means of attack, and military actions were doomed to take on a positional character. To effectively alter the relationship of forces to one's advantage, large armies were required; for the rulers to recruit these was difficult, and to maintain them over a long period, even harder.

One result of the widespread building of castles was a strengthening of the power of the feudal nobility over the peasants, while another was a weakening of the power of the king over the nobles. The feudal estate in the West, however, was now departing more and more from the classical model of the natural economy, and the inhabitants of the castles had fewer and fewer ties to their peasants in their interests and way of life. The exploitation of the peasants was intensifying precisely because the ruling class needed goods for exchange. Since the lands had all been divided up, and taking lands from one's neighbour was becoming increasingly difficult, the growth of the population was accompanied by an increase in the number of knights who had little or no land, and who were excluded altogether from the system of natural economy. One military-political consequence of this new situation was the Crusades. The expeditions by European knights to the Middle East were, however, merely part of a broader process. The idea of defending and spreading the faith provided a powerful ideological stimulus that aided the military and commercial expansion of Western Europe to the east and south. Henry the Lion of Bavaria conquered the territories of the maritime Slavs. Then the German knights, initially with the full support of the Polish kings, began seizing control of the Baltic coast, subduing and annihilating the Prussians, Livonians and Estonians. The Swedish kings organised Crusades against Finland. By the middle of the thirteenth century, territories that were 'unappropriated' in political or religious terms had ceased practically to exist.

THE 'MONEYLESS' PERIOD

In the ninth and tenth centuries Arab and Persian silver had stimulated the development of Russian and Scandinavian trade. By the eleventh century the influx of silver coins from the East had almost ceased. Then the flow of money from Byzantium stopped as well. Initially, the shortage of silver was made up by coins from Western Europe. Thanks to the Bohemian mines, silver was coming onto the markets there in substantial quantities. By the end of the twelfth century, however, German merchants were leaving fewer and fewer silver coins in Novgorod. Historians have explained this on the basis that as internal trade in Germany expanded, the internal demand for silver there increased markedly.[31] The reason, however, should probably be sought in reduced exports from the Russian lands. Earlier, exports had substantially exceeded imports; now there was equilibrium, which in the conditions of medieval trade favoured natural exchange.

One way or another, Rus was afflicted by an acute currency shortage. Some historians even talk of the beginning of a 'moneyless period'.[32] Coins were replaced by silver ingots imported from Germany, but these were ill-suited to act as currency, and as scholars acknowledge, could serve 'only for very large payments'.[33] Pelts, scraps of leather, and so forth, took the place of small change. In short, a primitivisation of exchange was clearly under way. With the growth of cities in Western Europe, Scandinavian trade was being reoriented as well. Meanwhile, the twelfth century saw a gradual decline in the economic vitality of Constantinople, at the same time as provincial centres were growing in importance. Russian trade as well was increasingly reoriented toward the provinces, but here, competition from Italians was already strong. In 1169 and 1192 the Genoese, to the envy of their Venetian competitors, concluded agreements with Byzantium that effectively gave them control of the Black Sea trade. It was Italian ships that transported foodstuffs and raw materials to Constantinople from Crimea. 'The monopoly privileges which Russian merchants had sometimes enjoyed', writes G. Litavrin, 'now passed to the Italian merchants.'[34]

With no need to make their way down to the Black Sea along the rivers, the Italians built larger, seagoing ships that were superior to the Russian vessels both in battle and for trade. Meanwhile, it was above all at sea that the Greeks at this time needed military help. As earlier, there was a Russian corps within the imperial forces, and recruiting to it was carried out in a massive way on the territories of the Slavic princes, but Slavs and Varyags were not the only people whom the emperor was able to hire. The Russian corps was increasingly 'diluted' with Anglo-Saxons.[35] In 1204 the Crusaders took Constantinople by storm, and established their own Latin empire there. It is significant that this was one of only a few 'international' events thought worthy of detailed description in the First Novgorod Chronicle. What was involved in this case was not only the sacking of the Orthodox capital by Catholics. The Russian chronicler described in detail how Orthodox Greeks and Catholic Varyags joined in defending the city. The Crusaders, as is well-known, sacked Constantinople at the instigation of the Venetians. For the Italian merchant republics, Venice and Genoa, an era of prosperity was beginning, an era when they would enjoy commercial mastery of the Mediterranean. The most important trade routes were under the control of Venice and, to some degree, Genoa. Goods from the south now reached Europe through Italy. Venice, it might have been said, was killing Kiev.

The Byzantine empire was later restored, but its decline was now irreversible. Since the Genoese had provided the Greeks with help in restoring the empire, their trading privileges were confirmed and expanded, while the positions of the Russian merchants grew still weaker. The route from the Varyags to the Greeks, as Pokrovsky writes, now ended in a 'commercial dead-end'. Instead of being 'staging posts on the high road of international exchange', the trading centres on the great river route had been turned into 'out-of-the-way trading villages on a backwoods track', and were ravaged by the Tatars.[36]

The princes who ruled in Vladimir controlled the trade routes that led along the Volga to the countries of the East, while at the same time maintaining their links with the West by way of Novgorod. Kiev, which lay on the route to Byzantium in the south, did not have the same value for the Vladimir princes as it had had for the Novgorodians in the time of Ryurik. As a result, Andrey Bogolyubsky not only subjected Kiev to plunder, but made no effort to rule in the city. After ransacking the 'mother of Russian cities', he placed one of his henchmen on the Kievan throne, and headed back to Vladimir.

In Western Europe at this time, new trade routes were being established between north and south. By way of the Rhine and other German rivers, goods from the Mediterranean countries were reaching the Netherlands, and going further still into England, Denmark and Sweden. The rapid rise of Netherlands' trade coincided with the decline of Novgorod. The commercial capital of the Russian north remained wealthy, but its strategic position was weakening.

THE GERMANS VERSUS THE NOVGORODIANS

The German expansion to the east in the early thirteenth century created a new situation in the Baltic. In the tenth and eleventh centuries, Novgorod and

Pskov had been the only trading centres in the eastern Baltic region. But late in the twelfth century the German knights, after defeating the Slavs, had founded their own cities. In 1143 the Count of Holstein, Adolf II, founded the city of Lübeck on the site of the destroyed Slavic settlement of Ljubech. With the help of Henry the Lion, Prince of Saxony and Bavaria, the shipowners of Lübeck established themselves on the island of Gotland, formally a dependency of Sweden. A Soviet text records:

Basing themselves on Gotland, the German merchants gradually increased in strength and organised a commercial union, the Hanseatic League. The Hansa merchants sailed the Baltic Sea in their kogge, rounded, high-sided, decked sailing vessels, which were more stable and capacious than the Scandinavians' long, oared vessels. The commercial dominance of the Hansa merchants in the Baltic, however, was probably due less to the superior construction of their ships than to the fact that the merchants were allies of the German feudal nobility in its Drang nach Osten [desire for eastward expansion].[37]

The relationship of the Crusaders with the Hansa in the north developed along the same lines as with Venice in the south. Lacking their own fleet, the knights became a tool for the commercial expansion of the traders.

In the thirteenth century, Lübeck became the main centre of German trade with Eastern Europe. From the middle years of the century, German merchants supplanted their Scandinavian competitors almost completely in the Baltic and Slavic countries. In the fourteenth century Lübeck headed the union of north German trading cities which from 1356 came to be called the German Hansa.[38]

Scandinavian historians note yet another important advantage which allowed the Germans to force the Danes and Swedes out of the Baltic trade. The German merchants had greater financial resources. They were able to put silver mined in Bohemia into circulation, and had extensive experience of operating in the new, quickly developing markets of Western and Central Europe. A stream of goods and money from Italy was flowing along the Rhine.[39] By the mid thirteenth century German merchants already enjoyed commercial privileges in the Scandinavian countries, just like the Genoese in the Greek territories. It was Germans who in the thirteenth century began the Baltic grain trade, destined to play such an important – and at times fateful – role in the history of Eastern Europe. In the Middle Ages, however, grain was not yet a key commodity. Far more important were timber and metals.

Novgorod carried on an active trade with the Hansa cities, but was unquestionably losing its role as the largest commercial centre in the region.[40] In 1201, the German port of Riga appeared at the mouth of the Western Dvina. In 1219 the Danes built the cities of Tallinn (Revel) and Narva on Estonian territory. In 1230 the Teutonic Order began subduing the Prussians. New commercial centres, Memel and Königsberg, arose. In western Finland, the city of Abo (Turku) grew up around a Swedish royal fortress, and in 1292, not far from Lake Ladoga, the fortress and port of Vyborg was established.

Relying on this settlement, the Swedes could exercise a dual control: over the Novgorians' most important maritime route, through the Gulf of Finland to the Baltic; and over their internal route through Lake Ladoga and up by way of Lake Vuoksa to the system of the Sajmen lakes and into the interior of the land of Sumi Em.[41]

If Venice and Genoa had forced Kiev out of world trade, the Hansa cities were turning Novgorod into their periphery.

The political configuration around the Baltic had changed as well. Until the middle of the twelfth century, the dominant power there had remained Denmark, whose interests had not directly clashed with those of Novgorod. Denmark was remote, controlling the western exit from the Baltic just as Novgorod sealed off the Baltic zone in the east. With the rise of German commerce, the situation changed. The German merchants not only turned the Livonian and Teutonic Orders into their military-political instruments, but in the northern part of the Baltic, found a patron in the King of Sweden. This partnership between the Hansa cities and the Swedish Crown proved astonishingly durable, lasting right up until the Thirty Years' War in the seventeenth century. The rise of Sweden continued throughout the twelfth and thirteenth centuries. It was not hindered even by the unification in 1397 of Denmark, Sweden and Norway in something like a federation, the Kalmar Union, under the Danish crown.

The seizure by the Swedes in the thirteenth century of Finland and part of Karelia put Novgorod on the defensive. Earlier, Finland had divided the Scandinavians from the Russians, and had suffered raids from both. Now, Novgorod shared a direct border with lands belonging to the Swedish king, and access to Finnish territory was closed off to Novgorodian bandits and merchants. The border conflict with Sweden continued for around a hundred years until it was ended in 1323 by a peaceful agreement, the Treaty of Noteborg. After this, the border did not shift until the end of the fifteenth century. It is significant that what the agreement of 1323 determined was not so much the division of the territories in the Karelian border region, as control over the river and lake routes. The agreement also allowed the Swedes and Novgorodians to make joint use of part of Karelia and Finland.

While the first era of European economic and political expansion founded Kievan Rus and enabled it to flourish, the second era weakened it and, ultimately, predetermined its downfall. In the ninth and tenth centuries, Western and especially northern Europe simply could not have developed without Rus. But in the thirteenth century, Western Europe no longer had much need of Rus, and following promptly on the commercial decline came the Tatar catastrophe. Pokrovsky is the only Russian historian prepared to argue that the devastation suffered at the hands of the Tatars in the thirteenth century was not the cause of the decline of the Old Russian state, but its consequence. The raid by Khan Batu was preceded by a 'process of decay of urban Rus between the tenth and twelfth centuries'.[42] The destruction of the unified economic space led to a steady weakening of central authority, to internecine war between princes, and to the military disorganisation which the Tatars exploited so successfully. Here, too, lies the explanation for the fact that the Tatar yoke lasted so long. Batu's

Horde also staged successful attacks on Poland and Hungary, but Russia's Western neighbours recovered considerably faster. Soviet historians repeatedly and quite correctly argued that Rus shielded the West by taking the main blow. Nevertheless, and whatever the strength of this blow, the shock it represented was by no means the only one in the history of medieval Europe. The attacks on Europe by the Hungarians were a genuine catastrophe. Later, the blows dealt by the Tatars against Hungary, Poland and Bohemia were no less appalling than those inflicted on Rus. The damage done to the West by the plague was no less than that which Rus suffered at the hands of Batu. It was not the insurmountable strength of the Horde that prevented the revival of Rus so much as the internal weaknesses of Russian society itself. In the thirteenth century, Rus had lost its initial forms of economic organisation, and could not find new ones.

3
Moscow and Novgorod

The thirteenth-century commercial decline, of which Pokrovsky supplies such a vivid description, played a fateful role in Russian history, weakening the country in the face of the Tatar assault. Nevertheless, the catastrophe was nowhere near so complete as Pokrovsky and many other historians have supposed. The eastern trade route continued to function satisfactorily, and the Black Sea trade did not come to a halt.

The fourteenth century even witnessed a revival of Russian trade with the coastal regions of the Black Sea, where new commercial cities were growing apace. Sudak-Surozh, under the control of the Genoans, was flourishing and becoming a major trading partner of Moscow. Commercial relations did not cease with Byzantium, which had recovered after being attacked by the Crusaders, but from now on imports and exports via the Black Sea would be conducted with the help of Italian intermediaries. Historians have noted that 'in Moscow there was a special corporation of Surozhan guests who carried on trade with the northern Black Sea region and with Constantinople. There was a Russian colony in the latter city during the fourteenth and fifteenth centuries.'[1]

During this period the Genoese colonies in the Crimea underwent rapid growth. Like many other trading centres of the time, these cities were centres of commercial and financial capital, parasitically exploiting the countryside – something that was also true to a significant degree of the urban centres of Kievan Rus.[2] The Tatar invasions of the thirteenth century were highly destructive, but did not lead to the collapse of the Crimean economy. Following the raids, life in these cities recovered relatively quickly, with everything resuming its former course. 'After making their raids the Tatars departed, and the city revived. Commerce was renewed, and trading caravans once again set off into the steppe.' It is true that not all the Tatars departed; scholars of Crimean history note that members of the Tatar elite settled among the Greeks and Italians, mixing with them and 'adopting the local Greek culture, many of them even becoming Christians'.[3]

PARTNERS OF MOSCOW: THE TATARS AND ITALIANS

While Batu's campaign of 1223 did not do the Black Sea region catastrophic damage, the raid by Khan Nogay in 1299 struck a far heavier blow. The traditional Greek centres fell into ruin, but new cities arose to take their place, especially Kafa and Sudak (Surozh). In Crimea in the fourteenth century Tatar murzy ruled directly over the Greek-speaking rural population, while feudal dues were collected in money form. In other words, the local economy remained firmly based on commodity production and the market. After the wars of the 1340s and 1350s, trade again flourished.

The river route made its way northward along the Don, while the caravans proceeded to Astrakhan. There the road diverged, with one route leading along the Caspian to Transcaucasia and Persia, the source of the silks that were so valued in the West, while the other route led to Central Asia, first to Saray-Batu, then to the mouth of the Ural River, then to Urgench and beyond to China.[4]

As historians observe, it was at this time that Moscow's trade with Kafa 'took on a systematic character, and began to figure in the everyday economic life of Muscovite Rus'.[5] To the south, Rus exported furs, linen and leather. From the Mediterranean, Italian merchants took soap, sugar, silk, almonds, pepper, cloves and other spices northwards. Russian artisans worked in Kafa, and as in most trading centres of the East, the city's population was an ethnic, cultural and religious mix. Greeks, Armenians, Jews, Tatars and Russians could be found living side by side with Italians. The Russians secured an important place in the ethnic division of labour; all the *skornyaki* (producers of fur clothing) in the city were Russians. In the year 1334 the Arab traveller Ibn-Batuta counted no fewer than two hundred ships in the port of Kafa, concluding that this was 'one of the great harbours of the world'.[6]

By comparison, data cited by Jacques Le Goff in *The Civilisation of the Medieval West* indicate that 'the overall number of "merchant galleys" servicing the three main trade routes in the 1320s was about twenty-five'.[7] Of course, if we add to this other trade routes, and other types of vessels based in different ports (especially in Crete), the Venetian fleet will appear somewhat more impressive. Nevertheless, a harbour containing as many as 200 vessels at a time would have made an enormous impression in those days. The prosperity of Kafa was not affected either by the city's difficult and at times even hostile relations with the Tatars, nor by the plague of 1348. Decline set in only after the seizing of Crimea by the Turks in 1475, and even then it was not immediate. Trade routes that were important for the prosperity of Moscow thus led through the territories of the Horde. It is usually considered that in the fourteenth century Moscow rose to prominence mainly as an administrative centre recognised by the Tatars; this is said to have been due to the cunning – and, to a certain degree, national betrayal – of Prince Ivan Kalita, who undertook to collect tribute from other Russian princes on behalf of the khan. However, the financial collaboration by the Moscow prince with the Horde developed against a background of no less active commercial interchange. Moreover, from the 1340s a period of discord began within the Horde. To an important degree, the subjection of Rus to the Tatars was becoming merely nominal. The Tatars were incapable of intervening actively in the internal affairs of the Russian princedoms. The fear of raids was diminishing. But Moscow's ties to the Horde were not weakened; shared interests bound the two states together.

It is well-established that before becoming a collector of Russian lands, the Moscow Prince Ivan Kalita was a collector of taxes for the Tatars. Kalita's

method was simple to the point of genius; princes who did not have the means
with which to pay tribute received loans from the Moscow ruler, but were forced
to pay back the debts with their lands. This means of acquiring additional
territories could, of course, work only on one condition: if the Moscow prince
always had cash available. As Pokrovsky writes:

At the beginning of the period we are discussing, the prince of Moscow was one of the
most petty and inconsequential, but he was in an extremely advantageous location. At
that time, two trade routes passed through Moscow. The older of them led from Smolensk
to the River Klyazma, from west to east. On the Klyazma stood what was then largest city
of feudal Russia – Vladimir. All the goods that were sent from the west to the territories
of Vladimir passed through Moscow. The other trade route led from north to south, from
the territories of Novgorod, which at that time had closer ties to Western Europe than any
other part of Russia, to the present-day *guberniya* of Ryazan, a region especially rich in grain.
From there, grain was exported to Novgorod, whose own harvest was rarely sufficient to
meet its needs.[8]

It was Ivan Kalita's control over the point of intersection of these trade routes
that provided him with money, and which ultimately made Moscow the capital
of a revived Russia. However, it was not only Russian internal trade routes that
met in Moscow. As noted earlier, Pokrovsky overestimated the decline that
affected the Black Sea trade in the early thirteenth century, while historians in
general have rarely assessed the eastern trade at its true worth.[9]

In the fourteenth century the economic links of Rus with the south were
developing rapidly, but conducting trade with the regions involved would have
been impossible if Rus had not maintained loyal relations with the Tatars.
Not only did the route along the Volga to Persia pass through the territories
of the Horde, but so did the route along the Don to Crimea, to the Genoese
possessions of Kafa and Sudak. As scholars have observed, in the fourteenth
century the Genoese colonies served as 'a sort of window on Europe, a direct
link between the Russian lands and the wealthy Mediterranean'.[10] With the
development of the Genoese colonies in Crimea, the 'Greek' trade shifted
from the Dnepr to the Don, exacerbating the decline of Kiev. From this point,
the developing cities of northern Russia – the already wealthy Novgorod and
Pskov, and the growing Moscow – were far less interested in the unity of the
territories of the former Kievan state. Loyal relations with the Tatars, however,
were to their advantage. This was a question not only of security, but also of
economic well-being.

Not only did the Tatars refrain from cutting off Rus from Europe; it might
be said that they acted as go-betweens, maintaining the links with Italy and
Greece. The political price that had to be paid for this mediation was, of course,
extremely high. Unlike Kiev in its time of greatness, the new Russia that was
taking shape beneath the Horde and its khans no longer controlled its trade
routes. The dominant position was held by Germans in the north, and by
Italians and Tatars in the south. But while formally under the 'Tatar yoke', Rus
in the fourteenth and fifteenth centuries was developing in relatively dynamic

fashion. No less important was the fact that it was developing in much the same manner as the West. The boyar aristocracy was gradually losing its influence, the princes were losing their independence one after another, and a unified state was being formed. If we consider the creation of such a state to be a crucially important precondition for entry into the new age, it must be recognised that in this respect the situation in Russia was developing more favourably than, for example, in Germany or Italy. The free citizens of the cities were yielding up their liberties to a centralised bureaucracy not just in Moscow, but also in France and England. The institutions of self-rule were of course preserved better in Western Europe, but in Rus as well traces of the republican system were visible, at least in Novgorod and Pskov, until late in the sixteenth century.

Without doubt, the Tatars exercised a huge influence on the creation of the Russian state, but it is quite wrong to interpret this as purely the extension of 'Eastern despotism' and 'barbarism'. Above all, the Tatar khans did not occupy the Russian lands, but founded their own state in the Golden Horde. Politically and economically, the Tatar yoke amounted to two requirements: the regular payment by the Russians of tribute to the Horde, and the khan's confirmation of the position of the Russian princes (the so-called 'badge of tsardom'). This meant that the Tatars did not have their own administration on the territory of Rus, and were compelled to act through Orthodox princes whose relation to them was that of dependent vassals. The collecting of tribute in such conditions required the creation of an efficient bureaucracy, which received precise instructions from the Horde as to the expected revenues, and which then had to report on the results of its work. Prior to the Tatars, the quantities of tribute which the princes received from their subjects amounted to what the latter handed over, or what the princes could appropriate by force. The dispute between Prince Igor and the Drevlyane over the extent and frequency of tribute collections had ended with the subjects simply doing away with their ruler.

The Tatars introduced a degree of order to these proceedings, setting approximate norms for each princedom. It is clear that the princes sought constantly to minimise these norms, while the wealth of the Moscow Prince Ivan Kalita stemmed from the fact that in collecting tribute for the Horde from his neighbours, he kept a substantial part of the sums received for himself. As Pokrovsky noted slyly, Prince Ivan Kalita was 'something like the khan's head bailiff'.[11] Not only did Ivan, like later Russian bailiffs, defraud his master to a degree, but he also possessed freely circulating funds, which he could lend to neighbouring princedoms. Unable to pay off the Kremlin usurer, the princes surrendered their domains. This was an important step in the direction of founding a modern state, and contrary to later notions of an 'all-national war' against the Tatars, a sort of alliance in fact developed between the princes and the Tatars, aimed at the joint exploitation of the Russian masses. An exception was Tver, where Prince Aleksandr sought to rely on the people in waging a struggle against the invaders; Moscow and the Golden Horde then joined forces in order to deal with him.

FEUDALISM IN RUSSIA

The decline of the cities, a trend that had begun even before the arrival of the Tatars, encouraged a slide back toward the natural economy. The Tatars, however, demanded that the Russians pay their tribute in money; and this had the effect of stimulating economic development. The relative calm of the Moscow princedom, and its remoteness from the Golden Horde, also permitted a steady growth of population. The wealth and influence of the local prince thus rested simultaneously both on trade and on the funds extracted from the agrarian population. It was this combination, together with a stable financial base, that made Moscow the ideal leader for the process of unifying the Russian princedoms. Overall, this unification took place according to the same logic as in other European countries. The war against the Tatars that began late in the fourteenth century was not a unique feature of Russian history either. The rise of the French monarchy was accompanied by constant war with English invaders; first the dynastic war of the Parisian Capet kings against the Anglo-Norman dynasty of the Plantagenets, and then the Hundred Years' War. Spain was a product of the Reconquista, a war against the Arabs that lasted for many centuries.

Comparing the social order in Moscow with that in the West, one finds that the notion of an 'absence of feudalism' and of a complete lack of rights for the population in the fourteenth and fifteenth centuries is not borne out by the facts either. Comparing documentary evidence on the situation in the German borderlands and in Russian rural society, the historian N.P. Pavlov-Silvansky noted 'the profound similarity of Russian and German medieval institutions'.[12] The rights and freedoms of the Russian rural community, which had existed in customary form, were reinforced in the fifteenth and sixteenth centuries through numerous deeds and charters. For example, a charter of 1488 granted by Ivan III 'to all the people of Belozersk' gave the local population such independence that in the enlightened nineteenth century it was necessary to abolish the remnants of these medieval freedoms, which were considered to render the government 'effectively powerless'. In Muscovite Rus, such liberties were not perceived as evidence of the weakness of the state; as in other European countries, they were quite normal. 'By Lake Beloe in the fifteenth century,' Pavlov-Silvansky writes, 'peaceful self-government retained all its ancient significance as the main bulwark of the state system.'[13]

The same applies also to relations of vassalage.

Just like his Western peers, our local boyar, the vassal and servant of the prince, had his own servants, who were subject to him on the same bases of military, free or contracted service. The boyar, like the Western vassal, was compelled to have his own military retainers, since he fulfilled his obligation of service completely only when at the command of the prince he 'mounted a horse', appearing not on his own, but accompanied in military accoutrement by a more or less numerous detachment of his own mounted servants and footsoldiers.[14]

The similarity of the Russian and Western European rights of that time is obvious. The population was no more lacking in rights in fifteenth- and sixteenth-century Muscovy than in Germany or France. Pokrovsky notes:

We need to understand clearly that neither the ruler of Novgorod the Great nor his fortunate rival, the Great Prince of Muscovy Ivan Vasilyevich, held sway over a herd of subjects who were uniform in their lack of rights, but over a motley feudal world of large and small 'boyardoms', each with its own ruler, who knew just as well how to defend his independence beyond the forests and bogs of northern Rus as did his Western peer behind the walls of his castle.[15]

The general processes that characterised Western Europe were also typical of Rus at the time when the Muscovite state was being formed. The fifteenth century, a period of rapid development in the West, was also a time of progress in Russia. It was not by chance that this period witnessed the artistry of Andrey Rublev, regarded by many as a Russian exponent of the proto-Renaissance. Russian culture in the fifteenth century indeed remained more 'medieval' than Italian. The same, however, might also be said of Sweden and even, with certain qualifications, of Germany. The art of Andrey Rublev clearly bears witness to the early stirrings of the Renaissance. The forms of social and political organisation were evolving in the same direction as in the neighbouring European countries.

While Kievan Rus had outstripped Western Europe in many ways, Muscovite Rus, as it had taken shape by the years during 1450–80, was by and large on the same level of development. Artillery and architecture were, at that time, among the foremost areas of technological development, and here the Moscow rulers strove to avoid falling behind the advanced countries of southern Europe. Diplomatic missions were sent to Venice in 1474, 1493 and 1499; on each occasion not so much for political ends as to secure experts. In 1489 a mission was sent to Austria, in order to bring skilled miners to Moscow. From Hungary, skilled foundry workers, silversmiths and architects were invited. The only noticeable lag was in book publishing; the first printing presses appeared in Moscow only in the sixteenth century.

Nor was Russia isolated from seaborne trade. Danish documents testify that Russian vessels appeared in the Baltic in both the fifteenth and sixteenth centuries.[16] The problem was not a lack of contacts, but the fact that there were no good ports. The Russian vessels, which set out to sea by way of the rivers, were therefore of low displacement, carried small volumes of cargo, and could not compete with the German ships.

The issuing of invitations to foreign artisans was evidence of a technical lag, but not of backwardness. Artisans were recruited in Italy and Germany not only by Russia, but also by Sweden, and even by England. This was a general European norm. In the Moscow Kremlin, cathedrals and fortifications were built by Italians. Anton Fryazin and Pietro Antonio Solario built towers in the years between 1485 and 1491, and Aristotel Fioravanti built the Uspensky cathedral in the years 1475–79. In 1505–08, on the site of an old temple built during Ivan Kalita's time, Aleviz Novy built the five-towered Arkhangelsky cathedral, clearly giving it, as art historians recognise, 'features characteristic of the Venetian palace architecture of the epoch of the renaissance'.[17] Modern scholars have explained that 'the creators of the heraldic seal of Ivan III, which for the first time in Rus depicted a two-headed eagle, were carvers from northern Italy'.[18] The origins of the Russian eagle in Byzantine heraldry are beyond doubt, but in Moscow it was not the Greek but the Italian design that was preferred.

There is no way that this Italian influence can be considered the result of backwardness. After all, it was Italians who in the fourteenth and fifteenth centuries were the best architects, engineers and artists in Europe. The Moscow princes invited architects from Italy itself, while the Scandinavians had as a rule to be content with Germans. The fact that Italians were appearing in the Kremlin is not evidence of backwardness, but rather of the fact that Rus was still living by the same rhythm as the rest of Europe, lagging behind the Mediterranean countries as they experienced the Renaissance, but by no means falling behind its closest Western neighbours. Foreign goods were becoming increasingly important in meeting the changing demands of the ruling-class consumer. From the sixteenth century, French wines were being imported into Rus.

In the south, the centre of attraction for Moscow was Italy, with its advanced technologies and cultural achievements, while in the north, Denmark had become the main partner. The more troubled the relations with Sweden became, the more the Moscow court sought to befriend the Danes. The diplomatic missions that appeared regularly in Moscow and Copenhagen discussed not only dynastic marriages and the possibility of military collaboration against the Swedes, but also trade. The pinnacle of these relations was the Copenhagen Treaty of 1562.

NOVGOROD: JUNIOR PARTNER OF THE HANSA

At the dawn of Russian history it was the Novgorodians, expanding southward, who unified under a single authority everything that later came to be called Kievan Rus. Throughout the whole Tatar period, however, Novgorod showed virtually no interest in the unification of the Russian lands. This, like the subsequent defeat of the Novgorodians by Moscow, is usually explained on the basis that the inhabitants of the merchant city had been spoiled by their prosperity, and had lost their warlike spirit. The real reasons were in fact much more profound. On the one hand, the interest of the Novgorodians in controlling the southern river routes disappeared as the route from the Varyags to the Greeks lost its importance; on the other hand, Novgorod itself was losing its earlier place in the world economy, and was going into decline. It is true that the Novgorodian lands yielded only meagre harvests, and that a constant exchange of goods with Russia's southern territories was essential. Grain and livestock were purchased in the 'lower reaches', while salt, furs and salmon were exported to these regions. Manufactured goods, however, were increasingly purchased from Hansa merchants. This changed the character of Novgorod's trade radically. Earlier, Russian merchants had transported products of the technologically more developed Byzantines, or their own goods manufactured using Greek techniques, to the backward West; now, they exchanged more simple agrarian produce for the manufactures of German artisans. Often, Novgorodian production even became more crude. Archaeologists note a decline of metalworking in Novgorod in the fifteenth century compared with the earlier period.

Novgorod's exports at that time consisted mainly of furs and wax. Among the European aristocracies of the period, the fashion for fur coats was spreading. In fourteenth-century England, the church had had to impose a special ban to stop nuns wearing furs. The English King Richard II shocked his contemporaries by paying a whole thirteen pounds for a fur coat! The sum was indeed considerable; at that time, it would have purchased a herd of 86 oxen. A certain quantity of furs came from Norway, but, as a Western historian notes,

by the end of the eleventh century most of the furs reaching Western Europe came from north Russia, not Scandinavia. Danes and Swedes could still exact tribute from people living around the Baltic, but they could no longer roam as freely in Russia as they had earlier. Russian princes then had more effective control over the region, and Novgorod took particular care to control Karelia. Merchants who wanted to obtain the best furs in large quantities had to buy them in the increasingly important market of Novgorod.[19]

In Pokrovsky's view, it was this 'near-monopoly domination of the market in furs' that secured Novgorod its place in the new system of European trade that took shape in the Baltic.[20] This domination, however, had to be fought for. In the thirteenth century, border conflicts with the Swedes were becoming commonplace, and in the fourteenth century the border was not stabilised. War with the German knights in the Baltic region also continued almost incessantly, with varying success. Soviet historians constantly stressed the defensive character of this struggle, arguing that, thanks to the campaigns of the Novgorodians, 'Rus did not become the prey of the German knights'.[21] The trouble was that although the Germans at times penetrated as far as Pskov, most of the battles took place on territory controlled by the Livonian Order, and which, in turn, Novgorodian forces regularly invaded. The main victories of the Novgorodians were won in Estonia. In 1234 Prince Yaroslav Vsevolodovich defeated the Germans on the River Embakh near Yuryev (otherwise known as Derpt, or Tartu). The famous battle on the ice of 1242, when Aleksandr Nevsky inflicted a decisive defeat on the German knights, took place while the Novgorodians were returning from a raid on Livonian territory. In 1269 the ferocious battle of Rakovor, which ended without a clear result, also took place on Estonian land. By the early fourteenth century the border in this region had also been stabilised. The Germans won the city of Yuryev (Derpt) from the Russians, but could advance no further. The Russians, for their part, abandoned their attempts to force the Danes and Germans out of northern Estonia.

On the whole, the final outcome of the thirteenth-century border conflicts was satisfactory for Novgorod. Meanwhile, research shows that the almost permanent state of war with the Livonian Order 'had no effect whatever' on trade with the German Hansa.[22] The merchants from the city of Lübeck were a major trading partner both of the Novgorodians and of the knights, and while the Novgorodians and the Order waged war on one another, the merchants conducted their business peaceably, formally speaking, on the territories of both contending sides. The struggle was in fact over the shares in this trade, and an end to the trade would have been equally catastrophic for both the Novgorodians and the 'dog-knights'.

In many ways, the struggle between the Novgorodians and the Germans in the thirteenth century recalls the seventeenth-century conflict between the British and Dutch. Like the Dutch, the Novgorodians mostly emerged victorious from the military clashes, but this proved insufficient to make up for the strategic advantages of the new, rising power. The Germans in the thirteenth century, like the British in the seventeenth, had substantial resources, and also a technological superiority that allowed them to stubbornly pursue their goal without regard for tactical setbacks. The upshot was that after a few decades of rivalry, the border was stabilised, and the Novgorodians, reconciling themselves to the loss of Yuryev (Derpt), turned into junior partners of the German merchants, just as Dutch capital ultimately became the junior partner of its British counterpart.

While the thirteenth century had been a time of almost uninterrupted war with the Germans, the fourteenth and most of the fifteenth centuries were exceptionally peaceful. Novgorod established trade relations not only with the merchants, but also with the knights. The Teutonic Order bought up furs wholesale in Novgorod, while at the same time supplying the merchant republic with the silver that was so necessary to it. In a sense, the wholesale deals with the knights were even more advantageous for the Novgorodians than the trade with the German merchants. 'Purchases in Novgorod were not as a rule paid for with goods,' notes the Swedish historian Artur Attman, 'but entirely with bars of silver, which were to a great extent carried to Novgorod by the servants of the Teutonic Order.'[23] It might be said that with the aid of silver, the Germans in the fourteenth and fifteenth centuries managed to acquire what they had tried unsuccessfully to gain through force of arms in the thirteenth century.

Archaeological studies show that in the early stages of development of the Novgorodian economy, the West's main role was as a supplier of raw materials.[24] The importing of raw materials did not cease even in later times, since the Novgorodian artisan production was almost entirely without its own resource base. Non-ferrous metals, alum, amber, silver, and so forth, were imported. It is significant, however, that the importing of non-ferrous metals from Western Europe reached its peak in the early thirteenth century, and then began to diminish. Until late in the tenth century, Novgorod obtained silver from the East, re-exporting it to the West (or, more precisely, to the north). After that, the flow of silver from the East dried up, while in the West the minting of silver coins increased. Novgorod began importing specie from Germany and England. In the thirteenth century the Germans began a Baltic trade in grain which a few centuries later would play a fateful role for all of Eastern Europe. As in the past, Novgorod obtained foodstuffs primarily from the south, via Torzhok, but if necessary it could acquire them from the Germans as well. The result was that the ties with southern Rus weakened still further.

Although the importing of raw materials did not stop, from the second half of the thirteenth century imports of finished goods began to increase, partly taking the place of the diminishing 'southern imports'. Wine was imported from Western Europe, as at times were weapons and horses. Cloth was purchased from Flanders, mainly from Ypres, Ghent and Bruges. A history of the city notes that:

Evidence of the scale of the imports of expensive cloth to Novgorod is provided by the fact that in 1410 the German merchants in the city held two hundred bales of cloth, or about eighty thousand metres. Meanwhile, a certain amount of the cloth imported that year had already been sold. Of course, not all the cloth, like other goods, which the Germans imported was consumed by the inhabitants of Novgorod and its territories; a significant proportion later reached the markets of other Russian cities.[25]

At the same time, archaeologists note the disappearance from the goods consumed by the cultured stratum of items that had earlier been brought from the Black Sea region. Goods that had previously come from Kiev were now being imported from Western Europe. The trade with the East was continuing; cloth from Bukhara continued to enjoy a market in Novgorod until the fourteenth and fifteenth centuries. It is curious that from the fourteenth century, manufactured goods also began arriving in Novgorod from the Golden Horde. Earlier, ceramics had been imported from Persia; now, they began to be imported from the territories of the Tatar khans.[26] This also indicates that the Horde was by no means the refuge of barbarism and savagery which many Russian historians have depicted. Also coming from the Horde were the silver coins that Rus sorely needed. Even the Russian word for money, *den'gi*, is of Tatar origin. In Russian historiography, the traditional explanation for the decline of the southern trade is that the Tatars' Golden Horde blocked it off. First the struggle with the Polovtsians 'paralysed the Volga trade route'; then, in the mid-thirteenth century, 'the Tatar-Mongol invasion for many years cut off the trade links between Novgorod and the south'.[27] Archaeologists, however, note that the southern trade was already 'fading' in the first half of the century; that is, before the arrival of the Tatars.[28] At the same time, Moscow chronicles and documents from the fourteenth century are full of complaints about the Novgorod bandits, the *ushkuyniki*, who systematically plundered trade caravans coming up the Volga from the south. The bandit raids were organised by members of the best boyar families. The victims were Tatar, Armenian and Arab merchants, but Russian cities also suffered from attacks.

Right up until the sixteenth century, or course, trade and brigandage were often interconnected. As a rule, the pirate bands gradually made the shift from plunder to more peaceful methods of commodity exchange. In the case of Novgorod, everything was reversed. In 1366, *ushkuyniki* with 150 ships attacked Nizhny Novgorod and sacked it. In 1371 and 1375, *ushkuyniki* twice stormed

Kostroma and plundered it. The sale of captives into slavery was normal practice; the centre of this trade was the Tatar city of Bulgar. The Moscow princes, by contrast, joined with the khans of the Golden Horde in trying to put a stop to the slaughter on the river routes. In 1366, the young Prince Dmitry Ivanovich of Moscow, the future victor at the battle of Kulikovo field, grew indignant at the behaviour of the Novgorodians, who 'sailed along the Volga and robbed my guests'.[29] The prince threatened to wage war on Novgorod, and it was only in the following year that a peace pact was signed. The raids by the *ushkuyniki*, however, did not cease. At Saray in 1375 the Tatars killed the participants in the sacking of Kostroma.

During the fourteenth and fifteenth centuries the Muscovites were repeatedly forced to join with the Tatars to fight against the Novgorodians. In other words, it was not the Tatars and Moscow that were blocking the trade of Novgorod, but the exact opposite; it was the Novgorodians who were impeding the trade of the Tatars and of Moscow. The latter states responded by joining forces to ensure the safety of the trade routes. For a time, they shared an objective interest. The relationship between them, however, gradually changed. From being a junior trade partner of the Tatars, Moscow began turning into an independent power; but at first not so much military as economic.

As Pokrovsky observes, the Volga trade route continued to function and develop throughout the whole of the fourteenth and fifteenth centuries, and it was Novgorod that linked this route to the markets of the Baltic. Here was one of the sources of the republic's wealth. The new situation, however, no longer required the political unification of the territories along the whole route. Moreover, with the passage of time, Novgorod was coming to play an increasingly parasitic role. The fact that a concern with ensuring the safety of trade was being replaced among the Novgorod elite by a desire for enrichment through plunder was a sign of the decline that was afflicting the northern republic.

WAS THERE A 'NOVGORODIAN ALTERNATIVE?'

A continual theme in liberal historiography in nineteenth-century Russia was regret that it had been Moscow, and not Novgorod, that had united the country. The fact is that the decline of Novgorod had been among the factors leading to the unification. Whatever the ambitions of the Moscow princes, a unified state could simply not be a reality so long as Novgorod led its own existence. In the ninth century, Novgorod – not yet a feudal trading republic – had acted to unite the territories along the trade route 'from the Varyags to the Greeks', but in the fourteenth century it no longer had any need for unity either with Kiev or with Moscow. Its commercial interests were oriented in a different direction. It had no interest in creating a unified national market, since its prosperity was based on its role as a commercial intermediary, not as a producer. To impose political control on the port cities of the Baltic region and the trading centres of the Volga was beyond its powers, while unification with the lands of southern Rus was not in its direct economic interest. Novgorod was thus perfectly satisfied with a role on the periphery of the German Hansa, acting as its advanced post in the east.

Almost never in history have trading republics been 'collectors of territories', trying to unite lands under single sovereign rule. In Italy and Germany, where the trading republics were strong, unification of territories into a single state simply did not occur between the fifteenth and seventeenth centuries. The Hansa cities, too, were interested not in the unity of Germany, but in the development of the Baltic trade, and to achieve this they relied more on the kings of Sweden and Denmark than on their 'own' German princes or emperor. In this respect the 'predatory' behaviour of the Novgorodian elites in the fourteenth and fifteenth centuries, when they often allied themselves with Lithuania against Moscow, corresponds to the general norm of behaviour of feudal trading republics. France, Spain and England were unified by kings with the support of the urban bourgeoisie, but their rulers were repeatedly forced to suppress not only revolts by the barons, but also separatism on the part of the traditional urban elites, who often summoned 'foreign' kings to their defence. The success of the royal authorities in these countries was predetermined by the fact that the cities were too weak to act independently.

The struggle to ensure the safety of the trade routes was conducted principally by Moscow, and to a significant degree was carried on against the Novgorodians. The advantage which Moscow enjoyed over Novgorod was founded not only on trade, but also on the powerful tax base furnished by the Tatars, and also on the control which Moscow exercised over a large population. At the same time, Moscow was no less interested in trade than Novgorod, though its focus was on the internal Russian market. For Moscow, the development of trade was closely tied to support for agrarian and artisan production on its own territory; without this production there would not have been a stable tax base.

With Novgorod the situation was quite different. Pokrovsky observes that Novgorod 'was a city not of artisans, but of merchants'.[30] While archaeological studies show that handicrafts were quite well-developed in the city, there are nevertheless no grounds for disagreeing with Pokrovsky. It was trade, not handicrafts, and certainly not agriculture, that represented the source of the republic's wealth. Even more importantly, this was transit trade. Novgorod traded in its own products only to an insignificant degree. Apart from fur coats, it produced little for export, and the furs arrived in the city as tribute paid by the northern territories. In other words, the fur trade did nothing to aid the growth of an entrepreneurial culture, of the development of bourgeois relations. The same can be said of the silver 'from beyond the River Kama' that reached Novgorod from the eastern (Urals) border of its territories. The Novgorodians did not work the mines themselves, but merely collected tribute. Foodstuffs reached the republic from the Volga region, or as the Novgorodians called it, 'downriver'. This was also where the largest market for the 'German' goods supplied by the Novgorod merchants was located.

The Novgorodian aristocrats became bourgeoisified, investing money in trading enterprises, while the merchants bought land and became feudalised. The result was that Novgorod, like the Italian trading republics of the fifteenth and sixteenth centuries, did not develop from feudalism to capitalism, but the other way round. The increase in wealth, Pokrovsky notes, led to feudalisation in Novgorod, not to democratisation. 'Feudalism, which outwardly seemed to move to Novgorod from Moscow, was prepared from within by the evolution of Novgorodian society itself.'[31] In their turn, popular representation and the *veche* (the people's assembly, which all free men were entitled to attend and had the right to vote) inevitably degenerated. The *veche* served 'merely as a battering ram, with the help of which the mercantile-capitalist bourgeoisie smashed the hereditary nobility'.[32] Once this aim had been achieved, and a new 'compromise elite' had taken shape in the republic, democratic institutions lost their former importance, which in turn later allowed the Moscow princes to finally do away with the democracy of the *veche*. It is significant that in the fifteenth century, when Moscow put an end to the democratic freedoms of the Novgorodians, the majority of the citizens of the city put up no particular resistance. 'The independence of Novgorod', Pokrovsky remarks, 'was defended mainly by the Novgorodian boyars, resting on the lower orders of the urban population; the Novgorodian merchants had an interest in maintaining good relations with those at the bottom of the social scale.'[33] After its victory, Moscow did not do away with the Novgorodian merchants, but transferred the head offices of the Novgorodian trading houses 'downriver'. Representatives of Moscow were sent to take the place of the heads of the old merchant families, an outcome which accorded on the whole with the aspirations of Novgorodian commercial capital itself.

The end of the Novgorodian *veche* did not by any means signify the wiping out of all forms of self-government in the Russian territories. There can be no talk of tsarist autocracy in Muscovite Rus. The boyar Duma played an important political role. The *oprichnina* of Ivan the Terrible was needed precisely in order to destroy the existing institutions of rule, and to do away with everything that limited the will of the tsar. This goal, however, was not achieved in full. Until the middle of the seventeenth century, the authorities periodically called in 'elected' people to resolve various problems.[34] Ivan the Terrible, in order to win support for additional taxes, was himself forced to appeal to a territorial assembly. The elevation to the throne of Mikhail Romanov, by the assembly of 1613, was possible precisely because the tradition of representation in the country had been retained. By the standards of the time, this representation was relatively democratic. As well as nobles and merchants, the participants in the assemblies of the seventeenth century more than once included representatives of the 'dark' (that is, free) peasants.

The defeat of the Novgorodian republic was in no way a defeat for the 'European' or 'Western' principle in Russian history. To the contrary, it signified that the Russian state was developing according to the same general logic as the rest of Europe, where absolute monarchies were also unable to unite their countries and impose order on them without putting an end to the remnants of medieval freedoms. The history of the flourishing and decline of the Russian trading cities is strikingly reminiscent of Italian history. This similarity is not due merely to chance. Novgorod in the fourteenth and fifteenth centuries was like Venice in the sixteenth century. It grew steadily richer, but had no prospects for commercial expansion. It developed with its 'face to the sea' and its 'back to the country'. The flowering of art, and the building of new temples and palaces, hid the decline of the state. Precisely because of this, the Novgorodians were rendered vulnerable. It was not the Tatar yoke, but the decline of the Mediterranean trade that played the fatal role in the history of Rus. The causes of the decline of Novgorod and Venice are not merely alike, but identical.

THE FALL OF CONSTANTINOPLE

Moscow did not unite the Russian lands; the lands united around Moscow later became Russia. This is why Russia in the fourteenth and fifteenth centuries seemingly shifted to the east. The lands of the earlier Kievan Rus, which were not of interest to the Moscow princes or were inaccessible to them, did not become part of Russia. These territories became Ukraine and Belarus, whose subjection to the Polish-Lithuanian crown no one contested. The historical and religious unity of Ukraine and Belarus with Muscovite Rus was recalled only in the seventeenth century, when the international grain trade began developing rapidly. The desire on the part of Moscow to establish its control over the Ukrainian black-earth lands would aid the unification of the Slavs no less than shared religious and ethnic roots. This, however, was to come later. By the end of the fifteenth century the trade route from the Varyags to the Greeks no longer existed, and the need for unity of the former territories of Kievan Rus therefore lapsed. Meanwhile, the Volga trade route continued to function.

In 1452, Constantinople fell to the blows of the Turks. After another 50 years almost all the eastern Mediterranean was under the power of the Ottoman empire. The eastern trading outposts of Venice were transformed into advanced lines of defence. In 1475, the power of the Genoese in Crimea also came to an end. The expansion of the Turks was eventually blocked, but the old trade routes finally lost their earlier importance. Naturally enough, it was precisely at this time that an intensive search began for alternative trade routes. The Portuguese pioneered the sea route to India around Africa, and the Spanish discovered America.

For centuries before this, people had navigated the Atlantic Ocean; the Vikings had reached America, and the Arabs had explored the African coast. These discoveries, however, had not been of decisive importance; economically, they had not forged a new system. Consequently, they remained known only to a few. In the fifteenth and sixteenth centuries, the situation changed radically.

At first, the fall of Constantinople and the decline of Mediterranean trade served to increase the importance of the Volga route, along which goods from the East might reach the Baltic and, from there, the markets of Western Europe. The world situation from 1450 to 1490 favoured Moscow. Not surprisingly, it was in the late fifteenth century that the Great Prince of Moscow took the decision to break with the Golden Horde. Moscow at this time, it might have seemed, had every possibility of rapid development.

It was at this time that Afanasy Nikitin, a merchant from the city of Tver, made his famous 'journey across three seas', eventually reaching India. Unlike the Portuguese voyagers of the same period, Nikitin discovered no new trade routes. He may not even have been the first Russian merchant to penetrate deep into Asia – as early as the eleventh and twelfth centuries, Indian sources mention 'armour from the land of the Rusi'.[35] But for the most part the trade with the East was carried on by Arabic and Jewish merchants, and by others from Bukhara; Nikitin merely followed their trade routes in seach of goods. Unlike the multitudes of other traders, however, he was also an explorer who left us a detailed written record, just like the sixteenth-century English merchants who left us a detailed description of Muscovy. In this respect, the journey of Afanasy Nikitin was a genuine part of the broader European movement to the East.

The conquest of the Volga region took place only in the sixteenth century. As they consolidated their state, the rulers of Moscow expended enormous efforts on establishing their control over the Volga and the adjacent territories. One after another, the Tatar trading cities – Kazan, Astrakhan and Saratov – passed under the control of Moscow. Not only were territories being seized from others; Russia itself was shifting to the east. The Volga was becoming a Russian river, known as the 'mother' and 'wet-nurse'. Just as a united power had arisen from the Baltic to the Black Sea during an astonishingly brief period in the ninth century, a new Russia was now arising. Not only were the lands of the Tatar khanates being seized, but the Tatar notables, many of them converting to Orthodoxy, hastening to become integrated into the Russian elite. A significant number of the boyar families of the seventeenth century had their origins in the Volga Tatar aristocracy, and many filled important state posts. Contrary to later ideas, it was during this period that Russians began mingling with Tatars in a massive way. It was not the Tatar invasion of Rus that led to the 'Tatarisation' of the Slavic population. Instead, the rapid shift of Muscovy to the east was accompanied by the widespread conversion of the local inhabitants to Orthodoxy, to their Russification and integration into Russian society. Moscow succeeded not only in seizing these vast territories in a brief period, but also in retaining them, precisely because the objective needed to maintain order on the Volga trade route required the unification of these lands under a single authority. This was no less obvious to the Tatar elite and to the Tatar merchants than it was to their Russian counterparts. Just as the Roman empire in ancient times unified the Mediterranean economic space and integrated the peoples inhabiting it into a single civilisation, Muscovite Rus formed itself as a nation by establishing a united authority over the river routes.

Like the Crusades and the Spanish conquest of America, Russia's eastward expansion was fed by the land hunger of the petty aristocracy. The peasants, too, appropriated new lands, as they sought to escape the power of the landowners. Nevertheless, the campaigns on the Volga, despite their success, came too late. At the very time when the Volga route came fully and definitively under the power of Moscow, world trade routes were shifting to the West. The discovery of America by Columbus not only opened a new era in European history, but also became the starting point for the formation of a world economic system. After Vasco da Gama had crowned the efforts of Portuguese navigators over many years by discovering a Western sea route to India, European commercial capital acquired quite new opportunities for development. The material and financial resources that were pouring into the West stimulated the growth of production and, most importantly, allowed entrepreneurship finally to take shape on a bourgeois basis. The exploitation of hired labour became profitable, and favourable conditions were established for the accumulation of capital. Although the 'prices revolution' that followed the vast influx of precious metals into Europe devalued money to a significant degree, the impetus gained by the Western economy was extraordinarily powerful. The Spanish Habsburgs, despite their initial successes, failed to transform the nascent world economy into a world empire. To subordinate the system to a single political authority was impossible, but bourgeois nations began to take shape. Overall, the global system started taking on the characteristic features which it has retained into the early twenty-first century. The nations which were most developed in the bourgeois sense became the 'centre' of the system, spontaneously transforming into their economic 'periphery' the rest of the world to which they had access.

These changes were far from passing Russia by. In the sixteenth century the Moscow tsardom was developing rapidly, and was engaging actively in trade. At the same time it fell further and further behind the West, which was changing even more rapidly. The river routes could not compare with the vast expanses opened up by seaborne trade. Moscow was running late, and from now on, as in Lewis Carroll's *Through the Looking Glass*, it would have to run very fast in order to stay where it was. The Moscow rulers were compelled to answer the challenge of the times. Located in the depths of the European continent, Russia had no direct access to the new trade routes. Gaining nothing from the flourishing of European trade that had begun after the discovery of America, Russia inevitably finished up on the periphery of world economic development, effectively dropping out of the world economic system that was taking shape. The late fifteenth and early sixteenth centuries thus formed a decisive boundary. It was at this time that Russia's subsequent fate – to struggle against backwardness and isolation – was determined.

It was not by chance that the slogan 'Moscow – the Third Rome' was proclaimed in 1517. Samir Amin considers this response 'brilliant'.[36] In fact, this slogan proved just as politically barren as it was entrancing to the imagination. It served as ideological compensation. The more Russia became in reality part of the periphery of the world system, the more it sought to declare itself the centre of the world on the level of culture and ideology.

But in the sixteenth century, the slogan 'Moscow – the Third Rome' was not meant to counterpose Russia to the West. On the contrary, it was an attempt, despite diminishing opportunities in the real world, to affirm the symbolic importance of Russia as a leading European power. The slogan traced Russia's origins to the same Roman empire to which many Western monarchs (starting with Charlemagne and the Holy Roman Empire, and ending with the empire of Napoleon Bonaparte) also appealed. In this respect, the sentiments of the slogan were not unique, or even anything novel.

MUSCOVY

The real challenges demanded an entirely concrete political response, one which had nothing in common with fantasies of a 'third Rome'. In theory, the discovery of America, which shifted trade routes in the direction of the Atlantic, could have provided Russian commercial capital with new opportunities. After all, the fifteenth and sixteenth centuries saw the beginning of rapid economic growth in northern Europe. The economic expansion had created a demand for grain (indispensable for the beginning of colonisation) and timber (essential for the construction of a fleet). In the fifteenth century, Novgorod was incapable of exploiting the new situation, since its Baltic trade was already controlled by Swedish and German intermediaries. In the changed situation, trading republics, whether Novgorod or Venice, could not maintain their trade routes independently, even when the economic possibility of their doing this still remained. The task now required strong armies and diplomacy. Novgorod lost its independence right at the point when the commercial situation was changing radically and definitively. Again, the cause lay not only in the power of Moscow, but also in the dramatic strengthening of the Muscovite party in Novgorod itself. The hereditary aristocracy still clung to the traditions of the feudal republic, but to large numbers of Novgorodian merchants it was already clear that in the broader reckoning there was nothing to defend.

Moscow met the needs of a changing period far better than commercial-aristocratic Novgorod. The Muscovite prince not only had his seat in a suitable location, where trade routes intersected, but also controlled a significantly greater population. The result was that it was Moscow, not the republic of Novgorod, that had the potential to develop the internal market. Without this, creating a European-style national state was impossible as well.

Klyuchevsky remarks with a certain puzzlement that 'so long as Rus was located on the black earth of the Dnepr, it traded mainly in the products of the forest and other such industries, and set about strenuously cultivating the soil when it migrated to the loams of the upper Volga'.[37] Grekov later wrote that Klyuchevsky had underestimated the development of agriculture in Kievan Rus. Nevertheless, Klyuchevsky posed the question in quite reasonable fashion; why was it in the period from the fourteenth to the eighteenth centuries that Russia abruptly 'set about cultivating the soil'? It is a fact that while Kievan Rus was located in the black-earth zone, in regions exceptionally suited to agriculture, the north-eastern territories where the Muscovite state arose have poor, boggy soils. Nevertheless, the dominant activity in Kievan Rus was intermediary trade, while Muscovy came to develop grain-growing. The expansion into Siberia, that began in the search for furs, also led quickly to colonisation and the rapid growth of agriculture.

The reason is simple. During the period of Kievan Rus the commercial demand for grain had been small. Moreover, the large cities of the eastern

Mediterranean had been able to obtain their foodstuffs from the nearby regions. The goods that were transported from one region to another were the products of artisanry. With the start of the modern era, by contrast, the demand for grain increased rapidly. Grain first became a traded commodity on the internal market, but this new situation was itself linked closely to the general dynamic of development. The flow of silver from America, and the 'prices revolution' that began in Europe in the sixteenth century, aided the development of commodity production. The cities were not only growing, and in need of food supplies, but could also pay for them. As grain became an object of world trade, Russia followed after Poland in becoming a world exporter. The development of the Russian grain trade, however, belongs to a much later period, and it is significant that this would occur against the background of the political and military decline of Russia's main rival, Poland. From the middle of the sixteenth century, Russia was drawn into a prolonged military conflict with Poland and Sweden. Poland was the leading supplier of grain to the world market, while Sweden controlled the Baltic Sea, by way of which this grain reached the West. For Russia, meanwhile, the struggle for the Baltic trade routes at first had nothing to do with the grain trade. Muscovy had sufficient grain for the development of its internal market, but not enough to allow the organising of regular exports. Timber and hemp were a different matter; Muscovy had surplus of both. In the sixteenth century the Moscow merchants competed with Poland in supplying raw materials for the growing shipbuilding industry, and this meant that Russia found itself at the centre of a political, military and commercial conflict that was convulsing Europe at the time.

4
The 'English Tsar'

Why was it precisely in the sixteenth century that Russia needed ports on the Baltic? For hundreds of years before this the Novgorodians had had an exit to the sea, but had not attempted to build fortresses or towns directly on the shore. Ivangorod was built opposite Narva only in 1492, and exclusively as a fortress. Control of the coast had a solely military significance. If the Swedes or Germans were to seize control of the mouth of the Neva, they could shut off Novgorodian shipping from access to the Baltic, and so bring Novgorod's trade under their control. The Swedes made two attempts to do this. It is significant that both times, the events concerned took place on the territory of the future St Petersburg. In 1240 they landed at the mouth of the Neva, but were attacked by the Novgorodians and forced to withdraw. It was in honour of this battle that the Novgorodian leader, Prince Aleksandr, came to be known as Aleksandr Nevsky. Sixty years later, however, the Swedish marshal Torkel Knutsson made a second attempt, sailing into the Neva mouth with a fleet of more than a hundred ships. This time, the efforts of the Novgorodians to drive the enemy into the sea were unsuccessful, and the Swedes established the fortress of Landskrona, as Karamzin notes, 'seven *versty* from present-day St Petersburg' (a *versta* being approximately one mile).[1] After the Swedish fleet had departed, the Novgorodians attacked the settlement, and in 1301 levelled it to the ground.

With the passage of time, however, the position of the Novgorodians was objectively growing steadily weaker. Between the eighth and eleventh centuries, river craft had differed little from seagoing vessels. In the twelfth century, however, the Italians and Germans were building ships with a substantially greater cargo capacity than those of the Russians and Scandinavians. With the start of the great geographical discoveries, a new trading fleet began to develop. The size and capacity of the ships steadily increased. The Novgorodian river fleet finally became uncompetitive.

THE ENGLISH 'DISCOVER' MOSCOW

In the early sixteenth century, the economy of the Moscow tsardom was developing much like those of other European countries. In 1534 Yelena Glinskaya, the mother of the future Tsar Ivan the Terrible, carried out a monetary reform, replacing the coins of various independent princedoms with a single monetary system. The conditions were arising for the formation of a common Russian internal market. Production and trade were growing. The paradox was that Russia's economic growth was accompanied by an increasing lag behind the West. This apparent contradiction arose from the fact that Russia, while drawn into a common process of development and socio-economic change, was located on the periphery.

As the economy grew, the borders of the state expanded. While Western European countries began founding colonies in America and on the African coast, Russia was spreading eastward. The first stage in this expansion was the conquest of the khanate of Kazan. As M. Pokrovsky notes, the trigger for this expansion was provided, as in Western Europe, by the parallel interests of the land-hungry nobility and of commercial capital. The nobility were growing in numbers and, as in the case of the Spanish hidalgos, lacked both land and peasants; commercial capital, meanwhile, was growing qualitatively, which enabled the financing of expeditions by the nobility in order to expand commercial interests. Such a situation had already emerged in Western Europe in the era of the Crusades, and by the end of the fifteenth century something analogous had occurred in both the East and the West of the continent.

This was superimposed on a crisis of the traditional feudal economy, caused by the development of the market. The landed estates were ceasing to be isolated. 'The transformation of grain into a commodity', Pokrovsky notes, 'meant that the land which yielded the grain became a commodity as well.'[2] The earlier relations of property and of mutual obligation had been placed in question. Nevertheless, the estates of the boyars were not sold or divided up, but remained family holdings.

Market relations were most rapidly assimilated in Russia by the monasteries. The large estates of the boyars were a brake on development; dividing them up or selling them off, however, was impossible because of the remaining political power of the boyar class. This also served to heighten the resemblance between the situations in Russia and Spain. In England, by contrast, the old aristocracy had largely been wiped out, and its political influence undermined, by the Wars of the Roses. Since expropriating the boyars would have been risky and politically difficult, external expansion became a reasonable choice; it offered a way of both obtaining land and putting grain on the market, without sacrificing the interests of the boyars. The war on the Kazan khanate, however, turned out not to be as easy as it had at first seemed. After the fall of Kazan, resistance from the local inhabitants continued in the form of partisan warfare for about six years. Victory was achieved only through settling the Volga region with large numbers of Russian colonists brought in from remote regions of the country. The peasants died in their thousands, but they changed the demographic situation to the benefit of the conquerors. The nobles, on the other hand, lost out: after six years of war they still had not managed to seize new estates for themselves, while there were even fewer peasants in the western provinces. The merchants had made greater gains; commercial capital had won access to waterways that led to Persia. However, this merely served to inflame the merchants' appetites.

Russia now sought to rid itself of a group of commercial intermediaries, the German merchants who controlled trade in the eastern Baltic region through the cities of Riga, Revel and Narva. Meanwhile, Russia was not the only country to be hindered by the operations of the German middlemen. In Western Europe, a new trading power was emerging – England. Britannia had not yet come to rule the waves, and a major problem facing the development of English commercial capitalism was the Spanish and Portuguese monopoly of the Atlantic. German domination of the Baltic, however, was also holding back the development of English trade. New markets and new sources of raw materials were needed; for English merchant capital, Russia promised to supply both.

In 1553 three ships set sail in the direction of Norway, officially to search for a northern sea route to China, Japan and India. The idea was utterly unrealistic. Even with the help of icebreakers in the Soviet period, a northern sea route around Siberia and Chukotka could not be established in any serious way. In the sixteenth century, however, thoughts of opening up such a route to China did not seem absurd either in England or in Russia. Thirty years after the failure of the English expedition, the merchant house of the Stroganovs mounted a second such attempt. In 1584, Dutch seafarers whom the Stroganovs had hired set out to achieve what had eluded the Englishmen, and naturally met with defeat.

In fact, the English expedition had from the first pursued a far wider range of goals. Its organisers were looking for new markets, since 'our merchants perceived the commodities and wares of England to be in small request with the countreys and people about us'.[3] The ships took with them a message from King Edward VI, addressed to no less than 'all kings, princes, rulers, judges and governors of the earth.'[4] This was not just an affirmation of the powers of the voyagers, who were at once merchants and official representatives of their country. 'The letter,' wrote the British historian T.S. Willan, 'explained the mutual advantages of foreign trade in terms which a nineteenth-century free-trader would have appreciated.'[5]

Two ships were wrecked, since the crews were not prepared for the conditions of the far north, and the expedition's chief, Hugh Willoughby, also died. But the third vessel, the *Edward Bonaventure* commanded by Captain Richard Chancellor, entered the mouth of the Northern Dvina. In February 1554, Chancellor, in the capacity of an English ambassador, was received in Moscow by Ivan the Terrible. The tsar granted the Englishmen commercial privileges in Russia, including the right to conduct duty-free trade throughout the country's entire territory.[6]

After this, Chancellor and his companions returned successfully to their homeland. A year later, the Muscovy Company was established in London. The importance of this move is suggested by the fact that this was the first such company whose founding was confirmed by Act of Parliament. In a sense, the Muscovy Company was not just the prototype for the commercial-political organsations set up in order to operate in the West and East Indies, but also a precursor of the transnational corporations of the twentieth century. The company's trading activity was intimately connected with diplomatic concerns. The English missions to the tsar's court defended the interests of the merchants, and the company's representatives conducted the business of the English Crown.

Once in Muscovy, the Englishmen did not waste their time. Unlike the letters of other travellers, the letters written by Chancellor and his colleague John

Hasse read above all like instructions for the commercial exploitation of Russia. The letters give a detailed description of the economic geography of Tsar Ivan's realm, listing what was produced and where, what could be purchased, and what could be sold in which places. Soon afterwards, the 'English court' appeared in Moscow. At first a single building, this later came to consist of a whole complex of residential, commercial and industrial structures, the remnants of which exist in Moscow to this day. A stone building on Varvarka Street was granted to the Englishmen as a gift from the tsar, 'as a mark of his special favour'.[7] As Russian sources noted, this did not suffice for the company, and 'the English foreigners built themselves wooden mansions'.[8] Before long, 'English houses' appeared in Kholmogory, Yaroslavl, Borisov, and other towns. The company had outposts in Novgorod, Pskov, Yaroslavl, Kazan, Astrakhan, Kostroma and Ivangorod. In Yaroslavl the Englishmen built large storehouses for goods that were later sent on to Asia. Protestant churches also appeared in Muscovy. The Moscow rulers were by no means passive onlookers where the Western reformation was concerned. 'Since the Russian government was extremely hostile to Catholics,' the historian I. Lyubimenko notes, 'it often showed great tolerance to protestants.'[9]

THE NORTHERN ROUTE

The new trade route was important not only to the English, but also to Muscovy. In 1556 a Russian diplomatic mission headed by the boyar Osip Nepeya arrived in England. Chancellor died while delivering him to London, but Nepeya completed his task, and went down in diplomatic history as having 'obtained in London the same benefits as the Englishmen had received in Moscow'.[10] Russian merchants, however, were unable to exploit these gains, since they lacked a fleet able to make long sea voyages. Regular trade along the northern route began in 1557. At first, these voyages involved numerous sacrifices. Six or seven ships would set out from England, and at times no more than half would return successfully. The navigation season was short, since the sea was frozen for five to six months each year. As the English seafarers gained experience of sailing in northern latitudes, these voyages became less risky. Nevertheless, the company complained periodically of losses: Tatar raids, pirates and northern storms all dealt blows to commerce. The attack on Moscow by the Crimean Khan Devlet-Girey caused the company losses of the then enormous sum of 10,000 rubles – which also gives an indication of the company's huge turnover. Around forty of sixty or so Englishmen then in Moscow perished in the fire. The Tatar attack evidently made a strong impression on the leaders of the company, since under Tsar Fyodor the Englishmen contributed £350 to the building of a new stone wall around Moscow.

The shareholders in the company were repeatedly called upon to make additional investments – of £50 per share in 1570, and £200 in 1572. However, they had no intention of shutting the business down. The reasons for this were not just the high profits that from time to time could be had from the trade with Muscovy, but also the importance these shipments had for England's overall military and political situation. The imports from Russia were comprised of not only goods from the north, but also strategic raw materials. As T.S. Willan observes, the Anglo-Russian trade of the sixteenth century 'was not unlike that which later developed between England and her colonies'.[11] From Russia, England imported timber, wax, hides, meat, fat, and at times grain, flax, hemp, whale oil, tar, ropes, and masts for ships. The tsar himself took part in the trade. As the English acknowledged, he was 'a great merchant himselfe of wax and sables'.[12] Wax was an extremely profitable commodity: it was used to make candles, vast numbers of which were needed to illuminate gothic cathedrals. This allowed the tsar to maintain that wax was not an everyday commodity, but a holy one that was 'reserved', and in which only tsars should deal. For other Russian merchants this monopoly was a real burden, and also cost the English dearly, but for Tsar Ivan it yielded extremely well. The tsar demanded the right of first purchase of goods imported from England, and was slow to pay. In this, he was no different from his contemporaries; Elizabeth of England was also reluctant to pay her debts. During the time of the *oprichnina*, the English company tried to obtain from the tsar money owed to it by boyars whom the tsar had had executed. The tsar heard the claims, but did not hand over the money, recommending that his English partners be more careful in lending money to Muscovites. Sometimes, on the other hand, even hopeless debts were returned. During the diplomatic mission of Ambassador Bowes, Ivan the Terrible suddenly ordered the repayment of 3,000 silver marks which the company had already written off.

THE MUSCOVY COMPANY

The English brought paper, sugar, salt, cloth, earthenware, copper, lead sheets for covering roofs, and luxury items to Moscow. In Russian markets, London cloth became known as '*lundysh*'. Also of importance were exotic goods from the Americas and Asia which reached Russia through the Muscovy Company. In the lists of the goods supplied we also find almonds, currants, horse harnesses, medicines, musical instruments, halberds, jewellery – and even lions. Church bells and precious metals were also brought in; these were banned from being exported from England, but by special order of the Crown, an exception was made for Russia. Particularly important for Moscow was the fact that the English ships also brought lead, gunpowder, saltpetre, sulphur and, from what we can tell, firearms.

The Muscovy Company did not, of course, have a monopoly on trade with the West. German, Dutch, Danish, and even Spanish and Italian entrepreneurs made their way to Moscow. However, in the sixteenth century it was the English who managed to raise commercial collaboration to the level of state policy.

In 1557 the English set up a rope-making works in Kholmogory. Vologda became another of the company's industrial centres. By 1560, local workers had mastered the technology, and most of the English tradesmen had returned home. While in Kholmogory, the English tradesmen were paid at the rate of £9 a year, of which £2 were invested on their account in England. These were excellent wages for the time, but the influx of precious metals from the Americas resulted in high inflation, and not only in Western Europe. Twenty-five years after the first English workshops had appeared in Russia, a certain John Finch, citing the price rises, demanded an increase in his wages to 42 rubles a year, some £28 in English money. As Willan correctly notes, this is evidence 'that the "price revolution" had been operating in Russia in the interval'.[13] In 1558, Muscovy Company representative Anthony Jenkinson received permission from the tsar to mount an expedition to Persia and Bukhara by the Volga route. Although many of the goods obtained were lost on the return journey, the proceeds were sufficient in commercial terms to justify the company's operations for a long time to come. While Jenkinson was in Persia, he also carried out a diplomatic assignment from Ivan the Terrible. The Moscow tsar was seeking an alliance with the Persians against the Turks.

At the dawn of the capitalist era, politics was openly intertwined with trade. The Azerbaijani scholar L.I. Yunusova observes that Jenkinson's commercial success was determined to a significant degree by the fact that he was 'not merely an English merchant, but an emissary of the Russian tsar'.[14]

Jenkinson's mission initiated a prolonged period of both rivalry and collaboration between English and Russian capital in the Caspian. Moscow, and later St Petersburg, needed foreign partners. Much of the trade with Persia was of a transportation character. The English helped to establish trade routes; Persian silks, together with other goods, were transported further into Europe on English ships, and later also on Dutch ships. On the other hand, the partners waged a fierce struggle with one another. Both were trying to seize the greatest possible share of the profits from the Persian trade for themselves.

In Persia, Jenkinson obtained commercial privileges similar to those in Moscow. English expeditions to Persia followed one upon another, in 1564, 1565, 1568, 1569 and 1579. This aroused fears in Moscow, where there was a reluctance to concede so profitable a trade route to foreigners. The tsar's court subsequently took steps to ensure that the Volga trade remained under its control, and restrictions were placed on the operations of the English in this area. Commercial expeditions to the south could be undertaken only jointly and with the permission of the tsar. For all the problems, the Persian trade was a veritable goldmine for the company. By the early seventeenth century, however, a simpler and safer route to Persia, via the Indian Ocean, was being established. The East India Company was starting to transport Persian goods to the West in significant quantities, lowering the commercial attractiveness of the Volga route. Nevertheless, trade with Persia through the Caspian continued, causing Astrakhan to flourish.

PARTNERS OR RIVALS?

Among Russian historians in later years, the activity of the Muscovy Company became a topic of heated discussion. The nineteenth-century historian N. Kostomarov turned his attention to the fact that the English merchants organised around the Muscovy Company had close ties to their government and acted in concert, often to the detriment of their compatriots who did not have political support in London. Kostomarov was convinced that the English had 'vast ambitions for political domination in Russia'.[15] Not surprisingly, this thesis was also extremly popular among Soviet historians, especially during the early years of the Cold War.[16] A number of Soviet historians set out to show that in Russia the English had found a backward country, and had 'set out to reinforce this backwardness in every possible way'; that they had 'prevented the Russians from studying and mastering advanced technology', and had 'taken the path of coercion and blackmail'.[17] Historians of the 'Westerniser' school, by contrast, have seen the English merchants as representatives of advanced civilisation, who brought knowledge to the backward Russian people.[18] It was only in the early 1960s that Ya.S. Lurye attempted to demythologise the history of Anglo-Russian relations in the sixteenth century.

The activity of the Englishmen in Russia was accompanied by numerous disputes between Russian and English partners. From the second half of the sixteenth century to the time of the first Romanovs, complaints about foreign competition were heard regularly from Russian merchants. In a petition against the 'English foreigners' presented to the tsar's government in 1646, much the same objections were voiced as in documents from an earlier period. The Russians accused the English of manipulating prices, while the English in turn complained of the unreliability of the Russian merchants, of frequent delays and of sharp practice. The complaints by Englishmen (and by foreigners in general) who were in Muscovy in the sixteenth and seventeenth centuries often seem quite comic. Foreigners thus objected to the fact that they were 'overfed', in a clear attempt to damage their health through excessive hospitality. In Muscovy at that time it was thought improper for guests not to become so inebriated at the host's table that they were incapable of standing and leaving by themselves, and if next day the guests did not complain of feeling sick from too much food and drink, the feast was considered a failure. In their dealings with Russian partners, the Englishmen found that the Russians did not keep their word, 'and if they start swearing oaths, they are probably out to trick you'.[19] Protestants could not fail to be astonished by the ability of the Russians to combine sharp wits and entrepreneurial flair with disorderliness and carelessness, but as Kostomarov notes, the claims and counter-claims of the Russian and Western merchants never stopped them from 'joining forces to deceive the government'.[20]

In fairness, it should be pointed out that situations always seem more dramatic in hindsight. Instances in which the various sides part company amicably leave fewer traces in the documentary record. It is when disputes arise that people start writing down complaints and appealing to various authorities, furnishing materials for future historians in the process. Paradoxically, it is the vast number of complaints, of all conceivable varieties, that testifies to the scope and intensity of the trading relations between the English and Russians.

In reality, of course, cultural differences were not the main problem. Making themselves at home in Muscovy, the English began trading on the internal market, competing successfully with local merchants. The English organised their own network of suppliers and system of wholesale purchases, providing credit to producers. This set-up, Kostomarov notes, 'was advantageous for petty traders and for the population in general, but ruinous for the Russian wholesale merchants'.[21] The law of mercantile capitalism is that the market is controlled by whoever has most capital at their disposal. With greater financial resources, the English were in a stronger position than their Russian rivals.

The actions of the English merchants in Muscovy aroused dissatisfaction not only in their Russian competitors, but also among numerous merchants in England itself. There was a belief in London that Russia had a corrupting influence on the company's agents. After arriving in Muscovy they quickly grew rich, built luxurious mansions such as the London shareholders could not permit themselves, and adopted local customs, keeping servants, dogs and bears. Like Moscow boyars, they began stuffing themselves with food until their stomachs ached.[22] It was thought in London that Russia led Englishmen astray through the temptations of excessive freedom, and that after living for a time in Moscow, they were reluctant to return to Puritan abstinence. Ambassador Bowes complained openly to Ivan the Terrible of his poverty ('my pitiful estate at home').[23] When agents of the company were recalled, they did everything possible in order to stay. To achieve this, some entered Russian service, and even converted to the Orthodox faith.

The trade with the English was so important to Ivan the Terrible that he ordered the boyar Boris Godunov, at that time the rising star of the Kremlin administration, to take care of them and keep a watchful eye on their affairs, so as to protect them from Russian bureacracy and corruption. The Englishmen accepted Godunov as a sort of protector. Conversely, an English astrologer, known in Moscow as Yelisey Bomeliy, enjoyed particular influence at the tsar's court. As well as foretelling the future, he also carried out more practical tasks for Ivan, preparing poisons for him, and collecting information on boyars suspected of treason. 'Bomeliy was so well known,' writes S.F. Platonov, 'and there was so much talk of his powers, that even a contemporary chronicle from a remote province refers to him in tones of the epic and fantastic.'[24] In the words of the chronicler, the 'fierce wolf' Bomeliy was to blame for all the misfortunes that befell the country during the reign of Ivan the Terrible. The English stargazer impelled the tsar to show 'ferocity' in dealing with his own subjects, and influenced him to the advantage of 'foreigners'.[25]

The question, however, is not how the English acted, but what the Russian government expected of them. Karamzin is certain that in establishing ties to England, the government of Ivan the Terrible made use of an opportunity to 'borrow from the foreigners what was most needed for civic development'.[26] Historians note that Ivan gave the foreigners such patronage as to deal 'great offence to his subjects, whom he readily humiliated before outsiders'.[27] The tsar's interest in foreigners, however, was thoroughly practical. In Queen Elizabeth of England, Ivan sought to find a military and commercial ally.

A STRATEGIC ALLIANCE

The fact that both the English and Russian governments gave preference to the organised merchants of the Muscovy Company over individual traders, whether Russian or English, is evidence that both sides were trying to achieve their goals on the state level. It was quite natural that Queen Elizabeth and Ivan the Terrible should feel a common interest. If the Swedes and Germans needed to preserve their commercial dominance in the eastern Baltic, the English, by contrast, needed to gain access to Russian resources independent of the Riga and Revel merchants. In just the same fashion, Muscovy also sought to find a direct outlet to European markets. However, the commercial goals of England and Muscovy could not be achieved by peaceful means. To understand why the state intervention by both London and Moscow was so intensive, it is enough to look at the list of goods the two sides were supplying to one another. The point is that what was involved was not so much commerce as collaboration in the field of military technology.

Individual arms shipments might be supplied by private traders, but even in the sixteenth century, the systematic procurement of military supplies was coordinated on a state level. Ensuring the effectiveness of this collaboration was the fact that arms sales were combined with the supplying of military materials and with exchanges of technology, the sending of experts, and so forth. Supplies from Russia were a decisive factor in the rise of the English navy. The collaboration between Russia and England was an element in the conflict between England and Spain. The Spanish King Phillip II was preparing to invade England, while Queen Elizabeth was urgently constructing her fleet. As the historian Ya.S. Lurye notes:

To cut off England and the Netherlands from the raw materials of Eastern Europe would have meant the destruction of these states. This was the goal that Phillip II was pursuing in Poland, Sweden and Russia. In the case of Poland his diplomats had only a certain success. In Russia, they met with complete failure.[28]

Russia's supplying of strategic raw materials to England played an enormous role in deciding the outcome of the military and political struggle that gripped Western Europe in the second half of the sixteenth century. A conflict between England and Spain over dominance of the Atlantic Ocean had become inevitable. For Elizabethan England, the creation of a powerful navy would be a question of life or death. 'The English fleet which was then built, and which defeated the Spanish Armada in 1588, was mainly rigged out with Russian materials', notes the Swedish historian Artur Attman.[29]

The Muscovy Company was an official supplier to the royal fleet. 'Russia had no monopoly of the supply of cables and cordage, which were also imported from the Baltic countries,' writes Willan, 'but the Russian source was of great importance to the Elizabethan navy, to which cables and cordage were as essential as oil to a modern fleet.'[30] The English seafarers acknowledged that the rigging obtained from Russia was 'the best brought into the country'.[31] Moreover, the cables and ropes from Muscovy were cheaper than those from elsewhere. As a result, Willan concludes, the northern trade 'was more valuable to England than to Russia'.[32]

For his part, Ivan the Terrible asked England for military supplies, weapons, engineers, artillery specialists, and architects familiar with the building of fortifications. When the Livonian War began in 1557, rumours flew about Europe of English weapons in the hands of the Muscovites. Poland and Sweden voiced protests. In Cologne and Hamburg, embargoes were placed on large shipments of weapons bought up by Englishmen, since the Germans feared that the equipment was in fact meant for the armies of Ivan the Terrible. Understandably, Queen Elizabeth denied everything. While reassuring other monarchs that there was no military collaboration with Muscovy, she also made a point of speaking disparagingly of the extent of the trade relations, maintaining that what was involved was a few merchant ships that had sailed into the mouth of the Northern Dvina almost by chance. The merchants, of course, were peaceable individuals whose exclusive concern was their commercial profits.

One particular episode shows just how 'peaceable' the agents of the Muscovy Company actually were. At the height of the Livonian War, in 1570, Swedish privateers attacked English traders who were transporting 'Russian' cargoes. In the ensuing battle the Swedish flagship was boarded and captured by the 'peaceable merchants'.[33] The story of this victory was promptly conveyed to Moscow by representatives of the company, and brought to the notice of the Russian authorities.

Nevertheless, Enlgish diplomats throughout Europe sought to refute the 'rumours' of military collaboration, and to this end, a special mission was sent to the continent. Meanwhile, weapons and other items of military technology suspiciously like those of the English were mysteriously appearing in the hands of Ivan's soldiers. In 1558, an agent of the company, Thomas Alcocke, who had been captured by the Poles, admitted that military materials were being delivered, but justified himself on the basis that 'only old, useless weapons were being supplied'.[34] This would hardly have met with the agreement of the engineer Lock, who boasted in his letters that with his help, the Muscovites had learnt to make weapons as good as any in Europe. Meanwhile, not only were English physicians and apothecaries arriving in Russia, but also architects, and builders skilled in 'the erection of stone structures'.[35] If it is recalled that Ivan several times wrote to London stating that he needed help with constructing fortifications, it becomes clear what kind of 'stone structures' were involved.

Surviving documents leave no doubt as to what was in the holds of the Muscovy Company's ships. They were carrying saltpetre, lead, sulphur and gunpowder for artillery pieces. Of course, nowhere near all the goods supplied were of strategic significance. The English, who did not produce wine themselves, nevertheless sent wine to Muscovy. The consumers there were not demanding, and the English hence dispatched 'various spoiled wines, sweet wines, and wines with a large admixture of cider'.[36] They may have sent a great deal else, since by no means all the deliveries have left traces in the documentary record. 'Although the English repeatedly assured other states that they were not supplying Russia with armaments,' writes the historian of Anglo-Russian trade, I. Lyubimenko, 'they repeatedly pointed out to the tsar himself what an important service they were doing him through their shipments of munitions.'[37] Since the munitions as a rule were had in exchange for wax, for which there was a strong demand in Europe, there was more to Tsar Ivan's taking personal control of deliveries of wax than just his desire to profit from a 'reserved commodity'.

The collaboration between England and Muscovy was as strategic as it was commercial. The trade of the sixteenth and seventeenth centuries was inseparable from war. In opening the route from northern Europe to the mouth of the Northern Dvina, the English quickly made it attractive to other Western countries. Russia's coastal region, however, possessed neither the technology nor the resources for the building of a substantial fleet. Moreover, creating a significant fleet in the Russian north was impossible in principle, even if the English had helped with its construction. This task required more than a great deal of timber and know-how. Experts could be recruited abroad, as Peter I was later to do. A strong navy, however, could only be based in large port cities. The Northern Dvina was too remote from the rest of Russia, and had too few resources and people, to compete with Riga. In any case, developing trade there was made difficult by the fact that the sea freezes in winter. Russian goods flowed for the most part through Revel, which was under German control, and through the Swedish port of Vyborg. The Muscovy Company was in fierce competition with these cities.[38] To gain access to new trade routes, Russia needed to establish its commercial position in the Baltic region, and hence the German merchants, who had been first the enemies and then the leading partners of the Novgorodians, again became enemies, though this time of Moscow. Russia needed its own large port on the Baltic, and with the beginning of the Livonian War, obtained it.

THE LIVONIAN WAR

In his work on the origins of the modern world economic system, Immanuel Wallerstein argues that during the Livonian War, Ivan the Terrible was seeking to 'establish autonomy of the Russian state from the European world-economy'. In this sense the tsar's policies, which led to the war, were not a failure but represented 'a gigantic success'. The result of Ivan's actions was that Russia 'was not pulled into the European world-economy', allowing the country to retain its developed national bourgeoisie, and subsequently to become a part not of the periphery of world capitalism, but of its semi-periphery.[39] It is curious how Wallerstein's ideas coincide with the official propaganda myth that held sway in the Stalinist period. The Livonian War was not just a military catastrophe, but resulted from the desire of the tsar's government to achieve inclusion in the embryonic world system at any cost.

At first glance, it might appear that during the sixteenth century Russia's integration into the world system was proceeding relatively successfully. As the Swedish historian Artur Attman notes, Russia maintained a positive trade balance with the countries of the West. 'As to the Russian market, since the Middle Ages and down to the middle of the seventeenth century at least, every country had to pay its trade deficit with precious metals.'[40] On the whole, Russia's situation was better than that of Poland, even though both countries often traded in the same goods (though Poland, unlike Russia, could not supply furs to the world market).[41]

Russia's trade in the sixteenth century was nevertheless a paradoxical phenomenon. On the one hand, it was marked by a positive balance and by a constant influx of ready money. In other words, Russia profited from world trade, and accumulated capital. On the other hand, the structure of this trade was clearly of a peripheral character. The resemblance which Willan notes to the American colonies was far from accidental. Russia was exporting raw materials and importing technology. It was competing on the world market with other countries and territories that made up the periphery of the rising world system. This combination of strength and vulnerability lay behind the inevitable aggressiveness of Moscow's foreign policy, and its subsequent failures.

In comparing Russia with Poland, and concluding that Ivan the Terrible was anxious to avoid the Polish fate of becoming an appendage to the European world system, Wallerstein is profoundly mistaken. The tsar was seeking precisely the opposite, trying unsuccessfully to seize for Russia the very place which Poland held in the developing world system in the sixteenth and seventeenth centuries. Contemporary figures were well aware that Russia and Poland were competitors on the world market. In the seventeenth century Dutch trade representatives in Moscow discussed these questions directly with the tsar, calling for an expansion of Russian grain exports.

Contrary to Wallerstein's view, Russia's rulers were not trying to resist Western expansion, but were seeking inclusion in the world system – as part of its periphery, but on their own terms. In the Livonian War, Poland and Sweden, which, by the mid sixteenth century, already occupied this place in the world economy, were defending their status.

Initially, the Livonian War went well for the Russian forces. In launching military operations, Ivan the Terrible made use of an absurd, deliberately contrived pretext, recalling the failure of the Bishop of Derpt to pay a tribute of which there had been no mention for 50 years. The Livonian Order had been undermined ideologically by the Reformation, and its forces were few in number. Unlike the situation in the conflicts of the seventeenth century, the weapons of the Russian army were not markedly inferior to those of their Western adversaries. Also of importance was the presence of English military experts. The Russians' artillery and metalworking were advanced for the times, and allowed the tsar's armies to score rapid successes during the early fighting. The Livonian Order suffered a crushing defeat. In May of 1558 the Russian forces captured Narva, the key port and fortress that opened the way to the Baltic.

For England, the capture of Narva opened up direct access to Russian raw materials. For the shareholders of the Muscovy Company, however, this was far from good news, since the northern route which the company had opened up with such difficulty now lost its attractiveness. After the Russians had taken Narva, English ships began arriving there. As a port, it did not have much to recommend it, and the conditions for doing business there were incomparably worse than in Revel. Nevertheless, it drew in Western traders. 'As with the north,' the American scholar Walther Kirchner notes, 'it was future expectations which the merchants connected with its acquisition by Russia rather than the reality which counted.'[42] During 1566 some 42 ships called at Narva, and trade boomed. Compared with this, the six or seven ships that took the northern route seemed an insignificant commercial operation. The Muscovy Company's monopoly did not extend to Narva, and anyone who wanted to could sail there. The company protested, complaining that traders who had no experience of working in Russia were bringing all sorts of rubbish to Narva, and were undermining the reputation of English goods. In the case of the northern sea route, authorities in London were completely on the side of the Muscovy Company, guarding its monopoly at all costs, but in the conflict surrounding the 'Narva navigation' the company was forced to yield. Here the trade had already reached such proportions that military and strategic considerations were inevitably overruled by commercial ones.

Queen Elizabeth, who had earlier given her full support to the Muscovy Company, was now reluctant to move against the Narva traders. The company had not only been a commercial enterprise, but also an instrument of English policy in Russia; with the capture of Narva, however, one of England's key political goals had been achieved. Of course, this did not mean that the policy had changed, especially since the compromise that was reached between the company and its competitors allowed the company to keep its dominant position. But now, all English merchants could enjoy the fruits of the company's efforts. The question of the Narva trade was discussed in the English parliament, and the monopoly was eventually confirmed. For the company, however, the form which the monopoly now took represented a Pyrrhic victory in commercial terms.

THE NARVA NAVIGATION

Prior to the Livonian War, Narva had been less a commercial port than a fortress blocking Russian access to the Baltic. After 1559, however, the Narva trade developed rapidly. As well as Englishmen, merchants appeared from Holland and other countries. Extensive building work began in the city, and business flourished. In 1566, 98 ships from Narva passed by Riga, while only 35 ships from Riga itself set off for the West.[43] Of English ships alone, no fewer than 70 set sail for Narva in 1567. With Narva in Russian hands, the port of Revel began falling into decline, and even after the end of the war, Narva continued to undermine Revel's position. The other German ports on the Baltic, Riga and Königsberg, suffered less, since Polish exports were passing through them. The Swedes tried initially to make up their losses by introducing duty-free trade in Vyborg for Russian merchants. At the same time, Swedish pirates terrorised the merchants heading for Narva.[44] Not even this, however, could secure the dominant position for Vyborg.

The commercial goals of the Livonian War had been achieved. In starting the war, however, Ivan had relied not only on the support of the merchants, but also on that of the land-hungry nobility. As Pokrovsky writes:

The bourgeoisie was satisfied, and for them there was no point in continuing the war. When a diplomatic mission from the Livonian Order came to Moscow suing for peace, it found support among the Moscow merchants. In military circles, however, the successes in the war had made a quite different impression. The campaigning in 1558 had yielded enormous booty; waging war in a rich, cultured country was quite different from battling foreigners in distant Kazan, or chasing elusive Crimeans about the steppes. The landowners now dreamt of making an enduring conquest of all Livonia, and of dividing up the rich farmsteads of the German knights. This latter process had, in fact, already begun. But the prospect of the entire south-eastern shore of the Baltic coming under Russian control brought all of Eastern Europe to its feet; neither the Swedes nor the Poles could allow this.[45]

Capturing Revel and Riga would have given Russia the chance to enter European trade without intermediaries. The Poles could not permit Riga to fall under the control of Russia, their main competitor on the world market. An era of trade wars had begun, something for which Muscovy was not ready, especially in diplomatic and political terms. After overpowering the Livonian knights, Ivan the Terrible came up against the united forces of Sweden and Poland, which, despite their conflicts with one another, could not allow a strengthening of Moscow's hand. Polish mercantile capital was in the same situation as its Russian counterpart, and Russian domination of the Baltic would thus be a catastrophe for Poland. In 1561 the Swedes occupied Revel, and the Poles annexed a large part of Livonia. Ivan tried to avoid a war with the Swedes, but it was already too late. Talks with the Swedish King Erik XIV failed as a result of a palace coup; the Swedish throne was then taken by Johann III, who categorically rejected any concessions to Moscow.

As Pokrovsky notes, the victories of the Russian forces in the first stage of the war 'were ensured only by a colossal numerical advantage; where the Order could field hundreds of soldiers, there were tens of thousands of Russians'.[46] With the entry into the war of Sweden and Poland, the relationship of forces changed. It was hard enough for Ivan's forces to cope with the Polish army, but when the superbly armed, organised and trained Swedish forces – arguably the best in Europe at the time – appeared on the battlefield, the situation of the Russians became catastrophic. Prince Kurbsky, the best of Ivan's military leaders, was defeated by 4,000 Poles near Nevel despite having 15,000 troops, and near Orsha in 1564 the Russian army was completely routed. The commanders were killed, and the enemy captured the cannon and the baggage train. Most importantly, the morale of the Russian army was shattered. In the coalition that had supported Ivan's reforms, a split took place.

THE *OPRICHNINA*

The tsar's room for manoeuvre was thus reduced. The Soviet historian R.G. Skrynnikov notes that:

In a context of foreign policy reversals, the tsar's allies advised him urgently to impose a dictatorship on the country, and to crush his opponents through violence and terror. In the

Russian state, however, not a single important political decision could be taken without the approval of the Boyar Duma. Meanwhile, the position of the Duma and of the church leaders was well known, and did not bode well for the enterprise.[47]

Trying to put pressure on the Duma, the tsar left Moscow, and declared that he had abdicated the throne. Before the country and its people, the tsar presented himself as the victim of injustice, driven out by the boyars from his own capital. The Duma was forced to reject the tsar's abdication, and came to him with professions of loyalty. Having undermined the political position of the Duma, the tsar declared that in order to protect his life he was forced to divide his entire land into the 'zemshchina' and 'oprichnina'. The zemshchina (the part of Russia which retained traditional administration during the oprichnina) remained under the control of the Boyar Duma, while the oprichnina was subject to Ivan's personal authority. Here everything was organised as if in a separate princedom. Administration was carried on by appointees of the tsar who were not of noble background. Low-born courtiers without ties to the boyar aristocracy were selected for these posts. Foreigners were eagerly recruited. Made up of such people, the forces of the oprichnina were a reliable weapon for the tsar in his struggle against internal opponents.

Moscow became the witness to bloody purges. Real and imagined enemies of the tsar were accused of conspiracy and mounted the scaffold. By Ivan's order, the chronicles were corrected in line with the changed political situation, and stories of boyar conspiracies, written to the dictation of the tsar's men, appeared in place of the non-existent investigative materials. The oprichnina, meanwhile, was not simply a terrorist organisation in the service of the tsar. It signified the beginning of a major land redivision. On the territory of the oprichnina, boyar estates began to be confiscated; they would then be used to provide for people whom the tsar had promoted. In waging war on Kazan and in the Baltic, the tsar had tried to satisfy the needs of land-hungry nobles and the mercantile bourgeoisie without infringing on the interests of the old aristocracy. But as Pokrovsky notes, since the defeats in Livonia continuing on such a course had been impossible, 'foreign policy no longer promised either land or money'.[48]

In Pokrovsky's view, the oprichnina was the only way out for a government that had become entangled in its own political manoeuvring. The tsar had twice attempted to satisfy the petty nobility's hunger for land, the first time with his Kazan campaign, and the second time during the Livonian War. In neither case was the goal achieved. There was only one solution: to expropriate the feudal aristocracy. What had now begun on the territory of the oprichnina was not only unrestricted terror against the old boyar families and their supporters, but also a redivision of the land. In the place of the feudal domains, there now appeared landowners' estates of much lesser extent. The domains of the boyars had been large enough to lead a closed, independent existence, sending only their excess production to market. The new estates, by contrast, were not self-sufficient; from the first, a substantial part of their output was produced in order to be exchanged.

The redistribution of property that occurred in the *oprichnina* lands was strikingly like that carried out by Henry VIII during the English Reformation a few decades earlier. The English aristocracy had largely been destroyed during the Wars of the Roses, and the vast monastery landholdings had been broken up. The 'new gentry' that set itself up on the confiscated lands laid the foundations for agrarian capitalism. The more the estates became oriented toward the market, the stronger the link became between the new gentry and the urban bourgeoisie. In the civil war of the seventeenth century, these two groupings fought side by side.

The redivision of landholdings imposed by Ivan the Terrible also received total support from mercantile capital. It is noteworthy that the *oprichnina* lands included all the main trading towns and trade routes. As the historian S.F. Platonov writes,

Of all the roads that connected Moscow with the borders, it was really only the roads to the south, to Tula and Ryazan, that escaped the attentions of the *oprichnina*. This appears to have been because the income they yielded in customs dues and from other sources was not great, and their whole extent lay in the troubled regions of the southern frontier.[49]

This cannot be explained by a concern for defence, since from a military point of view it was precisely the unsafe roads to the south that should have received primary attention. The *oprichnina*, however, was less a military than a socio-political organisation. As Platonov notes,

It was not without reason that the English, who were concerned with the northern provinces, asked to be also subject to the *oprichnina*, and it was no accident that the Stroganovs were inclined in the same manner. Commercial-industrial capital, naturally enough, needed the support of the administration that was in charge of the borderlands, and obviously was unafraid of the horrors with which we associate the idea of the *oprichnina*.[50]

In citing the above comment, Mikhail Pokrovsky makes the additional cutting remark: 'There was nevertheless much to be afraid of in the *oprichnina*, which this same capital had helped call into being.'[51]

Skrynnikov also stresses that Englishmen achieved serious economic success in the *oprichnina*. Within its territories they were allowed to prospect for iron ore and to 'build houses necessary for the production of iron'.[52] Moreover, unlike other regions, in the *oprichnina* territories there were no limits to the privileges granted to foreigners. Skrynnikov sees the *oprichnina* as 'the first example in Russian history' of foreign capital being granted such concessions.[53]

As Pokrovsky observes, the *oprichnina* involved the expropriation of the boyars by the petty nobility, oriented toward commodity production and above all toward the trade in grain. The *oprichnina*, Pokrovsky considers, 'lay in the natural line of economic development'.[54] In this respect, the *oprichnina* in Russia under Ivan the Terrible represented a step in the same direction as the creation of the new gentry in England under Henry VII. Not only were the goals similar, but also the methods. Henry did not hesitate to wreak vengeance on his opponents; supporters of the Catholic church were harshly repressed, and the monks were forcibly driven from their cloisters. But for all their resemblance to the measures enforced by Henry VIII, the steps taken by Ivan the Terrible differed in one very important respect: on a political level, they failed. Enacting reforms within the country, while at the same time waging a doomed war, was impossible. Ivan transformed the Moscow state, effectively setting it on its feet. In a context of military defeat, however, it proved impossible to consolidate what had been achieved.

Meanwhile, the Livonian War was irretrievably lost. Attacks were twice mounted on the Swedes in Revel, in 1570 and 1577, but each ended in a crushing defeat. In 1571 the Crimean Tatars reached Moscow, and wrought appalling devastation on the city. Contemporaries wrote of 800,000 dead and 150,000 captured and enslaved. Even if these numbers are exaggerated, the events involved were a disaster for a country with a population of no more than 10 million.

The *oprichnina* terror took on its 'pointless and pitiless' character against a background of military setbacks and a chronic lack of funds. The expropriations turned into habitual plunder, to the benefit not only of the treasury, but also of the *oprichnina* officials themselves. Discontent grew, and the authorities reacted by intensifying the terror. The height of the madness was the sacking by the tsar of Novgorod in January 1570. First the tsar and the *oprichniki* slaughtered almost all the local elite, including the women and children. The clergy were not spared the reprisals. Then the real massacre started. In the words of the historian R.G. Skrynnikov, the *oprichniki*

launched an all-out attack on the city. They looted the Novgorod warehouses, and divided the most valuable of the booty among themselves. The everyday goods such as fat, wax and flax were heaped in great piles and set on fire. In the course of the pogrom huge stores of goods meant for trade with the West were destroyed. Not only were the warehouses looted, but also the houses of Novgorod residents. The *oprichniki* tore down gates, smashed in doors, and broke windows. Townsfolk who tried to resist were killed on the spot. The tsar's henchmen showed particular cruelty toward the poor. As a result of famine, large numbers of beggars had gathered in Novgorod. During severe frosts, the tsar ordered them all driven out beyond the city gates. Most of these people died of cold and hunger.[55]

Despite the terror, and in significant measure because of it, the government's position remained precarious. In his letters of 1567, Ivan the Terrible broached the question of obtaining political asylum in England, should his enemies prevail in Russia. He also mentioned weapons, and architects for the building of fortresses. Still better would be the English fleet, for a war on Poland and Sweden. Queen Elizabeth promised asylum. The weapons, to judge from everything, continued to be supplied, though clearly not in the quantities on which Ivan was counting. However, the queen refused to openly enter the Livonian War. The cunning and wary Elizabeth, needless to say, would not agree to such a thing. This was not simply from fear of waging war on two fronts; a conflict was looming with Spain, and for England, a war in the Baltic would have been an impermissable luxury. The fleet that would one day rule the waves had not yet been built, and it was in order to build it that the English needed ropes and masts from Narva. Elizabeth, in any case, had another reason to be cautious. However important their interests in Russia, the English were also conducting an active trade with Poland, and were not about to sacrifice it. London found the existing state of affairs completely to its liking.

While refusing Moscow's plea to send the English fleet, Elizabeth did not totally ignore her partner's requests. In 1572 at least 16 English sailors were in Narva on the tsar's service. Some 130 years before Peter the Great, they were trying to establish a Russian navy in the Baltic, training people and helping them to build ships.[56]

In 1568 the diplomatic mission of Thomas Randolph impressed on the tsar that while the English would trade with Russia, they would not enter into an open military alliance. Ivan repeatedly let it be known that he was dissatisfied with this situation, but he was forced to accept the conditions the English had imposed, recognising that he had no alternative. In 1569 the privileges enjoyed by the Muscovy Company were reaffirmed in full. A new rope-making works was set up in Vologda, and the English began prospecting for metals in Russia, later undertaking their own mining operations.

In the words of Lyubimenko, the privileges of 1569 were 'undoubtedly the crowning point in the history of the successes achieved by the company with the Russian ruling power'.[57] Soon afterwards, problems began. In 1571, with the military situation in Livonia deteriorating, Ivan again tried to persuade the English to intervene directly. The tsar complained repeatedly that Queen Elizabeth was interested not in 'kingly matters', but in the 'mercantile' affairs of trade and finances. These complaints were clearly demagogic, since the tsar did not shun commerce either. But to use modern-day language, the purpose of such complaints was to shift the centre of discussion from commercial to political and military questions. Failing in this attempt, the tsar sought to exert pressure on English trading interests. The privileges were revoked, and English goods were seized. It is significant that this crisis in Anglo-Russian relations coincided with a crisis of Ivan's regime. The tsar, however, was in an unwinnable situation. In 1572 trade was resumed, on terms imposed by the English.

DISASTER IN LIVONIA AND SUCCESS FOR THE DUTCH

In 1581 Narva was lost, and along with it the Swedes also captured the old Novgorodian fortress of Ivangorod. For Moscow, the Livonian War had finally taken on a catastrophic character. A year later, the privileges enjoyed by the English in Russia were reaffirmed, but their extent was now more limited. Ivan the Terrible was again trying to use trade as the grounds for an open alliance, this time dynastic. He sought the hand in marriage of an English Tudor princess.[58]

This idea had been conceived as early as 1568, but only now did it become the topic of diplomatic talks. Lady Mary Hastings was presented to the Russian Ambassador Fyodor Pisemsky, but does not seem to have made any great impression on him. The English procrastinated, and in 1584 Ivan the Terrible died. The net result of Ivan's rule had been a lost war in Livonia and internal disorder. The struggle for the Baltic coast had turned into a complete rout for Russia, which had been forced not only to relinquish the ports it had seized on the Baltic, but also to surrender parts of its own territory. Polish forces under Stefan Batory had appeared beneath the walls of Smolensk, and had almost captured the city. The Muscovite state had been ruined by war and enfeebled. In the Baltic, Swedish hegemony had been consolidated for the next century or so. The Swedes had not only captured the trading centres of the Baltic, but later, would also seize the thinly populated strip of territory between Narva and Lake Ladoga. This territory was of no value in itself, but it's possession guaranteed the Swedes definitive control of the Novgorodian trade routes.

After its catastrophic defeat in the Livonian War, Russia was at risk not so much of finishing up on the periphery of the embryonic world system as of being outside its boundaries. Here was the tragic dilemma of the Russian state: the only real alternative to peripheral development was isolation and stagnation.

England, by contrast, achieved its goals, even if its triumph was not complete. It did not win free access to the Russian market, but during the most difficult period of its conflict with Spain, it was assured of systematic deliveries of the materials it required for the navy it was creating. In 1588 Spain's 'Invincible Armada' was destroyed, and the first decisive step was taken toward the day when Britain would indeed rule the waves. Nevertheless, Moscow's defeat in the Livonian War was also a major defeat for England in its struggle for direct access to Russian resources. Already in the late sixteenth century, Anglo-Dutch commercial rivalry was growing more acute. Allies not long before in the war against Spain, the English and Dutch bourgeoisies began quarrelling over control of markets. In the course of the seventeenth century this hostility was to breed unending conflicts, that would three times culminate in war. These struggles were also played out on the territory of Russia, since the Dutch, following in the footsteps of the English, were subjecting them to ever-greater pressure.

The first Dutch vessel entered the mouth of the Northern Dvina in 1578. This was not yet a serious threat to the English. The Swedes, French, Germans and even Spanish also took part in the northern trade, but none could seriously undermine the position of the London merchants. Soon, however, Dutch merchants fleeing from Danish pirates accidentally discovered a new site for a port that was better suited than the one used by the English. This landing place, near the Mikhaylo-Arkhangelskaya monastery, would later become the city of Arkhangelsk.[59] The Dutch asked to be allowed to transfer their trade there. The English objected, but cound do nothing more, and it was here that the main port of the Russian north was built in 1583 and 1584.

The port at Arkhangelsk was the best in the Russian north, but it was shallow, like most Dutch harbours, and ideal for the lighter Dutch ships. The draft of the English ships was significantly greater, and for the Muscovy Company to transfer its trade to Arkhangelsk thus involved additional problems. After the port of Arkhangelsk was opened, the rivalry between the English and Dutch intensified. Since defending its freedom in the struggle against the Spanish Crown, Holland had transformed itself into a leading maritime power. At the beginning of its fight for independence the Dutch bourgeoisie had needed the support of the English monarchy against their common foe, but subsequently the two most advanced countries in Europe had become first competitors, then enemies. One of the arenas for their rivalry was Russia. From Muscovy, the Dutch imported furs, caviar, hemp, flax, tar, fat, soap, and ships' masts. English and Dutch diplomatic missions to Moscow followed one after the other. The English sought unsuccessfully to block their rivals from penetrating into the interior of the country. During the English-Dutch wars, both sides tried to persuade the tsar to ban the supplying of masts – strategic raw materials – to their adversaries. The government in Moscow preferred neutrality, banning the export of masts to both of the warring states for the period of hostilities.

Accompanying the commercial rivalry and diplomatic intrigues was an ideological struggle. Contemporaries wrote that the Dutch 'tried to belittle and ridicule the English, drew caricatures of them, and made up lampoons'.[60] English representatives in Moscow complained that the Dutch 'deliberately placed a false English brand (a tailless lion with three upturned crowns) on their very worst cloth, in order to discredit British goods, while also spreading all sorts of libels about England'.[61] The most effective means of winning the sympathy of the Moscow elite, however, was the customary one of paying bribes.

In the course of the seventeenth century the position of the Muscovy Company grew weaker, while the Dutch merchants strengthened their presence in the Russian market. A Soviet researcher notes that

Their goods were of higher quality, as the English themselves admitted. The Dutch were also richer, and were better able to pay bribes, though they resorted to this only in extreme cases. Their gifts to the tsar, however, were more exotic and luxurious than those of the English. Finally, they managed from the outset to create for themselves the reputation of honest and unselfish traders.[62]

To this, historians often add that the Dutch acted more in a spirit of free enterprise, while the English were organised around the monopoly of the Muscovy Company in a commercial and political structure with close ties to the state. The setbacks suffered by the English in the seventeenth century were thus the result of the same factors that had ensured their impressive success in the mid sixteenth century. The Muscovy Company, with its close links to the royal court in London, was an ideal partner for Ivan the Terrible during the period when he was preparing for the Livonian War and while the war was in progress. During these periods, Lyubimenko takes delight in recording, the English ambassador 'made so bold as to enter the tsar's presence without removing his hat'.[63] After the defeat in the war, however, none of this was important any longer for the Moscow government. So long as Ivan the Terrible was alive, the earlier relationships continued, but with his death everything inevitably changed.

THE END OF THE 'ENGLISH TSAR'

On the eve of his death, Tsar Ivan arranged a meeting with the ambassador of Queen Elizabeth. Appearing in the Kremlin, the Englishman learned that the audience would not take place. 'Your English tsar is dead', the official, Andrey Shchelkanov, told him abruptly.[64] Shchelkanov's dislike of the English was by no means a personal characteristic, or at any rate not only a personal one. Shchelkanov was sympathetic to the Habsburgs, and later, to spite the English, he provided patronage to Dutch merchants. He belonged to that faction in the court which had put its stake not on a commercial and political alliance with distant England, but on joint action with the German emperor against Turkey.

Russia, even after it had lost the war in the Baltic, was by no means diplomatically isolated. But in Europe at that time, a decision to favour the English Tudors or the Austrian and Spanish Habsburgs was not simply a foreign policy choice. It represented a choice – an unconscious one, of course – in favour of the forces of bourgeois reform or feudal reaction. Fortunately for the English, neither Austria nor in particular Spain was able to offer Moscow anything of real benefit. The Dutch and Danes, for all their rivalry with the English, had no wish to strengthen the position of the Habsburgs. Ya.S. Lurye writes:

Even though the social order in feudal-absolutist Spain was undoubtedly closer to that in the Russia of Ivan the Terrible and Boris Godunov than to that in the Netherlands or even in England, and even though the participation of English merchants in state administration seemed to the Russian tsar to be a complete absurdity, Russia's position in international politics was objectively less agreeable to the Habsburgs than it was to their opponents.[65]

When the English lost their political influence, they were doomed to lose their commercial pre-eminence as well. Under Tsar Fyodor and Boris Godunov, they were finally stripped of the right to conduct retail trade, and lost the right to travel through Russia to Persia. The political relations between Moscow and London under Godunov no longer amounted to an alliance. From then on, Moscow saw England as only one of a number of possible trading partners, along with the Dutch and Danes. An alliance with the Danes was especially important, since it was in Denmark that Moscow hoped to find an ally against Sweden. To the venal Moscow bureaucrats, meanwhile, the generous Dutch were far more attractive than the English.

5
The Crisis of the Seventeenth Century

The incomplete and unstable character of the social transformation begun under Ivan the Terrible made the upheavals of the Time of Troubles inevitable. By the early seventeenth century all of Russia's social groups were more or less dissatisfied with their positions.

In the years from 1602 to 1604 the Muscovite state was afflicted by a terrible famine. The reserves of grain in the countryside ran out, and people were prepared to sell themselves into slavery in order to eat. It should be noted that Boris Godunov tried to limit the exploitation of the peasants, using the state's reserves of finances and grain to mitigate the food crisis. His moves, however, had no significant effect. A financial crisis now accompanied the food shortage. The collapse of the state grew still more catastrophic, and the nobility were angered. The reign of Boris Godunov ended with revolts and with the coming to Moscow of the impostor Grishka Otrepyev, who took the throne under the name Dmitry. The brief reign of the false Dmitry was interrupted by new revolts, followed by a chaotic series of military and political clashes, of urban and peasant rebellions, of foreign invasions, and of intrigues and treacheries. The Time of Troubles had begun.

THE RUSSIAN TROUBLES AND THE ENGLISH

The Troubles dealt Russia's foreign trade a catastrophic blow, but the merchants from the Muscovy Company did not abandon the country. In 1612, when Moscow was captured by the Poles, the company's head office was evacuated to Vologda. By this time, Vologda had become an important trading centre. Here, as I. Lyubimenko notes, a sort of international merchant association had arisen, uniting both Russians and foreigners.

In the winter of 1608–1609, Russian and foreign merchants were held up in Vologda because of the siege of Moscow by the Poles. Learning of this, Tsar Vasily ordered his commanders to organise the defence of the city, in which so many valuable goods had unexpectedly been concentrated. The foreign merchants, owners of the delayed goods, were also recruited to the defence effort. People chosen by them were to participate in leading the military actions, 'to be as one with the commanders and with the soldiers.' In this way, a sort of secular council was set up, running the general affairs of the city.[1]

In London, it was feared that a victory for Catholic Poland would lead to the complete loss by the English of their Russian market. At this time a certain Captain Chamberlain, who had served in the Russian army and had taken part in battles against the Swedes, sent the English Stuart King James I a proposal to intervene in Russia. The essence of the plan was that English forces should be landed in Arkhangelsk (where British troops also landed during the intervention in 1918), in order to defend the northern region against the danger represented by the Swedes. In the process, the English would also defend their own commercial interests. If the English forces were successful, they could continue further south, with the aim of liberating Moscow. The result would be the restoration of the Russian state, but this time as a protectorate of the House of Stuart. Chamberlain insisted that the intervention would not cost London any large sum of money – Russian merchants would pay for everything.

Soviet historians, while taking an extremely negative view of Chamberlain's plan, acknowledged that his proposal was indeed based on discussions with 'certain members of Russian society', and argued that the English were trying to 'exploit the fear felt by members of the aristocracy at the movement of the oppressed masses'.[2] Meanwhile, Chamberlain's proposal made quite clear that he was looking not to the aristocracy, but to the merchants. The proposal for English intervention was an obvious outcome of the 'defence of Vologda'.

If we consider that in Nizhny Novgorod at this time, the commercial bourgeoisie on the initiative of the merchant Minin were collecting money in order to set up a Russian militia, it is not hard to see that the social interests involved were identical. As Pokrovsky notes, the expedition led by Prince Pozharsky in 1612 with the goal of liberating Moscow was preceded by the 'hiring' of the nobles' army by the bourgeoisie.[3] After a series of catastrophes for Russian forces over almost 20 years, however, the confidence of the merchants in the nobles' army was at a very low ebb. Foreign mercenaries in any case made up a substantial part of the Russian army, and in military terms, the most effective part; consequently, the idea of hiring Englishmen seemed very attractive to the merchants, especially since there were shared commercial interests uniting Russian and English commercial capital.

The court officials in London treated Chamberlain's idea of an English protectorate as the fantasy of an adventurer, though it is significant that they did not by any means rule out the possibility of intervening. Nevertheless, too much remained uncertain. The London officials wanted to know in more detail who it was on the Russian side that was calling for English troops to be sent, and how representative these people were. John Meyrick, the chief agent of the Muscovy Company in Russia, was summoned to London, and then sent back with one of the company's directors, William Russell. In the accompanying documents, mention was made of a proposal that had been addressed to Meyrick the previous year by 'eminent and powerful figures' concerning questions of 'security', and there was also a reference to the restoring of peace 'with the help of our intervention'.[4]

John Meyrick was completely at home in the milieu of Russian bureaucrats and merchants. The son of William Meyrick, a leading official of the Muscovy Company, he had grown up in the English Court in Moscow, spoke Russian fluently, and had spent a considerable part of his life in the country. He was therefore an ideal intermediary, understanding and defending not only English interests, but also those of Russian commercial capital.

When Meyrick and Russell arrived in Arkhangelsk, they found that the question of sending an English expeditionary corps was no longer relevant; Moscow had already been taken by Prince Pozharsky's troops, and Mikhail Romanov had been chosen as tsar. England immediately recognised the new tsar, though as a Russian historian notes, 'the firmness of his hold on the position seemed doubtful to many'.[5]

In 1617, England acted as the official mediator in talks between Muscovy and Sweden. As might have been expected, this task was entrusted to John Meyrick. For Russia, the Peace of Stolbov that was concluded as a result of Meyrick's shuttle diplomacy was extremely burdensome but absolutely necessary. The Swedish claims – 'imprudent', in the view of the English – were rejected, but Russia finally lost its access to the Baltic, with the Swedes taking possession of the sparsely populated but strategically important strip of land between Narva and Vyborg. For England, the Peace of Stolbov was unquestionably favourable. 'Having established trade relations with Sweden by way of the Baltic Sea', Lyubimenko writes,

and with Russia by way of the White Sea, England could now carry on this trade under the old, favourable conditions, receiving from both countries the naval supplies needed by the Admiralty for the construction of the English fleet – hemp, ready-made ropes, timber for masts, pitch, and a multitude of other goods. During the sixteenth century receiving these valuable supplies had aided in... victory over the Spanish 'Invincible Armada', but they were no less necessary in the seventeenth century as well, since a struggle was looming with England's other seaborne rival, the mighty maritime power of Holland.[6]

THE ENGLISH REVOLUTION AND MUSCOVY

In 1618 the government of Mikhail Romanov turned to England for a loan, which was granted – though not by the royal treasury, but by merchants who had commercial interests in Muscovy. Only part of this money reached the tsar's treasury. Learning that Moscow was under siege by the Poles, the English Ambassador Dudley Digges, who had been sent with money contributed by the East India Company, turned back and took the money with him. The only sum that reached the tsar was 20,000 rubles that had been provided, it appears, by the merchants of the Muscovy Company. This episode weakened the influence of the English in Moscow and strengthened the position of the Dutch, who provided the tsar with an extremely important 'subsidy' in the form of munitions. After concluding a truce with Poland at Deulino in December 1618, the Russian government continued talks with London, seeking new loans and the conclusion of a military alliance against the Poles. The English, meanwhile, sought new commercial privileges and the right to trade with Persia by way of Russia. Here, the interests of Russian and English capital did not coincide, and despite all Meyrick's efforts, the Muscovy Company did not gain what it sought. Politically, the situation was made easier by the fact that in Europe the Thirty Years' War had begun, involving a direct clash between Catholic Poland and Protestant Sweden. Moscow and London put their stake on Sweden. This opened the way for a new military and political alliance, with the initiative this time coming from England.

The Thirty Years' War immediately dealt a blow to the traditional markets in which the English had traded. Following the defeat of Muscovy in the Livonian War, the bulk of Russian raw materials had reached the West through Estland, by way of the Swedish-controlled ports of Revel and Narva. The war, however, dramatically increased the difficulties of this situation. The demand for shipbuilding materials from the east rose sharply, while the supplies were under threat. Analysing English documents of the years 1618–22, Soviet historians found that in London the position had been regarded as critical.

The war cut England's traditional trade ties with the Baltic region, and made importing raw materials more difficult. From the earliest stage of the conflict the Estland market, which had been the main supplier of hemp, pitch and sailcloth for English shipbuilding, suffered enormously. The shortage of raw materials also had a severe impact on the English linen-weaving industry, not to speak of a dramatic reduction of exports of grain from Germany and the Baltic region. The English commercial bourgeoisie tried to make up for the curtailing of the Estland market by expanding their trade links with the Russian state. Consolidating their position on the Russian market became a question for them of life or death.[7]

The position was complicated by growing Dutch competition, by inefficient organisation and by disputes within the Muscovy Company. The Privy Council, the leading government organ of James I, was forced to intervene. In 1622 the Privy Council issued two orders requiring the Muscovy Company to step up its trading activity. To this end the company was guaranteed the patronage of the king and financial privileges. In accordance with the views of the time, the lack of efficiency was put down solely to the restricting of private initiative within the company. A decision was therefore taken to reorganise the firm; in effect, it was transformed from a joint-stock company into an association of independent merchants, trading with their individual capital and at their own risk.

John Meyrick spoke out emphatically against this reform. Citing his knowledge of Russia, he argued that this was a country where it was impossible to do business on the principle of 'every man for himself'.[8] He was opposed by a group of 'young directors' or 'new men' who had recently arrived in Muscovy. In Meyrick's view, these young gentlemen, who had not endured either Ivan the Terrible or the Troubles, understood nothing about the country in which they were seeking their fortunes; they were acting irresponsibly, and would cause the company to collapse. This time, Meyrick did not prevail. The young supporters of free enterprise may have known little about Russia, but they won the support of influential people in London.

Along with reorganising the Muscovy Company, the Privy Council prepared a draft for an Anglo-Russian treaty that not only would have expanded trade ties, but would also have drawn Russia into the Thirty Years' War on the Protestant side. For the first time, officials in London hit upon the idea that it was possible to wage war on the continent using not their own forces, but

Russian ones. In this fashion, Russia would later be drawn into a whole series of military campaigns, some of which even made Russian arms famous. In the years 1622–24, however, Moscow showed caution. The treaty was not signed.

As Meyrick had predicted, the reorganisation of the Muscovy Company was not crowned with success. The competition from Holland was not overcome, and increasingly the company fell apart into individual enterprises. There was dissatisfaction in Moscow, too. 'The number of Englishmen trading in Moscow increased, while the possibility of exercising control over their activity diminished. Customs revenues shrank, since the ambassadorial office began to issue charters for duty-free trade to all foreign merchants.'[9]

The latter move was not so much the result of an attachment to free trade on the part of the Russian functionaries, but rather the result of the chaos and perhaps corruption that reigned in the Moscow bureaucracy. The effective disintegration of the Muscovy Company deepened the confusion. In 1635 it became necessary to conduct a census of foreign merchants, and among them were discovered an inordinate number of 'illegals', said to 'conduct trade and purchase houses without the authority of the tsar'.[10] High-placed officials wrote threatening letters demanding explanations as to how such 'licence' had come about, and to know who in Moscow had illegally issued authorisations, if these had indeed been given out. As might have been expected, these enquiries yielded no serious results, and the confusion surrounding the customs duties did not cease either. In October 1638 the utterly bewildered officials in the Ustyug customs house sent a letter to Moscow asking for the situation to be clarified, but in the capital it took *two years* to compile a list containing the names of 23 merchants who had the right to commercial privileges. This was despite the fact that all 23 names were listed in English documents that had long been present in Moscow.

In the same year, 1638, the English for their part complained that senior local officials ignored the charters granted by the tsar, levied taxes illegally and, when the merchants refused to pay, inflicted 'even worse violence' on them.[11] Eventually, a new investigation followed. On orders from the capital, an enquiry was conducted. Local functionaries were interrogated and rebuked. But of course, there were no changes of any consequence.

The Englishmen nostalgically recalled the days of Ivan the Terrible, when order had been maintained in the country with an iron fist. On ascending to the English throne, Charles I wrote to Moscow and requested that the tsar appoint a special protector to safeguard the rights of the English residents, recalling that under the late Ivan IV this role had been played by Boris Godunov. In the court of the Romanovs, the reminder was clearly out of place.

In England itself, political conflict was increasing. Unlike the Tudors, the Stuarts were unwilling to defend the interests of the bourgeoisie as their own. The court was becoming oriented more and more toward the Catholic feudal powers, while the bourgeoisie were zealous in their support for the Protestants. As a result, England not only failed to play a serious role in the Thirty Years' War, but was also unwilling to support Russia's entry into it. Meanwhile, Moscow was not yet capable of defeating Poland unaided. In 1632, Charles

I agreed to allow 2,000 soldiers to be recruited in England for service in the Russian forces, and also to allow the purchase of 5,000 swords. In 1634 the war with Poland came to an end.

In England, revolution was imminent. The government of the Romanovs, who were still mindful of their experiences in the Time of Troubles, reacted with healthy class instincts to the events unfolding beyond the seas. The Russian Ambassador Gerasim Dokhturov, arriving in London at the height of the civil war, refused categorically to meet with the parliament, and demanded an audience with the king – who, understandably, was not in the capital. Trying to win the tsar's representative to their side, adherents of the parliament imprudently declared to the ambassador that all the merchants doing business in Moscow supported the parliamentary cause. For this, the English would be made to pay. After Charles I had been executed in 1649, a decree was issued by the tsar forbidding the English to trade with Russia. 'It has been made known to our great sovereign,' the decree stated, 'that the English have done evil by the whole land: they have put their sovereign King Carlus to death. We in the Muscovite state cannot support such an evil deed.'[12] Despite such clearly expressed displeasure on the part of the tsar, the government of Cromwell sought to repair relations with Moscow, sending two diplomatic missions to Moscow. However, there could no longer be any question of the former friendship. In 1650 the English royalists tried to restore relations with the Muscovite court, at the same time calling on the tsar to shut off access to Russia for merchants linked to the republicans. For the purpose of fighting the 'rebels', Moscow provided the Stuarts with a loan of 20,000 rubles – around £10,000 at the exchange rate of the time – though not in money, but in goods: furs, rye, and so forth. This, however, did not put a stop to the English revolution.

ENGLISH VERSUS DUTCH

The decline of Anglo-Russian trade in the seventeenth century was not due solely to politics. 'There is no doubt,' writes I. Lyubimenko, 'that the execution of Charles I was merely a pretext that was seized upon by Aleksey Mikhailovich in order to abolish the privileges enjoyed by the English, privileges that… cut across his entire economic policy.'[13] Significantly, the restoration of the monarchy and the crowning in England of Charles II (who even paid off his father's debt to the Muscovite tsar) did nothing to restore the privileged position of the English merchants in Russia. The decline of Anglo-Russian relations had two causes. First, the English lost their positions under the pressure of competition from Holland. Second, in the mid seventeenth century the whole character of Eastern European trade was transformed, and this could not fail to make a decisive impact on Russia's relations with the West.

As Lyubimenko observes,

The Dutch, who were trading in Russia as separate small companies, skilfully exploited the problems of the English. The capital they had invested in Russian commerce was calculated in 1642 at two million florins, that is, around four hundred thousand rubles.

It was thus about three times the sum the English had invested, and subsequently, this difference kept growing.[14]

With substantial funds at their disposal, the Dutch were ready to pay high customs duties, and hence were much more suitable partners for the Muscovite bureaucracy, which was acutely short of money throughout the seventeenth century. To Muscovy the Dutch merchants brought silver and gold (including coins), cloth, and weapons and munitions, including muskets, gunpowder and shot. They also helped with the hiring of officers for the tsar's forces. There were Dutch courts in Moscow, Kholmogory, Vologda, Arkhangelsk, Ust-Kola, Yaroslavl, Novgorod and Pskov. The normalisation of relations with Sweden also led to competition from Swedish and German merchants, who made use of the old Novgorodian trade routes through Revel and Vyborg. The privileges which Ivan the Terrible had granted to the English were the result of a strategic partnership which now belonged to the past. Russian commercial capital was now developed enough to play an independent role, the treasury needed funds which it had been receiving in inadequate amounts because of the duty-free trading of the English, and the Dutch had established direct links with the Russian merchants. The desire of the Muscovy Company to keep its privileges in the changed circumstances brought it into conflict with a united front made up of Dutch and Russian commercial capital, at a time when the Kremlin bureaucracy no longer viewed England as a political ally.

Still more important were the changes that had occurred in the world economic system. The victims of these changes included the countries of Eastern Europe and also the Muscovy Company, which had been founded in a different age.

It was the Dutch who began to play the leading role in the international relations of seventeenth-century Muscovy. They also became the country's main source of up-to-date technology. Dutch construction engineers built fortifications in Moscow, and with their help the Russian capital began its gradual transformation from a wooden city to one of stone. Dutch builders and architects were also recruited to work in two other important port cities, Arkhangelsk and Astrakhan.

For Holland itself, the trade with Russia might have seemed at first sight to have been of secondary importance. In the number of ships involved and their tonnage, the 'Russian route' was clearly less impressive than Holland's seaborne trade with Western Europe. Against a background of Dutch colonial trade, however, Muscovy appears in a quite different light; 20 Dutch ships a year were setting off for Russia, and only seven to India.

THE CRISIS OF THE SEVENTEENTH CENTURY

The first half of the seventeenth century was not only a time of military and political conflicts, but also a period when economic growth in the West slackened, and commercial competition grew more acute. From being allies, England and Holland became fierce enemies; Germany was devastated by the

Thirty Years' War; and Spain, despite the split in the ranks of the anti-Habsburg coalition, fell increasingly into decline. The British historian Eric Hobsbawm describes this siutation as 'the crisis of the Seventeenth century'.[15]

By the early years of the seventeenth century, the economic upturn which Europe had experienced since the late fifteenth century had exhausted itself. Everything was now placed in doubt – organisational structures, the method of rule and the dominant ideas. The state was changing in the most radical fashion of all. In England and Holland a parliamentary regime was taking shape, while in France the Bourbon dynasty was creating the model of an absolutist monarchy resting on a centralised bureaucracy. During the next century this system would serve as a model for most European countries, including Russia. Military reforms were going ahead as well; the feudal militias and detachments of mercenaries were being replaced by regular armies. In economic policy, no less important changes were occurring. As in later ages, the market could not solve the accumulating problems by itself. King Edward VI, when sending Chancellor and his companions on the northern expedition, had entrusted them with a message extolling free trade. In the Europe of a century later, quite different ideas held sway. The state was beginning to play a far more active role in both trade and production.

These changes, however, were not occurring spontaneously. The state was changing as a result of wars, uprisings and revolutions that were taking place against a background of almost permanent economic crisis. Europe was being shaken by political and social conflicts – the Fronde in France, and the revolution in England. Turbulent events were also unfolding in Russia, where political disorders had not by any means come to an end with the installing of the Romanov dynasty. In 1648 Moscow was shaken by a new political crisis. Then followed a reform of the church that split the country into two camps. In Hobsbawm's view, one of the causes of the economic crisis of the seventeenth century was the poverty of Eastern Europe, which was unable to buy Western commodities in large enough quantities. This is not, of course, to speak of luxury goods; 'the future industrialist required not an infinite willingness to keep scores of chefs, stucco artists and perruquiers employed, but mass demand'.[16] In reality, demand for Western manufactured goods and technologies grew in Eastern Europe during the seventeenth century, especially in Russia. The political disorders merely increased this demand, since weapons were being energetically exported from Western countries to the East. The actual source of the problem lay in the West itself.

In the sixteenth and early seventeenth centuries, the countries of the West had a trade deficit in relation to their Eastern European partners, just as they did with the countries of Asia. This deficit was financed by the American silver that was coming onto the European market in vast quantities. Around 1620, the flow of silver from the Americas started to dry up. This meant that commercial relations between Western and Eastern Europe inevitably had to change. In the mid seventeenth century the West could no longer use silver to pay for the goods that were being exported from Poland, Livonia and Russia. European manufacturers enjoyed no special demand in Asia, from which highly valuable commodities were being imported by the West. By contrast, the countries of Eastern Europe were prepared to purchase Western products, but only in limited quantities. The solution to the problem lay in maximising the development of trade with Eastern Europe, while at the same time lowering the prices of the goods that Eastern Europe was supplying. Russia, Poland and Livonia were thus in an obvious losing position. To have rejected these conditions of trade, however, would have made inevitable the collapse of the whole system of exchange in which the countries of Eastern Europe were by now deeply enmeshed, and in which they had no less an interest than the West.

A NEW COMPETITOR

Early in the seventeenth century, the first English colonies were established in North America. As T.S. Willan correctly observed, the functions performed by England's trade with Russia recalled those fulfilled later by trade with the American colonies. The settlers were able to supply the same goods, only in greater quantities. As a result, the importance of the northern sea route diminished. Risky and expensive, this route had been justified above all by the access it provided to strategic raw materials. Now, these materials were coming from America. With the appearance of the French colonies in Canada, a stream of furs also poured into Europe. Furs were also coming from the English colonies. The Muscovite goods that had been exported via the inconvenient northern route were simply unable to compete with those from America.

From the mid seventeenth century, all the countries of Eastern Europe suffered a deterioration in their terms of trade with the West. An unfavourable balance of foreign trade became the norm. The goods exported from Eastern Europe were cheap, while those imported were expensive. For Russia, however, an unfavourable balance of trade with the West finally became typical only around 1700 – in other words, only when the country, under the power of Peter the Great, turned its face fully toward Europe.

The constant worsening of the terms of trade required that this trade be just as steadily expanded. The less silver and gold could be imported from Western countries, the greater the difficulty in gaining access to foreign technical knowledge, and the greater the volume of raw materials that had to be exported. Dependence on foreign markets and technologies increased, and the need to absorb Western civilisation came to be felt more acutely.

A COUNTRY WHERE EVERYONE TRADED

Seventeenth-century Muscovy was crazy about trade. 'Every decision made in this country,' wrote a foreign traveller, 'is concerned with commerce and trade. This is clear from everyday experience, since everyone, from highest to lowest, is occupied exclusively in working out how they can get hold of this or that, and use it to make a profit.'[17] Western travellers meanwhile noted that the Russian bourgeoisie had little capital, and that the largest trading houses of Moscow seemed small by comparison with, for example, those of Amsterdam. Located

on the periphery of the emerging capitalist world system, the Russian entrepreneurial class were highly active in seeking to exploit the opportunities that
were opening up. But they could not manage the same levels of accumulation
as the bourgeoisie in the West.

In Muscovy, everyone – tsars, boyars and monasteries – was engaged in
trade. The local merchants were by no means the leaders in taking advantage
of the new market opportunities that had opened up as the local and world
economies changed. The merchants did not act as a new force opposing the
traditional elite and the state, but as their business partners, and junior partners
at that. The relationship that arose between Russian and foreign merchants
was no different.

Following the blows dealt by the Time of Troubles and the ensuing
depression, the merchants took many years to recover. The crisis of the
seventeenth century took its toll on Russian trade, as the data on the numbers
of merchant companies testify:

Toward the end of the sixteenth century the *gostinaya sotnya* had numbered 358 people;
in 1649, the figure was 171. The numbers in the *sukonnaya sotnya* also declined; in the late
sixteenth century there were 250 members, and in 1649, only 116.[18]

Not surprisingly, the Russian merchants had mixed feelings where foreigners
were concerned. On the one hand, the Dutch and English had far more capital,
and were able to put pressure on their Russian competitors. In Arkhangelsk
they controlled everything, and in Moscow as well their position was very
strong. Russian petty traders were jealous of the foreigners, and from time
to time complained to the authorities about them, hoping that government
intervention would alter the logic of the market. But Russian entrepreneurship
could not develop without the participation of foreign capital, and as time
went on, the dependency on this outside capital increased.

From 1617 the Muscovite merchants repeatedly appealed to the government
to open the door a little wider to foreign capital, since Russians needed to
learn 'crafts and trades' from the foreigners (with variations, this theme would
be repeated in an enormous range of documents, letters and articles over
the centuries). The success of the foreign entrepreneurs in Russia, however,
soon provoked alarm in the local merchants, and calls for the broadening of
free trade were replaced by the demand for protectionism. Contradictions
of this sort are typical of peripheral capitalism. On the one hand, it cannot
exist without the centre; that is, foreign influence provides it with the stimulus
necessary for development. But, on the other hand, the more that peripheral
capital develops, the greater its need to protect its own interests, or at least to
obtain better conditions for itself.

In the sixteenth century and the first half of the seventeenth century,
state regulation of business activity was not especially marked, but by the
middle of the seventeenth century the situation was changing. According to
the American historian Richard Hellie, 'Russian *homo economicus* was quite
capable of adapting and innovative on his own'; consequently, Hellie maintains,

a strong and economically active state was not only unnecessary, but would have been counterproductive.[19] Hellie clearly views the seventeenth-century Russian economy through the eyes of a late twentieth-century neoliberal, and even repeats with hindsight the same arguments: if the tsar's government had implemented privatisation and liberalisation (in accordance with the latest recommendations of the International Monetary Fund), Russian history would have unfolded in brilliant fashion. However, it is not only the Muscovite rulers and merchants of the early Romanov era who would have disagreed with such conclusions, but also their contemporaries in England or in the North American colonies. The second half of the seventeenth century was a period when the economic role of the state was growing everywhere. To later liberal historians, the rise in Muscovy of a 'strong' and economically active state appears to have been associated with continual foreign threats. Formed in order to resist hostile encirclement, this 'strong state' in the view of these historians later became self-sustaining, smothering the economy and stunting the development of *Homo economicus* (that is, the bourgeoisie). However, the Russian state in the seventeenth century was guided by the same principles as those of its Western neighbours. Authoritarianism was growing throughout Europe, as part of the very process of modernisation. A modern bureaucratic apparatus was taking shape, armies were being reformed and expanded, and a military-industrial complex was emerging (artillery workshops and shipyards were being built, weapons were being standardised, and army uniforms were being introduced). Russia was constantly at war, but its Western neighbours – Sweden, Poland, France, England, Austria and Holland – behaved in exactly the same fashion. From 1630, the wars that Muscovy undertook were offensive in character. The main aim of these expeditions was to win access to markets for the very same *Homo economicus* to whom the government, in the view of later scholars, was proving such a hindrance. In other words, not only did the 'strong state' pose no obstacle to the development of entrepreneurship, but, on the contrary, it also served the entrepreneurs' interests. Private capital needed just such a state, and supported it in every possible fashion.

Like most European countries, Muscovy in the mid seventeenth century was guided in its economic policies by the principles of mercantilism. In essence, mercantilism was a response to the prolonged crisis that had seized most European markets. Confidence in the advantages of free trade was being replaced by hopes of state support. From this time on, governments everywhere would strive to ensure a positive balance of foreign trade, encouraging the inflow of silver to their countries and trying to prevent its outflow. Along with most Western countries, the Muscovite state set out to achieve this goal using two methods. First, it sought to stimulate production; above all, in those sectors for whose output there was strong demand in other countries. Second, it increased the customs duties on foreign goods brought into the country. Foreigners were denied permission to deal on the internal market, and the state encouraged local capital, aiding the formation of commercial monopolies.

The Muscovite tsars were guided by the same principles as the 'Sun King' Louis XIV, who appointed the famous Jean-Baptiste Colbert, the theoretician of mercantilism, to oversee the economy. The decrees of the Muscovite state were infused with mercantilist ideas just as much as the decisions of the French court. The first step in this direction was represented by the Customs Statutes of 1653. These were followed by the New Trade Statutes of 1667, described by a Western historian as 'highly mercantilistically oriented'.[20] The privileges of foreign traders in Moscow were not abolished completely, but were seriously restricted. The local commercial capital that had arisen during the 100 years since Chancellor's journey was capable of independently organising import and export operations, of defending its own markets, and of appropriating new ones.

The New Trade Statutes strengthened state control over imports and exports, while at the same time doing away with numerous feudal restrictions on internal trade. A wide range of feudal dues vanished into the past. The laws became the same throughout the country. From now on, the goal of the tsarist customs system would be not only to provide revenues, but also to create a favourable trade balance for the Muscovite state. Customs duties from the export of raw materials and foodstuffs were collected by the Russian treasury in ducats and German talers. Western trade was becoming a vital source of silver for the internal market, and the taler, under the name *efimok,* circulated in Muscovy and would later serve as the prototype for the Russian silver ruble. The influx of German and Dutch silver aided the development of trade with Persia. The road to the East via the Caspian Sea had been known in Rus since the Middle Ages, but most of the trade had been conducted by merchants from Persia and Bukhara. In the fifteenth century, Afanasy Nikitin, a merchant from the city of Tver, followed the Caspian trade route and described it in detail; then in the sixteenth century Anthony Jenkinson conquered it commercially, for the Western trade. Russian merchant capital not only followed the trail of its English counterpart, but also reproduced the approach to trade introduced into Russia by the Muscovy Company. After beginning the commercial conquest of Persia alongside the English, it was not long before the Russian merchants took this business exclusively into their own hands. Foreigners were banned once and for all from trading with Persia by way of Russia. In 1664, Shah Abbas II provided the Russians in Persia with exactly the same commercial privileges as the English had obtained 100 years earlier from Ivan the Terrible. The same period saw Astrakhan flourish as a trading port, becoming a 'gateway to the East', just as Arkhangelsk was a 'gateway to the West'. The almost uninterrupted river route from south to north allowed the conduct of transit trade. Persian silks bought by Muscovite merchants in Astrakhan would be resold to the English and Dutch in Arkhangelsk.

In the 1650s, the Dutch took over the export of Caspian caviar to Western Europe. The Muscovite government in turn established its own monopoly on the trade in this commodity. In addition, the Muscovite rulers maintained their grip on the transit trade in Persian silks via Russian rivers: acting as a commercial intermediary was an extremely profitable undertaking.

The tsar's administration watched strictly to ensure that this trade remained in the hands of Russian merchants. Persians were not allowed further than

Astrakhan, or Europeans further than Arkhangelsk. The result was that the Arkhangelsk trade grew without let-up. In the mid seventeenth century, 30–40 ships were arriving in the city each year; in other words, the volume of navigation had increased by around seven times in the space of a century. At the same time, the northern trade was also continuing through Ust-Kola, another port that had begun to operate in the time of Ivan the Terrible. In addition, it was also in the seventeenth century that trade began with China by way of Siberia.

Nevertheless, the peripheral position of Russia in the nascent world system meant that in the seventeenth century, the Russian state could no longer get by without foreigners. The mercantilist policy of encouraging the local bourgeoisie made it possible to ensure that Russian entrepreneurs enjoyed the most favourable conditions within the framework of this system, but the main centres of capital accumulation were in the West. S.F. Platonov notes that after the Troubles, the influence of foreign capital in Moscow increased substantially.

Amid the general impoverishment of Moscow, foreign capital was the main force in the Russian market, and as the Moscow government sought to survive the economic crisis, it was inevitably obliged to forge close links with foreign commerical interests. The foreign merchants became the managers of Russian trade circulation, and the suppliers of silver (even of Russian coins) for Muscovite commerce. They took such a dominant position in Muscovite commercial life that the local merchant class began insistently seeking government protection, eventually winning some restrictions on the commercial privileges which the foreigners enjoyed.[21]

Moscow needed Western technology, and following after the technology came Western capital. The government, in full accordance with the requirements of mercantilism, supported the building of factories, but the local merchants were not ready to make use of the fruits of this policy. As A.D. Kuzmichev and I.N. Shapkin note in their history of Russian entrepreneurship, 'It was only later, in the early eighteenth century, that Russian merchants began to be drawn into the risky and unfamiliar business of manufacturing.'[22]

The state, by contrast, collaborated actively in the establishing of industry. In the area of foreign trade, the government had organised a system of official monopolies that succeeded in filling the tsar's treasury, but in industry the government acted as the principal customer. Even Richard Hellie, profoundly convinced that only private enterprise can yield positive economic results, is forced to acknowledge that 'the state was the prime innovator in the economy'.[23] It was the state that implanted new technologies, and at the same time, new capitalist relations (though in specifically Russian forms). As Pokrovsky observes:

For the first time, tsarist commerce took on the character of a large commercial enterprise. The industrial establishments of the tsar and his court were among the first examples of large-scale industry in Russia. Second place behind the tsar in the founding of mercantile capitalism in the Muscovite state was taken by the foreigners; apart from the tsar, they were our first factory-owners and major manufacturers. Like the foreign merchants, the foreign industrial entrepreneurs acted under the constant protection of the tsarist authorities, and in close alliance with them.[24]

THE FOREIGN INDUSTRIALISTS

Industrial production in seventeenth-century Russia was established either by foreigners or on the initiative of the government, with the state and foreign capital acting in tandem, as a rule. As in other societies where peripheral capitalism has taken shape, it was a partnership between the state and foreign capital that served as the basis for technological innovation.

An important proportion of foreign enterprise was oriented toward military needs. With official permission, the Dutchman Andrey Vinius in 1632 built an arms factory in Tula, promising to manufacture cannon, shot, gunbarrels and 'ironware of all types' at low prices. The enterprise used freely hired labour, as had been specifically stipulated in the decree on the establishing of the plant. In 1637, Vinius built a further three factories near Tula, founding a united production complex and laying the basis for the famous Tula armaments works, which were celebrated throughout the world in Soviet times.

As production developed, Vinius became a real Russian patriot, converted to Orthodoxy and, as Solovyev notes, 'felt more concern for the good of Russians than for his own compatriots'.[25] This, however, did not spare him from being attacked by Russian merchants complaining of 'German' domination. At first, the output of the Tula works was not noted for its high quality. Tula cannon that were sent to Holland for testing proved to be useless, and the government continued to buy muskets and artillery pieces in Germany. Production of armour could not be managed at all. Nevertheless, the Tula works turned out vast quantities of items of mass consumption – roofing iron, and metal doors and shutters. Another defence plant built by the Dutch turned out anchors; at a time when Russia did not possess a navy, these could not have had any military significance, but they were eagerly purchased by merchants navigating on the Volga and other rivers.

Vinius did not fare well with his business partners. Documents show that he was soon forced out of business by a Dane named Petr Marselis and by a Dutchman cited in Russian documents as Filimon Akema, both of whom Vinius had invited to join in his undertaking. Later, Vinius and Akema went to court against one another. It was while the case was under scrutiny that the poor quality of the weapons came to light. Vinius put the blame on the plant's new owners, but the enterprise remained in the hands of Marselis and Akema.

As they expanded the enterprise, Marselis and Akema encountered a labour shortage, and requested that the government assign peasants to the factories. The authorities obliged the entrepreneurs, and two rural districts administered by the tsar's court were 'attached' to the Tula and Kashira plants. It was thus 'civilised' Western investors who laid the basis for what was later considered a barbaric, and peculiarly Russian form of organisation of production

– the use of bonded serf labour in industry. This decision had far-reaching consequences. State enterprises soon came up against the same problem as the foreign investors; in Muscovy in the 1630s a shortage of free workers was being felt from time to time. The government followed an already well-worn path; for almost a century, numerous resolutions would be adopted and decrees issued broadening the use of serf labour in industry. The culmination of this process was a decree of 18 January 1721, which gave industrialists permission to buy whole villages for attachment to factories. At the same time, landowners acquired the possibility of setting up factories, to be worked by serf labour, on their estates. Pokrovsky describes this as the beginning of a 'capitalism of the landowners, of the serfholders'.[26] It is significant that after the foreigners, the next to set about establishing factories were not merchants but boyars. A relative of the tsar, Ilya Miroslavsky, and the sovereign's favourite, Boris Morozov, were both involved in producing metalware, but their businesses did not prosper. In 1656 Miroslavsky sold his factory to foreigners for 1,000 rubles, while Morozov's enterprise reverted to the state after his death.[27]

As early as the seventeenth century, a situation typical of Russia's subsequent development had thus been established: technological modernisation was not only associated with serfdom, but rested on it, while the strengthening of the country's military might was linked to dependency on foreign capital, which benefited directly from the state's efforts.

Foreign capital also established an international postal service in Muscovy. In 1663, Johann von Schweden founded a postal company which organised the regular dispatch of letters to Western Europe. A letter to Berlin took 21 days to arrive. In Soviet times, a letter to West Berlin also spent 21 days en route, but the delay was of course occasioned by the efforts of the intelligence services to study most if not all of the communications sent abroad. State officials in pre-Petrine Russia were not, of course, above such practices either, and the German postal company collaborated with the tsar's administration in these matters. All foreign letters were unashamedly opened in the ambassadorial offices. It is noteworthy that foreigners who visited Russia at this time took an approving attitude to this system, seeing it as proof that the Moscow government took an interest in international events. As Pokrovsky remarks, the notion of 'confidential correspondence' was then quite alien not only to people in Moscow, but also to their foreign teachers.[28]

By the seventeenth century, Russia's lag behind the West was especially marked in the area of metallurgy. Not a single blast furnace was built in Muscovy prior to 1636, although the first such installation had appeared in the West in 1443. On the periphery of the trade routes, Russia was also on the sidelines of the technological revolution of the fifteenth and sixteenth centuries; this in turn was responsible for the country's dependency on Dutch and English partners. Mercantilist ideology demanded that the transfer of technology be accelerated, and Western entrepreneurs were compelled to share their knowledge. In 1647, under pressure from local capital, the government transferred the Tula works to Russian entrepreneurs, but, as Lyubimenko notes, in Russian hands the works fell into decay, and in 1648 the factories were returned to the Dutch for twenty years. Soon afterward, the Protvino works on the Kaluga road were handed over for fifteen years, and also the Ugodsky works in the district of Malo-Yaroslavl. With the exception of the state-owned Pavlovo works, the entire industry of iron metallurgy thus became concentrated in Dutch hands.[29]

Dutch entrepreneurs also controlled the production of copper, glass and paper.

Even when employed in the same enterprises, skilled workers of Russian and foreign origin received different wages for the same work. In 1663–64, a foreign ironmaster at a blast furnace received 100 rubles a year, and his Russian colleague only 60 rubles. Meanwhile, wages were steadily falling. In Tula between 1647 and 1690, the wages of foreigners fell from 81 to 57 rubles a year, and those of Russians, from 22 to 18 rubles. This was despite the depreciation of the ruble that was occurring during this period.

The reforms of Peter the Great in the early eighteenth century led to the setting up of an extraordinary number of new manufacturing enterprises. Most of these were state-owned, or were established on the direct instructions of the tsar. The administrative enthusiasm of the great reformer, however, did not always yield the desired results. Many of his industrial undertakings proved unviable. Private initiative did not always make up for the inefficiency of state intervention; in fact, quite the reverse – it was the lack of any notable successes for the local bourgeoisie that set the government on the road to administrative entrepreneurship.

As Pokrovsky writes:

Nurtured on tsarist monopolies, and surrounded by the conditions of craft production, Russian commercial capitalism adapted very poorly to the wide field of action on which it found itself in the early eighteenth century. It came there not so much of its own free will, as driven by the pressure of Western European capital. Moreover, it was the latter that gained the lion's share of the profits.[30]

6
Empire of the Periphery

The delay in development that resulted from the shifting of trade routes (first in the twelfth and thirteenth centuries, and later in the sixteenth and seventeenth centuries) not only brought about a 'lag behind the West', but also caused Russia's social evolution to follow a qualitatively different trajectory. These Eastern 'peculiarities' were the consequence not of isolation from Western Europe, but, on the contrary, of the economic and political bonds that had been forged with the West. The more actively Russia was drawn into the world economy, the greater these 'specific differences' became.

It was in no way accidental that the 'second wave' of enserfment to which peasants in Eastern Europe were subjected proceeded in parallel with the establishing of slaveholder plantations in the Americas. The most active slaveholding relations generally arose where a dynamically developing capitalism experienced precisely this need. Robin Blackburn in his history of slaveholding shows that the three most advanced countries of the West – Britain, Holland and France – also played the decisive role in establishing the slaveholder economy in the New World.

CAPITALISM AND SLAVERY

Nor was it by chance that Holland, the most advanced bourgeois country during the seventeenth century, also led the development of the slave trade. During the period 1640–1750, slaveholding developed rapidly. The number of slaves rose apace, and in a number of Caribbean colonies their number came to exceed the figure for the white population. The first instance of this was on the British-controlled island of Barbados in 1645. Later, slavery began spreading quickly. 'Spain, the first and still the largest colonial power in the New World, ranked only fourth as a slaveholding power. Britain and France, which had no slave colonies in 1640, now possessed the most flourishing slave plantations in the New World.'[1] The nature of the plantations changed as well; they became larger, and more commercial in their orientation. 'The breakthrough to large scale plantation was made by British and French planters, backed by independent Dutch merchants in the Caribbean around 1640–1650.'[2] Gold mined by slaves in Portuguese Brazil was sent to the markets of London. Cotton and sugar were processed in France. Without European demand, the colonial plantation economy could never have developed. Meanwhile, Blackburn notes, the cheap colonial raw materials 'helped to make possible an enclave of accumulation that employed wage labour'.[3] The forced labour of the slaves on the plantations was an element in the primitive accumulation of capital.

The plantation revolution preceded industrialisation by at least a century. Whether or not some other path might have been possible or desirable, the actual transition to capitalist industrialisation was to pass through extensive exchanges with the slave plantations.[4]

The development of the slave plantations helped to overcome the economic difficulties which the West was encountering in the mid seventeenth century. In just the same fashion, the establishing of serf agriculture in Eastern Europe was an important aspect of the global changes that would allow the rapid growth of the world economy in the following century.

With the establishing of British and Dutch colonies in North America, the demand for supplies from Russia gradually diminished, and their prices fell. But as the traditional Russian raw materials were being devalued, a new market in foodstuffs was arising in the West. Accordingly, the nature of Eastern European trade underwent radical changes during the seventeenth century. Instead of the traditional goods, exports of grain now took first place.

The seventeenth century was the age of Dutch trade with Russia, just as the preceding century had been the time of English trade and influence. While the English had pioneered the exporting of Russian raw materials, the Dutch specialised in grain. On a world scale, the grain trade was concentrated in the hands of Dutch merchants. Until the mid seventeenth century, there was no surplus of grain in Russia. A century earlier, Western merchants had noted the possibility of a trade in grain, but had not seen it as the most profitable business available to them in Russia. It was only in the seventeenth century that Dutch representatives began trying to persuade the Muscovite tsar that a dramatic increasing of grain exports was desirable, since this would 'increase the sovereign's income from customs duties'.[5] From the tsar, the Dutch sought a monopoly on the exporting of grain. In principle, it was more profitable for the Dutch to purchase grain in Russia than in Germany, since in the East, grain could be had in exchange for Western manufactures: 'the ships that set out for Muscovy are laden with valuable goods, not with ballast like those that set sail for Danzig, Riga or France'.[6] In other words, it was the backwardness of production in Russia that made the country especially attractive to world commerce.

The Dutch needed grain above all to supply their domestic market. The agriculture of the United Provinces was oriented mainly toward products that yielded greater profits and were important to the development of industry. After starting to import food grain in large quantities from Eastern Europe, the Dutch merchants soon discovered that opportunities were opening up for them on the world market. Already in the seventeenth century thousands of ships were engaged in transporting grain, and Amsterdam had become the world centre of the grain trade.

The main supplier of grain was Poland. In the 1630s, however, Western Europe was experiencing acute food shortages, and the grain that was being shipped from Poland, Prussia and Livonia no longer sufficed. Moreover, Europe was in the grip of the Thirty Years' War.

Among the problems facing the Amsterdam trade were the Sund duties, imposed by Denmark on any goods shipped from the Baltic to the North Sea.

For some time, only the Swedes had been able to move goods into the North Sea by way of the Sund strait without paying duties to the Danish Crown. When Sweden captured the city of Malmö on the eastern shore of the strait, Denmark was finally transformed into a second-rate power. Meanwhile, the mouths of numerous German rivers and the trading cities of Livonia were controlled by the Swedish monarch. Only Swedish merchants, however, were allowed to trade through the Sund without paying duties, while German merchants from Riga, despite living under the Swedish Crown, did not enjoy this privilege. Riga was the largest city in the Swedish kingdom, and the government in Stockholm was extremely wary of the ambitions of its German subjects.

At the same time, the price of grain was rising in line with world demand. In 1606, one *last* (1.92 tons) of rye had cost 16 guilders in Danzig; by 1622 the price had risen ten-fold. After transport costs and the Sund duties had been met, the price was even higher. In Amsterdam in 1628, a *last* of grain cost as much as 250 guilders.

Russia was clearly of enormous interest to the Dutch. By putting large quantities of rye on the world market, Russia could drive down the price. In addition, the route from Arkhangelsk to Amsterdam bypassed the Sund strait. This made the route commercially attractive, despite all the difficulties of navigating the northern waters.

The Dutch representative in Moscow, Isaak Massa, prepared a memorandum for the tsar on the grain trade. In 1630 a diplomatic mission from the Netherlands appeared in Moscow, charged with concluding a special agreement on grain. From the tsar, the Dutch sought a monopoly on the export of Russian rye, even offering to plough up unused lands and to carry on production themselves.[7]

The tsar's government, however, was not to be satisfied with levying export duties. Before it was the example of Sweden, where the trade in grain was concentrated in the hands of the state. The Kremlin functionaries immediately drew up their own plans for establishing a tsarist grain monopoly. At the same time, they began trading with the Dutch, putting an end to the excessive prices before which all the horrors of the Sund duties faded into insignificance.

The plans of the Dutch were not realised, but a start had been made. Russian grain began moving westward in increasing quantities.

SERFDOM AND THE MARKET

Grain had also been exported from Russia in the sixteenth century, especially in years when there was famine in England. In this case, Russian rye was exchanged directly for silver. When there was famine in Muscovy, by contrast, the English imported grain to the country. This was the case particularly in 1571, when Russia was affected by a serious crop failure. In the early seventeenth century about 200,000 *chetverti* (quarters) of grain were exported annually by way of Arkhangelsk. In the 1630s grain began to be exported to Sweden in significant amounts. The shipments of Russian grain to Sweden in 1632 were related to military collaboration between the two countries; both Russia and Sweden were at war with Poland, and the Russian grain was in effect exchanged for weapons.

Russian rye also went to Amsterdam. After the tsar had established a monopoly on the trade in grain, the main concern of the government was to prevent prices from dropping. The grain exports brought the treasury huge revenues, but by the late seventeenth century the state had abandoned its grain monopoly for the sake of an even more profitable business pursuit. Selling grain abroad, it turned out, was less advantageous for the treasury than distilling it into vodka. The exporting of grain passed into the hands of private capital.

In order to become an export commodity, grain had to become an important commodity on the internal market. This occurred as early as the sixteenth century. The processes unfolding in Russia in this instance differed little from those taking place in Europe as a whole.[8]

In Russia in the seventeenth century changes were occurring that aided the development of the grain trade. If access to external markets was limited for the time being, on the internal market the trade in grain was expanding rapidly. It was by no means accidental that the increasing production of grain for the market went hand in hand with the imposing of serfdom.

Analysing the development of capitalist relations in Eastern and Western Europe, historians have discovered that serfdom not only failed to disappear beneath the pressures of modernisation, but on the contrary, strengthened its position. This in no way testifies to the weakness of capitalist development; market relations and private entrepreneurship were developing in parallel with the enserfment of the peasantry. Moreover, and like slavery in the Americas, serfdom stimulated the development of market relations and entrepreneurship. 'This remarkable growth in the use of unfree labor along the periphery of an expanding Europe,' notes the American historian Peter Kolchin, 'stood in marked contrast to its continuing decline in the more economically advanced nations of Western Europe.'[9] In Kolchin's view, 'both slavery and serfdom were labor systems that served to maximise the master class's access to market'.[10]

Kolchin also maintains that in the Russian countryside under serfdom, labour relations were even closer to the capitalist model than they were on the American plantations. Compelled to serve the tsar, landowners in seventeenth- and eighteenth-century Russia could not live in the countryside. They thus depended entirely on managers, who in turn could not devote themselves solely to maintaining order, but who had to transform agricultural production into money. The nobility's constant need for ready cash allowed their managers just as systematically to rob them, and also permitted a flourishing of mercantile capital, since control over the process of exchange lay in the managers' hands.

Long before Kolchin, Pokrovsky noted the same principle. Inasmuch as mercantile capital does not give rise to production, but exploits it, the American plantation and the Russian serfholder estate both proved to be ideal instruments for such exploitation.

The plantation is a manifestation of the capitalist economy, not the feudal economy. It is a sort of artificially established capitalism, thoroughly counterposed to industrial capitalism and to the factory in which free proletarians are employed, as totally opposite as can be imagined.[11]

The 'second wave' of enserfment of the peasantry did not simply represent 'feudal reaction', or a return to the past. What was involved was completely new forms of organising agriculture and exercising coercion. It was not only in Russia that serfdom was reconstituted in practice during the sixteenth and seventeenth centuries, reaching its culmination in the 'enlightened' eighteenth century. A similar process took place in East Prussia, and to describe the new relations of serfdom it was even necessary to introduce a new term, *Erbunter-tänigkeit,* in place of *Liebeigenschaft,* used to characterise the traditional feudal relations existing in the West. As the German historian Heide Wunder remarks, this new serfdom 'must be regarded as a radical innovation in the relationship between peasant and landlord'.[12]

The official historians of the Soviet period, who regarded serfdom as a relic of the Middle Ages, could not explain why the subjection of the peasantry to serfdom did not weaken during the sixteenth and seventeenth centuries, but on the contrary grew stronger. It was in the late eighteenth and early nineteenth centuries that the landowners sought to make the shift to a thoroughly 'plantation' economy, depriving the peasants of the remnants of their independence. The cultivators were transferred to the 'monthly' system, under which they were provided with their food and had their allotments taken from them. 'The landowner was then transformed into something like a plantation owner,' Pokrovsky concludes ironically, 'and the serf peasant into something like a negro.'[13] In Russia, however, this type of management remained the exception, 'an outside possibility'.[14]

The liberal tradition of the early twentieth century was inclined to explain serfdom by reference to the state's need to offload the costs associated with the country's accelerated modernisation onto the people. But this still does not explain why modernisation was accompanied by the retention and strengthening of medieval institutions in the countryside, instead of leading to their dissolution. In reality, serfdom was not a relic of the Middle Ages at all, but a product of the modern era. To the state, the link between the modernising of the country and the need to intensify the exploitation of the peasants was obvious, and no particular effort was made to conceal it. Meanwhile, the interests of the government and the landowners were backed up by the less obvious but no less important interests of commercial capital, both Russian and foreign. This mercantile capital, which set the agenda for the modernisers, required the use of bonded labour.

It is noteworthy that, as Kolchin remarks, serf relations developed primarily in the regions that were most suited to commercial agriculture, and which in this sense were most 'advanced'.

A region could be attractive either because of its good soil and relatively mild climate or because its location – for example, proximity to Moscow – provided a market for agricultural goods. Areas where the soil was poor or climate harsh, and where a sparse population produced no significant demand, were usually left to the state peasants, who eked out a living through subsistence farming and handicrafts.[15]

The first step toward enserfment was taken under Ivan the Terrible. Prior to this, the peasants had two weeks each year, from 20 November – St George's Day, when work was finished and they could leave a landowner and move to other landholdings. This departure was not entirely free; the peasants were obliged to pay the landowner a sort of tax in advance, the 'elder's ruble', a considerable sum for those times. During the years of the Livonian War, the authorities took the first steps toward abolishing this custom. As always, military necessity provided the ideal pretext for implementing 'unpopular measures' whose time, in the view of the ruling class, had come. This 'temporary measure' became permanent, a typical situation in Russian history. Historical sources mention the so-called 'commandment years' when the peasants' right to move was restricted. To judge from the evidence, these decrees were not in force throughout the country, but only in a few districts.[16] It is obvious that the economic consequences of the tsar's policies carried more weight than any official decisions. The devastation which the country suffered during the Livonian War meant that peasants who were moving to new lands were unable to pay the elder's ruble. In the hungry spring months they drifted from one landowner to another; and often the landowners themselves, equally oblivious to laws or customs, 'poached' peasants from their neighbours. As Skrynnikov writes:

By the early 1580s, a substantial section of the rural population had either scattered or died. The countryside was like a vast wasteland. The peasants were cultivating only a small area of the ploughland which had fed them earlier. Beneath the weight of the catastrophe, the old custom of moving on St George's Day fell completely out of use.[17]

However, the enserfment of the peasants, did not end after the Livonian War. On the contrary, the situation of the peasantry continued to worsen after the fighting ceased. The decisive steps toward consolidating the new system in law were taken by Boris Godunov, who had effectively ruled the country under Tsar Fyodr, and who later became tsar himself. Godunov did not find this decision an easy one. His government vacillated. Amid the famine of 1601–02 Godunov declared the St George's Day custom temporarily restored, though not throughout the whole country and not for all categories of landowners. In 1603, however, the policy was again tightened, and the peasants were definitively forbidden to move. This cost the tsar dearly; the mass hostility toward Boris, who had taken responsibilty for the final abolition of the St George's Day custom, was exploited by the impostor Dmitry in his triumphant march on Moscow.[18] As Skrynnikov states:

The civil war which unfolded in the Russian state in 1604 and 1605 was born primarily of the deep social crisis that resulted from the fracturing of the earlier social structure and from the imposing of the serf system. Boris Godunov tried in vain to lessen the acuteness of the problems by temporarily and partially restoring St George's Day. Resistance from the feudal landowners forced the authorities to return to the old serf-holding course. The 'great famine' of 1601–1603 hastened the explosion.[19]

The policy begun by Ivan the Terrible created the preconditions for the catastrophe of the Time of Troubles.

ENSERFMENT

The Livonian War, the terror of the *oprichnina,* the famine and the Troubles led to a huge collapse and to the flight of the population from the European regions of Russia. Throughout Eastern Europe, the situation during the first half of the seventeenth century was much the same. In Poland and various parts of Germany, massive depopulation had occurred following the Thirty Years' War and the series of military-political conflicts that continued even after the signing of the Treaty of Westphalia. By the mid seventeenth century, the demographic situation in Muscovy and other states of Eastern Europe was comparable to that in Western Europe after the plague. 'Serfdom,' writes Pokrovsky, 'grew quickly in Russia on the ruins that resulted from the Troubles, just as in Germany it arose on the ruins left behind by the Thirty Years' War.'[20]

The question presents itself: why did the depopulation of fourteenth-century England favour the development of free labour, while in Eastern Europe depopulation was followed by a directly opposite process, the 'second-wave enserfment' of the peasants? The American historian Robert Brenner sees this as resulting from the defeat of the peasant uprisings. The Bolotnikov uprising in the early seventeenth century was indeed finally defeated, as was the later revolt of Stepan Razin. The same, however, can be said of the fourteenth-century peasant revolts in Western Europe; the uprising led by Watt Tyler and the Jacqueries in France were also overcome. Peasant uprisings in general have always tended to end in failure. Moreover, in Western Europe after the plague, the feudal rulers also tried to limit wages or tie peasants to the land, but these attempts failed – not only due to massive resistance, but also for economic reasons, which cannot be said of Russian serfdom in the seventeenth and eighteenth centuries. Nor is the enserfment of the peasants to be explained as the result of the weakness of the bourgeoisie. Though backward by Dutch or English standards, the Muscovite merchants of the seventeenth century were stronger than the bourgeois strata had been in England 300 years earlier. Moreover, the serf system also grew stronger in Livonia, where the German mercantile bourgeoisie was unquestionably powerful. In reality, it was precisely the development of the international market and of bourgeois relations in the West that was the decisive cause behind the imposing of serfdom in the East. In the fourteenth century the need did not exist, either in England or France, for large-scale commodity production to satisfy external markets. Even the internal markets were extremely small. The cities were comparatively undeveloped. The sparseness of the population meant that people started purchasing in the market various goods they had earlier obtained through their own efforts within the framework of the 'natural economy'. The shortage of labour power thus led both to the formation of a labour market and to the development of the commodity market in general. By contrast, the East in the seventeenth century already possessed relatively developed and established markets, both internal and external. Because of the limited availability of labour power, these markets came to experience an acute shortage of commodities. The simplest way of increasing supplies – and perhaps the only way to achieve big increases in a brief period – was to intensify the exploitation of the peasants.

There was nowhere that Western European peasants, even free peasants, could go to escape the feudal authorities, since there was 'no land without its *seigneur*'. Russia was different; here there was no land shortage. The Russian people, Pokrovsky remarks, settled their land 'not through dispersal, but through resettlement'.[21] The periodic resettlement by the peasants from one place to another did not undermine the natural economy, since these shifts were occasioned less by feudal oppression than by demographic causes and by the exhaustion of the soil. Within the framework of the primitive peasant order, there were just enough people in any given locality to sustain both the peasants and the landowner. For commodity-based agriculture, this was no longer sufficient. Meanwhile, the resettled peasants on their new land reproduced the natural economy, thus limiting the development of the grain trade.[22] It is hence understandable that subjecting the peasants to serfdom should have become a 'necessary condition for production' in a context where ensuring a consistent supply of grain to the market was essential. 'Having crushed the feudal overlord in the name of economic progress,' Pokrovsky writes, 'the landowner himself quickly became an economically outmoded type; such is the paradox with which the history of the Russian economy of the epoch of Ivan the Terrible draws to a close.'[23]

In England, the agrarian revolution of the sixteenth century occurred in a setting marked by the transformation of commercial capital into a powerful social and political force, after the aristocracy had been destroyed in the Wars of the Roses. Similar processes were afoot in Russia during the time of Ivan the Terrible, but the needs of the market outstripped social development, and in this regard the rapid expansion of international trade played an enormous role. No less important is the fact that the creation of the agricultural market in Western Europe began long before the 'prices revolution', while in Eastern Europe the 'prices revolution' preceded the changes in agriculture, and to a significant degree stimulated them. The landlords needed to increase the commercial yield of their estates immediately, and with a minimum of available resources. Moreover, they needed to do this at a time when the currency was rapidly being devalued. 'It was necessary to tie down the unrestrained workers who were leaving the estate, but how could this be done without capital, without the "silver" through which the peasants could be secured?'[24]

The crisis that gripped all of Europe in the seventeenth century had directly opposite results in England and Russia. The outward symptoms of this crisis, and at times even specific events, seem at first sight to display a striking similarity. At the same time as England was being shaken by revolution, Moscow was undergoing its own social and political crisis. In 1648, revolts swept across the entire country. Not only did the population refuse to obey the orders of the authorities, but they also showed their discontent in organised form. As S.F. Platonov notes, after the Troubles, assemblies of the various social estates became an inalienable part of the political system. The elected representatives of the estates proclaimed their demands to the authorities. Of course, these forms of representation fell a long way short of the English parliament, but their power could not be ignored. The Romanov dynasty was obliged to the Zemsky Sobor (Land Assembly) for its very existence.

Platonov notes that,

> By the end of the reign of Mikhail Fyodorovich, the practice of making collective appeals to the authorities was firmly established, and along with this, it had become obvious that it was not within the powers of the government to satisfy all the wishes of the various social strata.[25]

And he likens the Moscow revolt of 1648 to a 'revolution'.[26] The political crisis unfolded against the background of a prolonged economic depression. Short of funds, the government followed the classical road of economic austerity. The boyar Morozov, who at that time effectively headed the tsar's administration, increased the taxes on salt and tobacco and reduced court spending, dismissing many of the servants and cutting the wages of those who remained. Not surprisingly, these measures deepened the economic depression in Moscow still further, and sparked an outburst of hostility to the ruler. Adding to the dissatisfaction with the government was the bourgeoisie's dislike of the clergy, who engaged actively in commercial dealings, and enjoyed all sorts of privileges while doing so. To the inhabitants of the merchant quarter, the church hierarchs were primarily competitors, and unfair ones at that.

The tax on salt that had been imposed in 1646 was abolished early in 1648, but the damage had already been done. Although the discontent was fundamentally of economic origin, the uprising by the Moscow populace took on a political character. The demands of the rebels resonated in striking fashion with the slogans that had inspired popular indignation in England. To the horror of the patriarch Nikon, the Moscow rebels were seeking equality of all citizens before the law, signifying an end to clerical privileges in the courts. Swedish emissaries wrote that the common people of the tsar's capital wanted 'good laws and freedom'.[27] In essence, a revolutionary situation had arisen in Russia. Foreign observers in Moscow wrote that the country was on the verge of a major revolt, and that the government might fall at any time.[28]

Just how alarmed the authorities were can be seen from the actions of the tsar, who sacrificed all the key people in his government. The head of the Land Office, Leonty Pleshcheev, was condemned to death, but the enraged crowd took its revenge on him before he could be brought to the place of execution. Morozov was dismissed and fled, and his house was ransacked. The court had so little trust in its own people that the tsar's guard was made up exclusively of foreigners; later, they were replaced with Russians, but under the command of Dutch officers.

The panicked state of the tsar's court is understandable if we consider that the revolt in the capital found echoes throughout the country. 'The warning spurred frantic activity', Klyuchevsky writes.

The court took fright, and began seeking favour with the soldiers of the capital and with the common masses. On orders from the tsar, the troops were plied with drink. For several days running, the tsar's father-in-law entertained in his home selected representatives of the tax-paying Moscow commoners. During the Procession of the Cross, the tsar himself addressed the people and called for forgiveness. With tears in his eyes, he pleaded with the multitude on behalf of his brother-in-law and beloved associate Morozov. Promises were given freely.[29]

The tsar sought humbly to justify himself before the people.

I promised to deliver Morozov to you, and I must confess that I cannot absolve him completely, but neither do I have the will to condemn him. That man is dear to me, he is the husband of the tsarina's sister, and to hand him over to his death would grieve me deeply.[30]

Nevertheless, for the tsar to limit himself to issuing promises and rearranging his officials was now impossible. On 1 September he was forced to convene the Sobor (Assembly) in order to adopt a new set of laws, the Code of 1648.

While the prehistory of the Sobor reads like a classical description of an early bourgeois revolution, the outcome of the crisis was a social order that differed dramatically from the one in Western Europe. On the one hand, the Code of 1648 abolished the privileges which the clergy had enjoyed in the legal system; in the words of Platonov, the Code 'established the principle of equality of rights between the middle layers of Muscovite society and the aristocratic elite'.[31] On the other hand, this same Code that affirmed democratic principles also consolidated the 'right' of landowners to the labour of their peasants. The destruction of the system of feudal privileges in Russia proved to be, not a step in the direction of civil freedoms, but rather a landmark on the road to the institutionalising of serfdom. There is no paradox here, since serfdom in Russia was born not of medieval barbarism but of the requirements of the emerging market economy.

As Platonov remarks, the new laws displayed 'all the features of conscious class work'.[32] The urban middle layers who revolted in 1648 were not linked to the rural population. Moreover, the rural estate-owners who made use of bonded labour were closer to the nascent Russian bourgeoisie than were the peasants. To the merchants, the landowners were partners, and now became political allies as well.

This alliance between the landed nobility and the mercantile bourgeoisie was victorious in 1648, dealing another blow to the privileges of the clergy and the old elite, while humiliating and once again restricting the monarchy. The events of 1648 are evidence not of backwardness, but of the considerable level of development of Muscovite society, which was able to organise itself and to obtain its due from the authorities. Here, however, the array of interests proved to be quite different from that in Western Europe. Paradoxically, the social bloc which triumphed in Russia was not so different in its make-up from the one that made a revolution in England during the same years. Cromwell's parliament was also dominated by an alliance between the bourgeoisie and the new gentry, an alliance cemented by the same shared interests as in the Muscovite Sobor. The principal difference, however, was that the commercial activity of the new English gentry, the activity which drove it into the embrace of the bourgeoisie, was based on the free hire of labour and on landlord–tenant relations, while in Russia the basis was the labour of serfs.

Russia and England both experienced the same global crisis, but each of these countries experienced it in its own fashion. If England furnished an example of a revolutionary outcome of the 'crisis of the seventeenth century', the example in Russia was of a reactionary outcome. In similar circumstances, the results were directly opposite. These results reflected not only different levels of socio-economic development and different political traditions, but, to a much greater degree, the different places which the two countries occupied in the emerging world system.

In the West, the Third Estate was victorious because it united the majority of the population in its ranks. The bourgeoisie, resting on the peasant masses and the urban plebeians, could not only permit itself to engage in conflict with the monarchy, but could also allow itself the luxury of revolutionism. From time to time the masses got out of control, which gave rise to bloody conflicts within the 'revolutionary' camp itself. In Russia, by contrast, the peasant majority was from the very beginning excluded from the political process.

In a certain sense, the failed revolution of 1648 determined the relationship of forces in all the subsequent social crises of Russian history until 1917. The 'middle layers' who were triumphant in 1648 and 1649 did not combine forces with the 'lower orders', but against them. It is perfectly understandable that for all their strivings to attain legal 'equality', these middle layers were incapable of democracy and needed strict authoritarian rulers to defend their interests. The bourgeoisie were tied body and soul to the landowners, and as a result were incapable of collaborating with the peasants. Modernisation could be implemented only from above, only under the supervision of the state's soldiers and bureaucrats, who would not give the rural masses any chance to intervene in the process. Tsarism survived until 1917 for the reason that, for all its drawbacks, it was better suited than democracy to the task of developing capitalism on the periphery. In 1905 and 1917, Russian Marxists explained the reactionary nature of the country's bourgeoisie as stemming from its fear of the aroused proletariat. But in 1648, when there could be no talk of a proletariat, the bourgeoisie acted according to the same logic as that of 250 years later.

Russian capitalism rested on landowner agriculture, on non-economic coercion, and on the ruthless exploitation of the rural majority. These were the phenomena that made Russian capitalism competitive on world markets, and which allowed it to develop in dynamic fashion despite the narrowness of the country's internal market. In Russia there could be no Third Estate, and consequently there was no bourgeois revolution. The imposing of serfdom in Eastern Europe, like slavery in the Americas, was in reality linked intimately with the development of capitalism in the West. The process of enserfment was stimulated by the ever-greater incorporation of the periphery into the new market economy, where the peripheral regions supplied the Western bourgeoisie with the cheap raw materials and foodstuffs that were essential for economic expansion.[33] It might be said that through their labour, the Russian serf and the plantation slave extended credit to Western European capitalism. This in turn gave rise to far-reaching differences in the way the bourgeoisies took shape. Capitalist relations were established both in the East and in the West, but in the West an industrial bourgeoisie emerged, while in Eastern Europe it was primarily commercial capital that developed. The Western bourgeoisie proved to be revolutionary, and viewed the surviving elements of feudalism as a brake on development. The bourgeoisie in the East, by contrast, lived in symbiosis with the landowner economy.

The economy of Russian serfdom was subject to the same dynamic as the American slaveholder plantations. Ivan the Terrible had restricted the rights associated with St George's Day, while Boris Godunov had finally abolished them, tying the peasant to the land. In the eighteenth century, peasants could be sold separately from land, just like plantation slaves. It was thus with the spread of the European enlightenment that human beings were definitively transformed into commodities.

FORCED LABOUR

'In the broadest sense,' writes the American historian Peter Kolchin, 'serfdom in Russia and slavery in America were part of the same historic process, despite the vastly differing societies in which they emerged.'[34] In Kolchin's view, these phenomena resulted from the combining of economic and geographic expansion with a shortage of labour power. Each of these factors was present in both Russia and America, but peasants were enserfed and slavery was restored even in regions where these problems were not especially acute. In particular, and as noted earlier, the peasantry were subjected to a 'secondary enserfment' in Poland and in Germany east of the Elbe. The reasons for the spread of forced labour on the periphery of the growing capitalist system lay far deeper, in the need of the expanding world market for cheap raw materials and foodstuffs. These latter were absolutely indispensable requirements if the use of free labour in the countries of the West was to be effective. If these conditions were to be met, labour power on the periphery had to be exceedingly cheap, available almost free of charge.

Unlike the feudal estate of medieval times, the North American plantation and the Russian serf agriculture of the period from the sixteenth to the nineteenth centuries were linked closely to the market. Production here was of a fundamentally commercial character. Ultimately, the forced labour on the periphery ensured the accumulation of capital in the centre, while of course guaranteeing the peripheral elites a worthy place among the world elites. This was particularly evident in the case of Russia, whose serf economy in no way prevented the country from holding an important place among the great powers of Europe.

An economy based on forced labour would have been impossible without a strong state. Agrarian development required the occupying of vast expanses, which had to be defended. On this level, there are again obvious parallels between the history of serfdom in Russia and that of slavery in America. Robin Blackburn notes that Holland was no match for Britain and France so long as it lacked the resources to maintain an empire based on slave labour. 'And in contrast to the Netherlands, Britain and France had been able to mobilise the requisite strength to defend their colonial conquests in the New World.'[35] Finally, it was essential to control the trade routes by which the products of the slave plantations reached world markets. Otherwise, these products would simply be devalued. Portugal, which had a vast colonial empire but lacked a strong fleet, was itself transformed into a semi-colony of Britain. Maintaining a plantation economy required the constant use of 'military, especially naval, strength'.[36]

The Russian state developed according to the same logic as the colonial empires founded by Britain and France. The main difference was not the fact that the Russian expansion of the seventeenth and eighteenth centuries was mainly across dry land. The struggle for sea routes remained among the chief preoccupations of the Russian state from the sixteenth to the eighteenth centuries, and to some extent even into the nineteenth century. A far more important difference was that Russia, having defended its self-determination during the years of the Troubles, developed as an independent state, on the one hand, while constituting part of the periphery, on the other. This peripheral empire was strong enough to solve on its own territory, through the use of its own power, the same problems that Britain and France confronted in their colonies. Russia was both an empire and the object of colonisation at the same time. This determined in advance many of the peculiarities of subsequent Russian history, not only in the political and economic fields, but also in the areas of culture and psychology. It might be said that from the seventeenth century the Russian state underwent 'self-colonisation'. The powerful state authority, based first in the Kremlin and then in the St Petersburg court, systematically enslaved its own population, while at the same time defending its borders against incursions and securing the trade routes by which products obtained through bonded labour were exported to the West. Russians became simultaneously an 'imperial' people, proud of their historic conquests, and an enslaved population, colonial in their essence.

THE CONQUEST OF SIBERIA

After recovering from the shocks of the Livonian War and the Troubles, Russia in the mid sixteenth century once again became actively integrated into world trade as a supplier of raw materials for developing Western capitalism. Compared to the time of Ivan the Terrible, however, the situation on world markets had changed substantially. Muscovy now had serious competitors in the form of the North American colonies, which were supplying more or less the same products. On the other hand, Russia in the seventeenth century was able to furnish considerably greater resources to world markets than a century earlier. The prime acquisition of the Russian state in the sixteenth and seventeenth centuries was Siberia. Significantly, the conquest of the vast expanses of Siberia began in parallel with the great geographical discoveries and the colonisation of America.

Why did the Russians not make their way to the east earlier? In the second half of the thirteenth century, this region was controlled by the Tatars. In the period when Kievan Rus had flourished, however, the area to the east had been a political vacuum. The Russian detachments had nonetheless persistently directed their course to the north and north-west, into territories not especially suited to colonisation, and quite useless for agriculture. There, they risked encountering (and did, indeed, constantly encounter) powerful Swedish forces who were heading in the same direction. The reason was simple: the north could provide furs and other goods able to be sold at a profit on European markets. From a commercial point of view, the east was unattractive. Grain was not yet a traded commodity; Russia fed itself, and so did the countries of Europe. The furs obtained from the north were quite sufficient, and were easier to transport along the rivers to the markets of southern Europe. The Siberian rivers flowed from south to north, or from west to east, and were not connected in any way to the great trade routes of the Middle Ages.

With the growth of cities and the colonisation of the New World, demand for grain on the European and world markets increased sharply. At the same time, the flood of silver from America also increased the demand for Russia's traditional export – furs, whose prices remained at the same levels as earlier. The volume of goods traded on the world market increased. In these circumstances, Russian commerical capital began taking more and more interest in the lands *za kamnem*, 'beyond the stone' – that is, beyond the Ural mountains.

Siberia became a source of essential goods. The expeditions into Siberia by Yermak and his comrades did not simply coincide with the campaigns of the conquistadors. They were part of the same world economic process. It was not the tsar's army that first set out for Siberia, but mercenaries funded by merchants. These expeditions were above all commercial enterprises; the expansion of the realm and military glory were merely by-products of this process. In 1574, Ivan the Terrible had given the Stroganovs vast territories beyond the Urals. The problem was that the lands which the Muscovite tsar had so generously granted did not belong to him, but were part of the domain of the Siberian Khan Kuchum. From the point of view of the Moscow bureaucracy, what had occurred was a simple clerical error. Once the Stroganovs had obtained their title deeds, however, they made haste to assert their property rights. Buying up the best weapons available at the time, they prepared a mercenary detachment headed by the Cossack ataman Yermak for service beyond the Urals.

The origins of the title deeds granted to the Stroganovs can scarcely be attributed to the naïvety and geographical illiteracy of the Moscow bureaucrats. The Soviet economist and historian S.G. Strumilin suspects that the arrangement was not concluded without resort to bribery.

It may be that the people in Moscow who granted title to foreign property did not know that the lands involved lay beyond our frontiers, inside the borders of the Siberian tsardom, with which Ivan IV was certainly not planning to provoke a dispute at that time. But bearing in mind that such 'gifts' were not to be had cheaply (given the well-known hunger for bribes of the Moscow officials), the Stroganovs must have known where they were seeking a gift, and what it consisted of. All this renders more believable a chronicle entry which suggests that the glorious conquest of Siberia by the freemen of Yermak Timofeevich should also be viewed as one of the ambitious commerical undertakings of the Stroganov trading house.[37]

Learning of Yermak's expedition, the Muscovite tsar and those around him realised what was afoot. A commotion broke out in Moscow, and furious letters were written to the Stroganovs demanding that the Cossacks be recalled. Threats were made that the participants in the expedition would all be hanged. But by the time the letters reached the Urals, Yermak had already succeeded in conquering the entire Siberian khanate, and seizing its capital Isker (now Tobolsk). The tsar's rage now turned to mercy, and from being a criminal, Yermak was hurriedly recast as a national hero, which is how Russians regard him to this day. The Stroganovs, however, were still punished. The lands conquered by Yermak were taken over by the state, and the trading house was compelled to write off the costs it had incurred in equipping its Siberian expedition.

Following commerical capital on the eastward trail came large numbers of peasants. The colonisation of the eastern Urals and Siberia had begun. The occupying of these 'new' lands by Russian settlers coincided with the incorporation of these territories into the world market. As early as the 1570s, the Stroganov merchants were exporting Siberian goods to Antwerp and Paris.

The conquest of Siberia had nothing in common with feudal expansion. Serfdom did not exist in the new lands. The local populations were at times ruthlessly exterminated, but were never turned into serfs or slaves. In the occupying of Siberia, the entrepreneurial initiative of the Stroganov merchants was crucially important. Having gained temporary possession from Ivan the Terrible of the lands on Russia's eastern border, the Stroganovs became the effective masters of 'the empty region below Great Perm'. They were able to recruit and arm 'hunting people' – that is, to form their own army – and to exact tribute from the Siberian Tatars.[38] In short, the powers of the Stroganovs were clearly reminiscent of the status of the British and Dutch merchant companies founded in order to take control of the West and East Indies.

It is significant that the expansion to the east by the Stroganovs should have dated from the granting of a charter by the tsar in 1558 – that is, the very year when the Livonian War began. Nevertheless, it was only in September 1581 that a Cossack detachment, recruited with the Stroganovs' money, led by Yermak and numbering fewer than a thousand men, penetrated deep into the territory of the Siberian khanate and established the first fortified village. It was only later that soldiers of the tsar were sent to the aid of the Cossacks.

The actions of the Stroganovs in Siberia were linked closely to the development of the world market. As historians have noted, the wealth of Anikey Stroganov had its origins in the fact that 'earlier than other Russians, he managed to reach the Ob, and there to exchange cheap "German" trinkets and other goods for valuable furs'. In the Altay Russian prospectors found gold and silver, which among 'men of business' stirred even greater interest in taking control of Siberia. Meanwhile, goods acquired in Siberia were reaching the West.

In order that the markets of Western Europe should be penetrated, commerical agents were selected from among captured 'Germans and Lithuanians' who were being held in the prisons, while experienced foreign sailors and shipbuilders were invited in.[39]

Throughout the seventeenth century, the prosperity and trade turnover of the Stroganovs steadily increased. In Arkhangelsk in the single year of 1671 their company purchased 'overseas goods' worth 30,000 rubles, a vast sum for the times. Meanwhile, wax, hides, silk, furs, the skins of sables and foxes, and the coats of arctic foxes were sold to the foreigners.[40]

While Columbus sailed across the Atlantic, hoping to find a route to India and China, the Russian conquerers of Siberia actually achieved this goal. Hence, in the seventeenth century, Chinese goods that had earlier been transported along the Great Silk Road further to the south reached Moscow by way of Siberia. The fact that trade routes had not passed through Siberia before this was no accident. Until the building of the Trans-Siberian Railway, organising successful trade through this region was impossible since suitable river routes were lacking.

It might be said that in socio-economic and cultural terms, the Russian conquest of Siberia was more like the British colonisation of North America than the conquest of South America by the Spanish and Portuguese. The consequences of the Siberian expeditions, however, were quite different from the outcomes of the Protestant colonial expansion. Moreover, the Russian economy in historical perspective has been closer to that of Latin America than to the North American economy. One can, of course, try to explain the differences by referring to the Protestant ethic or to its absence. The truth is, however, that another and much weightier cause was present. The European part of Russia was still subject to serfdom. The bourgeoisie was marginal in its social importance. It was in an effort to overcome this marginal status in relation to the tsarist state that the bourgeoisie mounted its expeditions to the east. But Russia's western provinces, where serfdom reigned, were simply incapable of apportioning either a sufficient number of settlers to assimilate the new territories or enough free capital.

In the sixteenth century, when the great movement to the east began, serfdom was far from universal among the population of Muscovy. The paradox was that the consolidating of serfdom in Russia's central regions was accompanied by the rise of free Cossack communities in the borderlands. The two processes were in effect different aspects of one and the same process: the development of commercial agriculture and the integration of Russia into the world market. Drzhinin writes:

Despite the intensive granting and spontaneous seizure of settled state lands, a layer of state peasants remained and gradually multiplied who were dependent in feudal fashion on the authorities, but who possessed their own personal freedom, officially recognised in law.

Alongside the enserfed peasants, great numbers of fugitives had settled in the forests of the Perm and Volga regions, on the broad expanses of Siberia, and on the southern steppelands, where they succeeded in avoiding organised searches, government censuses, and the coercive measures of the local organs of power. These people were not only the members of free Cossack communities, whose numbers rose continuously as peasants fled to join them, but also people who had spontaneously resettled; members of persecuted sects; and 'restless' elements who had managed independently to regain their lost freedom. So it was that in the serf-holding Russia of the sixteenth and seventeenth centuries, centres of free agricultural development arose, resembling the American squatter settlements that came into being due to the existence of vast unpopulated expanses with unappropriated natural wealth. The difference between these independent farming settlements and those of the squatters was that they arose within the bounds of a feudal-serfholding monarchy; the Russian settlers could not partake of the advantages of an established capitalist system, and lived under constant threat of persecution and destruction.[41]

There is, of course, another explanation for the differences between the Russian Cossacks and the North American colonists, as Druzhinin also observes:

As the Russian state advanced from the Urals into the remote regions of Siberia, it had at the same time to expect attacks from the south, and hence to establish forest strongholds and watch-posts, to maintain armed detachments on its borders, and to conduct delicate diplomatic manoeuvres in order to retain the expanses it had occupied. Danger also threatened from the west, from Livonia, Sweden and Poland. If Russia resembled the American colonies in terms of huge distances and the possibility of broad resettlement in various directions, the presence of a constant military threat was a sharp point of difference between Russia and Britain's transoceanic possessions.[42]

In reality, the British colonies in North America were also under constant military pressure, with the danger coming from the Indians to the East, from the French colonies to the north, and from the Spanish to the south. As Robin Blackburn remarks, it was the military aspect of colonisation that ultimately proved decisive. The ending of any serious external threat as a result of the British victory over France in the Seven Years' War encouraged the colonies to struggle for their independence; prior to this, they could not have defended themselves without the help of the metropolis.

THE COSSACKS

The Cossacks' problem was above all demographic. The 'self-colonisation' that was occurring in European Russia required an expansion to the east, and at the same time limited its prospects. Britain could apportion far more free citizens for colonisation than Russia, which faced an insoluble contradiction. On the one hand, Russia needed people to occupy new lands, while on the other, it needed them to produce commercial grain crops on the country's European territory. Both requirements were born of one and the same process; commercial capital needed ever-growing quantities of goods and resources for its expansion on the internal and external markets. But so long as the landowners remained the principal suppliers of cheap grain, the peasants had to remain in serfdom. It was not simply that the exploitation of the peasants in the western regions was being intensified, and that serfdom was moving gradually to the east. Under such conditions, colonisation required even more active state support than in America.

The Cossack communities were not just under constant pressure from the autocratic government. Located on the country's borders, these communities were subject to regular attacks from external enemies, with whom they could not have coped without support from the centre. The state in turn was forced to tolerate the Cossacks in the border regions to the extent that the Cossacks could be used to guard the frontiers. In the event, the Cossacks began to serve the very state from which they had fled. This collaboration, however, was not permanent, and relations with the authorities were fluid. From time to time the government took steps to tighten its control over the Cossacks, understandably provoking their resistance. During periods when the central authority was relatively weak, the Cossacks could effectively ignore the government and its commanders, taking orders exclusively from their atamans and from the 'Cossack circles', representative organs of military democracy that arose on the Russian borders. Collective land ownership, which prevented excessive property differentiation within the ranks of the Cossacks, allowed this variety of self-government to be maintained over a lengthy historical period. The Cossack detachments were self-governing communities that guarded their independence fiercely. Cossacks also played key roles in all the great anti-government uprisings that shook Russia from the sixteenth to the eighteenth centuries. The popular rebel leaders Bolotnikov, Razin and Pugachev were either Cossacks themselves or relied on Cossack support, though as a rule most of the rebels were enserfed peasants. The numerous impostors who laid claim to the Russian throne in the seventeenth century and in the second half of the eighteenth century also appealed to the Cossacks for help. Drawing a balance sheet of the political crisis that gripped Russian society in the early seventeenth century, a modern-day historian notes:

The Cossacks gave particularly steadfast support to the impostors who claimed to be the tsarevich (and later tsar) Dmitry Ivanovich, in whose victory they saw a guarantee of the honoured position held by the Cossacks in Russian society. The desire of the Cossacks to have their pretender crowned in Moscow was exploited in 1613 by the Romanov 'party'. The 'free' Cossacks were among the main forces that made possible the election by the *Zemsky Sobor* (Land Assembly) of Mikhail Romanov, whom they counterposed to the 'boyar' contenders for the Russian throne.[43]

For all the democracy of their military organisation, the Cossacks were in no sense bearers of progressive social relations. Nor were the Cossack households anything like those of the bourgeoisie or of family farmers. Having fled the country's central provinces for the frontier, the Cossacks set out to restore, in a new location, the old patriarchal order which government policy had undermined. As one historian puts it, the 'free' Cossacks of the Don, the Yaik and the Terek in the early seventeenth century were 'far more archaic in terms of their social development than the social organisation of the Russian state of the same period'.[44]

After lengthy struggles, the Cossacks finally won their freedom and a range of privileges. The liberties involved, however, were those of a medieval social estate, and it is therefore not surprising that by the mid nineteenth century the now-strengthened Cossacks had been transformed from a politically unreliable mass with a weakness for periodic revolts into a conservative force helping the regime to keep other social strata and groups in bondage. If the Protestant colonists in North America had initially been more or less loyal subjects of the king, only later turning into rebels, the Russian Cossacks evolved in the opposite direction. As early as the seventeenth century the Cossacks had periodically robbed peasants, subjecting them to all sorts of extortion. By the early twentieth century the Cossack units had become the main force (unlike the fickle troops of the regular army) on which the government could reliably count to suppress urban and rural revolts, strikes and uprisings.

THE STRUGGLE AGAINST POLAND

While the colonising of Siberia saw Russia's boundaries expand to the east, the wars against Poland achieved a good deal more than simply consolidating the Russian position in the west. When it annexed Ukraine, the Muscovite state seized the most important source of grain in Europe. In the sixteenth century, Russia had participated in the grain trade only episodically. By contrast, Poland in the sixteenth century was already actively involved in grain exporting. In the seventeenth century, the importance of grain on the world market rose dramatically. The more grain produced for the market, the greater the market value of land, and the greater the scale of agrarian conflict. The price of Ukrainian black-earth lands increased rapidly. Grain became an important commodity not only on the world market, but also on the domestic one. This led to active efforts to seize whatever land remained empty in the south, and also to an increasingly acute struggle for this land between the Polish aristocracy and the Ukrainian Cossacks. In the sixteenth century the Cossacks had played an active role in the campaigns by the Rzecz Pospolita against Muscovy, but in the following century the situation changed sharply. The conflict between the Polish landowners and the Cossacks in Ukraine intensified in direct proportion to the development of the grain market. Ultimately, this struggle served to undermine the Polish state, in the form which it had acquired by the end of the medieval period.

Meanwhile, the conflict between Russia and Poland also grew more acute as the grain trade developed. This time, the struggle was conducted not on the shores of the Baltic, but on the Ukrainian steppes, and it ended with the victory of Russia. The Ukrainian Cossacks, headed by Bogdan Khmelnitsky, were inclined to regard Moscow as a tactical ally from whom they would take their leave as soon as the question of the Poles was resolved. Russia, however, proved to be far more effective as a state than appearances might have suggested. The tactical agreement with the Muscovite tsar turned into the annexation, lasting for centuries, of Ukraine to Russia.

The paradoxical nature of the Russian empire was already fully apparent in the seventeenth century. On the one hand, Russia was a typical peripheral country, while on the other, it was a great European power. This paradox preordained the endless contradictions of Russian politics, the country's sublime ascents and painful downfalls, its imperialist ambitions and administrative helplessness, its building of a powerful army and its inability to overcome the chronic weakness of its economy.

The Russia over whose fate historians and philosophers have debated endlessly, the country of endless expanses and ever-unrealised potential, counterposing itself to the West and striving desperately to draw closer to it, at once self-satisfied and suffering from an inferiority complex, living beneath the constant weight of an autocratic regime, enforcing serfdom and also undergoing periodic explosions of 'senseless and pitiless' revolt – this Russia had its genesis in the seventeenth century. The conquest of Siberia dramatically altered the country's geography, and serfdom and autocracy became the basis of the social and political order. It was not the Tatar invasion of the thirteenth century, but the crisis of the seventeenth century and the changes which resulted from it and which culminated in the modernisation under Peter the Great, which inevitably made the Russian state authoritarian.

The seventeenth century was a time of crisis not only for Russia and Eastern Europe, but also for the Western world. The opportunities for economic and political expansion that arose along with the great geographical discoveries had been exhausted during the previous century. In order to continue developing, Europe itself had to change. It had to finally overcome the feudal order it had inherited from the Middle Ages, and to shape a new social order that met the demands of the modern era. This new order was established in painful fashion, through wars and upheavals. It was formed simultaneously in the West and East of the continent. In the West it took shape in the conquests of the English revolution; in Russia it became set in the form of the autocratic serf-holding regime that arose on the wreckage of the Troubles.

A HOME-GROWN BOURGEOISIE

The regime that became established in Moscow needed to define and justify itself in ideological terms. Here, it met with unexpected problems that came close to destroying the entire edifice of the new social and state system.

In seventeenth-century Moscow, the ideology was religion, just as it was religion that provided the ideological and moral prop for the state, but the ecclesiastical organisation of the Muscovite tsardom in the seventeenth century was extremely unstable. The church in Russia was not completely isolated from the outside world. Significantly, it was at the very time when the official church in the West was undergoing upheavals, and when the struggle was unfolding between Protestants and Catholics, that numerous 'heresies' first arose in Russia, to be followed by the beginnings of ecclesiastical reform.

As in the West, the slogan of the church reformers was a 'return to the old faith', but in fact this amounted to an attempt to adapt the church and the ideology to the conditions of the new era. The decisive factor here, of course, was not the influence of the Western Reformation, but the similarity in the conditions of social development. In both Western and Eastern Europe, parallel processes were under way. But here too, the 'peripheral' nature of Russian development made its effects felt.

Coming more than a century later than in the West, the Russian Reformation was similar to that of the West in some respects, but radically different in others, since the relationship and disposition of forces were now quite different. In Western Europe the 'royal' and 'popular' Reformations, despite periodic conflicts between them, were nevertheless interlinked. This was predetermined by the impossibility of completely destroying the old Catholic church organisation, and by the conflict – which had taken on an interstate and international character – between the bourgeois-Protestant north and the feudal-Catholic south. In Russia, by contrast, the old ecclesiastical system yielded its positions without a struggle, since Orthodoxy, unlike Catholicism, lacked an independent political organisation.

The clash between the 'popular' Reformation and the official 'ecclesiastical reform' thus took on the character of a struggle for the 'old faith', but it should not be forgotten that the archpriest Avvakum, the chief ideologue of the 'old rite', and the patriarch Nikon, who was leading the official reform, acted initially as allies against the traditional church. The conflict was not theological but social. On the surface, and in terms of dogma, the struggle might be perceived as having involved a collision between a 'conservative' mass of believers and reformist hierarchs. But in fact, the 'old believers' were defending a radical variant of church reform that extended to such extreme measures as doing away altogether with a special professional layer of priests, something also proposed by the most radical Protestant sects in the West.

Pokrovsky quite correctly describes the Old Believers as adherents of a 'peasant reformation'.[15] The distinctive feature of this religious revolt, however, lay not only in the resistance by the people to the ruling classes, but also in the fact that the movement 'from below', reformist in its essence though not in its slogans, took shape not in a struggle against the Old church, but against a reform 'from above'. To be more precise, both were occurring. The fact that Avvakum in his struggle made an appeal to old-time piety did not by any means make him conservative; Martin Luther and the leaders of the English Puritans acted in exactly the same fashion. The archpriest Avvakum and his radical supporters were forced to wage a fight against the old ecclesiastical organisation. This organisation, however, was not conservative, like the Catholicism of the early sixteenth century in the West, but on the contrary was actively reformist. Russian Orthodoxy had not wasted the century and a half that separated Luther from Nikon. It had assimilated both the lessons of the 'royal' Reformation and the experience of the Catholic Counter-Reformation.

Patriarch Nikon, who headed the official reform, not only corrected church texts on the basis of Greek models, but also strove for what might in modern language be termed the uniformity and standardisation of rites. The Greek church, as it happened, was not insisting on the rites being amended. Of crucial importance here were the needs of the state, and its desire to carry out modernisation from above. The church needed to be governed according to the same principles as the state bureaucracy, transforming itself and entering the new era as part of the system of rule. Not surprisingly, the church authorities supported such a reform, and tried to suppress Avvakum's supporters along with their ideas concerning the autonomy of communities.

The Old Believer schismatics in Russia were simultaneously a milieu that spawned successful entrepreneurs, and also the most consistent opponents of Western influences. In the merchant quarters they agitated continuously against foreign business rivals and Western 'heresies', bringing the enthusiasm of religious partisanship to commercial competition. The old believers accused Nikon of pandering to Western heresies, and viewed the government as a conduit for Western influences. Insofar as the government sought to impose 'German acts' on the people, it had to be rejected.[46]

It is easy to think of the Old Believers as obscurantists, reactionaries and enemies of progress. But their constant successes in the entrepreneurial field, lasting right up until the early twentieth century, clearly do not fit in with this picture. Liberal Russian historiography has felt an insurmountable antipathy for the Great Schism, or at best has shown a lack of interest. Meanwhile, the schismatics gave rise to numerous commercial and industrial dynasties, and their ideological views provided a sort of local analogue of the much-vaunted rotestant ethic. Similarly, in the epoch of Stalinist industrialisation, the place of the Protestant ethic as the moral organising principle was to be taken by communist ideology.

Because the liberal tradition associates everything progressive and modernising with Western influences, its adherents cannot even imagine that Russian society might have given birth to its own ideologies of modernisation, which were forced inevitably to compete with the ideas coming from the West. The more the ideology of the Old Believers resembled the Reformation in its general thrust, the more it had to counterpose itself to foreign influences and to the state that transmitted these influences. In the form of the Old Believer movement, Russia in essence witnessed an unconscious attempt to lay the base for a democratic bourgeois order, resting on its own strengths rather than on international trade and Western technology. Like the Protestant ethic, the Old Believer ideology viewed success in business as evidence of divine favour: 'Those who cleave to the old faith enjoy much greater riches than the followers of the new, and this shows that God blesses not the new faith, but the old.'[47] Similarly, the emigration of Old Believers from Russia had a good deal in common with the emigration of Calvinists from the Old World to the New. Of course, the forces involved were in no way comparable. This was not only because Western technologies and organisation in the seventeenth century were so much more powerful than those of Russia, but above all because Russian society itself, along with its elites, had already by that time taken on a peripheral form. The basis of support for the Old Believer movement was the same bloc of the urban commercial and artisan layer with the peasantry as in Western Europe. The events of 1648 showed, however, that in the Muscovite state, social history was not unfolding in line with the Western scenario. Most members of the nascent bourgeoisie linked their historical fate not with the peasantry, but with the nobility. The result was that a reformation and a Western-style bourgeois revolution were both impossible as a matter of principle. The aristocratic state was destined to become 'the only European in Russia', and the chief modernising force.

The defeat of the Old Believer movement put an end to the democratic tendencies that were evident in the seventeenth century. The radical heritage of the Time of Troubles was finally overcome. The 'peripheral' line of development of capitalism triumphed.

7
Peter the Great

The reforms begun by Peter I around the beginning of the eighteenth century are among the crucial topics of Russian history. We are concerned here not just with the absurd and essentially pointless romantic dispute between 'Westernisers' and 'Slavophiles', but also with far more important discussions carried on among scholars during the early twentieth century. The official literature, both during the tsarist period and under Stalin, viewed Peter the Great as a reformer and as a fighter against backwardness. The eminent historian S.F. Platonov wrote that historical research had 'long since consigned to the archives the old image of Russian life before Peter the Great as "stagnant" and "ossified"'.[1]

The philosopher Nikolay Berdyaev considered Peter the Great 'a bolshevik on the throne'.[2] Meanwhile, the liberal politician and historian P. Milyukov described Peter as a senseless bureaucrat, carried away with absurd projects, and as a result, destroying everything around him. In Milyukov's view the Europeanisation of Muscovy had been taking its natural course, and Peter effectively spoiled things with his excessively radical initiatives.

THE WESTERN INFLUENCE

In reality, Peter was not the ruler who implanted Western technology in the Muscovite state, or who established ties with Europe. Both processes had been under way long before Peter arrived on the scene. Indeed, ties with the West had never ceased to exist.

Contrary to the views of 'Westernising' writers in later times, Muscovy had never been isolated from the West, in either diplomatic or economic terms. Otherwise, the existence in Moscow of the well-known 'German quarter', where the young Tsarevich Peter learnt German and Dutch and acquired European manners, would have been unimaginable. It is true that the regime which came to power in Russia following the defeat in the Livonian War and the shocks of the Troubles consciously chose isolation. This, however, was isolation in cultural and ideological matters, not in economic ones. Increasingly dependent on Western technology, the state under the early Romanovs sought to compensate through cultural self-affirmation, through counterposing 'Muscovite piety' to Western mores. Russia was not being isolated from European culture, but was being counterposed to it. The reason for this counterposing was that Russians in the seventeenth century encountered various manifestations of Western culture on a continual basis.

V.O. Klyuchevsky writes:

The state grew confused amid the difficulties that were appearing. The government, which as a rule neither foresaw these problems nor issued warnings about them, began searching in society for ideas and people that might rescue it. Finding neither, it turned reluctantly to the West, where it beheld an old and complex cultural apparatus that was fashioning people and ideas. From the West, it hurriedly summoned artisans and scholars who might undertake something similar in Russia. It hastily built factories and established schools, into which pupils were herded.[3]

This combining of cultural isolationism with growing integration into the nascent world economic system serves to explain the contradictory, neurotic, almost schizophrenic state in which the ruling elites of Moscow found themselves at the time when Peter the Great took the throne. In Pokrovsky's view, the key to the Petrine reforms 'should be sought, ultimately, in the conditions affecting European trade in the seventeenth century'.[4] Nevertheless, the immediate cause of the events which shook Russia around the beginning of the eighteenth century was not the rapprochement with the West in itself, but the contradiction between this objective process and the political culture of the Muscovite tsardom under the early Romanovs.

Cultural conservatism was by no means the hallmark of all Russian history before the Petrine era. Nevertheless, Moscow in the second half of the seventeenth century certainly presented an odd spectacle. The closer Russia drew to the rest of Europe in technological terms, and the more it was drawn into general European politics, the more it sought to isolate itself culturally. As Platonov remarks, the cultural conservatism of the regime of the early Romanovs was above all a reaction to the Troubles. 'It seemed essential to return social thinking to the paths of old-time piety and national exclusiveness.'[5] To a significant degree, however, the very ideas of 'national exclusiveness' and 'old-time piety' were new ideological constructs, devised especially in order to satisfy the new requirements of the authorities.

Generally speaking, a conscious policy of cultural isolation was not pursued for very long, lasting only for the second half of the seventeenth century. During this period, Russia's lag behind the West steadily increased. The normalisation of life following the Troubles brought a massive demand for imported goods, from musical instruments to medicines. As noted earlier, the number of foreigners in Muscovy grew continuously throughout the seventeenth century. As early as the Livonian War, the Muscovite forces had been augmented with captured Germans, not to speak of the English 'experts' who were there in the background. Platonov observes that 'the foreign professional soldier, master artisan and merchant had become indispensable features of Moscow life'.[6] The foreigners were drawn into military service in especially large numbers. In the Moscow leaders, the failures of the Russian army during the Livonian War had created a firm conviction that only 'Germans' were capable of waging war professionally. The mass recruiting of foreigners began under Vasily Shuysky. The Moscow rulers soon found political benefits in this practice as well. In the unstable circumstances of the time, a guard composed of 'German' mercenaries was more reliable; it was not subject to sedition, would not join in revolts, and was indifferent to the swiftly changing course of social struggles. Foreigners were appointed to all sorts of command posts, and were rewarded with huge salaries and land grants. An infantry colonel received 250 rubles a month, and a cavalry colonel 400 – astronomical sums for those times. Under the Romanovs, the armed forces ministry was so dependent on Western mercenaries, both rank-and-file soldiers and officers serving as instructors and advisors, that it even set up a special institution, the 'foreigners' office'. The defence of national independence and state interests thus fell increasingly into the hands of outsiders. Numerous Western European adventurers in Russian service received vast incomes recruiting mercenaries, ordering weapons abroad, training soldiers, and establishing arms factories. In 1632, not only were muskets and bayonets for the war with Poland purchased in Holland, but even powder and bullets. The cost was unimaginably high. In the course of a single year the regimental infantry commander in charge of such matters, a certain Leslie, received a salary of 22,000 rubles.

Since the foreigners attracted by these conditions of service remained in Russia for long periods, a distinction began to be made between 'old' and 'new' 'Germans'. By the 1630s Muscovites were dividing the 'Germans' into 'old' and 'new' arrivals – that is, those who had come before the Time of Troubles, and those who had arrived since. The 'old' foreigners had quickly become Russified. A contemporary Western observer noted disparagingly that these 'old' arrivals were easy to pick; they 'went about in Russian dress', and were 'worthless in military matters'.[7] It was not self-isolation, however, that resulted in backwardness; to the contrary, it was Russia's peripheral position with relation to the emerging world economy which, as a peculiar reaction, gave rise to the policy of self-isolation. This reaction was ineffective, but perfectly understandable; it is enough to recall the similar attempts made by China and Japan between the seventeenth and nineteenth centuries to 'shut themselves off'.

Meanwhile, the isolationism of Muscovy in the seventeenth century was exclusively cultural. It did not presuppose a rejection of economic ties; indeed, to a signficant degree it was founded on them. Because the state was literally unable to exist without foreign technologies and experts, and even foreign mercenaries, it sought to preserve its political independence and to find ideological justification through constantly stressing its religious and moral superiority over the West. In the context of the cultural isolationism under the early Romanovs, the slogan 'Moscow – the Third Rome' also took on a new resonance. From this time on, the slogan would not affirm Russia's key significance for European and Christian history in general, but would assert the 'spiritual' superiority of Rus, against a background of the increasingly obvious technical superiority of the West.

Orthodox Christianity could not be the main reason for isolationism. Throughout most of the Middle Ages, religious discord had not put a stop to commercial and political contacts between the Russian princes and the Scandinavians, and later, Italians. In the eighteenth and nineteenth centuries Orthodoxy not only failed to prevent contacts with Europe, but also proved unable to avert the growing secularisation of society. Orthodoxy did not cause isolationism; it was the policy of isolationism that made stressing the religious differences between the Orthodox East and the Catholic-Protestant West unavoidable.

The social elite, which publicly proclaimed its fidelity to age-old customs and to the Orthodox faith, itself became more and more steeped in Western influences. In their daily lives, members of the elite imitated 'European comforts' in every possible manner, ordering expensive luxury items from abroad, and even inviting in German actors. Foreign furniture, clocks, carriages and other prestige goods were imported and purchased indiscriminately, without regard for taste or good sense. 'Foreign art', Klyuchevsky concludes ironically, 'was called upon to embellish the local vulgarity.'[8]

The embodiment of Russia's growing dependence on the West was the 'German quarter' in Moscow. The regime could not do without foreigners, but at the same time it feared them, and sought to isolate them. The 'Germans' lived apart, in their own little suburb. They were regarded with admiration and envy. In trying to protect their fellow citizens from temptation, the 'pious zealots' of Moscow achieved the very opposite; contrasting with the dreariness of everyday life in Muscovy, the flourishing German quarter came to seem more and more attractive, especially to young people from the privileged strata of society. In cultural terms, the West appeared at once alluring and repellent. The Muscovite rulers were in a hopelessly contradictory position. By proclaiming that the existing customs and procedures in the country would remain immutable, they condemned the 'corrupting influence' of the West; meanwhile, they depended on the West to an ever-greater extent. The more they strove to quarantine the 'Russian spirit' from the 'foreign pestilence', the less immunity society possessed to Western ideas. Peter the Great and his policies were a natural outcome of the Moscow of the late seventeenth century, thoroughly permeated by foreign influences, but refusing to admit this in public. As a member of the new generation, Peter was ready to take the decisive step. In the precise sense, this was a cultural revolution; its success was due to the fact that the thrust of Peter's policies was identical to that of the policies enacted by his predecessors. Peter did not alter the course along which Russia was proceeding, but he ensured the existence of the cultural and political conditions without which this course could not have been successfully pursued. Growing dependence on the West, and constantly increasing integration into the world economy, required a new attitude to Western culture, and the reorganisation of state structures.

THE EUROPEAN FAÇADE

Peter's fanatical desire to force the Russian ruling class to adopt the way of life of the European elite down to the smallest detail later drew ironic comments even from many Westernisers. The Petrine cultural revolution was intended to smash the resistance shown to Western ideas and norms by adherents of the 'old piety'. Naturally, the question of the virtues and shortcomings of Western culture itself was never posed; this culture was supposed to be adopted immediately and in its entirety, in just the same way as technology and forms of military organisation were adopted. Both Aleksandr Griboedov and Aleksey

Tolstoy wrote scathingly of the Western finery of the Russian nobility. Chaadaev in his philosophical letters waxed ironic over the prevailing belief in Russia that 'European progress', which had required centuries of slow development, could be 'mastered immediately, without us even taking the trouble to learn how it came about'.[9]

Peter's policies, however, were perfectly logical and well-founded. The Romanov state could not survive without Western Europeans, while at the same time it was trying to preserve its independence by fencing itself off from the foreigners in cultural matters. The more economically dependent Russia became, the greater its need for cultural isolationism – and in turn, the greater its dependence became.

Proceeding from the same logic, Peter found a different solution. If Russians could not do without Western Europeans, then the Russian nobles themselves would have to become foreigners. The tsar understood intuitively that the Western knowledge which all Russian tsars since Ivan the Terrible had made such efforts to obtain was the child of the corresponding culture. If Russia were not simply to acquire the products of Western science and technology, but to develop them itself, people were needed who had been raised in a cultural milieu analogous to that of the West. Even in the epoch of brilliant discoveries around the beginning of the eighteenth century, Western science was of course far from being the only model on the planet for the development of learning. It was, however, the only ready-made model accessible to the Russia of the time. By substituting Russians for foreigners, and by creating the cultural conditions in which Western technology could develop in Russia as well, Peter would seemingly have done everything needed to overcome the country's backwardness. If the problem had indeed been one of backwardness, by the mid eighteenth century it would have been resolved once and for all.

Peter's choice was thus to start a revolution from above. On the cultural level, the impact was truly massive. In the space of a single generation, one world was destroyed and another created. Cultural isolationism was replaced with openness, and fear of the West with an orientation to foreign models. Even the language changed, with an influx of German and Dutch words, designating a multitude of previously unknown concepts. In place of the old patriarchal system of rule, a new centralised bureaucracy was established on the German or French model. The army and navy were totally reorganised. A new system of education began to be implanted. Spelling was reformed, and the calendar was changed. New holidays appeared. The customs and daily life of the ruling class became Western. Architecture changed, and consequently the appearance of the cities changed too. The new capital of St Petersburg, constructed on the banks of the Neva where previously there had been nothing, became a symbol of modernisation and of Russia's new greatness. Successful wars consolidated what had been achieved, opening up access to the sea and making European politics without Russia unthinkable.

As with every revolution from above, the changes carried out by Peter contained numerous contradictions. The 'top-down' nature of the reforms, implemented by the government with bewildering speed, made them anti-popular in their essence.

In Peter's view, the new capital was built on vacant ground, but in reality it was built on a bog fertilised with the bones of thousands of peasants driven to this work in the name of the 'greatness of the empire'. The population of the new capital lived in completely unbearable conditions, suffering from the appalling climate and from frequent floods. It is recorded that

the first people to live on the banks of the Neva never built substantial houses, but only small huts. As soon as stormy weather approached, they immediately demolished these dwellings. Putting the planks on rafts, they tied the latter to trees, before themselves taking refuge on Duderhof Hill.[10]

A system that was founded through the efforts of a small Europeanised elite, and that was imposed on the country by a supreme ruler, could only be authoritarian. The paradox was that the more radical the reforms, the more violent, arbitrary and despotic the central power became. Bringing order to the state and giving it a European form, Peter in essence made it more barbaric.

Full of admiration for Peter I, Aleksandr Pushkin considered that by implanting European enlightenment in Russia the great reformer had created the preconditions for 'popular freedom'. At the same time, the poet conceded that Peter 'despised humanity', and that all layers of society, 'fettered without discrimination, were equal before his CUDGEL. Everyone trembled, and everyone obeyed unquestioningly.'[11]

There is a well-known remark by Voltaire to the effect that Peter eradicated barbarism using barbarous methods. Historical writers have delighted in depicting the great tsar personally beheading mutinous soldiers or shaving off the beards of boyars. However, it is not only the ruthlessness and crudity of the reformer tsar that is important, but also the nature of the new system which he set in place. Starting from a position of unqualified sympathy for the 'Westernising' tsar, nineteenth-century liberal scholars inevitably confronted the question: why had the empire which Peter constructed finished up so authoritarian? From the time of Klyuchevsky, the idea took root that after the Petrine reforms the Russian state became even less European in its internal organisation than before. As Klyuchevsky observes, 'beneath the forms of Western European culture, a political and civil life of a completely un-European type was taking shape'.[12] The peasantry had been definitively enserfed, and elements of local autonomy and self-rule had been banished.

Russian liberal historiography, of course, proceeded from a thoroughly idealised, grossly simplified notion of the West as a society of civil virtues and political freedoms. The colonial state built by representatives of this same 'Western civilisation' on the periphery of the new world system invariably remained outside the field of vision of Russian scholars.

In the traditional historiography, the accepted criteria for the success of Peter's reforms are his victory in the Northern War, and the foreign policy successes of the St Petersburg empire. However, the question immediately arises: what was the price of these victories? Subjecting the Petrine reforms to withering criticism, the eminent liberal historian and political figure of the early twentieth century, P. Milyukov, wrote:

New foreign policy tasks were heaped on the Russian population at a time when it still did not have the means of carrying out these tasks. The political growth of the state again determined its economic development.

In sum, Milyukov continues, 'Russia was elevated to the rank of a great European power at the cost of its ruination.'[13]

This manner of thinking is typical of Russian and Western liberal historiography, which conceives of the state as something self-sufficient, acting on the basis of its own internal needs. As a result, the state through its political ambitions and military demands deforms the 'natural' development of the economy and society. Klyuchevsky was still in this mindset when he declared that throughout Russian history 'the external territorial expansion of the state has been inversely proportional to the development of the internal freedom of the people'.[14]

It has scarcely occurred to scholars to examine the extent to which the political and military goals of the Russian state themselves reflected the existing economic situation, both national and global. The state did not 'deform' society and did not 'smother' it, but developed along with it, reacting to the stimuli of the external world. It was the needs of the nascent world economy, not the ambitions of Peter or some abstract 'state interest', that impelled Russia and Sweden into a deadly melee in the Baltic. Furthermore, it was the general laws that had become established within the new world system which determined that Russia's triumph would not lead the country to prosperity. 'The bankruptcy of the Petrine system,' Pokrovsky writes, 'did not consist in the fact that Russia was "elevated to the rank of a great European power at the cost of its ruination," but in the fact that despite the country's ruination, this goal was not achieved.'[15] The historical tragedy of Peter's reforms lies in the fact that while solving the problems of technical backwardness and cultural isolation, they incorporated Russia still further into the embryonic world system, confirming the country's peripheral status. The paradox is that it was necessary to fight even for this place in the world system. The Petrine reforms were responsible for Russia's final victory over Poland in this struggle.

The cultural reforms which Peter implemented gave Russia an enormous advantage over its Western neighbours, which experienced nothing comparable. The Polish ruling class was no less backward than that of Russia; its continual military defeats and uninterrupted political decline speak for themselves. More 'Western' in cultural terms, the Polish rulers nevertheless failed to grasp the extent of their own backwardness, and failed to set themselves the task of radical cultural reform. In Muscovy, by contrast, the officially declared cultural isolationism of the second half of the seventeenth century sharpened understanding of the problem and, as if by reverse action, prepared the way for the radicalism of the changes which Peter introduced. The inferiority complex which had taken hold of a section of the Russian elite by the beginning of the Petrine reforms was completely lacking in Poland. In Moscow around the end of the seventeenth century, this sense of diminished self-worth, together with an understanding of Russia's vast potential, provided a powerful stimulus to action.

THE EMPIRE EXPANDS

The military campaigns against Poland in the second half of the seventeenth century were successful, even though Russia under the early Romanovs was even more backward in relation to the rest of Europe than the Muscovy of Ivan the Terrible had been. Meanwhile, Poland was by no means among the advanced countries of Europe, with their rising bourgeoisies; it was just as peripheral as Russia, with a similar dynamic of development. Despite its external trappings of European culture, from Catholicism to the French fashions of its noblewomen, Poland on the whole was in decline. Its peripheral status meant that the Reformation failed, after initially enjoying considerable support. In the seventeenth century, Poland joined the camp of the Counter-Reformation. The combination of a peripheral economy with feudal reaction in ideological matters guaranteed that Poland's position in a changing world would grow steadily weaker. In military terms, however, it was not Russia but Sweden that dealt decisive blows to Poland, setting out to win control of the port cities through which Polish exports reached world markets.

For Russia, the steady rise of Sweden created new problems. In the mid seventeenth century, despite the Polish decline, Russia's position grew even worse, since up until the Livonian War German and Swedish trading cities had competed among themselves to attract Russian merchants. In the seventeenth century, all outlets to the Baltic for Russian goods were in the hands of a single power, Sweden, which now also controlled a significant portion of Polish exports. Dutch trade with Russia was limited by the low capacity of the port of Arkhangelsk.

Every year, as many as 500 Dutch ships set sail for Denmark and Norway, while the number setting out for Arkhangelsk was no more than 20–30. The tonnage of the Dutch fleet that plied the Arkhangelsk route was less than 1 per cent of the shipping that Holland had available to it in the Baltic. This, of course, exceeded the scale of the Dutch trade with Africa and Asia (ten ships set out for Guinea, seven for India, and only three for China), but the imports from Muscovy had to compete not with Asian goods, but with American ones.[16] Nevertheless, the small size of the Arkhangelsk trade should not lead one into error; to a large extent, and perhaps predominantly, the Baltic ports of Riga, Revel, Narva and Vyborg also traded in goods produced in Russia. It was this that lay behind the relative ease and speed with which Russian authority was imposed in the country's new Baltic provinces. After conquering Revel and Riga, the Russian government had no particular trouble maintaining its control over them until 1917. These successes for Peter provide a particular contrast with the difficulties of Ivan the Terrible, who was persistently unable to consolidate his hold on the Baltic territories. A great deal had changed since the time of the Livonian War. Not only had the Riga bourgeoisie grown rich on

Russian exports, but they viewed the Swedes as competitors. The government in Stockholm had not freed the merchants of Riga from the Sund duties, which Swedes did not have to pay, and the German nobles were gradually losing their privileges. Repeated efforts by the German elite in the Baltic region to win 'justice' from the Swedish king had yielded no results. Worse, in their attempts to undermine the position of the Germans, the Swedes had begun protecting the interests of the native population. Not surprisingly, the German barons and merchants greeted the arrival of the Russians in the Baltic in the early eighteenth century with relief.

The strengthening of Russia's armed might, and the country's emergence as a naval power in the Baltic, did not in any way alter the peripheral nature of Russian development. In this regard, the history of the Russian navy is instructive. Holland, Britain, and even Spain and Portugal needed powerful navies to support and defend their merchant fleets. By contrast, after winning an outlet to the sea, Russia swiftly built an impressive navy, but was unable to construct a significant merchant fleet by world standards until the revolution of 1917. Russia's trading partners, Britain and Holland, were themselves leading maritime powers. Moreover, the Navigation Act banned the importing of goods to British ports except in British ships. The growth of Russian exports, even in periods when the country enjoyed a positive trade balance with the West, thus aided primarily the development of British and Dutch commercial capital. Meanwhile, the Russian fleet in the Baltic was forced to protect the trade routes for British and Dutch vessels.

In his well-known pamphlet on secret diplomacy in the eighteenth century, Karl Marx noted that support for Russian military and political expansion in Europe became 'the openly professed and orthodox dogma of English diplomacy'.[17] Since Russian tsarism was seen in Marx's time as the main bulwark of European reaction, the author of *Capital*, dispensing with a more painstaking Marxist analysis, condemned the policy of British cabinets in the harshest terms. Meanwhile, it is noteworthy that the pro-Russian policy in London was pursued by the Whigs – that is, by liberals, supporters of free trade and bourgeois progress. Marx saw this as simply a manifestation of political shortsightedness and duplicity, and also as proof of Dutch influence; his main aim was to show that for more than a century, successive cabinets had implemented a policy that in no way reflected either Britain's national or its commercial interests. Here, Marx the radical commentator clearly overwhelmed Marx the scholar.

Examining the statistics for Anglo-Russian trade, Marx noted that in the course of the Northern War it grew to the same degree that Anglo-Swedish trade diminished. He therefore concluded that the growth was to be explained simply by the Russian empire's takeover of Swedens' former Baltic provinces. Marx, however, did not take account of the fact that to a significant degree, the Baltic ports were trading in Russian goods. British capital had now won direct access to the Russian market, without Swedish intermediaries or taxes. Overall, Russia's foreign trade under Peter the Great rose by a factor of eight to ten. Most of this increase fell to the share of Britain and Holland.

British and Dutch mercantile capital supported Russia's desire for modernisation, and encouraged Peter in every possible way as he strove to 'stand firmly on the seashore'. But the British and Dutch merchants, along with their countries' official diplomacy, showed no special delight at the outbreak of the Northern War between Russia and Sweden. The Russian historical tradition is inclined to view this British response as typically duplicitous behaviour on the part of 'perfidious Albion'. Marx detects the same treachery, but in relation to Sweden. In formal terms, Anglo-Swedish relations during the years of the Northern War were friendly, and until 1719 a mutual defence pact even existed between the two countries. 'Yet during almost the whole of this period,' Marx notes, 'we find England continually assisting Russia and waging war against Sweden, either by secret intrigue or open force, although the treaty was never rescinded nor war declared.'[18]

Although Holland had a commercial treaty with Sweden, and Britain a military one as well, the Dutch and British armed and trained Peter's forces. In 1715 Britain came close to openly joining an anti-Swedish coalition, when Hanover, linked to Britain by dynastic ties, aligned itself with Russia. In 1716 the British fleet appeared off the coast of Zeeland, supporting a Russian-Danish landing in preparation for an assault on Swedish territory. Ultimately, the Russian commanders rejected this risky scheme, the Russian forces returned to their homeland, and from 1718 British policy with regard to Russia changed dramatically. Sensing that Peter's empire was trying to achieve a dominant position in the Baltic, the British authorities began doing whatever they could to counteract this.

What motivated London and The Hague, as they pursued such an ambivalent policy toward Russia? The reason for the duplicity was the same as during the Livonian War. Sweden was an ally of France, the fierce enemy of the British and Dutch. British industry needed access to Russian markets, while Dutch merchants needed Russian grain. On the other hand, the British and Dutch assigned no less importance to Polish markets, access to which was provided by German commercial capital under the military and political patronage of the Swedish Crown. In other words, British diplomacy in the early eighteenth century encountered the same contradiction as during the Livonian War. The only difference was that during the Livonian War Muscovy had waged an independent struggle against the Polish armies, while during the Northern War the Rzecz Pospolita no longer played an independent role. From being a subject of international politics, Poland had become one of the objects, as Saxony, Sweden and Russia fought among themselves for influence within the country. The general economic situation, however, remained as before. The growing strength of Russia meant that Poland's decline deepened. In the seventeenth century the Swedes had systematically seized the mouths of the rivers along which Poland's exports reached the Baltic. Now, as Russian power increased, the Swedes were being forced out. Russia's growing influence in the Baltic not only opened up access for it to the sea, but also created the possibility of controlling the flow of goods coming out of Poland.

Both Russia and Poland had entered the world system as suppliers of cheap raw materials and foodstuffs. But precisely because this role did not, ultimately, promise major benefits, both countries were doomed to wage a furious struggle against one another, as they sought to maximise the few advantages that participation in world trade brought them. In essence, they were fighting for the same place in the world system. In the sixteenth century Russia had suffered a disastrous defeat in the first round of this struggle, finishing up on the verge of total catastrophe; in the eighteenth century Russia not only took its revenge, but also condemned Poland to economic and political decay, and later to the loss of its political independence as well. The rise of Russia was accompanied by the decline of Poland. During the Troubles, Polish troops had stood at the gates of the Kremlin, and the Polish Crown Prince had laid claim to the Muscovite throne. The era of trade wars culminated in the division of Poland and the annexation to Russia of its grain-producing provinces. In the nineteenth century, Warsaw passed under the control of the Russian tsar.

The division of Poland strengthened Russia's position in the world economy as the leading supplier of cheap raw materials and grain. 'With the incorporation of Poland,' Kirchner states with satisfaction, 'even the land routes had become free. Russia's struggle for direct connections with the West had been won, and both sides profited.'[19] Here the historian, defending the principles of free trade, shows an almost childlike naïvety as he expounds the benefits of destroying one of Europe's leading states. After their country had been divided up, Polish patriots for almost a century and a half appealed to the liberal West for aid, but were fobbed off with ambiguous promises. Sadly, and as romantics are prone to do, the fighters for Polish national rebirth paid far more attention to slogans and declarations than to business interests.

AUTOCRACY

The authoritarianism of the Russian state in the sixteenth and seventeenth centuries was far from unique. Ivan the Terrible might have been puzzled by the strange English customs under which his 'royal sister' Queen Elizabeth reconciled herself to parliamentary representation, but other European monarchs looked upon the English government with identical feelings. For that time, England was indeed an exception, and it was no accident that the new Stuart dynasty, on taking the throne, sought to recast the political system in the continental manner.

The situation was quite different in the eighteenth and nineteenth centuries, when the principles of political representation were breaking a path in Europe. In the West, bourgeois revolutions and political reforms were taking place, while in Russia autocracy not only survived, but was becoming stronger. It is not surprising that contemporaries saw this as proof of backwardness. This authoritarianism, however, was the inevitable result of serfdom, which in turn was by no means simply a survival from the past. The economy of the 'enlightened' eighteenth century was based on forced labour, which in turn ensured that Russia would be included in the system of European powers. Serfdom remained a key element of the whole St Petersburg 'project' of modernisation; it was the economic basis of Russian 'Westernism'.

The steadily growing incorporation into the world system required the modernising of Russian capitalism. Meanwhile, the Russian bourgeoisie, like its counterparts in most peripheral societies, not only lagged behind its 'class brothers' in the West, but was also unable to fully satisfy the demand of the world economy for Russian goods. For this reason, it was the state that from the first played the decisive role in shaping capitalist relations, while serving, in the first instance, the demands of the world rather than the local market.

Western travellers who visited Moscow on the eve of the Petrine reforms noted that Russians were extraordinarily interested in trade. There were more market stalls in the Russian capital than in any European city. These stalls, however, were 'small, and insignificant in their turnover'.[20] The bourgeois in the West differed from those in Russia not in possessing a more developed entrepreneurial culture, but primarily in having more substantial capital. 'Mercantile capitalism', Pokrovsky writes, 'came to us from the West; for Western Europe, we were even then that colony whose character, in many ways, we have retained to this day.'[21]

For the West, the serf-holding Russia of the eighteenth century remained a major supplier of agricultural produce, raw materials and semi-processed goods. Meanwhile, the lion's share of Russian exports went to bourgeois countries, Britain and Holland.

An active role in international trade was played by the Orthodox church. St Trifon, the founder of the Pechenga monastery, was unquestionably among the pioneers of mercantile capitalism, organising the export of grain to the Netherlands. Business was good, and the Pechenga brothers concluded trade agreements with partners in Antwerp, and later in Amsterdam. Although the volume of Russian trade rose sharply with the conquest of the Baltic ports, its structure remained much the same as in the previous century. Exports of timber continued. Industrial crops – flax and hemp – were sent abroad in vast quantities. As modern scholars have noted, market demand influenced the organisation of the landowner economy. The interest shown in industrial crops increased dramatically. 'The expansion of the areas sown to them, and the improved processing of the products were dictated in many ways by external demand.'[22] A part of the harvest was handed over to the landowner as dues in kind, and the rest was bought up by dealers. The bourgeoisie in Russia developed in a manner that saw it intertwined with the autocratic state and with the established system of landownership.

According to historians, the oldest merchant families in Moscow were

linked in the closest possible way, in terms of their activity, with absolutism and the feudal sector. They received privileges and loans from the government; were freed from accommodating billets, rendering services and paying taxes; enjoyed the right to monopolies on the production and sale of goods; and were allowed the use of forced serf labour.[23]

From the eighteenth century, numerous merchant families were ennobled, and hence acquired political rights.

In essence, Russia's historical tragedy was not that the people were unaccustomed to freedom or did not love it, but that the organised structures of civil society were absent. This was why Russia repeatedly won freedom, but could never consolidate it. The inclusion of Russia in the world economy and the development of ties with the West led not to the growth and flourishing of civil society, but to a strengthening of authoritarianism. A contradictory situation arose. On the one hand, the cultural and ideological influences that were coming from the West, and that were linked closely to the development of new relations of production, demanded the emancipation of the individual and the formation of civil institutions. On the other hand, the logic of the economic interdependence between Russia and the world system presupposed that an authoritarian system of rule would remain, not only in the state, but in society as well. This authoritarianism could not fail to permeate the entire range of social relationships.

In the nineteenth century, Slavophile historians furiously denounced Peter the Great for his reforms. This critique, however, was powerless to influence the dominant trend of historical thought. The reason was not just the obvious internal contradictions of Slavophilism, which despite angrily rejecting everything Western, was itself to a substantial degree the product of Western ideas, primarily German; without the influence of the aesthetic of romanticism and the philosophy of Schelling, Slavophilism would never have seen the light of day. More important is the fact that in seeing Russia's turn to the West exclusively from a cultural point of view, the Slavophiles looked on pre-Petrine Moscow as their ideal, without realising how dependent the Muscovite tsardom was on the West, or that the Russian history of the sixteenth and seventeenth centuries had prepared the way for the Petrine reforms and made them inevitable. Considering the course Russia had followed since the 1560s, these reforms were natural and legitimate, even the country's salvation. Their relative success, at least on the cultural and political plane, was determined precisely by the events that had gone before. The reforms did not represent a break from Russia's earlier trajectory of development, but rather its culmination.

Meanwhile, Western influences were not always a boon to Russia. In the sixteenth and seventeenth centuries Russia battled constantly, making enormous sacrifices, to be included in the world system which the West was establishing. During the same period, Japan was closed off from the West. According to the 'Westerniser' theories of development, the result for Japan should have been a historic catastrophe of unprecedented dimensions. For almost 200 years, while Russia lived alongside the West, traded with it, took part in its wars and adopted its technologies, Japan remained isolated – losing, as it would seem, nearly two centuries of development. Then late in the 1860s, when Japan finally opened itself up to the outside world, there proved to be nothing to stop the country from rapidly developing a capitalist economy, adopting new technologies and founding a modern state. In an astonishingly brief period Japan caught up with Russia, and early in the twentieth century dealt it a crushing defeat in the war of 1904–05. The victory of the Japanese was not determined by the genius of their commanders or by numerical superiority, but by their higher levels of technology and organisation. By the beginning of the twentieth century, the backward country was not Japan, but Russia.

For the Japanese empire, its self-isolation strategy proved to be more effective than the modernisation strategy undertaken by the St Petersburg empire. As an island nation remote from Europe, and with a completely different cultural tradition, Japan was of course able to choose isolationism. Russia, despite all the dreams entertained by enthusiasts for old-time piety, had no such choice, or at least, not in the seventeenth century. Nevertheless, the question thrusts itself upon us: could it be that the tragedy of Russian backwardness was the outcome not of remoteness and isolation from Europe, but of precisely the opposite – of Russia's closeness to the West and innumerable links to it? Was this backwardness due to the fact that whatever their wishes, neither Muscovite Russia nor its St Petersburg successor could escape the West's impact?

8
The Eighteenth-Century Expansion

Pokrovsky agrees with Milyukov in considering that 'the natural development of the early shoots of capitalism that existed in the seventeenth century would have yielded more than all the attempts to drive the Russian bourgeoisie into the capitalist paradise using a cudgel'.[1] A peculiarity of capitalism, however, is that it makes inconceivable any such 'natural development' in a single country taken on its own. Evolving as a global system, capitalism has drawn all societies into the world market, subjecting them to the same rules and 'infecting' them with the same maladies. In Russia, capitalism developed not so much as a result of natural internal processes, as under pressures from outside; the country had to modernise itself and become capitalist in order to satisfy the demands of the world economy. The first shoots of bourgeois development did of course exist in Russia. But the rapid incorporation of the country into the world market and the dizzying pace of modernisation, resulting from the need to participate in the political and economic life of Europe, did nothing to favour the development of these early manifestations of 'native' capitalism.

Bourgeois relations were developing in Russia, but at the same time their nature was changing. The characteristic structures of peripheral capitalism were being established, structures perceived by observers either as manifestations of backwardness, or as proof of Russia's 'uniqueness'. The government was not only the sole European in Russia (as Pushkin described it), but also the country's first capitalist. The court directed not only Russia's political life, but also its business affairs. Plunder by the state, both within and beyond its borders, proved extremely effective as a means of carrying out the primitive accumulation of capital. Simultaneously, a continual redistribution of wealth was also occurring, as state assets were partially privatised to the benefit of the St Petersburg elite. This privatisation took diverse forms, ranging from the granting of estates and the peasants living on them and the awarding of state contracts to the embezzling of treasury funds. Where the state plundered, its subjects practised theft.

THE ROMANOV STATE

In Pokrovsky's view, the empire of the Romanovs, as it became established in the seventeenth and eighteenth centuries, represented 'feudal tyranny in its pure form, but directed to new ends'.[2] These ends, however, were determined not by the Russian authorities, but by the overall character of world development and by the needs of the capitalist world system. The 'feudal' methods of mobilising resources served the modernisation of capitalism not only in Russia, but also in Europe. Western capital, Pokrovsky continues, needed Russia.

The country was necessary as a market, as an object of usurious exploitation, and simply as a military force. We took to repeating that in Russia during the eighteenth and nineteenth centuries the state 'marched ahead of society'. In technical terms, indeed, the state was always far more progressive than society, since its technology had international capital at its service. For international capital, supporting the Russian state – or more correctly, Russian feudalism – became a sort of profession.[3]

Unlike the crisis-ridden seventeenth century, the eighteenth century was a time of economic expansion for the world system. This could not fail to affect Eastern Europe. Throughout the eighteenth century the Russian state was not simply 'catching up' with the West, but was successfully integrating itself into the economic system which the West had established. To a significant degree, the successes of the St Petersburg empire in the eighteenth and early nineteenth centuries were linked with the effective service it rendered to this system. 'Here', Pokrovsky notes, 'is also to be found the source of the "westernism" of the eighteenth-century ruling class, a cast of mind as vulgar and naïve as its individualism....'[4]

Inasmuch as the 'feudal' form of the state was used to solve the problems of capitalist development, this was no longer feudalism in the sense in which it had existed in medieval France or Kievan Rus. Similarly, the slavery in America and Brazil in the mid nineteenth century had little in common with the slaveholding in ancient Greece. The world market needed Russian raw materials, while the Russian ruling class needed money in order to maintain 'European' standards. The more 'Western' the daily lives of the ruling class became, the greater the cost. The 'Europeanisation' of aristocratic life led, on the one hand, to the development of the commodity economy, and, on the other, to increasing exploitation of the peasants. The eminent Soviet historian N.M. Druzhinin notes that,

Throughout the eighteenth century, serfdom was gradually expanded so as to encompass new layers of the rural population, and to give the landowners unrestricted control over the labour power and all other aspects of the lives of the enserfed peasants.[5]

Between 1718 and 1721 an 'inspection' was conducted; in the context of a census of the population, all the various categories of bonded peasants were combined, and the status of all serfs was reduced to that of the *kholopy* – that is, of the group within the population that had fewest rights.

Under Peter I, the privileges of the old feudal aristocracy had also been definitively abolished. The boyars had lost their pre-eminence over the nobility, and the nobility itself had begun to be augmented with people from the most diverse social strata. It might have seemed that a radical democratisation of the social system was under way, but in fact something was occurring that was strikingly different from the processes taking place in the West.[6] In most European countries, 'democratisation' signified the abolition of feudal privileges, or an equalisation of social estates. In Russia, the doors of the ruling stratum were opened relatively wide; the system of privileges, however, was not only retained but strengthened. Over decades, the privileges of the nobility steadily expanded. Meanwhile, the privileged stratum, whose sole obligation was to render military or civil 'service', merged organically with the swelling state apparatus. In this way, Klyuchevsky states, 'the democratisation of rule was accompanied by a strengthening of social inequality'.[7]

In effect, the nobility dragged the countryside forcibly into the market. During the eighteenth century, the dues owed by the peasants increased by a factor of twelve. Peasant resistance was crushed in the most brutal fashion. A decree of 1765 permitted landowners to send offending serfs off to hard labour camps, and another of 1767 forbade peasants to address complaints about their masters to the sovereign.

It was not only the nobility that needed money, but also the government, whose 'European' ambitions were resulting in growing financial dependency on the West. In the eighteenth century, the obtaining of foreign credits became commonplace. In 1769, Catherine the Great took out a loan in Amsterdam for 7.5 million guilders to pay for her war with Turkey. The following year, money was borrowed in Genoa.

By the end of the empress's reign, sixteen foreign loans had been taken out, for a sum of 55 million rubles. Only 36 million rubles of this sum went to cover military expenses, while a total of 17 million was spent on paying off the loans themselves.[8]

On average, as much as 5 per cent of the state budget went on servicing these debts. Present-day historians generally console their readers by stating that this was 'a usual practice at the time'. Nor was anyone perturbed by the budget deficit. 'Despite all the innovations, the deficit was permanent, and it continually increased.'[9]

In the nineteenth century, such phenomena were regarded with less tolerance. As one of the economists of the period remarked, history knows of few examples in which 'the finances of an absolute monarchy were, if not in a flourishing condition, then simply in order'.[10] Trying to exercise control over court spending was a virtually hopeless endeavour.

The ambitious and spendthrift courts of Western Europe were, indeed, no better in this respect than the court in St Petersburg. There was, however, an important difference. The courts in the West borrowed from their own bourgeoisies – if not in their own countries, then at least within their own economic zone. The debts of the Western monarchs remained part of the economy of the 'centre', strengthening the position there of finance capital. The Russian debt, by contrast, served to pump money from East to West, aiding the development of the bourgeoisie not in Russia, but in the countries of the 'centre'. It was not simply that the expensive ambitions of St Petersburg were impossible to realise without foreign help; the very successes of the St Petersburg emperors also contributed to the development of a new world system in which Russia was far from being a dominant force.

These successes were quite genuine. The brilliant eighteenth century was not only a time of military and diplomatic achievements for the St Petersburg monarchy. It was also a period of rapid economic growth, in industry as well as agriculture. The fact that the advances of industry were stimulated not by rising internal demand but by the requirements of the world market and of international politics, was another matter entirely.

Britain remained Russia's main trading partner throughout this period. It is not hard to see a parallel between the creation of the British empire during this period and the achievements of the empire ruled from St Petersburg.

By the early eighteenth century Anglo-Dutch rivalry had dwindled to nothing. Having lost the military and political struggle with their British competitors, the Dutch bourgeoisie took to acting as their junior partners. This was evidenced in Russia as well; in place of the Muscovy Company came the Russia Trade Company, combining British and Dutch capital.

The decline of Holland as a naval power was accompanied by the development of Dutch finance capital, which lacked sufficient opportunities within Holland itself. The Dutch colonial empire could not be compared with that of Britain or even France. In Russia, however, Dutch capital found a promising field of investment. It was the Dutch who sent the first ship to the port of St Petersburg, and it was they who became the cultural model for Peter the Great. Most importantly, they regularly provided the funds that were essential for developing the St Petersburg empire. Marx wrote with obvious irritation that throughout the eighteenth century, Holland

remained the banker of Russia. At the time of Peter they supplied Russia with ships, officers, arms and money, so that his fleet, as a contemporary writer remarks, ought to have been called a Dutch rather than a Muscovite one.[11]

BRITISH CAPITAL

Nevertheless, it was British capital that played the decisive role in Russia's foreign trade. In the eighteenth century Britain accounted for almost half of the external trade of the Russian empire, and in the 1730s, for even more than half.[12] British merchants were also the main buyers of the so-called treasury goods – iron, copper, potash and rhubarb – whose sale brought direct proceeds to the St Petersburg government. As a rule, however, the balance of trade remained in Russia's favour. The shipments of Russian raw materials were strategically important to Britain. The only alternative available to the British was trade with its North American colonies, but the situation here was not promising. The government in London had sought repeatedly to expand the shipments from America, but without great success. As the Russian historian P.A. Ostroukhov observes, importing raw materials from Russia was a simpler and more profitable option. Despite enormous expenditures of money and effort, it proved impossible to increase the supplies of timber and other shipbuilding materials from New England substantially.

Efforts to increase the production of hemp were a complete failure. Equally unsuccessful were attempts by the metropolis to preserve the forest resources of the colonies as a permanent source of ships' timbers. These attempts met with resistance from the local population, for whom it was far more profitable to export timber to Portugal.[13]

The problem with the North American colonies, and particularly with New England, lay in the 'excessive' (from the point of view of the metropolis) development there of bourgeois relations. The colonists had their own business interests. They were not content with the role of suppliers of raw materials, and were prepared to compete with their historical homeland. Their ties with Britain were retained until the mid eighteenth century more for military and political reasons than for economic ones. Fear of the French presence in Canada forced them to look for their defence to the British Army and Navy. But as Ostroukhov notes, even before the Seven Years' War the North American colonies had begun to compete with the metropolis on the world market, producing 'the same products as were produced in Britain itself'.[14]

Far more suitable partners for the metropolis were the Southern slaveholding states, producing tobacco, cotton and rice. They did not compete with Britain, and supplied it with goods that could not be had from Europe. During the War of Independence, the political ties between the Northern and Southern colonies outweighed their commercial relations with the metropolis, but even after the rupture with Britain, the Southern states continued to provide a raw materials base for the British market, a situation which also contributed to the later conflict between North and South.

The American colonists needed raw materials for the development of their own industries. By contrast, Russia with its serf economy provided Britain with an ideal raw materials base. The more backward the Russian empire, the more successfully it was integrated into the world system. Exports to Britain rose steadily. The rapid economic expansion during the eighteenth century required constantly increasing supplies of raw materials. It was only in 1710 that Britain had a positive trade balance with Russia. But in the view of contemporaries, the strategic raw materials obtained from Russia served 'the spread of British trade to all countries of the globe, so that in essence, all the nations with which Britain trades pay for these raw materials'.[15]

To a significant degree, Britain's victory over its competitors in the Russian market was predetermined by the fact that Britain was the sole Western country that could permit itself a negative trade balance. Bringing into Russia the silver that the Russian government and St Petersburg elite sorely needed, the British shipped out commodities. The French, by contrast, invariably had a positive trade balance. It should be remembered that according to the mercantilist ideas of the first half of the nineteenth century, the export of silver from a country was regarded as a negative phenomenon, while an influx of silver was considered the main proof of a country's success in world trade. The result was that the French encountered numerous problems and restrictions from which their British competitors were free.

Nevertheless, the view in London was that exports to Russia could be substantially increased. The main task was seen as expanding shipments of wool and woven cloth, including for the purpose of providing uniforms for the

Russian army. The importing of British products to Russia, however, was by no means unproblematic. The government in St Petersburg imposed protectionist tariffs in order to defend its own manufactures. British goods were also subject to competition from Prussian and Dutch products. The rivalry between British and Prussian merchants was accomanied by the suborning of the Russian customs service, by the paying of bribes to the officials of the Russian defence ministry responsible for contracts, and so forth. The British sought a reduction of tariffs, and in 1731, during the reign of Anna Ioanovna, achieved their goal. The position of British capital was strengthened by the treaty 'On Friendship and Reciprocal Commerce between both Powers' of 2 December 1734. Although customs duties were lowered dramatically, this proved insufficient for the British, who demanded a further reduction. But not even the government of Anna Ioanovna and Biron, famous for its venality, could go this far. For the British, the most important outcome of the 1734 treaty was the fact that they were now permitted to carry out transit trade with Persia, something they had sought since the time of Ivan the Terrible. The opening to Russia of the Baltic ports provided a new stimulus to the transit trade via the Caspian. In the 1730s and 1740s, the volume of this trade increased sharply. Most of the turnover was in the hands of Armenian merchants. Armenians in Moscow and Astrakhan obtained goods from Holland, Britain and France which they then forwarded to the East. In principle, industrial products from Russia could also have been exported, but the government in St Petersburg had no wish to sell the goods that Russian industry was able to supply. In Persia and Bukhara, the demand was for Russian weapons, metals, and materials for naval construction; naturally, the authorities in St Petersburg were unwilling to help their southern neighbours to strengthen their armed forces. The Persian campaign mounted by Peter I had been a pointless adventure, but in St Petersburg, the idea of a new thrust to the south had by no means been ruled out.

The result was that Russia's Caspian commerce remained heavily weighted toward transit trade. From Astrakhan, raw silk was brought to St Petersburg. In the 1730s the value of these goods averaged 116,700 rubles per year, a figure which increased in the 1740s to 292,100 rubles;[16] in the space of a decade, the volume of this traffic more than doubled.

It is not surprising that British capital came to see a direct presence in the Caspian as highly desirable. The treaty of 1734 opened new markets to British expansion; the British could now use Russian territory as an additional staging ground for increasing their commerical, political and even military influence in Persia, Central Asia and India. The stipulation was made that British traders would have to transport goods along the rivers in Russian vessels, a condition that violated the British Navigation Act. A special decision of parliament, in 1741, was required in order to allow the Navigation Act to be bypassed in the case of the Caspian. A further initiative was the establishing of a British shipyard on the Caspian. In the view of Soviet historians, this move resulted from the British 'wanting to be independent of Russia'.[17] In fact, the main reason was the need to fulfil the requirements of the Navigation Act.

BRITISH IN THE CASPIAN, FRENCH IN ST PETERSBURG

After talks with the Russian authorities, it was decided to build ships, on the Volga, that would be used in the Caspian; the vessels would sail under the British flag, but the crews would be Russian. The first such ship, with a displacement of 180 tons, was launched at the government shipyards in Kazan in August 1741. In November 1742 construction was begun of a second ship, to which the British gave the flattering name *Empress Elizabeth*. The ships were also equipped with cannon and powder from the government stores. Russian ships were ordered to render the British vessels all necessary help while at sea. Also in 1742, the Governor of Astrakhan, and the commanders in Tsaritsyn and Saratov, received a resolution of the senate instructing them to see promptly to the needs of British subjects and their agents.[18] The Azerbaijani historian L.I. Yunusova notes correctly that the Russian authorities were themselves equipping the fleet of their commercial competitors.

Depending on their construction, the carrying capacity of Russian merchant ships in the Caspian up to that time had been from three to five thousand *pudy* (48 to 80 tons). The relationship between the Russian ships and the planned British vessels, and accordingly of the prospects for trade using these ships, thus becomes clear.[19]

In London, conflict flared between the Russian and Turkish companies. Both now traded with Persia, and each defended its own interests not only in the local markets, but also in representations to the British authorities. The Russian Company set out to show that its chosen trade route, though somewhat more complicated, was also safer, and therefore cheaper. Ultimately, the two companies agreed to operate jointly in Persia.

Despite all sorts of extortion, and the irresponsibility and boorishness of Russian officials, Russia for the British remained an unusually easy and safe country in which to do business. At least in military respects, everything was predictable; there was no need to fear either bandit attacks or corsair raids. If necessary, the Russian authorities sent soldiers to accompany British trading caravans. There was, of course, a price to be paid for this; the military detachments that carried out this task were provided 'at the cost of the merchants'.[20] The government of Anna Ioanovna saw no particular problem in supplying its personnel for the service of the British. It was agreed that the British would receive soldiers from Russia, and, as Pokrovsky remarks, 'it was not thought necessary even to specify who they would fight against'.[21]

There was not, in fact, any particular mystery here. The axis of international politics in the eighteenth century was the rivalry between France and Britain; the British empire needed Russia not so much as a business partner as a military ally in its global conflict with the French. This was apparent in the Caspian as well. With Russian help, British factories were being set up in Azerbaijan. British cloth was being exchanged for Persian silk, the transaction yielding a profit of as much as 80 per cent. The Russian government imagined that the presence of foreign capital would open up new possibilities for the development of Russian trade. Russian merchants would thus gain from the hiring by the British of river boats for transporting goods, and would also 'form companies with the British' to conduct business in Persia.[22] Even if the Russian merchants ended up losing money, this should be tolerated 'for the good of the state'.[23] In practice, things worked out somewhat differently. Russian capital quickly began to be forced out of the Caspian zone. With far greater financial resources than the Russians and with considerable experience in Eastern matters, the British needed the Russians as military and political collaborators, but not as commercial partners.

Karl Marx, who hated the St Petersburg regime, complained that in developing ties with Russia, British politicians and entrepreneurs became tools for 'realizing the plans of Peter I and his successors'.[24] Russian historians and commentators in turn complained of foreign dominance during the first half of the eighteenth century. The question, however, is not of who was using whom. Both the government in St Petersburg and its foreign partners were participating in a common process, incorporating Russia into the expanding world system.

The government of Anna Ioanovna, consisting mainly of Baltic Germans, was notorious for its venality and neglect of Russian national interests. The domination exercised by foreigners in all fields of St Petersburg life aroused indignation in Russian society. It is significant, however, that, as Pokrovsky notes,

the foreigners to whom the German government sacrificed Russian interests were not Germans, but British. Biron did not serve the people who could talk with him in the same language, but those who paid him more and better.[25]

As the main rival of the ascendant British empire, France also had its candidate in St Petersburg. This was Yelizaveta Petrovna, the future Empress Elizabeth. When a conspiracy against Anna Ioanovna and Biron was hatched in the Russian capital, the French embassy supported it enthusiastically. The patriots and opponents of foreign domination, who had united around the candidacy of Elizabeth, in turn supported close relations not only with the French, but also with the Swedish court, which was plotting a war on Russia. As Pokrovsky remarks ironically, the 'patriotism' of those times 'was of a quite peculiar variety'.[26]

Events did not unfold quite as the conspirators had foreseen. The Swedes' military campaign ended in defeat, a fact which Elizabeth was later to exploit; having promised to reward Stockholm for its help by making territorial concessions, she reneged on this pledge. The British sought to bring the conspiracy undone by informing Biron and his associates of the danger, but Biron's government was doomed. On 9 November 1740, Biron was arrested. The struggle was resolved by the Guard, which placed Elizabeth on the throne. The triumph for France, however, proved short-lived. The objective course of events favoured Britain. London's representatives had to bear the expense of bribing the officials of the new administration, but the decisive factor was still that of economic influence. Britain was incomparably more important to Russia's trade than France. In 1742 a new Anglo-Russian agreement was signed.

The British gradually regained the major positions they had held under Anna Ioanovna, and which they almost lost in 1740. Even the supplies of cloth for the Russian army were organised from Britain. In London, liberal observers stressed that the links between the Russian and British empires were 'formed by nature and inviolable'.[27]

It was only on the question of the Caspian that Empress Elizabeth's government took an intransigent position. Those who were to blame for this, however, were the British themselves, who not only had forced Russian merchants out of the Caspian, but had also created military and political problems for Russia in the region. Establishing themselves in Persia's Caspian ports, British entrepreneurs had forged links with the local authorities, and had started building a navy for the shah. One large vessel and a number of smaller ones had been launched, and several others laid down. Crews for them were being recruited from among Englishmen, and also from among fugitive Russian bandits who had taken refuge in Persia. With fittings for the ships in short supply, the Persians tackled the problem with oriental directness, and set about stripping Russian vessels that arrived in Derbent, taking 'superfluous' anchors and cables from them.

It remains unclear whether the British merchants and shipbuilders were motivated simply by thoughts of commercial gain, or whether they were colluding with officials in London. The latter, naturally enough, denied any involvement in the matter. Whatever the case, the authorities in St Petersburg could not be indifferent to such developments. In the senate, a report was drawn up stating that if Persia's Caspian fleet were to 'multiply', this would lead to an arms race, and that the Russian government would 'inevitably be forced to maintain another fleet there, at no small cost to the treasury'.[28] It was decided to take steps to ensure that British military and naval experts did not accompany merchants to Persia, and British ships were ordered to be detained in Astrakhan. Even after this, however, British participation in the building of the Persian fleet did not cease. In 1746 Russia once more banned the British from the transit trade with Persia. The relevant article in the treaty of 1734 was annulled. At the same time, the St Petersburg authorities set about finding someone to blame. Since it was impossible for the officials themselves to accept responsibility for the decision, they decided to make a scapegoat of Astrakhan governor V.N. Tatishchev. The governor, it was said, had 'dealings in common' with the British.[29]

THE RUPTURE WITH BRITAIN

A new crisis in Anglo-Russian relations erupted in the 1750s, and was connected with the Seven Years' War. This was the first conflict that might have been described as a world war. The battles were fought on land and sea, in Europe, America and India, and by the coasts of Africa. The military actions began with a raid on a French outpost in Canada; dismally unsuccessful, this exploit was organised by a young British officer named George Washington. During the conflict, the future first President of the United States distinguished himself solely by his extreme cruelty to prisoners of war.

In the Seven Years' War, Britain and Russia unexpectedly finished up in hostile coalitions. The reason was the familiar duplicity of British policy in Eastern Europe. As in earlier times, London had cultivated relations with Russia while simultaneously pursuing its interests in countries that were Russia's competitors. The global conflict became superimposed on regional rivalry. In this particular case, a choice had to be made between Russia and Prussia. The Prussian army, headed by Frederick the Great, was needed by the British empire because it could strike a blow against the French forces on the European continent, leaving Britain's armies free rein in India and Canada. Meanwhile, St Petersburg, fearful of a strengthening of Prussia, took the side of Paris.

At first glance, the Seven Years' War was a success for Russia. The Russian armies emerged victorious from one battle after another, and Königsberg and Berlin were taken. It was at that point that Frederick the Great uttered his famous phrase, 'Everything is lost – except honour!'

It is significant, however, that this war did not become part of the national myth, in the manner of the campaigns of Peter the Great and Suvorov. It receives only passing mention in school history textbooks, and few scholarly works are devoted to it. The reason, of course, is not simply that the victories cost the Russian forces an unbelievably high price. The losses were monstrous, but in other wars, too, Russian generals took no special pity on their peasant infantry. From its very beginning, the Seven Years' War was not especially popular among educated society in Russia, and most importantly, it was not understood. For the economy, the war was catastrophic. Vast military expenditures were added to the losses associated with the ending of trade with Britain. 'By the time of Elizabeth's death,' Pokrovsky writes, 'the position was such that any reasonable government would have made haste somehow or other to extricate itself from the conflict.'[30]

Frederick had expected that the first to conclude a peace would be the Austrians, on whom he had inflicted serious defeats. The court in Vienna, however, held out to the last, while St Petersburg offered peace to Prussia on extremely advantageous terms. Peter III, after inheriting the throne from Elizabeth, promptly ceased military actions. This peace was viewed in hindsight as traitorous, since all the conquests of the Russian army were handed back to Frederick. Until his elevation to the Russian throne, Peter III had been a Prince of Holstein, and did not conceal his admiration for the Prussian monarch. It was not, of course, simply a matter of Peter's sympathy for the 'enlightened monarch' in Berlin, nor of the personal enmity which Elizabeth had nourished for the 'Voltarian' Frederick. The country simply could not carry on fighting, and had no wish to do so. Russian society was aroused to indignation not by the peace with Prussia, but by the intention of the young tsar to immediately start a new war, this time in alliance with Frederick. Another coup followed; Peter III was driven from power, and soon killed. The throne was assumed by his wife, a German princess who was to go down in Russian history under the name of Catherine the Great.

Unlike her unfortunate husband, Catherine was considered a wise ruler. She pursued the same policies as Peter III, but in a more considered and cautious fashion. Even before Peter III was crowned, Catherine had emerged as one of the leaders of the 'pro-British' party, and as a leading opponent of war. She was not, of course, distinguished by any real love of peace, and unlike her husband, displayed no sentimental admiration for Prussia. She was motivated by specific political and economic interests.

In essence, Catherine continued the policies of Anna Ioanovna, but from now on, St Petersburg would not be dominated by short-term favourites or upstarts with dubious pasts. A more or less stable elite was becoming established, an elite which, despite the diversity of its pedigrees, was becoming conscious of itself as a national aristocracy. This political class was capable of ruling effectively. Anna Ioanovna's government of Baltic Germans had served foreign interests in minute detail, for the sake of bribes and short-term benefits, while ignoring the claims of the Russian nobility; now, the St Petersburg rulers were starting to think strategically. Under Catherine, a compromise solution that suited both Anglo-Dutch commercial capital and the Russian elites was at last taking shape.

Catherine's reign was a time of uninterrupted war. From now on, however, Russian policy would have a different thrust. In attacking Turkey the government in St Petersburg was trying to open a new trade route, and to win new markets in the south, by breaking through into the Mediterranean. The opportunities in the Baltic that had seemed so enticing in the time of Peter the Great no longer sufficed for the growing stream of Russian exports. The Baltic trade route, like the Arkhangelsk route before it, was a sort of trap. It stimulated Russia's involvement in world trade and incorporated the country in the international division of labour, but at the same time Russia was persistently unable to obtain the benefits that were expected to result. Since the virtues of world trade were not in doubt, the only solution was through expansion – a dramatic broadening of exports, the conquest of new markets and, most importantly, of new trade routes that were not controlled by intermediaries.

INDUSTRIAL DEVELOPMENT

While the seventeenth century had been a time of crisis throughout Europe, the eighteenth century was a period of rapid economic growth. An element in this expansion was the impressive rise of the St Petersburg empire under Catherine. Estate agriculture was being radically transformed. It was becoming increasingly organised and efficient, and its links with the world market were becoming more durable. In the view of Pokrovsky, the economic life of Russian landowners in the seventeenth century amounted to 'an orgy of naïve people who had glimpsed commercial agriculture for the first time.' By the eighteenth century things were different. For Russia, the economic growth in the West meant 'a flourishing of landowner entrepreneurship'. Meanwhile, estate agriculture in Russia was growing stronger 'the closer its ties with Western Europe became'.[31]

Within Russia, foreign commercial capital worked directly with the nobility, and Russian merchants received only a minor share of the profits. The inevitable cultural consequences of this were the cosmopolitanism and Westernising views of the nobles, and the provincial-minded patriotism of the merchants, shut up in the domestic market. There were of course exceptions. Large-scale industrialists such as the Stroganovs and Demidovs integrated themselves quite successfully in the world market. However, they themselves were serf-owners, and later joined the ranks of the aristocracy.

By the middle of the eighteenth century the European part of Russia had not only recouped the monstrous population losses that had resulted from the wars and reforms of Peter the Great, but also faced the problem of agrarian over-population. The excessive numbers of peasants controlled by the landowners gave the latter the chance to try their hands at industry. Serf-holding estate owners, possessing both money and labour, had the chance to set up productive enterprises on their lands, enterprises that were relatively advanced for the time. In Russia, building factories was an undertaking not so much of the bourgeoisie, but of large landholders.

Under Peter the Great, active efforts to establish new manufacturing had required the use of freely hired labour. Skilled workers had to be brought from abroad, or trained there. By the middle of the eighteenth century the situation had been 'normalised', and the share represented by serf labour was steadily growing. The earnings of skilled workers, in decline throughout the seventeenth century, continued to fall after the Petrine reforms, with the sole difference that the wages of foreigners and Russians were gradually drawing level. In 1723 the wages of a master iron-smelter had been 36 rubles; by 1772 this figure was only 26 rubles. It is not hard to see why this decline occurred; free workers were increasingly having to compete with serfs.[32] It could be said that in the period when the development of production was stimulated mainly by military and political needs, labour was more free than in the middle years of the century, when enterprises had begun orienting themselves primarily toward demand on the world market.

Of course, it was not only serfs who were employed in industrial labour. The peasant mineworkers of the Urals were not serfs in legal terms, but neither was there any question of their being freely hired. People 'attached' themselves to industrial enterprises, seeing factory labour as a means of working off their poll tax obligations to the state. The result was that in the Urals, where serfdom had not existed earlier (just as feudal estates had not existed either), it arrived in the eighteenth century along with the development of advanced industry.

From time to time, factory workers rebelled. The greatest outpouring of resistance was the Pugachev revolt which, by analogy with German history, was described in Soviet times as the 'Peasant War'. In fact, the revolt was by no means exclusively peasant in nature. The rebels included Cossacks, members of a military stratum within society. Others who joined the uprising were workers 'attached' to factories. It was these workers who provided the rebel army with artillery. In the mid eighteenth century, landowners were building plants to weave cloth and canvas, setting up distilleries and excavating mines. Serf labour lay at the heart of the rapidly growing metallurgical industry. Metallurgy, meanwhile, was one of the sectors most thoroughly integrated into the world economy.[33]

As Druzhinin notes, neither the implanting of industry by an absolutist state nor government support for local entrepreneurs was unique to Russia.

The same was done in Britain under Cromwell, and in France in the time of Colbert; later, the practice would be repeated in Prussia. 'But in Russia,' the historian continues,

the implanting of large-scale industry met with two difficult obstacles: a lack of private capital, and an acute shortage of free labour power. Despite the developing unequal exchange and wealth of furs in vast, newly-conquered Siberia, Russia did not have colonies as rich as those possessed by Britain and France during the period when capitalism was emerging; the rural population of an agrarian country was tied to its allotments, and fewer people left their native surroundings than nascent industry required.... Forcing the pace of development of large-scale industry, especially in the Urals region with its mineral deposits, the government and private industrialists resorted to an economic measure unknown in Western Europe: tens of thousands of state peasants were forcibly assigned to industrial enterprises. The entrepreneurs were given permission to buy peasants and to employ them in industrial production. The peasants – assigned, temporary, 'granted in eternity', or purchased – had to work off their dues as serfs in the newly established and multiplying plants and factories.[34]

In examining the Russian factories of the eighteenth and the first half of the nineteenth centuries, the Soviet academician S.G. Strumilin encountered a problem of methodology. Clearly, what he was studying was not classical capitalism, since the labour it employed was not free. On the other hand, it was clearly not feudalism either; it featured neither a natural economy, nor systems of personal obligations passed down by inheritance. Ultimately, Strumilin soothed himself and his readers by referring to the 'transitional' nature of this phenomenon.[35] Strangely, however, this 'transitional' phenomenon existed for a century and a half, leaving its mark not only on Russian capitalism, but also on the world economy. Moreover, M. Tugan-Baranovsky remarked that what occurred as industry grew in the Russian empire was not a transition from serf to free labour, but, on the contrary, a strengthening of the constraints on workers. The position of workers deteriorated in direct proportion to the development of the Russian factory. Since there were both free and serf workers in plants at the same time, the factory-owners sought persistently to put the rights of these two categories of toilers on an equal footing, by ending the freedoms of all. This was achieved in 1736, when an imperial edict was issued to this effect.[36]

The logic behind this and many other paradoxes of Russian history must be sought in the development of the world system. 'Semi-free' labour is a normal phenomenon on the capitalist periphery. This was not only the case in the early stages of the history of capitalism, but remains so in the early twenty-first century. Restricting the freedom of workers is the price which the periphery pays for successful integration into the system; it is the periphery's competitive advantage. 'Free' labour hire in the centre is not only combined with far harsher forms of exploitation on the periphery, but is an important element in the global division of labour.[37]

RUSSIAN METAL

The Northern War led to rapid growth of the metallurgical industry in the early eighteenth century. Previously, Russia had obtained a significant proportion of its iron from Sweden. With the beginning of the war against the Swedes, these shipments naturally stopped. Peter the Great, meanwhile, needed metals in growing quantities to equip his armies. To meet the wartime needs, new plants were established in the Urals and in European Russia, and old ones were expanded. Not only were workers brought there by force, but entrepreneurs were also compelled to join companies organised by the tsar. In the Urals the plants were mainly private, but in western Russia, close to the theatre of war, state-owned blast furnaces were built. Despite all the drawbacks of Peter's methods, results were achieved. By the 1720s, an important metallurgical industry had been created, most of it concentrated in the Urals.

With the end of the war, it was found that productive capacity exceeded demand on the internal market many times over. Meanwhile, as if from inertia, the growth of state-owned plants continued, including in the Urals. Production could now be developed only on the basis of the external market. Already by the end of the Northern War, Russia was exporting an average of 35,000 *pudy* (one *pud* was equal to roughly 16 kg) of iron per year to Britain. After the war, exports grew rapidly. In 1723, a total of 360,177 *pudy* of iron was sent abroad.[38] Thanks to serf labour, selling Russian iron on Western markets was extremely profitable. In addition, world prices were steadily rising. In 1720 a *pud* of bar iron cost 0.45 rubles in St Petersburg, and 0.89 rubles in London. The corresponding figures in 1766 were 0.72 and 1.81 rubles, and in 1798, 1.16 and 2.90 rubles.[39] With the beginning of the industrial revolution in the 1770s, demand for iron in Britain grew rapidly, and this was naturally reflected in prices. Under Catherine the Great, Russia held first place in the world for iron production. Internal demand, however, was extremely weak. In 1769, the problem of overproduction in the metallurgical industry was being discussed at court. As well as going to Britain, Russian iron was being exported to France, where rival producers were complaining that the competition was ruining them. Iron was also exported through the port of St Petersburg to Holland, Spain, and even North America. The only alternative on the world market was Swedish iron, but this was noticeably dearer. Contemporary scholars observed that in the eighteenth century Britain could 'no longer get by without supplies of Russian iron'.[40] Between 1754 and 1793, 55–74 per cent of Russia's iron exports went to Britain. Even the Russian producers, however, were thoroughly dependent on the British. Not only was Britain the main purchaser, but British merchants held a virtual monopoly on the exporting of iron from Russia.

In eighteenth-century Russian metallurgy, state and private interests were closely intertwined. The Demidov and Stroganov plants in the Urals were private, but operated on the basis of state monopolies. Oriented to the world market, metallurgy became one of the most important sources of funds not only for the government, but also for the aristocracy. Periods of state construction alternated with waves of privatisation, when state enterprises were transferred to prominent dignitaries on the pretext of their inefficiency. Needless to say, this did nothing to increase the output of the plants or to raise their efficiency.

The list of owners of metallurgical enterprises is like a register of the higher St Petersburg nobility, with princes side by side with counts. Strumilin writes:

The truth is that this glittering cavalcade of the nobility never gilded their chosen industrial plants with their brilliance. These people were not builders, but dilettantes. Benefiting from the favours of loving tsarinas, they eagerly acquired factories as gifts or on credit, or as dowries for wealthy brides. But while pilfering virtually all the state enterprises in this manner, they multiplied their indebtedness, and having lost their factories, in almost all cases found themselves once more in financial strife.[41]

As in the 1990s, privatisation had an ideological basis. Court experts argued enthusiastically that state-owned industrial plants were inefficient, poorly managed and 'failing'; they could only be saved, it was said, by transferring them to private hands. Then, when the privatised enterprises with their new owners in turn started to fail, the need arose for the state to support and save them.

It was precisely the state enterprises that were the main exporters. They sent two-thirds of their production off to the world market, while the proportion for private plants was barely a third. In the 1750s the share represented by the private sector in deliveries of Russian metal to the world market began steadily to rise, though the reason for this was not so much an increase in production as the privatisation of state property.

In government circles in eighteenth-century Russia, an obvious struggle was occurring between various currents. The strongest positions were held by supporters of increased exports of raw materials and semi-processed goods. Meanwhile, the dominant view was that treasury revenues could best be increased through expanding deliveries, and not through a rise in the prices of sale. Also making their voices heard were supporters of a concerted development of the defence industries, to the point where they could themselves turn the country's raw materials and semi-processed goods into finished products. However, it was the current favouring raw materials in the export trade that prevailed.[42]

Russian serf-owners were perfectly familiar with the ideas of free trade. Nevertheless, Catherine the Great was perturbed by the lack of competition on world markets. She therefore addressed a letter to the College of Commerce, insisting that a search be made for new markets for Russian iron. In her view, the metal could be exported not only to Britain, but also to Mediterranean Europe, thus subjecting the British purchases to competition. The tsarina considered that if need be, iron could even be sold at a loss, so long as competition was created. But when the College of Mines and the College of Commerce saw the letter from the empress, they disagreed with her suggestions. As they saw it, the decline in returns from selling Russian iron was not linked to the monopolisation of export operations by the British. It was simply that the production of Russian state and private enterprises was 'continually multiplying'. In short, the problem was a typical crisis of overproduction, that had nothing to do with the way the international economic order was structured. 'The more iron there was in the port to be shipped, the more its price fell.'[43] The College of Mines suggested making up for the losses from falling prices by expanding exports. The devotion of the Russian bureaucracy to the ideas of the free market proved insuperable, and the empress was forced to yield. The success of her project was also blocked by political factors; the exit to the Mediterranean was in the hands of the Turks. Consequently, it was difficult for Russia to trade with Italy and Spain. The demand in these relatively backward European countries was limited and, as the bureaucrats correctly noted, it was necessary to ship other goods there besides iron. Meanwhile, the demand in Russia for goods from these countries was minuscule.

It is significant, however, that it does not seem to have entered the heads either of the enlightened monarch or of her opponents that it might have been possible to develop domestic demand as well, and not only on the basis of defence production. The narrowness of Russia's internal market was linked to the serf-holding system, which meant that the overwhelming majority of the population exercised no effective demand. However, it was precisely this system which gave Russia its distinctive competitive advantage on the world market. The metal smelted by serfs was cheap. For the elites that had arisen in post-Petrine Russia, the super-exploitation of their own population was a means of economic and cultural integration into Europe, the basis not only of their prosperity, but also of their country's status as a great European power.

For the 'free' economy of Britain in turn, obtaining cheap raw materials and semi-finished products from Russia and America was very important. Precisely because British labour was free, and hence relatively expensive, a special significance attached to supplies of cheap iron, cotton and other goods produced by serfs in Eastern Europe or by slaves on American plantations. Russia was not only modernising itself on the basis of serfdom, but was also making its contribution to the development of European capitalism. There was only one way in which the cheapness of Russian exports could be made up for – through increasing the volume of sales. This could be ensured only by constant expansion; not so much economic as military and political. Although Catherine's plans concerning the metals trade in southern Europe remained on paper, she did not cease her interest in the Mediterranean.

THE DRIVE TO THE SOUTH

As a great power in military terms, Russia naturally sought to dominate its economic zone. It is noteworthy that the expansionism of Russian monarchs did not meet with serious Western resistance either in the eighteenth century or in the first half of the nineteenth. Russia was compelled periodically to take part in Europe-wide wars, but this was not the result of any desire by the country's Western neighbours to restrain its territorial expansion. On the contrary, the situation stemmed from the desire of Russia's political and economic partners in the West to draw Russia into the wars they were fighting against one another, exploiting the vast military potential of the Russian empire for their own purposes.

Russian expansionism in the eighteenth century was supported by Britain, Holland and even Prussia above all because it answered the objective needs of the developing world economy. Dominating Eastern Europe, the Russian empire assisted in maintaining order in the region, and helped integrate it into the world market. This was why the Western powers did nothing to obstruct the gradual swallowing up by the St Petersburg rulers of Poland and the Baltic region, but took pains to ensure that Russian expansion did not extend beyond the bounds of the peripheral zone to which the empire itself belonged. Hence during the Russian-Turkish Wars of the eighteenth and nineteenth centuries, Russia's Western partners did not prevent the court in St Petersburg from widening its domains at the expense of the 'sick man of Europe', but never allowed the Russian monarchs to force the matter to its conclusion. Plans to finally dismember Ottoman Turkey were nurtured in St Petersburg for a century and a half, but each time they had to be abandoned. Catherine II was compelled to bury her 'Greek project' – a plan to create a Greek state under Russian control, with its capital in Constantinople and with a Russian Grand Prince Constantine at its head. At that point, the main opposition to Russian interests was coming from France, but Russia's allies, Britain and Austria, were not willing to support the empress's plans either.

The war with Turkey ended in the Peace of Kuchuk-Kaynardzha, on terms that were very favourable for Russia, but which at the same time represented the total collapse of Catherine's 'Greek' ambitions. Andrey Zorin, a student of eighteenth-century Russian political life, notes that this resistance on the part of Christian powers to Russian plans with regard to the Muslim Turks aroused genuine puzzlement among the Russian elites, and laid the basis for 'the mythology of a world-wide conspiracy against Russia'.[44] Meanwhile, French policy was viewed in St Petersburg not simply as hostile, but as an attempt 'to exclude Russia from the system of European states'.[45]

If we are to regard Catherine's 'Greek project' as an attempt to restore the route from the Varyags to the Greeks, it is obvious that this was a utopia in the era of Atlantic trade. Nor can the symbolic importance of Constantinople as the centre of the Orthodox world have been of much concern to Catherine – a German, educated in the writings of the French enlightenment. Nevertheless, the effort by St Petersburg to broaden its influence in southern Europe was not rooted exclusively in a desire for territorial conquests.

The states of Eastern and southern Europe, which like Russia were part of the peripheral zone of the world economy, were doomed in one way or another to fall under the influence of the empire. The more 'backward' these countries became in the process of development, and the more dependent they became on the West, the greater the influence on them of their Eastern neighbour. In ideology, causes and consequences will often swap places, and hence the economic 'backwardness' of the region has been ascribed in hindsight to Russian influence, while the situation in practice was very much the reverse. This misconception also helps explain the hope (particularly characteristic of the Polish elites in the nineteenth and twentieth centuries) that liberation from Russia and the forging of political ties with the West would help the countries of Eastern Europe to solve their problems. It also lies behind the near-unbroken series of 'betrayals' on the part of the West, which periodically handed over its freedom-loving admirers to the mercy of the Russian autocracy. A classic example of this was the notorious indifference of the West to the Polish uprisings of the nineteenth century. The partitions of Poland, the Congress of Vienna and the Russo-Austrian alliance against the Hungarian revolution of 1848–49 successively strengthened the role of the regime in St Petersburg as the gendarme of Eastern Europe. In this role, Russia acted with the complete approval of the Western powers, and in the interests of the developing international economic order.

9
The Granary of Europe

In the 1780s and 1790s, grain became an exceptionally profitable commodity, and the growth of demand was accompanied by the modernisation of agriculture. Although rye had been exported from Russia since the time of Ivan the Terrible, the country's main agricultural export was not grain, but industrial crops. In the eighteenth century first place had been held by hemp, followed by flax. Hemp was needed for sails and ropes, without which the ships of the time could not have functioned; it was as much a strategic material as coal was in the second half of the nineteenth century, or oil in the twentieth century. Top-grade Russian hemp went to Britain, while material of lesser quality was supplied to the French. The Russian peasants produced hemp for their own use only in minuscule quantities, and on the internal market demand for it was small. But landowners, oriented toward demand on the world market, induced their peasants systematically to sow hemp in the fields.

The question of how important grain exports were to the Russian economy was already the topic of lively debate in the nineteenth century. Some writers argued that the exporting of grain played a key role in the country's development, while others set out to show that no more than a tiny proportion of the grain produced was exported, and that as a result there could be no talk of agriculture being export-oriented. Both sides were able to put forward persuasive arguments to support their point of view, which is not surprising if one considers that the volume of grain exported varied widely depending on the harvest and the state of the world market. What is really important, however, is not how much grain was shipped abroad in one year or another, but the fact that world grain prices gradually began to determine the prices on the internal market. This was because nowhere near all the grain produced in Russia was meant to be sold. In a country where most of the population lived in the countryside, the internal market was not especially large. Exports might have been small compared to the overall quantity of grain produced, but if we take account only of the grain produced for sale, the picture changes radically. Agriculture was becoming export-oriented to the same degree in which it was becoming commercial and market-driven.

Pokrovsky noted that the two types of grain produced in Russia corresponded to the social hierarchy. Rye was a 'peasant' crop, while wheat was the grain of the gentry. The growth in wheat production was linked closely to the growth of commercial agriculture and to its integration into the world market. The variations in wheat prices in Russia throughout the nineteenth century reflect world trends. But the prices for rye also reflect the same dynamic, though with a certain delay. The influence of the world market was gradually beginning to affect not only landowner agriculture, but also that of the peasants.

In the post-Petrine era, grain exports from Russia were restricted by the fact that while there was a surplus of grain in the south of the country, there was, as a document of the period observes, 'no port close to those regions'. In citing this remark, Pokrovsky concludes ironically that with these words, 'a modest, unremarkable individual from an out-of-the-way place set forward the philosophy behind all the Russo-Turkish wars of the eighteenth century'.[1]

GRAIN AS STRATEGY

Throughout most of the eighteenth century, the main doors onto the world economy remained Riga and Arkhangelsk. The policy of Peter the Great, and of the following generation of imperial rulers, was aimed at encouraging the use of the port of St Petersburg in every way possible. From the point of view of economic geography, however, the capital had been built in a completely inappropriate place. Politically, St Petersburg might have been a window on Europe, but not for the reason that it was located on the Baltic; constructed from the very beginning as the capital of a great European power, it embodied the architectural-bureaucratic utopia of the eighteenth century. St Petersburg was never intended to be anything except a capital. The only other function it was capable of fulfilling was a military one. Pushkin was entirely correct when he put into the mouth of Peter the words, 'A city will be founded here to spite the haughty neighbour', and 'from here we shall menace the Swede'. St Petersburg closed off the mouth of the Neva, and in this respect was located in a very important strategic position. As early as the thirteenth century the Swedes had tried to establish the fortress of Landskrona on the site, and in the seventeenth century had seized this patch of ground from Muscovy, a piece of territory of no special value for them in itself, but very important militarily. Russia ultimately acquired a great city that was to come under military threat, or attack, in the course of almost every major European war. But unlike Moscow, situated in the very heart of Russia, the city which Peter ordered to be built on Russia's outskirts has never once been captured by an enemy.

The presumption that once the port of St Petersburg had been established 'all flags would visit us' nevertheless turned out to be false. The policy of favouring St Petersburg did enormous damage to Arkhangelsk and impeded business in Riga, but still yielded no results. The restrictions on the Arkhangelsk trade were lifted in 1727, but the harm they had done was so great that the city never recovered its status as a major port.

The greatest gains from Peter's victories were made by the German city of Riga, which became one of the largest cities in the Russian empire. Riga, however, did not trade only in Russian goods. Grain was exported through Riga from Lithuania and Belarus, which at that time were still under Polish rule. Though an important export, grain was not the main one, and the authorities in St Petersburg had trouble formulating a consistent policy with regard to it.

Periods of free trade alternated with periods of strict government regulation. In 1701 Peter gave permission for grain to be 'sent overseas unhindered'.[2] The stipulation was made, however, that exports would be restricted if the price of rye in Moscow province exceeded four rubles per *chetvert*. Making use of their political influence, or by simply paying bribes, particular foreign merchants had themselves exempted from these rules.

In 1705 the policy changed radically, and the trade in grain became a state monopoly. Predictably, this policy was also repeatedly breached. In 1713 the decision was made to return to the laws of 1701, from 1718 to 1720 grain exports were banned altogether, in 1721 they were again permitted, and from 1722 to 1727 a new ban was in place. It was only in 1763 that restrictions on grain exports were finally lifted. It was not so much the vagaries of politics that were to blame for this inconsistency so much as the extreme instability of Russian agriculture. Even though both the Russian government and Western capital took every opportunity to organise exports, Russia's northern provinces were poorly suited to crop-raising, and the harvests were insufficient to ensure that shipments abroad would be dependable. The bulk of Russian grain exports went to the Dutch, who had initiated this trade in the seventeenth century. From the Dutch point of view, competition between Russian and Polish grain was essential if the rise in food prices was to be restrained.

In the eighteenth century, Poland remained the principal grain supplier. The need for Russian grain was not especially great, and Russian exports played a subsidiary role. In addition, landowners often found it more profitable to sell grain to distilleries. By the late eighteenth century, however, the demand for grain on the world market was rising steeply. The political consequences were not long in making themselves felt. Russia, Austria and Prussia began dividing Poland among themselves, with St Petersburg gaining control of the main grain-producing districts. Meanwhile, war broke out with Turkey.

Taking over the grain lands of Polish Ukraine, the Russian state also took over the corresponding niche in the world economy. The decisive factor in the development of grain exports, however, was the victories achieved in the Black Sea region. 'It was only the opening to wheat-growing Russia of the gates to the Black Sea,' Pokrovsky writes, 'that could make grain exports the basis for the Russian balance of trade.'[3]

Victorious military campaigns followed one upon another. Legendary Russian cities, Odessa and Sebastopol, appeared on the Black Sea coast. But as in the Baltic, the victories for Russian arms 'did far more to help develop the Black Sea shipping of every other country than they did to aid Russian shipping'. Sebastopol became the base for the Russian navy's Black Sea fleet, and a 'city of Russian renown', but unlike its predecessor, the Byzantine city of Khersones, it did not become a flourishing commerical port. The grain was exported primarily on British merchant ships. Nevertheless, the goal was achieved; 'Russian grain was to proceed in massive quantities along the new road to the West.'[4] By the 1780s a rapid growth of exports was turning Russia into the 'granary of Europe'.

The rise of Russian grain exports coincided with a period of great turmoil in Europe. Among advanced French thinkers, the Russian empire was considered an enlightened monarchy, distinguished by a much greater liberalism than the French regime with its foolish and incompetent kings. When revolution erupted in France, however, the enlightened government in St Petersburg joined with the liberal elite of Britain in opposing it. Understandably, the St Petersburg bureaucrats were not delighted by the ideas of the Jacobins, but the principles of British parliamentarism were alien to them as well. Ideological hostility to revolution was in this case superimposed on economic interests, and reinforced by British gold.

The result was that Russian armies turned up in the most unexpected corners of Europe. Admiral Ushakov joined with Nelson in defeating the French fleet in the Mediterranean, and attacked the island of Corfu. Suvorov fought in Italy, and then crossed the Alps. None of these victories for Russian arms yielded the country an inch of new territory. They were the price paid for the Anglo-Russian alliance, with all the benefits that flowed from it for Russian bureaucrats and landowners. In 1798, when French troops under the command of the young Napoleon Bonaparte landed in Egypt, the British government even discussed whether to hire a Russian army to defend India.[5] Even the conservative patriot Danilevsky was forced to admit that in the wars of the late eighteenth and early nineteenth century, the armies sent by Russian emperors to the West fought 'with varying degrees of success, not for Russian interests but for European ones'.[6] Danilevsky saw the reason for this solely in the 'nobility' of the Russian government, always ready to come to the defence of European peoples suffering from French aggression. This 'nobility' on the part of St Petersburg was of course paid for generously with British gold, and was linked closely with the general commercial interests of the two empires. The attempt by Catherine's heir Paul I to alter the direction of Russian foreign policy ended in a *coup d'état*. Paul's plans to end the alignment with Britain, and his decision to join with the French in waging war on the British, were regarded by the St Petersburg elite as obvious proof of derangement; in the same category was the new tsar's anxiousness to improve the situation of rank-and-file soldiers at the expense of the nobles who made up the officer corps. The image of Paul as a mad emperor has been cemented so firmly into the national historical tradition that in the period since, only a few scholars have tried seriously to examine his actions.

THE CONTINENTAL SYSTEM

Even the progressive elements in the Russian elite were strongly convinced that it was necessary to stick with the British. The future Decembrist Denis Fonvizin wrote:

The break with Britain dealt enormous harm to our foreign trade. Britain supplied us with manufactures and with goods from its colonies, in exchange for the raw materials produced by our soil. This trade represented the sole route through which everything Russia needed flowed into our country. Through the export of grain, ship's timbers, masts, lard, hemp, flax and so forth, the nobility received reliable incomes from their estates. The rupture with Britain shattered the material well-being of the nobility, and strengthened the hostility to Paul which his harsh despotism had in any case aroused. The conviction became almost universal that by some means or other, Paul needed to be removed.[7]

Needless to say, by Paul's 'despotism' was implied his populist measures, aimed at defending peasants and soldiers from the tyranny of the nobility. For the educated Russian public of the time, such steps amounted to violating the 'liberties' of the ruling layer. In essence, anyone who did not belong to this stratum was also outside of society. The conspirators were promised a 'subsidy' from Britain. The plan at first was to remove Paul from power by reason of his 'madness', as had been done with George III in Britain. Then, a more straightforward and familiar path was followed: the imperial populist was simply killed. Peace was promptly concluded with Britain, the Cossacks whom Paul had sent to conquer India were recalled, and Admiral Nelson's squadron, without waiting for an official decision on the cessation of hostilities, put into Revel to stock up on fresh water and supplies. This stirred panic in the city's commander, who had not been briefed on high-level political matters, and who decided that the British were trying to seize Estland.

Immediately after the enthronement of the new tsar, Paul's decrees banning imports of diverse types of foreign manufactures were rescinded. Thanks to a *coup d'état* and an act of regicide, free trade had triumphed.

The new emperor was Alexander I, the favourite grandson of Catherine the Great, a man who had been raised on the literary works of the French enlightenment, and who was sympathetic to liberal initiatives. This was 'the brilliant beginning of the Alexandrine era', when people in St Petersburg dreamt of reforms in the spirit of British parliamentarism, or of representation on the Swedish model. The young people surrounding the tsar hoped to interest their British allies in their progressive undertakings. Russian representatives in London explained that St Petersburg was ready to be included once again in the anti-French coalition, but that the war had to be fought not in the name of restoring the old order, but rather under the slogans of freedom and legality. To the Bonapartism and Jacobinism of the French, there needed to be counterposed something along the lines of the British constitutional model, adapted to the conditions of continental Europe.[8]

None of this aroused the slightest interest in London. The British response to the Russian proposals was to start talking about war subsidies. The business-like British needed to know precisely what the price would be of engaging the Russian army for the next campaign against the French. Subsidies were provided, but they proved insufficient; this was reflected in the unfortunate manner in which, for the Russians, the war unfolded. As Pokrovsky notes, this alliance was dictated by economic necessity, 'and more on the Russian side than on that of Britain'.[9] The peripheral position of the Russian empire made it hostage to the wars of others, and forced it to pay with the blood of its soldiers for its 'economically inescapable' international obligations.

Alexander's first campaign in Europe ended in defeat at Austerlitz. The subsequent battles were not as catastrophic for the Russian army, but overall, things did not go well for the Russians. The chronic failures of the Russian, Prussian and Austrian armies in the struggle against Napoleon led London to conclude that it was pointless spending money to maintain continental allies. After the Russians had lost the battle of Friedland in 1807, St Petersburg still had the armed forces needed to continue the fight, but money had run out. To a plea for a new loan of £6 million, London replied with a categorical refusal. 'The resources were not there to wage war any longer,' Pokrovsky concludes, 'and willingly or unwillingly, peace had to be made with the "enemy of humankind".'[10] Alexander was forced to sign the Peace of Tilsit. The victorious French demanded that St Petersburg not only withdraw from the war, but that it also join the continental blockade, breaking its trade ties with Britain. Under the impact of military defeats, Alexander was forced to follow the same path as his unfortunate father.

For Russian exporters, this was a grievous blow. As a contemporary writer put it, 'they viewed the closure of the harbours to British ships as a ban imposed on the produce of Russia'.[11] Observing this, French emissaries in St Petersburg appealed to Napoleon to substitute French shipments for the British ones. The trouble was that France could neither buy nor sell goods in the same quantities as Britain. Inflation rose sharply, and the paper money quickly became devalued. In 1809, a one-ruble currency bill exchanged for only 33 silver copecks.

The continental blockade also had its positive aspects. It encouraged the development of domestic industries aimed at replacing imports. Some entrepreneurs managed to forge direct links with French, Dutch and Danish partners. More than a few merchants grew rich on contraband. Many of the factories built during the period of the continental blockade were destroyed in the Moscow fire of 1812. Nevertheless, the positive effects of the blockade were felt until 1819, when a new customs tariff again ensured complete freedom of trade in Russia for British importers. Russian merchants told one another that 'there were many celebratsions in London on this account'.[12] Unable to withstand British competition, numerous Russian factories fell derelict.

Ultimately, the continental blockade proved ruinous not so much for the bourgeoisie as for the landowners. The emergence at this time of Michael Speransky, with his projects of reform, was no accident. 'The argument was between industrial and commercial capitalism', Pokrovsky writes.

The continental blockade was advantageous for the former, but for the latter it spelt disaster. Speransky was on the side of the industrialists.... For him, the political freedom of Russia flowed from the country's industrial development. His understanding of this point was entirely bourgeois; he regarded a juridically free worker as the sole conceivable basis for 'industrialism'.[13]

The 'continental system', reinforced through the customs tariff of 1811, became the topic of heated discussions in educated society. Opinions at court were divided. The finance ministry took an extremely negative view of any limitations on freedom of trade. But State Chancellor Count Rumyantsev, himself a major factory-owner, supported the ban on imports of British manufactures. Rumyantsev argued that without protectionism expanding national industry would be impossible, and that the general population, engaged exclusively in agriculture, would be doomed 'to remain forever in poverty and ignorance'.[14]

From the government, the disagreements spread to the court, and then to all of educated society. In his history of Russian factories, Mikhail Tugan-Baranovsky later wrote:

In the history of our social development, the second decade of this century was curious for the arguments over protectionism and free trade that engaged public consciousness to an extraordinary degree. Since the overwhelming majority of educated people at this time were connected in one way or another with the agriculturalist class, it is understandable that protectionists, or more precisely supporters of the system of trade bans, did not enjoy public sympathy. The number of pamphlets written in defence of the existing tariff was very small compared with the pamphlets and articles favouring free trade.[15]

In his reference to agriculturalists, Tugan-Baranovsky was, strictly speaking, incorrect; the agriculturalists of that time did not write pamphlets or take part in debates. Nevertheless, the landowners were keenly interested in questions of international trade.

The Russian bourgeoisie was too weak, backward and primitive to take advantage of the situation that had arisen. Speransky's reforms had no solid basis in society, and his plans dangled in the air. By 1810 the continental blockade had effectively collapsed so far as Russia was concerned. Contraband had become a massive phenomenon, and no one was mounting a serious struggle against it. The discontent of the nobility made continuing with the earlier policy impossible. The fall of Speransky and the effective disintegration of the continental system took place simultaneously.

The war of 1812 became a key national myth, and in many ways it was a turning point for Russian history. From the very beginning this war was perceived as patriotic; in other words, the goal was to save the homeland from foreign conquest. However, the French invasion was in no way aimed at conquering Russia. Bonaparte was certainly not mad; having captured Moscow, he waited in vain for emissaries from the emperor in St Petersburg, in order to conclude an honourable peace. Bonaparte's great army had proceeded into the depths of Russia because France simply had no other way left of forcing St Petersburg to return to the continental blockade. The outcome of Anglo-French rivalry was perhaps decided to an even greater degree in the battles of Borodino and Tarutino than on the field of Waterloo. The victor was Britain.

THE MANCHESTER NOBILITY

How important was the world economy to the development of Russia in the eighteenth and nineteenth centuries? It is obvious that only a tiny proportion of the country's resources finished up on the world market. The peasants and landowners in a remote province from which 'you would ride for three years without encountering any sort of state' had only an extremely dim notion of what the world market amounted to. In St Petersburg, however, people understood the world market very well, even too well. Precisely because they understood these matters, they drove the peasants and the landowners to war at the point of a gun, forcing them to take part in endless incomprehensible conflicts, sometimes at the other end of the continent. Either the Russian forces were to take Berlin, or they were to conquer Crimea, or cross the Alps; eventually, they reached Paris. Russian society was uniformly proud of these victories, but the majority of the population, including the provincial nobility, rarely had any comprehension of the purpose of these campaigns. The war of 1812 was the first conflict since the time of Peter the Great that ordinary people had understood; it was this that earned it the name the 'Patriotic War'.

In the early twentieth century, when no one was yet prepared to talk of the positive role of serfdom in history, Lenin argued that the serf-holding landowners had tried unsuccessfully to fence Russia off from the West, to 'impede the growth of commodity exchange between Russia and Europe', in order to ensure the survival of the 'old, decaying economic forms'.[16] Lenin here was clearly reiterating the standard positions of liberal commentary. In reality, the serf-holding economy had a vital interest in the foreign market, and served as a sort of agent drawing Russia into the world system. Pushkin in the 1830s coined his well-known remark to the effect that the government, despite its crudity and cynicism, was 'still the only European in Russia'.[17] The poet, of course, was not referring to the cultural achievements of the St Petersburg bureaucrats, but to their involvement in wider European affairs and to their resulting wish to 'modernise' the country.

For all its authoritarian bureaucracy, St Petersburg was for Pushkin a source of dynamism, a force impelling the country into motion and causing it to participate in world affairs. It would be naïve, however, to explain this behaviour of the authorities solely on the basis of their political ambitions. The Europeanism of the authorities was predicated on the involvement of the elites in the international economy. The Russian capital needed the money and goods to be had from the world market. The higher the position of a social group in the St Petersburg empire, the stronger its ties to Europe – or, in other words, to the emerging bourgeois world system. It is true that the people drawn into this system made up only a tiny minority of Russia's inhabitants. But it was this minority that ruled the country and, in essence, owned it.

In the late 1770s the Russian writer Denis Fonvizin travelled about Europe with his ailing wife, and left us an extremely revealing set of observations. Europe, living with a presentiment of future revolutionary shocks, appalled the Russian writer with its coarseness. Everywhere, Fonvizin saw backwardness and barbarism. In the eastern regions of Germany he encountered abominable roads, revolting food, an unreliable postal service, drunkenness, rudeness and inefficiency. A journey by mail coach was akin to torture.

Generally speaking, the postal institutions of His Prussian Majesty are not worth a farthing. His posts at their fastest are much slower than our foot-messengers. In Saxony things are a little better, but also quite bad.[18]

Only the western regions of Germany met with the traveller's approval. Having crossed the French border, Fonvizin recorded,

When we entered the city we were met by a revolting stench, so that we could no longer doubt we had arrived in France. To be brief, they have not the slightest conception of cleanliness here. People are allowed to pour anything out of the windows onto the street, so of course no one opens their windows unless they want to suffocate.[19]

The streets in France were narrow; in Lyons, 'the widest would not serve as an alley-way in Russia, and they are wretchedly maintained'.[20] In the middle of a city, the Russian writer notes, 'the French allow people to singe pigs! Just think whether they would find anywhere to singe a pig in Millionaya Street, and whether our police would let them do it!'[21] Even the customs of the French aristocracy evoke Fonvizin's condemnation:

The table napkins in France are so filthy that the ones used by the nobles on feast-days are incomparably worse than the ones that in Russia are put out on weekdays in poor homes. They are so coarse, and so poorly washed, that wiping your mouth is a vile business.[22]

Things in Italy were even worse. The poverty was such that 'on fertile soil, the people suffer from hunger'.[23] All around, there was 'an enormous amount of swinish behaviour'. Meanwhile, 'the floors are of stone, and dirty; the linen is filthy, the bread is such that the poor in Russia would not eat, and they consider to be clean water what we would regard as slops'.[24]

On top of everything, Russia in Fonvizin's view was a much freer country than Italy. In St Petersburg and Moscow people freely read Voltaire, Diderot and Rousseau, while in Rome these writers were strictly forbidden. In short, the Russian traveller on returning to his homeland came to the firm conclusion that 'life in St Petersburg is incomparably better'.[25]

One of the few people in Paris whom Fonvizin found genuinely interesting was Benjamin Franklin, United States Ambassador and one of the Founding Fathers of American history. There is something to ponder in this meeting of two heartsick enlighteners, one of them representing a slave-owning republic, and the other a serf-holding monarchy.

If we are to believe Fonvizin, eighteenth-century Russia had far outstripped the West in all respects. The same era, however, has left us another literary memento, Aleksandr Radishchev's *Journey from St Petersburg to Moscow*. The picture drawn by this traveller was so gloomy that the book was banned and its author was exiled to Siberia.

Fonvizin made two journeys about Europe, the first in 1777 and 1778, and the second in 1784. Radishchev's book was published in 1790. In other words, the rapture of Fonvizin and the horror of Radishchev relate to one and the same period. The first traveller looked on the road before him with the eyes of a St Petersburg nobleman. It never occurred to him that there was no need to ban the books of Voltaire and Rousseau in an empire where most of the population was illiterate, and where most of those who could read were satisfied with the existing order. In Europe he was everywhere confronted by ordinary people, appearing with their uncouth manners before his haughty gaze. In Russia, the police would not permit such an outrage. The local aristocrats bore no comparison with those in Russia, since they were short of cash. From the bearers of noble titles, money had passed to the bourgeoisie. Radishchev, by contrast, sought to look at his road through the eyes of the peasants and common people. His Russia was not mighty and brilliant, but god-forsaken and sinister.

However, neither the moral indignation of Radishchev nor the well-meaning recommendations of the French enlighteners influenced the policies of the St Petersburg government. This was not only because the government rested above all on nobles with an interest in serfdom, but also because it saw no other path it might have followed. Even the Pugachev revolt failed to shake the conviction of St Petersburg that for Russia, being a European power and being a serf-holding country were one and the same thing. Numerous French books on the rights of the individual crammed the libraries of St Petersburg aristocrats to whom it never occurred that all this might have some bearing on the lives of enserfed peasants. This situation only changed in the early nineteenth century. The reason was not only that the new generation of young people who had grown up in Moscow and St Petersburg read the books of Voltaire and Rousseau more attentively than their parents. Russia after the Napoleonic Wars was a country on the rise.

This was not only because the campaign of 1812 took on the character of a victorious popular war, following which Russian forces reached Leipzig in 1813 and Paris in 1814. Nor was it only because of the hopes aroused in society by these victories and by the liberal promises of Alexander I. In economic terms as well, Russia at this time was achieving a great deal. The results of the modernising efforts of the eighteenth century were finally starting to have an effect not only in St Petersburg and Moscow, but in the provinces as well. The prospects for agriculture looked highly pomising, while industry, which had received a powerful stimulus during the years of the continental blockade, continued to develop rapidly. Manufacturers were taking their products onto the world market, and in Europe the demand for Russian iron remained relatively high. Western Europe needed constantly increasing quantities of Russian grain, and the ports of southern Russia began to develop rapidly. Odessa, which had been founded in 1794, grew apace. Described by nineteenth-century economists as 'the commercial capital of the Black Sea coast region', Odessa flourished thanks to the grain exports.[26] In 1802 the city had a mere 400 buildings, and at most, 8,000 residents; by 1812 the number of buildings was 2,600, and the population had reached 35,000.

In the years from 1813 to 1817, Russian grain exports increased by a factor of five. As the industrial revolution in Britain continued, Pokrovsky writes, the Russian landed estate was transformed into a ' grain-producing factory'.

A genuine revolution occurred in the landowner economy. Output of grain for the market had to be raised quickly and massively.

This change had already been in evidence in the late eighteenth century, but it made its effects felt with particular force immediately after the Napoleonic Wars... in the middle of the second decade of the nineteenth century.[27]

Serf labour was relatively unproductive, but cheap, and could be extremely profitable so long as the market was more or less stable. When the need appeared for a sharp increase in labour productivity, however, the inefficiency of the serf system became apparent. This was clear both from the point of view of the landowners and in terms of the general developmental needs of the world system. Grain was in short supply. Prices in London rose rapidly, from 50 shillings a quarter in the late eighteenth century to 90 shillings at the end of the Napoleonic Wars. Not surprisingly, the Russian nobility increasingly became imbued with the spirit of free trade, in the spirit of the Manchester school of British economists. Pushkin with a degree of irony records that his hero Onegin has read Adam Smith, and Marx later took satisfaction in quoting fragments from *Evgeny Onegin* that in his view bore witness to an exemplary grasp of political economy. This enthusiasm on the part of Pushkin's hero was perfectly understandable to the poet's contemporaries. Pushkin's novel, including its account of the economic views of the nobility of the time, was indeed 'an encyclopedia of Russian life'.

An enthusiasm for the ideas of free trade was typical of the landowners of that period. Unlike the nobility and aristocracy, Russian industrialists favoured protectionism, but it was not they who set the tone in the capital. Describing the moods of the St Petersburg elite in the early nineteenth century, Tugan-Baranovsky turned his attention to the universal enthusiasm for the ideas of Adam Smith. As we see, Pushkin's Onegin was far from being an isolated case: 'If we look through the *St Petersburg Journal,* the official organ of the Interior Ministry in the early years of the century, we are struck by how much space in this publication is devoted to the preaching of the Smith school.'[28]

It was none other than that favourite of the tsar, Count Aleksey Arakcheev, who drew up the next proposal for the emancipation of the peasants. Yet Arakcheev was to enter Russian history as a symbol of harshness and despotism! Pokrovsky speaks repeatedly of 'Manchester nobles'. It is significant that such sentiments should have held sway among the inhabitants of the 'nests of gentlefolk' at this time, when the conjuncture on the world market was especially favourable. On this same world market, however, import changes were taking place. It was only at first that the industrial revolution in Britain and the ending of the wars on the continent brought a sharp increase in the demand for Russian raw materials; later, demand began to decline. The technology employed in British metallurgy was being modernised, and shipbuilding was also gradually changing. As the fleet made the shift to steam power, demand lessened for the hemp, sailcloth and masts which the Baltic coast had earlier supplied to British and Dutch shipyards. Finally, the ending of hostilities made it possible to buy grain unhindered in the most diverse markets. Competition between sellers increased, and prices fell. These processes did not, of course, begin operating immediately, and their results did not really begin to be felt in Russia until the late 1820s and early 1830s.

During the first half of the 1820s a unique situation arose in which the Russia Empire was already beginning to feel the impact of the changes, but still had enough money and resources to continue developing successfully. For the impulse received early in the century to continue, radical changes were needed, changes affecting not only the internal structures of the empire, but also its place in the world. The economy needed to be reoriented toward the internal market, which could grow only on the basis of a shift to freely hired labour and a rise in the cost of labour power. This would also have signified the transformation of Russia from a peripheral empire into an economically independent country, for which internal rather than external goals were paramount. By the early 1820s, the material resources for this transition were present. The numerous proposals for reform voiced during the period testify to the fact that Russian society also contained people who understood the problem. But the political will was insufficient, and the question of whether the social basis for change existed remained unresolved.

It was the specific nature of this period (a period, incidentally, which has been very little studied by historians) which explains the revolt of 14 December 1825.

THE DECEMBRISTS

The revolt of the Decembrists was to become a seminal myth for Russian culture. Some people see in this episode a romantic story of noble aristocrats who, infused with the ideas of the enlightenment and proceeding about Europe in a victorious campaign, decided to renounce their class privileges. The revolutionaries of the second half of the nineteenth century declared the Decembrists their direct predecessors, and not even Lenin rejected this heritage. Here, however, the Marxist tradition encounters a serious problem. On the one hand, we are faced with a movement voicing demands that were clearly revolutionary. On the other, the leaders of this movement and most of its participants belonged to the traditional elite of society.

Despite their aristocratic origins, Mikhail Pokrovsky explained a century later, the Decembrists were genuine revolutionaries. In terms of the ideas of the age, theirs was an extremely advanced political organisation. The Decembrists had 'proceeded to the utmost limit of revolutionism that is attainable by non-proletarian classes'. More could not have been demanded of them, since 'there was no proletariat whatever in Russia at that time'.[29]

What induced these brilliant aristocrats to resort to 'the utmost limit of revolutionism'? At first glance, the image of the Decembrist revolt as doomed, as premature, as having been plotted by people who were ahead of their time, is confirmed by the general picture of the reaction that held sway in Russia after the movement collapsed. The words of Aleksandr Griboedov, commenting ironically on an attempt by 100 ensigns to turn the country upside down, have remained in popular consciousness. So too has Lenin's well-known formula: 'The circle of these revolutionaries was narrow, and they were terribly remote from the people.' For Lenin, the revolt of 1825 was not of significance in and of itself. It did not represent an opportunity that was let slip. Rather, it was an essential first step, after which a second would naturally follow: 'Their exploit was not in vain. The Decembrists aroused Herzen. Herzen expanded the revolutionary agitation.'[30]

Every subsequent generation of revolutionaries was more radical, more democratic ('popular') and more effective. After Aleksandr Herzen came the *narodnik* populists, whose agitation was broader and more profound, and finally there appeared the Marxist social democrats, at the head of 'the only thoroughly revolutionary class', the proletariat. The activity of Lenin's Bolshevik party represented the culmination and completion of a century-old process. This scheme, completely in line with the Hegelian tradition, looked convincing at the dawn of the twentieth century. The real story, however, was far more complex and dramatic.

The image of the Decembrists as a 'small circle' is quite debatable. Of course, they were not a large group compared with the mass parties of the twentieth century, but both the Union of Prosperity and the Union of Salvation were relatively serious organisations for their time. Even the materials of the official investigation provide us with a picture of a distinctly impressive conspiracy, by no means restricted to a narrow circle of St Petersburg malcontents. Beyond the scope of the investigation there remained thousands of sympathisers who were not, of course, prepared to join in the conspiracy, but who would cheerfully have attached themselves to the rebels had the latter been victorious. Naturally, the defeat of the Decembrists was not a matter of chance. But neither was their attempt to transform Russia a baseless adventure. Indeed, their enterprise was absolutely in keeping with the times.

Secret societies began to be formed immediately the Napoleonic Wars ended. First were the Russian Knights (1814), then the Union of Salvation (1817), followed by the Union of Prosperity in 1818. By 1821 a fully-formed conspiracy had arisen, and had drawn into its orbit not only a considerable section of the St Petersburg elite, but also provincial officers from the impoverished nobility, who provided the backbone for the Southern Society and the Society of United Slavs, representing the extreme left of the movement. In the unique political and economic situation of the years from 1815 to 1825, the boldest and most enlightened section of the Russian ruling class saw a historic opportunity opening before the country. Once the social order had been modernised, the logic of peripheral development could be broken, and Russia could be turned into a fully-fledged European power, possessing not only a large army, but also a strong and independent economy. The military and political outcomes of the years 1812–14 needed to be consolidated on the level of social development, or they would be irretrievably lost, as indeed happened under Nicholas I.

The Decembrists were not merely aristocrats, but in the first instance constituted a military elite. In this respect the conspiracy of 1825 was fundamentally unlike the European revolutions of the nineteenth century, instead representing a prototype of the numerous conspiracies, coups and revolutions which throughout the twentieth century were to be engineered by military officers with modernising views in the countries of the periphery. A significant number of these coups, at times prepared and executed much less ably than the revolt of 14 December 1825, were completely successful, at least in the sense of taking power. How well the victors used this power is a different question.

The revolt of 1825 was tragic not because it represented a first heroic step that was obviously doomed, but for another reason: it was a historic opportunity – real, even if let slip – for Russia to leave the road of peripheral development. Just how extraordinary the situation in the early 1820s had been, and how inconceivable the prospect that it would be repeated, had become clear by the end of the decade. While taking his revenge on the Decembrists, Nicholas I did not at first reject all thoughts of reforms, or even of emancipating the peasants. But with every year it became more obvious that for the government in St Petersburg, following such a path was not a practical possibility.

THE AGE OF REACTION

'The social history of Nicholas's reign', Pokrovsky writes, 'cannot be understood if we lose sight of the fact, prosaic but with enormously important consequences, that the 1820s and 1830s were a period of exceptionally low grain prices.' This decline of the price of grain on the domestic market was merely a reflection of a broader world trend: 'Throughout all Europe it was the same.'[31] Along with the fall in prices came an end to the growth of exports, 'and together with it, a freeze in the development of the landowner economy which had held out such glowing prospects for the agricultural producers of the Alexandrine epoch'.[32]

In Britain around the turn of the nineteenth century, the industrial revolution was continuing. The need for raw materials was growing, but the structure of this demand was changing. The transformation taking place in Britain had a particular impact on Russian metallurgy. At first, the demand for Russian iron had grown dramatically, but by the beginning of the nineteenth century new technologies had permitted such an increase in the productivity of British metallurgy that it had become cheaper to produce iron in Britain than to import it from Russia, despite the cheapness of serf labour. The bonded labour employed in Russian enterprises had aided the development of the industrial revolution, but these enterprises then fell victim to the changes that had occurred. As Strumilin notes, 'Russian metallurgy, which had fed its iron to British machine-building and quickened the pace of the industrial revolution in Britain, felt the consequences of this revolution in especially painful fashion.'[33]

In the eighteenth century Russia had been the world leader in metals production, outstripping Britain, France and Sweden. But by 1805 Britain already smelted more cast iron. The development of British industry was of course stimulated by military needs – weapons were needed for the struggle against Bonaparte – but technological innovations nevertheless played the decisive role in this expansion. The further the industrial revolution in the

West developed, the more Russia felt the constraints of its peripheral position. Initially, the falling-off of exports to Britain was compensated by the growth of purchases by the countries of continental Europe, but then Russia began to lag behind these countries as well. As exports declined, the narrowness of the internal market made its effects felt. The growth of output slowed, and the sector began falling into decline. By 1825 Russian metallurgy had been overtaken by that of France and North America, and in 1855 Russian output of cast iron was less than that of Germany and Austro-Hungary. By the mid nineteenth century Russian industry needed to import cast iron from Britain.

In the new conditions, the reform projects which the court had found so captivating in the time of Alexander I were quite unrealistic. Nicholas I was by no means a committed supporter of serfdom; various proposals for the emancipation of the peasants continued to be discussed in St Petersburg throughout his reign. Enacting these proposals against the background of an extremely unfavourable market conjuncture, however, would have meant ruining the landowners. Consequently, the plans for making the shift to freely hired labour and for modernising agriculture no longer seemed so attractive economically as during the previous reign.

Even in the absence of reforms, the landowners were starting to have problems with money. Large numbers of estates were mortgaged, with the state bank, as the Marquise de Custine noted, acting as the main creditor to the nobility. The government thus obtained an additional instrument of control over 'enlightened society'.

The reign of Nicholas I was not, however, a period of total economic stagnation. Industry, which had received an impulse to its development during the years of the continental blockade, contined to grow, and at quite rapid rates. The narrow internal market was by now insufficient for the Russian factory-owners. In order to maintain industrial growth, the government resorted to protectionism, defending the Russian market against British competition; meanwhile, new markets needed to be sought. There was obviously no serious possibility of exporting Russian industrial products to Europe. That meant that markets had to be secured in the East – in Turkey, Persia and Central Asia. Out of necessity, Russian foreign policy was becoming expansionist.

The growth of Russian industry had put in question Russia's place in the international division of labour. The mutual understanding between Britain and Russia, based on the traditional eighteenth-century community of interests between British capitalists and Russian landowners, had been broken.

The restructuring of the world economic order which the industrial revolution brought about created a new situation, which Russia tried actively to exploit in order to win a more exalted place in the world system. For the St Petersburg empire, however, the chances of success in this endeavour were minuscule. The internal structure of Russian society doomed the effort to failure, and the last possibility of radical reform was lost with the defeat of the Decembrist uprising.

The Russian empire was left with no choice except to expand to the east. Russian influence was growing in Turkey and Egypt; the country was methodically conquering the Caucasus, and was beginning an offensive in Central Asia, conducted for the time being through trade and diplomacy. As Pokrovsky explains,

the interests of Russian industry were the starting-point for a whole series of diplomatic moves; in a process of which the actors themselves were not always aware, but which was always evident to any attentive outside observer, these moves gradually formed themselves into a definite political line. At the end of this line was Sevastopol.[34]

According to Pokrovsky, the British economy by the 1830s had far less need of Russian goods than earlier.

As luck would have it, the main commodity which Britain sought on the Russian market – that is, grain – was cheap in Western Europe at this time. This on its own meant that Britain no longer needed Russia. With the growth of Russian industry after 1812, Russia became – or at any rate, appeared – dangerous and threatening.[35]

Recent research, however, paints a far more complex picture. As one Soviet historian puts it, Britain in the mid nineteenth century was for Russia simultaneously both its 'main trading partner, and a rival'.[36] For all the political conflicts, economic ties between Russia and Britain were intensive. As before, politics and commerce went hand in hand; the British consul in St Petersburg was also the representative of the London-based Russian Company. In the mid nineteenth century Britain accounted for about a third of Russia's imports, and approximately half of its exports. As well as grain, Russia exported timber, flax, hemp, lard, wool, and pig bristles, while gradually increasing its purchases of British industrial equipment. By the 1840s Russia was supplying Britain with two-thirds of its needs for raw flax and hemp, and 80 per cent of its flax and hemp seed.[37] It is noteworthy here that in Russia itself, output of linen goods was falling, a development not unrelated to British competition.

As Britain's fleet of steamships expanded, demand in the country for Russian hemp declined, but this did not happen immediately; for some time, old and new technologies coexisted. Russian timber served the British 'railway fever' of the 1840s, just as Russian metals 30 years earlier had been used in the mechanisation of the 'workshop of the world'. Now, however, raw materials were coming from all directions – from Australia, South America and Canada. The further the capitalist world-system expanded, and the richer the sources of raw materials became, the wider the choice for the 'centre', and the fiercer the competition between the countries of the 'periphery'. As a source of imports to Britain, Russia at this time held second place, behind only France, and it led the field as a supplier of raw materials and foodstuffs to the 'workshop of the world'. Among the countries to which Britain exported goods, Russia occupied fourth place. Moreover, a substantial proportion of the goods which Russia exported to Germany and Holland finished up eventually on the British market. In the re-export of colonial goods, Russia shared first place with the Hanseatic cities of Germany. The Russian market took on special importance in years of industrial crisis. In 1841 and 1842, imports to Russia of British goods continued growing against the background of an overall decline in world trade.

Britain was not only the greatest trading partner of the Russian empire, but also its main creditor. British capital participated in seven of the ten foreign loans concluded by the tsarist government between the 1840s and the 1860s.[38] Although most of the funds were obtained on the London financial market, the tsar also contracted debts with the bankers of Berlin and Paris.

The first Russian railway, linking St Petersburg with Moscow, was built with the help of foreign loans. Foreign credits were also required for the building of a railway line to Warsaw. Most of the money was obtained in 1840 in Berlin, though British and Dutch capital was also involved in financing the project. Since Russian railway construction depended increasingly on the Berlin financial market, Prussia used its influence when plans for a railway to Lithuania were being discussed in St Petersburg. This railway could have subjected Prussian trade to serious competition, and under pressure from Berlin, the tsar's government was forced to reject the proposal.

Despite active Prussian participation, it was British capital that played the decisive role in the first wave of Russian railway construction. According to calculations by Soviet historians, 'at the time of subscribing, British capital accounted for approximately half of the total sum of all the loans for financing railway construction'.[39] The money borrowed by the Russian government often remained in the West, where it was used to buy railway equipment in Britain and America. In order to maintain its creditworthiness, the government in St Petersburg was forced to sell its gold to the Bank of England.

During the crisis of 1847, the financial markets in London and Paris themselves felt the need for Russian money. The crisis of European industry had an extremely severe – though not immediate – effect on Russia. At first there was a sense that as an exporter of agrarian produce and raw materials, Russia was in a better position than the Western countries that had been hit by the industrial downturn. Russian raw materials and foodstuffs had been purchased before the crisis struck; the result was that the Western industrialists were left with mountains of unsold products, and their Russian suppliers with ready cash. The tsar's government found itself unexpectedly with a surplus of money, and began actively playing the market, buying up French, British, Dutch, Austrian and Prussian stocks. The industrial downturn of 1847 restored Russia's reputation in Europe as a wealthy country, but as Marx observed ironically, this reputation 'had to be bought with cash'.[40] In addition, the purchasing by the Russian government of securities in London and Paris took place against the background of a flow of British capital out of Russia. In sum, Strumilin argues, a substantial part of the Russian gold that poured onto the London market during the crisis belonged 'not to the Russian tsar, but to British capitalists who had long since penetrated Russia, and was withdrawn from Russia at a moment of danger in order to save the capitalists' own country from monetary crisis'.[41]

The following year showed that the 'advantages' which the Russian economy possessed were fanciful. Following the collapse of demand for industrial products came a catastrophic fall in demand for raw materials. According to Strumilin's calculations, Russian exports suffered an immediate decline of 40 per cent. Such a blow, Strumilin remarks, 'could not pass off without leaving its mark on Russian trade and industry'.[42]

The country was experiencing all the delights associated with its 'peripheral' position in the world economy. Under conditions of depression, foreign investments began to be repatriated to the countries of the 'centre', where an acute need for money had arisen. The demand for raw materials declined, while the need for imports of industrial products remained at relatively high levels. The excess of money was replaced by catastrophic shortage. In 1848 the Russian budget ran a deficit of 32 million rubles. The reserves of gold held in the vaults of the Petropavlovsky Fortress melted away, declining by 17 per cent in a single year.

The most important historical consequence of the industrial crisis of 1847 was the wave of revolutionary struggles that rolled across Europe during 1848–49. The government of Nicholas I viewed these developments as a direct threat, and was willing to take an active part in putting down the Western revolutions. War, however, costs money, and none was to be had. Then London once again came to the aid of St Petersburg. The defeat of the Hungarian revolution of 1848 was carried out by Russian bayonets, but using British money. The funds for the Hungarian campaign were provided by Barings Bank, traditionally linked to the British government and court. The bank lent the tsar the £5 million (35 million rubles) needed for the war.

CONFLICT WITH BRITAIN

Consequently, it cannot be said that in the mid nineteenth century there was any sharp decline in Britain's need for Russian raw materials, or in Russia's need for British money. Nevertheless, the situation changed substantially. The strategic importance of Russian supplies diminished as the fleet made the transition from sail to steam. Meanwhile, competition increased; the goods that had been supplied from Russia could be obtained elsewhere. As markets for the sale of British goods, however, Russia and the countries of the Near East came to mean far more to British capital than in earlier decades. But standing in the way of these commercial ambitions was Russian industrial protectionism.

The protectionist policies of the Russian government were a serious problem for British exporters not only in Russia itself, but also in the countries which in one fashion or another fell within the sphere of Russian influence. The possibility that the Russians might capture the Black Sea straits was a genuine nightmare for British capitalists operating in the Near East. War was in the air as early as the 1830s and, as Pokrovsky notes, Russia appeared 'in the role of the attacking side'.[43] Here is how the notorious 'Eastern question' arose.

Fierce competition between British and Russian industrial suppliers emerged in Central Asia. As British India expanded to the north, British goods came increasingly to penetrate nearby markets. In Bukhara and Khiva, British goods began forcing out Russian ones. As usual, commercial competition was combined with political rivalry. While the Afghans fought back against British attempts at conquest, the Central Asian khanates tried to preserve their independence by appealing to the Russian tsar to defend them.

Acting as the protector of Slavs and Orthodox Christians, the government in St Petersburg was trying to establish its control – if not overt, then at least indirect – over the territories in south-eastern Europe that were still formally subject to the Ottoman empire. Russian protectionism also stood in the way of British goods en route to Persia. The conquest of the Caucasus closed off yet another potential market to British industry.

In the early 1830s, Russian influence on Turkish affairs was so great as to cause panic in London. The Ottoman empire was trying desperately to keep Egypt under its control, but was suffering one defeat after another. In 1832, forces of the Egyptian ruler Muhamed Ali advanced on Istanbul. The entire Ottoman political system was in danger of collapse. Under these conditions the sultan had no alternative but to appeal for help to his age-old enemy, the Russian emperor, who provided Turkey with the necessary guarantees, and who in extreme circumstances was also ready to provide military assistance. The agreement of 1834 gave Russia enormous privileges on the territory of the Ottoman Porte.

Predictably, Britain regarded these developments as extremely undesirable. As recently as 1827, the Russian and British navies had fought alongside one another against the Turks at Navarino,[44] and now the London press was writing about the possibility of military conflict with Russia. Nevertheless, direct conflict was avoided. Reforms that had begun in Turkey meant that its political alignments shifted toward Britain. 'In the second half of the 1830s,' wrote the modern-day scholar V.N. Vinogradov,

Russian influence in Istanbul declined dramatically, while that of the British, by contrast, was in the ascendant. The reformers, for obvious reasons, turned their gaze not to a backward autocratic state, but to the countries that were impressive for their economic might, naval power, political stability, and flexible system of rule.[45]

The decisive role, however, was not played by ideological sympathies, but by trade. Between 1825 and 1835, British exports to Turkey more than doubled, making the Turkish market especially important for Britain in a period when other European countries, having established their own industries, were increasingly resorting to protectionism. In 1838 an Anglo-Turkish convention was signed, creating still more favourable openings for British capital. As Vinogradov puts it, 'on a backward, somnolent country, "free trade" was imposed with the foremost industrial power of that epoch'.[46]

Influenced by the British Manchester school, the reformers were convinced that free trade would lead Turkey to prosperity. The anticipated prosperity, however, failed to eventuate. Not only Turkish but to some degree Russian industry as well fell victim to the new system. The competition from the stream of British goods that poured onto the Turkish market was too great for the Russians. Just as important was the fact that the British entrepreneurs had more money. Both in Turkey and in Central Asia, they could sell goods at 'giveaway' prices (according to Russian sources, even at a loss), provided they won a commanding position in the market. Vingradov concludes:

The reason for the growing eclipse of Russian influence is to be found in the irresistible force of circumstances. Tsarism had nothing with which to counter British naval and financial might, or the varied range of Western industrial goods, or the attractiveness of bourgeois ideology to the Turkish reformers. It lost the battle without having put up a fight.[47]

Britain had no need to go to war with Russia in the 1830s, since it could achieve its goals by peaceful methods. But the conflict was not exhausted. British industry was desperately seeking new markets and fighting to retain existing ones, while the crises followed one after another. After the crisis of 1836 came the depression of 1841–42, which was succeeded by a short-lived upturn in 1843. Then in 1847 a new slump began.

It is obvious that under such conditions the struggle against Russian protectionism became one of the most important foreign policy tasks which London faced. British diplomats repeatedly called on St Petersburg to review its customs tariffs. Prussia, too, sought a lowering of Russian customs duties, with Berlin enjoying more success than London. The Liberal-Whigs headed by Viscount Palmerston had traditionally sought to collaborate with Russia, but they were unable to win the required concessions from St Petersburg. The customs tariff of 1841 did not improve access to the Russian market, and Britain immediately began seeking its abolition. The agreement of 1842 ensured both countries most favoured nation status in their reciprocal trade, but did not satisfy London.[48] Russia continued to defend its industry through protectionist measures, while Britain campaigned against these provisions. Soon after the signing of the agreement, the British Conservative Prime Minister, Robert Peel, held a very informative discussion with the Russian envoy, F.I. Brunnov. If we are to believe the report which the diplomat sent to the minister K.N. Nesselrode in St Petersburg, the British leader lectured his interlocutor on the evils of industry. Peel argued that

Russia was destined by nature itself to be an agricultural country, not a manufacturing one. Russia should have factories, but it does not follow that it should summon them into life artificially, through the permanent protection of Russian industry.[49]

After this, the Prime Minister set about complaining of the ingratitude of British entrepreneurs, who never appreciated the concern the government showed for them.

The efforts of British diplomacy yielded at least a partial result in the form of a lowering of customs duties in 1846, but this could not satisfy British industrial capital, which had encountered another crisis of overproduction. Tariffs were again lowered in 1850, but once more, London was not satisfied. British textiles were meeting with growing competition in the Russian market, and prices were falling. In such conditions, even reduced tariffs were a relatively heavy burden for British industrialists.

For its part, the government in St Petersburg was prepared to reduce tariffs only gradually, keeping imports, in the words of contemporaries, 'within the bounds required by the condition of Russian factories'.[50] On the whole, this approach was relatively effective. The government defended national manufacturers, but did not let them rest on their laurels. This was especially true in the case of the textile industry, which was involved in fierce competition with its British counterpart. 'The reduced profits of the cotton textile factories in connection with the tariffs of 1850', a Soviet scholar notes, 'would force them to step up their activity in Eastern markets.'[51] Not surprisingly, this approach aroused little joy in London. Not long before the Crimean War, Brunnov informed St Petersburg that Britain would even reconcile itself to a Russian conquest of Turkey, 'were it not afraid of Russian tariff'.[52]

THE REPEAL OF THE CORN LAWS

During the 1830s a struggle was unfolding in British society whose outcome would do much to decide the next shift in the course of Russian history. This struggle was between supporters and opponents of the Corn Laws. These laws had been adopted in 1815, when the Tory Party was in power and was steadfastly defending the interests of landowners. In its efforts to protect British agriculture, parliament introduced high customs duties which restricted imports of foreign grain to the United Kingdom. In essence, this move represented a compromise. The Corn Laws were in no sense a ban on imports; Britain's rapidly developing economy could no longer have got by without foreign foodstuffs. The resulting price levels, however, left space on the market for both importers and local producers.

This situation changed radially in the 1830s. One after another, the countries of continental Europe were setting out on the road of industrial revolution. British goods were subject to increasing competition. Industrial crises were affecting output. Entrepreneurs were trying to reduce their costs, while the need for imported food supplies was growing as urbanisation proceeded.

The only way that British industrialists had of cutting wages, or at least of restraining their growth, without provoking massive resistance from workers was through the abolition of protectionist tariffs. During the industrial crisis of 1836–37, tariffs had been reduced, and in 1846 they were finally abolished. The repeal of the Navigation Acts followed in 1849 and 1850. From now on, the interests of industry would be of more importance to Britain than maintaining a commercial monopoly. Capitalism was entering a new era.

For Russia, the repeal of the Corn Laws and the triumph of the 'free trade system' meant the possibility of dramatically increasing exports. The expectations of the economists of the 'free trade school', which had prophesied that a fall in prices would follow swiftly on the abolition of protectionist tariffs, were not borne out. Agriculture depended not only on the market, but also on the weather. The crop failure of 1847 in Western Europe was an unprecedented stroke of good fortune for Russian landowners. Prices and the volume of sales rose simultaneously. Twenty years of stagnation were replaced by rapid growth. The granaries of the Russian landowners contained large quantities of grain, which they had not been able to sell for years. At a stroke, 10.5 million *chetverti* of grain flooded onto the world market. In the late 1840s and early 1850s, the share of Russia's exports represented by grain almost doubled. Referring to statistical data, Marx during the Crimean War argued that Britain's dependence on Russian grain had been greatly overestimated. However, he was misled by the imprecision of the documents, which defined the place of origin of the grain not as the country where it was grown, but as the one where it was loaded onto a ship. In other words, Russian grain loaded in Königsberg or Amsterdam for shipment to Britain changed its nationality.

Between the 1820s and the early 1860s, prices on the Berlin grain exchange rose by 74 per cent for wheat and by 90 per cent for rye. In 1838, 20 million *pudy* of wheat were exported from Russia; the corresponding figure in 1851 was 22 million, and in 1853, no less than 64.5 million.[53] World demand for grain was so strong that even rye, which in Russia was considered 'peasants' grain', and which was grown for the peasants' own use or for the local market, was readily sold abroad. As the export trade developed, grain prices rose within Russia as well. The 'golden rain' that was pouring down on the country opened up new opportunities for the development of industry. Russia had already begun importing industrial equipment in previous decades, but now machinery imports took on a massive character, with equipment coming not just from Britain, but also from France and Belgium. All the signs were present of an incipient industrial revolution. Import substitution was taking place; instead of importing manufactured items, Russians were beginning to buy equipment, and to set up production locally.

At the same time, competition on the world market was also growing dramatically. In 1854 the official journal of the Interior Ministry stated that 'competition for Russian ports, and especially for those in the south' had 'intensified to an extraordinary degree'.[54] The international division of labour was changing once again. The industrial revolution was beginning to make an impact on agriculture. For producers in the 'centre', the possibility had now arisen of producing, at low prices, goods which in the past had been obtained more cheaply from the 'periphery'. The list of grain-exporting countries began growing quickly. The Danube principalities, Egypt and the US were now shipping grain abroad; soon they would be joined by Canada and Argentina. Pokrovsky writes:

Russia's place in the European grain market was contested by a whole series of bourgeois countries, both European and non-European, and the rivalry with them was leading to an inescapable conclusion: the necessity of making the shift to bourgeois relations within Russia itself.[55]

10
The Crimean War and the World System

The Crimean War resulted from an attempt by the Russian empire to alter its place in the world system. With the aid of an expansionist foreign policy and military conquests, Nicholas I sought to do what the Decembrists had tried to achieve with the help of political and social reforms. This expansionist strategy was implemented, however, against a background of internal reaction that doomed the country to failure. Conservative regimes are typified by attempts to solve internal problems through actions in the external field. Meanwhile, the government in St Petersburg felt extremely confident in matters of international politics. Since 1812, Russia had been considered beyond question the major military power in Europe, and the ruling elites in the West, with an interest in employing the 'Russian gendarme' against the revolutionary movement on the continent, backed these ambitions of the tsar in every conceivable way. Nicholas's government did not want war with Britain and France, but when it became clear that his plans to partition Turkey were encountering firm resistance from these countries, it was decided in St Petersburg that Russia had quite enough military strength to cope with this problem as well. In any case, the Russian authorities did not believe that Britain and France would mount serious military actions on land.

In hindsight, the defeat of Russia in the Crimean War was inevitable; the two most advanced countries of Europe were bound to prevail over a backward empire. The government of Nicholas I, however, reasoned differently. Russia had been preparing for war since the 1830s. The navy had been expanded, and fortresses had been rebuilt. In 1812 and 1815, Russia had managed to defeat France, an incomparably more developed country. Why could Russia not win a conflict with Britain as well? It was no accident that Nicholas, in his correspondence with his adversaries, constantly reminded them of 1812. Moreover, a land war was anticipated only with the Turks, who were not expected to present any special difficulties.

Unfortunately, the problem for Russia in 1853 turned out not to be backwardness as such, but the industrial revolution that was unfolding at the other end of Europe. The invention in the 1840s of screw propulsion for steamships brought about a naval revolution that rendered worthless all the previous efforts by St Petersburg to strengthen its fleet. Russia was not in any condition to build a completely new navy and bring it into operation. Nor was it prepared to re-equip its land forces with new-generation firearms. During the siege of Sebastopol the defenders suffered their worst losses not from the enemy artillery, but from rifle fire. Finally, Russia's lack of a developed railway network was a crucial factor in the war. The allied armies were able to reach Crimea unhindered by sea, but after penetrating to Sebastopol along appalling Russian roads, the tsar's forces were in a terrible state, having lost large numbers of men and horses along the way. Nicholas had been right to recall the experience of 1812; this time, however, it was not a foreign invasion that was brought undone by the vastness of Russia, but his own troops. 'Neither energy nor prudence was lacking', Pokrovsky writes.

What was lacking was technology. But the technology of a particular country is always determined by its level of economic development. The key to the disaster suffered by Russian foreign policy in the first half of the nineteenth century, and to this policy itself, has to be sought in the economy.[1]

THE GRAIN QUESTION

In analysing the reasons behind the Crimean War, Karl Marx noted that all the clashes between Russia and Turkey 'were in part the result of commercial competition between the provinces of southern Russia and the Danube principalities, as well as Bosnia, Serbia and Bulgaria, which traded along the Danube'.[2] It was not by chance that the latest conflict had begun with the occupation of the Danube principalities by Russian forces and their complete control over the mouth of the river. Nevertheless, the explanation offered by Marx is clearly inadequate. It is not merely that Nicholas's ambitions were far greater – he aimed to take control of Istanbul and of the Black Sea straits. Plans to capture Constantinople had, of course, been nurtured in St Petersburg from the time of Catherine the Great. Russia had already launched repeated incursions into Turkish territory, arousing disapproval in London and irritation in Paris. Even though St Petersburg never concealed its desire to partition the Ottoman 'mpire (the 'sick man of Europe'), Russian diplomacy was always perfectly aware that conquering Turkey was impossible without foreign help. As the authorities in St Petersburg drew up their plans, they therefore made genuine efforts to take into account the interests of Britain, and also of Austria and France, viewing these countries not so much as rivals but rather as potential partners in the partitioning of Turkey. An analogy was drawn with the dividing of Poland in the eighteenth century; there, the acts of partition had been carried out jointly with Prussia and Austria.

This time, Russia not only failed to win the support of its traditional allies, the Austrians and British, but also encountered growing resistance from them. Quite against its expectations, the Russia of Nicholas I found itself in conflict with all of Europe. The narrowness of the internal Russian market was a decisive obstacle to the growth of industry, an obstacle for which no degree of protectionism could compensate. Russian protectionism, however, was by now arousing the irritation not just of Britain, but also of other European countries which had set out on the road of the industrial revolution. Prussia had long complained of St Petersburg's customs policies. Austria was unnerved by the Russian efforts to assert control over the Danube principalities, and consequently over the Danube trade as well. France had followed the Dutch road, and by the mid nineteenth century had been transformed from the main rival of Britain to its junior partner.

One of the results of the industrial revolution in France had been the development of modern transport, on both land and sea. French capital had found a highly effective form of symbiosis with its British counterpart. British firms produced goods for the world market; French entrepreneurs took charge of supplying these goods to the consumers, while also providing financial services. Railway construction, merchant shipping and bank credits became the main specialties of French capital. As the industrial revolution developed, the British elite was increasingly less alarmed by the competition it encountered from foreign merchant navies. Now, it no longer mattered whose ships transported the raw materials and finished products; the main thing was that export markets should be guaranteed.

ECONOMIC CRISIS

Why, then, did this situation lead to a major war precisely in 1853? Tensions between Britain and Russia over the 'Eastern question' had begun as early as the 1830s, but somehow everything had been settled. This time, a political crisis broke out suddenly and developed apace.

As Marx observed, 1853 was the last pre-crisis year, a time of 'feverish prosperity' when the 'overheating' of the economy in Europe and America was unmistakable. 'In other words, the economic cycle had again reached the point where overproduction and excessive speculation are replaced by crisis.'[3] Also in 1853, world grain prices reached a peak. By this time, there were clear signs of a crisis of overproduction.

Marx noted ironically that in the first half of 1853, against the background of a still-continuing industrial expansion, the 'Eastern question' was something like a 'remote little cloud' on the horizon.[4] But by the end of the year, when industry had become fully aware of the impending difficulties, the disagreements between Britain and Russia suddenly took on the form of an irreconcilable conflict.

As Kirchner observes, Russia from the 1840s was experiencing the same economic cycles as all the other countries that were part of the world system. Even earlier, economic booms and busts in the West had of course impacted directly on life in Russia. Now, however, this link was becoming far stronger. The fluctuations of grain prices on the internal market, for example, now 'corresponded to those in the West'.[5] To the competition from the Danube principalities, Moldavia and Wallachia, there was now added the increase in grain exports from other countries, including even Egypt. In the market for wheat, this competition appeared so threatening that, as an official St Petersburg journal put it, 'the Russian heart was gripped with unwitting fear'.[6]

As the crisis drew near, the nervousness and aggressiveness of the main players increased, not only in the economic field but in politics as well. For both Russia and Britain, a war seemed, unexpectedly, the simplest way of resolving all the problems. The St Petersburg authorities decided to make use of the favourable situation to deal with Russia's competitors on the Danube, imposing Russian control over the main flows of grain onto the market, and if the war were a success, taking control of the straits as well. What Nicholas's government did not understand was that the impending crisis had made London even less open to persuasion than usual. For the Russian authorities, the harsh response of the British to the 'Eastern question' thus came as a complete surprise.

The contradictory nature of British policy with regard to Russia, something that was already evident in the time of Ivan the Terrible, emerged with particular acuteness in the 1850s. As the government in St Petersburg prepared for another war with Turkey, it expected that the British would at least remain neutral, even if they did not provide active support. Secret talks on the partitioning of the Ottoman empire were conducted between British and Russian diplomats. Once again, however, the interests of British capital in Russia came into conflict with the interests of British capital in neighbouring countries – in this case, those of the Near East. London would have liked an expansion of Russian grain exports, but not at the cost of effectively destroying Turkey. Because St Petersburg could no longer make concessions, the British government was forced to choose. The choice turned out to be in favour of Turkey; London's interests in the Middle East were a higher priority.

Turkey in 1851 and 1852 purchased far more British goods than Russia, though the latter was both richer and more populous. The historian E.V. Tarle notes that

The more Russia's protective tariff policy restricted British sales in Russia, the more insistent the desire became in the British commercial world to be done with the need to pay an annual 'tribute in gold' to the Russian imperial treasury, to the Russian landowning class and to the Russian export merchants for grain, and British businessmen naturally showed an ever greater inclination to expand their operations in the two grain-producing provinces – Moldavia and Wallachia – that were still numbered among the domains of the sultan.[7]

Turkey was also of exceptional importance for the transit of British goods to Persia. An expansion of the tsar's possessions threatened to extend the control of the Russian customs service to this route as well. From the point of view of the elites in Victorian Britain, Turkey in this period was a country of free trade, open to British goods and influence. Russia was a protectionist country. In other words, the loss of the Russian market if there were a war would, of course, be a misfortune, but because of Russian protectionism the British risked losing this market even without a war. Meanwhile, to retreat on the 'Eastern question' meant losing both Russia and Turkey. Such was the reasoning in London. The government in St Petersburg was confident in turn that the old commercial ties between the two countries were of such scope and importance that the British would not go to war in any circumstances, but would prefer to negotiate.

While the war became a disaster for St Petersburg from the very moment the British and French entered into it, for the Western countries the Eastern War served initially as a way to postpone the onset of the crisis. As Marx noted:

Particular sectors of industry, such, for example, as the production of leather, iron and woollen goods, and also shipbuilding, received direct support thanks to the demand occasioned by the war. For a short time, the fear aroused by the declaration of war after forty years of peace paralysed speculation. Thanks to the loans concluded by various European states in connection with the war, interest rates were so high as to provide an obstacle to the excessive development of industrial production, and thus delayed the crisis.[8]

According to a Soviet historian,

The Crimean War showed the falseness of many diplomatic forecasts on both sides concerning the role of the economic factor in British-Russian relations. The fact that economic ties were at stake did not prevent the conflict, but it proved stronger than the inclination to do without trade with Russia, and to impose a full economic blockade.[9]

It was quite obvious that Victorian Britain had no intention of waging a serious war on tsarist Russia. This infuriated radical nineteenth-century writers who, like Marx, saw the Russian empire as the main prop supporting European reaction. Marx therefore consistently sought to expose the approach which the cabinet in London was taking to the Crimean conflict, showing that the British empire was merely making a show of waging war, and had no serious desire to crush the power of the tsar's army. This, of course, was correct; the British government was not in any way aiming at a comprehensive rout of the Russian forces. Still less was it intent on bringing about the collapse of tsarism and the abolition of serfdom.

From the British viewpoint, the Russian government was clearly not going to be content with Russia's poor standing in the world system at that point in time. Consequently, it had to be taught a lesson. To this end, a limited contingent of British troops was sent to Crimea. The appearance of British squadrons in the Baltic and off the Solovetsky Islands, and even an ill-fated landing on Kamchatka, served the same purpose. The British empire was not about to go to war in the Far East or in the Baltic; it was simply demonstrating its power and its readiness to inflict blows in the most unexpected places. As Pokrovsky notes, this tactic proved extremely effective. The Russian government was forced to disperse its forces across an enormous territory, without knowing where the main blow would fall. To a considerable degree, meanwhile, the landing in Crimea was a surprise for the Russian government, which had been distracted by the operations of the allies in other regions.

Military actions were not mounted in the sole place where Russian and British possessions shared a common border – in Alaska. This territory, then known as Russian America, was practically undefended in military respects, but no invasion took place. Instead, an agreement was concluded between the Russian-American Company and the British Hudson Bay Company under which Alaska and the western part of Canada were declared neutral territories for the duration of the war. The events of the Crimean War, however, showed beyond doubt that Russia was incapable of defending its American possessions, and prepared the way for the transfer of these regions to the United States. It was during the period of the Crimean campaign that the idea of buying Alaska began to be discussed in the US. At first, St Petersburg refused, especially since there was no direct British threat to the territory. Nevertheless, the first step had been taken, and some time later Russian America ceased to exist.

The fighting in Crimea was extremely fierce, but neither Russian interests nor those of the allies would have been served by a full-scale war. Russia's foreign trade was conducted on foreign vessels, primarily British ones. The Crimean War put this system in jeopardy. As became clear, Britain as well as Russia suffered from the halting of trade. British industrialists had an interest in maintaining uninterrupted supplies of raw materials and foodstuffs, irrespective of how events turned out in the East. In an address to parliament, J. Ricardo, the son of the distinguished economist, warned that production would otherwise suffer serious damage. The year 1853 saw record purchases of Russian goods by British entrepreneurs, who were clearly anxious to build up reserves of indispensable raw materials in case of war. Champions of free trade argued for the preserving of ties to Russia whatever the circumstances. A solution was found when the British cabinet recognised the right of neutral ships to transport goods from Russia during wartime. This was an unprecedented step, which ran counter to all previous British practice.[10] The United States offered its services as an intermediary. The problem was that the US in the 1850s did not possess a sizeable merchant fleet that could have made up for the ending of direct trade between the 'granary of Europe' and the 'workshop of the world'. In fact, the scale of Russian-American trade during the war even diminished. Exports of Russian goods across the land border with Prussia increased, however, and from Prussia they went by land to Western Europe. While shipping Russian goods from the Prussian port of Memel, the Americans at the same time offered their ships to the British and French for the transporting of troops, the evacuation of wounded, the supplying of munitions, and so forth.

In the United States itself, the greatest sympathy for Russia was felt, understandably, by Southerners. The plantation-owning aristocrats and serf-holding landowners were united by something akin to class solidarity. In St Petersburg, it was thought that the conservative slave-owning South, rather than the democratic industrial North, was an ally in the conflict with liberal Britain. In reality, the situation was not so simple. Like the serf-holding agriculture of Russia, the plantation economy of the American South was far more bound up with British capital than the North, and was far more oriented to the world market. By contrast, the industrial North sought with the aid of protectionism to shut itself off from British goods, and it was from this that the strength arose that in time would allow the United States to overtake Britain as the leading power in the world capitalist system. The Crimean War represented one of the first moves in this direction, though not of course a decisive one. As Marx observed, in the US the war stimulated 'an unprecedented rise in shipbuilding and maritime trade, and ensured markets for several types of raw materials which earlier had been supplied mainly or exclusively by Russia'.[11] Particular benefits were enjoyed by traders in grain (also principally Northerners), who made up for the lack of Russian grain on British markets. It is hardly surprising that in the US, the news of peace between Britain and Russia was received, to use the words of a Russian diplomat, 'not without a certain displeasure'.[12] For many Americans, the ending of the war meant the end of high commercial profits.

Prussian entrepreneurs also grew fat on the Crimean War, transporting Russian raw materials and foodstuffs by land. Flax, hemp, tallow and other goods passed through Prussia on their way to Britain. During the war the tsar's government continued to float its loans on the European money markets, where it carried on its dealings alongside Prussian, British and French finance capital. Russia's pre-war loans were still quoted freely on the London securities exchange. The Russian government in turn continued to service the old loans it had obtained from its enemies. It is understandable that St Petersburg officials should have remarked in astonishment that the British trade blockade existed 'only on paper'.[13]

OUTCOMES OF THE WAR

The main negative result of the Eastern War for the tsar's government was the loss of its fortresses and naval fleet in the Black Sea. For the Western allies, the main positive outcome was the ending of Russian industrial protectionism – the opening of the Russian market, and free access to the markets of the Near East. It is not surprising that the later efforts of Russian diplomacy, aimed at doing away with the negative consequences of the Peace of Paris, were brilliantly successful. The credit here was due not to the exceptional talents of Prince Alexander Gorchakov, who headed the Russian diplomatic service after the Crimean War, but to the fact that in the 1860s and 1870s neither Britain nor France saw Russia as a serious threat to their economic interests, even though problems remained in their relations with St Petersburg. Neither the rebuilding of the Black Sea fleet nor even a new conflict between Russia and Turkey changed anything in this respect.

Britain's victory in the Crimean War was sealed not only by the Peace of Paris, but also by the new Russian trade tariffs that came into force in 1858. Russia finally accepted the 'free trade system'. The next British-Russian trade agreement was drawn up in the same spirit, and the drafting of the tariff provisions began immediately after peace was concluded. By February 1857 a draft had been prepared that accorded fully with the recommendations for the new Tsar Alexander II that the London *Times* and *Economist* had publicly set out on their pages. Nor did the authorities in St Petersburg conceal the fact that the tariff was meant to 'satisfy, as far as possible, the numerous requirements in this area both of our own trading community and of foreign governments'.[14]

Commercial relations with the West again began developing rapidly. Russia's foreign trade turnover quickly came to exceed the pre-war level. Crop failures in Europe followed one upon the other; grain prices rose, and along with them, Russian grain exports. Among European exporters to the British market, Russia immediately assumed first place; among all the sources of British imports,

Russia was second only to the United States. British exports to Russia also expanded rapidly. In 1867 they reached £4 million, and in 1873, £9 million.[15]

French banks and experts came to Russia along with the railway loans. The former enemies began collaborating in the very area whose weak development had played such a fateful role for Russia during the war. 'Beneath the walls of Sevastopol,' Pokrovsky concludes, 'French capitalism had won for itself a new field of expansion.'[16]

11
The Age of Reforms

The defeat in the Crimean War was viewed by Russian society, including the ruling groups themselves, as proof of the country's hopeless backwardness. For the Russian state, the army had always been not just a means to an end, but something close to an end in itself. During centuries of struggle against invasions from East and West, a state tradition had taken hold according to which the viability and authority of the ruling apparatus was linked intimately to its military might. Nowhere was backwardness felt so painfully by the government itself as in the military field. The Russian military machine was the most important part of the state organism, and this conviction was shared by both the popular masses and the ruling class. The people were ready to accept the existing state system as necessary and inevitable, for all its obvious injustice, so long as this system could ensure the battle-readiness of the army. The ruling elites in turn sought constantly to justify their rule through genuine or imaginary military successes. The defeat of the Swedish army at Poltava, and the victory over Charles XII in the Northern War, signified the irreversible triumph of the Petrine system not only in the international arena, but also, most importantly, within the country. From this time on, Peter's reforms, despite their appalling cruelty and obvious anti-popular nature, were vindicated so far as the masses were concerned. Under Catherine II the capture of Crimea and the asserting of Russian dominance over the Black Sea were seen as proof of the success of modernisation, though the enemy by this time was different; Peter had waged war against the outstanding general Charles XII, who headed one of the best armies in Europe, while Catherine had fought the backward and declining Turkey. The triumph over Napoleon in 1812–14 was viewed in the same positive fashion as Catherine's victories.

To be defeated on the field of battle in Russia had always been an ideological catastrophe. In the eyes of the lower social orders – and of the ruling layer itself – the state lost its main justification, the reason for its existence. A lost battle or catastrophic losses might have been explained, but to lose a war, even the most minor one and even in a remote and useless borderland, created serious tensions in society.

Nevertheless, to explain the abolition of serfdom and subsequent reforms as the results of a lost war, as many Russian historians have done, is to confuse the instigation with the cause. The defeat at Sebastopol created an exceptionally favourable set of conditions in society for political and social reforms, but these reforms themselves were the outcome of far deeper processes taking place not only in Russia, but also in the world at large.

THE SECOND INDUSTRIAL REVOLUTION

The world economic crisis that had been postponed by tbe Crimean War broke out immediately after the war ended. It began in America, and from there spread to Western Europe and Russia. In a period of crises, Russia felt the disadvantages of its peripheral status in the world system with particular acuteness. 'As our statistics show,' Strumilin writes, 'every world crisis brought drastic reductions in the overall value of commodity exchange with Russia, due to the lowering of effective demand and prices.'[1] For the government in St Petersburg, the downturn of 1857–58 exacerbated the problems associated with the defeat in the Crimean War. This damage was partly made up by continuing rises in world grain prices. On the global scale, however, it signified the beginning of important changes from which Russia could not remain isolated.

The British historian Willie Thompson describes the 1850s as the time of 'the second industrial revolution'.[2] Unlike the first industrial revolution, which had begun in Britain and had made it the 'workshop of the world', the new industrial revolution encompassed and in one way or another affected the entire world economic system, giving rise not only to new technologies, but also to radical changes in the political geography of the planet. Capitalism was becoming global not only as a unified commercial form of organisation, but also as a productive, social, cultural and ideological system.

Technological innovation affected both existing technologies, and more importantly, produced an entire new range. Steam engines and steel production methods were revolutionised, as were certain textile manufacturing processes. Industrial chemistry entered a new era. Even more significant, however, was the emergence of new power sources in the form of the petrol engine and electricity with its multitude of possible applications; communications in a variety of dimensions from telephones and the sound phonograph to the motor vehicle and cinematography.[3]

The demand for raw materials and resources for growing and changing industries ensured new international conflicts. The world order which had seemed to be firmly established, which was reinforced by the Holy Alliance of Russia, Prussia and Austria and which had withstood the revolutions of 1848 and 1849, was vanishing into the past. The allies of the recent past were becoming adversaries.

Industrialisation was becoming a global process, and at the same time the crises of overproduction were becoming increasingly profound. These developments entered economic history as the 'great Victorian depression', which, as Thompson notes, 'in spite of its name did not affect Britain only'.[4]

The Crimean War had shown that Russia could not succeed in conquering foreign markets. It was necessary to expand the internal market. The abolition of serfdom in Russia was seen by 'enlightened society' as an indispensable step toward overcoming technical and social backwardness. This step, however, was wonderfully attuned to the worldwide processes occurring at this time.

At the beginning of the 1860s neither slavery in America nor serfdom in Russia could be called productive systems in decline. In the Russian empire, another rise in world grain prices had brought a new surge of reforming moods to the urban nobility. In the slave-owning states of America, things were also going well: 'The southern economy was booming, with per capita production actually increasing at a slightly faster pace than in the industrializing North.'[5] The profitability of Russian serf-holding estates also remained high, and labour productivity was continuing to rise.[6] In other words, emancipation was not the result of an internal crisis of the landowner-planter economy, but a consequence of pressures on it from outside. Industry had an acute need for new markets, for labour power and for consumers. On both the national and international scale the capitalist economy was, to use Kondratyev's term, entering a period of reconstruction.

Following on the changes in the world economy during the 1860s, a restructuring of international politics was also beginning. New powers were making their presence felt. Everywhere, social and political reforms were beginning. Germany was being united under the power of Prussia, which in turn was modernising rapidly. Italy was being unified as well. Austria-Hungary was being transformed into a federative state on the basis of a compromise reached between the Hungarian elites and the court in Vienna. In Japan the Meiji revolution was under way, and a rapid development of capitalism was beginning. In the US, the Civil War had broken out; it would end with the emancipation of the slaves. In Russia, serfdom was being abolished.

All this took place in the course of a single decade. In the 1870s the world economic depression reached its nadir, and was overcome with the help of a new burst of colonial expansion. The Western European powers set about conquering Africa, and Russia seized Central Asia.

The world system was changing. Parts of the periphery were being integrated, and were swallowed by the centre, while other parts were being subjected to increasingly ruthless colonial exploitation. It could be said that in the 1860s and 1870s both centre and periphery expanded. The gap between Britain and other countries of the centre shrank dramatically, but by contrast, the gap between the centre and periphery grew apace. Meanwhile, countries and regions that earlier had not been part of the world system, or which had had contact with it only episodically, were drawn into it.

From the point of view of Russian history, the key question is why tsarist Russia, which had actively participated in this process, ultimately met with defeat, while Germany, the US and Japan, which entered the list of great powers only later, succeeded in modernising.

RUSSIA IN THE GLOBAL RECONSTRUCTION

If we compare Russia with Germany and the US, it can readily be seen that in the 1860s and 1870s the 'backward', 'peripheral' regions of both countries were successfully integrated into a unified political and economic space, becoming part of the centre. In Russia, by contrast, the underdeveloped 'backwoods' acted as a brake on modernisation. The country seemed too big, too heavy to lift, too stagnant. In reality, the problem was not Russia's 'limitless expanses', but the level of development of industrial capitalism.

By the time their modernisation began, both Germany and the US possessed a 'critical mass' of industrial capital, which was also the main motivating force of the changes that were occurring. It was in the interests of industrial capital that the model of development was formulated. Colonial and industrial expansion ensured the advance of the system to new frontiers; the centre seized hold of a new periphery in place of the integrated one, and it was this process that yielded the resources needed for integration. Latin America was taken over by North American capital, while German colonies were founded in Africa. All this occurred together with, and to some degree as a result of, the modernisation of the American South and of Germany east of the Elbe. Russia, however, did not possess a developed industrial capitalism. The two-centuries-old rule of commercial capital was not shaken by revolutions.

According to Pokrovsky, the main preconditions for the peasant reform of 1861 were rapid price rises on the world grain market, accompanied by the steady growth of Russian grain exports. 'The peasant "liberation" was a direct response to the high grain prices that had prevailed in Western Europe since the 1840s.'[7] This trend was evident before the outbreak of the Crimean War, and continued after it ended. The growth of prices persisted even in the context of the crisis of industry that had engulfed Europe. To a certain extent it was also due to the Crimean War, which destabilised the Black Sea trade zone from which the West obtained a significant proportion of its grain. 'In Russia's overall exports on the eve of the abolition of serfdom,' a Soviet historian reports, 'the share made up by grain exceeded 35 per cent, and represented around a fifth of the overall volume of grain that was traded.'[8]

It is noteworthy that once the landowners had money, their indebtedness did not diminish. But if their funds had earlier been spent on consumption, on maintaining 'a way of life worthy of nobles', money now began to be invested in agriculture. Serf-holding estates were starting to take on the features of normal bourgeois enterprises. The more the landowners needed money, the greater became their interest in reform – but in the kind of reform that would force the peasants to buy their own land and, in the process, to finance the development of landowner agriculture. In essence, what was involved was transferring the debts of the landowners to the peasants. Reform was needed in order to help the landowners turn themselves into bourgeois. The goal of reform, Pokrovsky concludes, was 'not in any sense to create a free and independent peasantry, but to replace bonded labour with hired labour, and the enserfed peasant with the paid farm-hand'.[9] The more bourgeois the landowner became, the less chance the peasant had of turning into a farmer. 'The transformation of the landed estate into a capitalist enterprise was thus purchased at the cost of delaying bourgeois development in the countryside.'[10]

In reality, what resulted was not simply a delay, but a qualitatively different type of development, radically different from that in the West. In order to participate in the new economic relations, it was not necessary to refashion the whole rural system in the spirit of capitalism. Moreover, reconstructing Russia in this way would have been too costly both for Russian capital, and for the world system. Russian agrarian capitalism remained peripheral, and unmistakably backward. But it was this backwardness that provided its main competitive advantage on the world market, guaranteeing cheap products and simple management.

AGRARIAN CAPITALISM

While the British and French armies defeated their Russian counterparts in the Crimean War, Russian industrial capitalism was defeated by agrarian capitalism. For Russian industrial capital the new customs tariffs were an unquestionable defeat, for which the new opportunities associated with the emancipation of the peasants and the building of railways were only partial compensation. The rapid growth recorded by industry in the 1830s and 1840s was replaced by stagnation.

The industrial depression of 1857 affected Russia even more than the countries of the West. Strumilin explains this on the basis that in Russia the world crisis of overproduction coincided with 'a crisis of the entire system of serf agriculture'.[11] But as we see from the agricultural statistics, the position of landowner agriculture at this time was improving. More likely, we are confronted here with a particular case of a general rule of the capitalist market: in times of crisis, suppliers of raw materials suffer more than sellers of finished products, peripheral countries more than those of the centre, and weak economies more than strong ones. In 1857, as now, the greatest losses from the crisis were borne by Russian suppliers of industrial raw materials to Western markets. Meanwhile, the shift to the 'free trade system' in the heat of the crisis dealt industry a heavy blow.

The emancipation of the peasants in 1861 did not have a stimulating effect on industry. In 'liberated' Russia, Pokrovsky states, industry developed more slowly than at the height of serfdom under Nicholas I.[12] The 'era of stagnation' under Nicholas had seen industry and culture develop rapidly (it is enough to recall Pushkin, Belinsky, Gogol and Herzen), while the succeeding 'era of great reforms' was marked by the exceedingly slow growth of industry, by the rule of political mediocrities, and by far less impressive results for Russian culture.[13] The only sector of industry that developed impressively during the 1860s was railway construction. For this activity the free trade tariffs were unquestionably a boon, since they expedited the importing of machines and metals from abroad. A significant proportion of the machinery that was imported to meet state and private orders was brought in duty-free.

The building of the railways, Pokrovsky writes, 'provided the most powerful impulse to the development of capitalism that Russia experienced throughout the entire nineteenth century'.[14] Without this, a new wave of industrialisation and modernisation would have been unthinkable; without railways, the traditional commercial capitalism and the agrarian capitalism of the landowners could not have developed. Not least, the building of railways aided integration into the world economy. Railways were needed for the export of grain, and there was no question of waiting until Russian industrialists accumulated the necessary capital; the world market demanded grain promptly. Western credits played an important role in the peasant reform, but in the railway programme of the 1860s, their role was simply crucial.

The 'railway fever' was accompanied by a 'chartering fever' in the banking sector. Between 1868 and 1873, 26 banks were founded (for purposes of comparison, the overall number of banks in Russia reached just 34 by 1894). With a shortage of funds for financing major construction projects, the Russian banks were forced to turn to the West for credit, and later to sell their shares on the Berlin and Paris markets.

Taking part in the building of railways were not only foreign financiers, but also Russian aristocrats. In the lists of company founders we find some of the country's most distinguished names. It was easier for nobles than for ill-educated provincial merchants to forge relationships with foreigners, and to obtain support in St Petersburg for projects. As the railways failed to yield the expected profits, they were gradually transferred to the hands of the state. The main basis for agrarian capitalism in the second half of the nineteenth century was not the 'national bourgeoisie', but the nobility and its government, in alliance with foreign capital.

THE PEASANT QUESTION

The main question agitating the St Petersburg government and, thanks to *glasnost*, debated heatedly in the press, was not whether to free the peasants, but how to free them – with land, or without. Later, V.I. Lenin was to sum up the alternatives before Russian society as a choice between the 'Prussian' and the 'American' roads to the development of capitalism in agriculture. The 'Prussian road' foresaw the existence of a free but landless peasantry. With all the land remaining in the hands of the landowners, the better-off peasants would be transformed into tenants, while the poor peasants would be turned into hired workers, becoming farm-hands or moving to the towns and filling the ranks of the industrial proletariat. According to this strategy, the country would receive a large quantity of labour power for capitalist production, both in the towns and in the countryside. The landowning junkers would transform their estates into large agrarian enterprises which would produce goods for the market and form a natural continuum with the rapidly growing urban factories. This model of development allowed the rapid growth of Germany's economic capacity in the 1880s.

The 'American road', by contrast, proposed the complete abolition of the system of landed estates (in North America, of course, there had been nothing to abolish, since feudal relations had never existed there). Peasant households on free land would then, it was supposed, turn into highly productive family farms, competing among themselves and creating the basis for the development of capitalism in the countryside. As small farms would gradually fall into ruin, the flow of labour power to the cities would be assured, along with the growth of productivity in the agrarian sector of the economy. Meanwhile, the enrichment of the rural elite would create a stable demand for industrial goods.

In Lenin's view, Russia chose the 'Prussian road', but the truth was that the tsar's government was unable or unwilling to follow the German example. Forced to choose between 'emancipation without land' and the dividing up of the landowners' estates, the government chose something in between. The peasants received land, but their allotments were minuscule. Carrying on efficient, independent commodity production on this basis was impossible. Worse still, the peasants were obliged to pay for the land they received, or to work on the landowner's estate.

Implementing the Prussian model required the presence of a relatively strong urban bourgeoisie, able to quickly employ the mass of labour power that had been freed up, and to collaborate in modernising the landowners' estates. By the second half of the nineteenth century the German bourgeoisie already had a long history, and possessed substantial capital and entrepreneurial experience. Nothing comparable existed in Russia. Under Russian conditions, the 'Prussian road' could lead to nothing except mass unemployment and a rapid increase in social tensions – to numerous revolts in both city and countryside, something which had no place in the plans of the reformers. Meanwhile, the 'American road' undermined the position of the landowners, that is, of the very class on which the Russian state had traditionally rested. Since there was no strong bourgeoisie in Russia, the authorities simply had no one else to base themselves on, even if the bureaucracy in St Petersburg had decided to break with the old privileged layers. The dividing up of the holdings of the landowners would have created a social vacuum, whose result would undoubtedly have been the crisis and collapse of the whole political system.[15]

Liberal and radical thinkers could argue as they might about the advantages of various Western models, without giving a thought to the consequences of implementing them. By contrast, the St Petersburg bureaucrats, who had little interest in theories and models, instinctively chose the solution that was least painful, and in its way most sensible. The result was that the country made another rapid advance – not, however, along a 'Prussian' or 'American' road, but pursuing its own Russian course. There was nothing particularly attractive about this line of march. The elements of capitalism in Russia were not simply – to use Lenin's expression – doomed to coexist with medieval, barbaric and 'Asiatic' structures and practices. They were directly linked to and intertwined with these structures and practices, together with which they had evolved. Even in 1912, Lenin was forced to speak of the 'predominantly serf form of present-day Russian agriculture'.[16] The autocratic-landowner state had an interest in the rise of urban capitalism, and aided this rise in every possible way. But the Russian capitalism that came into being in such circumstances differed strikingly from that of Western Europe. Its base of support in the countryside was neither the farmer nor a British- or Prussian-style landowner-entrepreneur. The Russian model of agrarian capitalism rested on the peasant communities and on landowners who had made little progress since the time of serfdom.

Studying the processes that were actually taking place in the Russian countryside, the noted Russian economist of the early twentieth century, A.V. Chayanov, found that from the point of view of bourgeois political economy, the peasants were behaving incorrectly in the marketplace. Statistics showed that in years of high grain prices the peasants reduced their deliveries to the market, while in years when prices were falling they suddenly poured still more grain onto the market. In terms of market logic such actions were completely ruinous, but despite this, peasant agriculture remained relatively stable. When the peasants sold grain, they were guided by a quite different logic. Unlike farmers, who produce goods exclusively for sale on the market, the peasants had traditionally sold their surplus grain in order to satisfy their needs. These needs changed little over time. Consequently, peasants in a 'good' year were in a position to sell less grain, leaving themselves with a reserve against hard times in the future. In a 'bad' year, the peasants had to sell more. Farmers work in order to accumulate capital and maximise their profit; the traditional peasant household, by contrast, restricted itself to meeting its own internal requirements. From this, Chayanov concluded that 'the structural peculiarities of peasant family agriculture force the peasants to reject the mode of action dictated by the usual formula for the calculation of capitalist profit'.[17]

The peasants could not remain outside the market, but to an important degree, the way in which they interacted with the market was not bourgeois. Unable to develop commodity production on a broad scale, the peasant households were oriented primarily toward supplying their own needs. For the landowners, meanwhile, exploiting dependent peasants on small allotments was clearly more profitable than developing capitalist agriculture. The result, Chayanov notes, was that throughout the period 1861–1917, capitalist production in the countryside not only failed to drive out other modes of operation but itself collapsed. The *kulaki,* the better-off peasants whom the Bolsheviks later viewed as a Russian version of the rural bourgeoisie, in fact had little in common with large-scale farmers in the West. To a significant degree, the *kulaki* prospered through usury, lending grain, equipment or money to their less-fortunate neighbours, and not through developing their own production.

In reality, the picture was, of course, far more complex than the interpretations provided by economists, whether of the liberal, Marxist or populist schools. Agrarian capitalism in post-reform Russia at times advanced, and at other times retreated. These rises and declines of bourgeois development in the countryside were linked intimately with the fluctuations of the world market. The state, with its interest in the timely payment of taxes, helped maintain the communal village structures that kept the peasants bound in a 'mutual guarantee'. The village preserved the patriarchal system. Hundreds of thousands of people who were unable to support themselves through agriculture were taken on as factory workers, but often retained their links to the village communities, as was still evident even in 1917 and 1918. Many – even those living in the cities – returned to the countryside to perform seasonal work. Because of this, there was almost no unemployment in Russia during crises of industry; when people lost their jobs, they set off for the countryside.

Projecting the experience of Western Europe onto Russian history, liberal economists in the late nineteenth century – and orthodox Marxists in the early twentieth century – expected rural entrepreneurship to develop out of the household of the peasant smallholder. These economists' knowledge of the processes unfolding in the countryside was extremely limited, and their understanding of the history of the West was equally scant. Western capitalism did, indeed, germinate in the countryside as well as in the towns. There is no question that bourgeois production arose out of petty commodity production, including that of peasant households. However, this took place in the specific circumstances of Western Europe in the fifteenth and sixteenth centuries. Both before and after this, smallholdings were able to exist for centuries without becoming bourgeois. In precisely similar fashion, the bourgeois system would have been impossible without primitive accumulation, which, as Marx stressed, presupposed the mass ruin of petty producers, the expropriation of the assets of traditional proprietors and the destruction of the old order. Petty producers everywhere desperately resisted this pressure from capital.

The distinguishing feature and, as it were, advantage of the peripheral economy was that capital could acquire significant resources for the local and world markets without destroying the accustomed order. This meant that there was no need to overcome the desperate resistance of small producers. However, it also meant that the accumulation of capital proceeded extremely slowly, and that capital itself became set in its early 'archaic' form.

MARKET DEPRESSION AND POLITICAL REACTION

By the 1860s the rapid growth of the world grain trade was slowing down, and in the 1880s the European grain market became saturated. Prices once again began to fall. In nineteenth-century Russian novels and in the late plays of Aleksandr Ostrovsky, the 1880s appear as a time when Russian capitalism was flourishing. This sense that the 'bourgeois ethic' had triumphed, however, had its roots in the fact that economic conditions were noticeably worse than earlier, and that as a result, behaviour had become more ruthless. This harshness that entered into people's relations signified not so much that Protestant rationality had finally been attained in Russia, as that money was simply lacking for traditional Russian sentiments. The late nineteenth-century writers who attributed the impoverishment of the nobility to the reform of 1861 were also quite mistaken. When the ruin of the 'nests of gentlefolk' became widespread in the 1880s, it was against the background of the agrarian crisis. The fluctuations of the world economy were directly reflected in the state of Russian society. According to calculations by Strumilin, the overall decline in trade between Russia and the West that resulted from the crises during the period between 1861 and 1908 amounted to 2 billion rubles.

This enormous blow to exports during the crisis years was mainly due to lower prices for grain, butter, eggs, flax, hides and other products of the Russian countryside. These billion-ruble sacrifices by the working people of Russia to the Moloch of world capitalism could not, of course, fail to affect the state of the domestic market. Selling a substantial proportion of its commodity production at a discount because of world crises, or unable to sell it at all, the Russian countryside in turn cut its demand for printed fabrics, sugar, kerosene, iron and other products of national industry. If we also recall the particularly direct dependency of Russian industry on imports of foreign machinery, cotton, dyes, and a whole series of chemical and other products, the mechanism through which global cycles affected the development of our industry will become clear.[18]

One of the key results of the peasant reform was an increase in the production of rye. Despite receiving no more than a highly conditional freedom, and tiny plots of land, the peasants became a problem for the development of the market. The Soviet scholar of the 1920s, P. Lyashchenko, wrote that after the reform of 1861 the growing economic importance of the peasant households did not bring about a sharp decline in commodity production, but saw a shift in the Russian countryside 'from such globally traded commodities as wheat to the Russian peasant product, rye'. This shift in turn constituted 'one of the main reasons for our agrarian crisis in the 1880s'.[19] At the beginning of the decade the 'peasant's grain' appeared to be showing its superiority over the 'landowner's grain', wheat. The price for wheat, which was more subject to the fluctuations of the world market, fell more quickly than that for rye; consequently, the initial phase of the agrarian crisis saw the relationship of forces in the countryside begin to change. The peasants grew stronger while the landowners fell into decline. The rental and purchase of estate lands by peasants became widespread.

Unfortunately, rye could be sold profitably on the world market only during a grain boom. Indeed, the trade in rye was declining even in good years. In 1850, 376,000 tons of wheat were exported, and in 1870, no less than 1,573,000 tons; for rye, the picture was quite the opposite, with 900,000 tons exported in 1850 and only 442,000 in 1870.[20] While the 'peasant's grain' responded only after a delay to the signals of the world market, it could not ignore these signals. The growth of the world grain trade in the mid nineteenth century was accompanied by increasing competition, but the demand in Europe was so great that there was room in the market for everyone. As demand stabilised, the competition grew more acute. By the 1870s the wheat produced by American farmers was beginning to supplant not only the wheat supplied to the European market by Russian landowners, but also the peasant's rye. The world market was also seeing an increasing role played by such 'new' countries as Argentina, Canada and Australia.

Another competitor for Russia on the grain market was British India. Russian economists in the 1870s complained that cheap Indian exports were 'proving a barrier in the major markets not only to us, but also to the Americans'.[21] Nevertheless, it was the United States that represented the main threat to Russian suppliers. The Americans were not only winning on the basis of prices. Russian experts noted that America was forcing Russian suppliers out because it possessed 'an incomparably better organised trade, an abundance of capital, and superb grain processing'.[22] Moreover, the ports of southern Russia at the time were notorious for fraud, with low-quality grain sold under the guise of the high-quality product. In sum, it was stated,

our wheat is considered better by nature than that of the Americans, but in recent years we have done everything to undermine its good reputation, while the Americans with a whole series of improvements have raised the quality of their grain to the point where on European markets it continually attracts a higher price than ours.[23]

By the period 1898–1902, Russia was supplying the world market with only a quarter to a third as much grain as the United States. Russia's less technically developed agriculture suffered more from crop failures. It was not simply that the American grain-producing states were in climatic zones far better suited to crop-raising than the Russian provinces that competed with them. Agriculture in the US was also expanding on a massive scale onto previously uncultivated territories. In Russia, it might have seemed, there were both previously unploughed lands and people to work them. But the population was concentrated in the old agrarian provinces. Dispatching large numbers of people to the virgin lands would have meant undermining landowner agriculture, and at the same time destroying the institution of the village community which allowed the government to extract both taxes and soldiers from the countryside. In sum, this would have meant doing away with the entire traditional system on which both the landlords and peasant society was based.

By the mid 1880s the monetary resources of peasant agriculture were exhausted. The crisis was affecting rye even more than wheat. The peasants who suffered worst were those who had previously been serfs; they became more dependent on the market, but could not make the transition to farmer-style commercial agriculture. The nobility for their part, immediately drew the conclusion that the peasants needed to be 'put in their place', that labour power in Russia was excessively expensive. For Russia, according to Lyashchenko, the fall in world grain prices 'took on the nature of a catastrophe'.[24]

The 1880s ended with measures to restore the system of class distinctions and the privileges of the nobility. The political reaction and the stagnation of the grain trade coincided in entirely natural fashion. 'The rise in grain prices on the European market turned the landowners of the 1850s from supporters of serfdom into liberals', Pokrovsky states. 'The strong prices of the next two decades then sustained the "bourgeois mood" of the Russian nobility under Alexander II.' Sadly, nothing lasts for ever, especially grain prices, and in the 1880s the situation changed dramatically. 'When Russian producers exported their grain, they received less and less for it.'[25] The crisis of the 1880s turned both landowners and St Petersburg officials into reactionaries.

The countryside witnessed the beginning of a sort of counter-reform. The peasants could not be deprived of their personal freedom, but, on the economic level, efforts could be made to restore as much as possible of the old order. The free peasants finished up tightly controlled by the landowners. After the reforms, landowner agriculture rested on the *otrabotki,* a system of debt-bondage in which the feudal dependency of the peasantry had changed only in appearance.

In the course of the 'liberating reforms', the landowners had lost part of their holdings; now the peasants were forced to compensate their former owners for this loss. According to Druzhinin, the large estates in Russia had

already in the 1860s and 1870s turned into a base of support for survivals from the era of serfdom. The estates were rented not to capitalist farmers but to impoverished peasants, on conditions that included burdensome share-cropping arrangements, exploitative payments and the expiation of debt through labour. Where the new leaseholders were merchants or well-off peasants, the rented lands were divided into small plots and sublet at extortionate rates to needy village communities, peasant associations or half-ruined farmers.[26]

By the 1880s, semi-serf forms of organisation had not only failed to vanish into the past, but, in the conditions of the agrarian crisis, had come to play an increasingly important role in the life of the countryside. Traditional pre-capitalist agrarian relations were most clearly expressed in the *otrabotki*, under which the peasants, in order to pay for the land they had received, were forced to work without pay on the lands of the estate-owner. In principle, and as Pokrovsky stresses, this was free labour; no one could force the peasants to work off their debts, and they could, of course, simply renounce their claim to the land. Significantly, it was small and medium landowners who most often resorted to the *otrabotki*. The larger the landholding, and the greater the landowner's financial resources, the easier it became to employ free labour. 'The feudalists adapted more readily to the bourgeois environment than the petty landowners', Pokrovsky notes ironically.[27]

The only way Russian producers had of maintaining their position in the world market was to systematically lower their prices. It was in this era that Russia began to live by the slogan 'We shall go hungry, but we shall export!' The landowners could still somehow survive this situation, but for the peasants, real misery ensued. Once again, the domestic market was sacrificed to its world counterpart, and the peasant household to the interests of commercial capital. The profits of grain traders were maintained at the expense of the producers. The poorer a village was at the beginning of the crisis, the worse its ruin by the time the crisis ended. As Lyashchenko writes,

The decline of grain prices, and along with it, the whole weight of the competitive struggle waged by Russian grain on the world market, was loaded onto these impoverished groups to the most intense and ruinous degree. The well-known formula 'We shall go hungry, but we shall export!' was merely a concise and quite unabashed official expression of this situation. The only people who were forced to go hungry in order to export were, of course, those who were forced by necessity to lower their prices on the world grain market. Only on these terms could commercial capital act as an intermediary between these producers and the world market, and only on these terms did it agree to do so.[28]

POPULISTS AND MARXISTS

As Pokrovsky puts it, the formula for the development of post-reform Russia can be summed up in the formula 'Absolutism and the rejection of political freedom, together with a maximum of civil freedom, as the indispensable condition for further capitalist development without revolution.'[29] This formula would have been quite clear to people in the late nineteenth century, since it was already obvious that the development of capitalism was not only failing to weaken the domination of the countryside by the landowners and of the cities by the autocracy, but, on the contrary, was reinforcing this domination.

The worse the situation on the world grain market became, the less inclined the landowners were toward liberalism. But as reaction triumphed in the countryside, it met with resistance in the cities, which were undergoing modernisation and were used to living by new rules. The emancipation of the peasants was accompanied by an unexpected spread of socialist moods within the intelligentsia. The year 1876 saw the founding of the first populist (*narodnik*) organisation, Land and Freedom. Three years later, Land and Freedom split to form the radical People's Will party, which took the road of anti-government terror, and the more moderate group Black Redivision. Later, émigré members of the moderate wing of populism, headed by Georgy Plekhanov, would set up the Marxist group Liberation of Labour.

This sudden popularisation of socialism in a country where an industrial proletariat still barely existed led the Marxist thinkers of the next generation into a dead-end. Such a turn of events, however, was quite natural for a peripheral country. The Russian bourgeoisie, unlike its counterparts in the West, was not only failing to show any desire for democratic change, but was not even inclined to liberal opposition. Russia's capitalists were quite satisfied with the social order which the autocracy guaranteed them. The opposition of the 1880s, Pokrovsky notes, 'had only a left wing'.[30] With no natural buffer of moderate liberals between the authorities and the radicals, the democratic opposition was bound inevitably to become revolutionary, and later, terrorist as well. The government in turn could combat its opponents using police measures, but not political ones.

In a situation such as this, democratic ideology could not fail to be simultaneously anti-bourgeois, and the anti-bourgeois protest could find a positive programme only by turning to European socialism. During the twentieth century something similar occurred repeatedly in other peripheral countries, from China to Cuba and South Africa. Meanwhile, orthodox Marxists of the late nineteenth and early twentieth centuries regarded the populist understanding of socialism as a curious political misapprehension, an ideological delusion that had arisen because the thinking of the *narodnik* intelligentsia had combined an interest in advanced Western ideas with a desire for anti-monarchic revolution. Russian Marxists saw no objective connection between *narodnik* ideas and the reality of the peasant economy, especially since the peasants themselves at first reacted with extreme caution, and often hostility, to the *narodnik* propaganda.

Plekhanov, the founder of Russian Marxism, was firmly convinced that after the peasant reform the triumph of capitalism in agriculture was inevitable. As he saw it, the penetration of market relations into the countryside would lead inevitably to the decay and disappearance of all pre-capitalist forms of social organisation. All that held back this process was 'the force of inertia, which at times makes its presence felt so painfully on all the forward-thinking people of any backward agricultural country'.[31]

The decay of the traditional modes of life in Russia in the late nineteenth century was an obvious fact. It would be premature, however, to conclude from this that the 'outmoded forms' were replaced by new, European types of organisation. Furthermore, the problem did not, of course, lie simply in the 'backwardness' and 'inertia' of which the 'advanced thinkers' complained so much. Karl Marx held quite different views. From the mid 1870s, Russia occupied an increasingly important place in his works. Marx had not merely overcome the Russophobia which, it must be acknowledged, characterised him in the 1850s. He was also starting to see Russia as a country which it was necessary to understand in order to have a grasp of the modern world in its entirety. As he continued to work on *Capital*, Marx made plans to use the historical experience of Russia in the third volume, just as he had used the experience of Britain in the first.[32] At the same time, he was starting to show an interest in populist ideas. If the Russian *narodniki* were studying the author of *Capital*, the thinking of Marx himself was to an increasing degree developing under the influence of Russian populism. He devotedly studied the Russian language, and diverted himself with the works of N.G. Chernyshevsky, whom he spoke of (perhaps with a certain exaggeration) as 'a great Russian scholar and critic'.[33]

In the 1850s, Marx viewed Russian society as an unrelieved reactionary mass of humanity. He even regarded the émigré dissident and socialist Aleksandr Herzen, then living in London, as part of the same aggressive imperial and provincial world; this was a response to Herzen's pan-Slavist sympathies. In the 1870s Marx saw Russia in a totally different light. The Paris Commune had been defeated, and the West at this time was not a place to look for the triumph of progressive principles. As Theodor Shanin has noted,

At the turn of the decade, Marx became increasingly aware that alongside the retrograde official Russia, which he so attacked as the focus and the gendarme of European reaction, a different Russia of revolutionary allies and radical scholars had grown up, increasingly engaged with his own theoretical work. It was into the Russian language that the first translation of *Capital* was made, a decade before it saw light in England. It was Russia from which news of revolutionary action came, standing out all the more against the decline in revolutionary hopes in Western Europe after the Paris Commune.[34]

Marx began attentively reading the works of the Russian populists, and found in them not only ideas that accorded with his own, but also questions to which, as a scholar of social development, he felt compelled to respond. As the populists analysed the Russian past, they threw down a challenge to both of the dominant trends of national thought, the Slavophiles and Westernisers. The *narodnik* writers rejected the ideas of the Westernisers, who saw the future of Russia as repeating the 'European road', but in the same way they also rejected the Slavophile myth of Russian uniqueness. To the contest of myths in Russian social consciousness they counterposed their historical and sociological analysis, which to a substantial degree was based on the ideas of Marx. The *narodnik* thinkers suggested that Russia would be able to avoid repeating the path of European capitalism. As Shanin notes, their anti-capitalism had nothing in common with anti-Westernism. 'That possibility resulted, however, not from Russia's uniqueness, exalted by the Slavophiles, but from Russia's situation within a global context, which had already seen the establishment of capitalism in Western Europe.'[35]

The Russian populists were, in essence, the first to sense the specific nature of peripheral capitalism. They discerned that in Russia it was not the national bourgeoisie but the autocratic state, integrated into the world system, that was the main agent of capitalist development. Consequently, a blow against the government was inevitably a blow against capitalism as well. Within the context of the world system, meanwhile, Russia had the status of an exploited nation. Not only the proletariat, but all the country's working strata were subject to exploitation, though in varying forms. The world system benefited from this situation, but the main tool of exploitation nevertheless was not foreign capital but Russia's own authorities. From this stemmed the alliance between the Russian revolutionary movement, seeking to base itself on the intelligentsia and the peasant masses, and the proletarian movement in the West. Russia's peripheral status in the world system meant that pre-capitalist structures, above all the peasant communities, were preserved in the country. The peasant communities were subject to exploitation by the state, which used them as a tool for extracting taxes; by the landowners; and by finance capital in association with the government. This exploitation made the peasantry a potential threat to the system, and the village communities themselves a possible point of support for future change. The result was that Russia's peripheral status and 'backwardness' might unexpectedly prove to be an advantage from the point of view of revolutionary struggle.

At the core of the theoretical discussion was the question of the peasant communities, which the one-time moderate populists, now transformed into orthodox Marxists, viewed as survivals from the past. Declaring themselves the interpreters and advocates of Marxism in Russia, Plekhanov and his supporters launched an irreconcilable ideological battle against populism.

Meanwhile, the views of Marx himself were developing in the opposite direction. Like the revolutionary populists, the author of *Capital* did not deny the archaic origins of the peasant communities. However, his dialectical approach forced him to see in one and the same phenomenon both a relic of the past, and a potential prototype of the future. When asked for his opinions on this topic by an adherent of Plekhanov's group, the Russian revolutionary Vera Zasulich, Marx backed the populists in no uncertain manner. He repeated the same conclusions in a letter to the journal *Notes of the Fatherland*.

The deeper the author of *Capital* immersed himself in questions of Russia's history and economy, the more clearly he perceived that the question could not be reduced to the future of the peasant communities. The real issue was the degree to which the world outside Europe and North America was doomed to repeat the 'Western' road of development. In *Capital*, Marx had written that the more developed countries displayed for the less developed a map of their future. He asserted this, however, in comparing Britain with Germany. In this case, he was correct on the whole; for all its national peculiarities, German capitalism, like that of other countries of the centre, did not transgress the bounds of the general Western model first established in Britain and North America. Russia was different; in comparing it with Britain, Marx concluded that the 'historical inevitability' of the processes of capitalist development he had described was 'limited strictly to the countries of Western Europe'.[36]

This does not mean that capitalism fails to affect the countries of the periphery, but that in these countries everything happens differently. In any case, there is no reason to see human history as a pre-programmed process in which social formations succeed one another in mechanical fashion. In essence, Marx here entered into a polemic with those of his followers who were trying to use his theories as a universal master-key. These followers, Marx objected, invariably found it necessary to

turn my historical sketch of the rise of capitalism in Western Europe into a historical-philosophical theory of a general road along which all peoples, whatever the historical conditions in which they find themselves, are fated to proceed, in order to arrive ultimately at that economic formation which ensures both the supreme flourishing of the productive forces of social labour and the fullest development of humanity.[37]

It was by no means true that the incorporation of Russia into the world market, and even the development of bourgeois relations there, would necessarily lead to the rise of the same sort of capitalism as in the West. 'Events which are strikingly analogous, but which take place in a different historical setting, have led to quite different results.'[38]

The sharp polemics here were so obviously directed against the orthodox Marxism then taking shape, that it is easy to see why Plekhanov and his co-thinkers did not publish these two letters of Marx, even though they had the texts. They were not persuaded to print them even by a recommendation from Friedrich Engels, who looked after Marx's affairs during the latter's illness and after his death. The letter to the editors of *Notes of the Fatherland* was published in 1886 in the *Herald of the People's Will,* while the letter to Vera Zasulich came to light only in 1924, due to the efforts of David Ryazanov. The latter, who was director of the Institute of Marx and Engels, was later repressed by Stalin.

In their refusal to take note of these texts, the orthodox Marxists were as one with the irreconcilable critics of Marxism who throughout the twentieth century insisted that Marx had set forward his theory of social development as a universal schema, to be applied mechanically in all circumstances. In fact, and as Shanin correctly observes, Marx himself in his polemic with the orthodox Marxists clearly articulated 'neo-Marxist' positions. In the last years of his life he was preoccupied with the very questions that were at the centre of Marxist discussions in the twentieth century. In other words, he not only spoke as the founder of Marxist theory, but also anticipated its development by a good half-century.

The question of peripheral development lay at the centre of discussions by sociologists and economists in the final third of the twentieth century. For Marx, meanwhile, Russia provided the material that allowed him to grasp the unevenness of the development of capitalism as a world system. Along with the experience of Russia, he studied the history of other peripheral countries, even studying Eastern languages and encouraging Engels to do the same. It was, however, analysis of the events unfolding in Russia that was crucial for him. Shanin's remarks are instructive here:

While the experience of India or China was to Marx's generation of Europeans remote, abstract and often misconceived, Russia was closer not only geographically but in the basic sense of human contact, possible knowledge of language and of availability of evidence and analysis, self-generated by the natives. It was not only the difference in extent of information which was at issue, however. The Russia of those times was marked by political independence and growing international weakness, placed on the peripheries of capitalist development, massively peasant yet with rapidly expanding industry (owned mainly by foreigners and the crown) and with a highly interventionist state.[39]

The combining of all these factors made a powerful social explosion in Russia inevitable. Because of the peripheral nature of Russian capitalism, however, the impending revolution was clearly going to differ radically from the proletarian movements of the West. The agrarian revolution and the seizure of the landed estates by the peasants placed in question the very existence of the Russian model of capitalism and its integration into the world system.

The populists described the transfer of the land to the rural masses as the 'black [that is, peasant] redivision'. From the point of view of the orthodox Marxists, there was nothing anti-capitalist about such an agrarian movement. Had not the Western bourgeois revolutions begun with the abolition of landed estates? Indeed, in the long term such a 'black redivision' might have led to the development of rural capitalism. But in the short term, it would have led to the peasants quitting the market, which would have been a catastrophe for capitalist development.

In *Capital,* Marx stressed that the expropriation of petty producers was a precondition for capitalist accumulation. In imperial Russia, however, this expropriation was carried out by commercial capital with help from the landowners. Meanwhile, because of its ties to the landowners, peasant agriculture was not done away with completely but was subordinated to the requirements of the market. This is why the 'black redivision' was a catastrophe from the point of view of the accumulation of capital. Its impact on the world economy was even more severe. The time was no longer the sixteenth century, and large volumes of capital were required for development. The small-scale accumulation by the 'solid proprietors' was being drawn out over decades; it was of no use either for the building of railways, or for the payment of international loans.

Russian capitalism could no longer develop without the exploitation of the peasantry by the landowners. Therefore, an agrarian revolution would inevitably turn into an anti-capitalist overturn, and the effort to radically improve the position of the peasantry was inseparable from the question of changing the character of the entire Russian state.

In one of the drafts of his letter to Vera Zasulich, Marx wrote:

The question at issue here is no longer therefore of the problem that needs to be solved, but quite simply of the enemy that needs to be crushed. To save the Russian peasant community, a Russian revolution is needed. In the event, the Russian government and the 'new pillars of society' are doing everything possible to prepare the masses for such a catastrophe. If the revolution occurs in timely fashion, if it concentrates all its strength in order to ensure the free development of the village community, this latter will soon become an element in the rebirth of Russian society, and will provide it with an advantage over those countries that are beneath the yoke of the capitalist system.[40]

RUSSIAN COLONIALISM

From the 1870s, the Russian empire, having recovered after its defeat in Crimea and fortified itself with reforms, again set out on the path of foreign expansion. To outside observers this appeared to be a rebirth of Anglo-Russian rivalry in the East, an attempt to settle old scores with Turkey, and an effort to regain for the tsar the aureole of defender of Slavic interests. Like all international developments of the nineteenth century, however, the new military campaigns of tsarist Russia had profound economic roots.

Russian industry was gradually starting to revive. It is significant that the 'free trade' customs tariff was abolished in 1877, at the very time when Russian foreign policy was once again asserting itself in the Balkans and Central Asia. A distinguishing feature of a peripheral society is the narrowness of the internal market. Lenin was convinced that Russia suffered simultaneously from capitalism and from its insufficient development. If we look at the size of the Russian internal market, however, we find that in these terms the development of capitalism was not merely sufficiently great, but was excessive and disproportionate when compared with domestic demand.

The development of Russian capitalism was dictated not only by internal requirements, but also by the logic of the world market. For capital, being on a 'modern' level meant being part of the world system. The Russian domestic market, however, was too small for this. In nineteenth-century Britain, an extensive domestic market allowed mass production and the possibility of conquering foreign markets. Russian industrialists, by contrast, could make up for their weakness only through government support and through expansion into foreign markets. To compete abroad was difficult, requiring low prices and the military-political support of the state. The Russian population was obliged to pay for both. It was forced to pay high prices for local and imported goods in a protected market, and also to maintain the army and the bureaucracy, which was growing constantly as a result of the new tasks required of it. The population was compelled, ultimately, to go to war in order to conquer or defend markets for the 'national commodity producers'. Industry was demanding expansion, an empire, war. Economic weakness required a maximum of political effort. Russia, as a great power, had to stand on the same level as the other colonial empires.

At first, the victory of agrarian over industrial capital that followed Russia's defeat in the Crimean War returned Russian foreign policy to its accustomed pro-British course. However, the earlier collaborative relations could no longer be restored. On the one hand, increasing influence was being exerted on Russia by Germany, which had been united in 1870 under the domination of Prussia. On the other, the Russian empire was continuing to advance into Turkestan. From the outset, this offensive had had a simple and understandable goal: to 'cordon off Central Asia for Russian manufactures, since here there are God knows how many competitors'.[41]

Despite the expansion of the Russian empire, the country's dominant classes were unable to effectively shift the economic frontier and to accumulate sufficient resources in the colonies to allow the modernisation of the metropolis. Russian commercial capital arrived in Bukhara, which had lured Moscow merchants since the time of Afanasy Nikitin. In itself, this conquest did not yet provide a powerful stimulus for industrial development. Nevertheless, the type of expansion was changing. Earlier, the authorities in Moscow or St Petersburg had tried to make any conquered territory a part of Russia. Now, Turkestan was turned into a colony. It was organised to an important degree on the model of British India, with its local elites and with its clear division into European and Muslim societies, existing in parallel with one another.

For the British entrepreneurs who had begun penetrating to Bukhara and Khiva this was bad news, since the Russian troops were followed immediately by Russian customs duties. The change in the geopolitical situation aroused even greater concern. When Paul I had tried to send Cossacks on a campaign to India, this was no more than an adventure. Now things were different. The British land forces in India were not large, and the arrival of Russian armies in Central Asia could not be welcomed in London. While rejecting fears among his countrymen that the Russians were planning to conquer India, the British diplomat Lord Curzon nevertheless observed that ever since the notorious adventure by Paul I, officials in St Petersburg had dreamt of repeating such a campaign. For a century, 'the possibility of striking at India through Central Asia had been present in the minds of Russian statesmen'.[42] Of course, the threat was imaginary, and so the conflict did not go beyond the bounds of diplomacy. British India urgently set about reinforcing its northern frontier, intensifying its penetration into Afghanistan. Over several decades, forays into Afghanistan by the Anglo-Indian army met with serious defeats and heavy losses, but by the early 1880s had achieved their goal; a government loyal to London had been installed in Kabul. The Russians, meanwhile, defended their own interests in Afghanistan, trying to incite the emirs in Kabul against the British, and offering them aid while avoiding open conflict with London.

This struggle as it unfolded acquired the name of the 'Great Game', but on the scale of global politics it was no more than a game. British officials understood perfectly that for the government in St Petersburg, 'the real objective was not Calcutta but Constantinople'.[43] The real problem for the British empire was not the concentrating of Russian forces in Turkestan, but the growth of German industry. Britain was also losing its positions in the Russian market, mainly because of German competition rather than as a result of the growth of Russian industry. The rapprochement between St Petersburg and Berlin, however, did not lead to a stable alliance. The two empires were competitors on the world grain market, and this was of far more importance than any number of colonial misunderstandings with the British.

BACKWARDNESS? OR PERIPHERAL DEVELOPMENT?

For 200 years, the Russian elites had viewed the problem of peripheral development as one of 'backwardness'. For Russia, the second half of the nineteenth century was a period when the authorities and the opposition, conservatives and liberals, bureaucrats and intellectuals, were seized by a single, shared idea: catching up with the West. The Crimean War had put a question mark over the place of the Russian empire in Europe. This place had to be regained and consolidated with the help of reforms, diplomacy, military construction, the building of railways and the expansion of education. In Russia's twin capitals the liberal public was well aware that an autocratic state could act as a tool for modernisation, but that the authoritarianism that was effective in exceptional circumstances was not conducive to healthy development or to the consolidation of successes that had already been achieved. Russia had taken on Western forms, but without becoming part of the West. The problem was clear and simple, but for liberal minds, the solution to it was maddeningly elusive. Russia's problem was not backwardness, but something else. Backwardness was delayed development; Germany had been a backward country compared to Britain. Russia was part of the periphery, and this represented a quite different variant of development. Attempts to overcome the development gap rapidly through a 'burst' of progress created fresh problems and new dangers unknown to the 'advanced' countries.

The modernisers were invariably convinced that their own countries would pass through the same stages, in orderly sequence, as the 'advanced states' of the West, only with a certain delay. As a result, the problem was reduced to the speed of development. How could the advance along the road of progress be accelerated? In reality, different speeds of development inevitably gave rise to different economic and socio-political structures, and this in turn altered the character of the processes that were occurring. The outcome was quite different from what had been intended. One society cannot repeat the path of another, quite different one.

Pyotr Chaadaev was the first Russian thinker to recognise this contradiction.

In my view, anyone who argued that we were doomed somehow to repeat the whole long train of lunacies committed by peoples in less favourable situations than us, and once again to undergo all the calamities they have experienced, would be displaying a profound incomprehension of the role which fate has allotted us.[44]

According to Chaadaev, Russia's backwardness was not only fraught with appalling catastrophes, but also harboured certain advantages. These, however, could be brought into play only when the country rejected attempts to copy the experience of the West. When Marx wrote to Vera Zasulich on the future of Russia, he used almost the same words. The ideologues of Russian populism addressed the same question in the late nineteenth century.

The supporters of such ideas, however, were always a minority. Meanwhile, the modernisers, captivated by their own illusions, dreamt of solving all the problems with a fresh and even more rapid burst of progress. In the eighteenth and nineteenth centuries the majority of Russian progressive intellectuals shared totally in the illusion of the authorities that Russia's backwardness could not prevent it from following the path of the rest of Europe. The only difference was that the bureaucracy was oriented toward implanting Western technology and methods of organisation, while the opposition intellectuals dreamed in addition of Western civil liberties. From the time of the enlightenment, both liberals and revolutionary democrats were united in seeking to accelerate progress along the Western path. Also with their origins in this process were the first Russian Marxists. All the members of these currents were convinced that it was necessary only to eradicate those 'relics of the Middle Ages', autocracy and serfdom (or later, large landholdings), for everything then to proceed smoothly. To their shame, they kept silent about the fact that under Peter the Great autocracy and serfdom had been tools of modernisation. In the form which these institutions assumed in the nineteenth century, they were no longer in any sense relics of the Middle Ages. On the contrary, they could more accurately be described as by-products of Westernising reform. Since the days of Peter I, serf labour and state despotism had made it possible to erect beautiful palaces, to found universities, to build factories, and to introduce civilisation to the remote ends of a vast country. Such was the model of development that had been chosen.

Whether adhering to the government camp or to that of the opposition, the ideologues of modernisation reduced Russia's problems to the conflict of the old and the new. On at least several occasions in Russian history, the sense was genuinely present that the task of 'catching up with the West' had almost been accomplished, and that it remained only to put in a finishing dash for Russia to enter the category of highly developed countries. The reforms of Peter I ensured an extraordinarily rapid pace of development, and by the time of Catherine II the Russian empire was viewed in Europe as a perfectly 'normal' state, barely lagging behind its Prussian and Austrian neighbours. The French enlightenment thinkers Diderot and Voltaire held serious hopes that the methods of rational state administration which they propounded, and which had not been implemented in France or Prussia, would be adopted in Russia. Catherine's empire had universities that conceded little to those of the West in the number of their students and the quality of the teaching; factories that produced goods to match any of the period; a superbly equipped army and navy that inspired fear in neighbouring states; and agriculture that produced grain for export. Voltaire and Diderot notwithstanding, there was no need for political reforms or emancipation of the peasants for all this prosperity to be attained; thanks to the efforts of a despotic central authority, it was achieved on the basis of slavery and autocracy.

In the late nineteenth century the feeling was once again arising that Russia would soon stand as an equal alongside the 'advanced' countries of Europe. But the latest round of modernisations, that had begun with the reform of 1861, could in no way guarantee this. The Russian empire was only one of the countries that underwent rapid changes in the final third of the nineteenth century, and of these countries, it was in the least favourable position.

Making use of hindsight, many historians stress the high growth rates in Russia in the 1890s and on the eve of the First World War, trying to prove that capitalist development was proceeding successfully, and that only the war and the revolution that followed it prevented Russia from 'catching up' with the West. In reality, the situation was far less favourable. The late nineteenth and early twentieth centuries were a period of rapid industrialisation in most of the states of the capitalist world, including even such colonial or semi-colonial countries as India and China. Germany, the United States, Austria-Hungary and even Japan, which not long before had lagged behind Russia, were developing overall at significantly more rapid rates. Russia was clearly falling behind, and this meant that in the new international division of labour that was taking shape, it would finish up in a distinctly disadvantageous position. There were unquestionably more factories in Russia than earlier, and they were turning out more modern products, but dependency on exports, and on foreign technology, loans and capital investments, had grown as well. As in the 1850s, all was not well on the defence front; Russia could not re-arm itself as quickly as its rivals. For a state in which armed might had traditionally meant far more than economic prosperity, this could not fail to become a serious problem.

In the world system, the success of some countries had traditionally led to the decline of others. While capitalism was experiencing its latest 'reconstruction', the Russian empire was having to endure increasingly fierce competition from countries whose positions were incomparably more advantageous. Germany and the United States had entered the period of modernisation at the same time as Russia. Both countries had also undergone political transformations. Germany had been unified in a single state, while in the course of a ferocious civil war the United States had overcome the division between North and South.

The advantage that the US and Germany possessed over Russia was that despite being relatively backward countries, they had nevertheless belonged from the first to the 'centre' of the capitalist world system. The triumph of North over South in the US was not simply the victory of the industrially developed part of the country over the agrarian part, but also the victory of the centre over the periphery. The Southern states were doomed to fight a war not only because their slave-owning system was incompatible with the liberal institutions of the North, but also for the reason that as a peripheral society, they had far stronger ties to the world market for raw materials than to the American internal market. The North needed the raw materials and labour power of the South for its own development. The Southerners were lucky. After losing the war, they finished up integrated into the centre of the capitalist world system, something their local elite had strenuously resisted.

In similar fashion, unification allowed Germany to overcome the gap between the more developed and the relatively backward parts of the country, and to organise a single labour market, a common education system and a transport network.

Finally, Japan, which was integrated into the world system in approximately the same period, was not weighed down by the baggage of the past. It entered the capitalist world without being part of capitalism's periphery, at the very moment when highly favourable conditions had arisen for it. Japanese capital did not serve the process of accumulation in the West, but on the contrary, was able to exploit the fact that European colonial and commercial expansion had opened the markets of the Far East to foreign penetration.

The modernisation of Germany and the US thus saw peripheral regions that were part of the same political space as the centre, 'gravitate' into it, while the modernisation of Japan represented a unique case in which a country burst into the world system from the outside. Russia, by contrast, was still a country of the periphery, even though a relatively developed one. For this reason, Russia's efforts to 'catch up' with the West did not extend outside the framework of the general rules dictated by the world system.

12
The Flourishing of Russian Capitalism: From Witte to Stolypin

Even though participation in the world grain trade was ruining the countryside, during the 1880s this trade remained a crucially important source of funds for industrialisation. Capitalism, as Lyashchenko puts it, survived the crisis of the 1880s 'at the price of the destruction of the petty commodity producer'.[1]

By the early 1890s these efforts were starting to bear fruit. The growth of the cities had brought with it the development of the internal market, including that for Russian agricultural produce. As Russia had overcome the consequences of the Crimean defeat, its customs policies had become more protectionist. Russian industry was beginning to recover from stagnation.

The year 1894 saw prices on the Russian and world markets reach their low point. After this, a sustained rise began. The flow of capital into agriculture made production commercially profitable, at least under certain circumstances. Wheat increasingly took the place of rye, and grain exports almost doubled. Exports of grain during 1900–14 were worth 7.3 billion rubles, compared to a mere 8.6 billion rubles during the previous 30 years.[2]

In Lyashchenko's view, the income which Russia obtained from grain exports around the beginning of the twentieth century was comparable to the export earnings which in America created 'the preconditions for the brilliant development of capitalist industry'. Why then, this historian asks, did nothing similar occur in Russia? The reason, he maintains, lay in 'the backward social and economic conditions which this flow of wealth encountered in Russia'.[3] The development in Russia of these 'backward social and economic conditions' was not, of course, divorced from the impact on the country of the world market or of the established international division of labour. As we shall see, Russia's entry into the industrial era did not by any means signify that 'backwardness' had been overcome. In a certain sense, the flow of wealth not only stimulated 'progressive development', as interpreted by both the liberal and Marxist economists of the period, but also had the contrary effect of strengthening the 'backward relations' which liberals and Marxists were united in condemning.

THE WITTE ERA

The proceeds from the grain trade allowed increased investment in industry and encouraged industrial growth, but were not enough to ensure that this growth would be maintained. The 'grain' income was followed by investments from the West. As Pokrovsky puts it, the industrial upturn of the 1890s was accompanied by 'the conquest of Russia by foreign capital'.[4]

During 1856–87, a total of 15 foreign companies had been established in Russia, with a combined capital of 71.1 million rubles. Between 1888 and 1894, 22 companies were set up, with a capital of 62.9 million rubles. Between 1895 and 1902, the number of companies reached 90, with a capital of 253 million rubles.[5] Western capital was quickest of all to seize the dominant positions in the banking sector. Russia's growing industries were acutely short of credit. Contemporaries noted that the delayed industrialisation had created a disproportion between the level of development of production and the state of Russian banking. In the West, wrote the Marxist scholar of the 1920s, S. Ronin, the accumulation of capital had 'proceeded in step with the development of industry and with the growth of its requirements for credit'. In Russia, by contrast, the industrialisation called forth by the new international division of labour outstripped the accumulation of local capital. In sum, Russian industry was 'to a large extent indebted to foreign capital' for its rapid growth rates.[6]

The problem which Russia encountered in the 1890s has reappeared many times in countries of the 'periphery' which have set out on the road to industrialisation. The creation of modern industries has demanded high levels of accumulation from the first, while the 'natural' development of capitalism has presupposed a gradual 'ripening' of the financial sector, as occurred in the West. The countries of the periphery, whose resources have financed accumulation in the centre, have unexpectedly encountered a shortage of money. A positive trade balance has not been enough to solve the problem. The more quickly industry grows, the more acute its shortage of capital investment. The result is the inevitable rise of the cult of the foreign investor as a force driving the economy forward. The shortage of funds also implies an exceedingly important role for the banks, acting not only as creditors to the industrialists, but also as intermediaries between local commodity producers and the world financial markets.

In the West, an obvious crisis of overaccumulation was apparent at this time. Credit was relatively cheap, and the owners of capital had nowhere to invest it profitably. In such settings, peripheral countries invariably take on a particular attractiveness. Russia in Witte's time was attracting capital through state orders and through rates of profit so high as to be inconceivable in Europe. It was not surprising that Western capital entered most enthusiastically into those sectors whose prosperity was guaranteed by government decisions.

Count Sergey Witte, who at that time was the main architect of St Petersburg's economic policy, had an acute awareness of the opportunities which at that time were opening up before Russia. Thanks to the reforms he enacted as Minister of Finance, the ruble became a sought-after hard currency on European markets. In the liberal journalism of the late twentieth century, one finds constant references to the 'former glory' of the ruble, highly regarded in the West. In reality, the ruble throughout most of its history has been an extremely weak currency. The St Petersburg government made no apology for this, since a cheap ruble, worth even less in Europe than at home, was advantageous for exporters. Under Witte, however, this situation changed. Industry needed equipment and capital. On becoming finance minister in 1892, Witte restored the circulation of precious metals. One paper ruble was equal to 66 silver copecks, but at the same time the amount of paper money in circulation was reduced and the silver coins were reminted. The exchange rate of paper and silver money then became one paper ruble to one silver copeck, and was fixed at this level. The financial reform, carried out against a general background of inflation in Europe, led to a sharp appreciation of the ruble, which for the first time in its history came to be valued more highly than gold in the West. The exchange rate of the Russian currency was now as elevated as it had earlier been depressed. Nevertheless, the system worked.

A positive trade balance could only be maintained by exporting grain. In the mid 1880s, 17 per cent of total Russian grain production went abroad, and in the early 1890s, no less than a quarter. Meanwhile, world prices were declining. The growth of exports was supposed to compensate for the lower prices, but the increasing Russian exports themselves put pressure on the world market, exacerbating the problem. In the 1880s, Russia had run balance of trade surpluses of 100–150 million rubles a year, but by 1899 this figure was only 7.2 million.[7] In the first years of the twentieth century the position improved somewhat, with world grain prices again rising. However, this was accompanied, by an increase in domestic prices and a rise in the price of labour power. Naturally, this created favourable conditions for the growth of the workers' movement, which gave a serious account of itself in 1905.

Despite holding only the post of finance minister, Witte concentrated enormous powers in his hands, powers that far exceeded his official authority. The secret of his success lay in the fact that, while taking advantage of exceptionally favourable market conditions, he managed at the same time to strengthen the national currency and dramatically increase state spending. At the same time, the treasury's printing press was run at full capacity; the lower orders of Russian society were forced to pay the growing costs of the government.

Large sums were poured into railway construction, ensuring a flood of orders for the metallurgical and, to some degree, machine-building industries. The return to protectionism stimulated local production. Under Witte, Russian customs tariffs were among the highest in the world. Despite this, machines and equipment were imported in huge quantities; the growing Russian market was attracting foreigners, and the 'strong' ruble allowed technology to be imported relatively cheaply.

With the ruble strengthened, the government in St Petersburg was able to sharply increase its borrowings on international financial markets. To Western investors, Russia seemed a country of unique opportunities. Circumstances had coincided, it appeared, in an extraordinarily fortunate manner. In Russia there was a strong ruble, while Western financial markets were suffering from a surplus of 'excess' money. 'All this', Ronin writes, 'poured like a river of gold into railway construction and into industries that were shielded from foreign competition by the high protective tariff of 1891.'[8]

The industrial expansion of the 1890s and early 1900s was genuinely impressive. Between 1890 and 1899, output in the chemical industry grew by 274 per cent; in mining, by 372 per cent; and in metallurgy, by 793 per cent.[9] According to data cited by Strumilin, the overall growth of industrial production in the years 1895–1900 came to 59 per cent; if 1892 is taken as the base year, the growth by 1899 amounted to 73 per cent.[10] Even in this setting, the pace of development of the railway network was dizzying. The programme of railway construction drawn up in the last years of the nineteenth century created a furious demand for the products of the metallurgical industry. Between 1860 and 1870, the length of Russia's railway network grew from 1492 *versty* to 10,090, which was considered an impressive success. Between 1870 and 1880, it again doubled, reaching 21,236 *versty.* But the years from 1890 to 1900 witnessed a new 'railway fever', with the length of track reaching 48,565 *versty,* mainly due to the Trans-Siberian Railway.[11] By inflating the demand for metals and other products, this latest burst of railway construction created the conditions for the expansion of other industrial sectors. This demand was underwritten by state programmes, so it is not surprising that the completion of the Trans-Siberian Railway was a real catastrophe not only for Russian capitalists, but for French ones as well. Russian industrialists complained constantly of the government's unsystematic and inconsistent approach to railway construction, but as the economist I. Vavilin later remarked, these reproaches were misplaced:

The Tsar's government built railways using money from the pockets of the French, British and German bourgeoisies. Consequently, it could not have its own plan for building railways. Instead, it built them when the European bourgeoisies provided money, and did not build the lines needed to satisfy the requirements of the economy, but those that corresponded to French military commands.[12]

Indeed, the French government repeatedly told the Tsar's administration that the tracks should be constructed on the basis of strategic considerations. In 1901 the French general staff insisted that credit provided to Russia should be used for the building of a strategic double-track line from Bologoe to Sedlec. Witte argued that for this to happen, St Petersburg would have to be provided with a new loan; meanwhile, the officials in Paris were convinced that the funds already borrowed would be quite enough. In the end, a new loan was made available. In 1912 and 1913 the French finance ministry twice declared that a condition for the providing of credit was the building of a railway network in western Russia that would allow troops to be moved there rapidly in the case of a war with Germany. The official French representatives acted in close collusion with private banks such as Crédit Lyonnais, incidentally disproving the argument that French entrepreneurs were apolitical. The Russian population was told informally that 'the French government can aid in the regular placing of Russian stocks on the market, but as compensation it has to receive military aid from its Russian allies'.[13]

INDUSTRIALISATION IN SOUTHERN RUSSIA

The years around the beginning of the twentieth century were a time of rapid industrialisation in southern Russia. Numerous metallurgical and metalworking plants were built in the region. The overwhelming majority of these enterprises were established by foreign capital – first British, and then French and Belgian. The initial step was taken by the Englishman John Hughes, who founded the Novorossiysk Coal and Rail Production Company. Soon afterward, the Southern Dnepr Metallurgical Company was set up by the Belgian firm Cockerill. This was then followed by the French Krivoy Rog Iron Ore Company, by the Russian-Belgian Metallurgical Company, and many others. Virtually all scholars of the early twentieth century acknowledge the role of foreign investment in the economic boom of that period. 'The exceedingly rapid growth of industry that took place in Russia in the late nineteenth and early twentieth centuries', Vavilin notes, 'was due in significant measure to an influx of capital from the countries of Europe.'[14] This thesis was embraced by both Marxist and liberal economists.

The measures that Witte used to strengthen the ruble drew foreign capital to Russia at a time when a crisis of overaccumulation was gathering strength in the West. Profits were in decline, and attractive investment projects were lacking. As Tugan-Baranovsky remarks, in the 1890s there was 'an abundance of available capital on the Western European market'.[15] The crisis of overaccumulation was especially severe in Britain and France. In 1895, capital invested in Paris yielded 2.2 per cent; in London, 2 per cent; and in Berlin, 3.15 per cent. Two years later, the yield in Paris was 2 per cent; in London, 2.78 per cent; and in Berlin, 3.84 per cent.[16] In Germany, where industrialisation had begun later, the average return on capital was higher. In conditions of acute Franco-German rivalry, investing money in the development of German industry presented problems for French financiers. By contrast, Russian enterprises were ready to pay unimaginable returns, while the strong ruble made it possible to accumulate funds and to repatriate them at any convenient time. Belgian capital – usually the junior partner to its French counterpart – had an important part to play in the industrialisation of Russia. Belgian entrepreneurs owned a disproportionate number of newly established enterprises in diverse sectors. In particular periods the share of Belgian capital on the Russian market was almost equal to that of French capital, and in terms of direct investment the Belgians outstripped the French. This was due to the fact that unlike the French investors, who brought with them only their financial assets, the Belgians much more often brought technology with them as well. In the early years of the twentieth century, Belgium, a smaller-sized nation, was one of the most industrially developed countries on earth. Belgian industry, however, had quickly reached the natural boundaries of growth within its own country, and Belgian capital was setting out to conquer new territories in Eastern Europe.

The major investments by foreigners were in the south of Russia, where steelworks, engineering plants and tube-rolling mills were established. As Tugan-Baranovsky writes,

These plants yielded huge profits of the kind to which foreign capitalists had long been unaccustomed, and shares in the enterprises commanded such high prices on foreign markets that it was enough to add the words 'Dnepr' or 'Donetsk' to the name of a firm to ensure the ready sale of its shares abroad.[17]

The Russian tube-rolling mills, which were under German control, were combined into a syndicate that waged a fierce struggle with its French and Belgian competitors. In their turn, French and Belgian capitalists founded syndicates in the coal industry of southern Russia. Prior to the arrival of foreign capital, this part of the country had been almost untouched by industrialisation. By 1895, however, the south had outstripped the Urals, the cradle of Russian industry, and by 1900 was smelting more cast iron than all the rest of the empire together. By 1900, some 70 per cent of Russia's cast iron was being produced in this region.

Of the 18 industrial joint-stock companies that were set up in Russia during these years, twelve were completely foreign-owned, while the other six were of mixed ownership. Foreign enterprises accounted for 67 per cent of the locally produced cast iron, and for 58 per cent of finished manufactures.[18] With the help of foreign investment, electrical generating stations, machine-building works, and locomotive and wagon-building plants were constructed. Describing the trade in Russian securities 'behind the scenes' of the Paris stock exchange, Professor Levin wrote in 1918: 'It would not be an exaggeration to say that it was Parisian stock-jobbers who founded our heavy industry.'[19]

The dominance of foreign capital was felt acutely in the 'high technology' of that period – in the energy industry, and in the production of electrical goods and chemicals. The investors were mainly German. Scholars recognise that in the Russian electrical goods industry, German capital held an 'almost monopolistic position'.[20] Of the two companies specialising in the production of resins, one, Provodnik, was French; while the other, Treugolnik, was German. In the tobacco industry, the leading position was held by the British-owned General Russian Tobacco Corporation.

American companies invested in goldmining, oil wells and insurance. Between 1900 and 1915, their investments increased almost fifteen-fold, from 8 million to 114 million rubles.[21] American firms also set up in business producing agricultural machinery. Once entrepreneurs from the US had established themselves in Russia, the historian M.Ya. Gefter notes, 'they became ardent supporters of the introduction of protective tariffs'.[22] Production of copper also fell increasingly under the control of British and French capital, and 90 per cent of platinum production was in foreign hands. Foreign investments were also made in the coal industry of the Donetsk basin, and in iron ore mining.

Unlike French capital, which was concentrated in the south, the more conservative British investors preferred to put their money into Urals metallurgy. But of special importance for Russian industry was, of course, the Swedish firm Nobel, which undertook oil extraction on a massive scale in Baku. The Nobel Brothers partnership had been founded as far back as 1879.

Before the formation of this first foreign oil company, oil production by local entrepreneurs had been increasing, but had employed very primitive technical methods. The firm of Nobel Brothers immediately put its enterprise on a solid footing. No expense was spared to optimise production; the company introduced technical improvements, established special laboratories, and fundamentally transformed the methods used in oil refining. Oil pipelines were laid to transport oil from the well-head, and huge tanks were built for oil storage. Tanker ships and barges began to be used for river and sea transport, while on the railways special tank wagons were introduced, specially equipped for carrying oil. The refineries were connected to the docks by kerosene pipelines.[23]

The Nobels were followed to Baku by other Western investors. The flood of capital quickly transformed the out-of-the-way town into one of the great industrial and cultural centres of the empire. By the end of the century, Russia was outstripping the US in oil output. Baku oil was of increasing interest to the British. At that time, the British empire lacked sufficient proven resources of oil on its territory, and the importance of this strategic resource was growing rapidly. At a time when conflict with Germany was in the offing, control over the Baku oilfields was becoming a crucial question not only from an economic point of view, but also from a military and political one. The British company Shell arrived in Baku, establishing the Russian General Oil Corporation for the specific purpose of operating in the country. Together with Nobel, Shell came to control more than half of oil extraction in Russia, and 75 per cent of the trade in Russian oil. In the years 1910–14 alone, British investments in the field amounted to 134.6 million rubles, compared to a mere 9.58 million rubles of Russian capital (this, moreover, was in a period when Russian capital was enjoying a boom period).[24] By this time, the Russian General Oil Corporation had outstripped both Shell and Nobel.

The history of the Grozny oilfields resembles that of Baku. Development of this resource was begun by Russian entrepreneurs, but it soon emerged that they lacked both capital and technology. In 1894, the joint-stock firm I.A. Akhverdov and Company, which controlled the oilfields, tried to find investors in Britain. The British in turn approached Belgian and Dutch banks, with the result that the joint-stock company Pétroles de Grosnyi was founded in Brussels a year later. Eventually, the whole enterprise was taken over by Belgian interests. Other Grozny enterprises suffered a similar fate.

Foreign capital played a considerable role even in such seemingly internal Russian matters as the development of urban transport. In Moscow there were two companies running horse-drawn tramways. The 'First Company' was under Russian control, while the 'Second Company' was Belgian. In 1891 they concluded an agreement on joint use of the lines. 'Under this agreement, the technical administration of both enterprises would be carried out locally by the Russian company, and the financial management by the Belgian firm, which received several places on the board of the former.'[25] Later, the transition from horse to electrical traction on the tramlines of Russia's first capital was made with the help of German capital.

The situation in other cities was analogous. Horse-drawn and electric trams, a Kharkov observer complained in 1908, were a highly profitable commercial undertaking. 'This is why hordes of foreign capitalists descend like vultures on every city where the question of building tramways is even raised.' As calculated by this observer, the Belgian tramway concession in Kharkov, Kremenchug and other centres had served to enrich foreigners, while 'leaving the cities as dirty, ill-lit and badly run as before'.[26]

Having unmasked the self-interest of the foreign investors who were taking their profits out of the country, the author of the above-cited pamphlet appealed to his home city to start building and operating tramways, and to spend the proceeds on improving the city.[27] This compelling decision, it seemed to him, was impeded only by a lack of imagination and entrepreneurialism on the part of his fellow citizens, who at every step let obvious benefits slip through their fingers. In reality, the inability of Russian entrepreneurs and bureaucrats to get by without the help of foreigners had far more profound causes. Unlike the Kharkov citizen who tried to defend the city of his birth from Belgian tramway operators, most economists of the time saw no problem with the influx of foreign capital.

IMPORTED CAPITALISM

When people spoke to Witte about the problems that might be associated with foreign capital, he simply replied that to be alarmed on these grounds meant 'to be ignorant of your own great history, to not believe in yourself and in your own great strength'.[28] In Russia, references to the country's 'great history' have traditionally meant that the government is trying to conceal the fact that it lacks any other argument. Official economists in later times have also argued along these lines. In 1990, when attracting foreign capital was once again proclaimed as state policy, A.G. Dongarov published a brochure entitled *Foreign Capital in Russia and the USSR* which aimed to prove that the effect of Western entrepreneurs on the Russian economy had been exclusively favourable. 'It was Russia that exploited foreign capital in the interests of its development, and not foreign capital that dictated goals in its own interests, for example, the extraction of raw materials for export.'[29]

What foreign capital was seeking in Russia early in the twentieth century was not raw materials, which could be had readily enough from other sources, but profits that substantially exceeded European norms. This was well understood by the prominent economist M. Tugan-Baranovsky, who was acutely aware that the Western capital that was entering Russia was seeking 'colonial' super-profits: 'The markets that Britain seeks thousands of *versty* off in remote countries of Africa and Asia is opened up for the Russian manufacturer in his immediate neighbourhood, thanks to the railway line.'[30] The movement of capital from 'old' bourgeois countries to 'new' ones is a natural phenomenon, the basis of global progress and development. Tugan-Baranovsky was perfectly aware of the source of the exceedingly high profits to be had in the 'new' markets:

Russian industrial capital feeds not only on the juices of the workers whom it exploits, but also on the juices of other, non-capitalist producers, above all peasant agriculturalists. The peasant who buys a plough or a scythe for a price twice the cost of production contributes even more to the high rate of profit of Hughes, Cockerill and other owners of metal goods factories than do their own workers. It is this chance to shear the sheep twice, so to speak, to burn the candle at both ends, that is the secret behind the attractiveness of Russia to foreign capitalists.

It follows that in practice, the arguments about the narrowness of the internal market in the Russian empire make no sense either.

For capitalist industry, the market is even more attractive in those countries in which, as in Russia, natural wealth is present in abundance, while the mass of the population has not yet broken with the previous archaic economic forms.[31]

Tugan-Baranovsky was, of course, convinced that with the progress of capitalism this superior attractiveness would necessarily be lost.[32] In other words, the super-exploitation of the local population would lead in the end to the development of 'normal' capitalism, which would banish such disproportions and create the conditions for a more just society. As early as the beginning of the twentieth century, however, the experience of the 'remote countries of Africa and Asia' was giving cause for doubt as to whether this conclusion was correct. Contrary to the arguments of liberal economists, 'development' does not by any means necessarily lead to prosperity. Paradoxically, the undistinguished citizen of Kharkov fared better at revealing the essence of the matter than many professors in the capital. The trouble with foreign investments is that you have to pay for them. Where there are imports of capital, there must also be exports of profits. The super-profits obtained in Russia served the process of accumulation of capital in France and other countries of the West. In circumstances where dividends reached 40 per cent in Russia,[33] while the average return on capital in France was barely 2 per cent, it is not hard to see that in parallel with industrial development, a vast redistribution of resources was taking place from the poorer country to the richer. In Paris at the time, it was said that Russia was becoming 'France's Wild West', in recognition of the fact that for French capital, investment in Russia was opening up the same kind of limitless possibilities as the 'gold fever' in California had done for America.[34]

The thesis on super-profits is disputed by Dongarov, who cites far lower figures. According to his calculations, the average rate of profit for foreign commercial-industrial capital 'amounted to 12.9 per cent between 1887 and 1913'.[35] It is obvious, however, that the data cited by Dongarov are akin to 'the average temperature of the patients in a ward'. These data include the period of upturn from 1888 to 1894; the economic boom from 1895 to 1902, when profits reached their peak; the crisis years from 1903 to 1905, when profits fell sharply and Western investment declined just as dramatically; and the subsequent revival of the economy from 1906 to 1913. In the peak periods, when most of the capital arrived in Russia, profits of 12–13 per cent were considered rather inferior; and during the industrial downturn, capital flowed out of the country. But even if the rate of profit on foreign investments in Russia did not exceed 13 per cent, it would still have been considered extraordinary for European industry, exceeding the French indices approximately six times over. How were these results achieved?

The 'dual exploitation' of producer and consumer described by Tugan-Baranovsky may have made the situation more agreeable for foreign entrepreneurs, but it could not have failed to slow the development of the internal market, with all the consequences that flowed from this. How was it possible to maintain high prices for almost two decades, while industry expanded rapidly? The country was developing, but political tensions abroad and social tensions at home grew more rapidly than the national economy. Contrary to the views of Tugan-Baranovsky, the main source of super-profits was not the peasantry but the government. The gigantic loans taken out by the Russian government on financial markets in Paris and elsewhere were related in the most direct way to the profits of Western entrepreneurs. The state debt increased, since it was necessary to pay for the huge government orders that were attracting foreign capital. While maintaining these state orders, it was necessary meanwhile to sustain the 'strong ruble'. The government was obliged to intensify its financial pressure on the population, forcing them to pay for development. The peasantry did, indeed, subsidise the industries that were being built with Western capital, but not so much through the purchase of goods as through paying taxes to the treasury. Because this revenue was nevertheless inadequate, new credits were required. Russia, in sum, was made to pay twice – to pay dividends to foreign investors, and to pay off the state debts from which these profits were being financed.

Even at the time, it was remarked that Witte's policy of attracting foreign capital was ruining the countryside, which was ultimately required to provide the funds both to service the foreign debt and to build the railways. One St Petersburg bureaucrat remarked bitterly:

The finance minister is a dashing horseman, but his steed is ill-fed and worn-out. It is simply a peasant horse, true, very hardy and patient, but however much you spur it on and scourge it with the whip, it cannot reach the speed of a thoroughbred.[36]

The readiness to 'spur on' and 'scourge' the 'peasant horse' gave rise to tensions which, as they gradually accumulated, created the preconditions for a social explosion. The economic successes of the years from 1895 to 1900 prepared the way for the political shocks of 1905.

In Russia in the late nineteenth and early twentieth centuries, the relations between 'centre' and 'periphery' that became typical for Latin America only from the mid 1970s were tested for the first time. After a crisis of overaccumulation of capital in the 'centre', a debt crisis on the 'periphery' inevitably followed. From 1847, every serious crisis in the West was accompanied by an outflow of capital from Russia. As early as 1861–66, according to Strumilin's calculations, no less than 455 million gold rubles was taken out of Russia.[37]

Around the turn of the twentieth century, this problem began taking on even greater dimensions. According to a modern scholar, Russia between 1881 and 1913 paid a sum of more than five billion rubles in interest and principal on its state loans, that is, half as much again as it received. In practice, it did not import capital, but exported it. In this respect, however, Russia was no different from the other countries that made up the periphery of world capitalism in the late nineteenth century.[38]

Strangely enough, this statement is reassuring to liberal historians, for whom the very fact that a country is part of world capitalism is an indisputable achievement. Moreover, the share of the expenditure side of the budget represented by payments to foreign creditors had diminished somewhat by 1913, and the overall total of these payments, which had reached a peak in 1910, had begun to decline. However, this merely reflected the general dynamic of the world financial markets, subject as ever to fluctuations. In periods of growth the position of debtors tends to improve, creating the illusion of a 'strengthening of independence'; with the onset of the next crisis, however, this position again deteriorates. The data referred to above, moreover, refer only to the outflow of funds from Russia via state channels. As explained earlier, most of the loans went to pay for orders that had gone to Western investors. A substantial proportion of the profits was reinvested in Russia. The 'Western investments', it follows, were often entirely of Russian origin. The large-scale repatriation of capital against a background of international economic downturn explains the fact that by the end of the crisis period, Russian industry had begun to appear more 'national'; the Russian bourgeoisie had, to some degree, taken the place of the departed foreign investors. Once growth resumed, however, the relationship of forces between Russian and foreign proprietors again changed in favour of the latter.

Meanwhile, the government, as it tried desperately to attract 'foreign capital', became increasingly enmeshed in debt. The mechanism of financial exploitation of the country was gradually picking up speed. Even though the growth of Russian industrial entrepreneurship was an obvious fact, there was no question that it would force out foreign investors. 'The history of foreign investments,' a Soviet scholar remarks, 'is a history of the growing, not decreasing, role of external capital in the Russian economy.'[39] It would appear that the Russian bourgeoisie grew along with industry. Nevertheless, foreign investors managed without any particular effort to secure the key positions in the banking sector, and to exert a powerful influence in the productive sphere. While holding only a third of the shares in Russian banks and an even smaller share in industry, Ronin asserts, French, Belgian and German groups 'contrived to take control of the whole Russian economy, and of the Tsar's government to boot'.[40] If this is an exaggeration, it is not a particularly huge one.

By the early 1890s, the major Russian banks were selling substantial proportions of their shares to German, French and – less frequently – British partners. Foreign capital was invested mainly in the very largest banks with close ties to the government. The most influential French and Russian banks formed a so-called 'Russian syndicate' to finance industry within the empire. Because the Russian partners were chronically lacking in their own funds, they made regular use of Western credit. Supplying Russian banks with circulating capital, German and French financiers came to play an increasingly large role in the Russian market.

According to Ronin's calculations, 'on average, about 40 per cent of the shares of eighteen Russian banks, whose founding capital made up about 75 per cent of the capital of all the forty-six commercial joint-stock banks operating in 1914, were held by foreigners'.[41] Western investors also began to play a growing role in provincial financial markets. French banks aided in share issues by the Merchant Bank in Rostov-on-Don, and by the Siberian Bank. In the Russian-Asian Bank, French capital made up about 60 per cent of the total.[42] French capital also played a considerable role in the Russian-Chinese Bank, which opened in 1896 in connection with the building of the Trans-Siberian Railway. The same bank also financed the construction of the Manchurian Railway. The dominant position of the French in these projects aroused the concern of Witte, on whose initiative the State Bank acquired a substantial proportion of the shares in that credit establishment. Even after the intervention of the government, however, French influence in the enterprise remained particularly strong.

German capital also took part in the railway programmes, but on a much lesser scale than its French counterpart. The position of German investors in the sector gradually declined, while the presence of British capital in the market for railway securities began to grow.

Around the turn of the century, the links between Russian industry and the Paris stock exchange became strong and self-perpetuating. Among the host countries for British investments, Russia was only in tenth place, and in 1911 was behind both Peru and Uruguay. For French capital, however, the Russian empire had become a key area of expansion. In 1897, 6 million francs were invested in Russia; and in 1902, according to various estimates, the figure was around 9–10 billion francs – constituting almost half of all the French capital invested in Europe.[43]

THE RUSSIAN GOVERNMENT AND FOREIGN CAPITAL

Whatever the importance of foreign investment, the most important source of funds for Russian industry was the government itself, distributing orders and credit on a wide basis. It was state orders that made it profitable for French and Belgian capital to invest in metallurgy and metals fabrication in southern Russia. 'When plants were set up, they were provided with state orders for several years', Tugan-Baranovsky states.[44] These orders in turn were backed by credit taken out on financial markets in Paris and elsewhere.

Numerous official industrial departments founded their own enterprises in all areas of the economy. 'Public' plants were responsible for a substantial part of the overall volume of production. No other European state in the late nineteenth and early twentieth centuries had such a large number of official institutions regulating economic life. All sorts of commissions, chancelleries, ministries, committees, chambers, councils, and so on, played key roles in deciding literally any question. Entrepreneurs and their organisations in turn collaborated closely with these institutions, and took part in their work. In 1911, the Ministry of Trade and Industry stated that

In Russia, the government is one of the main consumers, and the fate of many branches of industry depends to an important degree on state orders. Aside from the metal industry, which supplies the state railways and the artillery and naval departments, there are also, for example, the textile, leather and other sectors of industry.[45]

The state railway programmes played a decisive role in the formation of a unified internal market. Until the completion of the Trans-Siberian Railway, it was only possible to speak conditionally of a single national market, encompassing the whole territory of the empire. Economic ties between regions were sustained, to a significant degree, by the functioning of the state system, and collapsed every time the state was in crisis. A paradoxical situation arose in which the bourgeoisie had closer ties to the world market and to the national government than to a unified domestic market. It was these links with administrative structures, rather than operations in a single market, that united the Russian bourgeoisie on the national level.

Neither under Witte nor later under Stolypin was the government in any way a force resisting foreign influence. A witticism of the times described the St Petersburg banks as 'Russian in their appearance, foreign in their capital, and ministerial in their risk-taking'.[46] In fact, the amount of Russian capital invested in the banks was also substantial, but it was foreign investors who held the strategic positions in the financial sector. Meanwhile, the St Petersburg government was forced to serve the interests of the foreign banks, since they were playing the decisive role in the establishing of a 'national' credit system.

Vast sums that had been pumped out of the Russian economy accumulated in the accounts of the St Petersburg government in Paris and Berlin. Some of this money would later be reinvested in the Russian economy, but in the form of foreign credits and investments. The more St Petersburg came to depend on foreign financial markets, the more it protected foreign investors. Having accepted responsibility on behalf of the foreign banks for the well-being of their Russian branch offices, Ronin stresses, the Ministry of Finance was obliged to attend constantly to their interests, 'in order to avoid rebukes'.[47] The government was forced to intervene regularly in banking matters, protecting the foreign owners from the mishaps which might befall them on Russian financial markets. The country's investment rating had to be maintained. Unfortunately, these interventions drained the treasury and led to increases in internal debt, which in turn increased the need for foreign loans. Such a system, as contemporaries recognised, inevitably required 'attentiveness and compliance in the area of foreign policy'.[48] The price of this compliance became fully apparent only in 1914.

Out of patriotic feeling, the Russian government sought in whatever way possible to understate the significance of foreign investments. What the focus on this patriotic statistic led to can be judged from a single example. According to data for 1898, the total number of foreign enterprises that were opened in

Russia that year was 24. Meanwhile, the Belgians alone reported setting up a total of 35 enterprises in the country in that year. 'It might be supposed', a contemporary observer noted ironically, 'that foreigners are more readily able to find out which enterprises they have put their savings into, and what belongs to them.'[49]

THE CRISIS OF 1899–1900

Benefits would continue to flow from this situation only so long as the strong ruble and high grain prices kept pumping capital into Russia, and while a protectionist tariff underpinned the growth of industry. For this model, the next slump in the world economy proved fatal. This time, the Russian empire was not only a victim of the global disorder, but also one of the sources. As noted by contemporaries, the world economic crisis of 1899–1900 began with an 'overheating' of the Russian economy, and only then 'spread little by little throughout Europe'.[50] The completion of the great railway projects in Siberia and the Far East brought a sharp contraction in orders for the metallurgical industry; then, in a chain reaction, demand fell in other sectors as well. This hit foreign investors hard, who then began to curtail their activity in Russia. Inevitably, the effect was felt on the Paris stock exchange.

Spilling over into a world crisis, the economic downturn devastated world prices for raw materials. As soon as world grain prices began to falter, a shudder passed through the edifice of the St Petersburg state apparatus.

An 'overheating' of the economy had already been apparent in Russia in 1898 and 1899. The funds that were borrowed on the French financial market were insufficient to maintain growth. The St Petersburg government tried to obtain money from Britain and the US, but without great success. In London, Russia was still viewed as a rival power threatening the interests of the British empire in Asia. On the Berlin stock exchange, large quantities of ready money were simply not available. Moreover, the moment was extremely inopportune. In 1898, the first signs of an impending crisis had been felt on the European money market, and credit had become more expensive. The situation in 1899 was even worse.

In 1900, faced with a financial crisis, foreign holders of Russian securities began dumping them. The French alone sold securities worth approximately 100 million rubles, and roughly the same sum in gold was taken out of Russia.[51] To restrain the flight of capital, Witte was forced to introduce more and more favourable terms for the foreign owners of Russian securities. This led to new problems. When the Russian authorities in 1901 decided to float a new 4 per cent loan in Paris, they met with open political pressure. The French government demanded concessions, mainly in the economic field. The funds borrowed in Paris had to be spent at least in part on orders placed with French factories or with companies owned by French capital. St Petersburg replied to these demands with a formal refusal, but in fact fulfilled them. Foreign enterprises that had been in a difficult position because of the economic crisis that was sweeping the country began receiving new orders. This, however, was no longer enough; the demands of the French became still more harsh. Witte justified himself by reminding his partners that in line with the principles of a liberal economy, 'every industrialist who undertakes business stands to gain or to lose'.[52] Unfortunately, Western leaders who zealously preach liberalism to credulous natives are invariably deaf to such appeals when these are aimed in their own direction. The dependence of St Petersburg on Paris was by now so great that in each specific case Witte was forced to yield. He consoled himself, while informing Paris of another concession, by reminding the French Minister of Finance, J. Caillaux, that the decision did not 'accord with the sound principles of banking policy which I am charged with defending'. Witte was taking this step 'solely in order to please you, my dear colleague, and the French government'.[53]

THE REVOLUTION DRAWS NEAR

The starting point for the 1905 revolution was the defeat suffered by St Petersburg in the Russo-Japanese War. But this conflict itself had profound causes, rooted in the maturing crisis of the world system and in the contradictory role played within this system by Russia. In Pokrovsky's view, this war was a 'skirmish around the forward posts' of Anglo-American and German imperialism.

The interests of Russian imperialism itself had a secondary significance in all this, just as they played a secondary role even in the conflict of 1914. To the extent that Russian capitalism was active here, it was as an old commercial capitalism, not as a new financial or even industrial capitalism.[54]

The rivalry between Germany and Britain in fact manifested itself long before the First World War, in the most unexpected places and in the most unusual forms. The first skirmish between German and British interests was the Boer War. The behaviour of the Boers, who had shown unexpected toughness in a dispute with the mighty British empire, and who in effect were the first to begin hostilities, cannot be explained without taking into account German military aid and diplomatic promises which they had received in Berlin. The strategy of the Boers was founded on expectations of a great war that would soon begin in Europe, and which would undoubtedly distract the British forces. At that point, however, the German empire was not ready for a direct conflict. When this finally became clear even to the most radical Boer military leaders, they not only made peace with London but also turned themselves into consistent defenders of British imperial interests in Africa.

Russia's war with Japan unfolded against a background of the world economic crisis that had been precipitated by the ending of Russian railway construction in the Far East. The British empire stood clearly with Japan, which, with British help, had succeeded not only in building a first-class navy, but also in training its sailors. Berlin, on the other hand, did everything it could to encourage St Petersburg to go to war. Nevertheless, to view the Russo-Japanese conflict simply as a manifestation of Anglo-German rivalry would be grossly simplistic.

It is worth noting that in another text, the same Pokrovsky provides a far more detailed explanation of the causes of the war. Russia's ambivalent position as a semi-peripheral, or more precisely, as a peripheral empire, was especially obvious in the area of colonial policy. On the one hand, Russia's own economic development depended on processes occurring in the West. On the other hand, the Russian state, as an empire, was sufficiently strong – at least in military respects – that it could take part in the European colonial expansion. Here, Russian capital simultaneously defended its own interests and acted as a bearer of Western influence, helping to draw more and more new territories into the world system. In the process, Russia both served the interests of the nascent global 'centre' and competed with it.

This ambivalent and contradictory nature of Russian capital explains the problems encountered by Russian colonial policy, which was completely successful only where it did not meet with serious resistance from other world powers. In Central Asia, China, Korea, Mongolia and Persia, Russian expansion developed alongside the expansion of other empires, with which St Petersburg at times competed and at other times collaborated.

Beginning in the 1870s, a feverish race to acquire colonies unfolded against a background of stagnation in the European and North American markets. The impulse which the industrial revolution had provided to the world economy was now to a significant degree exhausted. The development of technology had become evolutionary; as a result, qualitatively new products and new markets were no longer appearing. The growth of capitalism now depended on the ability of the leading powers to expand their empires. Russia participated in this process alongside Britain, France, Belgium and Germany, playing a subordinate role but zealously protecting its own interests. In the 'Great Game', the Russians had ultimately been forced to renounce ideas of expanding into Afghanistan, but the British empire was now also forced to reckon with the presence of a new military force on the very borders of India. In competing with the British in Persia, the Russian government tried to emulate its rivals, but the resources available to the two sides were unequal. As a Soviet historian noted, 'while stubbornly pursuing a policy of "capitalist conquest" of Persia, the Russian autocracy took this policy to the most absurd lengths'.[55] Instead of deriving benefits from its expansion, St Petersburg was forced to spend ever-greater sums for minimal results. The rivalry with Britain proved futile. The situation was redeemed by the Anglo-Russian Agreement of 1907, which provided for a dividing-up of spheres of influence in Persia, Afghanistan and Tibet.

In the same fashion, Russian expansion in the Far East, backed by railway projects and French investments, began to falter in the early twentieth century as it encountered resistance from Japan, behind which stood the might of Britain. The completion of the Trans-Siberian Railway opened up the possibility of incorporating Siberia fully in the world market system. But now as never before, ice-free harbours were needed in the Far East. Japan became Russia's enemy not because it was competing with Russia for colonial mastery over Korea and China; the real reason was that Japan, through this rivalry, impeded the access of Siberian grain and other resources to world markets. To quote Pokrovsky, Japan 'stood in the road'.[56]

Meanwhile, the situation in Russia itself was becoming increasingly tense as the crisis conditions brought the contradictions in Witte's policies to the surface. A small but victorious war was needed so that the internal tensions could be relieved.

The ending of construction work on the Trans-Siberian Railway coincided with the bottoming-out of world grain prices. Thereafter, the situation improved. As Pokrovsky notes,

It is typical that Siberia as a colony began to interest the Russian government and Russian capitalism precisely in the period when grain prices were at their lowest, when it was exceedingly important for Russia to find some way of increasing the amount of raw produce it was pouring onto the grain market, because this produce was bringing lower and lower returns, and new regions had to be found from which to extract it....[57]

THE STORM OF 1905

If the tsarist regime felt Russia's lag behind the 'old' empires of Britain and France to be something normal and irremediable, the rapid rise of Japan signified the collapse of all the Russian government's hopes of playing a more weighty role in the world, and testified to the failure of the path to modernisation that the Russian authorities had chosen. The identity of the foe was clear, but the funds needed for victory were now lacking. The defeat suffered by the Russian fleet in the battle of Tsushima was not principally the result of talent on the part of the Japanese Admiral Togo, or of incompetence on the part of his opponent Admiral Rozhestvensky, but of fundamentally different levels of military technology. The entire Japanese fleet was made up of ships of a single generation, while the Russian squadron, along with its three modern battleships, included obsolete vessels incapable of seriously resisting the Japanese. Leading a flotilla of old, slow vessels, the new Russian dreadnoughts could not exploit their superiority since they were unable to operate at full speed or to manoeuvre effectively. In addition, it later emerged, the Russian naval gunners had been supplied with defective shells that were incapable of doing any serious damage. Precisely the same occurred as at the Battle of Alma; the enemy stood off at a safe distance, and bombarded the Russian squadron as if its ships were targets on a firing range.

Tsushima could be interpreted as a symbol of the bankruptcy of the Russian government's entire modernisation strategy. Rapid development in particular sectors, and the establishing of modern enterprises, could not by themselves make up for overall backwardness. Ultimately, this ballast of underdevelopment sank the advanced elements of the economy. While Western societies developed in more or less even fashion and at the same pace, in Russia every attempt to speed up 'movement along the road of progress' simply increased the disproportions and made the problems more intractable. The old did not prevent the rise of the new, but it was the old that imposed its logic and rules. Modern social layers and structures were fastened to a system of archaic social relations, and could not reveal their potential to the full. By the beginning of the twentieth century, Russian society as a whole resembled Admiral Rozhestvensky's ill-fated squadron.

The country was on the brink of revolution. To resolve the accumulated contradictions without radical social and political change was impossible, and modernisation of the economy, begun but not completed during the years of peasant reform, remained on the agenda. Not only did radicals talk of the impending revolution, but liberals as well. The officials of the state administration took this threat very seriously as well. It is striking, however, how dimly the character of the looming revolution was perceived by most of the future participants in this historic drama.

Liberal society dreamt of a successful 'Europeanisation' of the state, of the abolition of tsarism and of the introduction of 'normal' capitalist modes of operation. However paradoxical it might seem, Russian liberals, who traditionally had by no means been hostile to socialism, referred in this case to Karl Marx; in Marxism, they saw proof that the universal triumph of capitalism over patriarchal and feudal structures was inevitable. If all countries were bound to pass through capitalism, backward Russia was destined also to travel the 'Western road' and to catch up with the advanced countries of Europe. Revolution was essential in order to do away with the 'relics of serfdom', and to clear the way for the new liberal-bourgeois Russia. Only one thing remained unclear: what were the social forces that would carry out this salutary overturn?

The real Russian bourgeoisie showed no particular signs of being a revolutionary class. The big capitalists of St Petersburg had close ties to the central bureaucracy; the state was their business partner and main source of orders. The Moscow entrepreneurs, the owners of the textile mills, were more radical-minded; they had an interest in broadening the internal market, and this would require an increase in the purchasing power of the peasantry, the main consumers of textile products. For these entrepreneurs, reforms that would improve the situation of the peasants were indispensable. Even this more left-wing faction of the bourgeoisie, however, was not at all inclined to revolution. Meanwhile, the provincial capitalists often outstripped even the local landowners and government officials in their barbarism and reactionary views. Finally, all sections of the bourgeoisie had begun to sense the danger from the growing working class, and consequently felt the need to be defended by the state.

Unlike the situation in England and France, where during the revolutionary period the bourgeoisie led a broad popular movement, the Russian capitalists grew increasingly conscious of the difference between their interests and those of the masses. The Russian entrepreneurs depended on foreign credit, guaranteed by the government, and consequently on political stability. It is quite understandable that these entrepreneurs should have been conservative. The political position of the Russian bourgeoisie in the late nineteenth century was thus 'the diametrical opposite of the classical models of Western history'.[58] The petty and middle bourgeoisie, living on their sales to the domestic market, were weak, provincial and ill-educated, while the upper bourgeoisie were dependent on foreign capital and were 'tied hand and foot to the landowners'.[59]

In such circumstances, any political crisis hit directly at the interests of the entrepreneurs. The intertwining of bourgeois and landowner interests thus occurred at a whole range of levels. The money obtained through the semi-serf exploitation of the peasantry was deposited in the banks and was used to finance private industry. In the countryside, landowner agriculture was the main partner for urban capital. In the West, the ending of feudal exploitation in the countryside had preceded industrialisation, but in Russia, to a significant degree, industrialisation took place on the basis of funds acquired through the exploitation of rural labour using patriarchal and semi-serf methods. In Britain, the aristocracy and bourgeoisie had become intertwined as the changes wrought by the revolution had been consolidated; in Russia, the same process occurred prior to and 'in place of' a bourgeois revolution. There, capitalism and bureaucratic, quasi-serf-holding autocracy were, so to speak, Siamese twins. With its characteristic bureaucratic inefficiency, autocratic rule of course acted as a brake on the development of the country – or more precisely, on the development of 'modern', 'advanced' forms of capitalism – but the bourgeoisie could not do without it. Russian capitalism was so intimately linked to the patriarchal order and to the authoritarian state that for the country's bourgeois the collapse of the autocratic regime meant inevitable catastrophe. The leaders of British industry might allow themselves a certain democratism, but Russian entrepreneurs needed a harsh state authority. Where the Western bourgeoisie would readily compromise, their Russian counterparts had no option except to appeal to the government.

Chaadaev once observed ironically: 'Russian liberals are like midges swarming mindlessly in a ray of sunlight. The sun, in this case, is the sun of the West.'[60] This 'cowardice' of Russian liberalism, this inability of bourgeois 'progressives' to resist government policy, was stressed constantly by socialist writers, including not only Lenin and Plekhanov, but also people of far more moderate views. 'The further east you go in Europe, the more weak, base and cowardly the bourgeoisie becomes in political terms', Engels once declared, and in Russia these words were repeated by none other than the young Pyotr Struve, later to become a leading ideologue of the counter-revolution and an active figure in the White movement.[61] Pokrovsky reacted to this formula with irony: 'What, is ever-increasing baseness some mysterious, mystical property of the Eastern bourgeoisie?'[62] It was, of course, no accident that many liberal politicians including Struve regularly revised their outlook, and moved further and further to the right. The bankruptcy of liberalism in Russia was predicated on the weakness and organic dependency of the Russian bourgeoisie itself. Describing the Russian merchants of the late eighteenth century, who resorted constantly to help from the state, had neither the skills nor the desire to participate in free competition, and who exploited serf labour, a modern-day scholar notes that these people still had not 'attained the level of bourgeois morality'.[63] The early twentieth century had brought few changes to this picture. Historians have been forced to state that the image of the Russian industrialist, 'shielded from competition by the protectionist system, employing the crudest forms of exploitation, endlessly importuning the authorities for privileges, and politically intertwined with tsarism, was indeed unattractive'.[64]

In 1903–05, the bourgeoisie, to use Pokrovsky's expression, 'played at making revolution'.[65] Russian industrial capital was forced to speak out against the autocracy, but could neither be consistent in this struggle nor lead it to victory. During the October political strike of 1905, many factory-owners continued to pay their striking workers. The limited freedoms which the tsar's October Manifesto conceded under pressure from the workers could never be considered even the beginning of constitutional monarchy in Russia; clearly, the struggle for democracy was far from reaching its culmination. The events of the revolution, however, quickly changed the bourgeoisie's way of thinking.

The 'backwardness' of Russia did not signify by any means that once the 'progressive forces' willed it so, the country could pass through all the stages that Western civilisation had already traversed, and at an accelerated rate. While the French bourgeoisie in the eighteenth century had seen nothing but support coming from further down the social scale, the Russian entrepreneurs could not fail to perceive a danger.

Not only the proletariat, but the peasants as well were hostile towards capitalism to a significant degree. The modern city stood counterposed to the patriarchal village, the rich to the poor, and private property in all its forms to the communitarian tradition. The young Lenin, polemicising in his book *The Development of Capitalism in Russia* against the *narodnik* populists and their belief in the special destiny of Russia, had sought to show that the small peasant households were gradually becoming part of the capitalist economy, and that capitalist agriculture was being born in the depths of the Russian countryside. Lenin's book, which was passed by the tsarist censors, met with warm approval from the liberal intelligentsia; in it, the Westernisers found the very picture they wanted of the Russian countryside. The debate, however, was by no means over. For Lenin, all commodity production, and in fact any contact with the market, was a sign of capitalist development; Chayanov, however, recognised that forced contact with urban capitalism was not enough to turn a peasant into a capitalist farmer.[66] What was happening was the destruction of peasant agriculture under the impact of the new market relations, rather than the successful bourgeois transformation of the countryside.

If capitalism were to score a complete triumph in the cities, capitalist relations would of course sooner or later emerge victorious in the countryside as well. However, it was precisely the lack of a developed rural capitalism in Russia that blocked any possibility of the development of bourgeois relationships 'of a European type' in the cities. The overwhelming mass of peasants felt no ties whatever to the 'progressive bourgeoisie'. A Third Estate in the Western sense simply did not exist.

While a Third Estate uniting the bourgeoisie with the ordinary masses did not exist in Russia, the peasants were linked very closely to the workers, and what united them was not so much hostility to the autocratic state as a shared dislike for 'city moneybags'.

In 1905, Pokrovsky wrote, the countryside gained the upper hand over the cities, 'imposing rural ideals on the urban revolution'.[67] The hatred that had built up over decades was a symptom not so much of an impending revolution, as of an inevitable social catastrophe. Even if the bourgeoisie were not fully conscious of this fact, they could not help but feel a sense of threat. If liberal politicians prior to 1905 could still have illusions concerning the possibility of a popular bourgeois-democratic bloc, the events of the first Russian revolution clarified everything once and for all. With practical experience now of revolutionary turmoil, the bourgeoisie turned rapidly to the right. This was the case not only with liberal intellectuals, who, as the former 'legal Marxist' Sergey Bulgakov put it, felt 'the breath of the antichrist'.[68] Large-scale capital in Russia had never shown any particular interest in democratic change, and after October 1905, it began to cool to the idea of constitutional reform as well.

In *Vekhi* – a collection of articles published immediately after the revolution by Pyotr Struve, Sergey Bulgakov and other prominent, highly talented commentators of liberal bent – the rightward turn was declared openly: better a compromise with the autocracy than an uncontrolled social explosion. The more acutely the need for radical change made itself felt, the more counter-revolutionary the bourgeoisie became. For Marxist thinkers who had been raised on the textbooks of German social democracy, this situation came as a complete surprise.

Analysing the Russian experience of 1905, Max Weber came to the pessimistic conclusion that capitalist development did not, in and of itself, automatically give birth to bourgeois democracy; indeed, it represented an obstacle to democracy arising. Political freedom had appeared in the West 'in unique circumstances' involving great geographic discoveries, the rise of the urban culture of the late Middle Ages, the Reformation, and so forth. These circumstances would never again be repeated, and capitalism was being shaped by quite new and different social conditions.

It would be quite ridiculous to hope that present-day capitalism (this inevitable outcome of economic development), as it has been imported to Russia and installed in America, is somehow connected with 'democracy' or even with freedom (in any sense of this word). The question is quite different: what, in these circumstances, are the chances of democracy, freedom, and so on surviving in the longer term? They will survive only if the nation shows a decisive *will* in its determination not to be a herd of sheep.

Ultimately, according to Weber, the fate of democracy depends on political culture and on the decisiveness of 'the champions of freedom in Russia, irrespective of the 'tendency' and 'class' to which they belong'.[69] One cannot help noting that in the way he poses this question, Weber is far more dialectical, and far closer to Marx, than the theoreticians of orthodox Marxism. But the practical politicians who had founded a workers' party in Russia could scarcely have been pleased by the pessimistic general conclusions of the German sociologist.

At first, Russian Marxism differed little from liberalism in its assessments of the country's future. It was no accident that in Russia all the leading theoreticians of liberal progress had passed through a phase of enthusiasm for Marxism, and for the social democrats, through the experience of collaborating with liberals. For both liberals and social democrats, the 'legal Marxism' of the early years of the century was a common ideology of modernisation. The founder of Russian social democracy, G.V. Plekhanov, assigned the workers' movement the role of the radical left wing in the bourgeois-democratic revolution, while the main work of reordering Russian society would be carried out by the bourgeoisie. More radical socialists stressed the contradictions between factions of the bourgeoisie, calling on the proletariat to maintain its own independent organisation and to collaborate only with the 'progressive' wing of the capitalist class. The problem lay in finding this 'progressive' wing. Where Lenin surpassed his comrades in Russian social democracy was in his readiness to break with the schemas of the orthodox Marxism which he himself had zealously defended in the early days of his political career. The flawed nature of these schemas had become clear to him right at the beginning of the 1905 revolution. Once the country felt the need for bourgeois-democratic change, and the progressive bourgeoisie effectively deserted the struggle, the role of the pre-eminent revolutionary force would have to be assumed by the proletariat. Born out of capitalist development and modern industry, but deprived of elementary civil rights and oppressed both by the entrepreneurs and by the autocratic state, the Russian working class had a greater interest than other classes in the modernisation of society. This was the source of Lenin's famous thesis on the hegemony of the proletariat in the bourgeois-democratic revolution.

Nevertheless, Lenin did not answer one of the most important questions. If the working class were really interested in modernisation, this still did not mean that it would fight for the bourgeois-democratic vision of the future. There was no reason why the proletariat, once it had taken real power, should set up a bourgeois-democratic regime rather than some other that corresponded to its own concepts of freedom and justice. Lenin in 1905 still did not imagine any process of modernisation apart from a capitalist one. The question, however, was already being posed in all its tragic sharpness.

Trotsky held more radical views. In formulating his theory of 'permanent revolution', he effectively began where Lenin had left off. Seizing power in the course of the bourgeois-democratic revolution, the proletariat in Trotsky's view would inevitably go beyond the boundaries of capitalist modernisation and would begin to implement its own programme, corresponding to its own ideology and interests. Taking into account how backward Russian society was, and how unprepared it was for socialism, Trotsky called for this problem to be solved through permanent revolution.

The socialist transformation in Russia would inspire workers in the West, and in Trotsky's view it would be the triumph of socialism in the developed countries of Europe that would give the Russian workers' republic its eventual form. How all this would occur in practice was not fully clear to Trotsky, but even Kautsky, at the beginning of the century, had written that revolutions in

Eastern Europe might serve as a detonator for transformations in the West. Ultimately, a revolutionary explosion in so vast a country as Russia could not fail to affect the rest of the world, and Trotsky's reasoning was far from groundless. The problem was simply that the real historical process proved to be more complex, 'deceitful' and tragic than even the most penetrating theoreticians had expected.

THE AGE OF REACTIONS AND REFORMS: THE GOVERNMENT OF STOLYPIN

The revolution of 1905 shook the regime, but did not bring about its overthrow. To the surprise of many, tsarism made concessions relatively quickly. The mass political strike in October culminated in the tsar's manifesto 'granting' freedom of speech and of the press, and legalising opposition parties. The regime manoeuvred, trying not only to lower the temperature of the revolutionary struggle, but also to adapt at least somehow to the new requirements of capitalist development.

The St Petersburg bureaucracy gave the country a whole series of clever and well-educated administrators who, to one degree or another, recognised the necessity for modernisation. The most outstanding figures of this era were Witte and Stolypin, the two heads of the Russian government who were in office during the years of revolution and of the reaction that followed.

Within the bureaucracy, Witte and Stolypin were almost polar opposites. Witte drafted the October Manifesto that established the State Duma – a feeble half-measure, but nevertheless a functioning structure of representative power. Stolypin, while limiting the already weak influence of the Duma, implemented agrarian reform. Witte put his stake on political liberalisation as an indispensable precondition for overcoming backwardness, while Stolypin tried to substitute economic reforms for political changes. Both supported a restricted liberalism, but in practice their strategies were fundamentally different. Witte helped the regime to adapt to the revolutionary crisis, while Stolypin used repressive measures to smash the revolutionary movement. Both, however, were able to carry out their reforms only because of the pressure from the revolutionary forces. Both sought to ensure that modernisation would continue within the framework of the old regime, and both with the help of reforms did their utmost to avoid revolution.

Comparing the trends in world grain prices and the problems in the life of nineteenth-century Russian society, Pokrovsky found an obvious interdependence. Grain prices in the markets of Berlin and London had only to rise, and the Russian elites were possessed by a desire for liberal and reformist initiatives. But when grain prices fell, the yearning for change of the ruling groups declined as well. The times of depressed prices invariably coincided with periods of reaction.

In this respect, the Stolypin reforms were the culmination of the 'grain' cycles of Russian public life. The government took decisive steps to accelerate development and to modernise the country according to the Western model. But unlike previous periods of reform, the Stolypin years combined liberal initiatives in the economy with consistent reaction in the area of politics. Contemporaries understood this as being natural and necessary. While politicians from the 'party of popular freedom' (the Cadets) might complain from inertia about the anti-democratism of the authorities, the most profound thinkers of Russian liberalism, grouped around *Vekhi,* now viewed the government's reactionary policies as an essential condition for development. After all, any democracy in Russia would turn inevitably into an uprising by the anti-bourgeois masses. Russian liberalism had come full circle, reaching a peculiar culmination in Stolypin's programme.

In Pokrovsky's view, Stolypin's reforms amounted to 'a compromise, a genuine agreement between industrial and commercial capital'.[70] In this sense as well, the reforms serve as a summary of the outcomes of the revolution.

Implemented against a background of fierce political repression, Stolypin's agrarian programme was meant to create a prosperous, independent peasantry in Russia, capable of becoming a genuine agent of capitalist development in the countryside. As Stolypin himself noted, 'the government, which had resolved not to permit even attempts at peasant violence and disorder, had a moral duty to show the peasants a lawful way out of their needy condition'.[71] Offering them the right to leave the peasant communities, and encouraging them to resettle themselves on unoccupied land, Stolypin sought desperately to transform the rural *kulak* into an independent, modern proprietor, something like a farmer in the West. Lenin described Stolypin's reform as 'the last valve that could be opened without expropriating the estates of the landowners'.[72] Nothing good would come of this, since 'the step in the direction of the new was made by the old, while retaining its universal authority', and the result would be 'the administering of bourgeois agrarian policy by the old serf-owners, retaining all their land and powers'.[73]

In formal terms, this definition was completely correct. However, the essence of the Stolypin reforms did not consist solely of this. In effect, the regime had been forced to state that in the 50 years that had passed since the abolition of serfdom, the capitalist transformation of the landowners' estates had not taken place, that the 'Prussian road' had not worked, that in the Russian countryside there were no bourgeois forces in the proper sense, and that they would have to be created artificially.

Stolypin tried to alter the social relationships in the countryside by abolishing the forcible ties that bound the peasants to their communities, and in the process, as he put it, to do away with 'the enserfment of the individual, something that is incompatible with the concept of the freedom of human beings and of human labour'.[74] The internal contradiction of the reform lay, however, in the fact that in destroying the peasant communities, the government made possible not only the embourgeoisement of one section of the rural population, but also the proletarianisation of another. As was to be expected in a backward country, proletarianisation proceeded far more rapidly than the formation of a new bourgeoisie. In this respect, Stolypin's reform not only failed to solve the regime's problems, but also prepared the way for a new and even more powerful social explosion, which occurred in 1917.

Despite the growth of industry, the available workforce increased more rapidly than the ability of urban and rural capital to provide people with purposeful and productive work. The industrial proletariat increased in numbers. But as Pokrovsky notes, the number of landless peasants was also growing 'like a snowball'. By early in 1915, when the reform finally expired under the impact of the war, some 30 per cent of the peasants who had left the communities had sold their allotments.[75] In other words, instead of becoming Western-style farmers, people had been turned into day-labourers, rural proletarians and lumpenproletariat. On the other hand, the increased supply on the labour market, clearly outstripping the growth of industry, restrained the growth of wages. Social discontent increased, and political tensions in society rose. In other words, Stolypin's reform had the same consequences as many other attempts at modernisation in the countries of the periphery: while somewhat increasing the rate of development, it simultaneously created new sources of social tension.

Stolypin tried to relieve this tension by introducing state programmes to support peasant households – a move which, as he himself acknowledged, 'might recall the principles of socialism'. It was true, he added, that if this was a principle of socialism, then it was of 'a state socialism which has been employed repeatedly in Western Europe, and which has had real and substantial results'.[76] Such are the ironies of history; even Stolypin, the state official who perhaps put more effort into ensuring the capitalist transformation of Russia than anyone before or since, could not implement capitalist modernisation without resorting to 'socialist' methods.

Stolypin's reform ended with a marked increase of social stratification in the countryside and the appearance of a mass of impoverished people who, after being given guns in 1914, in 1917 became the mass base of support not only of the Bolshevik party, but of all the more radical forces of the Russian revolution. The rise of a rural bourgeoisie did not do away with the landowners or their estates, and new problems and contradictions were piled onto the unsolved ones from the past. The *kulaks* created an internal market for Russian industry; purchases of agricultural machinery increased and demand for consumer goods expanded. Nevertheless, the growth of *kulak* households was limited, and as a result the new rural entrepreneurs never provided a base of support for the regime. The attitude of the *kulaks* to the landowners was extremely aggressive. Earlier, it had been possible to speak of conflict between peasants and landowners; now, the peasants still hated the landowners, but no longer felt a sense of solidarity with one another.

The increased grain prices of the 1900s were followed by another deterioration in market conditions after 1911. The record for exports was reached in that year, when 824 million *pudy* of grain were exported.[77] After this, the situation grew steadily worse. Strangely, the onset of the new period of economic difficulties coincided with Stolypin's resignation and disgrace. As well as problems with trade, there were now political ones; because of the Balkan War and the conflict between Turkey and Italy, the Turkish government closed the Bosphorus, dealing a heavy blow to exporters of Russian grain. Competition from Germany was also increasing. Thanks to high productivity, East Prussian agriculture was able to sell grain profitably on the world market, despite paying more for labour. In 1912, 114 tons of German rye were imported into Russia! 'The Russian grain-importing provinces, mainly those of the north-west, Pskov, Novgorod, and so forth, found it cheaper to bring in low-priced German rye than to buy the expensive Russian product', Pokrovsky reports. 'This was a real scandal.'[78] In this instance, patriotic appeals on their own would no longer suffice; restrictive tariffs had to be imposed on German grain.

Favourable conditions in the world grain market were crucial for the success of the Stolypin reforms. Strictly speaking, it was such conditions that had made the reforms possible. Now, the situation was changing literally before people's eyes.

Growing industry required new investment. During the crisis of 1900, industrial capital in Russia had become more 'national', since French investors had repatriated their funds. Now, however, Russian entrepreneurs were faced with the small size of the internal market. In the countryside, Stolypin's reforms had given rise to a layer of well-off peasants able to buy not only consumer goods, but sometimes also agricultural equipment. This layer, however, was extremely narrow. Moreover, and despite protectionism, the dependence of the Russian empire on imports was constantly increasing, and the trade balance was deteriorating. Drawing a balance sheet of the pre-war years, Tugan-Baranovsky stated: 'In Russia, the industrial upturn led to a significantly more rapid growth of imports than of exports.'[79] By 1913 it was obvious, as economic journals of the time testified, that the limits of growth had been reached.

The crisis of the 'Stolypin model' struck in 1914, when, after several years of solid economic growth, the situation 'unexpectedly' worsened and barricades again appeared on the streets. To many people in St Petersburg, the war with Austria-Hungary and Germany did not seem such bad news. In any case, it seemed the best, if not the only, way to avert the looming revolution.

1907–14: THE BATTLE FOR RUSSIA

The liberal historical tradition of the twentieth century was inclined to view the First World War as an annoying episode, a political catastrophe that interrupted the proper and on the whole successful development of Russia. Accordingly, the revolution of 1917 was also just 'an appalling misprint of history, which crept in for no legitimate reason, and which might just as well not have been'.[80] Politics once again 'obstructed' socio-economic development; 'interests of state', by demanding participation in European coalitions, overturned the generally favourable course of history, and brought to nothing the efforts of Witte and Stolypin.

Unfortunately, Russia was far from being an accidental participant in the war of 1914–18. The course of events that preceded the First World War – events, moreover, that were primarily economic in nature – had made both the war itself and Russia's participation in it inevitable.

There was no serious antagonism on the part of the St Petersburg government towards Germany, but the logic of events drove the Russian rulers into conflict with Berlin's main partners, Austro-Hungary and Ottoman Turkey. The desire of the Russian empire to seize control of the straits that connected the Black Sea with the Mediterranean, already the cause of several wars in the eighteenth and nineteenth centuries, remained unchanged in the early twentieth century. In the words of Pokrovsky, the conquest of the straits was 'a cardinal question for Russian commercial capital'.[81] In earlier times, Britain had invariably stood in the way of this Russian ambition. By 1914, however, the situation had changed radically. Until 1905, fears had been held in London that Russia would invade India. When an Anglo-Russian Agreement governing relations between the two powers on colonial questions was signed in 1907, the British diplomats discovered, not without astonishment, that officials in St Petersburg were no less afraid of British penetration into Central Asia via Afghanistan than the British were fearful of a Russian attack on India. The British 'solemnly promised not to undertake anything of the sort, and to see to it that no threat came from Kabul either'.[82]

Since 1902 an Anglo-Japanese treaty had been in force, guaranteeing the security of India in the case of such a turn of events. But after the catastrophic defeat suffered by Russia in its war with Japan, the British elite finally realised that their fears had been completely unjustified. A warming of Anglo-Russian relations began. If Japan had ensured the defence of British interests in Asia against Russia, then Russia would defend the interests of the British empire in Europe against Germany. A 'heartfelt agreement' with France completed the building of the coalition. In this entente, each partner had its own particular interest. Russia's concern was the straits, which the British promised to take from Turkey. It should be said that in this case London made an honest effort to fulfil its promise; in 1915 the Australian and New Zealand Army Corps (ANZAC) landed on the Turkish coast. However, the operation to seize the straits ended in defeat.

Nevertheless, the desire to take possession of the straits was not the sole, and perhaps not the main cause impelling Russia not merely to enter into the world conflict, but to be one of its main instigators. A Franco-Russian military alliance against Germany had been concluded as early as 1893, against a background of the massive loans supplied to the tsar's government by Parisian bankers. In the words of the Soviet historian B.V. Ananyich, the loans which St Petersburg obtained on the Paris money market from the late 1880s were 'the foundations on which the edifice of the Franco-Russian alliance would soon be erected'.[83] In 1888 the sum of 500 million francs was borrowed; in 1889, two new loans for 2 billion francs were obtained; and in 1890 and 1891, another five loans totalling 1.5 billion francs. At first, the Paris officials were extremely unenthusiastic about the floating of Russian loans in France. Gradually, however, an understanding began to dawn of the valuable political opportunities that were opening up as the debt owed by the Russian empire increased. In 1894, the French government did everything it could to complicate the procedure for allowing Russian securities to be quoted, arguing that even without this move, the local financial market was overloaded with them. This, indeed, was completely correct; data for 1897 show that on the Parisian stock exchange,

Russian securities totalling 8 billion francs were in circulation. In allowing loans to be floated, the government in Paris invariably made the point to St Petersburg that what was involved was a show of goodwill, to which the Russian side was expected to respond with reciprocal political and military moves.

The goodwill in Paris was not exhausted even during the period of the 1905 Russian revolution, when many in the West believed the tsarist regime to be on the verge of collapse. By the turn of the century, France had become St Petersburg's largest and most reliable creditor; as contemporaries noted, 'no political developments in Russia could shake the French confidence in the tsar's government'.[84] The political loyalty which French capital showed to tsarism provided a guarantee for Paris of strategic advantages. In this respect, the loan of 1906 was decisive; according to a French scholar, it 'allowed French capital to strengthen its position in Russia in the face of German competition, with the self-interested support of British capital, which by now held a strong position in the oil industry of the Caucasus'.[85] The St Petersburg government also obtained some funds from Germany in 1902 and 1905. The German loans had a clear political purpose; Berlin was trying to undermine the position of Paris. These efforts, however, were not crowned with success; the Russians took the money but did not repudiate the alliance with France.

The twentieth century began with a severe economic depression, which affected both Russia and the West. Against the background of this depression, a fierce rivalry unfolded between the capitalists of various countries. On the Russian investment market, bitter clashes occurred between French and German interests. Although the tsar's government had for years maintained close ties with the Paris financial market, in the private sector a battle raged between German and French bankers.

During the first decade of the new century the feeling arose in Russian society that industrial capital in the country was becoming 'national'. This point of view was shared even by Pokrovsky, who cited a generally accepted statistic according to which the shares in enterprises set up using French or Belgian money had begun to be transferred in large numbers to the hands of the Russian bourgeoisie. In reality, the picture was more complex. The influx of foreign investment between 1900 and 1909 did, in fact, decline sharply; in the first place because of the economic crisis, and second, because of political instability. But as soon as a new economic upturn began in Russia in 1909, the flow of capital from abroad resumed as well, and along with it, the relationship of forces between foreign and 'national' proprietors began changing as well. Even in the crisis period from 1903 to 1905, eleven new foreign companies were established with a combined capital of 9.5 million rubles, and between 1906 and 1913, a further 88 companies, with a total capital of 168.6 million rubles.[86] As Vavilin notes,

the decline in the flow of foreign capital was not apparent in all sectors by any means, and together with previous investments, the funds coming from abroad continued to occupy almost the same dominant position as in the late nineteenth century. The time when Russian capitalism would be freed completely from foreign dependence was still a long way off.[87]

It is significant that even in the period of crisis, foreign investment in Russia did not come to a halt. At the same time as money invested in industry was returning to the West, French capital was pressing ahead with its efforts to take over the banking sector.

The battle by Western capital for the Russian financial market began in the nineteenth century, and was waged with variable success. The rivalry with the British empire in Central Asia created problems for Russian access to the British financial market, and the rapid growth of German industry consumed such quantities of money that in Germany almost no uninvested capital remained. Moreover, in 1887 Bismarck forced the Berlin banks for political reasons to cease holding Russian state bonds. The result was that Russian securities came to be traded almost exclusively on the Paris stock exchange. In the period immediately before the Russo-Japanese War, however, the German financial market was again opened to Russia, reflecting the geopolitical situation of the time.

In 1898 and 1899 the Russian government sought to reduce its dependency on France and tried to secure money in London and New York, but without success. As Ananyich notes,

Consequently, the main and almost the only creditor of tsarism once again remained the French bourgeoisie. Because the success of Witte's economic programme depended on a constant inflow of capital, the direct result of tsarism's failed attempts to take out loans on the international market had to be, and indeed was, a further increase in the dependency of Russia on the French stock exchange.[88]

The revolution of 1905 provided the Paris banks and finance ministry with a new opportunity to strengthen their position in Russia. Amid the political and military catastrophes that were shaking the country, the Russian government was acutely short of money. The necessary sums were found in diverse places throughout Europe. In 1906 a banking pool was formed, involving financiers from Britain, Holland and Austria, but the decisive role was again played by France. Private initiative, meanwhile, went hand-in-hand with the support of the French government, without whose participation the bankers would never have resolved to dispatch their money to a country wracked by revolution. In sum, a government that had clearly lost the confidence of its own people was supplied with a loan of 843.75 million rubles. Witte described this loan as 'the salvation of Russia'.[89] The French scholar R. Girault summed up the result of this operation in far more pragmatic fashion: 'For at least two years, the tsar's government lost its financial independence.'[90]

The loan of 1906 was a sort of political guarantee extended by Paris to St Petersburg. Such gifts, of course, had to be paid for. According to Ronin,

It is extremely significant that the initiative for the large-scale investment of French capital in Russia was not taken by Russian but by French banks. After the defeat of the 1905 revolution and Stolypin's 'stabilisation', the Parisian bankers regained their faith in the opportunities to be had in Russia. From this point began the organised assault of French financial capital on the Russian economy.[91]

While the tsarist government needed French loans to preserve stability, industry needed money for development. Arriving in Russia, however, French bank capital found that to a significant degree the site was already occupied. Until the mid 1900s, German investors were dominant in Russia. Now, a veritable battle for Russia unfolded between French and German financiers. As Vavilin has noted,

From their earliest origins, the Russian banks developed with the direct participation of foreign capital. In the 1860s and 1870s more than ten banks in Berlin, Hamburg, Frankfurt, Königsberg and elsewhere took part in organising Russian banks. When the foreign banks lent their capital, they appointed their representatives to the boards of the Russian banks in order to exert direct control over the banks' affairs. The helplessness of the Russian banks and their need for foreigners is evident from the fact that all their main official functions were carried out by foreigners. There were not yet any Russian banking specialists, so it was necessary to invite experienced Germans and to learn from them. Hence the first Russian bank assembled its staff on the recommendations of the Berlin banking house Mendelson and Company, and of Rothschild in Paris.[92]

In the six largest St Petersburg banks of that period, foreigners owned more than half the shares. In Russia's 22 largest establishments, foreigners again owned about half the shares, and in the six largest, more than half.[93] In all these institutions, the dominant position was held by Germans. Ronin notes that

French capital only made a decisive entrance onto the scene late in 1907. With a noticeable recovery under way, it sought to gain a strong foothold for itself in the Russian banking system. Since the largest banks were in the German orbit, French capital set about reorganising second-ranking banks in the largest cities, and within a few years transformed them into first-class establishments. Still later, and in a more modest degree, British capital started showing an interest in Russian banking. Thanks to the combined efforts of Paris, Berlin and London, the Russian banking system on the eve of the war was overwhelmingly controlled by European financial capital.[94]

The relationship of forces, at first extremely unfavourable to the French, changed steadily to their advantage. In 1907–08, a total of 81.5 per cent of the shares of all newly opened Russian banks were held in Germany, and only 18.5 per cent in France. In the years 1910–12, the German financial market held only 38.8 per cent of the shares in all the major banks, while the French accounted for 56.8 per cent, with the British holding 4.4 per cent. On this basis, Pokrovsky concluded that by 1914, 'French capital had clearly taken the upper hand'.[95]

In 1912 and 1913, Russian cities began placing their securities on Western markets. In 1912, Moscow issued bonds for 36 million rubles, Nikolaev for 6.5 million, and Vilno for 4.2 million. In 1913, loans were floated on the financial market by St Petersburg and Kiev. A fierce struggle unfolded between Paris,

Berlin and the City of London over the placing of these loans. Ultimately, they were placed in Britain, and in the view of contemporaries this was a 'major victory' for the British.[96] These British successes, however, no longer had any independent significance. In the Russian market, the British were increasingly acting in a single bloc with French and Belgian investors.

In its rivalry with the German banks, French capital was victorious, according to scholars, because it was 'highly concentrated'.[97] The French banks were closely interconnected, supported one another, and avoided competition among themselves. In addition, the Paris money market was simultaneously a source of funds both for the Russian government and for the private sector. The increasing influence of French banks in Russia made an impact on politics, while the growing political closeness strengthened the economic ties.

Contemporaries also saw 'subjective' reasons for the success of the French. In the view of Professor Levin, who in 1918 published a history of investment in Russia, the failure of the Germans was in large measure due to the peculiarities of their business culture. British, Belgian and French capital came in 'impersonal' form, while from Germany came 'not only capital, but also people.' These people were not always to the liking of local entrepreneurs, especially since the German banks, which had close ties to industry, invariably sought to 'combine the export of capital with the export of goods'.[98]

The view in Russia was summed up as follows: 'The Germans regard the placing of capital abroad as a means of expanding their economic and political influence, and go to extreme lengths in their enthusiasm for this.'[99] Experience in fact showed that French investments were by no means politically neutral either. Still less could this be said of the long-standing British business presence in Russia. The problem, of course, lay not only in a clash of cultures, but in the fact that the structures of financial capital in France and Germany were different. The French *rentiers* were not burdened by obligations to their industries, while the German model combined financial and industrial capital in a unified whole. It was this that lay behind the rapid growth of the German economy in the late nineteenth century. In the Russian market, however, these same features of German business became a weakness. Russian industrialists perceived German investors as competitors, while Franco-Belgian capital became dissolved in the Russian business environment, and was regarded almost as local.

The fierceness of the rivalry between French and Germans in Russia constantly increased. After 1910, Europe was clearly divided into two opposing blocs, the Anglo-French entente and the German-Austrian alliance of the central powers. A clash between them was inevitable. By the beginning of the war, capital of British and Franco-Belgian origin was dominant both in Russia's financial sector and in its industry. As Vavilin remarks, by 1914 the total sum of French capital invested in the Russian empire was 'more than the capital of all other nationalities'. If we take into account the make-up of the international coalitions, the picture becomes even clearer.

The countries of the entente (France, Britain, Belgium, America and Italy) accounted for 1,681,085,600 rubles, that is, for 75 per cent. The share of German and Austrian capital came to 449,143,200 rubles, or only 20 per cent. This huge preponderance of entente capital over its German and Austrian counterpart reveals with particular clarity the material basis for the foreign policy of the tsarist autocracy. In the war of 1914 to 1917, Russia had inevitably to be on the side of the entente.[100]

In many ways, the battle for Russia waged by French and German capital in the early twentieth century recalls the Anglo-Dutch rivalry in the seventeenth century. In both cases, the clash that unfolded in the Russian market was merely part of a global conflict. The Dutch gained the upper hand in Russia, but the results of this victory were finally annulled by the overall defeat suffered by Holland in its struggle with the British. The victory of French over German capital determined the role that Russia would play in the First World War. The fruits of this victory, however, were brought to nought by the military defeats which Russia suffered, and by the revolution of 1917.

13
The Revolutionary Explosion

Both the Russo-Japanese War of 1904 and the First World War were natural results of the accumulating contradictions between the leading world and regional powers. Rivalry between the 'old' and 'new' empires inevitably led to armed conflict. People had been waiting for this clash ever since the 1880s. Germany, Japan and other powers that had been too late to participate in dividing up the world, but which had accumulated a formidable industrial and military potential, sought to put the situation right with the help of force. The 'old' empires, which now included Russia, were obliged to defend themselves. Several times the diplomats managed to postpone the war, but preventing it was not within their power.

Lagging behind its more dynamic rivals in terms of economic development, but still an important military power, Russia found it advantageous to hasten the conflict. The aggressive behaviour of the Russian government in the Far East in 1904 led to the war with Japan; later, Russian actions in the Balkans in 1912 and 1914 brought increased tension to relations with Austria-Hungary, and ultimately provided the trigger for the world war. In neither case were these simply chance errors of tsarist diplomacy.

For Russia, the war brought catastrophic military defeats, which shook not only the state but society as a whole to its foundations. After three years of uninterrupted military failures, and more than 1 million dead, the Russian army was transformed from a traditional support for the regime into a demoralised mass that readily assimilated revolutionary propaganda. Tsarism collapsed, and as it seemed, buried Russia itself beneath its fragments. The bourgeoisie survived the autocracy by only a few months. Backward capitalism and the tsarist bureaucracy were doomed to perish together, neither of them able to survive any longer without the other. The bourgeoisie was incapable of building a new order on the ruins of the old; it could not prevent social, economic and political chaos. In short, it had not become a ruling class in the full sense.

The democratic republic that arose on the ruins of tsarism did not manage to last out the year. It was replaced by the 'republic of the Soviets', which owed its rise far more to elemental revolutionary forces than to the political will of the victorious Bolshevik party. The 'republic of the Soviets', meanwhile, could not exist for long in its original form, giving way to the party dictatorship of the Bolsheviks. The 'power of the Soviets' became the 'Soviet power'.

With the transfer of the capital from St Petersburg to Moscow and the shifting of the government to the Kremlin, a symbolic balance sheet was drawn up of the entire period of Russian history that had begun with the Northern War of Peter the Great and ended with the defeat in the First World War. The strategy, pursued over two centuries, of integrating Russia into the capitalist world system had led ultimately to a revolution aimed against both the Russia of St Petersburg and the entire world system of which Russian tsarism had been part. In summing up the lessons of the revolution, Lenin wrote:

What if the complete hopelessness of the situation, multiplying tenfold the strength of the workers and peasants, has opened up for us the possibility of a different approach to setting in place the basic premises of civilisation, an approach different from that taken in all the states of Western Europe?[1]

In reality, both the revolution itself, and the coming to power of the Bolsheviks whom Lenin headed, were outcomes of the crisis of the world-system and of the downfall of the Russian elites who had been incorporated into this system.

BOLSHEVISM

With their tight organisation and faith in their historic mission, the Marxist-Bolsheviks were in essence the only party capable of restoring order in a country that was experiencing the disintegration of its economic and social system. Compared to the Mensheviks, the Bolsheviks were not simply the more ideologically radical wing of social democracy (ideological radicalism was a characteristic of many Menshevik leaders as well). The strength of the Bolsheviks lay in their ability to act in the interests of their social base, without reflecting on theoretical subtleties – to act quickly, and often harshly.

In Russia, social democracy from the very first represented an alternative variant of modernisation. If the liberals sought to base themselves on the relatively civilised section of the elites, the Marxists found support in the most modern section of the lower orders – industrial workers in the large urban centres, and the urban intelligentsia. Born of the development of industry and the spread of European forms of culture, these social layers at the same time – and unlike the bourgeoisie – were without ties to the old regime; consequently, they were far more ready to head up the new modernisation.

This explains both the strong and the weak sides of the Bolsheviks' politics. On the one hand, the Bolsheviks were determined defenders of urban interests; on the other, they showed mistrust and hostility to the patriarchal countryside. It took about a year of civil war, accompanied at first by severe defeats for the Bolsheviks, before the new government saw the peasants not as savages requiring to be civilised, if necessary with the help of cannon and machine-guns, but as allies in the social revolution. The Bolsheviks were a party of the cities, and their rule during its first months was not so much a dictatorship of the proletariat, aimed against the overthrown bourgeoisie, as a dictatorship of the city over the countryside.

The rise of the Bolsheviks to power was entirely to be expected, but it does not follow from this that the Bolsheviks themselves were ready for power. To an important degree, four years of unprecedentedly savage civil war, economic ruin and social chaos had disorganised the camp of the victors. The economic policies which the party of Lenin and Trotsky pursued years from 1917 to 1919 were more a reaction to existing circumstances than the implementing of a project that had been thought through and formulated in advance. The Bolshevik economist Yevgeny Preobrazhensky stressed that the nationalising of industry in conditions of collapse was a measure which to a substantial degree had been forced on the government. Pokrovsky makes the same point. In fact, the disintegration of the market and the rapid rise of food prices had made any industrial production unprofitable. As Preobrazhensky noted, 'there were cases in which the commercial value of production was lower even than the wages'.[2] Under such conditions private industry could not exist, and production had to be transferred to an owner who not only had no need of profits, but who could feed the workers in any case. This owner could only be the state. Nationalisation was the only means through which Russia's technological and productive potential could be preserved, and the workers maintained. In turn, the forcible extraction of grain from the countryside had become the only way of maintaining the cities.

It is not surprising that the first proposals of this type had been made back in the days of the tsarist government, when it had become clear that the war had thrown the established economic mechanisms into chaos, and that food supplies to the cities were under threat. Neither the tsarist administration, nor the Provisional Government during its few months of existence had resolved to take this step, and it was this that largely guaranteed their downfall. Power finished up in the hands of the only party that was prepared, without the slightest hesitation, to requisition food. In later times, liberal Soviet historians would repeatedly pour scorn on the policy of 'war communism' pursued in the years from 1918 to 1920, viewing it as a prototype for Stalin's terror or simply as the outcome of utopian fantasies. Meanwhile, Lenin's work *The Immediate Tasks of the Soviet Government*, written immediately after the first Bolshevik government was formed, demonstrates that war communism had not in any way been planned in advance. Lenin early in 1918 had still hoped that order could be restored to the economy by relying on market methods analogous to those which the Bolsheviks employed later, in the 1920s. Predictably, this attempt failed. The monetary system was in total collapse, the demand for industrial products (with the exception, of course, of weapons) had fallen to a minimum, and commercial exchange between the cities and the countryside had become impossible.

'Carrying out the task of supplying the population with bread in a huge country with poor means of communication and with a dispersed peasantry was extraordinarily difficult...', Lenin wrote in 1919. 'Looking back over all the sessions of the Soviet of People's Commissars, I can state that there was not a single task on which the Soviet government worked as persistently as on this one.'[3] Characteristically, Lenin in this case departed from his accustomed class categories and spoke not of the proletariat, but of the population in general. But what population did he have in mind? It is clear that he was not referring to the peasants, who supplied themselves with grain, but to the city-dwellers.

In essence, the civil war of 1918–21 was fought not only and not so much between Reds and Whites as between the city and the countryside.

In order to feed the urban population, food had to be extracted from the countryside, relying on the military superiority of the cities. Otherwise, the urban economy would simply have ceased to exist, as was predicted in Chayanov's *Peasant Utopia*. Meanwhile, the methods employed on the 'barbaric' countryside by the 'modern' and 'civilised' cities were so crude and harsh that they resulted in massive numbers of peasants crossing over to the anti-Bolshevik forces, to an escalation of the civil war, and in sum, to the need for an even harsher dictatorship. In other words, the cruelty and violence that stemmed from economic necessity was exacerbated by the incompetence and prejudices of the urban revolutionists themselves. The Bolsheviks were saved by the fact that the White Guard leaders, who lacked a clear understanding of the processes unfolding in the countryside, and who tried to restore the privileges of the old ruling layers, also alienated the peasants. Of two evils, the countryside chose the lesser, and by the end of 1919 most of the peasants had gone over to the now incomparably wiser Bolsheviks.

The catastrophic military defeats of 1918 taught Lenin and his government a great deal. They began taking the peasantry into account. Nevertheless, the peasants remained an alien and potentially hostile force for the Bolshevik leaders, a force with which a common language might be found, but with which the Bolsheviks could never unite completely. Ultimately, the urban workers and intelligentsia, who at the cost of extraordinary effort and sacrifice had ensured the success of the Bolsheviks in the civil war, themselves became social hostages to the military-bureaucratic apparatus. This apparatus, set up in order to ensure the dictatorship of the city over the countryside, swiftly acquired its own independent interests, and came to dominate the 'advanced' urban layers for whose defence it had been created. By the early 1920s the expanding bureaucracy had become both the core of the new regime and its main point of support.

THE NEW ECONOMIC POLICY

Emerging victorious from the civil war, the Bolsheviks made the transition to the New Economic Policy (NEP), envisaging a combination of centralised management of state industry with the development of the free market, especially in agriculture. In the years from 1918 to 1920 the peasants, after receiving the land, had found that they could not dispose of what they produced on it; the city, through the 'surplus appropriation' system, took everything it needed by force. The NEP, when it succeeded war communism, began by replacing 'surplus appropriation' with a tax in kind on food. Most of the grain now remained in the hands of the peasants, and could be traded on the market. The peasant proprietors had finally gained what they had been fighting for; both the land and its produce now belonged to them. The transition to a market economy in 1921 and 1922 under the banner of the NEP not only failed to stop the bureaucratisation of the regime, but accelerated it.[4] Under war communism the power of the Bolsheviks at the local level had been despotic, but not bureaucratic. The entire apparatus of a local revolutionary commissar might consist of a few sailors with a machine-gun, and the sum total of their functions might be to seize grain from the peasants and supply it to the hungry cities. In one place their behaviour might be savage, and in another extremely liberal, depending on their disposition. Often there were no written instructions, and if there were, no one read or followed them. The questions of account-keeping and of administrative correspondence simply did not exist. Sometimes, with hindsight, local revolutionary leaders were shot for arbitrary excesses. Or they might be promoted and transferred to the centre, sometimes for the very same actions. Decisions taken in Petrograd did not apply in Moscow, and those taken in Moscow did not have force in Kiev. A number of soviet republics had been established immediately on the territory of the former Russian empire, often with different political rules.[5] Intensified persecution of enemies of the revolution was accompanied not only by sharp discussions within the party, but also by the legal activity of various groups of opposition socialists – left Mensheviks, sections of the anarchists, communist-revolutionaries, Ukrainian *borot'bisty*, and so forth. Non-government newspapers were shut down, then reappeared; censorship was introduced, then again abolished.

With the shift to the NEP, a stop was put to all this. Factions within the Bolshevik party were banned, and the legal opposition in the Soviets was suppressed. A wave of repression against opposition socialists in 1921 and 1922 was the first sign that political life was being 'normalised', and that the repressive apparatus was being assigned new tasks. It was not the struggle against counter-revolution that now took centre stage, but the crushing of dissidents and inconsistent followers within the revolution's own camp. The apparatus sensed its power, and sought to consolidate it. Along with the Transcaucasian Federation, the independent soviet republics of Ukraine and Belarus lost their formal self-determination, and in 1922 were officially incorporated into a single Soviet Union, though even the local communist parties doubted the wisdom of this decision. Lenin's project of a federation of equal partners was unquestionably much more democratic than that of Stalin, who called for turning the former independent states into autonomous territories within the framework of Russia, completely subordinating these national regions to the power of Moscow. Nor is there any doubt that a natural desire for unification existed; the workers and peasants of Ukraine and Belarus who supported the Bolsheviks during the civil war had understood perfectly that victory for the 'Reds' would mean reunification with Russia. The creation of a single union apparatus, however, was an important landmark on the road to the formation of a new bureaucratic elite.

The party apparatus was also put in order. At the outset of the revolution the Leninists, who had broken definitively with social democracy, renamed themselves; from being the Russian Social Democratic Workers' Party (Bolsheviks), they became the Russian Communist Party (Bolsheviks). In the 1920s the party was again renamed, from 'Russian' to 'All-Union'. Every change of name reinforced the changes in the internal state of the organisation. The new All-Union Communist Party (Bolsheviks) possessed a far more rigid structure than the clandestinely organised Russian Social Democratic Party (Bolsheviks), or the revolutionary Russian Communist Party (Bolsheviks). An organisation had been established that was tightly bound up with the state apparatus and with the system of economic management.

The founding of the USSR brought with it a dramatic centralisation of administrative power in Moscow. The apparatus of government put itself in order and grew. The NEP permitted a strengthening of the bureaucratic structure. Unlike in the period of war communism, the focus now was not on compulsion but on 'accounting and control'. This required the formation of numerous departments. It was necessary to levy taxes and to keep track of the enforcing of laws in a unified way throughout the whole territory of the country. This represented a natural transition to the normal functioning of state mechanisms, but at the same time it could not fail to strengthen the position of the bureaucracy. In this respect, Lenin's project of a 'market without democracy' created the preconditions for Stalin's 'dictatorship without the market'.

As before, the main historic task – the modernisation of the country – remained unfulfilled. The restoring of order in the 1920s made it possible to approach the pre-revolutionary levels, and in some sectors even to exceed them. Gross industrial production in 1926 amounted to 11,083 million rubles, compared to 10,251 million rubles in 1913, while in heavy industry the pre-war level was exceeded by 16.5 per cent.[6] It should be remembered, however, that even in years of economic upturn the 'achievements' of tsarist Russia had been impressive only in relative terms, and that the 13 years that had been lost to economic development would somehow have to be made up.

SOVIET RUSSIA AND THE WORLD MARKET

By excluding Russia from the world system, the revolution of 1917 paradoxically transformed it from a peripheral country into merely a backward one. The idea that 'backwardness' was at the core of the problem assumed the need for an 'acceleration' of development, which in turn required a more active involvement in the world economy and an expansion of the sale of resources on the world market. But this in turn would simply intensify the country's dependency. To its ideologues, modernisation represents a kind of race, in which, naturally, there are those who get first place and those who get last place. In such a contest, as at the racetrack, one can always speculate as to why one of the runners has sprinted ahead or lagged behind. The relations between the centre and the periphery, however, are formed according to a quite different principle. The resources furnished by the periphery serve to speed up the 'run' of the centre. The histories of Russian ferrous metallurgy in the eighteenth century, and of grain production in the nineteenth, provide obvious examples. The more actively the periphery competes, the further it lags behind, and the more it helps the West to sprint ahead. Furthermore, while the countries of the periphery pass through all the same phases as the West, they do so not so much with a delay as in a different fashion. In other words, the relationship in this case is not the one between two independently running participants in a race, but is more like the relationship between horse and rider. Both of these arrive at the same place, reach the same goal, but do so in a different state. The horse can neither choose its goal nor outrun the rider, unless it throws him off. The modernisation in the Soviet Union was in essence just such an attempt to throw off the rider, while continuing the race in the same direction as before.

Soviet industry no longer served the accumulation of capital in the West, but the question arose of where it would obtain the resources it needed in order to catch up with the 'advanced countries'. The theoreticians of Bolshevism were faced with a dual question: how to carry out modernisation, while at the same time pursuing the party's ideological goal of making the transition to socialism. The Marxist tradition had assumed that socialism would triumph in the developed industrial countries, while the practice of the Russian revolution had made it necessary to approach the problem from the other end. Modernisation and the transformations involved in creating socialism would not follow one after the other, but would have to proceed simultaneously.

Nikolay Bukharin, who quickly became the main ideologue of the party following the death of Lenin, proposed that socialism could be built – gradually and relatively painlessly – in a single backward country. The main enemies of the revolution had already been defeated, and the new social problems that had arisen in Russia since the Bolshevik victory, Bukharin maintained, were not especially serious. Citing Lenin, he argued repeatedly that conflict between the working class and the peasantry was 'by no means inevitable'.[7] The familiar pressure on the countryside needed to be continued in order to obtain additional resources for industrialisation, but the main stimulus for industrial development should become market demand. Light industry, according to Bukharin, should receive priority for development, but the pace of industrialisation should depend on the capacity to absorb goods of the domestic market, with its mainly peasant purchasers. In other words, Bukharin hoped to retrace the road travelled during the rise of industrial society in Britain and the United States, and with minimal conflicts. Britain, however, had developed under the conditions of a worldwide monopoly; it had almost no competitors, and for a whole era outstripped its competitors, remaining the 'workshop of the world' throughout almost the entire nineteenth century. Toward the end of the nineteenth century, Germany and the US caught up with it. The pace of economic development accelerated as international competition grew more acute, and technology came to be renewed more often. Countries that expanded their industrial capacity more slowly were doomed to chronic 'structural' backwardness. The most important thing was no longer the number of industrial plants, but their quality – that is, the technology applied in them.

The concentration of financial resources in the state sector allowed growth rates to be accelerated. Britain had needed more than a century to create its economic capacity; Russia might move two or three times as fast, but even this was not enough in the twentieth century. Meanwhile, the historical circumstances provided few chances to repeat the 'Western road'.

Later, Soviet ideologues would argue for high rates of industrialisation on the basis of the military threat from the West. The danger of war was quite real, as subsequent events would confirm. The international situation in the 1920s, however, did not suggest that a new world war was inevitable. Fascism had not yet triumphed in Germany, and a united front of left forces might still have prevented Hitler from coming to power. Even if there had not been a military threat, however, the pace of industrialisation needed to be accelerated. This was required by the very social basis on which Bolshevism rested.

After the defeats in the First World War and the subsequent revolution, the new state that was founded on the territory of Russia possessed not only a new ideology and a radically altered elite. As a political current, the Bolsheviks had emerged from the Russian progressive movement, and viewed the goal of social development as 'overcoming backwardness'. Unlike their bourgeois predecessors, however, the Bolsheviks had an excellent grasp of the limited nature and ineffectiveness of all previous attempts at modernisation. If these attempts had not failed, the Bolsheviks would never have come to power.

The social base of Bolshevism was the working class, and in the broader sense, the industrial city, whose interests the Bolsheviks defended fiercely and without compromise in the years from 1917 to 1920. As a result, the Bolshevik leadership was faced with the need to continue the industrialisation that had been begun by Witte and Stolypin, resting on the new sectors that had been established at the beginning of the twentieth century, but doing this through completely different methods and at a quite different rate.

THE PROBLEM OF ACCUMULATION

The revolution of 1917 was accompanied by the exclusion of Russia from the world economy.[8] Such a development had never been foreseen by the Bolsheviks. The world system, however, had been thrown into disarray by the world war. With Russia's customary economic life now impossible to maintain, the old system of relations between city and countryside collapsed, and participation by Russia in the international division of labour was reduced to a minimum. The repudiation by the Bolsheviks of the debts of the tsarist regime ruined large numbers of the French petty bourgeoisie, but the financial markets in Paris and London understood perfectly that these debts could not be repaid in any case. One way or another, they would have to be written off along with the other costs of the war.

In order to accelerate its development, Russia was compelled to review the nature of its relations with the world system. Paradoxically, the events of the war had made this task easier. Russia did not tear itself loose from the world system, but merely refused to return to its previous place when the system began to be reconstructed in the early 1920s.

The Bolshevik revolution, the nationalisation of industry and the repudiation of the tsarist debts excluded Russia from the global process of capital accumulation, but not from the world market. Indeed, participation in the world market was integral to the hopes of accelerated industrialisation held by the country's leaders. When Russia set out on this road, it would not be able to get by without technology transfers and purchases of equipment. During the

1920s Russian grain reappeared on the world market, but Bolshevik economists lamented the 'still minuscule scale of exports'.[9] The exporting of grain was required to finance the acquisition of essential technology. Meanwhile, the cutting off of the Soviet Union from the world capital market made it possible to stop the draining of resources from the country, and to concentrate all the available means on the principal tasks. In essence, all the leaders of the party were united around this programme, not only the 'centrist' Stalin and the 'right-wing' Bukharin, but even the Left Opposition of Trotsky, which saw no alternative to venturing onto the world market. The only disagreements concerned the question of how to get hold of the grain. While Bukharin, supported at that point by Stalin, sought to develop the independent peasant holdings, Trotsky by contrast warned of the threat posed by the formation of a rural bourgeoisie, and called for obtaining the grain through 'pressure on the *kulaks*'.

The main economist among the leftists was Yevgeny Preobrazhensky, who advanced his own theory of 'primitive socialist accumulation'. In his view, industrialisation could not proceed without the extracting of resources from the countryside. In relation to the 'socialist' cities, the 'petty bourgeois' countryside would have to play the same role as the periphery in relation to the centre during the period of primitive accumulation under capitalism.

The more a country making the transition to the socialist organisation of production is economically backward, petty-bourgeois and peasant in composition, and the smaller the inheritance which the proletariat of this country receives for its socialist accumulation fund at the time of its social revolution, the more socialist accumulation will be forced to rely on the exploitation of pre-capitalist economic forms....

In other words, 'the state economy cannot get by without exploiting petty production, without the expropriation of part of the surplus product of the countryside and of artisan producers'.[10] In practice, this 'expropriation' was carried out through railway charges, monetary emission, the credit policies of state banks, and most importantly, through trade. Preobrazhensky in this case rested his arguments on the practice that already existed in Russia during the NEP period. The market in foodstuffs was divided into planned and private sectors. Part of the grain was purchased by the state from the peasants and collective enterprises at fixed prices, while the peasants were able to sell the rest independently. Not surprisingly, the state purchases were made at low prices, as was recognised both by the Left Opposition and by the supporters of Bukharin. Naturally, the peasants tried to compensate for the low prices in the planned sector of the economy by raising prices on the free market, but here as well the state held the advantage; by raising the prices of manufactured goods, it took back part of the funds which the peasants had obtained in the private sector. This was described as the 'price scissors', or simply as the 'tribute' which the village had to pay to the city in the name of industrialisation.

Preobrazhensky stressed that the prices policy in the state sector had to be constructed in such a way that when the peasants bought manufactured goods, they subsidised industry. In turn, 'socialist protectionism' had to defend national enterprises, while the monopoly of foreign trade would make it possible to sell cheap agricultural produce at world market prices, and so to obtain 'surplus income'. In this way, foreign trade would subject petty rural production to 'the pump of socialist accumulation'.[11] These formulations aroused the indignation of Bukharin, who declared that describing the relations between city and countryside as 'exploitation' meant to 'call the proletariat an exploiter class'. To talk in such terms meant to 'miss the whole essential character of the process, not to understand its objective significance, to play at analogies', and also to expound views that threatened to 'destroy the worker-peasant bloc'.[12]

For all this, Bukharin made no suggestion as to where else the funds for developing industry might be obtained. Once the discussion turned to the 'price scissors' between agricultural and industrial products, he showed an unexpected ease in agreeing with Preobrazhensky: 'Yes. There is no doubt whatever about that.'[13]

For Bukharin, the problem lay not in politics but in ideology. It was possible to act, but not to talk about what one did. Funds could be expropriated, but it was unacceptable to call this 'exploitation'. Resources could be redistributed from the countryside to the cities, but declaring this to be a strategy of the state was inadmissible.

Nor, for his part, did Preobrazhensky insist that the products of the countryside be expropriated on a massive scale. To do this, as the radical economist saw it, would be to kill the goose that laid the golden egg. To the contrary, petty production needed to be supported, so that it could provide the resources on the basis of which industry could be developed over a prolonged period. Comparing 'primitive socialist accumulation' with the primitive accumulation of capital, Preobrazhensky stressed that the proletariat would behave far better toward the countryside (the internal periphery) than the bourgeoisie behaved in relation to its colonies.

Here the task of the socialist state does not consist in taking less from petty-bourgeois producers than capitalism took in the past, but in taking more out of the greater income that will be ensured to petty production by a general rationalization, including of the country's small-scale economy.[14]

A close study of Preobrazhensky's text reveals that he was not proposing any radical new measures. In essence he was merely summarising, and substantiating in theoretical terms, what was being done in any case by the Soviet authorities, and with Bukharin's full approval. The discussion between left and right therefore touched not so much on the main principles of economic policy as on its radicalism and ideological foundations. The right called for caution and moderation, while the left called for the same line to be implemented more firmly. The right sought to influence the peasants with persuasion and promises, while the left was more inclined to try to intimidate them (including through openly and honestly characterising its actions as 'exploitation'). Neither side, however, saw any alternative to this policy.

Although Bukharin spoke of building 'socialism in a single country', while the leaders of the left categorically rejected this way of posing the question, both sides in the discussion clearly proceeded on the basis that Russia would have to solve its problems independently, without expecting a world revolution to change the nature of the global system. Meanwhile, it was obvious that neither strategy could do without the world market. The produce extracted from the countryside had to be sold, and turned into machines, equipment, technology, and metals for industry. Doing this on a massive scale was possible only through the world market.

At the same time, processes destined to change Russia's situation drastically were once again under way in the world economy. The Great Depression was approaching.

FROM AUTHORITARIANISM TO TOTALITARIANISM

At the Fifteenth Congress of the party in December 1927, Bukharin's line was clearly dominant. The congress resolutions stated that the middle peasant had become the central figure in the countryside. If bourgeois development in the countryside had led to polarisation within the rural population (with one section of the peasantry being impoverished and turned into proletarians, while another section grew rich), Soviet rule had created a situation in which the poor peasants, having received land and support from the state, had begun to improve their holdings, and were becoming middle peasants. While proclaiming the goal of the party in the countryside to be the struggle against the *kulaks*, viewed as members of the rural bourgeoisie, the congress resolutions did not prefigure any coercive measures. To the contrary, the resolutions spoke of the gradual development of cooperation among the middle peasants, with only the longer-term prospect of a transition 'to large-scale collective agriculture, on the basis of technical reconstruction and the unification of the scattered peasant holdings'.[15]

The congress resolved that 'it would be incorrect to reject the deriving of funds from the countryside for the construction of industry', but to be overzealous in this regard would mean to precipitate 'a political break with the peasantry', threatening the development of the internal market and the raw materials base of production.[16]

In agriculture, the state performed mainly a 'planning and regulatory role', based on 'the growing influence of the socialist elements within the countryside itself'.[17] Meanwhile, it was stressed that the technical backwardness of agriculture had to be overcome; because of this backwardness, the country lacked sufficient grain for the exports that were 'the basis for the import operations that are essential for the rapid industrialisation of the country and for the further development of agriculture itself'.[18]

The resolutions of the Sixteenth Party Conference in April 1929, shortly before the beginning of the Great Depression in the West, were still more moderate. They stressed that there was no question of any forced unification of the holdings of the middle peasants.

The large-scale collective farm is not counterposed to the individual holdings of the poor and middle peasants as a force hostile to them, but creates bonds with the peasants as a source of assistance, as an example of the benefits of large-scale farming, and as an organiser of collaboration in gradually uniting them in large-scale agriculture.[19]

The conference resolutions spoke repeatedly and in detail about the 'help' provided by the state and the collective farms to the individual enterprises of the middle peasants.

The Soviet authorities were thus forced to strike a balance and to seek compromise decisions, trying to hold fast to a 'golden mean' between the developing of industry and keeping the loyalty of the countryside. In such a situation, sharp differences could not help but arise within the leadership. The factional struggle grew fiercer, ending in the defeat of the Left Opposition. Nevertheless, the views of the left continued to exert a substantial influence within the party.

The First Five-Year Plan, finally approved in April 1929, was quite radical, foreseeing a sharp acceleration of industrialisation, but it too made no mention of dramatic changes in the countryside. Almost immediately, however, events forced corrections to the plans of the Soviet leadership. These events were domestic as well as international. The precarious balance of the NEP system had collapsed beneath the blows of a dual crisis.

THE CRISIS OF GRAIN COLLECTIONS

By the late 1920s, the policy of levying 'tribute' from the countryside in order to fund industrialisation had begun to show serious signs of breaking down. The further the state lowered the purchase prices for grain, the harder it became to meet the plan targets for grain collection. The peasants reduced their grain-sowings, changing to other, more profitable crops. The result was not only shortages of food in the rapidly growing cities, but also a shortage of foreign currency. However acute the grain problem, it would not have been so painful for the Soviet authorities had grain not been the country's main export. As Bukharin pointed out, for industry to be developed, imports of equipment had to be paid for using 'agricultural foreign currency'.[20] As a result, the Soviet leadership could afford neither to sharply increase the purchase prices, nor to allow a substantial fall in the production of wheat.

In 1927, a grain collections crisis broke out. Grain prices on the private market increased rapidly. This turn of events could have been expected. Throughout 1925–28 the Bolsheviks had regularly lowered the state purchase prices for grain, forcing out resources for export. In 1928, crop failure in the North Caucasus led to marked shortages of rye and wheat. Purchase prices were raised, but even then they remained 4 per cent lower than in 1925–26. Prices in the planned sector were now less than half those on the private market.[21]

Analysing the grain collection crisis many decades later, the economist Andrey Kolganov noted a clearly unfortunate coincidence that was, however, the natural result of earlier policy:

These circumstances might not have had such an appreciable effect on the situation with grain collections, had it not been for two factors. In the first place, although the reduction in the turnover of grain in the state sector and in the amount of grain supplied by the state to the urban population was not significant, this occurred at a time when industry and the urban population were growing rapidly, presenting a growing demand for food. It was this that caused the jump in prices on the private market. The second factor was the fall in grain exports that was associated with the acute shortage of supplies for the internal market. In 1928–29, grain exports were only 3.27 per cent of the level in 1926–27.[22]

Exports of grain were indeed falling sharply, from 2.18 million tons in the 1926–27 season to 344,400 tons in 1927-28. Worse still, to maintain food supplies to the cities it proved necessary to import 248,200 tons of grain from abroad, spending the equivalent of 27.5 million rubles in foreign currency for this purpose.[23] Accordingly, the programme for the importing of machinery and equipment, on which the success of industrialisation depended, was not fulfilled.

The crisis of grain collections led to new divisions in the party. Bukharin recognised that the failure was 'connected with an incorrect prices policy, with the huge gap between prices for grain and for other products of agriculture'.[24] Stalin's group, by contrast, accepted the arguments of the left, who declared that the main problem was 'sabotage' by the *kulaks*, who were hiding grain.

Nevertheless, the crisis of grain collections would not have been fatal to the social and political equilibrium that had been reached in post-revolutionary Russia, had it not coincided with completely opposite processes in the world economy. At the same time as grain prices were rising rapidly on the internal market, on the world market they were falling just as fast. The 'scissors' were working in reverse. The nearer the West drew to the beginning of the Great Depression, the lower world grain prices became. Back in 1926 Kondratyev had stated that during a 'declining wave' on the world market, 'agriculture experiences a more profound depression, agricultural commodities fall more markedly in price, and their purchasing power declines in relative terms'.[25]

The strategy for Soviet industrialisation was based on the expectation that by exporting grain, the state could acquire equipment and technology. Taken together, the combination of falling world grain prices, rising prices on the domestic market, and reduced exports led to a critical situation. The industrialisation programme was threatened with collapse.

By the beginning of 1928, the shortfall in grain collections amounted to 128 million *pudy* compared to the previous year. In the capital, no solution was found except to use repression against the countryside. Stalin summed up the problem in the clear, simple terms that were characteristic of him: 'It is better to put the screws on the *kulak* and to extract his grain surplus... than to spend foreign currency that has been put aside in order to import equipment for our industry.'[26]

In January 1928 the Politburo of the All-Union Communist Party (Bolsheviks) voted for 'the use of emergency measures with regard to the *kulaks*, in relation to the grain collection campaign'.[27] It is significant that this decision was also supported by the rightists, Bukharin, Rykov and Tomsky. They also voted for emergency measures at the April Plenum of the party's Central Committee. Naturally, they stressed that such measures should be exclusively of a temporary nature, and should not in any circumstances be turned into a system. But here as well, their position was not radically different from the views expressed at that time by Stalin.

The 'emergency measures' adopted in 1928 yielded the expected result: despite a poor harvest in the main grain-producing regions in the 1928–29 season, only 2 per cent less grain was collected than in 1926–27. However, another result of this policy was the breaching of the delicate compromise that had been achieved between the cities and the countryside at the end of the civil war: 'Force applied to extract grain in 1928 gave a measure of success,' wrote the historian Moshe Lewin, 'but boded ill for the results of the next agricultural and procurement campaign; and rationing was to be introduced very soon to meet the food-supply "stringencies".'[28]

The forcible collecting of grain in the countryside shattered the precarious social and political equilibrium on which the Soviet model of the 1920s had rested. The peasants lost their faith in the Bolshevik cities, and this created the need for still harsher measures in order to retain control of the situation. In 1928, the emergency measures had been applied in a limited and selective manner, but in 1929, with the world depression already beginning, the Soviet leaders were forced to resort to the broad-scale confiscation of grain and to the 'dekulakisation' of landholders producing for the private market.

In sum, the emergency measures that had been introduced on a temporary basis had to be repeated again and again, turning into a permanent practice. The impossibility of carrying on in this fashion, however, was obvious to everyone. In the conditions of the civil war, the 'food requisitions' might have achieved their goal for a time, but in conditions of peace a different solution was needed. The widespread grain seizures of 1918 had fanned the flames of the civil war. Implementing such a policy on a permanent basis meant that sooner or later, the country would suffer another outburst of civil conflict, in the course of which the Soviet government might well collapse.

There was no longer any going back. The NEP had collapsed, having failed to withstand the impact of the Great Depression. Since it was no longer possible to maintain control over the foodstuffs market with the help of periodic confiscations, new slogans were coined – 'complete collectivisation' and 'liquidation of the *kulaks* as a class'. In essence, what was involved was the possibility of controlling agriculture directly, from within, by uniting all the producers in collective farms subject to the state. The possibility thus appeared of bypassing the market, and of using administrative methods to extract from the countryside as much grain as the state needed, at any time and without any emergency measures.

THE 'GREAT TURNING POINT'

The Bolshevik leaders did not have a ready-made plan. As late as the summer of 1928, Stalin had written that it was 'impossible to wage a struggle against the *kulaks* by means of dekulakisation', and that talk of abandoning the NEP was 'counter-revolutionary chatter'.[29] By the autumn, however, the situation had changed fundamentally. There was an urgent need to come up with a solution, and one was duly found: 'complete collectivisation'. The *kulaks* would be repressed; other malcontents would be declared to be '*kulak* sympathisers', and sent after them; the private peasant holdings would be abolished; the implements and livestock would be seized, and everyone would be herded into collective farms under the control of the state.

Significantly, the sharp change of course at first evoked total disbelief in the supporters of Trotsky and other activists of the Left Opposition. The decisions that had been made contradicted everything that Stalin had said and done in the preceding years. 'The struggle that has been proclaimed against the right-wing deviation and against conciliatory attitudes to it', the *Bulletin of the Opposition* wrote, 'is just as much a parody of real struggle as the celebrated self-criticism was a parody of criticism.'[30] The assessments by the oppositionists were dictated by their ideological standpoints, but also by the experience of the 1920s. In the course of this period Trotsky had come to a firm conclusion: 'The politics of the Stalin leadership consist of short zigzags to the left and profound ones to the right.'[31] In 1927, oppositionists had been beaten up in the streets for trying to take part in a demonstration commemorating ten years of the revolution while carrying placards that stated: 'Turn the fire to the right – against the *kulak*, the nepman and the bureaucrat.'[32]

The shift by the Stalinist majority in the party leadership in 1928 and 1929 from supporting a balance between city and countryside to launching a fierce attack on the peasants did not flow logically from the 'centrist' course that Stalin and his associates had been pursuing. It is only with hindsight that historians have been ready to chart elegant schemes in which the leadership would first take its revenge on the left, then deal a blow against the right. In reality there was no plan prepared in advance, and could not be, since Stalin and his comrades-in-arms had foreseen neither the grain collection crisis nor the Great Depression. The Trotskyists in their publications were thus completely correct in describing the course followed by the leadership as dictated by necessity. What the oppositionists failed to recognise was how profoundly the new circumstances would change not only the course of the party, but also the very nature of the Soviet regime. The decision which Stalin and his closest associates took amid the danger of an economic catastrophe contradicted not only the views of Bukharin and other 'moderate' leaders, but also the Five-Year Plan, the decisions of the party's Fifteenth Congress and Sixteenth Conference, and the positions expressed earlier by Stalin himself. The party chief was forced to acknowledge this. However, he declared, the situation had changed, and the earlier decisions had to be 'laid to one side'.[33]

In his own fashion, Stalin was correct; the situation really had changed. The change, however, had not come in the Russian countryside, where the peasants had no wish to be drafted one and all into the collective farms, and where they resisted collectivisation in whatever way they could, but in the world system. The Great Depression not only altered the rules of the marketplace, but also heralded massive international shocks. The spectre of a new world war was becoming more and more easy to make out. Consequently, the programme of industrialisation had to be speeded up, whatever the cost. The Great Depression in the West helped propel Russia to the 'Great Turning Point'. Collectivisation, accompanied by the widespread slaughter of livestock, the disintegration of farm enterprises, and later by the deaths of massive numbers of people, threw production in the Soviet countryside into turmoil for decades. Nevertheless, it created the conditions for the rapid growth of industry.

The cost of 'progress' turned out to be appalling. According to official Soviet figures, more than 1 million 'dekulakised' peasants were banished to places little suited to supporting human life. Those who actively resisted were shot or sent to prison camps. The problem of acquiring grain for industrialisation, however, was solved:

Each year from 1928, the gross harvests of grain declined, if we do not count the unusually favourable year of 1930. Nevertheless, grain collections and exports increased. In 1930, 77.2 million tons of grain were harvested, and 4.8 million tons were exported; in 1931, when only 69.5 million tons were harvested, exports were 5.2 million tons.[34]

The official history of the Soviet economy states that throughout the whole period of the Great Turning Point, the main source of foreign currency receipts remained grain exports.

In the years from 1929 to 1932, Soviet grain exports reached their highest levels of the entire period before the Second World War.... From the exporting of grain, the Soviet government gained foreign currency to the value of 444.5 million rubles.[35]

The old slogan 'We shall go hungry, but we shall export!' had once again become a guide to action.

The growth of exports was combined with a sharp increase in the urban population. By contrast, agricultural output declined following the shocks of collectivisation. There was also a shortage of consumer goods, which continually grew more expensive, something which had a particular impact in the countryside. By 1930 and 1931 the threat of famine had become very real, and when the grain-growing regions were affected by drought in 1932, the 'food supply difficulties' turned into a genuine tragedy.

In line with bureaucratic logic, grain was invariably collected where the original plans had decided, with no regard for the situation in the various localities or even for the drought. The result was the famine of 1932–33. At this time the country was producing enough grain to avoid catastrophe. The grain was collected, however, precisely in the regions which in the original plans had been designated as fertile, and which were now suffering from drought. At the height of the famine, documents testify to above-plan deliveries of rye and other types of grain for export.[36]

By no means everyone approved of the choice that had been made in favour of exports. Documents in the Russian State Economic Archives show that in 1930 some officials argued that it was essential to reduce food exports 'in connection with the food supply problems in our country', and that 'the people in charge of Soviet foreign trade had definite doubts concerning the advisability of exporting foodstuffs even in 1931'.[37] Such views, however, were regarded as mistaken.

As a result of the global economic crisis, world trade turnover fell by two-thirds. Prices declined as well. To Stalin, this represented a historic opportunity.

A real chance had appeared for the Soviet state to obtain machinery, equipment and metals on the world market in the quantities required. It was also clear that the new opportunity to expand imports could not last long.[38]

Equipment prices did indeed decline, but very unevenly. Prices for construction equipment fell by 4–6 per cent, but for some types of machinery the decline was as much as 30 per cent. The Soviet organisations that imported technical goods stated that the prices for electrical equipment had fallen by 17.5 per cent. Meanwhile, the prominent German firm Karl Zeiss had begun charging 10 per cent less for its optical goods, and 13 per cent less for its measuring instruments, while also extending the time allowed for payment of its credits.[39]

The trouble was that the prices for Soviet exports were falling even more rapidly than the prices of imported equipment. Receipts of foreign currency from exports came to only 60.5 per cent of the sum projected in the Five-Year Plan, while in terms of physical volume 95 per cent of the plan targets had been met.[40] The unique 'opportunities' provided by the worldwide crisis had turned into monstrous costs. The official Soviet sources as well were obliged to recognise this.

It is a well-known fact that during the period of crisis the prices for agricultural products fell by more than the prices of industrial goods. As a result, the Soviet state during those years lost 1,873 million rubles on its exports, while saving 772.6 million on its imports. Consequently, our country lost 1,100.4 million rubles in foreign currency as a result of the fall in prices on the world market.[41]

The lower the price of grain, the greater the requirement to export it. The main importer of Soviet goods during that period was Britain. Despite the lower prices, the overall value of British imports from the Soviet Union rose after the beginning of the depression from £21.1 million in 1927 to £34.2 million in 1930.[42] According to figures from the Soviet trade office in London, the USSR in 1930 accounted for 13.3 per cent of the wheat imported into Britain. In the first nine months of 1931, the Soviet share reached 24.5 per cent.[43] To compensate for the fall in prices, it was necessary not only to increase grain exports (which caused prices to fall still further), but also to expand the range of exported goods. The Soviet government was prepared to export anything that could be sold, at any price and in any quantity. As well as grain, the USSR exported oil products, timber, iron ore, flax, hemp, tow, asbestos, manganese, precious stones, handicrafts, carpets, matches, caviar, lard, fresh and dried fruits, vegetables, and so forth. Prices, however, declined for virtually all types of products. The index of wholesale prices in Britain declined from 177.9 in 1925 to 129.3 in 1930, and continued falling, reaching 101.6 in August 1931. In the US it fell from 152.3 in 1925 to 125.1 in 1930, and in August 1931 stood at a mere 100.4. In Germany the corresponding fall was from 130.2 to 103.8, and by August 1931 the index stood at 101.3.[44]

During the years 1929 and 1930 the price of butter fell by 39.8 per cent, and in 1931 by another 11.9 per cent.[45] The decline of prices in 1931 was so marked that despite an increase in butter exports of 10 per cent, the value of exports was down on the previous year by 13 per cent.[46] The price of eggs fell by 44.3 per cent, and then by a further 10.4 per cent. For oil products the fall in prices averaged 4–6 per cent, followed in 1931 by a fresh decline, this time of 10–15 per cent. The price of asbestos fell by roughly a third, then by a further third. Fox furs from Tobolsk declined in price by 38.7 per cent, then by another 33 per cent. In the depression conditions, ermine pelts from Yakutsk sold for 58 per cent less; then in 1931 the price dropped a further 21 per cent. Carpets from Bukhara fell in price by 8.9 per cent, then by another 17.5 per cent.[47]

Such losses could be coped with only through the pitiless exploitation of the countryside and of the selfless toil of urban workers living in appalling conditions. Western newspapers accused Soviet exporters of dumping, which was true only in part. Goods really were being sold at less than their value, but the Soviet government had often obtained them for next to nothing. Soviet documents of the period frequently mention discrepancies 'between the delivery prices and the actual cost'.[48] Kolganov calculates that 'the costs exceeded the procurement prices for grain approximately two to three times over. The relationship between prices and costs in livestock production was even worse.'[49] The situation with industrial crops was somewhat better.

Despite the crisis, the minuscule prices for which the state was acquiring agricultural produce meant that profitable sales could be made abroad. Even if goods had often to be sold on the world market at an outright loss, this was no longer of fundamental importance; what was needed was foreign currency. Since there was a shortage of money for machinery imports in any case, the importing of raw materials ceased almost completely. Everything that could be obtained within the country was called into play. Agriculture underwent a massive reorientation toward industrial crops, sacrificing foodstuffs such as potatoes, vegetables and meat that did not have export potential. The countryside was required above all to serve the needs of industrialisation and exports, in the second instance to supply the cities with food, and only in the third instance to feed itself. 'As a result,' Kolganov writes, 'the economy of the collective farms took on a suspicious resemblance to certain features of the feudal estate.'[50] The survival of the peasants was their own concern; the collective farms were charged first and foremost with solving the problems of the state as a whole.

EVERYTHING FOR SALE

'The statistics for foreign trade', Trotsky wrote in 1931, 'are increasingly becoming the determining figures where the plans and tempi of socialist construction are concerned.'[51] Despite the shortage of foreign currency, the plan for imports of machinery was even overfulfilled (at 105.6 per cent of the projected figure), while for imports as a whole the level was only 48.6 per cent. The share of imports represented by means of production was as high as 90 per cent.

By the end of the Five-Year Plan the Soviet Union held first place in the world for imports of machinery and equipment. In 1931 around a third, and in the following year around half of all world exports of machinery went to the USSR.[52]

Metals were imported in large quantities, making up for around 20 per cent of expenditures of foreign currency. There was a particular shortage of high-quality steel, which had to be purchased abroad. Since foreign currency was in chronic short supply, the state was prepared to export anything and everything, from gold, oil and furs to the pictures in the Hermitage Museum. Postage stamps, coins and antiques were sold. The trade encountered difficulties due to a shortage of expert personnel. The Soviet trade office in Berlin explained that it was in acute need of an auctioneer, but that it had no such person.[53] The Berlin firm of J.H. Stolow tried to monopolise the sale of Soviet postage stamps in Germany, but its relations with Moscow proved erratic. The owners of the company, the Stolov brothers, maintained that in the conditions of the depression their clients were short of money and that it was necessary to provide them with goods on credit. In return, the Stolovs tried to engage the attention of their Soviet partners by promising that they could 'easily put an end' to contraband, since they knew all the smugglers personally. Their account of the brilliant prospects for the struggle against contraband ended with a specific request: 'We ask you to send us an acknowledgement in which you guarantee to keep all our denunciations secret.'[54] The reaction in Moscow to these suggestions was unenthusiastic, since the Soviet authorities had developed their own, unique method for waging the fight against contraband. From now on, new Soviet postage stamps would first appear in foreign philatelic shops, and only after a certain period in Soviet post offices. In this way, the Soviet officials concluded, they could 'saturate the foreign market, without facing any competition'.[55]

At the height of the world crisis, and amid the shocks of collectivisation, measures were taken to attract foreign tourists to the USSR. Despite the 'unfavourable conjuncture in the world tourism market', the People's Commissariat of Foreign Trade considered the prospects for attracting tourists to be reasonably good.[56] In practice, the successes were insignificant, not only because of the generally difficult conditions, but also because of lack of personnel and resources. To obtain goods for export, the official accounts reported proudly, special conferences were convened in the union republics and provinces, while 'shock brigades of Young Communists were organised, along with mass month-long campaigns'.[57]

In the Russian State Archives of the Economy (RGAE), some of the minutes of the export conferences have been preserved, and provide us with an idea of the desperate confusion that reigned at the local level. The obtaining of products for export was described in military terms such as the 'autumn–winter campaign' and the 'spring campaign'. Resources were procured through a combination of political mobilisation, material incentives and repression. The awarding of prizes to export brigades, and the introduction of special rates of payment for production meant for export, were a commonplace matter. Special importance, however, was assigned to agitation. It was essential to impress on the workers that what they were involved in was a state task of the first order, the mobilising of 'the collective farm members and especially, the Young Communists for a decisive struggle to fulfil the annual export targets'.[58] As well as one-month and two-week campaigns for the procurement of export goods, cells were established for the purpose of assisting in export activity. Trade unions, party organs and the press were to take part in the propaganda campaign.

The search for goods suitable for export led the officials in charge to adopt some quite unexpected measures:

In view of the fact that 90 per cent of dogs have coats suitable for the fur trade, the People's Commissariat of Foreign Trade should be requested to propose to the People's Commissariat of Supply of the USSR that state purchases of dogs should be transferred to the fur industry.[59]

The results of this initiative were soon felt, as can be seen from a protocol of the Central Black-Earth Province: 'To note the marked acceleration by the hunting union of the killing of dogs during the summer, with the aim of obtaining skins.'[60] However, it was found that summer was the least suitable time for hunting dogs. The quality of the skins declined. Consequently, it was decided to adopt a special resolution 'on the struggle against stray dogs, aimed at killing the maximum number of dogs during winter, and maintaining their population during the spring and summer periods'.[61]

Cats were not spared either; it was explained that their skins could be exported too. The massacre of animals reached such a scale that measures had to be taken to regulate the slaughter. 'In order to maintain the basis for fur production' it was decided to stop 'the catching of dogs and cats during the period from 1 April to 1 November'.[62]

Small wild animals fared no better. A conference in the Central Black-Earth Province discussed the question 'of the autumn procurement of moles, hamsters and mole-rats'.[63] It was proposed that 'exportable breeds of rabbits' be developed; at the same time, it was found that 'diseases of rabbits, and measures for dealing with these illnesses' had not been studied.[64] It was noted that the state purchasers were required to hand over to the People's Commissariat of Foreign Trade 'all waste material suitable for fur and other production'.[65]

The participants in the conference were charged with compiling 'a plan for research into new types of export', and with 'thoroughly investigating the question of offal'.[66] In the North Caucasus, efforts were made to organise exports of beer, fruit juices and mineral waters. Here too, however, there was no progress for months. In order to find a niche in the world market, it was necessary to study the varieties of Soviet beer that were available. Unfortunately, by the time the beer arrived in Rostov, where the decision was to be made, it had spoiled and 'become worthless'.[67]

The list of export commodities included horsehair, starch, glycerine, frozen meat scraps, dressed poultry, fish glue, honey, preserved strawberries and blackcurrants, sunflower and castor oils, and eggs.[68] The state purchasers complained that eggs for the British market could not be got ready in sufficient quantities because of hot weather and the lack of refrigerators, although everything was being done 'in accordance with the relevant decrees'.[69] There were other problems as well. 'The village soviets do not feel any responsibility concerning the state procurement of eggs for export.'[70] It was necessary to impose 'a strict target for eggs on the *kulaks* and the better-off elements in the villages'.[71]

Charcoal, bacon, preserved tongues, furs, undressed pelts, bristles and rags were exported. The list was endless – apples, nuts, pickled cucumbers, lace, willow twigs, baskets, tobacco, wool, potash, paraffin, cement, industrial waste materials, cotton, medicinal herbs, poppy seed, railway sleepers, planks, parquetry, feathers, down, hooves and horns. The conference in the Central Black-Earth Province even mentioned 'the failure of procurements for Spanish Fly'.[72]

It was found that crab meat could be sold on the world market, and a resolution was adopted: 'To conduct extensive information work among the fishing population on the importance and necessity of catching crabs.'[73] There were also more useful suggestions, such as providing the fishers with the necessary tackle. Ultimately, the measures taken were ineffective, and the plan was not fulfilled. Explaining the reasons for the failure, the participants in the conference explained that a multitude of errors had been permitted, and that the work had 'not been satisfactorily organised'. There was, it is true, a further cause: 'The fact that crabs were not coming into the gulf.'[74]

It is hard to say how big the catch would have been with better organisation, given that there were no crabs in the gulf anyway. Recognising that there was a certain contradiction here, the conference resolved that before the guilty were punished, the objective problems had to be taken into account. In exactly the same way, the plan for bacon exports was not met, since there were not enough pigs. Disparities between the plans and the actual situations featured constantly as the main reason for failure. In the North Caucasus, officials were compelled to recognise that the plan for exports had not been fulfilled 'because of the lack of sufficient resources in the territory'.[75] In other words, the goods being sought simply did not exist in the territory, or at least, not in the quantities that were demanded. As a result, figures for plan fulfilment of 5–10 per cent were commonplace.

The search for scapegoats was accompanied by mutual rebukes between state bodies. Those in charge of the export organisations, it was argued, had 'devoted too little study to all the reasons responsible for the non-fulfilment of the plan' and had mounted 'only a feeble struggle against all the obstacles in the way of fulfilling the plan'.[76] Exports of beer and fruit juices from the North Caucasus territory, it was said, did not go ahead because of the 'utterly disgraceful attitude' shown by the agro-industrial body Sevkavkazselprom. It was also thought necessary to note 'the completely unacceptable attitude of the territory office of Vseutilsyrye', to put a stop to 'the abnormal actions of Kraykolkhozsoyuz, both in the territory and in the regions', and so forth.[77] In Crimea an export conference 'failed to sufficiently involve the broad masses of collective farm members in export activity'.[78] In the Central Black-Earth Province the organisation Legtekhsyrye performed poorly in running the procurement campaign, as was shown by 'the lack of information and by the pressure placed on the state purchasers while agreements were being concluded with them'.[79] Documents note 'the incorrect ideas entertained by Okhotsoyuz', as a result of which the performance of the fur industry was 'unacceptably weak, bordering on failure'.[80]

Criticism was not the whole story; executive chiefs were subjected to outright repression. When the Krasny Aksay agricultural equipment plant failed to meet its export plan, a decision was taken to 'hand the matter over to the prosecutor for investigation and for the bringing to justice of those at fault'.[81] Special attention was devoted to ensuring that goods meant for export did not finish up on the internal market. When a consignment of chairs (apparently meant for export, but unsuitable because of their poor quality) was sold locally, a scandal erupted: 'For the violation of the export plan for chairs the appropriate individuals from the factory administration have been handed over to the courts.'[82] The minutes of the conference note as a serious problem the fact that some export enterprises were continuing to fill 'particular orders for the internal market'.[83] In the course of discussion on 'the breaching of the plan for purchases of berries' and 'the catastrophically low level of fulfilment of the plan for strawberries', it was resolved to undertake special measures 'to prevent any diversion of berries onto the internal market'.[84] In Crimea the export conference called for 'taking measures against the diverting of fresh fruits of export quality onto the internal market'.[85] In addition, it was decided to do everything required to promote 'the struggle against the accumulating of tobacco in the regions where state purchases are being carried out'.[86] To be fair, it should be noted that as compensation, the participants in the conference suggested bringing tobacco of lower quality into the province to meet local demand.

When goods were nevertheless obtained, a further problem arose; the transport system was unable to cope. The managers of the railways had been issued with a decree 'on the acceptance of all export freight for loading out of order'.[87] However, the ports and railways were overloaded with export shipments, there were insufficient elevators for the grain that was to be exported, and 'a threatening situation' had arisen.[88]

The minutes of the export conferences are littered with complaints about the failure to meet plan targets and about the poor quality of goods. The quantities of defective products, innumerable reports state, had reached 'colossal dimensions'.[89] Chairs made using specially imported equipment were unfit for sale abroad. 'Offal of low quality', the records state, was being sent for export.[90] The Soviet trade office in London complained that by all measures, the goods had 'deteriorated significantly'.[91]

The reasons for this deterioration can readily be grasped if we take the example of poultry production. Conference participants reported that the poultry processing works were unable to function normally, since 'the feeding pens were severely overcrowded'; as a result, birds were killed 'without having been fattened, despite having been in the feeding pens for thirty days'.[92]

The poor-quality work was due to the difficult situation in which the workers found themselves. 'The living conditions of the workers are quite impossible', it was reported.

There are no hostels, no political study areas, no dining-rooms. The food supply is inadequate, which affects the availability of labour power.[93]

The conferences called for increasing the material stimuli for workers to improve output, and for 'putting an end to irresponsibility, ill-discipline and wage-levelling'.[94]

The rates at which products were unloaded were 'catastrophically low'. On page after page, the conference minutes acknowledge 'the catastrophically low level of fulfillment of the plan for export deliveries' or the failure of a 'two-week export campaign', and so forth.[95] At times, a philosophical mood seizes the authors of the documents, and they include in the records such remarks as that 'if the supply situation does not improve, the prospects will be dismal'.[96] Not surprisingly, 'a mood of disorganization' was observed among the workers of Sovkavpushnina, and the administrative heads of other departments were called upon to 'do away with the demoralised mood that has arisen'.[97]

In 1932, only eight of out of 23 provinces that had been assigned export targets fulfilled them. Nevertheless, the overall goal was attained. At the cost of vast effort and desperate, poorly organised, inefficient work at the local level, the industrialisation programme received the foreign currency it needed.

THE SUCCESS OF INDUSTRIALISATION

To some degree, Soviet industry made up for the shortage of funds for purchasing the goods that were required. In the conditions of drastic worldwide economic decline, import substitution was a necessity. The Soviet Union thus became the first country in the world to produce synthetic rubber on a large scale. The development of the chemical industry made it possible to replace, or reduce to a minimum, imports of acids, fertilisers, dyes, plastics, coke and nitrates. Exploration for new mineral deposits was begun, followed by the development of discoveries.

In many cases, programmes such as these had not been foreseen in the original plan. The more machinery was imported, however, the more the Soviet Union needed to replace other types of imports. In other words, the 'exclusion' of the Soviet Union from the world market and the creation of a 'closed economy' was largely the result of the processes taking place in 1929–32 in the world market itself. In 1931, the same chaos that reigned in other sectors prevailed in the departments concerned with importing equipment. The officials in charge recognised that in the question of planning, there was 'no clarity and no possibility of establishing whether plans had been fulfilled'.[98] People did not understand how to work with Western firms; officials of the People's Commissariat of Foreign Trade were warned 'to observe closely the actions of representatives of foreign firms, and not to permit them such things as to wander about our institutions finding out in advance what we are going to order from them'.[99]

By the end of 1931 the situation had begun to improve somewhat. Prices for goods exported from the USSR had begun to rise, as had the efficiency of the Soviet foreign trade organisations. Because the conditions of the depression meant that a substantial proportion of goods were sold on credit (and the conditions of the credit became more advantageous the worse the situation of the company), the Soviet foreign trade organisations were able to settle their debts and place new orders.

From 1932, imports of equipment steadily declined as the output of the Soviet machine-building industry expanded. The new Soviet industry was constructed on the basis of the most advanced technology of its time. The main importer of Soviet goods, political obstacles notwithstanding, was still Britain. During the depression years it remained ahead of Germany in this capacity; between 1929 and 1931 the British took 23.7 per cent of Soviet exports, with the Germans accounting for 21.4 per cent.[100] The United States, by contrast, imported very few Soviet goods. It was the US, however, that became the main supplier of equipment. In 1930 it accounted for 31.2 per cent of all technical goods imported to the Soviet Union, and in the first quarter of 1931, for no less than 42.8 per cent.[101]

The Soviet leadership had made its choice in favour of the country that possessed the most modern technology. By the mid 1920s the United States not only held first place for the technical re-equipping of industry. The conveyer-belt production methods first introduced in the plants of Henry Ford, along with the forms of organisation of labour that corresponded to them, had dramatically increased efficiency and had brought about genuine mass production. Most sectors of Soviet industry were set up from the start on the basis of Fordist technologies, without passing through earlier phases.

The accelerated growth of industry bore fruit during the Second World War. Comparing the results of the industrialisation between 1928 and 1940 with the growth of industry from 1900 to 1913, the liberal sociologists L.A. Gordon and E.V. Klopov concluded that Stalin's modernisation was far more successful than the reforms of Witte and Stolypin.

Each of these periods of equal length was followed by an armed conflict between our country and one and the same foreign enemy. The war acted as a sort of examiner, testing the results of what had been achieved. In the second case, moreover, the examiner was far more 'strict' than in the first. Throughout the First World War Germany and its allies were fighting on two fronts, and could direct only a minor part of their armed strength against Russia; the majority of their forces remained in the Western theatre of military operations. For three of the four years of the Great Patriotic War, the Soviet Union waged what was virtually a one-on-one struggle against fascist Germany. Not a third, as in the years from 1914 to 1918, but approximately three-quarters of the German armed forces were concentrated against us from 1941 to 1945. Nevertheless, pre-revolutionary Russia suffered military defeat, while the Soviet Union crushed fascism.[102]

In both cases, the industrialisation was based on the exporting of grain and the exploitation of the countryside, though Stalin's measures for their harshness and effectiveness were in a quite different league from either the financial pressures of Witte or the repressions of Stolypin. But was this forcible extraction of funds from the countryside the main condition for success? Unquestionably not; the achievements of the First Five-Year Plan were predetermined not by the repression directed against the peasants, but by the fact that Soviet Russia was not a participant in the international process of capital accumulation. It was this disassociation from the world system, or delinking, to use the term employed by Samir Amin, that made it possible to concentrate the USSR's resources on the priority task of industrialisation. It was this independence of the world capital markets that allowed Soviet industry to record thoroughly respectable growth rates as early as the mid 1920s.

By contrast, the repression aimed at the peasantry, the universal collectivisation and the shift to totalitarianism in 1929–32 were to a significant degree (though not exclusively) the result of the worldwide economic crisis that affected Soviet Russia differently from Germany or the US, but no less fatefully.

It is obvious that no 'external circumstances' can exonerate the people who exiled and killed peasants, who later wrought massive vengeance on party activists, 'Old Bolsheviks' and the intelligentsia, and who in the 1940s sent whole peoples into exile. The triumphant bureaucracy pursued its own ends, which had less and less in common with the socialist ideals proclaimed by the revolution. The formation of a bureaucratic elite in Russia and its political victory were accomplished facts by the end of the 1920s. The turn toward a 'Soviet Thermidor', of which Leon Trotsky spoke, was already in full swing under the NEP. Nevertheless, it was the world crisis from 1929 to 1932 that lent Stalinism the form in which it entered history. It was this crisis that gave birth to totalitarianism in the USSR, just as it resulted in the victory of Nazism in Germany. But unlike German Nazism, Stalinist totalitarianism represented the continuation of a revolution, and even during its most appalling years still bore the traces of a human face. It was thanks to this that the later softening of the regime, the famous 'thaw' of the 1960s and the new flowering of 'initiative from below' in all spheres of life, eventually became possible.

THE SOVIET 'THERMIDOR' AND SOVIET BONAPARTISM

Trotsky characterised the consolidation of the bureaucratic system in the USSR as a 'Soviet Thermidor', and the Stalinist regime as a 'bloc of Thermidorean-Bonapartist forces'.[103] The analogy with the French Revolution was readily understood by all the participants in the political struggle of the 1920s. The Thermidorean overturn in France signalled the end of participation by the masses in determining the fate of the republic, and marked the triumph of the new elite. Born of the revolution, this elite had no intention whatsoever of rejecting the revolution's conquests. It completed the revolution and secured its results, but did this not in the interests of the masses, but in its own interests. In the same fashion, Trotsky considered, the Soviet bureaucracy had politically expropriated the proletariat, and had appropriated to itself the results of the proletariat's struggle.

As early as the beginning of the 1920s there was talk in Russia of the possibility of a 'Thermidorean' counter-revolution, and Trotsky was not the first to utter these words. Lenin noted that such a turn of events was not excluded. The Mensheviks prophesied it, and the White émigrés waited for it to happen. During this period, however, everyone imagined the future Thermidorean regime in terms quite different from the reality of the 1930s.[104]

The Left Opposition which Trotsky headed in the party saw the basis for the Soviet Thermidor in a bloc of the party-economic bureaucracy with the *kulaks*, that is, with a rural bourgeoisie which to a significant degree had arisen thanks to the achievement of the 1917 revolution in doing away with estate landholding. In the countryside of the 1920s, the *kulaks* were by no means the same proprietors who had played this role in the pre-revolutionary period. Significant numbers of the new 'substantial farm enterprises' had arisen as a result of the seizing and dividing up of the landowners' estates and other possessions. In this sense, and despite the intentions of the Bolsheviks, the *kulaks* finished up among those who benefited from the revolution.

A bloc between the bureaucracy and the *kulaks* seemed a perfectly real prospect in the 1920s. The Stalinist regime of the 1930s, however, did not resemble this prognosis; it took shape through the smashing of the *kulaks* – and, indeed, of the peasantry in general – through the forced collectivisation. It is usually considered that Trotsky in this case was mistaken, and during the 1930s he plainly rethought his concept of the Soviet Thermidor.

But were the people who were already predicting a Thermidor in the early 1920s equally mistaken? The evolution of the party during that period had a clearly expressed Thermidorean character, as the repressions levelled against the Left Opposition plainly confirmed. But around the beginning of the 1930s something happened that abruptly altered the development of the Soviet regime; a rupture occurred which not even those who took part in it had anticipated or predicted.

The anti-communist tradition does not see any fundamental difference between the Bolshevik dictatorship of the 1920s and the Stalinist regime that became established during the 1930s. To be more precise, no one can deny that the regime became much harsher, that repression began on a massive scale, and that a wave of terror swept across the country. Nevertheless, the transition from authoritarianism to totalitarianism that took place between 1929 and 1932 is depicted as something natural and inevitable, flowing automatically from the very essence of the revolution and of communist ideology. Even if this were true, the question would remain unanswered of why this transition occurred precisely at this time, and assumed such a form; of why it was so abrupt and unexpected, catching everyone involved, including Stalin himself, quite unawares.

Collectivisation proved to be a decisive stage in the transforming of the Soviet system from an authoritarian to a totalitarian one.[105] The rural Soviets, which had earlier retained a certain autonomy with relation to the party organs, finally lost all their independence. The last serious opposition, the group of Bukharin, Rykov and Tomsky, was smashed. Open discussions within the party came to an end. The cult of Stalin the individual rapidly took shape. The cult of the great leader is a characteristic trait of Bonapartist regimes, and during the twentieth century it was incorporated into the ideological arsenal of totalitarianism.

After collectivisation, the economy of the Soviet Union was completely statised; the formal independence of the collective farms concealed administrative control which at times was even more rigorous than in the official state sector. Any form of private or collective administrative activity that was not included in the system of centralised management was eliminated. It was in the years of the 'Great Turning Point' that the Soviet economy took on its closed character, separating itself off from the world market. To a significant degree, this transition to a 'closed economy' was of a forced nature. It resulted from the chronic shortage of funds and from the oppressed condition (following collectivisation) of agriculture, which earlier had played the role of the main export sector.

During the civil war the dictatorship of the Bolsheviks had been harsh, but inconsistent; massive repressions had been mounted against 'counter-revolutionary elements', at the same time as relatively free discussions had been held with Mensheviks, anarchists and other opposition groups. With the transition to the NEP, the power of the Bolshevik party had become far more consolidated; this was when the opposition parties were finally banned. But even when the Soviet power finally took on the form of a one-party dictatorship in 1921–22, it was not yet totalitarian. The Soviet regime corresponded fully to a type of revolutionary authoritarianism that was well known in the history of Western Europe. Lenin was perfectly correct when he compared the Bolsheviks to the Jacobins. Neither group had any regard for the rules of formal democracy. Nevertheless, this was still something short of total domination, penetrating all the pores of society and subordinating to itself all forms of public life.

The society of the 1920s was based on a compromise between the cities, which were in the hands of the Bolsheviks, and the countryside, which retained a good deal of economic independence. The power of the Communist Party was limited, as was its ability to exercise economic control. Numerous political forces during the 1920s therefore had reason to hope for a softening of the authoritarianism and for a democratisation of the Soviet regime. The Left

Opposition, which warned its supporters of an impending Thermidor, and the moderate émigrés[106] who dreamed of such a Thermidor, of course saw the future evolution of the regime quite differently.

Both groups, as has been explained, were mistaken. Nevertheless, their expectations were not baseless. The members of these groups had simply not been able to foresee the shift experienced between 1929 and 1932 not only by Russia, but by the entire world.

The link between the Great Depression and the rise of the Nazi regime in Germany is a generally acknowledged historical fact, but the rise of the totalitarian system in the Soviet Union is viewed by most scholars exclusively as the result of internal processes, with no connection to world events. The fact that the Soviet regime underwent a dramatic transformation precisely in 1929–32 is seen as a chronological coincidence at most (Russian history, as has already been noted, positively teems with such strange 'coincidences').

Meanwhile, the importance of the changes that occurred is impossible to overestimate. The entire social and economic structure of Soviet society, the way of life and the rules of politics, all changed radically as the country witnessed the rise of what journalists and historians have termed 'Stalinist totalitarianism'. Soviet society in the 1930s not only underwent a shift from authoritarianism to totalitarianism. The post-revolutionary elite, after passing quickly through the Thermidorean stage of its development, passed on rapidly to Bonapartism. The Soviet Union began taking on the features of an empire, a change which on the cultural level was finally confirmed during the Second World War with the return of the old ranks and officers' epaulettes, with the cult of the great leader, with the reconciliation with the church, and with the rewriting of history. Russian Bonapartism took the form of a totalitarian regime.[107]

As befitted a Bonapartist regime, the Stalinist system put a stop to the revolution and at the same time reinforced its consequences. The country had changed radically, and stood on the same level with the leading powers of the West. Nevertheless, the main victors in the tragic period of the first half of the twentieth century were not the ordinary masses, who had made a heroic leap into the future, but the bureaucratic elite, who had secured themselves a monopoly on power and control.

14
The Soviet World

In the twentieth century the United States replaced Britain as the world's leading capitalist country. The rise of the US as a world power is usually considered to have begun during the First World War, when the US was transformed from a debtor to a creditor country, and its armed forces played a decisive part in the victory of the entente over Germany in 1918. No less important for the world system, however, were the consequences of the Russian Revolution of 1917. For two centuries Russia had played a substantial role in the development of European capitalism; as a supplier of raw materials, as a market, as an importer of 'free' capital, and as a debtor country. With the departure of Russia from the world system, a great deal changed.

At the same time as Western European capital was 'losing' Russia, US capital was finally assimilating Latin America. Unlike Britain or France, the US had important resources of raw materials. These resources were on the territory of the US itself, not in remote colonies, and there was no need to defend them constantly. Moreover, the US possessed an enormous internal market and had its 'own' Latin American periphery, located immediately to the south of the Rio Grande. With the departure of Russia from the world system, these advantages of the US became far more obvious. When the Soviet Union also gradually quit the world grain market after collectivisation, the US was left as the unquestioned leader in this area as well. The American elites, unlike the German ruling class, did not pursue a course of struggle against the 'old' world power, that is, Britain. To the contrary, the US acted as a force guaranteeing, up to a certain point, the survival and inviolability of the British empire. The old world power stood in increasing need of this support as the external threats it faced grew more serious. Ultimately, the partners changed places. The Second World War transformed the US into the leader of the West. Nevertheless, the US was only able to consolidate and shape this leadership thanks to the Cold War with the USSR.[1]

THE COLD WAR

That the coalition partners would turn on one another after defeating Germany in 1945 was not hard to predict. Nevertheless, it was far from obvious in the spring and summer of 1945, when the foundations of the post-war world system were being laid, that this hostility would develop so rapidly, that it would take so acute a form, or that it would result in the rigid division of the planet into two blocs headed by the two superpowers.

The Soviet Union was neither intent on a new confrontation, nor ready for it. The destruction wrought by the war with Germany had been too great. During the meetings in Yalta and Potsdam, Stalin had not concealed his intention to keep within his sphere of influence the Eastern European countries liberated (or occupied) by the Soviet army, but at that time Moscow's ambitions did not extend any further. This is why Moscow in 1946 and 1947 displayed caution and a readiness to make concessions, while the US behaved with increasing assertiveness.

In the post-war period, an exception on the European continent was Finland, which to an important extent ended up under the influence of the Soviet Union, but which retained its Western social, political and economic institutions. This situation was possible because Finland, unlike Eastern Europe, was not under occupation. But if we look at the policies implemented by Moscow and by the communist parties under its control in the 'liberated countries', we find that at first it was not very different from what was happening in Finland. In Bulgaria the communists declared that they were entering a government which, if we are to believe its protestations, had 'no intention of establishing a communist regime'.[2] In Romania a popular-democratic government was established with participation by liberals, and the king remained on the throne. The police and state security organs, controlled by colleagues of the Soviet authorities, even persecuted opponents of the monarchy, and on 8 November 1946 the communist newspaper *Era Nuoa* stated that 'the people of Romania have faith in their king'.[3]

In Hungary, multi-party elections were held in November 1945, with the Communist Party receiving only 17 per cent of the votes. In the governing coalition, the Communists received only four cabinet portfolios out of 15. In subsequent elections in July 1947, the communists achieved somewhat better results, but still won the support of only 21.5 per cent of voters.

In Poland in 1945 an administration was formed with the participation of supporters of Moscow and of representatives of the émigré government which during the war had been based in London. In Czechoslovakia, the most developed of the countries occupied by the Soviet Army, the policies of the pro-Moscow Communist Party were also conspicuously moderate, even though the communists had considerable influence. A coalition government was set up, with liberal forces included. Nationalisation decrees, that had the support not only of the left but also of a significant part of the political centre, did not affect medium-sized businesses. Workers' councils began operating in the enterprises. On 26 May, free elections were held, and the Communists received 38 per cent of the votes. In Slovakia, 62 per cent of the votes went to the Democratic Party, which was running against the communists. The latter could rule only in coalition with the Social Democrats, who held nine government portfolios out of 26.

Naturally, the Eastern European republics in 1945 and 1946 were by no means model democracies. The Soviet representatives paid very close attention to the foreign policy of their new allies. From time to time, people who had fallen out of favour with the new authorities were persecuted (these latter often included left-wing politicians who demanded a more radical course). This persecution, however, bears no comparison with what ensued in Eastern Europe after the Cold War began in earnest.

Late in 1947, against the background of a rapid deterioration of Soviet-US relations, a sharp turning-point was reached in Eastern Europe. The territory of occupied Germany was divided into two states. Arising in the west was the Federal Republic of Germany. In response to the 'splitting policy of the Western powers and of German reaction', a German Popular Congress was held in the Soviet Zone, and on 11 October the formation was announced of the German Democratic Republic, 'the first workers' and peasants' state in German history'.[4]

That autumn proved fateful for all of Eastern Europe. In Czechoslovakia the state security organs, controlled by people loyal to Moscow, began a struggle against 'conspirators', a category to which the most influential opponents of the Communist Party were assigned. Purges and reshuffles began in the structures of power, culminating in February 1948 in the formation of a new government that was a coalition only in name. Similar events occurred throughout the Soviet sphere of influence. Opposition parties were dispersed and outlawed, while dissidents were repressed or banished to the West. Virtually all sectors of production were nationalised; Polish agriculture was an exception, with the peasants continuing to stubbornly resist collectivisation. Systems of centralised economic management, closely replicating the Soviet one, were constructed. Before long, the victims of the mass repressions included communists as well. After the Yugoslav Communist Party under Josip Broz Tito declared its independence, reprisals began against 'Titoists' throughout the Soviet sphere of influence. There were not in fact any Titoists in these countries, but Moscow's representatives single-mindedly exterminated or exiled all local communist leaders who enjoyed authority among the masses – in the process dealing a preventive blow aimed at ensuring that the 'Yugoslav scenario' was not repeated.

Moscow's logic was simple; the Cold War needed political consolidation. Ideologues from the communist parties declared that the harsh measures were in response to the policies of the US in Western Europe, policies that amounted to an attempt to 'go on the offensive against the forces of democracy and progress, headed by the Soviet Union'.[5]

The truth was that both in the dividing of Germany into two states, and in the creation of two opposing military blocs on the territory of Europe, the first steps had been taken by the United States. It was the US that had first developed a nuclear weapon, and that had used it against Japan. The monetary reform carried out in the Western occupation zones of Germany, the proclaiming there of the Federal Republic, the founding in April 1949 of the North Atlantic Treaty Organisation (NATO) and the establishing of other military blocs along the borders of the USSR were clear provocations to Moscow to adopt corresponding measures. Meanwhile, the people in the Kremlin were far from being pacifists either. The Soviet reaction was not only quick in coming, but in its severity exceeded anything that anti-communist ideologues might have dreamed of. By mid 1948 all the steps taken by the West had received retrospective moral and political justification, though many intellectuals continued to the last to hope for some softening of the Soviet system following the war.[6] After the founding of the German Democratic Republic (GDR), deliberate work began on establishing the Soviet bloc, which sought to become a sort of alternative world system. January 1949 saw the founding of the Council for Mutual Economic Assistance (CMEA, or Comecon), which united the Soviet Union and its new allies in a single trading organisation.

Meanwhile, the Soviet leadership continued to display a certain hesitancy on the 'German Question' until the mid 1950s. It is enough to recall Stalin's famous note of 10 March 1952, in which the Soviet leader suggested that the process of unifying Germany should begin. As historians who have studied declassified archival documents have observed, Stalin's note aroused 'consternation' in the GDR leaders, while Western diplomats remarked on Moscow's 'readiness to hold new elections, and thus to allow a rejection of communism in the Soviet zone'. In return, Stalin demanded only the 'neutralisation of Germany'.[7]

Archive documents linked to the preparation of Stalin's 1952 note also reveal sharp disagreements within the Soviet leadership, with the roles disposed in a fashion quite different from that which subsequent events might suggest.

The Soviet Foreign Ministry had to deal with relatively open resistance from military circles to even the most limited plans to shift the stance on the German question away from the rigid repetition of old slogans and ideas. The affair reached the point of fierce disputes between Stalin and representatives of what came later to be called the military-industrial complex.[8]

Stalin's conciliatory position was supported by the all-powerful head of state security, Lavrenty Beriya, while N.S. Khrushchev, who was later to inspire the 'thaw', argued for a hard line.

The Soviet line on the 'German Question' was finally settled only after Stalin's death, when a mass uprising by workers in Berlin was put down in June 1953. On Khrushchev's initiative a consistently hard line, aimed at bringing about a complete break with the West, was pursued from that point. Eastern Europe was transformed into a single military and political bloc, which took formal shape in 1955 within the framework of the Warsaw Pact. In 1961 the demarcation between the two parts of the continent came to be embodied physically in the Berlin Wall.

Ultimately, the Cold War suited both sides. It allowed the Soviet Union to consolidate its domination of Eastern Europe. For the US, its consequences were even more important. The more tense the stand-off, the more solid was 'American leadership', and the more Western Europe needed the US economically and depended on it politically. Within the context of the Cold War, it became possible for the US to invest money in restoring its former military adversaries and trading competitors, from Germany and Japan to Britain and France, with no need to fear new challenges from their direction.

The Soviet leaders in turn had realised by the late 1950s that the only way their rival could be weakened was through a rapprochement between the USSR and Western Europe. The peak of the confrontation between the two systems was the Cuban missile crisis of 1962, when, in response to the stationing of American missiles in Turkey, the Soviet leadership tried to install its own missiles in Cuba, which had experienced revolution not long before. The Caribbean crisis put the world on the brink of a new war, in circumstances where the position of the USSR was clearly weaker than that of its 'potential adversary'. After the crisis had been resolved by diplomatic means, the inevitable conclusions were drawn in Moscow. While the USSR continued to expand its weaponry, seeking parity with the US (this was achieved by the early 1970s), it also put its stake on the policy of 'peaceful coexistence', later to be renamed the 'policy of relaxing international tensions', or, more succinctly, détente.

Although the slogans of peaceful coexistence and détente were addressed formally to the entire capitalist world, in practice the main addressees were the countries of Western Europe. Achieving a rapprochement with them was, of course, simply impossible without entering into negotiations with the US. The process of détente reached its apogee during work on the Agreement on Security and Cooperation in Europe. In July 1973 the Finnish capital, Helsinki, saw the opening of a conference aimed at preparing this document. For many years, Soviet diplomacy had been seeking such a pact. Taking part in the discussions, alongside representatives of the European countries, were delegations from the US and Canada. In 1975 the work of the conference culminated in the signing of the Final Act, which proclaimed the principles of peaceful coexistence and of the inviolability of borders on the European continent. The same document, however, also mentioned the need to respect the fundamental rights and freedoms of citizens; from this time, dissidents in the Soviet Union were able to refer to the obligations which the Kremlin had officially undertaken, but which it was refusing to fulfil.

The Soviet leadership declared triumphantly that from then on, an atmosphere of 'mutual trust and confidence in the free, independent and peaceful development of each country' would take shape in Europe.[9] Behind these optimistic assessments lay concealed a hope that the countries of Western Europe, feeling themselves secure, would gradually begin taking their distance from the US.

EFFORTS AT REFORM

By the early 1970s, the Soviet Union could unquestionably consider itself a successfully developing state. At the very least, the tasks which had confronted the country in the previous period had been successfully resolved. Industrialisation had been carried through, the war had been won, nuclear 'parity' with the US had been achieved, universal literacy had been brought to the population, and what was arguably the world's best system of education and advanced science had been established. Since 1953, moreover, mass terror had been brought to an end. At the Twentieth Congress of the Communist Party of the Soviet Union the party's new leader, Nikita Khrushchev, not only revealed the crimes of Stalin. By criticising his predecessor, he provoked a long-lasting political discussion and gave rise to a whole generation of people for whom rejection of Stalinism was linked intimately to faith in the Soviet system, on the basis that the system had proven its ability to correct its 'mistakes'. However limited the freedoms of the Soviet population might be, the changes in comparison to Stalinist times were thoroughly real; the system had evolved from totalitarianism to authoritarianism. Although most of the institutions of authority and control that had been founded in the 1930s remained in place, the pressure they exerted on society was clearly weaker.

Nevertheless, and despite the obvious successes, the Soviet Union as early as 1959 was encountering growing difficulties. The growth rates of the economy, though still impressive, had begun a steady decline. The consumer demand that had awakened under peacetime conditions was not being satisfied. Living standards were rising more slowly than the party had promised, and most importantly, the ideological foundations of the regime were increasingly being placed in doubt.

Paradoxically, the Soviet Union was the victim of its own success. The centralised system and mobilisational economy set in place in the 1930s as the Soviet answer to the challenge of the Great Depression had been effective in the times of industrialisation and war. Now, when the country had already been industrialised, and life had settled into a peaceful pattern, these methods were simply failing to work. The political reforms of the 1950s and early 1960s had proven insufficient. They had freed people, creating the conditions for open or semi-open discussion of the problems, but had not created a mechanism for solving these problems in practice.

The need for new reforms was not denied by the party hierarchs who, in 1964 and 1965, after Khrushchev had been replaced, announced that they would pursue a course aimed at creating a more flexible and decentralised system of economic management.

Leonid Brezhnev and his associates, who headed the Communist Party of the Soviet Union in 1964, came to be viewed in hindsight as a group of inveterate conservatives, who sought in every possible way to block the processes of democratisation of society and to prevent changes to any aspect of life. In the first years of their rule, however, they behaved quite differently. Even the sacking of Khrushchev from his post as party leader can be viewed in a certain fashion as proof of democratisation; for the first time in Russian history the country's leader was removed by peaceful means, and, having lost power, did not suffer repression. Supporters of democratisation continued to be published in the journal *Novy Mir.*

The economic reforms were planned as a new and important stage in the changes, one that would lead not only to increased efficiency in production, but also to a broadening of democracy. It is usually considered that the reforms of 1964 and 1965 were aimed at ensuring a 'harmonious' combination of plan and market in the economy. Elements of market relations, however, had existed in the Soviet system ever since the ending of 'war communism'. The main task of the reforms was not to implant market elements in the Soviet economic order, and not even to expand the sphere of action of these market relations; above all, it was to make use of market mechanisms in order to decentralise and democratise the planning process. But this programme, which corresponded to the interests of the growing layer of middle-level Soviet managers – and indeed of the work collectives in general – was fraught with a weakening of the party bureaucratic elite.

Just how serious these problems could be emerged in the spring of 1968, when in Czechoslovakia the process of economic reform that had had been initiated on the Soviet model turned into a political crisis. Czechoslovak society began changing rapidly, taking on the features of a democratic socialism strikingly different from the Soviet model of the 1930s. For some time the leaders of the USSR hesitated, but by the summer of 1968 it had finally become clear that a continuation of this process would mean serious changes throughout the Eastern Bloc, and then within the Soviet Union as well. The reforms in Czechoslovakia were crushed using military force, and their supporters were forced into silence. Meanwhile, the leaders of the Communist Party of the Soviet Union reached the firm conclusion that implicit in any serious changes was a loss of political control.

THE ERA OF STABILITY

The intervention in Czechoslovakia by Soviet forces in August 1968 showed how much the party leaders in the USSR feared reforms and the political risks associated with them. Only in hindsight, however, was it possible to say that the rejection of reform was final. The situation in 1968 and 1969 was by no means so clear. Even in Czechoslovakia, the Soviet leaders were not resolved on using force to remove the leaders of the Communist Party from their posts. An ambiguous situation remained for almost a year, with the reformers retaining their jobs, the occupation forces exerting pressure on them, and the workers' councils in the factories and the student movement continuing to insist on a continuation and even radicalisation of the changes.

In Hungary the economic reforms and the liberalisation of the regime were allowed to continue, on the condition that they would not affect the political monopoly of the party. In Poland in 1970 the Soviet leaders permitted the overthrow of the party leadership in the course of workers' strikes. The instigators of the strikes suffered repression, but the Polish government was forced to justify itself before the workers, and to alter course.[10] The situation remained ambiguous within the USSR as well. The conservative sector of the leadership unquestionably strengthened its positions, but the economic reforms were not officially reversed. The opposition journal *Novy Mir* continued appearing in print runs of millions of copies, though its editor Aleksandr Tvardovsky now reiterated that every issue published was the last. Dissidents began to be persecuted, but on the other hand, the authorities now showed they were able to tolerate some of them remaining free, which earlier would simply have been inconceivable. In short, the victory of the conservatives was far from definitive.

The rejection of reform was consolidated politically only in the mid 1970s. This period marked the beginning in the Soviet Union of the era of 'stability', or 'stagnation' as it was later termed. The triumph of the policy of 'stability' became possible thanks to changes that were occurring in the world capitalist economy.

The turning point came in 1973 when, during the latest Arab-Israeli War, oil prices rose sharply. The Arab countries tried to exert influence on the West, which supported Israel, through the mechanism of an oil embargo. In political terms, this strategy was a complete failure. With the rise in oil prices, the importance of Israel as an outpost of the West in the Middle East even increased. In economic respects, however, the position adopted by the Arab countries in the autumn of 1973 had far-reaching consequences.

The dramatic rise in oil prices was not just the result of political decisions. On the contrary, these political decisions were based on long-term trends in the world economy, trends which finally surfaced in the early 1970s. During the Great Depression and the Second World War the Fordist economic model had triumphed in the West. This was a system of conveyor-belt technology and mass consumption in which workers acted not only as the producers of goods, but also as their consumers. In the absence of rising working-class living standards, the industrial growth risked choking on itself. State regulation, the redistribution of income to the benefit of the most deprived sections of society, and programmes of social welfare and education for the masses became an economic necessity, a guarantee against a repetition of crises of overproduction such as the one which had shaken capitalism in 1929–32. The regulation of markets, proposed in the late 1920s by the renowned British economist J.M. Keynes, became normal practice for most governments irrespective of their ideological orientation. In place of the state, acting as the 'night watchman' of capitalism, came the welfare state, in which moderate leftists held strong positions.

This system, however, had obvious limitations. While preserving the stability of capitalism, it cost the capitalists more and more dearly. The bourgeois elite had to buy social peace at the cost of concessions to the workers, and in the eyes of the capitalists, this cost was becoming excessive. After the former colonial countries had won their independence and become the 'Third World' (in distinction to the 'First World' of the rich West and the 'Second World' of the communist states), the situation grew still more complex. Along with the latest 'reconstruction' of capitalism in the mid twentieth century, relations between the centre and the periphery changed as well. Western agriculture was modernised. Exporting foodstuffs ceased gradually to be the lot of the 'peripheral' countries, which instead were called upon to supply ever-increasing quantities of industrial raw materials.

The Third World sought to improve its position in the world system by using the same methods of regulation that had been tried out in the West, and also through revolutionary overturns. Earlier, the prosperity of the advanced countries had been maintained by a flow of cheap resources from the colonial world; now, the relations between 'centre' and 'periphery' entered a crisis.

By the early 1970s the latest cycle of global economic upturn was coming to an end. The technological potential of Fordist production was essentially exhausted, and growth was beginning to peter out. A side-effect of the Keynesian model was the continual growth of state spending, leading to increased inflation. 'Weak financial discipline' became the Achilles' heel of the system. So long as the growth rates of production exceeded the rates of inflation, no one suffered especially as a result of the budget deficit. But from the early 1970s, the situation changed radically. Growth rates started to decline, and trying to maintain them, governments flung ever-new financial resources into the furnace of the economy. But this was not enough; the devalued money had no effect. 'Stagflation' set in, combining economic stagnation with high inflation.

In 1973, during the Middle East war, the Arab countries tried to make use of oil as a weapon. World prices for oil increased rapidly. The stream of inflationary funds that had banked up in Western Europe and the US during the years of Keynesian policies surged in a single direction.

This served to enrich a section of the 'peripheral' elites. But with no possibility of investing their capital profitably at home, and no mechanism that would allow them to keep their funds in their own countries, the oil elites began making deposits in Western banks. The result was a crisis of overaccumulation. The banks had no idea what to do with the money that was pouring into their accounts. There was an urgent need for the funds to be invested somewhere, so as to bring a return. For potential debtors, it seemed that an exceptionally favourable situation had arisen. Money could be borrowed at interest rates that were lower than the rate of inflation. The bankers simply had no alternative; any other approach would have meant that the 'free' capital would have remained unused, with the financiers incurring a direct loss.

For the Soviet Union, the changes occurring in the West represented a unique chance. At one and the same time, the possibility had appeared of obtaining additional funds from the sale of oil at increased prices, and of using cheap credits to buy technology and equipment. For Western creditors in turn, the USSR seemed almost the ideal debtor. Possessing developed industries and a relatively modern society, the country could launch major investment projects, and these would require credits. The Soviet Union could successfully 'absorb' Western technologies. Meanwhile, the USSR had oil; consequently, there was every reason to hope that the debts would be repaid regardless of how effectively the credits were employed.

THE STRATEGY OF COMPENSATION

The authors of an official Soviet study have noted that,

Between 1970 and 1975, the foreign trade turnover of the USSR increased by a factor of 2.3 in current prices. Such a rapid growth of foreign trade had not been observed in any of the post-war five year plans, including in the years when the initial level of trade turnover had been low, and when achieving high growth rates had been much easier.[11]

However, the growth was due mainly to the increase in energy prices, and also to dramatically increased exports of raw materials and semi-finished products. The structure of Soviet exports accurately reflects the specialised role which the country was taking on in the international division of labour. In 1970, machinery and equipment had made up 21.5 per cent of these exports; by 1987 this figure had fallen to 15.5 per cent, consisting, moreover, mainly of sales to developing countries and to allied states. Imports of machinery and equipment had risen from 35.6 per cent to 41.4 per cent. Exports of energy, meanwhile, had increased over the same period from 15.6 per cent of total Soviet exports to 46.5 per cent.[12] Sales of raw materials to the West had also become an important source of income for other Eastern Bloc countries, following in the wake of the USSR. By the early 1980s, the CMEA countries were supplying 8 per cent of the energy consumption of Western Europe, after almost doubling their sales of energy on the world market compared with the 1960s. The share of energy sources in the exports of the CMEA countries to the West reached 58.8 per cent in 1979, after amounting to only 14.5 per cent in 1971–75. The greater part of this energy, naturally, was exported from the Soviet Union.[13]

The USSR was developing according to the principle 'If we have oil, we don't need reforms'. Meanwhile, Soviet industry was rapidly becoming more dependent on imported machinery and technology, and in some cases, on imported raw materials as well. Between 1971 and 1975, imports were used to meet approximately 15 per cent of the demand for new industrial equipment.[14] This figure would not have been particularly significant for another country, but for the Soviet Union, which for many years had relied on its own strength, it signified the beginning of dramatic changes. Moreover, imports were playing a growing role in supplying the country with advanced technology, not because Soviet science was incapable of developing this technology, but because the Soviet economy was more and more often unable to put its own innovations to work. In just the same way, the Soviet leaders put their stake on increased imports 'as a way of raising the living standards of the Soviet people'.[15] In the process, they effectively recognised the inability of the Soviet economy to cope with the task of producing consumer goods and of coming up with products that would satisfy the country's own population. At the same time, and against a background of failed efforts to improve agriculture, the USSR's dependence on food imports steadily increased.

According to official figures, foreign trade rose 'at a noticeably more rapid pace than had been set down in the overall plan projections'.[16] In this area, unlike the case with other sectors, the figures were not overstated, and as a result Soviet statistics even understated the growth rates of foreign trade compared with the economy in general. In the same fashion, the importance of Western countries as partners of the Soviet Union also increased. In 1970, trade with the West had accounted for 21.3 per cent of overall Soviet foreign trade turnover; by 1976, the figure was already 32.9 per cent.[17] Soviet ideologues began talking of a 'turn by the economy toward the foreign market'.[18]

From the point of view of abstract theory, this turn did not pose any serious threat to the Soviet Union. By signifying that a more open economy was in formation, it also held out the prospect of a more free society. In practice, however, everything was far more complex. The turn to the foreign market was not the result of processes of democratisation in the USSR, but on the contrary, of an attempt to slow down these processes and to substitute for them. In similar fashion, collaboration with the West provided a way of maintaining the old system of authority and administration, thus acting as a substitute for the economic reforms that had been frustrated by the bureaucracy. In these circumstances, the effect of international cooperation was not so much to stimulate the Soviet economy and society, as to speed their disintegration.

As early as the 1970s, it was clear to experts that the 'strategy of compensation' that had been chosen had serious drawbacks. It was not cheap to develop mineral deposits for export, and to transport raw materials overland for vast distances. The extraction and transporting of oil from the USSR to the West required major investments, far more than if it were obtained from the Middle East. 'As a result,' Soviet experts acknowledged,

any expansion of the country's energy and raw materials complex will inevitably draw off part of the funds that might have gone to the knowledge-intensive sectors, to manufacturing industries that show high rates of growth and of labour productivity. Moreover, the likely brevity of the boom in energy and raw materials prices should be taken into account, even though this boom ensures certain gains in the short term.[19]

All these problems, however, seemed of secondary importance. The chosen strategy of 'compensating' for internal problems through developing external ties simply left the Soviet leadership with no alternative.

COMPENSATION DEALS

The rapid growth of Soviet energy exports aroused disagreements between the United States and the countries of Western Europe. In 1978 and 1979, West Germany and the USSR signed agreements which opened the way for extensive shipments of Soviet gas to Europe on a basis of compensation. Gas had begun to be supplied to the West in the 1960s, when Austria had begun to receive Soviet energy. Finland followed suit in 1971. It is worth noting that both these countries, though part of the capitalist world, were neutral in political and military terms. After the 'oil shock', however, military and political considerations on both sides gave way definitively to economic ones. From 1973 Soviet energy supplies were flowing to the Federal Republic of Germany, after another year to Italy, and from 1976 to France. As the crisis in the Middle East grew more acute, the European countries showed more and more interest in such projects. Soviet gas could to a degree take the place of Arab oil. The gas was cheaper, and depending on supplies from the 'predictable' Soviet Union now seemed a lesser evil than obtaining energy from 'unpredictable' and unstable regions of the Third World. The growth of energy supplies from the USSR continued unabated. In 1982, Italy received from the Soviet Union more than a third, West Germany 14 per cent, Austria 67 per cent, and Finland 100 per cent of the gas it consumed. France obtained 14 per cent of its gas needs from this source, with the flow increasing rapidly to approach one-third.[20]

Meanwhile, the sources of the gas were shifting steadily eastward. When the Soviet Union had begun supplying gas to Austria in the 1960s, this fuel had come from the Western Ukraine. Later, deposits in the Eastern Ukraine had been exploited, then in Western Siberia, and finally, in the far north. To a significant degree, the development of the Siberian resources was now occurring on the basis of Western credits and technology, and was aimed from the first not at the needs of the Soviet Union's own industries, but at exports. Transporting energy over vast distances from such remote regions required the building of huge pipelines. The Soviet Union began taking out credits against supplies of raw materials. Massive purchases of expensive equipment were begun. The energy sector underwent hypertrophic development.

In this situation, collaboration with West Germany took on special importance. As early as the 1960s, the Soviet Union had begun working with Austria and West Germany on the principle of 'compensation deals'. Gas was supplied in exchange for pipes, through which the same gas was pumped across to Europe. By the early 1980s, virtually all the gas exports were conducted on a compensation basis. Already in 1970 the Ministry of Foreign Trade of the USSR had concluded 60 major contracts, aimed principally at the development of extractive industry.

The collaboration was not limited to gas. West German firms, operating on a compensation basis, were included in the building of large chemical complexes. Japan expressed interest in developing oil deposits on the Sakhalin shelf. France was also included in the process. In exchange for gas, the French too supplied pipes and equipment. In exchange for technology required by paper and cellulose combines, they received cellulose, and so forth.

There was something symbolic, almost Freudian, in the fact that 'compensation deals' became the preferred form of external ties for the Soviet leadership. Officials in Moscow continued to console themselves with the thought that once the shipments of raw materials were under way, Soviet industry would start making a breakthrough ono the world market, and the conditions would appear 'for making export sales of Soviet machinery and equipment'.[21] Unfortunately, this had no part in the plans of the Western partners, who were interested mainly in raw materials and semi-finished products. The Soviet Union was returning to the international division of labour to take up the same place once occupied by pre-revolutionary Russia. Even the main partners, Germany and France, were the same.

In the late 1970s talks began on a massive Soviet-German project. West Germany was to receive gas in exchange for pipes and equipment needed for the construction of the Urengoy-Uzhgorod gas pipeline, through which this raw material was to be supplied. The agreement took its final form early in 1981. In the same year, at a meeting of Western leaders in Ottawa, President Reagan demanded that German Chancellor Helmut Schmidt reject the project. The German leadership, however, did not give way, and the 'contract of the century', as Soviet propagandists described it, was signed in December 1981. In the mid

1980s, Soviet experts observed, not without surprise, that economic ties with Western Europe were broadening 'despite the worsening of the international situation'.[22] In fact, the question of Soviet energy supplies to the West was the setting for a clash of two strategies, neither of which promised anything good for the Soviet system. The United States, especially after the coming to power of the conservative Reagan administration, was seeking to isolate the USSR, to limit trade with it, and in this way to force it to make political concessions. By contrast, the French and German rulers calculated that the development of trade cooperation, and a growing Soviet dependence on Western technology and credits, would ultimately have a far greater impact on the political evolution of their Eastern neighbour.

The Soviet leaders, meanwhile, did their best to exploit the disagreements in the Western camp. An official Soviet study of the period states:

Unlike American companies, which often propose unacceptable conditions, the Western European partners have expressed a willingness to supply equipment not only for gas export pipelines, but also for internal gas mains. The credit conditions have also been more favourable.[23]

From the mid 1970s, Eastern Europe became an important sales market for German and French companies. In 1975, 22 per cent of the production of the West German machine-building industry was sold here.[24] Along with West Germany and France, a key Soviet partner was Finland; not only because of its geographical proximity, but also thanks to its 'intermediate' political status this country acted as a broker between the two blocs, supplying goods and technologies which could not be sold directly.

From the point of view of the Soviet leadership, the compensation contracts were supposed to provide proof of 'the advantages of the international division of labour', and an example of how 'mutually beneficial cooperation with the developed capitalist countries' should be established.[25]

What was ultimately fatal for the USSR was the combination of increasing military and political pressure from the US and of constantly growing economic dependency on Western Europe. The greater the dependency became on goods and technology from Germany, France and Finland, the more painful were the trade restrictions imposed on the Soviet Union by the US. The greater the involvement in the world system, the more strongly the country's leadership suffered from an inferiority complex due to the fact that within the framework of this system, they were not perceived as belonging to it.

THE DISINTEGRATION OF THE EASTERN BLOC

The world crisis of overaccumulation of the 1970s created the preconditions for the debt crisis of the 1980s. Oil prices eventually stabilised at a new level. The 'free' capital was invested in one fashion or another. Credit started to become more expensive. The corporate elites, meanwhile, took advantage of the destabilisation of the Keynesian model to launch a social and political counter-offensive. The welfare state was declared to be excessively expensive, and the political positions of the social democrats were shaken.

Within the capitalist system, the time had come for another 'reconstruction'. The era of Fordism had drawn to a close. New technologies which had come into the hands of the ruling class had created the possibility of a more flexible control over labour power. Thanks to the new means of communication, it had become possible to transfer production to remote countries, to disperse it without having it become unmanageable.

The changing world economy created the preconditions for political changes, including changes in the relations between states. The global system, however, could not become radically different so long as the Soviet Union remained as a superpower and as the centre of an alternative world system. Meanwhile, the Eastern Bloc itself was losing its monolithic character under the impact of the changes that had been occurring. As early as the late 1970s, the 'strategy of compensation' that had been devised by the Brezhnev leadership of the USSR as an alternative to internal reforms had begun to break down. The stabilisation of world raw materials prices that had begun at that time coincided with a sharpening of the internal crisis in the USSR and the Eastern Bloc. The growth rates of the Soviet economy were continuing to fall, while growth in the 'fraternal countries' depended increasingly on Western credits and markets. Within the planning system, bureaucratic entropy reigned; the yield from investments steadily diminished. Projects accordingly became increasingly expensive; it was necessary to invest more and more funds, and the outcomes were invariably worse than had been planned. At the same time as the Western countries were preparing for another 'reconstruction', involving a leap into the era of information technology, the Soviet Union was increasingly orienting itself toward the production of raw materials for traditional industry.

The 'energy question' played a particular role in the disintegration of the Eastern Bloc. The countries that were part of the CMEA were at first protected against the impact of the oil crisis. The Soviet Union continued its shipments of raw materials, and energy prices did not rise either in 1973 or in 1974. In 1975, however, Moscow demanded that its partners pay more. The review of prices was accompanied by a tense negotiating process, and by growing disagreements between the allies.

The crisis of overaccumulation in the world economy had for the most part been overcome by the beginning of the 1980s, but it was replaced by a debt crisis. The 'excess' money had been placed more or less successfully by the Western banks in the form of credits to the countries of the Third World and of Eastern Europe. After oil prices had stabilised, inflation in the developed capitalist countries continued from inertia. However, there was no longer a surplus of ready cash. Economic growth rates fell, and capital became more expensive. In conditions of stagflation, the banks began experiencing an acute need for available funds. Accordingly, they needed to get back the capital that had been invested in the form of international credits. The question of how effectively this money had been placed took on a sharp importance. The interest rates which the debtors were paying began rising rapidly, and the credit conditions grew dramatically worse. For Eastern Europe, the combination of debt crisis and of the stabilisation of oil prices proved fatal. Receiving less for its oil shipments to the West, the Soviet Union started demanding that its partners in the CMEA pay more for their supplies. The West, meanwhile, demanded higher interest payments on the credits it had extended. As the American scholar William M. Reisinger notes, the 1980 crisis in Poland and other Eastern European countries was due not only to the inefficiency of the system, but also to external factors: 'Western "stagflation" made it extremely difficult to repay the loans.'[26]

By the early 1980s, the prices the CMEA states were paying for energy were approaching world levels. Responding to protests from the 'fraternal countries', Soviet experts noted that the energy and raw materials base of the Eastern Bloc was 'not isolated from the world economy or from the changes occurring in it'.[27] Against the background of stabilising world resource prices, the danger arose that the prices paid within the framework of the CMEA, prices that had been set on the basis of medium-term agreements, could even exceed those on the free market. The political results of the crisis were not slow in making themselves felt.

In 1980 a workers' revolt began in Poland, the result of which was the fall of the communist government of the time and the appearance on the scene of the free trade union Solidarity. The Soviet leadership vacillated between the need to 'restore order' in the 'fraternal country', and a reluctance to repeat the Czechoslovak scenario of 1968. In the conditions of Poland, which had old traditions of anti-Russian resistance, such an occupation was fraught with the danger of a real war, a prospect that was especially unwelcome when military conflict had already begun in Afghanistan.

A solution was found when in December 1981 the Polish armed forces themselves staged a coup, introduced censorship and banned opposition trade unions. The 'normalisation' of Poland, however, diverted the energy and attention of the Soviet leadership from less dramatic but no less important events that were occurring in the other 'fraternal countries'. No longer able to support the economies of these countries with supplies of cheap resources on the former scale, and unable to impose tight political control on them, Moscow was forced to reconcile itself to the fact that its partners were falling increasingly into debt dependency on the West. These partners, accordingly, reoriented their foreign ties; exports to the Soviet Union were seen increasingly as a burden preventing these countries from achieving their principal goal of selling goods to the West in order to obtain the hard currency needed to pay the international bankers. The local elites as well reoriented themselves to the West. Reisinger notes that paradoxically, the collapse of the CMEA was caused not by political pressure from the Soviet Union, but by the fact that the USSR's partners made use of their extensive economic independence. By the early 1980s, however, Moscow simply did not have the strength or resources to pursue any other policy.

DEBTS

For the Soviet Union, increased trade with the West was accompanied by growing foreign debts. It might seem that the changes in world prices in the

1970s would have benefited Soviet exports. The USSR's balance of trade, however, steadily deteriorated. In 1970, according to official figures, the trade deficit with the developed capitalist countries had amounted to 0.36 million rubles; in 1976 the corresponding figure was 3 million.[28] The problem was that the higher energy prices ultimately affected the prices of imported machinery, industrial products and foodstuffs as well. While international trade ties were booming, hard currency was in chronic short supply. The shortage of foreign currency made it necessary to resort to barter deals, but this did not solve the problem. The more the USSR became integrated into world trade, the more acutely the shortage of funds was felt. The only way out was through foreign loans. With a crisis of overaccumulation in the West, interest rates were low, and the deals seemed highly advantageous for both sides. As delighted Soviet commentators noted,

For the banks of capitalist countries, against the background of a crisis in the capitalist monetary system and in conditions of general economic instability, credits and loans advanced to the member countries of the CMEA, and especially to the Soviet Union, represent operations in the reliable placement of their uncommitted funds, since as the entire Western bourgeois press recognises, the socialist countries have impeccable financial reputations.[29]

Initially, Soviet officials were firmly convinced that the growth of the foreign debt was not a serious problem. In the view of the country's leaders, the strength of the Soviet economy was such that paying off the credits would not be difficult even in the most unfavourable circumstances. Moreover, the foreign trade deficit was regarded as a temporary, transient phenomenon, associated with the current stage of the technical re-equipping of industry. In the final analysis, the USSR had already resorted to massive imports of foreign technology in the 1930s, and this had merely strengthened its independence. The 'contract of the century' with West Germany was supposed to prove the effectiveness of the chosen strategy.

Once gas deliveries have paid off the credits which have been advanced, the Soviet Union will acquire a large new source of hard currency which will be used to finance imports of machinery, equipment and other products from the capitalist states.[30]

In reality, the prospects were nowhere near so rosy. The flow of hard currency increased, but the debts and the need for foreign equipment grew even more rapidly. As the West neared the end of its crisis of overaccumulation, credit became more expensive as well. Many investment projects which in the era of cheap credits had seemed fully justified in commercial terms thus proved unexpectedly to be highly expensive, and ineffective from a financial point of view.

The debt crisis in Eastern Europe broke out in 1980 and 1981, a few years before an analogous crisis shook Latin America. Within the Soviet Bloc, Poland became the epicentre of the crisis. The inability of the Polish government to meet its debt obligations to the West drove it to try to solve its financial problems by raising prices and lowering real wages. The result was massive strikes and the rise of the Solidarity trade union.

By 1981, Poland's debts amounted to $24 billion. Those of the Soviet Union were $12.4 billion; of East Germany, $12 billion; of Romania, $9.8 billion; and of Hungary, $6.9 billion. Following the political catastrophe in Poland, the other Eastern Bloc countries took desperate measures to reduce their indebtedness before it took on a critical nature. To some degree this was successful; by 1984 the debts of the Soviet Union had fallen to $4.2 billion; of Romania, to $6.5 billion; of East Germany, to $6.7 billion; and of Hungary, to $5.1 billion. It was only in Poland, where control over the economic situation had been completely lost, that the debt continued to grow, reaching $28.1 billion.[31]

These efforts, however, also had their downside. Less money remained for investment programmes, economic growth slowed still further, and living standards stopped rising; in many cases they actually fell. While there was still enough money for industry and social welfare, the effects on the infrastructure were grim. The greater the sums that went to repay the debts, the greater the need became for foreign currency. Products that earlier had been aimed at the CMEA market were now exported to the West, if there was any hope they might be sold there. The result was a weakening of the ties between the Eastern European countries and a deepening of the commodity famine. By contrast, the dependence on the world market of all the Eastern European countries, including the USSR, increased sharply.

All this had dire effects on the development of the Soviet system during the second half of the 1980s. Against the background of stabilising oil prices, economic growth steadily slowed, and the foreign debt once more began rising. The economist Sergey Glazyev noted that,

Amid the structural crisis which had been rapidly worsening since the early 1970s, the reliance on foreign trade increased dramatically. Meanwhile the export base, which had expanded sharply with the entry into operation of the new oil and gas facilities, later grew only slowly, and consumed more and more resources. When programmes for increasing the output of foodstuffs and consumer goods were adopted in the early 1980s, the burden that had been placed on exports exceeded their potential. Obvious evidence of this was provided by the failed 'acceleration' programme; it shattered against the resource limitations of the export industries. The accumulation of disproportions in the economy exceeded the possibility of compensating for them through an expansion of energy exports.[32]

The strategy of 'export compensation' that lay at the basis of Brezhnev's policy of 'stability' served to postpone the crisis, but allowed the problems to accumulate. By the time the crisis broke out anyway, the problems were so severe that the system could no longer cope with them through its accustomed methods. Changes did not come as a result of the goodwill of the country's leaders, whose minds were not suddenly smitten with enlightenment (as it seemed to many intellectuals and even dissidents), but as the inevitable outcome of the previous policies, which had been aimed at preventing any changes whatsoever.

FROM STAGNATION TO *PERESTROIKA*

By the 1980s, the transformation of one of the world's leading industrial powers into a raw materials supplier and an international debtor was gradually coming to be perceived within the country as a humiliation. Soviet economists recognised that the situation was

the natural consequence of the strategy of structural development that had been followed during the preceding years – an orientation toward the possibility of compensating, through developing the country's 'cheap' raw materials, for a lack of attention to the need to prioritise the development of high technology and the consumer complex.[33]

But the reform policies that were initiated in the Soviet Union around the end of the 1980s, and which reached their culmination in 'independent' Russia, failed to solve the problem. In fact, they made it still worse.

When the USSR's new leader, Mikhail Gorbachev, announced the beginning of *perestroika* in the second half of the 1980s, optimists immediately began drawing a parallel with the changes wrought by Peter the Great. Indeed, the country's leadership had once again turned its face to Western culture and proclaimed the need to borrow from Western experience. On the cultural level, Gorbachev encountered many of the same problems as Peter I. Breaking the resistance of conservative elements within the ruling elites, both of them strengthened Russia's ties with Europe. Rejecting traditional values, they made the country more open to the outside world. Here, however, the similarities end. Peter the Great founded an empire, while Gorbachev destroyed it. Peter conquered new lands on the Baltic, while Gorbachev lost them. Peter transformed his country into a mighty European power, built a fleet, and forced the outside world to reckon with Russia. Gorbachev turned a superpower into a dependent, ruined swathe of territory.

In the final reckoning, Gorbachev did more to destroy the achievement of Peter than any of Russia's other rulers. This was quite understandable, since the underlying principles of Peter's reforms and of Gorbachev's *perestroika* differed radically from one another. Under Peter I, open access to information and growing collaboration with the West were combined with a firm and even aggressive military and political stance. Regardless of the objective relationship of economic forces, the aim of Peter's reforms was to compel Europe to accept Russia as a new political force. While becoming part of the periphery of the capitalist world system, the St Petersburg empire at least mounted a consistent defence of its special political role within that system. By contrast, the rulers of the USSR in the 1980s sought only to join 'world civilisation', at any price. To achieve this, they sacrificed the country's national sovereignty and economic interests, and ultimately, even the very existence of their state. So far as they were concerned, this was merely the price that had inevitably to be paid if they were to become part of the world ruling class.

Gorbachev's policies were, in essence, policies of capitulation. This became still more obvious when Russia's ruling elite came to be headed by Boris Yeltsin.

The disintegration of the Soviet Union, which Gorbachev's administration had sought to avoid, was declared by the new leadership to be its most important achievement. In place of the once-unitary state there now appeared 15 new republics, most of which had not even sought independence. Russia returned to its borders of the early seventeenth century, with the only difference that the North Caucasus, subdued by tsarist generals after decades of bloody wars and ethnic cleansing, remained part of the country.

The economic reforms that were begun on Gorbachev's initiative were not only slow and inconsistent. Far more important was the fact that the reformers themselves did not have a precise strategy or a clear goal. The result was that the course of the changes itself became the object of struggle between various groups, each of which inserted its own content into the process. Most of society took the slogans which *perestroika* proclaimed – of democratic socialism, struggle against privileges, economic decentralisation and labour self-management – in all seriousness. By contrast, the bureaucratic elite which was responsible for implementing these principles came increasingly to see in them merely a sort of transitional programme that would allow to make a smooth shift to the complete restoration of capitalism, without losing control of the situation or surrendering their privileges. It was this course that the Western elites in turn supported with enthusiasm.

The last Soviet leadership was forced to try to deal with the consequences of the 'policy of compensation' which the previous generation of leaders had followed. As the flow of petrodollars dried up, the country experienced ever-greater difficulties. The Kremlin officials tried to deal with snowballing problems by borrowing money from the West. As Sergey Glazyev notes, the last Soviet government during its five years in office 'borrowed more than fifty billion dollars from outside sources, while at the same time spending the reserves of gold and foreign currency'.[34] The cost of servicing the foreign debt reached a third of export earnings. The political dependency on the West increased.

A heavy blow to the USSR was the disintegration of the Eastern Bloc in 1989. The CMEA collapsed along with Soviet political hegemony in Eastern Europe. The former partners took to trading in convertible currency at world market prices.

The less hard currency was available, the fewer goods were on sale. By the beginning of the1990s a full-scale supply crisis had broken out. Shops welcomed their customers with empty shelves. This nightmare, however, was in no way the inevitable result of the Soviet system as such. A shortage of consumer goods had existed throughout all of Soviet history, but the situation had previously been kept under control, and in the second half of the 1960s the situation even improved. The collapse of the consumer market in 1990 and 1991 was the result of the complete exhaustion of the hard currency reserves which had earlier been used to mitigate the problem. This was not just the collapse of the Soviet distribution system, which for all its shortcomings had managed to survive for seven decades, but also the dismal outcome of the 'strategy of compensation' which had blocked internal development.

Glazyev notes that

The rigidity of the economic structures, the lack of flexible mechanisms for its adaptation to changing realities, and also the corrupting influence of the flood of petrodollars effectively blocked any stimuli to economic development once the influx of 'easy' foreign currency began to peter out. Economic growth became choked off in 1990 and 1991, giving way to rapid decline in virtually all sectors. This was accompanied by a no less rapid decline of exports both because of less favourable conditions for the extraction of raw materials, and also because investment in the extractive sectors was inadequate. Between 1989 and 1991 exports fell by more than a third, returning to the level of 1981. The most painful blow was dealt by the decline in oil shipments, the earnings from which fell by more than half. Over the same period imports diminished by 43 per cent, which in turn had a negative impact on internal production and exports.[35]

It was then that the International Monetary Fund (IMF), which had performed its work successfully in Latin America, appeared on the scene. The approach adopted by the IMF was simple and effective. The Fund helped debtors cope with their short-term financial problems, but in return for this it demanded unswerving fulfilment of its recommendations in the field of economic and social policy. What this amounted to in practice was that in return for the restructuring of its foreign debt, the country had to renounce part of its sovereignty. While entering into relations with the IMF, the Soviet leadership still vacillated, defending its honour as a superpower. But the days of Gorbachev and his team were already numbered. They were replaced by the team of Boris Yeltsin, on whom most of the bureaucratic elite had placed their stake.

In striking fashion, the Soviet bureaucracy managed to turn even the crisis and collapse of their own system to their own advantage. The disintegration of the Soviet Union and the chaos that accompanied it created ideal conditions for the bureaucratic elite, converting power into property, to join the global ruling class.

This was a programme of restoration, following the same historical logic as the restorations in seventeenth-century England and nineteenth-century France. The restoration did not simply mean the return of the old order which the revolution had overthrown. Its social significance lay in the reconciling of the new elites born of the revolution with the traditional ruling class that still held sway within the framework of the world system.

Boris Yeltsin, the former Sverdlovsk Province party secretary who in the space of a few months had turned himself into a convinced anti-communist, was ideally suited to this role. So too were his associates – people with impeccable party histories, often in the capacity of ideologues. The Yeltsin team's main economic strategist, Yegor Gaidar, was one such hereditary member of the ideological elite, belonging to the third generation.

The prominent journalist Oleg Davydov wrote that 'with regard to the three generations of Gaidars, speculation about "heredity" and "genes" is not just empty talk. There really is something in this – something is handed on'.[36] And indeed, the grandson destroyed the conquests of the revolution with the same unquestioning, reckless decisiveness with which the grandfather had wrought vengeance on the enemies of this revolution (during the civil war he was distinguished by his ruthlessness even by the standards of that terrible period). It is striking to note, however, that neither Gaidar nor other hereditary members of the elite uttered a single word to condemn their ancestors, the consequences of whose actions they now fought against so desperately. On the contrary, they continued to show pride in their pedigrees.

In fact, this apparent contradiction expresses the very essence of the restoration. The only people able to see a contradiction here are the victims of the authorities, those who fell beneath the wheel of Stalinist collectivisation or, on the other hand, of the liberal reforms of the 1990s. From the point of view of the elite, there is no contradiction present. In dealing with the enemies of the Soviet regime, wiping out the old elite, subduing the peasants and 'disciplining' the workers, the leaders of the past cleared the way for a new elite which could then take over the country. Without a revolution, there could not have been a restoration. There would have been no possibility of seizing and dividing up property. This very property, created with the sweat and blood of the generations drawn into the revolutionary drama, would not have existed.

The bureaucratic elite, which rapidly turned itself into a new entrepreneurial stratum, was in sum the main beneficiary of the Soviet experiment. Following a 70-year pause, it was able to return the country to the world system, after seizing hold of immensely rich resources, privatising the fruits of the revolution and putting them up for sale. How effectively this transformed and bourgeoisified elite could manage the wealth it had appropriated was another question entirely. As the Hungarian historian Tamas Krausz notes,

This may seem strange, but both the rise and the fall of the Soviet Union had causes in common. The emergence and the collapse of the 'land of the Soviets' were both linked organically not just with historical precedents reaching back many centuries, but also with the question of integration into the world system, or to be precise, with the specific problems of isolation. The 'semi-peripheral model', struggling for its own survival, could not free itself from the pressure of the general laws of capitalist accumulation. It was no accident that this model collapsed, just as it was no accident that it had been victorious.[37]

15
After 1991: The Peripheral Capitalism of the Restoration Era

In the 1990s, Russian journalists and politicians were fond of reminding people that the country was wealthy, since its subsoil contained almost all the elements of Mendeleev's Periodic Table. This mineral wealth, however, had not been a secret in earlier periods of Russian history, and had been accessible then as well. The resources had in fact been explored and developed during the era of Soviet industrialisation. Official Russian sources admit that 'following the collapse of the Soviet Union not a single (!) geological expedition was sent out to explore for new mineral deposits in our country'.[1] Even the exploitation of Russia's natural resources, which served as the basis for the post-Soviet 'open economy', thus became possible only thanks to the efforts of the preceding period.

The decade of reforms that began with the disintegration of the Soviet Union and the coming to power of Boris Yeltsin, and which culminated in the presidency of Vladimir Putin, saw a fall in productive output unprecedented in peacetime. Industrial production and gross domestic product (GDP) shrank by more than half. This substantially exceeded the losses suffered by the Russian economy as a result of the First World War and the revolution, and even of the damage wrought by the Second World War.[2] This was not, however, simply a decline in production. Against the background of the destruction of industry and the fall of living standards, a redistribution of property was taking place, together with a radical restructuring of the economy. By the mid 1990s, Russia was already radically different from the Soviet Union.

The internal market, undermined by the impoverishing of the population and by the shortage of funds available to enterprises, contracted sharply. The importance of the external market, in which Russia as before figured mainly as a supplier of energy sources and other raw materials, increased accordingly. Foreign debt grew rapidly, but unlike the situation in Soviet times it was exacerbated by capital flight, which became the favourite sport of the new owners of Russian enterprises. The economy was privatised almost completely. The result was the rise of a narrow stratum of self-satisfied, irresponsible *nouveaux riches*, who, thanks to the facile touch of journalistic commentators, came to be known as 'new Russians'. Arising in parallel was a new middle class, quite satisfactorily paid but few in number, and concentrated almost exclusively in Russia's two capital cities.

By the end of the 1990s, Russia's economy had become capitalist only in part. Still present were the features of 'Soviet corporatism'. Workers in many cases depended more on their enterprises for their existence than on the market for their labour. The bureaucracy remained a self-sufficient force, able if need be to spoil the lives even of the wealthiest citizens, and property which had been seized illegally could not be effectively defended even by the law.[3]

From the point of view of liberal ideologues it was this incompleteness, this unfinished character of the new Russian capitalism, that was the source of all the problems. Invariably, however, the attempts to 'complete' reform, undertaken with striking persistence over ten years, either failed or exacerbated the very problems they were supposed to solve. Russian society on the threshold of the twenty-first century, for all its post-Soviet peculiarities, had taken on all the characteristic traits of peripheral capitalism, and was obeying the logic of this system. The dependent position of workers, the miserable wages and weak internal market represented competitive advantages for the raw materials monopolies that operated on the world market. Russia's financial problems became inseparable from the processes unfolding in the global economy. Corruption was a natural reaction by the state apparatus to social stratification.

The resemblance between Russia and the countries of the Third World grew stronger as the structural reforms, enacted according to the prescriptions of the International Monetary Fund, went ahead. In the early 1990s the world system was being reconfigured under the aegis of the sole remaining superpower, the US. The new economic programme clearly expressed the interests of finance capital and the transnational corporations, whose power had been enhanced under the new conditions. The ideological basis of the new programme was neoliberalism, proclaiming a return to the free market values that had prevailed in Britain in the late eighteenth century. Its political formula became the 'Washington Consensus', supported with greater or lesser enthusiasm by the elites of almost the entire world. The social formula of the Washington consensus was a consolidation of the ruling class on a transnational level beneath the leadership of the United States. The economic programme foresaw a single set of measures for all – privatisation, deregulation, liberalisation of prices and the freedom to export capital. These prescriptions were urged by Western experts with identical zeal in every country, from Zimbabwe to Russia. The programme did not bring any benefits to the peoples of Africa or Latin America, but its effect was unquestionably to make Russia more similar to Zimbabwe.

The Russian economy was now fully incorporated into the world system, included in the global division of labour that reflected the interests of the transnational corporations that held sway in the new, changed world that followed the collapse of the USSR. The dream of the reformers that Russia would be integrated into the world economy and the global community had been realised. Russia had once again become a source of raw materials and financial resources for the West.

FOREIGN DEBT

Throughout the 1990s, the government had made servicing the foreign debt one of its most important priorities. Accordingly, the IMF and the World Bank had become the main partners and consultants of the new administrative elite. Vice-Premier Yegor Gaidar, the member of Yeltsin's team who held responsibility for economic reform, did not conceal the fact that his programme matched in full the recommendations coming from the Western experts. The first document to formulate the economic policy priorities of the new Russia was the Memorandum of 27 February 1992, addressed not to the Russian population, but to the heads of the IMF in Washington. American scholars note that in taking this step, 'the Russian government was acknowledging the West's leading role as a participant in reform planning. The Western approach had prevailed in the Kremlin'.[4]

The formal reason behind the government's action was the catastrophic state of Russian finances, and the inability of the authorities to pay off the foreign debt. Collaboration with the IMF, however, did not bring the anticipated quick relief. In their book *The Tragedy of Russian Reforms,* Peter Reddaway and Dmitri Glinski write:

Gaidar's priority was clearly to obtain foreign financial support, not domestic political backing. But even this task was not successfully fulfilled, since what Russia got in early 1992 was IMF conditions in exchange for (at least initially) no money.[5]

The government's need for money was undoubtedly acute, but the alliance which Yeltsin and Gaidar made with the IMF also solved another problem they faced, a problem which in strategic terms was arguably far more important. Collaboration with the West and the fulfilment of its demands were indispensable conditions if the changing Russian elite were to join the world ruling class. The decision to carry out privatisation was not in any way the result of pressure from the IMF or the World Bank. The Russian leaders themselves were intent on seizing property, and needed no prompting from across the ocean in order to do this.

Nevertheless, collaboration with Western financial institutions was essential if the property that was seized during the orgiastic plunder of national assets that began in 1991–94 was to be recognised in law, and if the new owners were to be rendered respectable. With the help of the IMF this goal was achieved to a considerable extent, though, as later experience showed, not fully. With the Yeltsin regime beginning to totter, and amid growing danger that the leader himself would fall, reports of Russian corruption began appearing in the Western press. Attempts began in Europe and the US to bring to justice Moscow figures who were implicated in money-laundering; the culmination of these efforts was the arrest in the US of Pavel Borodin, the former head of Yeltsin's presidential administration. But the passions in the West abated once President Putin had taken office in Russia, and the political situation again took on an appearance of stability. Through this process, the Russian elites learnt a lesson that had long been familiar to elites in the Third World: their status in the global community depended not only on the amount of property they had managed to steal, but also on their ability to effectively control their country, while supporting its participation in the world system.

Where foreign debt was concerned, the intervention of the IMF did nothing to ensure salvation. As in other peripheral countries, foreign debt turned into.

a long-term structural problem. While Russia experienced a certain relief in the first years of the new century, the reason for this was not the success of the debt-restructuring measures, but favourable conditions on the world market. According to figures cited by Deputy Finance Minister Sergey Kolotukhin, Russia's foreign debt on 1 October 2002 stood at $120.1 billion. During 2003 it fell somewhat as a result of high oil prices, which were allowing the government to build up its reserves of foreign currency.[6]

THE ENERGY ECONOMY AND THE EXPORTING OF CAPITAL

By the late 1990s the oil and gas complex was providing approximately 20 per cent of Russia's gross domestic product, around 45 per cent of exports, and 60 per cent of foreign currency earnings.[7] The energy industry also remained the principal creditor of the other sectors of the economy. As world prices for oil and gas rose in the first years of the new century, the importance for Russia of the 'energy export economy' even increased. By this time the revenues from oil extraction within the country were put by experts at

between 75 and 89 billion dollars per year, of which less than a quarter represented the cost of labour and capital. The rest consisted of natural rents, redistributed to the benefit of capital. The state, despite owning the source of the rents, received less than 30 to 35 per cent.[8]

Throughout the entire period of the neoliberal reforms the already-devastated Russian economy also suffered from a chronic lack of investment. Equipment became worn out, and was not replaced. Items of infrastructure broke down. Personnel no longer had their training upgraded. Not even the oil industry received capital investments in the quantities needed for it to develop. The situation improved only a little after economic growth resumed in 1999.

The exploitation of the country's natural wealth was accompanied by the exporting of capital on a massive scale, a situation thoroughly typical of peripheral capitalism. Throughout the 1990s there had been almost no investment in industry and infrastructure. Modernisation had affected only those sections of the infrastructure essential for the integration of Russia into the world economy. Of course, certain sums were invested in the economy, and technological modernisation continued. But here as well, the development of Russian capitalism had an obvious peripheral character.

By the year 2000 the number of digital-based international telephone lines had reached 48 times the number at the end of the Soviet period; meanwhile, the number of internal intercity lines had multiplied by a factor of only 2.6.[9] 'In the tempo and scale of its development,' the political scientist Alla Glinchikova concludes, 'external informational integration thus outstripped its internal counterpart by more than eighteen times.'[10] It should be noted that this happened in a country which, during the Soviet period, had also suffered from a shortage of telephone connections. By 1998, Russia had one telephone line for every six people, compared with one per 1.5 people in the US. The total number of Russian telephone lines barely exceeded 25 million, while the American figure was 182 million. Not surprisingly, access to the internet developed as a privilege of the capital cities and of those social strata that in one way or another had been drawn into the world economy, or which had participated in the redistribution of power and property.

Wage levels also differed qualitatively, depending on whether workers were linked to the export sector or not. In Soviet times it had been possible to talk of such things as 'the average wage in industry'. In the new Russia such categories lost all meaning. The average wage of a gas industry worker in the late 1990s was 392 per cent of the national average. In non-ferrous metallurgy the figure was 192 per cent; in science, 82 per cent; in light manufacturing, 51 per cent; and in agriculture, 46 per cent.[11] Scientists and scholars in turn were divided into a narrow group who received Western grants and an impoverished majority whose work was not of interest to Western institutions, or who lacked ties to potential sponsors. The few 'stars' enjoyed a prosperous existence and agreeable conditions of work thanks to their fame in the West. By comparison, the dire state of the research institutes that survived by renting out their premises appeared even more catastrophic. Even if many of these bodies had been thoroughly ineffective and in need of reorganising, their decline hit hard at the entire system for the training of scientists and scholars, since there was nothing to take their place. University graduates either sought work abroad or found jobs in more or less prosperous companies that had nothing to do with their areas of specialisation.

Just like social stratification, the inequality between regions also became more marked. The incomes of the population in the most prosperous regions were ten times higher than in those that lagged futhest behind. Not surprisingly, the most prosperous zones included the capital cities, and also the provinces in which export production was concentrated.[12]

In the other sectors, a profound desolation reigned. Machinery wore out and buildings fell into disrepair, while housing and communal services fell into decay. Money ceased being spent on raising the qualifications of industrial workers. As the 1990s neared their end, and industry began to revive, enterprises found themselves almost completely lacking in young workers with adequate levels of training. Overall, the scientific and industrial workforces were ageing.

The shortage of investments, however, was not due to a lack of funds. The fact that there was enough money in the country was shown by the scale on which the new Russian property owners and the subsidiaries of foreign companies were sending capital abroad. Assessing the outflow of capital across the country's borders, Andrey Kolganov writes:

This outflow exceeded all the foreign investments and loans received by Russia during the reform period many times over. During the 1990s it was estimated at one to two billion dollars per month, and various experts put the total sum that was taken out of the country illegally at between 150 and 250 billion dollars. During the period of economic growth in 1999 and 2000, the drain of capital even increased somewhat.[13]

Experts put the scale of capital flight from Russia during the second half of the 1990s at around 30 per cent of exports, with a peak value of between $20 billion and $25 billion per year. Contrary to the impression created by the press, even the capital that was exported illegally was not, for the most part, criminal in origin. Those who owned it did, however, evade Russian taxes. The funds taken out of Russia represented 'a cheap source of capital for the world economy'.[14] A significant proportion of the 'foreign' investments in Russia around the beginning of the new century also represented the return of part of the capital which had taken flight. This explains the fact that a good deal of this money came from Cyprus, which was favoured by Russian businessmen as an offshore zone. As scholars observed,

such capital obviously did not bring with it to Russia any significant managerial, scientific or technical experience. In practice, it was simply a means of providing credit from abroad to Russian enterprises (given the weakness of the banking system), or represented a strengthening of control by its effective owners over Russian enterprises.[15]

In the view of most experts, the fluctuations of the Russian political climate and the financial collapse of 1998 did not have any obvious impact on the exporting of capital from Russia. For the most part, the outflow of capital had nothing to do with unfavourable economic conditions. Quite the reverse; in the year 2000, when the Russian economy achieved record growth rates for the post-Soviet period, exports of capital increased in proportion. Between 1999 and 2002, exporters of energy, and later also of metals, received vast sums for the goods they sent abroad, but this had little effect on the investment climate within Russia. Something like an investment boom was of course observed, but exports of capital did not cease. Successful Russian companies set about investing money in acquiring foreign firms, turning themselves into transnational corporations. As Kolganov notes,

Even the most solidly established of them, such as Gazprom made very limited productive investments. The economic growth of 1999 and 2000, which was accompanied by a significant growth of investments in the oil and gas sector, failed even to make up for the inadequate investment during the preceding period.[16]

Kolganov concludes from this that the oligarchy had no serious interest in modernising the Russian economy. This, of course, was perfectly true. The problem, however, was not only with the interests of the oligarchy. So long as the model that was established in the 1990s for integrating Russia into the world system remained, any serious attempt at modernisation would be doomed to encounter insurmountable obstacles.

In the 1990s Russia began to serve the international process of accumulation; like other peripheral countries, it redistributed funds to the benefit of the centre. According to Interior Ministry figures, exports of capital from Russia in 2000 amounted to approximately $11.5 billion, with as much as 80 per cent of this sum sent to the US. Meanwhile, total foreign investments in the Russian

economy came to $7.9 billion. Most of the foreign investments came from
offshore zones.[17]

DEINDUSTRIALISATION

As was noted by Mihkail Delyagin, an economic adviser to the government of
Yevgeny Primakov and Mikhail Kasyanov, 'a raw materials orientation in the
long term is not a diagnosis but a condemnation'.[18] Such a system, as Delyagin
observed, is 'doomed to fail because of the innate lack of stability of raw
materials markets, which unlike the markets for highly processed goods are not
controlled by the seller, on whom they ultimately have a destabilising effect'.[19]
Delyagin urged that a solution be sought through developing high technologies
and through modernising the industries serving the internal market. By the
beginning of the new century, however, the raw materials orientation was
not simply an economic policy for the Russian elites, but the basis for their
existence and their means of integrating themselves into the world system.
Accordingly, there could be no solution to the problem that did not affect the key
interests of the Russian oligarchy, and that did not come into conflict with the
neoliberal world order (that is to say, with capitalism) as a whole. The attempts
by Primakov's government in 1998 and 1999 to stimulate industry through state
regulation through raising the purchasing power of the population and through
investment programmes yielded quick and obvious results. Unfortunately, these
measures brought a chorus of condemnation from Western 'Russia experts', as
well as desperate resistance from the oligarchs, resulting in the political defeat
of the cabinet. After a mere eight months Primakov's government was forced
out of office, leaving behind it glowing recollections and uncompleted tasks.

Not only were enterprises shut down during the 1990s in Russia and other
post-Soviet republics, but millions of people who earlier had worked in industry
were forced to look for new jobs – as petty traders, security guards, servants of
the 'new Russians', and so forth. The abrupt shift to an open economy meant
that Soviet producers, who had been used to quite different conditions, were
helpless before the world market. Whole sectors of the economy perished.
The reformers sought to justify themselves by recalling that many of the failed
enterprises had been inefficient, and had produced goods of low quality. This
was of course true, but instead of providing stimuli to these enterprises to
operate more effectively, the reformers created conditions in which not even
the strongest survived.

Around the end of the 1980s, the experts of the IMF, while forecasting
an inevitable decline of Soviet industry under the conditions of 'structural
perestroika', prophesied that agriculture would develop successfully. In practice,
agriculture suffered a decline no less grievous than industry. In 1998, output in
this sector stood at a mere 43.4 per cent of the 1990 level.[20]

The results of 'ten years of Russian reforms' are best illustrated by the GDP
data. According to this index, Russia's position in the world economy at the
beginning of the twenty-first century was worse than in the Soviet era, and
worse even than in 1913 (Table 15.1). Not only had many conquests of the

post-revolutionary period been lost, but also what had been achieved under Witte and Stolypin.

Table 15.1   Russian share of world GDP (%)

	1913	1960	1980	2000
USSR/Russia minus Poland and Finland	9.07	14.47	11.71	3.80
Russia within the boundaries of the Russian Federation	6.80	8.94	7.08	2.10

Source: *Mirovaya ekonomika. Global'nye tendentsii za 100 let.* Moscow, Yurist, 2003, pp. 509–10.

The deindustrialisation in the republics of the former Soviet Union has differed qualitatively from that which has taken place in the West. In the West, industrial output has declined at the same time as new technologies have been developed. What has occurred in Russia has been a technological degradation. Most of the jobs that have been lost in industry have either not been made up for at all, or have been replaced by jobs in the 'informal sector', where there can be no talk of modern technology. Equipment has often been stolen, while in cases where production has been maintained, the machinery is gradually wearing out. The industry workforces themselves have begun rapidly growing older, since the training of personnel has ceased and new workers are no longer being recruited.

The degradation of production has also impeded the development of the country's technological potential. Most of the innovations devised by Russian engineers and scientists since the 1980s have not been applied to the productive process. Many of the ideas and techniques have simply been stolen. 'Russia's lag behind world standards in the area of technology,' Mikhail Delyagin stated gloomily in 2000, 'took on an irreversible character in the mid-1990s....'[21]

THE OLIGARCHIC STATE

The initial stage in the plunder of Russian assets gave rise to the grotesque breed of the 'new Russians' – semiliterate businessmen, often with a criminal past and invariably with bandit habits. These comical individuals, however, never really controlled the country's life. Real economic power gradually became concentrated in the hands of the new elite that controlled the largest oil, gas and metallurgical companies. Emerging from the ranks of the old bureaucracy, this elite transformed itself, topping up its ranks with 'fresh blood' and changing its culture and behaviour.

By the mid 1990s the process of transition was essentially complete. Serious entrepreneurial clans, their leaders dubbed 'oligarchs' by the press, had taken shape. The origins of their capital lay in their control over the exporting of raw materials and semi-finished goods to the world market. Exports of resources grew in proportion as Russian industry collapsed; in this respect, the crisis and decline represented an important condition for the successful accumulation of capital.

Control over exports, combined with a catastrophic fall in the exchange rate of the ruble, guaranteed that 'real' financial resources would be concentrated in the hands of the oligarchs. The devaluation of the ruble led to the dollarisation of the economy, and this in turn meant that the dominant positions in Russia would be held by firms which received a steady flow of Western currency. The entrepreneurial clans that had taken over the exporting of raw materials dictated the rules of the game not only in the economy, but also in politics, culture and the mass media.

The oligarchic brand of capitalism that had been established in Russia by the mid 1990s was linked closely to the peripheral nature of the economy. The one would have been impossible without the other. The inclusion of the Russian Federation in the world economic system as a supplier of raw materials and as a market for the transnational companies presupposed the formation of a corresponding oligarchic elite, its power and wealth based on the parasitic exploitation of the country's resources and of what remained of the productive potential created by Soviet industrialisation. Meanwhile, the power of the oligarchy made attempts to implement any other scenario of development economically and politically impossible.

The state, which had been given its constitutional form by the coup of 1993, when the legally elected parliament had been shelled by tanks, could only have been authoritarian. The 1993 constitution not only bolstered the overweening ambitions of Yeltsin, who sought to be both an autocrat and a 'democratic' president at once, it also created a political system agreeable to the oligarchic and bureaucratic elites, a system in which the people had almost no ability to influence the authorities, whoever might hold office. The new state structures combined the authoritarianism of an executive power that rested on electoral fraud with the legal existence of a parliamentary opposition and with real freedom of the press; neither of the latter had any influence on 'serious politics'. In this respect, the Russian state took on once again the features of the tsarism of 1905–14, with the sole difference that the formal restoration of the monarchy (repeatedly discussed within the Russian elite) was not found necessary. The old model of the monarchy had been replaced by a more 'modern' oligarchic republic.

THE DEFAULT OF 1998

Throughout most of the 1990s, the Russian leaders conscientiously fulfilled all the recommendations of the IMF. After the inflation rate was more or less stabilised late in 1993, a clearly overvalued ruble exchange rate was established. This change coincided in odd fashion with the completion of the first stage of privatisation, in the course of which Russia's main resources became concentrated in the hands of new owners. After this, the 'new Russians' retreated into the shadows, and the oligarchs came to the forefront.

The exporting of raw materials was now combined with support for an overvalued ruble. At first glance this might have appeared illogical, since the oligarchs depended on exports, and the high exchange rate left exporters disadvantaged. The important consideration, however, was not the needs of Russian industry, which was being smothered by this policy, but the interests of raw materials exporters. For them, the decisive factor was not the ruble exchange rate, but the world price of oil. Russia was inundated with cheap imports, and local industry, unable to withstand the competition, was expiring. But as the distinguished American economist Joseph Stiglitz correctly noted, the elevated exchange rate, though catastrophic for the country as a whole, was 'a boon' for the elite.[22] The privileged layers could purchase luxury items at advantageous prices, while also sending money abroad. The largest exporters were at the same time the owners of the main banks, which invested money in financial operations, the exporting of capital, and the importing of goods.

The elevated exchange rate therefore ultimately suited the oligarchy. The overvalued ruble was even more agreeable to the transnational corporations which shipped goods into the impoverished country, and to financial speculators dealing in Russian state bonds. 'The IMF worried that a devaluation of the ruble would set off a new round of inflation,' Stiglitz writes. 'Its insistence on Russia maintaining an overvalued currency and its supporting that with billions of dollars ultimately crushed the economy.'[23] Despite the unswerving fulfilment of the recommendations of the Western experts, the promised economic growth did not ensue.

Thus, at the time of the East Asia crisis, Russia was in a peculiar position. It had an abundance of natural resources, but its government was poor. The government was virtually giving away its valuable state assets, yet was unable to provide pensions for the elderly or welfare payments for the poor. The government was borrowing billions from the IMF, becoming increasingly indebted, while the oligarchs, who had received such largesse from the government, were taking billions out of the country. The IMF had encouraged the government to open up its capital accounts, allowing a free flow of capital. The policy was supposed to make the country more attractive for foreign investors; but it virtually was a one-way door that facilitated a rush of money out of the country.[24]

The flight of capital and the decline of industry left the government without money. The country's leadership, which consciously served the oligarchs (and which at times consisted of members of the oligarchy) did not see any great tragedy in this. Some state spending, however, had still to be financed, especially since this was demanded by business itself, seeking to enrich itself out of state revenues whenever the slightest opportunity appeared. The state deficits were covered by borrowing on both the external and internal markets. Russia's internal debt turned into a gigantic financial pyramid, the collapse of which became only a question of time.

By the late 1990s the policies of the free market, pursued on a global scale on the basis of the Washington Consensus, had led to their predictable result – a world crisis of overproduction. This crisis began in the countries of East Asia, to which a significant proportion of world industry had now migrated. The contraction of output in Asia was accompanied by a growth of monetary instability in the global economy, and by a fall in demand for oil. Both had an impact before long on Russia. Because of its clearly overvalued exchange rate, the ruble became an ideal target for international financial speculators, while the fall in oil prices undermined the incomes of the state and of private companies. As a result, pressures on the ruble in the financial markets increased sharply, while the funds available for maintaining its exchange rate became significantly less.

By early 1998 the price of oil had fallen to such an extent that the proceeds from its sale did not cover the costs of its extraction and transportation. Then in the summer the crisis which had begun in Asia reached Russia. In June 1998 the American corporation Goldman Sachs hired the vast House of Unions, where the funerals of Lenin and Stalin had once been held, to glorify Russian capitalism and to celebrate the opening of the new Goldman Sachs offices. To delight the guests, the Americans brought former US President George Bush to the gathering. Two months later Russia declared itself in default on its internal debt, devalued its currency, and aroused panic on international financial markets.

After the government defaulted on its borrowings in August, a chain reaction of crashes spread through the banking sector. Foreign financial speculators who had traded in Russian securities lost billions of dollars. The crisis then shifted to Latin America, where the Brazilian currency reached the brink of collapse. But here, unlike the situation in Russia, the currency was devalued in timely fashion, and the fall in the exchange rate for the Brazilian real did not take on the same catastrophic form as the crash of the ruble.

KEYNESIANISM RUSSIAN-STYLE

The collapse of the ruble, which demoralised the oligarchic elite, proved a blessing for the economy. Imports fell rapidly, and Russian enterprises felt more confident as the cheaper ruble increased their competitiveness. Meanwhile, Western firms, seeing no possibility of exporting products to Russia but fearing the loss of their markets, started investing money and transferring technology in order to produce within the country. This spontaneous import substitution brought a noticeable revival of industry. With the oligarchs in confusion and the population embittered, President Yeltsin was left with no choice but to appoint a government capable of implementing a real change of economic course. The new Prime Minister was Yevgeny Primakov, with Yury Maslyukov as his vice-premier in charge of the economy. Both were determined opponents of neoliberalism.

Instead of struggling to maintain the ruble exchange rate, the new cabinet set about stimulating production and developing the internal market. The huge wage debts that had accumulated in the state sector began to be paid off. To the amazement of the neoliberal experts, inflation grew much more slowly than the increase in the volume of paper money. Prices on the market had been unjustifiably high, and as cash appeared in people's hands, prices even started falling, adjusting their levels to meet effective demand. Industry in Russia began to expand. The defence industries restored their output to some extent, exporting weapons to China and India. Also helping to create an illusion of prosperity was a rise in world energy prices which began in 2000. The economies of the countries of East Asia, recovering from the downturn, were once again demanding raw materials.

At the same time, a considerable potential for inflation had built up in the US and Western Europe. Thanks to the credit and stock market inflation that had occurred in the US over the preceding 15 years, vast sums had been taken out of the 'real economy' throughout the world, and had migrated into the area of financial speculation. Here Russia was in the front ranks, sending vast sums to the US that had been stolen from industry. The redistribution of funds from industry to finance capital, a shift which in Russia took the form of unconcealed plunder, occurred in Western countries as well, though in more 'civilised' form.

As Russian researchers note,

the lion's share of the credit growth went into the stock market, contributing to its unjustifiably rapid rise. Instead of inflation in the consumer market, there was inflation of financial assets.[25]

This pumping-up of the economy with credit led to massive stock market speculation, destabilising the world system. Governments that were faithful to the Washington Consensus limited their spending, but no one took steps to restrain credit and stock market speculation. Over ten years, paper money did not become cheaper, but speculative financial capital grew out of all proportion to the increase of production. The devalued 'non-cash' money could for the time being be converted freely into perfectly valid cash. All that was needed was some mechanism that would allow this to be done, and one such mechanism was the rise of oil prices in 2000 and 2001. A sort of 'inflationary overhang' had appeared in the economies of the West; now the 'superfluous' money poured into the oil market. As this shift proceeded, the dollar 'overhang' collapsed.

Having become an 'oil currency', the ruble unexpectedly strengthened, and a stream of cheap dollars poured into Russia, supporting the growth of production and the illusion of prosperity. But this growth, which in 1999 and 2000 had shown impressive results, was extremely unstable. Enterprises resumed production, but there was almost no investment. As Delyagin notes, the revival of industrial production after the crisis 'was in many respects "purchased" at the cost of a deterioration of the situation in other areas, above all through a fall in the real incomes of the population and a complete collapse of the financial sector'.[26]

Recovering from the shock it experienced in 1998, the oligarchy quickly re-established its position. Primakov's government, with its Keynesian measures, had effectively saved its political opponents. As soon as the improvement in the economy became obvious, the oligarchy regained its self-confidence. A decision by Yeltsin resulted in the Primakov government being sacked. Then in January 2000 a new president took office in the Kremlin – Vladimir Putin, who had been chosen by Yeltsin as his heir.

THE SECOND 'STABILITY'

The political project mapped out by the new administration was uncannily reminiscent of the course selected in the early 1970s by Leonid Brezhnev. While acutely aware, since the crash in 1998, of the weaknesses of the Russian economy, the ruling groups had no intention of fundamentally altering it, especially since Russian society, demoralised and confused by the changes of the preceding years, posed no serious danger to the elite. So long as oil prices favoured the country, Putin and his team could avoid taking any initiatives, while at the same time convincing the people – and the members of the elite themselves – that Russia was entering a new era of order and stability. At first glance, everything seemed to be going well. The gold reserves of the central bank were increasing, the foreign debt was being paid off, and industry was continuing to grow, though at markedly slower rates.

Closer examination, however, revealed a darker side to this success. The growth of industry was not linked to any serious investment. The new owners were still using the equipment and technology bequeathed to them by the Soviet state. All that was happening was that the production which had been sharply curtailed in the 1990s was being resumed. Even here, the achievements were not brilliant. In 2003, after four years of growth, the rate of utilisation of industrial capacity was only 55 per cent. Only in the energy sector and metallurgy, the leading areas of development, were the rates of utilisation better, at 79 per cent and 70 per cent respectively.[27]

The Russian authorities considered one of their major achievements to be the renewal of grain exports in 2002. While the Soviet Union had regularly imported grain, the new post-Soviet Russia, despite having lost the grain-growing provinces which had become part of the independent Ukraine and Kazakhstan, was able to enter the world market as an exporter. This would indeed have been an important success, had it not been for one thing: this victory had been achieved not so much because of a sharp rise in output, but rather because of a decline in internal consumption. The Moscow newspaper *Rodnaya Gazeta* stated: 'Our agriculture has returned to the hallowed old model... of 1913. Russia is again sending abroad the "excess" grain from undernourished provinces.'[28]

In Soviet times the main reason for the imports was a shortage of feed grain for stock. The numbers of stock, which had fallen dramatically during the collectivisation period, were restored only after the Second World War, and with immense difficulty. During the years of neoliberal reform another massive slaughter of stock began, exceeding even what had happened during the collectivisation years. The areas sown diminished as well. The large cities did not feel the effects of these developments, since the gap in supplies was immediately filled by imports. But the countryside, the small towns and the poorest layers of society felt the consequences immediately.

The Chief Sanitary Inspector of Russia Gennady Onishchenko has testified that the food intake of Russians has fallen by a thousand calories from the figure of 3200 that was projected during the well-fed 1980s. An authoritative state commission has acknowledged that the main cause of high death rates is an inadequate and unbalanced diet – more simply, malnutrition.[29]

Even at such a price, Russia was unable to consolidate its place on the world grain market; in 2003 the exports fell sharply. But at the same time, Russia had come to the fore as an arms exporter. Throughout the 1990s, experts close to the government had explained the failure of the reforms on the basis that

the structure of production in the Soviet Union was weighted to an unusual degree in favour of the defence sectors. Under the new economic conditions, such a serious collapse was inevitable.[30]

However, it was precisely those provinces where production was oriented toward consumption by the population that suffered the worst losses after the shift to the policies of the open market. While arms production also suffered from the changes, it maintained its position, since during Soviet times this sector had already been accustomed to direct and indirect competition on the world market. Defence orders from within Russia fell to a minimum, but arms shipments continued to India, and later to China as well. Paradoxically, defence production survived relatively intact at a time when Russia's defensive capability was in decline.

In the world economy of the early 1980s, the Soviet Union had specialised in supplying energy and weapons. Exactly the same specialisation remained, and was even strengthened, after the restoration of capitalism. In other words, the transition to an open market not only failed to help overcome the disproportions typical of the late Soviet economy, but intensified them.

The only substantial difference with the Soviet period was the entry of Soviet metallurgy onto the world market following the default. As in the eighteenth century, falling internal demand (due to the cutting of defence orders to a minimum) led to a freeing-up of productive capacity, while the cheapness of labour power made Russian metals thoroughly competitive. Here, too, the increase in output was due not so much to development and modernisation as to old productive capacity dating from Soviet times.

MOSCOW BETWEEN BERLIN AND WASHINGTON

The weakness of Russia's position was revealed fully in the spring of 2003, during the war in Iraq. This conflict, which had begun as a clash between the US and the Arab world, culminated in a diplomatic stand-off between Washington and a German-French coalition opposed to unleashing war. To the surprise of many observers, and to its own considerable astonishment, the Putin administration in the Kremlin came down strongly on the side of Germany. During the first days of the Iraq conflict, Russian official declarations and the tone of the television broadcasts reminded many people of the anti-American propaganda of Soviet times. These harsh words, however, came not from the leaders of a superpower but from the cautious leadership of a poor country looking around constantly at its influential European neighbours.

The decisiveness of the Russian leadership was not the result of a clear grasp of the country's national interests, or of any considered strategy. During the 1990s a system had been established under which Russia depended politically on the US, and economically on Germany. The importance of Germany is obvious if we examine the structure of the investments that foreign capital had made in Russia by the first years of the new century.

On 1 January 2003, according to official data, total foreign investments in Russia amounted to $43.93 billion. German investments amounted to $8.15 billion, while the US held third place with $5.52 billion. Second place was held by Cyprus, with $5.63 billion; it was through circulation in Cyprus that Russian money was able to avoid taxes.[31] It is noteworthy, meanwhile, that the German investments were directed mainly into production, which cannot be said of the operations by American capital in Russia. Still greater was the importance of Germany for the Russian raw materials and energy sector, the bulk of whose export production went to German buyers.

It was the US that dictated the political agenda to Russia, but among foreign investors in Russia and the foreign partners of Russian firms, German capital gradually came to occupy the leading positions. This system worked well so long as Germany sought to remain inconspicuous in its international dealings, and, at least verbally, expressed solidarity with the US. In the early years of the new century, however, the unfolding crisis of the world system undermined this precarious equilibrium. The situation grew more acute with the appearance on the world market of a new global currency, the euro. As many scholars have justly noted, the unification of European currencies (effectively on the basis of the German mark) represented something more than an attempt at expansion on the world financial market. There are abundant grounds for 'regarding the introduction of a single European currency as a geopolitical project'.[32] After the American-German contradictions surfaced, the Moscow leadership was thrown into confusion. Once it became clear that Germany and France would obtain a majority on the United Nations Security Council even without Russia, President Putin made haste to issue a decisive declaration in order to prove to the European partners that they needed him.

The Kremlin's radicalism perplexed the Russian elite, and by the summer of 2003 Moscow was trying to go into reverse, doing its utmost to show its loyalty to Washington. But as in previous world conflicts, Russia was not a free agent; it was being squeezed between opposing blocs. The Russian market and Russian resources were playing too important a role in Berlin's European strategy. As the political weakness and economic instability of European integration were revealed, it became increasingly vital to consolidate a firm 'core' of a united Europe. The global economic downturn that had begun with the new century had placed the dominant neoliberal models in question. The competition between capitals was growing more acute. The Cold War had finally ended, and together with it, undisputed American leadership had vanished into the past. The new European Union had entered into competition with the US, and Russia in turn had become the raw materials base and geopolitical 'rear' of the European coalition. From the moment when the US set out to seize the oil of Iraq and to bring the resources of the Middle East under its control, the importance for Western Europe of Russian energy multiplied many times over. It was not important that the oil extracted in Siberia and the far north was expensive. It remained a global strategic resource.

As in the early twentieth century, Russia was being drawn into global rivalry, not as an independent force but as a hostage country without the ability to influence events. Compared to tsarist times, the position of the new Russia was even weaker. The Russian elite had far less capacity for action; its self-confidence was much weaker, and it enjoyed far less support within society.

AN UNFINISHED NATION

In Russian society, the collapse of the Soviet Union was accompanied by an acute demoralisation and 'crisis of identity'. All the 'accursed questions' of previous Russian history came suddenly to the forefront, but in far more painful form, since whatever the approach adopted, there were no obvious resources available for solving the problems. From the point of view of cultural self-determination, Russia in the nineteenth century had clearly been an 'unfinished nation'; though one of the great European powers, it remained part of the periphery. The result was that the national self-consciousness of the inhabitants of the empire was extremely contradictory. Throughout the whole of the St Petersburg period, a constant puzzle remained of where the 'empire' (whether in the old, Byzantine, or new colonial sense) ended, and where the 'nation' (in the Western sense of the word) began. Russia had to be everything at once. The peripheral position of the Russian state created a need for national self-assertion, just as in other countries of the periphery, from Mexico to India. The existence of the empire, however, placed its stamp on Russian nationalism, giving it manifestly reactionary features. The suppression of minorities within the empire was viewed as an indispensable requirement of the struggle against the 'machinations of the West'.

The 1917 revolution appeared to resolve these contradictions in a fundamental manner. The problem of external dependency was resolved not by a struggle against 'foreigners', but through a social transformation within the country. Meanwhile, the imperial-national question was dealt with through the founding of a new state in which 'a new community of peoples', the Soviet people, was supposedly to arise. The 'Soviet Thermidor' modified the results of the revolution, but did not reverse them. The social liberation proved to be restricted, and limited to the 'equal' participation of all citizens in industrial society. In the absence of political freedom, equal rights were incomplete and conditional, and the formation of a new bureaucratic elite went ahead at full speed. In the Soviet 'family of peoples', meanwhile, the features of the old empire were increasingly clearly perceptible.

The collapse of the USSR, however, drove Russia backwards not only in relation to the real achievements of the Soviet period, but also compared to tsarist times. The St Petersburg empire, for all its peripheral character, had nevertheless been capable of playing an independent role in world politics. The new Russia which arose amid the ruins of the Soviet experiment had no such ability. In a certain sense, it managed to synthesise all the worst traditions of both the St Petersburg period and the tsarist era. It inherited the imperial mentality without the empire, and the national inferiority complex without the enthusiasm for social change. Within the new Russia an elite took shape that despised its own country to a degree that took on comic elements. At least initially this elite was consistently 'defeatist', in the sense that it was the failure of the Soviet Union in the Cold War that ensured the elite access to new privileges and allowed it to integrate itself into the world ruling class. This was an elite typical of those that exist during restoration periods – self-satisfied, devoted to the search for immediate pleasures, and irresponsible. Opposing it, however, was an opposition that drew its inspiration from the darkest periods of Russian history and from the most retrograde ideologies, both home-grown and imported. Uniting the leaders of the official opposition was a sort of ideological compromise that combined clericalism, nostalgia for the totalitarian aspects of the Soviet past, ethnic nationalism and Islamophobia. Political discussion was reduced to disputes between an elite that was incapable of modernising the country, and an officially recognised 'counter-elite' that had no wish for modernisation.

This situation was extremely advantageous for the oligarchic capitalism that triumphed in Russia in the 1990s. The situation persisted, however, not only because it suited the authorities, but also thanks to the severe psychological depression that gripped society after the catastrophe it had suffered. This depression began slowly to be overcome only around the turn of the new century. The years of economic growth, for all their limitations, did not pass in vain. An indication of the changes was provided by the labour conflicts of 2002 and 2003, which above all affected the sectors that were among the most 'globalised' and integrated into the world economy, such as air transport and the mining of nickel and rare metals. The new situation was recognised by the press, in reports such as the following:

in Russia, thanks to the connivance of the authorities and the exceptional greed of the property-owners, the conditions have arisen for the development of a genuine trade union movement. The workers in the successful enterprises, understanding the scale of the profits they are bringing their corporations, have shown a readiness to fight in order to raise their social status.[33]

And among the middle class in Russia's capital cities, left-wing views became fashionable.[34]

By the end of 2003 it had become clear that the 'stabilisation' brought by the high prices on the oil market would not last indefinitely. Putin's associates recognised this better than anyone. The Kremlin's answer to the imminent problems was to 'tighten the screws', increasing the degree of authoritarianism. The system of 'managed democracy' became increasingly less democratic and more managed. At the same time, blows were aimed at the oligarchic clans that refused to accept the new rules (above all, at the company YUKOS, whose leaders finished up in prison or abroad). This 'struggle against the oligarchs', however, did not change the structure of the economy in any way, and neither did it alter the character of Russia's relations with the world system. In the best national traditions, Russian capitalism transformed itself from oligarchic in nature to bureaucratic, without ceasing to be backward and peripheral.

LIVING BEYOND THEIR MEANS

In the early 1990s the scientific intelligentsia had seen themselves as a potential counter-elite, that might succeed the dying party bureaucracy. Individual members of 'educated society' did in fact achieve impressive heights in government and business, but most of the intelligentsia saw their position decline catastrophically. Alla Glinchikova notes that

Some perceived the liberal slogan of privatisation in the name of freedom, progress and the overcoming of stagnation as a path to weakning and doing away with informational and administrative inequality and privileges. Others, by contrast, saw it as a means of consolidating inequality and privilege. Both elites put their stake on economic and technological change, expecting positive results for themselves.[35]

It was more than obvious who prevailed in the 1990s, but how complete and definitive this victory would be remained unclear. Russia's peripheral integration into the world economy, and the oligarchic model of social and political organisation that corresponded to this integration, had brought the country to such an acute crisis, and to such obvious and insoluble problems, that a new round of social conflict was inevitable.

Russian society turned out to be too educated for the economy that arose in Russia on the basis of the neoliberal reforms of the 1990s. Despite a dramatic fall in living standards, Russia was 'living beyond its means', since the newly established social system could not supply the population with even the minimal conditions for a civilised existence. On the other hand, neither the state bureaucracy nor the oligarchy could allow themselves to 'take the reforms to the logical limit'.

In the early 1990s, Russia experienced a social catastrophe, expressed in a sharp fall of living standards for the majority of the population, accompanied by an equally dramatic rise for the property-owning layers. The decline of consumption on the internal market was the clearest indicator of the changes that were occurring. In 2003 the liberal newspaper *Novaya Gazeta* reported that in the 1980s, 'consumer spending per citizen amounted to $500 per month. The figure now is $60.' According to data cited by the same newspaper, 'a sum of $1.5 trillion of Russia's working capital' had been 'burned up by the "reforms"'. These resources, it was reported, had been 'siphoned off abroad'.[36]

In such conditions, not even the completely irresponsible elite that held power in Russia at the beginning of the new century could risk a second catastrophe. It was clear that the appeal for Russians to 'live within their means' signified a demand for the final liquidation of all the social and cultural gains of the twentieth century, gains dating not only from the Soviet period, but also from the times of Witte and Stolypin. Post-Soviet Russia had finished up as a country in which the majority of the population had a miserable standard of living, sustained only through state subsidies and grants. The same also applied to the existing level of education and qualifications of the workforce. The struggle around the surviving elements of the systems of education and science took on a drawn-out character, a sort of positional warfare. Attempts to overcome the crisis of these systems invariably failed, but equally ineffectual were efforts at the definitive 'reform' (that is, liquidation) of the systems, which had clearly become 'redundant' for a peripheral economy. The question of reform of the military was also left hanging.

In the early twenty-first century, Russia again faced a parting of the ways. Ahead lay either a rapid new advance, aimed at overcoming the country's peripheral position in the world system, or renewed decline, fraught this time with the decay of society and with national disintegration.

Conclusion

In the late 1980s and early 1990s, the propaganda of the triumphant restoration argued persistently that the sacrifices made by the Soviet population during the twentieth century had been pointless, and that their achievements had been insignificant. The sacrifices were indeed monstrous, and by no means always essential. But they were not pointless. The achievements of the Soviet period were entirely real. This does not justify Stalinism, just as the changes that occurred in Europe in response to the Napoleonic Wars do not, on the moral plane, justify authoritarianism and aggression.

The tragedy is that the restoration has not in any way set right the consequences of the crimes and errors committed by the revolutionary and postrevolutionary regimes. It was the catastrophe of the 1990s that proved in hindsight the positive significance of the Soviet experience. Paradoxically, it was the destruction of the results of the Soviet modernisation during the period of neoliberal reforms that really put the results of the twentieth century in question, and which threatened to render pointless all the sacrifices that had been made. Objectively, therefore, the actions of the reformers represented not the overcoming of the crimes of Stalin, but an aggravation of them. To resurrect those who died in the *gulag* is no longer possible. But to destroy most of what was created, and which was paid for in blood, in millions of lives and in millions of mutilated fates – the reformers proved fully capable of this.

The historical self-consciousness of Russians has consistently been centred on searches for a 'golden age', for a splendid past. For the Muscovite tsardom, this splendid past was Kievan Rus, and the Byzantine empire that became fused with it into a single cultural myth. Peter the Great sought to cast out this myth, turning for inspiration to the culture of the West. But his era itself became a cultural myth for succeeding generations. In identical fashion, imperial St Petersburg represented the lost golden age for many people in the Soviet period, and after the collapse of the USSR the Soviet experience itself entered the category of the 'splendid past'. History was transformed into myth, which has to be subjected to criticism at least so that its real roots can be understood.

At the same time, and even while rejecting mythological exaggerations, one cannot help seeing something strikingly tragic in Russian history. The St Petersburg period represented a 200-year-long attempt by the Russian elites to occupy a fitting place in the world system, while playing by the prescribed rules. Properly speaking, this attempt began not with the founding of St Petersburg, but much earlier, with the policies of Ivan the Terrible – in effect, from the very moment when the capitalist world system arose. All of this culminated in the disaster of the First World War and in the revolution of 1917. The collapse of tsarist Russia and the triumph of Bolshevism were in no way accidental. They were prepared not only by the whole course of previous Russian history, but also by the whole history of the world system.

At the basis of the Soviet experiment lay an understanding – partly rational, partly intuitive – by the new post-revolutionary elite of the causes that had brought about the downfall of their predecessors. For approximately 50 years, the Soviet system therefore retained a single dynamic, independent of the zigzags of the political course and the evolution of the system itself. This dynamic amounted to an attempt by the Soviet system to counterpose itself to the world system, to break away from it, and to establish its own international order around itself. To the degree that the revolutionary impulse was lost, the bureaucracy, appropriating to itself the fruits of the heroic efforts of the people, became more and more conservative. The impact of the masses was replaced by the organised work of the apparatus, and workers' democracy by bureaucratic centralism.

Ultimately, the 'new world' that had formed around the USSR began to acquire the distinct features of a 'world empire'. Such world empires had already met with defeat in the sixteenth and seventeenth centuries, as they entered into conflict with the rising bourgeois world system. The same fate overtook the Soviet alternative. The collapse of this system was a natural process, but it became inevitable from the moment the bureaucratic elite employed a turn to the world system as a defensive reaction against the 'reformist threat' that was maturing within Soviet society itself. The trade in raw materials during the 1970s prepared the way for the political self-liquidation of the Soviet empire in the 1990s. The restoration of capitalism resulted not simply in the return of Russia to the world system, but also in a return on conditions incomparably worse than those on which tsarist Russia had existed within the system. The same restoration was also a tragedy of global scale for the countries and peoples of the world periphery who had linked their hopes of changing their role in the world with the Soviet Union. It also prefigured severe defeats for the Western left, including those forces that had never had any illusions about Stalinism.

Like any tragedy, the collapse of the USSR was a natural and understandable development. Nevertheless, if one draws up a balance sheet of the desperate sprint forward which Russia carried out in the twentieth century, the capitalist restoration in itself turns out to be unstable and incomplete. This incompleteness is an inherent trait of all restorations that follow great revolutions. The truth is that only the actions of the masses themselves can totally refashion society. Restoration that is imposed on the people from above, like all historical action that is limited by the narrow egoism of an elite, is incapable of social creativity. Without this creativity, the founding of a stable social system is impossible.

In Russian society, the catastrophic results of the restoration are calling forth a persistent, though not always conscious, demand for changes of a type that cannot fail to affect Russia's situation in the world system. A repeat of the Soviet experiment, however, is now impossible, since history has moved far beyond the situation in the early twentieth century, not least because of the Soviet experiment itself. The results of the 70 Soviet years were far more impressive, though also far less enduring, than the results of the St Petersburg period. Meanwhile, the fruits of the Soviet experiment have not been done away with entirely, despite all the efforts of the reformer-restorationists. Any attempt at democratic change in Russia inevitably comes up against the need to define the country's relation to the world system. The experience of Russian history shows that remaining within the framework of the system means to condemn oneself to degradation, while to pursue salvation through separating oneself from the system becomes a sentence of isolation. But does this mean that Russia, like most of the rest of the world, is forever doomed to perform the role of the periphery, hoping only for some insignificant improvement of its lot during the next Kondratyev cycle?

Russia during the twentieth century came close to breaking out of the world system. But 'coming close' does not count. For Russia in the twenty-first century, as for all of humanity, there is only one way out: to change the world system. Russia must transform itself in such a way that, at the same time, the outside world is also changed.

How successful such attempts will be is no longer a question of theory, but a question of practice. Here, our journey into the depths of Russian history comes to an end.

One can complain as much as one likes about the unfortunate past, or dream of a great future. Both these courses are best suited to ideological neurotics. Those who choose action need to remember a very simple truth. The fate of Russia is inseparable from the history of humanity, and we can struggle for a better world for ourselves only through trying to build a better world for everyone. And this, of course, can also be said of any country.

Notes

INTRODUCTION

1. P. Chaadaev, *Polnoe sobranie sochineniy i izbrannye pis'ma*, vol. 1. Moscow, Nauka, 1991, p. 330.
2. Ibid., p. 534.
3. *Malaya sovetskaya entsiklopediya*. Moscow, OGIZ RSFSR, 1939, p. 386.
4. *Pravda*, 12 January 1939.
5. M.N. Pokrovsky, *Russkaya istoriya v samom szhatom ocherke (ot drevneyshikh vremen do kontsa XIX stoletiya)*, parts 1 and 2, 7th edn. Moscow and Leningrad, GIZ, 1929, p. 3.
6. Samuel Huntington, *The Clash of Civilizations*. New York, Simon and Schuster, 1996.
7. N.Ya. Danilevsky, *Rossiya i Evropa*. Moscow, Izvestiya, 2003, p. 42. It is curious that in the foreword to this edition of Danilevsky's book his theories are directly counterposed to the Marxist understanding of the world system. Meanwhile, the superiority of the 'civilisation approach' is argued in extremely odd fashion. It turns out that the world system approach, by revealing Russia's peripheral character, arouses pessimism, while Danilevsky's ideas put Russians in an optimistic frame of mind. Theories of society, it seems, should not be evaluated on the basis of how truthfully they explain reality, but according to the mood they evoke in the reader. Meanwhile, it is not out of place to recall that pessimism and optimism are subjective matters. World system theory does not in any way assert that the countries of the periphery are doomed inevitably to dependence on the West. This theory merely explains why these countries cannot solve their own problems without changing the world system as a whole.
8. Ibid., p. 54.
9. Ibid., p. 45.
10. Ibid., p. 55.
11. Ibid., p. 50.
12. For a brilliant description of the Crusades as a clash of Western barbarism with Eastern enlightenment, see Tariq Ali, *The Clash of Fundamentalisms. Crusades, Jihads and Modernity*. London and New York, Verso, 2003.
13. Andre Gunder Frank, *ReOrient*. Berkeley, Los Angeles and London, University of California Press, 1998.
14. Here we should recall the point made by Robert Brenner, one of Wallerstein's main critics, that it was agrarian capitalism, and not the rise of a new world system, that lay at the basis of the early bourgeois revolutions.
15. Especially notable here is the work of William Robinson on the transnational bourgeoisie (see, for example, his *Transnational Conflicts: Central America, Social Change and Globalization*. London, Verso, 2003).
16. Within the framework of the school of world-system analysis, a discussion has unfolded on 'pure' and 'impure' capitalism. While Rosa Luxemburg, like most of the later members of this current, stresses the presence of 'non-capitalist' elements within the world system, Wallerstein by contrast calls for all these relationships to be considered bourgeois on the basis that they have been 'inserted' into capitalism. Such an approach fails to reveal the actual contradiction of the system, which gains from the possibility of using unfree labour and other 'cheap' methods of exploiting people and resources, while these relations on the other hand represent a brake on the development of peripheral countries, placing the local bourgeoisie in a notoriously ambiguous and weak position (as became clear in the course of the revolutions of the twentieth century).
17. M. Pokrovsky, *Ocherki po istorii revolyutsionnogo dvizheniya v Rossii XIX i XX vv*. Moscow and Leningrad, GIZ, 1927, p. 10.

18. Ibid., p. 8.
19. Among Marxists, Kondratyev's theory found both ardent supporters and categorical opponents. Most Soviet economists of the 1920s met it with fixed bayonets; a significant reason for this had to do with Kondratyev's populist past. Like the other outstanding economist of the time, A.V. Chayanov, Kondratyev could not be considered fully at home among the Marxists in ideological and methodological terms. In Western Marxism, by contrast, the theory of long waves found support, influencing the ideas of Immanuel Wallerstein and Ernest Mandel. Kondratyev perished in the Stalinist repressions, and was finally rehabilitated in the Soviet Union in the mid 1980s. The prominent Soviet economist Stanislav Menshikov, calling on his colleagues to arm themselves with the theory of long waves, argued that 'the roots of Kondratyev's theory of long waves lie in Marxism' (S.M. Menshikov and L.A. Klimenko, *Dlinnye volny v ekonomike. Kogda obshchestvo menyaet kozhu*. Moscow, Mezhdunarodnye Otnosheniya, 1989, p. 23). One can agree with this only in part. Kondratyev's conclusions were based on his summarising of empirical material, something that is perfectly possible without the help of Marxism. Meanwhile, an explanation of the nature of long waves does indeed need to be incorporated into the Marxist theoretical arsenal.
20. Even if we suppose that all the people born in a particular period have something in common, we are nevertheless unable to explain what this 'something' is, or to predict the future of the people concerned. To refer to the 'influence of the stars' is merely to make a spectacle of our impotence. Just as unsustainable is the attempt by Andre Gunder Frank to detect Kondratyev cycles in remote history. The economies of ancient Egypt or China were unquestionably cyclical, but the meaning of these cycles should be understood not according to Kondratyev, but in line with the views of the biblical Joseph; agrarian production depended on natural climatic cycles, which beset society as if from outside, in the form of floods, droughts, overpopulation, the exhaustion of soils and other calamities summarised in the marvellous image of the lean cows. By contrast, Kondratyev's cycles are determined by the internal logic of capitalist development, by the exhaustion of the potential of the dominant technological model, by the limits to the development of the market, and by the overaccumulation of capital. Even though Kondratyev's cycles are uneven in duration (and because of this, make chronological forecasts meaningless), an especially important point is that Kondratyev himself saw the extent to which the transition from one cycle to another is linked to major upheavals.
21. N.D. Kondratyev, *Problemy ekonomicheskoy dinamiki*. Moscow, Ekonomika, 1989, pp. 199–200.
22. Menshikov and Klimenko, *Dlinnye volny v ekonomike*, p. 24.
23. Ibid., p. 33.
24. See Ibid.
25. Kondratyev, *Problemy ekonomicheskoy dinamiki*, p. 200.
26. Ibid., p. 211.
27. Ibid., p. 219.
28. Ibid.
29. Ibid., p. 207
30. Ibid., p. 205.
31. *Oprichnina* was a term for both a regime of direct (emergency) rule, introduced by Ivan the Terrible in some Russian provinces which were exempt from traditional law, and for the organisation formed to actually run these provinces, in practice through intimidation and terror, recognising no rules or limits to the tsar's power.
32. *Notes on Russia by Marquis de Custin*. Moscow, 1990, p. 127.

CHAPTER 1

1. It is curious that Russian historians, relying above all on the data from the chronicles, should assign fundamental importance to the trade with Byzantium. Western authors, basing

themselves on Russian sources, are also convinced that all the trade was with Constantinople, while 'relations with the Orient were sporadic and isolated' (D. MacKenzie and M.W. Curran, *A History of Russia, the Soviet Union and Beyond*, 4th edn. Belmont, Calif., Dorsey Press, 1993, p. 43). Meanwhile Scandinavian scholars, relying on archaeological data, have come to the directly opposite conclusion that the trading relations of Rus were 'with Muslims rather than Byzantines' (B. Sawyer and P. Sawyer, *Medieval Scandinavia. From Conversion to Reformation, circa 800–1500*. Minneapolis and London, University of Minnesota Press, 1993, p. 146). The point is that Byzantine coins are very rare in Scandinavian hoards, while Arab ones are numerous. Large numbers of Arab coins have also been found in Russian hoards of the same period. The truth is obviously that the 'Arab' and 'Greek' commercial currents reinforced one another.

2. N.M. Karamzin, *Istoriya gosudarstva rossiyskogo*, Book 1, vols I–IV, St Petersburg, Zolotoy Vek, 1997, p. 98; V.P. Adrianova-Perets (ed.), *Povest' vremmenykh let*, 2nd edn. St Petersburg, Nauka, 1996, p. 13.

3. Karamzin, *Istoriya gosudarstva rossiyskogo*, Book 1, p. 98.

4. S.M. Solovyev, *Sochineniya*, Book 1. Moscow, Mysl', 1988, pp. 240–1.

5. M. Pokrovsky, with N.M. Nikol'sky and V.N. Storozhev, *Russkaya istoriya s drevneyshikh vremen*, vol. 1. Moscow, Mir, 1913, pp. 109, 95. The importance of trade to Kievan Rus has been the topic of heated historical discussions. Klyuchevsky assigned it fundamental significance, while in the Soviet period the accepted approach was to stress the agrarian nature of the Old Russian economy. For Soviet authors, it was important to demonstrate the similarity between Rus and Western Europe, and so once again to prove the unity of the historical process. The question is not, in fact, how widespread agriculture was in Kievan Rus (there is no doubt that it was the land that fed the bulk of the population), but the relative importance of trade and agriculture for the formation of the state. On its own, medieval agriculture simply could not have produced a surplus product in the quantities needed to support wealthy cities and the powerful Kievan state over a prolonged period. It is significant that in polemicising with Klyuchevsky, the leading Soviet scholar of the Kievan period, B.D. Grekov, did not deny the importance of trade, but merely argued – in thoroughly convincing fashion – that Russia possessed relatively developed agriculture and stock-raising. Meanwhile, Grekov acknowledged that 'the wealth of princes, boyars and merchants did not lie in grain' (B.D. Grekov, *Kievskaya Rus'*, Moscow and Leningrad, GIPL, 1953, p. 54). The American historians MacKenzie and Curran also remark that 'the bulk of the population derived a livelihood from agriculture', while trade was vitally important for 'princes and their retinues' (MacKenzie and Curran, *A History of Russia*, p. 47).

6. B.A. Rybakov, *Kievskaya Rus' i russkie knyazhestva XII–XIII vv.* Moscow, Nauka, 1982, p. 5.

7. Arab sources record of the Volga Bulgars that in 922 they 'had officially adopted Islam, were pursuing a settled way of life, lived in towns, and as well as occupying themselves with trade, were also engaged in agriculture' (N.I. Ashmarin, *Bolgary i chuvashi*. Kazan, 1902, p. 119). The case with the Khazars is somewhat more complex. The French historian René Grousset writes: 'Although they never adopted a sedentary or agricultural way of life, as sometimes said, they had built a coherent state, enriched by trade and with a relatively high culture, thanks to their contacts with Byzantium and with the Arab world' (R. Grousset, *The Empire of the Steppes: A History of Central Asia*. New Brunswick, Rutgers University Press, 1991, p. 180). Arab sources, however, testify to the Khazars making the transition from herding to agriculture. If early references to the Khazars describe them as herders, in later ones it is stated that in spring the population of the largest Khazar city, Itil, 'went out into the fields to perform agricultural work' (*Mezhdunarodnye svyazi Rossii do XVII veka*. Moscow, AN SSSR, 1961, p. 45). The question, however, is not simply one of how life in Itil was organised. It is impossible to construct an enduring state without a settled population. Meanwhile, it is of course true that in medieval states, beginning with those of the early Arabs and Turks, the agrarian population were not always members of the ruling national group.

8. See M.N. Tikhomirov, *Drevnerusskie goroda*. Moscow, Izdatel'stvo politicheskoi literatury, 1956.

9. It is indicative that despite using 'Marxist' terminology, most historians of the Soviet period showed little interest in the question of how the economy of Kievan Rus functioned; of how production was organised; and of what technologies were employed. Grekov devotes particular attention only to the organisation of the feudal estates, though he acknowledges that it was not to these estates that the princes and boyars owed their wealth. Trade and manufacturing receive almost no attention, and culture is examined at more length than technology. N.Ya. Froyanov, while providing detailed studies of the role of the princes, of the organisation of the armed retainers and of the situation of the peasants, has nothing whatsoever to say about the merchants. In describing the medieval cities, he fails to touch on either trade or manufacturing, limiting himself to the political role of the cities and their links with the countryside. Economic and technological development is a matter of even greater indifference to I.N. Danilevsky, who is writing in the post-Soviet period, and hence is free from even the ritual requirements of 'Marxism'.

10. A.V. Nazdratenko, *Drevnyaya Rus' na mezhdunarodnykh putyakh. Mezhdistsiplinarnye ocherki kul'turnykh, torgovykh, politicheskikh svyazey IX–XII vv.* Moscow, Yazyki Russkoy Kul'tury, 2001, p. 78.

11. Pokrovsky, *Russkaya istoriya s drevneyshikh vremen*, vol. 1, p. 104.

12. Ibid., p. 119.

13. Sawyer and Sawyer, *Medieval Scandinavia*, p. 149.

14. G.G. Litavrin, *Vizantiya i slavyane*. St Petersburg, Aletaya, 1999, p. 442.

15. V.O. Klyuchevsky, *Sochineniya*. Moscow, Mysl', 1988, vol. 1, p. 167.

16. Pokrovsky, *Russkaya istoriya s drevneyshikh vremen*, vol. 1, p. 109.

17. Klyuchevsky, *Sochineniya*, vol. 1, p. 168.

18. *Polnoe sobranie russkikh letopisey*, vol. 2, St Petersburg, 1908, p. 97.

19. See Solovyev, *Sochineniya*, Book 1, p. 695.

20. Litavrin, *Vizantiya i slavyane*, p. 425.

21. Cited in Solovyev, *Sochineniya*, Book 1, p. 154.

22. Karamzin, *Istoriya gosudarstva rossiyskogo*, Book 1, p. 136.

23. *Russkiy istoricheskiy sbornik*, vol. VI, Moscow, 1843, p. 357.

24. Rybakov, *Kievskaya Rus' i russkie knyazhestva XII–XIII vv.*, p. 382. See also G.I. Os'kin and N.N. Marichev, *Izuchenie boevogo proshlogo nashey Rodiny.* Moscow, Prosvechenie, 1971.

25. Quoted in Solovyev, *Sochineniya*, Book 1, pp. 154–5.

26. Ibid., p. 155.

27. See Rybakov, *Kievskaya Rus' i russkie knyazhestva XII–XIII vv.*, pp. 380–3.

28. See M.I. Artamonov, *Istoriya Khazar.* St Petersburg, Lan', 2001.

29. Grousset, *The Empire of the Steppes*, p 181.

30. Artamonov, *Istoriya Khazar*, p. 361. According to Artamonov, it was the adoption of Judaism which resulted in the decline of Khazaria, since the hereditary religion of the 'chosen people' could not unite Khazar society. 'The Khazar Jews failed to take account of the fact that religion acts as a powerful factor for social unification even when the economic base has no need of it' (ibid., p. 624). Here, the principles of national consolidation which emerged in Europe in the modern era appear to Artamonov to be self-evident and universal. In fact, these principles have nothing in common with the ethno-political system of the medieval East, where religious and ethnic diversity did nothing to impede the founding and development of empires. Rus, which defeated the Khazars, was also a heterogeneous society. The decline of Khazaria was predetermined by the fundamental inequality of forces in the struggle which the khanate was forced to wage simultaneously against Kiev, Byzantium and the Turkic tribes.

31. Ibid., p. 364.

32. Ibid., p. 586.

33. Ibid., p. 587.

34. Grousset, *The Empire of the Steppes*, p. 182.

35. Quoted in Sawyer and Sawyer, *Medieval Scandinavia*, p. 148.

36. Karamzin, *Istoriya gosudarstva rossiyskogo*, Book 1, p. 145.

37. Quoted in A.L. Yakobson, *Srednevekoviy Krym.* Moscow and Leningrad, Nauka, 1964, p. 55.

38. The Scandinavian name for Rus, *Gardarika,* means 'land of fortresses', or 'land of towns'. See A. Grishin-Almazov, *Zolotoy vek ili neskol'ko statey po istorii Kievskoy Rusi.* Moscow, 1998, p. 73.

39. L.V. Zvorikin, N.I. Os'mova, V.I. Chernyshev and S.V. Shukhardin, *Istoriya tekhniki.* Moscow, Sotsekgiz, 1962, p. 66.

40. See M.N. Tikhomirov, *Drevnerusskie goroda.* Moscow, Gospolitizdat, 1956; *Mezhdunarodnye svyazi Rossii do XVII veka.* Tikhomirov stresses that by no means all towns were located on trading routes; some were on the sites of old tribal centres. This, however, does not alter the general picture. The towns ensured military and administrative control over the rural population, that is, the extraction of the surplus product that was indispensable for maintaining the commercial economy of Kievan Rus. As a rule, the rise of towns in the absence of trade was inconceivable during the Middle Ages, whether in Russia or in Western Europe.

41. N.Ya. Danilevsky, *Drevnyaya Rus' glazami sovremennikov i potomkov (IX–XII vv.).* Moscow, 1998, p. 84.

42. T.M. Kalinina, *Drevnya Rus' i strany Vostoka v X v. Srednevekovye arabo-persidskie istochniki o Rusi.* Moscow, Otkrytoe Obshchestvo, 1976, p. 15.

43. Ibid., p. 17.

44. C. Brinton, J.B. Christopher and R.L. Wolf, *A History of Civilization. Volume 1, Prehistory to 1715.* Englewood Cliffs, NJ, Prentice-Hall, 1956. Here the American authors attribute the development of the market in Russia exclusively to the influx of Byzantine silver. As we see from other sources, this is not entirely correct. More significant is the fact that the authors follow Russian historians in ascribing the subsequent decline of Rus to Byzantine influences and to the Tatar invasion.

45. Noting the large number of Arab coins that arrived in the Viking lands from Rus, P. Sawyer remarks that this is not necessarily evidence of trade; the coins might simply have been stolen. This, however, cannot explain why the flow of silver from Rus was so marked during a period when there were no major wars between Slavs and Scandinavians. The robbery of traders was commonplace in medieval Europe, but even more typical was robbery for the sake of trade, as for example when the peoples of the north were robbed so that their furs could be sold at a profit in the south. Moreover, the traders did not carry large amounts of silver with them. The only way to seize large numbers of coins at any one time was by capturing a town. Russian towns were well fortified (old Ladoga already had stone walls in 860), and on the whole, neither Russian nor Scandinavian sources record the capture of Russian towns by Vikings in the tenth and eleventh centuries. More credible is Sawyer's suggestion that the silver was 'the pay of mercenaries' (P. H. Sawyer, *Kings and Vikings.* London and New York, Methuen, 1982, p. 113). Byzantine coins reached the north in similar fashion, but it is important to recall that in Rus, unlike in Byzantium, the Vikings were not only mercenaries but also part of the local feudal elite. Consequently they received not only wages, but also a share of wartime plunder, and a portion of the various feudal dues and taxes.

46. V.L. Yanin, *Denezhno-vesovye sistemy russkogo srednevekov'ya.* Moscow, 1956, p. 293.

47. Nazdratenko, *Drevnyaya Rus' na mezhdunarodnykh putyakh. Mezhdistsiplinarnye ocherki kul'turnykh, torgovykh, politicheskikh svyazey IX–XII vv.,* p. 113.

48. See Pokrovsky, *Russkaya istoriya s drevneyshikh vremen,* vol. 1.

49. Karamzin, *Istoriya gosudarstva rossiyskogo,* Book 1, p. 125.

50. See V.N. Smirnov, *Ekonomicheskie svyazi Drevney Rusi s Vizantiey i Severnym Prichernomor'em v VIII–XV v.* Leningrad, 1980, p. 8.

51. Yakobson, *Srednevekoviy Krym,* p. 77.

52. Artamonov, *Istoriya Khazar,* p. 609.

53. Solovyev, *Sochineniya,* Book 1, p. 243.

54. Pokrovsky, *Russkaya istoriya s drevneyshikh vremen,* vol. 1, p. 97.

55. Smirnov, *Ekonomicheskie svyazi Drevney Rusi s Vizantiey i Severnym Prichernomor'em v VIII–XV v.*, p. 8.
56. Sawyer, *Kings and Vikings*, p. 122.
57. This is not, however, evidence of barter trade. The great quantity of Eastern silver that circulated in Russia also allowed the Greek trade to proceed on a monetary basis.
58. Litavrin, *Vizantiya i slavyane*, p. 427.
59. It could even be said that in the initial period their residence rights were restricted, since their numbers in Constantinople were limited by the Greek administration.
60. Smirnov, *Ekonomicheskie svyazi Drevney Rusi s Vizantiey i Severnym Prichernomor'em v VIII–XV v.*, p. 3.
61. Os'kin and Marichev, *Izuchenie boevogo proshlogo nashey Rodiny*, p. 15.
62. See N.Ya. Froyanov, *Kievskaya Rus'*. Leningrad, 1980, p. 197. Froyanov considers the 'large-scale' production of standardised weapons to be proof that the general population in Kievan Rus was armed. However, this production is better seen as evidence that the princes' retainers were well organised, and that the city militias had a high level of 'mobilisational readiness'. In the Middle Ages, 'popular' weaponry was neither standardised nor present in large quantities. The standardisation of armaments testifies precisely to the professionalisation of the military structures, and to their remoteness from the common people.
63. See I.G. Spasskiy, *Russkaya monetnaya sistema*. Leningrad, Avrora, 1970, pp. 52–4.
64. V.F. Andreev, *Severnyy strazh Rusi*. Leningrad, Lenizdat, 1983, p. 64.
65. See Litavrin, *Vizantiya i slavyane*, p. 512; Smirnov, *Ekonomicheskie svyazi Drevney Rusi s Vizantiey i Severnym Prichernomor'em v VIII–XV v.*, pp. 8–9.
66. *Mezhdunarodnye svyazi Rossii do XVII veka*, p. 17.
67. See Grekov, *Kievskaya Rus'*, p. 51.
68. The Soviet historian V.N. Smirnov notes that despite the general recognition of the importance of Russian-Greek relations, little study has ever been devoted to 'the economic aspects of these relations, although it was these which to a significant degree determined the stability of the contacts between Rus and Byzantium over many centuries, a stability which endured even amid frequent political and religious disputes between the two medieval states' (Smirnov, *Ekonomicheskie svyazi Drevney Rusi s Vizantiey i Severnym Prichernomor'em v VIII–XV v.*). The economic ties between the two societies have been examined by historians 'only in passing' (ibid., p. 2). This is especially surprising because huge quantities of archaeological data were obtained during the twentieth century, and because new opportunities appeared for studying Greek materials. These developments, however, had little impact on the main trends of historical thought. If the 'Greek' aspects of the 'route from the Vikings to the Greeks' received a certain amount of study (an example is the dissertation by Smirnov), the 'Viking' elements attracted much less. Most crucially, historians devoted almost no attention to the interaction between the 'Greek', 'Viking' and 'Eastern' markets; as a specific economic phenomenon, the 'route from the Vikings to the Greeks' was never the subject of detailed examination. One might even cite, as a curiosity, a pronouncement by V.A. Rybakov to the effect that no route from the Vikings to the Greeks ever existed, and that everything written on this topic was 'a Normanist conjecture' (Rybakov, *Kievskaya Rus' i russkie knyazhestva XII–XIII vv.*, p. 294). Rybakov's hostility to the 'Normanist theory' was so great that he denied even the theoretical possibility that Vikings might have travelled along the Russian rivers en route to Constantinople, supposing perhaps that the Slavs imposed border controls like those in Soviet times.

CHAPTER 2

1. N.M. Karamzin, *Istoriya gosudarstva rossiyskogo*, Book 2. St Petersburg, Zoloty Vek, 1997, pp. 196–7.
2. Ibid., p. 197.
3. L.V. Zvorykin, N.I. Os'mova, V.I. Chernyshev and S.V. Shukhardin, *Istoriya tekhniki*. Moscow, Izdatel'stvo sotsialno-ekonomicheskoy literatury, 1962, p. 64.

4. M. Baring, *The Russian People*. London, Methuen & Co., 1911, p. 90.

5. K. Marx, *Secret Diplomatic History of the Eighteenth Century, and the Story of the Life of Lord Palmerston*. Edited with an introduction by L. Hutchinson. London, Lawrence and Wishart, 1969, p. 121.

6. See Karamzin, *Istoriya gosudarstva rossiyskogo*, Book 2; M. Pokrovsky, with N.M. Nikol'sky and V.N. Storozhez, *Russkaya istoriya s drevneyshikh vremen*, vol. 1. Moscow, Mir, 1913.

7. N.M. Karamzin, *Istoriya gosudarstva rossiyskogo*, Book 1. St Petersburg, Zoloty Vek, 1997, p. 318.

8. *Khristianskiy mir i 'Velikaya mongol'skaya imperiya'. Materialy frantsiskanskoy missii 1245 goda*. St Petersburg, Evrasiya, 2002, p. 278. For a full translation of the report by Giovanni de Piano Carpini, see G. Del' Plano Kapini, *Istoriya mongolov. G. de Rubruk, Puteshestvie v vostochnye strany*. Moscow, Kniga Marko Polo, 1997.

9. *Khristianskiy mir i 'Velikaya mongol'skaya imperiya'. Materialy frantsiskanskoy*, p. 381. See also *Drevneyshie gosudarstva na territorii SSSR. Materialy i issledovaniya. 1986*. Moscow, Nauka, 1988, pp. 207–9.

10. *Khristianskiy mir i 'Velikaya mongol'skaya imperiya'. Materialy frantsiskanskoy*, p. 278. See also P. Pelliot, *Recherches sur les Chrétiens d'Asie Centrale et d'Extr me-Orient*. Paris, Fondation Singer-Polignac, 1973, pp. 73–4; *Drevneyshie gosudarstva na territorii SSSR. 1987*. Moscow, Nauka, 1989, pp. 302–3.

11. R. Grousset, *The Empire of the Steppes: A History of Central Asia*. New Brunswick, Rutgers University Press, 1991, p. 267.

12. D. MacKenzie and M.W. Curran, *A History of Russia, the Soviet Union and Beyond*, 4th edn, Belmont, Calif., Dorsey Press, 1993, p. 81.

13. See R. Hilton (ed.), *The Transition from Feudalism to Capitalism*. London, Verso, 1992, p. 161.

14. J. Le Goff, *Tsivilizatsiya srednevekovogo Zapada*. Moscow, Progress-Akademiya, 1992, p. 103.

15. Karamzin, *Istoriya gosudarstva rossiyskogo*, Book 1, p. 584.

16. K.O. Morgan (ed.), *The Oxford History of Britain*. Oxford and New York, Oxford University Press, 1989, pp. 187, 188.

17. R. Strong, *The History of Britain*. London, 1996, p. 107.

18. Henry Knighton's chronicle, cited in ibid., pp. 106–7.

19. Morgan, *The Oxford History of Britain*, p. 187.

20. Karamzin, *Istoriya gosudarstva rossiyskogo*, Book 2, p. 203.

21. *Znamya*, 1988, no. 8, p. 166.

22. Pokrovsky, *Russkaya istoriya s drevneyshikh vremen*, vol. 1, p. 221.

23. M. Pokrovsky, *Russkaya istoriya v samom szhatom ocherke (ot drevneyshikh vremen do kontsa XIX stoletiya)*, parts 1 and 2, 7th edn. Moscow and Leningrad, GIZ, 1929, p. 33.

24. Karamzin, *Istoriya gosudarstva rossiyskogo*, Book 2, pp. 201–2.

25. In the first chapter of his narrative, Rubruck tells of Surozh (also known as Sudak or Soldaiya): 'All the merchants come there, both those coming from Turkey and heading for the northern countries, and also those coming back from Russia and the northern countries, and wanting to cross into Turkey. Some bring ermine and squirrel skins, and other precious furs, while others bring cotton cloth, fustian, silk materials and sweet-scented roots' (Kapini, *Istoriya mongolov. G. de Rubruk*, p. 89).

26. See V.N. Smirnov, *Ekonomicheskie svyazi Drevney Rusi s Vizantiey i Severnym Prichernomor'em v VIII–XV v.* Leningrad, 1980, p. 11.

27. *Mezhdunarodnye svyazi Rossii do XVII veka*. Moscow, AN SSSR, 1961, p. 63.

28. See Kapini, *Istoriya mongalov. G. de Rubruk*, pp. 134–5, 139–40. See also Grousset, *The Empire of the Steppes*, pp. 276–7.

29. The thesis that identifies the Tatar yoke as the cause of backwardness is appearing less and less convincing even to 'Westerniser' historians who continue to think within the framework of the old 'corrupting Asiatic influence' paradigm. A search is therefore beginning to be made for 'eastern-Asiatic causes' already present in pre-Tatar Rus. The 'flaw' of Kievan Rus is seen in the fact that in the time of Prince Ryurik or Prince Vladimir a strong state

existed there along with 'collective feudal property', while in the West 'the development of individual feudal property was apparent' (*Aktual'naya istoriya: Novye problemy i podkhody*, Samara, SAMGU, 1999, p. 25). It is clear that everything 'collective' and 'Asiatic' is seen as bad, while the 'individual' is identical to the 'European', and is good. The trouble is that such writers compare ninth-century Rus with France in the fourteenth century. If we take the Carolingian empire, which existed in the same historical era as the Kievan state, we find that there, as well, feudalism was developing on the basis of state power and collective property. Moreover, feudalism could not as a matter of principle develop on any other basis, since feudal relations took shape on the basis of the gradual 'privatisation' of administrative authority by the tribal elite – by the margraves in Carolingian Europe, and by the princes and boyars in Rus.

30. Pokrovsky, *Russkaya istoriya s drevneyshikh vremen*, vol. 1, p. 140.
31. See I.G. Spassky, *Russkaya monetnaya sistema*, Leningrad, Avrora, 1970, p. 60.
32. See E.A. Rybina, *Arkheologicheskie ocherki istorii novgorodskoy torgovli X–XIV vv.* Moscow, MGU, 1978; Spassky, *Russkaya monetnaya sistema*; A. Attman, *The Russian and Polish Markets in International Trade, 1500–1650*. Gotheborg, Institute of Economic History, 1973.
33. Spassky, *Russkaya monetnaya sistema*, p. 62.
34. G.G. Litavrin, *Vizantiya i slavyane*. St Petersburg, Aletaya, 1999, p. 513.
35. See ibid., p. 517.
36. Pokrovsky, *Russkaya istoriya s drevneyshikh vremen*, vol. 1, p. 148.
37. I.P. Magidovich and V.I. Magidovich, *Istoriya otkrytiya i issledovaniya Evropy*. Moscow, Mysl', 1970, p. 155.
38. Ibid.
39. See B. Sawyer and P. Sawyer, *Medieval Scandinavia. From Conversion to Reformation, circa 800–1500*. Minneapolis and London, University of Minnesota Press, 1993, p. 161.
40. German purchases in Novgorod began earlier than in Scandinavia. In the sixteenth century, according to archaeological evidence, German coins first appeared in Novgorod, and only from there spread further north (see P. Sawyer, *Kings and Vikings*. London and New York, Methuen, 1982). With regard to the Novgorodians, however, the role of the German merchants was already quite different; unlike the Scandinavians and Arabs, they arrived with both weapons and cash simultaneously, and hence acted as a dominant force.
41. Ibid., pp. 158–9.
42. Pokrovsky, *Russkaya istoriya s drevneyshikh vremen*, vol. 1, p. 143.

CHAPTER 3

1. V.N. Smirnov, *Ekonomicheskie svyazi Drevney Rusi s Vizantiey i Severnym Prichernomor'em v VIII–XV v.* Leningrad, 1980, p. 13.
2. Cf. M. Pokrovsky, *Russkaya istoriya v samom szhatom ocherke (ot drevneyshikh vremen do kontsa XIX stoletiya)*, parts 1 and 2, 7th edn. Moscow and Leningrad, GIZ, 1929.
3. A.L. Yakobson, *Srednevekoviy Krym*. Moscow and Leningrad, Nauka, 1964, p. 104.
4. Ibid., pp. 108–9.
5. Ibid., p. 109.
6. Cited in Smirnov, *Ekonomicheskie svyazi Drevney Rusi s Vizantiey i Severnym Prichernomor'em v VIII–XV v*, p. 109.
7. J. Le Goff, *Tsivilizatsiya srednevekovogo Zapada*. Moscow, Progress-Akademiya, 1992, p. 203.
8. Pokrovsky, *Russkaya istoriya v samom szhatom ocherke*, p. 40.
9. For the sake of fairness it should be pointed out that in his work *Russkaya istoriya s drevneyshikh vremen*, Pokrovsky also notes the links between Moscow and Genoa, and the continuation of active trade with the East by way of the Volga route. Strangely, however, he does not analyse the significance of this trade, limiting himself merely to a reference to the Italian participation in the building of the Kremlin.

10. Smirnov, *Ekonomicheskie svyazi Drevney Rusi s Vizantiey i Severnym Prichernomor'em v VIII–XV v*, p. 15.

11. M. Pokrovsky, *Russkaya istoriya v samom szhatom ocherke*, p. 41.

12. N.P. Pavlov-Sil'vansky, *Feodalizm v Rossii*. Moscow, Nauka, 1988, p. 178.

13. Ibid., p. 211.

14. Ibid., p. 104.

15. M. Pokrovsky, with N.M. Nikol'sky and V.N. Storozhez, *Russkaya istoriya s drevneyshikh vremen*, vol. 1. Moscow, Mir, 1913, p. 94.

16. See W. Kirchner, *Commercial Relations Between Russia and Europe, 1400–1800*. Bloomington, Indiana University Press, 1966, pp. 31, 34.

17. L. Pisarskaya and A. Rodimtsev, *Moskovskiy Kreml'*. Moscow, Moskovskiy rabochy, 1976, p. 46.

18. *Rossiyskaya Federatsiya segodnya*, no. 24, 2000, p. 85.

19. B. Sawyer and P. Sawyer, *Medieval Scandinavia. From Conversion to Reformation, circa 800–1500*. Minneapolis and London, University of Minnesota Press, 1993, p. 154.

20. Pokrovsky, *Russkaya istoriya s drevneyshikh vremen*, vol. 1, p. 184.

21. V.F. Andreev, *Severnyy strazh Rusi*. Leningrad, Lenizdat, 1983, p. 109.

22. E.A. Rybina, *Arkheologicheskie ocherki istorii novgorodskoy torgovli X–XIV vv*. Moscow, MGU, 1978, p. 71.

23. A. Attman, *The Russian and Polish Markets in International Trade, 1500–1650*. Gotheborg, Institute of Economic History, 1973, p. 106.

24. Rybina, *Arkheologicheskie ocherki istorii novgorodskoy torgovli X–XIV vv*, p. 11.

25. Andreev, *Severnyy strazh Rusi*, p. 72.

26. See ibid., p. 79.

27. Ibid., p. 78.

28. It is noteworthy that Rybina, in *Arkheologicheskie ocherki novgorodskoy torgovli*, while making the usual reference to the 'Tatar factor', cites statistics that clearly contradict this thesis. The dynamic of imports and exports begins to change from the early thirteenth century, when people in Rus had not even heard of the Tatars.

29. Andreev, *Severnyy strazh Rusi*, p. 119.

30. Pokrovsky, *Russkaya istoriya s drevneyshikh vremen*, vol. 1, p. 203.

31. Ibid., p. 200.

32. Ibid., p. 197.

33. Pokrovsky, *Russkaya istoriya v samom szhatom ocherke*, p. 49. Pokrovsky remarks that 'the Old Russian freedom was a freedom of the cities, and it fell along with the cities' (ibid., p. 32). The collapse of the trading cities was the result of their internal contradictions. It was this, and not the despotism of Moscow, that put an end to the old rights of the population.

34. The importance and political weight of representative assemblies was different in various countries. While in England the parliaments gained a high degree of political influence, the estates-general in medieval France played an insignificant role. In this sense the Russian assemblies fit perfectly in the general European picture, while the Land Assembly of 1613 had a degree of power and authority which no English parliament enjoyed until the beginning of the revolution.

35. *Mezhdunarodnye svyazi Rossii do XVII veka*. Moscow, AN SSSR, 1961, p. 58.

36. *Review of Fernand Braudel Center*, vol. XXI, no. 2, 1998, p. 213.

37. V.O. Klyuchevsky, *Boyarskaya Duma drevney Rusi*. Petrograd, Narkompros, 1919, p. 11.

CHAPTER 4

1. N.M. Karamzin, *Istoriya gosudarstva rossiyskogo*, Book 1. St Petersburg, Zoloty Vek, 1997, p. 531.

2. M. Pokrovsky, with N.M. Nikol'sky and V.N. Storozhez, *Russkaya istoriya s drevneyshikh vremen*, vol. 2. Moscow, Mir, 1913, p. 77.

3. Cited in T.S. Willan, *The Early History of the Russia Company, 1553–1603*. Manchester, Manchester University Press, 1956, pp. 2–3.

4. Ibid., p. 4.

5. Ibid.

6. Perhaps influenced by Chancellor's expedition, Tsar Ivan after a period sent his own expedition to China, but by a land route. In 1567 he dispatched the Cossack ataman Ivan Petrov with a letter 'to unknown peoples'. Together with the Cossack Burkash Yelichev, Petrov travelled from the Urals to Beijing, in Mongolia receiving a letter granting him passage through the 'iron gates' of the Chinese wall. He later compiled a description of the lands he had seen.

7. I. Lyubimenko, *Istoriya torgovykh snosheniy Rossii s Angliey*, vol. 1: XVI vek. Yuryev, 1912, p. 37.

8. *Drevnyaya Rus' i slavyane*, Moscow, Nauka, 1978, p. 312.

9. Lyubimenko, *Istoriya torgovykh snosheniy Rossii s Angliey*, vol. 1, p. 63.

10. I.P. Magidovich and V.I. Magidovich, *Istoriya otkrytiya i issledovaniya Evropy*. Moscow, Mysl', 1970, p. 178.

11. Willan, *The Early History of the Russia Company*, p. 54.

12. Cited in ibid., p. 14.

13. Ibid., p. 40.

14. L.I. Yunusova, *Torgovaya ekspansiya Anglii v basseyne Kaspiya v pervoy polovine XVIII veka*. Baku, AN AzSSR, 1988, p. 29.

15. N. Kostomarov, *Ocherk torgovli Moskovskogo gosudarstva v XVI i XVII stoletiyakh*, 2nd edn. St Petersburg, 1889, p. 24.

16. See A.S. Samoylo, 'Proval popytki angliyskoy kompanii zakhvatit' russkiy rynok v XVI i pervoy polovine XVII veka', *Uchenye zapiski Moskovskogo oblastnogo pedagogicheskogo instituta*, vol. 22, 1955; N.T. Nakshidze, *Russko-angliyskie otnosheniya vo vtoroy polovine XVI veka*. Tbilisi, 1956; A.I. Ivanov, 'K voprosu o nachal'nom etape anglo-gollandskogo torgovogo sopernichestva v Rossii', *Uchenye zapiski Komi gosudarstvennogo pedagogicheskogo instituta*, vol. 34. Syktyvkar, 1968. There is also a good deal that is ironic about the changes in the position expressed by I. Lyubimenko. In her pre-revolutionary works she takes a very positive view of the activity of the English in Russia in the sixteenth and seventeenth centuries. In her works of the Stalinist period, however, she characterises the same actions as attempts by colonisers to seize the country. (See E.A. Kosminsky and Ya.A. Levitsky (eds), *Angliyskaya burzhuaznaya revolyutsiya XVII veka*. Moscow, Izdatel'stvo Akademii Nauk SSSR, 1954, p. 2.).

17. Ivanov, 'K voprosu o nachal'nom etape anglo-gollandskogo torgovogo sopernichestva v Rossii', p. 83; Nakshidze, *Russko-angliyskie otnosheniya vo vtoroy polovine XVI veka*, pp. 153–4.

18. See Lyubimenko, *Istoriya torgovykh snosheniy Rossii s Angliey*, vol. 1, pp. 64–6.

19. Ibid., p. 98.

20. Kostomarov, *Ocherk torgovli Moskovskogo gosudarstva v XVI i XVII stoletiyakh*, p. 37.

21. Ibid., p. 33.

22. See Lyubimenko, *Istoriya torgovykh snosheniy Rossii s Angliey*, vol. 1, pp. 54–5.

23. Ibid., p. 57.

24. S.F. Platonov, *Moskva i Zapad v XVI–XVII vekakh*. Leningrad, Seyatel', 1925, p. 26.

25. See Ibid.

26. N.M. Karamzin, *Istoriya gosudarstva rossiyskogo*, Book 2. St Petersburg, Zoloty Vek, 1997, p. 672.

27. Lyubimenko, *Istoriya torgovykh snosheniy Rossii s Angliey*, vol. 1, p. 36.

28. *Mezhdunarodnye svyazi Rossii do XVII veka*. Moscow, AN SSSR, 1961, p. 442.

29. A. Attman, *The Russian and Polish Markets in International Trade, 1550–1650*. Göteborg, Institute of Economic History, 1973, p. 6. Other Western historians also recognise the enormous role played by deliveries of strategic raw materials. See C. Brinton, J.B. Christopher and R.L. Wolf, *A History of Civilization. Volume 1, Prehistory to 1715*. Englewood Cliffs, NJ, Prentice-Hall, 1956, p. 413.

30. Willan, *The Early History of the Russia Company*, pp. 280–1.
31. Cited in Lyubimenko, *Istoriya torgovykh snosheniy Rossii s Angliey*, vol. 1, p. 87.
32. Willan, *The Early History of the Russia Company*, p. 281.
33. Lyubimenko, *Istoriya torgovykh snosheniy Rossii s Angliey*, vol. 1, p. 97.
34. Ibid., p. 115.
35. Ibid., p. 130. See also Willan, *The Early History of the Russia Company*, p. 14.
36. *Uchenye zapiski Komi gosudarstvennogo pedagogicheskogo instituta*, vol. 11. Syktyvkar, 1963, p. 143.
37. Lyubimenko, *Istoriya torgovykh snosheniy Rossii s Angliey*, vol. 1, pp. 80–1.
38. For a more detailed treatment, see Attman, *The Russian and Polish Markets in International Trade*, p. 25. Attman notes that until the Livonian War most of Novgorod's exports went through Revel, and that, in essence, Revel had grown and flourished as a transit port for Novgorod (see p. 35).
39. See I. Wallerstein, *The Modern World System I*. San Diego, etc., Academic Press, 1974, pp. 315, 319.
40. Attman, *The Russian and Polish Markets in International Trade*, p. 160.
41. Wallerstein considers that the policies of Ivan the Terrible helped the Russian bourgeoisie and monarchy to avoid 'at least for the moment, the fate of their Polish counterparts' (Wallerstein, *The Modern World System I*, p. 319). The paradox is that Russia and Poland both laid claim to one and the same place in the world system, and in this sense the failure of the tsar to conquer Livonia can be seen with hindsight as a stroke of good fortune. In reality, however, the military defeats suffered by Moscow in no way isolated it from the world system, but merely forced it to become integrated on less favourable terms. Meanwhile, the struggle between Poland and Russia for a place in the world system continued until Poland disappeared from the map of Europe.
42. W. Kirchner, *Commercial Relations Between Russia and Europe, 1400–1800*. Bloomington, Indiana University Press, 1966, p. 11.
43. Ibid., pp. 70, 77.
44. Attman notes that throughout the sixteenth and seventeenth centuries, the Vyborg trade was a matter of concern to Swedish kings. They deliberately pursued policies aimed at directing Russian trade through Swedish ports. In 1550, Gustav Vasa prepared a study of the Russian market designed to serve this end. In 1640, the Swedish Peter Loofeldt, resident in Moscow, prepared a new study in which he turned his attention to the growing activity of the English and Dutch in Arkhangelsk, and suggested measures for strengthening the Swedish position in the Russian market.
45. Pokrovsky, *Russkaya istoriya s drevneyshikh vremen*, vol. 2, p. 108.
46. Ibid., p. 109.
47. R.G. Skrynnikov, *Ivan Groznyy*. Moscow, Nauka, 1983, p. 101.
48. Pokrovsky, *Russkaya istoriya s drevneyshikh vremen*, vol. 2, p. 111.
49. S.F. Platonov, *Ocherki po istorii smuty v Moskovskom gosudarstve XVI–XVII vekov*. St Petersburg, 1910, p. 141.
50. Ibid., p. 140.
51. Pokrovsky, *Russkaya istoriya s drevneyshikh vremen*, vol. 2, p. 115.
52. Quoted in Skrynnikov, *Ivan Groznyy*, p. 170.
53. Ibid.
54. Ibid., p. 79.
55. Skrynnikov, *Ivan Groznyy*, p. 152.
56. See Willan, *The Early History of the Russia Company*, pp. 80–110.
57. Lyubimenko, *Istoriya torgovykh snosheniy Rossii s Angliey*, vol. 1, p. 44. T.S. Willan and other writers share this point of view.
58. In popular historical literature, the assertion is often made that the tsar sought the hand of Elizabeth herself. However, there is nothing in the documentary record to confirm this.
59. J.W. Veluwenkamp, *Archangel*. Amsterdam, Uitgeverij Balans, 2000.
60. Kostomarov, *Ocherk torgovli Moskovskogo gosudarstva v XVI i XVII stoletiyakh*, p. 37.

61. A.D. Kuzmichev and I.N. Shapkin, *Otechestvennoe predprinimatel'stvo. Ocherki Istorii,* Moscow, Progress-Akademiya, 1995, p. 25.
62. Ivanov, 'K voprosu o nachal'nom etape anglo-gollandskogo torgovogo sopernichestva v Rossii', p. 103.
63. Lyubimenko, *Istoriya torgovykh snosheniy Rossii s Angliey,* vol. 1, p. 65.
64. Ibid., p. 48.
65. *Mezhdunarodnye svyazi Rossii do XVII veka,* p. 442.

CHAPTER 5

1. I. Lyubimenko, 'Plany angliyskoi interventsii v Rossiyu v nachale XVII stoletiya', *Sovetskaya Nauka,* 1941, no. 2, p. 25.
2. E.A. Kosminsky and Ya.A. Levitsky (eds), *Angliyskaya burzhuaznaya revolyutsiya XVII veka,* vol. 2. Moscow, Izdatel'stvo Akademii Nauk SSSR, 1954, p. 93. I. Lyubimenko has no doubts that the proposal concerning the sending of English troops came 'from a section of the Russian nobility' (*Sovetskaya Nauka,* 1941, no. 2, p. 20). Elsewhere, however, she suggests that the plan for English intervention originated among merchants who had business ties to the Englishmen in Vologda (see ibid., p. 25).
3. See M. Pokrovsky, with N.M. Nikol'sky and V.N. Storozhez, *Russkaya istoriya s drevneyshikh vremen,* vol. 2. Moscow, Mir, 1913, p. 215.
4. Cited in Kosminsky and Levitsky, *Angliyskaya burzhuaznaya revolyutsiya XVII veka,* vol. 2, p. 93. See also I. Lyubimenko, 'Novye raboty po istorii snosheniy Moskovskoy Rusi s Angliey', *Istoricheskie Izvestiya,* 1916, no. 2, pp. 14–25; I. Lyubimenko, 'Proekty anglo-russkogo sojuza v XVI i XVII vekakh', *Istoricheskie Izvestiya,* 1916, nos 3–4, pp. 29–53; I. Lyubimenko (ed.), 'Letters Illustrating the Relations of England and Russia in the Seventeenth Century', *English History Review,* 1917, vol. 32, no. 125, pp. 92–103; I. Lubimenko, 'A Project for the Acquisition of Russia by James I', *English History Review,* 1914, vol. 29, no. 114, pp. 246–56.
5. Kosminsky and Levitsky, *Angliyskaya burzhuaznaya revolyutsiya XVII veka,* vol. 2, p. 94.
6. Ibid., p. 95.
7. *Uchenye zapiski Komi gosudarstvennogo pedagogicheskogo instituta,* vol. 11. Syktyvkar, 1963, p. 147.
8. See ibid., p. 149.
9. Ibid., p. 164.
10. Cited in ibid.
11. Cited in ibid., p. 166.
12. Cited in A.D. Kuzmichev and I.N. Shapkin, *Otechestvennoe predprinimatel'stvo. Ocherki Istorii,* Moscow, Progress-Akademiya, 1995, p. 20.
13. I. Lyubimenko, 'Moskovsky ryinok, kak arena bor'by Gollandii s Angliyey', *Russkoe Proshloe,* 1923, vol. 5, p. 4.
14. Kosminsky and Levitsky, *Angliyskaya burzhuaznaya revolyutsiya XVII veka,* vol. 2, p. 114.
15. E.J. Hobsbawm, 'The Crisis of the Seventeenth Century', in T.H. Ashton (ed.), *Crisis in Europe: 1560–1660.* London, Routledge, 1965. See also E.J. Hobsbawm, 'From Feudalism to Capitalism', in R. Hilton (ed.), *The Transition from Feudalism to Capitalism.* London, Verso, 1992, p. 162.
16. Ashton, *Crisis in Europe,* p. 46.
17. Cited in Kuzmichev and Shapkin, *Otechestvennoe predprinimatel'stvo. Ocherki Istorii,* p. 12.
18. Ibid., p. 13. The *gostinaya sotnya* (guild) united the merchants (*gosti*) based in Moscow, while the *sukonnaya sotnya* did the same for provincial traders who had offices in the capital.
19. R. Hellie, *The Economy and Material Culture of Russia, 1600–1725.* Chicago and London, University of Chicago Press, 1999, p. 643.

20. A. Attman, *The Russian and Polish Markets in International Trade, 1550–1650*. Göteborg, Institute of Economic History, 1973, p. 183.

21. S.F. Platonov, *Moskva i Zapad v XVI–XVII vekakh*. Leningrad, Seyatel', 1925, pp. 57–8.

22. Kuzmichev and Shapkin, *Otechestvennoe predprinimatel'stvo. Ocherki Istorii*, p. 21.

23. R. Hellie, *The Economy and Material Culture of Russia*, p. 641.

24. Pokrovsky, *Russkaya istoriya s drevneyshikh vremen*, vol. 2, p. 290.

25. S.M. Solovyev, *Sochineniya*, Book 5, Moscow, Mysl', 1988, p. 459.

26. Pokrovsky, *Russkaya istoriya s drevneyshikh vremen*, vol. 2, p. 302.

27. See S.G. Strumilin, *Izbrannye proizvedeniya. Istoriya chernoy metallurgii v SSSR.*. Moscow, Nauka, 1967, p. 93.

28. See Pokrovsky, *Russkaya istoriya s drevneyshikh vremen*, vol. 2, p. 273.

29. Lyubimenko, 'Moskovsky ryinok, kak arena bor'by Gollandii s Angliyey', p. 17.

30. Pokrovsky, *Russkaya istoriya s drevneyshikh vremen*, vol. 2, pp. 302–3.

CHAPTER 6

1. R. Blackburn, *The Overthrow of Colonial Slavery, 1776–1848*. London and New York, Verso, 1988, p. 5.

2. Ibid., p. 11.

3. Ibid., p. 5.

4. R. Blackburn, *The Making of New World Slavery. From the Baroque to the Modern, 1492–1800*. London and New York, Verso, 1997, p. 515.

5. Quoted in M. Pokrovsky, with N.M. Nikol'sky and V.N. Storozhez, *Russkaya istoriya s drevneyshikh vremen*, vol. 2. Moscow, Mir, 1913, p. 87.

6. Quoted ibid., p. 86.

7. See ibid., p. 14.

8. B.D. Grekov observes that prior to the sixteenth century, the grain trade in Rus was undeveloped. It was only in the sixteenth century that grain began to play a noticeable role on the internal and at times, external markets, 'in connection with the changes that had occurred in the economic life of all Europe, and of Rus in particular' (B.D. Grekov, *Kievskaya Rus'*, Moscow and Leningrad, GIPL, 1953, p. 54). See also B.D. Grekov, *Glavneyshie etapy v istorii krepostnogo prava v Rossii*. Moscow and Leningrad, Sotsekgiz, 1940; B.D. Grekov, *Krest'yane na Rusi s drevneyshikh vremen do XVII v*, Part 2. Moscow, AN SSSR, 1954.

9. P. Kolchin, *Unfree Labor: American Slavery and Russian Serfdom*. Cambridge, Mass. and London, Harvard University Press, 1987, p. 2.

10. Ibid., p. 360.

11. M. Pokrovsky, *Ocherki po istorii revolyutsionnogo dvizheniya v Rossii XIX i XX vv*. Moscow and Leningrad, GIZ, 1927, p. 9.

12. T. Astin and C. Philpin (eds), *The Brenner Debate*. Cambridge, Cambridge University Press, 1988, p. 99.

13. Pokrovsky, *Ocherki po istorii revolyutsionnogo dvizheniya v Rossii XIX I XX vv.*, p. 9.

14. Ibid., p. 10.

15. Kolchin, *Unfree Labor*, p. 27.

16. Historians do not agree entirely on the question of the 'commandment years' under Ivan the Terrible. The actual decree has not survived, either in the original or in quotations. B.D. Grekov considers that during the years of the Livonian War the peasants were enserfed everywhere, while Academician S.B. Veselovsky has suggested that only particular regions were affected. For a more detailed treatment see R.G. Skrynnikov, *Rossiya posle oprichniny*. Leningrad, LGU, 1975, pp. 178–80.

17. R.G. Skrynnikov, *Boris Godunov*. Moscow, Nauka, 1983, p. 96.

18. As Pokrovsky notes ironically, Tsar Boris was doomed by the same quandary that has brought undone many other politicians who have tried to normalise autocracy, bringing it within the framework of laws and regulations: 'All police states have broken their heads on

the insoluble problem of combining "justice" with a complete lack of rights for the subjects' (see Pokrovsky, *Russkaya istoriya s drevneyshikh vremen*, vol. 2, p. 158).

19. R.G. Skrynnikov, *Sotsial'no-politicheskaya bor'ba v russkom gosudarstve v nachale XVII veka*. Leningrad, LGU, 1985, p. 324.

20. Pokrovsky, *Russkaya istoriya s drevneyshikh vremen*, vol. 2, p. 221.

21. M. Pokrovsky, with N.M. Nikol'sky and V.N. Storozhev, *Russkaya istoriya s drevneyshikh vremen*, vol. 1. Moscow, Mir, 1913, p. 73.

22. Later, this conflict between market demand and the needs of the peasant economy was analysed brilliantly in the works of A.V. Chayanov.

23. Pokrovsky, *Russkaya istoriya s drevneyshikh vremen*, vol. 2, p. 127.

24. Ibid., p. 135.

25. S.F. Platonov, *Moskva i Zapad v XVI–XVII vekakh*. Leningrad, Seyatel', 1925, p. 106.

26. See ibid., p. 107.

27. Cited in ibid., p. 108.

28. When it expelled the English merchants from Moscow, the government of the Romanovs was not, of course, guided exclusively by ideological considerations. The news of the execution of King Charles in London must, however, have had unpleasant associations for the Russian rulers, who had just survived the events of 1648.

29. V.O. Klyuchevsky, *Sochineniya*, vol. 3. Moscow, Mysl', 1988, p. 125.

30. Quoted in S.M. Solovyev, *Sochineniya*, Book 5. Moscow, Mysl', 1988, p. 464.

31. Platonov, *Moskva i Zapad v XVI–XVII vekakh*, p. 108.

32. Ibid., p. 109.

33. For a more detailed discussion, see M. Postan, 'The Rise of a Money Economy', *Economic History Review*, 1944, vol. 14. This view is disputed by Robert Brenner, who, like most Soviet writers on the topic, argues that serfdom was exclusively a manifestation of feudal backwardness. In Brenner's opinion, the development of trade was simply not capable of undermining the personal dependence of the peasant on the landowner; consequently, the market had, as it were, an existence in and of itself, and serfdom likewise (see Astin and Philpin, *The Brenner Debate*, p. 26). Brenner's judgement, however, is not borne out by the factual material. As already noted, the Russian peasants prior to the end of the sixteenth century had simply not known the forms of personal property that became established in the course of the Time of Troubles and the Petrine reforms. Brenner and other proponents of the 'backwardness' theory cannot explain why serfdom not only failed to weaken as commodity relations developed, but grew radically stronger, or why the situation of the Russian peasants in the sixteenth century had been more or less identical to that of their class peers in the West, while in the time of Catherine the Great it differed little from that of plantation slaves. Moreover, it is significant that Brenner, like the Soviet historians, never examines the parallels in the development of the landowner and plantation economies, even though these parallels are striking.

34. Kolchin, *Unfree Labor*, p. 30.

35. Blackburn, *The Overthrow of Colonial Slavery*, p. 5.

36. Blackburn, *The Making of New World Slavery*, p. 515.

37. S.G. Strumilin, *Izbrannye proizvedeniya. Istoriya chernoy metallurgii v SSSR*. Moscow, Nauka, 1967, p. 109.

38. Quoted in I.P. Magidovich and V.I. Magidovich, *Istoriya otkrytiya i issledovaniya Evropy*. Moscow, Mysl', 1970, p. 202.

39. A.D. Kuzmichev and I.N. Shapkin, *Otechestvennoe predprinimatel'stvo. Ocherki istorii*. Moscow, Progress-Akademiya, 1995, p. 15.

40. See ibid.

41. N.M. Druzhinin, *Sotsial'no-ekonomicheskaya istoriya Rossii. Izbrannye trudy*. Moscow, Nauka, 1987, p. 336.

42. Ibid., pp. 330–1.

43. A.L. Stanislavsky, *Grazhdanskaya voyna v Rossii XVII veka*. Moscow, Mysl', 1990, p. 243. It is interesting that foreign candidates were also proposed. Some delegates preferred Archduke

Maximilian of Habsburg, others the Swedish prince, Karl Phillip (see G.L. Freeze (ed.), *Russia: A History*. Oxford and New York, Oxford University Press, 1997, p. 63).
44. Ibid., p. 244.
45. Pokrovsky, *Russkaya istoriya s drevneyshikh vremen*, vol. 2, p. 155.
46. Ibid., p. 148.
47. Quoted in M. Pokrovsky, with N.M. Nikol'sky and V.N. Storozhev, *Russkaya istoriya s drevneyshikh vremen*, vol. 3. Moscow, Mir, 1913, p. 221.

CHAPTER 7

1. S.F. Platonov, *Moskva i Zapad v XVI–XVII vekakh*. Leningrad, Seyatel', p. 59.
2. See N. Berdyaev, *Istoki i smysl russkogo kommunizma*. Paris, YMCA Press, 1955.
3. V.O. Klyuchevsky, *Sochineniya*, vol. 3. Moscow, Mysl', 1988, p. 11.
4. M. Pokrovsky, with N.M. Nikol'sky and V.N. Storozhez, *Russkaya istoriya s drevneyshikh vremen*, vol. 2. Moscow, Mir, 1913, p. 251.
5. Platonov, *Moskva i Zapad v XVI–XVII vekakh*, p. 56.
6. Ibid., p. 58.
7. Ibid., p. 129.
8. Klyuchevsky, *Sochineniya*, vol. 3, p. 255.
9. P. Chaadaev, *Polnoe sobranie sochineniy i izbrannye pis'ma*, vol. 1. Moscow, Nauka, 1991, p. 332.
10. M.I. Pylyaev, *Staryy Peterburg*. St Petersburg, Izdaniye A.S. Suvorina, 1889, p. 110.
11. A.S. Pushkin, *Polnoe sobranie sochineniy*, 2nd edn, vol. 8. Moscow, AN SSSR, 1958, p. 126.
12. Klyuchevsky, *Sochineniya*, vol. 3, p. 367.
13. P. Milyukov, *Gosudarstvennoe khozyaystvo Rossii v pervoy chetverti XVIII stoletiya i reforma Petra Velikogo*. 2nd edn, St Petersburg, Tipografiya M.M. Stasyulevicha, 1905, p. 546.
14. Klyuchevsky, *Sochineniya*, vol. 3, p. 7.
15. M. Pokrovsky, with N.M. Nikol'sky and V.N. Storozhez, *Russkaya istoriya s drevneyshikh vremen*, vol. 3. Moscow, Mir, 1913, p. 4.
16. See E.A. Kosminsky and Ya.A. Levitsky (eds), *Angliyskaya burzhuaznaya revolyutsiya XVII veka*, vol. 2. Moscow, Izdatel'stvo Akademii Nauk SSSR, 1954, p. 116.
17. K. Marx, *Secret Diplomatic History of the Eighteenth Century and the Story of the Life of Lord Palmerston*. Edited and with an introduction by L. Hutchinson. London, Lawrence & Wishart, 1969, p. 61.
18. Ibid., p. 86.
19. W. Kirchner, *Commercial Relations Between Russia and Europe, 1400–1800*. Bloomington, Indiana University Press, 1966, p. 21.
20. Quoted in Pokrovsky, *Russkaya istoriya s drevneyshikh vremen*, vol. 2, p. 252.
21. Ibid., p. 256.
22. *Materialy po istorii sel'skogo khozyaystva i krest'yanstva v SSSR*. Compendium IX, Moscow, AN SSSR, 1980, p. 254.
23. A.I. Aksenov, *Genealogiya moskovskogo kupechestva XVIII veka*. Moscow, AN SSSR, 1988, p. 133.

CHAPTER 8

1. M. Pokrovsky, with N.M. Nikol'sky and V.N. Storozhez, *Russkaya istoriya s drevneyshikh vremen*, vol. 3. Moscow, Mir, 1913, p. 25.
2. M. Pokrovsky, with N.M. Nikol'sky and V.N. Storozhez, *Russkaya istoriya s drevneyshikh vremen*, vol. 2. Moscow, Mir, 1913, p. 307.
3. Ibid.
4. Pokrovsky, *Russkaya istoriya s drevneyshikh vremen*, vol. 2, p. 306.

5. N.M. Druzhinin, *Sotsial'no-ekonomicheskaya istoriya Rossii. Izbrannye trudy.* Moscow, Nauka, 1987, p. 335.

6. This 'democratism' of the Russian nobility was stressed repeatedly in the works of conservative Russian thinkers, from primitive members of the 'native soil' current to F.M. Dostoevsky.

7. V.O. Klyuchevsky, *Sochineniya*, vol. 3. Moscow, Mysl', 1988, p. 365.

8. V. Vorontsov ('V.V.'), *Gosudarstvennyy byudzhet i gosudarstvennye dolgi Rossii.* St Petersburg, 1908, p. 70.

9. A. Kamensky, *Rossiyskaya imperiya v XVIII veke: traditsii i modernizatsiya.* Moscow, NLO, 1999, p. 243.

10. Quoted in Vorontsov, *Gosudarstvennyy byudzhet i gosudarstvennye dolgi Rossii*, p. 68.

11. K. Marx, *Secret Diplomatic History of the Eighteenth Century and the Story of the Life of Lord Palmerston.* Edited and with an introduction by L. Hutchinson. London, Lawrence & Wishart, 1969, p. 93.

12. See Pokrovsky, *Russkaya istoriya s drevneyshikh vremen*, vol. 3, p. 49.

13. P. A. Ostroukhov, *Anglo-russkiy torgovyy dogovor 1734 g.* St Petersburg, 1914, p. 27.

14. Ibid., p. 28.

15. Ibid., p. 43.

16. See A.I. Yukht, *Torgovlya s vostochnymi stranami i vnutenniy rynok Rossii (20-60-e gody XVIII v.).* Moscow, 1994.

17. L.I. Yunusova, *Torgovaya ekspansiya Anglii v basseyne Kaspiya v pervoy polovine XVIII veka.* Baku, AN AzSSR, 1988, p. 55.

18. Quoted in Ostroukhov, *Anglo-Russkiy torgovyy dogovor 1734 g.*, p. 131.

19. Yunusova, *Torgovaya ekspansiya Anglii v basseyne Kaspiya v pervoy polovine XVIII veka*, p. 61.

20. Quoted in Ostroukhov, *Anglo-russkiy torgovyy dogovor 1734 g.*, p. 131.

21. Pokrovsky, *Russkaya istoriya s drevneyshikh vremen*, vol. 3, p. 58.

22. Quoted in Yukht, *Torgovlya s vostochnymi stranami i vnutenniy rynok Rossii*, p. 86.

23. Quoted in Ostroukhov, *Anglo-Russkiy torgovii dogovor 1734 g.*, p. 111.

24. Marx, *Secret Diplomatic History of the Eighteenth Century*, p. 126.

25. Pokrovsky, *Russkaya istoriya s drevneyshikh vremen*, vol. 3, p. 49.

26. Ibid., p. 61.

27. Quoted in Marx, *Secret Diplomatic History of the Eighteenth Century*, p. 15.

28. Quoted in Ostroukhov, *Anglo-russkiy torgovyy dogovor 1734 g.*, p. 136.

29. Yunusova, *Torgovaya ekspansiya Anglii v basseyne Kaspiya v pervoy polovine XVIII veka*, p. 86.

30. Pokrovsky, *Russkaya istoriya s drevneyshikh vremen*, vol. 3, p. 84.

31. Ibid., p. 125.

32. See S.G. Strumilin, *Izbrannye proizvedeniya. Istoriya chernoy metallurgii v SSSR.* Moscow, Nauka, 1967, p. 176 and passim.

33. Pokrovsky, who did not yet have full access to British and Russian documents relating to the export of Russian iron, nevertheless concluded correctly that this sector had 'enormous international importance' (Pokrovsky, *Russkaya istoriya s drevneyshikh vremen*, vol. 3, p. 135).

34. N.M. Druzhinin, *Sotsial'no-ekonomicheskaya istoriya Rossii. Izbrannye trudy.* Moscow, Nauka, 1987, p. 338.

35. See Strumilin, *Istoriya chernoy metallurgii v SSSR*, pp. 226–7.

36. See M. Tugan-Baranovsky, *Russkaya fabrika v proshlom i nastoyashchem*, vol. 1. Kharkov, 1926.

37. It is not surprising that the question of Russian manufacturing in the eighteenth and nineteenth centuries, a question often examined in isolation from its world context, proved beyond the grasp not only of Strumilin, but also of Pokrovsky. The latter saw in bonded factory labour a typical example of feudalism in the service of capitalism. In analysing the industrial initiatives of the Petrine era, however, Pokrovsky followed Milyukov in seeing them as entirely misconceived, as examples of bureaucratic ineffectuality. Tugan-

Baranovsky insisted that factories based on bonded labour had nothing in common with capitalism, and operated extremely inefficiently. Strumilin made use of Pokrovsky's weakness in this instance to try to demonstrate the unsustainability of Pokrovsky's entire approach to economic history. The Soviet academician recognised that 'the inner content of the hybrid form was totally capitalist' (Strumilin, *Istoriya chernoy metallurgii v SSSR*, p. 232). The principal question, however, remains unanswered: why did the development of capitalist forms of production in Britain require free workers, and, in Russia, a workforce made up largely of serfs? Furthermore, why did the rapid expansion of Russian industry stimulate the development of advanced forms of capitalism not in Russia, but in the West? Without an understanding of the general laws of development of the world economy, the nature of Russia's 'hybrid' form of capitalism cannot be understood either.

38. See Strumilin, *Istoriya chernoy metallurgii v SSSR*, p. 195.
39. See ibid., p. 193.
40. *Russko-britanskie torgovye otnosheniya v XVIII veke. Sbornik dokumentov.* Moscow, RAN, 1994, p. 9.
41. Strumilin, *Istoriya chernoy metallurgii v SSSR*, p. 169.
42. *Russko-britanskie torgovye otnosheniya v XVIII veke*, p. 12.
43. Ibid., p. 48.
44. A. Zorin, *Kormya dvuglavogo orla... Literatura i gosudarstvennaya ideologiya v Rossii v posledney treti XVIII – pervoy treti XIX veka.* Moscow, NLO, 2001, p. 65.
45. Ibid., p. 82.

CHAPTER 9

1. M. Pokrovsky, with N.M. Nikol'sky and V.N. Storozhez, *Russkaya istoriya s drevneyshikh vremen*, vol. 3. Moscow, Mir, 1913, p. 142.
2. *Materialy po istorii sel'skogo khozyaystva i krest'yanstva v SSSR*, Collection IX. Moscow, AN SSSR, 1980, p. 246.
3. Pokrovsky, *Russkaya istoriya s drevneyshikh vremen*, vol. 3, p. 143.
4. Ibid., pp. 143–4.
5. See P. Hopkirk, *The Great Game: On Secret Service in High Asia.* Oxford, Oxford University Press, 1990, p. 25.
6. N.Ya. Danilevsky, *Rossiya i Evropa.* Moscow, Izvestiya, 2003, p. 43.
7. Quoted in Pokrovsky, *Russkaya istoriya s drevneyshikh vremen*, vol. 3, pp. 267–8.
8. Pokrovsky takes an extremely negative view of Alexander's liberal initiatives, regarding them simply as an attempt to deceive European public opinion. There are not, however, any reasons to doubt the sincerity of the young tsar and in particular, of the educated young noblemen among his associates. It is noteworthy that in Western Europe as well as Russia, many people saw the wars against Napoleon as a liberating process, expecting that victory would be followed by social change. This sentiment united the future Decembrists in the Russian army with General Wilson, who in 1812 represented the British on Kutuzov's staff. The disappointment that set in after the victory of 1814 put Wilson on the road to conspiracy, just like the Russian officers together with whom he had fought against Bonaparte.
9. Pokrovsky, *Russkaya istoriya s drevneyshikh vremen*, vol. 3, p. 288.
10. M. Pokrovsky, *Diplomatiya i voyny tsarskoy Rossii v XIX stoletii.* Moscow, 1923, p. 19.
11. Quoted in Pokrovsky, *Russkaya istoriya s drevneyshikh vremen*, vol. 3, p. 290.
12. Quoted ibid., p. 300.
13. Ibid., p. 334.
14. Quoted in M. Tugan-Baranovsky, *Russkaya fabrika v proshlom i nastoyashchem*, vol. 1. Kharkov, 1926, p. 215.
15. Ibid., pp. 215–16.
16. V.I. Lenin, *Polnoe sobranie sochineniy*, vol. 20. Gosudarstvennoye izdatel'stvo politicheskoi literatury, p. 173.

17. A.S. Pushkin, *Polnoe sobranie sochineniy*, vol. 10, Moscow, AN SSSR, 1958, p. 654.
18. D.I. Fonvizin, *Izbrannye sochineniya i pis'ma*. Moscow, OGIZ, p. 246.
19. Ibid., p. 212.
20. Ibid., p. 214.
21. Ibid., p. 215.
22. Ibid., p. 223.
23. Ibid., p. 265.
24. Ibid., p. 262.
25. Ibid., p. 215.
26. M.P. Fedorov, *Khlebnaya torgovlya v glavneyshikh russkikh portakh i v Kenigsberge*. Moscow, 1888, p. 105.
27. M. Pokrovsky, *Ocherki po istorii revolyutsionnogo dvizheniya v Rossii XIX i XX vv.*, Moscow and Leningrad, GIZ, 1927, p. 14.
28. Tugan-Baranovsky, *Russkaya fabrika v proshlom i nastoyashchem*, vol. 1, p. 213.
29. Pokrovsky, *Ocherki po istorii revolyutsionnogo dvizheniya v Rossii XIX i XX vv.*, p. 20.
30. Lenin, *Polnoe sobranie sochineniy*, vol. 21, p. 261.
31. M. Pokrovsky, with N.M. Nikol'sky and V.N. Storozhev, *Russkaya istoriya s drevneyshikh vremen*, vol. 4. Moscow, Mir, 1918, p. 14.
32. Ibid., p. 15.
33. S.G. Strumilin, *Izbrannye proizvedeniya. Istoriya chernoy metallurgii v SSSR*. Moscow, Nauka, 1967, p. 174.
34. Pokrovsky, *Russkaya istoriya s drevneyshikh vremen*, vol. 4, p. 32.
35. Ibid., p. 38.
36. L.S. Semenov, *Rossiya i Angliya. Ekonomicheskie otnosheniya v seredine XIX veka*. Leningrad, LGU, 1975, p. 3.
37. See G.P. Nebolsin, *Statisticheskoe obozrenie vneshney torgovli Rossii*, vol. 2. St Petersburg, 1850, pp. 25–7, 139.
38. The sources disagree in their calculations of the total financial obligations of the Russian Empire. According to A.D. Druyan, between 1841 and 1853, some 70.1 million silver rubles were received in new loans, while 149.3 million rubles were spent on paying the interest and principal on previous loans (see A.D. Druyan, *Ocherki po istorii denezhnogo obrashcheniya Rossii v XIX v.* Moscow, 1941, p. 44). According to other calculations, loans amounting to 101 million rubles were taken out in the period 1840–49 alone (see Semenov, *Rossiya i Angliya. Ekonomicheskie otnosheniya v seredine XIX veka*, p. 82). Of particular interest is the highly involved story of the so-called 'Dutch loan'. At the Congress of Vienna, Britain undertook to pay off a proportion of the debts contracted by the tsar's government on the Dutch financial market during the Napoleonic Wars. London and St Petersburg promised to continue payments even if war should break out between the two countries. The King of the Netherlands also undertook to cancel part of the debt, but only on the condition that Belgium, which had been annexed to his possessions by decision of the congress, would remain under his power. After the cecession of Belgium, the Dutch government stopped making payments, but the British continued fulfilling their obligations. Marx believed that the money the tsar saved as a result went towards suppressing the Polish revolt.
39. Semenov, *Rossiya i Angliya. Ekonomicheskie otnosheniya v seredine XIX veka*, p. 89.
40. K. Marx and F. Engels, *Sochineniya*, vol. 7. Gosudarstvennoye izdatel'stvo politicheskoi literatury, p. 226.
41. S.G. Strumilin, *Ocherki po istorii ekonomiki Rossii*. Moscow, Gosudarstvennoye izdatel'stvo politicheskoi literatury, 1960, p. 469.
42. Ibid., p. 470. For Strumilin, the crisis of 1847 posed a serious methodological problem. This development, he concluded, was 'unquestionably a reflection of the world capitalist crisis within serf-holding Russia' (ibid., p. 475). This dependency was to be explained by the existence of elements of capitalism within the 'serf-holding system'. Strumilin stresses, however, that these elements of capitalism were secondary. For the Soviet academician, it was ideologically impossible to acknowledge that this was not simply a matter of 'bourgeois

elements', but that the serf-holding system itself was profoundly integrated into world capitalism, and made up an important part of it.

43. Pokrovsky, *Russkaya istoriya s drevneyshikh vremen,* vol. 4, p. 38.

44. Pokrovsky notes ironically that 'at Navarino a Russian squadron under the command of a British admiral set fire to a Turkish fleet' (ibid., p. 35).

45. V.I. Vinogradov, *Britanskiy lev na Bosfore.* Moscow, Nauka, 1991, p. 59.

46. Ibid., p. 60.

47. Ibid., p. 62.

48. The treaty between Britain and Russia signed in 1842 is also interesting as a step towards abolishing Navigation Acts because they didn't cover Russian ships any more. This had very little practical significance because Russian trade was carried mainly under foreign flags. However, it set an important precedent.

49. Semenov, *Rossiya i Angliya. Ekonomicheskie otnosheniya v seredine XIX veka,* p. 31.

50. Nebolsin, *Statisticheskoe obozrenie vneshney torgovli Rossii,* vol. 2, p. 364.

51. *Voprosi genezisa kapitalizma v Rossii.* Leningrad, LGU, 1960, p. 179.

52. Quoted in Semenov, *Rossiya i Angliya. Ekonomicheskie otnosheniya v seredine XIX veka,* p. 40.

53. See Pokrovsky, *Russkaya istoriya s drevneyshih vremen,* vol. 4, p. 51.

54. Quoted in ibid., p. 48.

55. Ibid., p. 47.

CHAPTER 10

1. M. Pokrovsky, *Ocherki po istorii revolyutsionnogo dvizheniya v Rossii XIX i XX vv.* Moscow and Leningrad, GIZ, 1927, p. 40.

2. K. Marx and F. Engels, *Sochineniya,* vol. 10. Gosudarstvennoye izdatel'stvo politicheskoi literatury, p. 605.

3. Ibid., p. 602.

4. Ibid., vol. 9, p. 340; for the English original, see the *New York Daily Tribune,* no. 3892, 7 October 1853.

5. W. Kirchner, *Commercial Relations between Russia and Europe, 1400–1800.* Bloomington, Indiana University Press, 1966, p. 22.

6. *Zhurnal ministerstva vnutrennykh del,* January 1854, section III, p. 3.

7. E.V. Tarle, *Krymskaya voyna,* vol. 1. Moscow and Leningrad, AN SSSR, 1950, p. 52.

8. Marx and Engels, *Sochineniya,* vol. 10, p. 604.

9. L.S. Semenov, *Rossiya i Angliya. Ekonomicheskie otnosheniya v seredine XIX veka.* Leningrad, LGU, 1975, p. 48.

10. It is noteworthy that this was the second instance (after the Caspian undertaking of the 1730s and 1740s) in which the interests of the Russia trade had forced British leaders to diverge from their own maritime rules of practice.

11. Marx and Engels, *Sochineniya,* vol. 10, p. 602.

12. Quoted in *Istoricheskie zapiski,* issue 110, Moscow, 1984, p. 272.

13. Quoted ibid., p. 241.

14. Cited in Semenov, *Rossiya i Angliya. Ekonomicheskie otnosheniya v seredine XIX veka,* p. 150.

15. See Pokrovsky, *Ocherki po istorii revolyutsionnogo dvizheniya v Rossii XIX i XX vv.,* p. 38.

16. M. Pokrovsky, with N.M. Nikol'sky and V.N. Storozhev, *Russkaya istoriya s drevneyshikh vremen,* vol. 4. Moscow, Mir, 1918, p. 43.

CHAPTER 11

1. S.G. Strumilin, *Ocherki po istorii ekonomiki Rossii.* Moscow, Gosudarstvennoye izdatel'stvo politicheskoi literatury, 1960, p. 465.

2. W. Thompson, *Global Expansion: Britain and its Empire, 1870–1914.* London, Pluto Press, 1999, p. 9.

3. Ibid.
4. Ibid., p. 10.
5. P. Kolchin, *Unfree Labor: American Slavery and Russian Serfdom*. Cambridge, Mass. and London, Harvard University Press, 1987, p. 370.
6. This thesis, expounded by Kolchin, contradicts the official view found in Soviet historiography. The research by Russian historians that has been published since 1991, however, generally confirms Kolchin's ideas. Contrary to the thesis of Soviet historians in the 1950s, serf agriculture remained profitable at the time when the peasant reforms began, and labour productivity was rising. In this respect, one cannot speak of inefficiency or of the 'exhaustion' of the internal possibilities of the serf system. See Boris N. Mironov, 'When and Why was the Russian Peasantry Emancipated?', in M.L. Bush (ed.), *Serfdom and Slavery: Studies in Legal Bondage*. London and New York, Longman, 1996, pp. 346–7.
7. M. Pokrovsky, with N.M. Nikol'sky and V.N. Storozhev, *Russkaya istoriya s drevneyshikh vremen*, vol. 4. Moscow, Mir, 1918, p. 99.
8. L.S. Semenov, *Rossiya i Angliya. Ekonomicheskie otnosheniya v seredine XIX veka*. Leningrad, LGU, 1975, p. 155.
9. Pokrovsky, *Russkaya istoriya s drevneyshikh vremen*, vol. 4, p. 66.
10. Ibid., p. 111.
11. Strumilin, *Ocherki po istorii ekonomiki Rossii*, p. 476.
12. Pokrovsky, *Russkaya istoriya s drevneyshikh vremen*, vol. 4, p. 112.
13. See M. Pokrovsky, *Ocherki po istorii revolyutsionnogo dvizheniya v Rossii XIX i XX vv.* Moscow and Leningrad, GIZ, 1927, p. 39. See also Semenov, *Rossiya i Angliya. Ekonomicheskie otnosheniya v seredine XIX veka*, pp. 150–5.
14. Pokrovsky, *Ocherki po istorii revolyutsionnogo dvizheniya v Rossii XIX i XX vv*, p. 12.
15. The 'American road' could be followed only if what took place in the country was not a reform but a revolution, and if the only social layer capable of seizing and holding power amid conditions of universal collapse was the intelligentsia, increasing rapidly in size during the relevant years. More than likely, the form in which the intelligentsia exercised power would be a terrorist dictatorship. Marx and Engels warned clearly of the type of social order that could arise as a result of such a revolution. For all the divergence in their views, the most influential ideologues of the Russian revolutionary movement of that era, P. L. Lavrov and P. N. Tkachev, agreed that the new order would be implanted using terror. It is pointless to seek the reasons for this agreement in the bloodthirstiness of revolutionaries. Tkachev foresaw a progressive, authoritarian state power in Russia, along the lines of the Jacobin dictatorship in eighteenth-century France, while Lavrov, who hated the state and believed in the liberation of the individual, argued that terrorism should be used by the masses themselves under the leadership of a 'Socialist Union'. As an example to be imitated, he cited the American 'Lynch law'.
16. V.I. Lenin, *Polnoe sobranie sochineniy*, vol. 16. Gosudarstvennoye izdatel'stvo politicheskoi literatury, p. 17.
17. A.V. Chayanov, *Krest'yanskoe khozyaystvo. Izbrannye trudy.* Moscow, Ekonomika, 1989, p. 121. The degree to which independent peasant agriculture is capitalist is a question with importance not just for Russia. As the American economist John Roemer notes, the success of the peasantry in Western Europe in their struggle against feudalism did not by any means lead automatically to capitalism. Rather, it led to the rise of an economy based on small-scale holdings, and using part of the land in common (J. Roemer, *Free to Lose*. Cambridge, Mass., Harvard University Press, 1988, p. 121). Robert Brenner examines the same phenomena (see T. Astin and C. Philpin (eds), *The Brenner Debate*. Cambridge, Cambridge University Press, 1988). As American scholars analysing the experience of Mexico have noted, the 'Chayanov' model of non-commercial peasant production cannot of course be stable when the survival of the household depends on buying and selling goods on the capitalist market (S. Cook and L. Binford, 'Petty Commodity Production, Capital Accumulation, and Peasant Differentiation: Lenin vs. Chayanov in Rural Mexico', *Review of Radical Political Economics*, vol. 18, no. 4, 1986, p. 24). The problem, however, lies on a completely different plane. As peasant agriculture decays, it becomes incorporated into the

peripheral model of capitalism, which needs commodity production but which does not by any means necessarily presuppose a thoroughgoing development of bourgeois relations in the countryside.

18. Strumilin, *Ocherki po istorii ekonomiki Rossii*, p. 465.
19. P. Lyashchenko, *Russkoe zernovoe khozyaystvo v sisteme mirovogo khozyaystva*. Moscow, Izdaniye Kommunisticheskoi akademii, 1927, p. 8.
20. Pokrovsky, *Ocherki po istorii revolyutsionnogo dvizheniya v Rossii XIX i XX vv*, p. 13.
21. M.P. Fedorov, *Khlebnaya torgovlya v glavneyshikh russkikh portakh i v Kenigsberge*. Moscow, 1888, p. 405.
22. Ibid., p. 413.
23. Ibid., pp. 412–13.
24. Lyashchenko, *Russkoe zernovoe khozyaystvo v sisteme mirovogo khozyaystva*, p. 278.
25. Pokrovsky, *Russkaya istoriya s drevneyshikh vremen*, vol. 4, p. 229.
26. N.M. Druzhinin, *Sotsial'no-ekonomicheskaya istoriya Rossii. Izbrannye trudy*. Moscow, Nauka, 1987, p. 347.
27. Pokrovsky, *Russkaya istoriya s drevneyshikh vremen*, vol. 4, p. 107.
28. Lyashchenko, *Russkoe zernovoe khozyaystvo v sisteme mirovogo khozyaystva*, p. 286.
29. Pokrovsky, *Russkaya istoriya s drevneyshikh vremen*, vol. 4, p. 77.
30. Ibid., p. 170.
31. G.V. Plekhanov, *Sochineniya*, vol. 2. Moscow, GIZ, 1923, p. 271.
32. See T. Shanin, (ed.), *Late Marx and the Russian Road: Marx and the 'Peripheries of Capitalism'*. London, Monthly Review Press, 1983, p. x.
33. K. Marx and F. Engels, *Sochineniya*, vol. 19. Gosudarstvennoye izdatel'stvo politicheskoi literatury, pp. 118–19. Marx's writings on questions of Russian populism are published in Shanin, *Late Marx and the Russian Road*. See pp. 134–5.
34. Shanin, *Late Marx and the Russian Road*, p. 7.
35. Ibid., p. 9.
36. Marx and Engels, *Sochineniya*, v. 19, p. 250. In English, see Shanin, *Late Marx and the Russian Road*, pp. 123–4.
37. Marx and Engels, *Sochineniya*, vol. 19, p. 120. In English, see Shanin, *Late Marx and the Russian Road*, pp. 136–7.
38. Marx and Engels, *Sochineniya*, vol. 19, p. 121. In English, see Shanin, *Late Marx and the Russian Road*, p. 137.
39. Shanin, *Late Marx and the Russian Road*, p. 19.
40. Marx and Engels, *Sochineniya*, vol. 19, p. 410. In English, see Shanin, *Late Marx and the Russian Road*, pp. 99–122.
41. *Delo*, 1880, no. 12. Quoted in M. Tugan-Baranovsky, *Russkaya fabrika v proshlom i nastoyashchem*, vol. 1. Kharkov, 1926, p. 434.
42. Quoted in P. Hopkirk, *The Great Game: On Secret Service in High Asia*. Oxford, Oxford University Press, 1990, p. 446.
43. Ibid.
44. P. Chaadaev, *Polnoe sobranie sochineniy i izbrannye pis'ma*, vol. 1. Moscow, Nauka, 1991, p. 534.

CHAPTER 12

1. P. Lyashchenko, *Russkoe zernovoe khozyaystvo v sisteme mirovogo khozyaystva*. Moscow, Izdaniye Kommunisticheskoi akademii, 1927, p. 293.
2. See ibid., p. 313.
3. Ibid., p. 373.
4. M. Pokrovsky with N.M. Nikol'sky and V.N. Storozhev, *Russkaya istoriya s drevneyshikh vremen*, vol. 4. Moscow, Mir, 1918, p. 370.
5. See A.G. Dongarov, *Inostrannyy kapital v Rossii i SSSR*. Moscow, Mezhdunarodniye otosheniya, 1990.

6. See S. Ronin, *Inostrannyy kapital i russkie banki*. Moscow, Izdaniye Kommunisticheskoi akademii, 1926, p. 2.

7. See M. Pokrovsky, *Ocherki po istorii revolyutsionnogo dvizheniya v Rossii XIX i XX vv.* Moscow and Leningrad, GIZ, 1927, p. 105.

8. Ronin, *Inostrannyy kapital i russkie banki*, p. 25.

9. Ibid., p. 26.

10. See S.G. Strumilin, *Ocherki po istorii ekonomiki Rossii*. Moscow, Gosudarstvennoye izdatel'stvo politicheskoi literatury, 1960, pp. 486–90.

11. See I. Vavilin, *Inostrannye kapitaly v Rossii*. Leningrad, Priboy, 1925, p. 39.

12. Ibid., p. 43.

13. R. Girault, *Emprunts Russes et Investissements Français en Russie, 1887–1914*. Paris, Librairie A. Colin, 1973, p. 564.

14. Vavilin, *Inostrannye kapitaly v Rossii*, p. 23.

15. M. Tugan-Baranovsky, *Russkaya fabrika v proshlom i nastoyashchem*, vol. 1. Kharkov, 1926, p. 274.

16. Vavilin, *Inostrannye kapitaly v Rossii*, p. 51.

17. Tugan-Baranovsky, *Russkaya fabrika v proshlom i nastoyashchem*, vol. 1, p. 269.

18. See Vavilin, *Inostrannye kapitaly v Rossii*, p. 59. Dongarov cites the same information, with minor differences: 'There was scarcely a single enterprise in southern Russia in which foreign capital was not involved. Of eighteen joint stock companies in the region, the shares of sixteen were quoted on foreign stock exchanges' (Dongarov, *Inostrannyy kapital v Rossii i SSSR*, p. 22).

19. I.I. Levin, *Germanskie kapitaly v Rossii*. Petrograd, 1918, p. 56.

20. Dongarov, *Inostrannyy kapital v Rossii i SSSR*, p. 24.

21. P. V. Ol'. *Inostrannye kapitaly v narodnom khozyaystve dovoennoy Rossii*. Leningrad, Vsesoyuznaya akademia nauk, 1925, pp. 15, 29.

22. *Istoricheskie Zapiski*, 1950, no. 35, p. 63.

23. Vavilin, *Inostrannye kapitaly v Rossii*, pp. 65–6.

24. See ibid., p. 67.

25. *Monopolii i inostrannyy kapital v Rossii*. Moscow and Leningrad, AN SSSR, 1962, p. 211.

26. D.I. Visochin, *Bel'giyskie kandaly*. Kharkov, 1908, pp. 2, 187.

27. Ibid., p. 188.

28. S.Yu. Witte, *Konspekt lektsiy o gosudarstvennom i narodnom khozyaystve*. St Petersburg, Typographia Brokgauza i Yefrona, 1912, p. 142.

29. Dongarov, *Inostrannyy kapital v Rossii i SSSR*, p. 36.

30. Tugan-Baranovsky, *Russkaya fabrika v proshlom i nastoyashchem*, vol. 1, p. 291.

31. Ibid., pp. 292–3.

32. Ibid., p. 293.

33. See ibid., pp. 274–5.

34. Girault, *Emprunts Russes et Investissements Français en Russie, 1887–1914*, p. 451.

35. Dongarov, *Inostrannyy kapital v Rossii i SSSR*, p. 37.

36. Quoted in *Monopolii i inostrannyy kapital v Rossii*, p. 305.

37. See Strumilin, *Ocherki po istorii ekonomiki Rossii*, p. 485.

38. *Rossiya vo vneshneekonomicheskikh otnosheniyakh. Uroki istorii i sovremennost'*. Moscow, 1993, p. 11.

39. L.Ya. Eventov, *Inostrannye kapitaly v russkoy promyshlennosti*. Moscow and Leningrad, OGIZ, 1931, p. 19.

40. Ronin, *Inostrannyy kapital i russkie banki*, p. 17. An analogous view was expressed by Pokrovsky, who declared that because they possessed ready capital, the Western banks were 'commanders of the Russian banks, and with them, of all Russian industry' (Pokrovsky, *Ocherki po istorii revolyutsionnogo dvizheniya v Rossii XIX i XX vv.*, p. 153).

41. Ronin, *Inostrannyy kapital i russkie banki* p. 81.

42. See ibid., pp. 73, 74, 67.

43. See Vavilin, *Inostrannye kapitaly v Rossii*, p. 13.

44. Tugan-Baranovsky, *Russkaya fabrika v proshlom i nastoyashchem*, vol. 1, p. 270.

45. Cited in L.E. Shepelev, *Tsarizm i burzhuaziya v 1904–1914 gg.* Leningrad, Nauka, 1987, p. 249.
46. Cited in Ronin, *Inostrannyy kapital i russkie banki*, p. 104.
47. See ibid., p. 93.
48. *Birzhevye Izvestiya*, 1907, no. 222.
49. L. Voronov, *Inostrannye kapitaly v Rossii.* Moscow, 1901, p. 24.
50. Zh. Leskor, *Obshchie i periodicheskie promyshlennye krizisy.* St Petersburg, 1908, p. 248.
51. See B.V. Ananyich, *Rossiya i mezhdunarodnyy kapital. 1897–1914.* Leningrad, AN SSSR, 1970, p. 51.
52. Quoted in ibid., p. 57.
53. Quoted in ibid., p. 59.
54. Pokrovsky, *Ocherki po istorii revolyutsionnogo dvizheniya v Rossii XIX i XX vv.*, p. v.
55. *Monopolii i inostrannyy kapital v Rossii*, p. 308.
56. Pokrovsky, *Ocherki po istorii revolyutsionnogo dvizheniya v Rossii XIX i XX vv.*, p. 107.
57. Ibid., p. 106.
58. Pokrovsky, *Russkaya istoriya s drevneyshikh vremen*, vol. 4, p. 376.
59. Ibid., p. 377.
60. P. Chaadaev, *Polnoe sobranie sochineniy i izbrannye pis'ma*, vol. 1. Moscow, Nauka, 1991, p. 469.
61. *Perviy S"ezd RSDRP. Dokumenty i materialy.* Moscow, Gosudarstvennoye izdatel'stvo politicheskoi literatury, 1958; *KPSS v rezolyutsiyakh i resheniyakh s"ezdov, konferentsiy i plenumov TsK*, 9th edn, vol. 1. Moscow, Gosudarstvennoye izdatel'stvo politicheskoi literatury, 1983, p. 16.
62. Pokrovsky, *Ocherki po istorii revolyutsionnogo dvizheniya v Rossii XIX i XX vv.*, p. 113.
63. A.I. Aksenov, *Genealogiya moskovskogo kupechestva XVIII veka.* Moscow, AN SSSR, 1988, p. 143.
64. Shepelev, *Tsarizm i burzhuaziya v 1904–1914 gg*, p. 257.
65. Pokrovsky, *Ocherki po istorii revolyutsionnogo dvizheniya v Rossii XIX i XX vv.*, p. 111.
66. It is not surprising that towards the end of his life, Lenin, having gained practical experience of ruling in a patriarchal-peasant country, became highly interested in Chayanov and began studying his writings intently.
67. Pokrovsky, *Russkaya istoriya s drevneyshikh vremen*, vol. 4, p. 403.
68. S. Bulgakov, *Agoniya.* Paris, 1946, p. 76.
69. M. Weber, *Politische Schriften.* Published in Russian in *Sintaksis*, no. 22, Paris, 1988, pp. 94, 93, 96.
70. Pokrovsky, *Ocherki po istorii revolyutsionnogo dvizheniya v Rossii XIX i XX vv.*, p. 117.
71. P. A. Stolypin, *Nam nuzhna velikaya Rossiya.* Moscow, Molodaya gvardiya, 1991, p. 52.
72. V.I. Lenin, *Polnoe sobranie sochineniy*, vol. 16. Gosudarstvennoye izdatel'stvo politicheskoi literatury, p. 18.
73. Ibid., pp. 21, 20.
74. Stolypin, *Nam nuzhna velikaya Rossiya*, p. 52.
75. See Pokrovsky, *Ocherki po istorii revolyutsionnogo dvizheniya v Rossii XIX i XX vv.*, p. 122.
76. Stolypin, *Nam nuzhna velikaya Rossiya*, p. 95.
77. See Dongarov, *Inostrannyy kapital v Rossii i SSSR*, p. 13.
78. Pokrovsky, *Ocherki po istorii revolyutsionnogo dvizheniya v Rossii XIX i XX vv.*, p. 139.
79. M.I. Tugan-Baranovsky (ed.), *Voprosy Mirovoy voyny.* Petrograd, Pravo, 1915, p. 292.
80. A. Goryanin, *Mify o Rossii i dukh natsii.* Moscow, Pentagraphic Ltd, 2002, p. 185.
81. Pokrovsky, *Ocherki po istorii revolyutsionnogo dvizheniya v Rossii XIX i XX vv.*, p. 140.
82. P. Hopkirk, *The Great Game: On Secret Service in High Asia.* Oxford, Oxford University Press, 1990, p. 520.
83. Ananyich, *Rossiya i mezhdunarodnyy kapital. 1897–1914*, p. 12.
84. Vavilin, *Inostrannye kapitaly v Rossii*, p. 27.
85. Girault, *Emprunts Russes et Investissements Français en Russie, 1887–1914*, p. 450.
86. These figures are cited by Dongarov in *Inostrannyy kapital v Rossii i SSSR.*
87. Vavilin, *Inostrannye kapitaly v Rossii*, p. 90.

88. Ananyich, *Rossiya i mezhdunarodnyy kapital. 1897–1914*, p. 49.
89. Cited in ibid., p. 171.
90. Girault, *Emprunts Russes et Investissements Français en Russie, 1887–1914*, p. 446.
91. Ronin, *Inostrannyy kapital i russkie banki*, p. 54.
92. Vavilin, *Inostrannye kapitaly v Rossii*, p. 46.
93. See ibid., pp. 48–9.
94. Ronin, *Inostrannyy kapital i russkie banki*, p. 60. In the period described, the disposition of forces was as follows. Of the largest Russian banks, the Bank for Foreign Trade and the International Commercial Bank were controlled by German capital. The Azov-Don Bank, the Russian-Asian Bank, the Commercial-Industrial Bank and the Private Commercial Bank were controlled by the French.
95. Pokrovsky, *Ocherki po istorii revolyutsionnogo dvizheniya v Rossii XIX i XX vv.*, p. 154.
96. Levin, *Germanskie kapitaly v Rossii*, p. 17.
97. Ronin, *Inostrannyy kapital i russkie banki*, p. 121.
98. Levin, *Germanskie kapitaly v Rossii*, p. 48.
99. Ibid., p. 51.
100. Vavilin, *Inostrannye kapitaly v Rossii*, p. 92.

CHAPTER 13

1. V.I. Lenin, *Polnoe sobranie sochineniy*, vol. 45. Gosudarstvennoye izdatel'stvo politicheskoi literatury, p. 380.
2. *Voprosy Ekonomiki*, 1988, no. 9, p. 123.
3. Lenin, *Polnoe Sobranie Sochineniy*, vol. 38, p. 63.
4. The political scientist Alla Glinchikova points out that after the revolution only four People's Commissariats were established to take the place of the former ministries, but that 'in the 1920s a dramatic expansion of the administrative apparatus began' (*Mir Rossii*, 2003, no. 1, p. 114).
5. The most 'liberal' political regime was in the Republic of the Far East, where as late as 1922 non-Bolshevik socialist parties not only functioned openly, but also took part in the system of government. Lenin proposed a coalition of Bolsheviks and Mensheviks as a political solution for Georgia after it had been occupied by the Red Army, but failed to win support among the leadership of his own party.
6. See *Istoriya sotsialisticheskoy ekonomiki v SSSR*, vol. 2. Moscow, Nauka, 1976, p. 268.
7. N.I. Bukharin, *Izbrannye proizvedeniya* Moscow, Izdatel'stvo politicheskoi literatury, 1988, p. 88.
8. In this case it would be more precise to use the term *delinking*, as employed by Samir Amin. A brief exposition of Samir Amin's views on questions of global development may be found in his article 'The New Capitalist Globalisation', *Links* (Australia), nos 7 and 8.
9. P. Lyashchenko, *Russkoe zernovoe khozyaystvo v sisteme mirovogo khozyaystva*. Moscow, Izdaniye Kommunisticheskoi akademii, 1927, p. 358.
10. *Voprosy ekonomiki*, 1988, no. 9, pp. 126, 110.
11. Ibid., p. 117.
12. Bukharin, *Izbrannye proizvedeniya*, pp. 90, 91, 86.
13. Ibid., p. 90.
14. *Voprosy ekonomiki*, 1988, no. 9, p. 111.
15. *XV s"ezd VKP(b). Rezolyutsii i postanovleniya*. Moscow, Partizdat, 1932, p. 126.
16. See *XV s"ezd VKP(b), Dekabr', 1927, stenograficheskiy otchet*. Moscow, Gosudarstvennoye izdatel'stvo politicheskoi literatury, 1962, p. 1443.
17. *XV s"ezd VKP(b). Rezolyutsii i postanovleniya*, p. 119.
18. Ibid., pp. 113–14.
19. *XVI konferentsiya VKP(b). Rezolyutsii*. Moscow, Partizdat, 1932, p. 28.
20. Bukharin, *Izbranniye proizvedeniya*, p. 406.

21. A.N. Malafeev, *Istoriya tsenoobrazovaniya v SSSR (1917–1963)*. Moscow, Mysl', 1964, pp. 119–21.
22. A.I. Kolganov, *Put' k sotsializmu: tragediya i podvig*. Moscow, Ekonomika, 1990, p. 107.
23. See *Istoriya sotsialisticheskoy ekonomiki v SSSR*, vol. 3. Moscow, Nauka, 1977, p. 328.
24. Bukharin, *Izbrannye proizvendeniya*, p. 404.
25. N.D. Kondratyev, *Problemy ekonomicheskoy dinamiki*. Moscow, Ekonomika, 1989, p. 221.
26. I.V. Stalin, *Sochineniya*, vol. 12. Gosudarstvennoye izdatel'stvo politicheskoi literatury, p. 92.
27. *Voprosy ekonomiki*, 1988, no. 9, p. 97.
28. M. Lewin, *Russia/USSR/Russia*. New York, The New Press, 1995, p. 106.
29. Stalin, *Sochineniya*, vol. 11, pp. 124, 15.
30. *Byulleten' oppozitsii*, 1929, no. 3, p. 13 (letter from Kh.G. Rakovsky).
31. Yu. Fel'shtinskym (compiler), *Kommunisticheskaya oppozitsiya v SSSR. Iz arkhiva L. Trotskogo*, vol. 4. Benson, Vermont, Chalidze Publications, 1988, p. 254.
32. Ibid., p. 253.
33. Stalin, *Sochineniya*, vol. 12, pp. 181–2.
34. Kolganov, *Put' k sotsializmu: tragediya i podvig*, p. 123.
35. *Istoriya sotsialisticheskoy ekonomiki v SSSR*, vol. 3, p. 309.
36. See Russian State Archives of the Economy (RGAE), fund 413, schedule 13, file 207, pp. 144–5, etc.
37. Ibid., fund 413, schedule 13, file 203, p. 21. It is noteworthy that in 1930 and 1931, articles appeared in the Western business press arguing that it was not to the advantage of the Soviet Union to reduce its exports of foodstuffs, since this would result in the loss of the markets that had been difficult to conquer.
38. *Istoriya sotsialisticheskoy ekonomiki v SSSR*, vol. 3, p. 309.
39. See RGAE, fund 413, schedule 13, file 233, p. 6. See also RGAE, fund 413, schedule 13, file 242, p. 15.
40. See *Istoriya sotsialisticheskoy ekonomiki v SSSR*, vol. 3, pp. 310–11.
41. Ibid., p. 311.
42. See RGAE, fund 413, schedule 13, file 227, p. 3.
43. See ibid., p. 6. Soviet figures show overall imports by Great Britain from the USSR in 1930 as having a value of £34,245,419 (see ibid.). Britain at this time was the main importer of products from the USSR. The Soviet trade office in London monitored prices very attentively; this may also have been linked to the 'representative' character of the British market from the point of view of world market conditions.
44. See RGAE, fund 413, schedule 13, file 227, p. 14.
45. See ibid., pp. 8–11.
46. See RGAE, fund 413, schedule 13, file 203.
47. See RGAE, fund 413, schedule 13, file 227, pp. 8–11.
48. RGAE, fund 413, schedule 13, file 208, p. 23.
49. Kolganov, *Put' k sotsializmu: tragediya i podvig*, p. 127.
50. Ibid., p. 128.
51. *Byulleten' oppozitsii*, April 1931, no. 20, p. 4.
52. *Istoriya sotsialisticheskoy ekonomiki v SSSR*, vol. 3, p. 313.
53. RGAE, fund 413, schedule 13, file 216, p. 6.
54. Ibid., p. 13.
55. Ibid., p. 15.
56. RGAE, fund 413, schedule 13, file 203, p. 1. Here we may recall an episode from the Ilf and Petrov novel *The Golden Calf*. While on the road, the heroes encounter some Americans travelling about the countryside with an Inturist translator. Tormented by the Prohibition then in force in the US, the Americans are seeking the recipe for *samogon*, Russian home-distilled vodka.
57. *Istoriya sotsialisticheskoy ekonomiki v SSSR*, vol. 3, p. 310. Numerous records of the export conferences testify to the ineffectiveness of these methods. As a rule, the month-long

campaigns proceeded 'very feebly, without yielding any significant results' (RGAE, fund 413, schedule 13, file 207, p. 84).

58. RGAE, fund 413, schedule 13, file 208, p. 69.
59. Ibid., p. 16.
60. RGAE, fund 413, schedule 13, file 207, p. 72.
61. Ibid.
62. Ibid., p. 108.
63. Ibid., p. 62.
64. RGAE, fund 413, schedule 13, file 208, p. 19.
65. RGAE, fund 413, schedule 13, file 207, p. 108.
66. RGAE, fund 413, schedule 13, file 208, p. 7.
67. RGAE, fund 413, schedule 13, file 208, p. 45.
68. The memoirs of Victor Serge include the following episode. 'In Belarus, seeing that horses were having their hair clipped and sent for export, and knowing that the animals would die as a result, a group of women surrounded Goloded, the head of the local administration (who was shot or committed suicide in 1937), and with unexpected fury pulled up their sarafans, beneath which they were naked. "Now, you swine, take our hair if you're brave enough, but you won't get the hair from the horses!"' (V. Serzh, *Ot revolyutsii k totalitarizmu: Vospominaniya revolyutsionera.* Moscow and Orenburg, Praksis and Orenburgskaya Kniga, 2001, p. 298. French original: V. Serge, *Mémoires d un Révolutionnaire.* Paris, 1978). The truth of this story is in some doubt; it is hardly likely that the head of the government (Soviet of People's Commissars) of Belarus Nikolay Goloded would personally have taken part in the state purchasing of horsehair. Nevertheless, Serge's memoirs convey the atmosphere of those times to perfection.
69. RGAE, fund 413, schedule 13, file 208, p. 10.
70. RGAE, fund 413, schedule 13, file 207, p. 110.
71. Ibid.
72. Ibid., p. 68.
73. RGAE, fund 413, schedule 13, file 208, p. 12.
74. Ibid., p. 47.
75. Ibid., p. 5.
76. Ibid., p. 4.
77. Ibid., pp. 6, 7, 8.
78. Ibid., p. 40.
79. Ibid., p. 68.
80. Ihid., p. 2.
81. Ibid., p. 43.
82. Ibid., p. 36.
83. Ibid., p. 74.
84. Ibid., pp. 28–9.
85. RGAE, fund 413, schedule 13, file 207, p. 44.
86. Ibid., p. 42.
87. Ibid., p. 109.
88. RGAE, fund 413, schedule 13, file 208, p. 82.
89. Ibid., p. 36.
90. Ibid., p. 25.
91. RGAE, fund 413, schedule 13, file 227, p. 52.
92. RGAE, fund 413, schedule 13, file 207, p. 25.
93. Ibid.
94. Ibid., p. 65.
95. RGAE, fund 413, schedule 13, file 208, pp. 1, 5, 72.
96. Ibid., p. 22.
97. Ibid., pp. 8, 9.
98. RGAE, fund 413, schedule 13, file 233, p. 8.
99. Ibid., p. 2.

100. See RGAE, fund 413, schedule 13, file 227, p. 3.

101. See RGAE, fund 413, schedule 13, file 233, p. 16.

102. L.A. Gordon and E.V. Klopov, *Chto eto bylo? Razmyshleniya o predposylkakh i itogakh togo, chto sluchilos' s nami v 30-40-e gody.* Moscow, Politizdat, 1989, pp. 67–8.

103. *Byulleten' oppozitsii,* April 1930, no. 20, p. 14.

104. For an analysis of the concept of the 'Soviet Thermidor', and of the predictions that it would occur, see the book by the Hungarian historian Tamas Krausz, *Sovetskiy Termidor. Dukhovnye predposylki stalinskogo perevorota 1917–1928.* Budapest, Hungarian Institute of Russian Studies, 1997.

105. In twentieth-century literature the term 'totalitarianism' has often taken on a speculative character. The counterposing of totalitarianism to democracy frequently conceals an inability (or reluctance) on the part of the author to make a more precise analysis. Here, the term signifies the techniques of the exercise of power described in the works of writers such as Hannah Arendt and Erich Fromm.

106. The views of this wing of émigré society were expressed most consistently by the group Smena Vekh (Change of Landmarks).

107. Against the background of the bureaucratic degeneration of the Soviet regime, a polemic naturally unfolded among Western leftists concerning the degree to which the system that had arisen in the USSR was 'socialist'. Later, *samizdat* publications in the Soviet Union took up the same debate. A discussion of this topic lies beyond the bounds of the present study. It is enough simply to note that neither Marx nor Lenin considered the formal nationalisation of industrial plants a sufficient basis for talking of socialism, still less of socialism 'in one country taken in isolation'. At the same time, the Soviet experiment cannot be separated off from the history of socialism, if only because socialist principles were proclaimed by the 1917 revolution, and not only by the Bolsheviks. Lenin himself saw the Russia of the 1920s as combining various systems – socialism, state capitalism, petty commodity production, and capitalism proper. It is clear that elements of socialism that had arisen out of the revolution continued to exist and develop within Soviet society right up until the collapse of the USSR in 1991, and to some degree even after this. It does not, however, follow from this that a 'socialist system' had been constructed in the USSR in the fashion that the party propaganda used to assert, and since 1991 the official slogans to the effect that socialism had triumphed 'completely and definitively' have sounded quite ludicrous. It may be that Lenin provided the best formulation of the essence of this question when he declared that 'the term "socialist Soviet republic" signifies the determination of the Soviet power to carry through the transition to socialism, not a recognition of the new economic order as socialist' (Lenin, *Polnoe sobranie sochineniy,* vol. 36, p. 295). An overview of the discussions among Russian leftists on the nature of Soviet society can be found in a number of publications, including B. Kagarlitsky, *Dialektika nadezhdy.* Paris, Slovo, 1988; N.A. Simoniya, 'Stalinism protiv sotsializma', *Voprosy Filosofii,* 1989, no. 7; and A.V. Buzgalin (ed.), *Kriticheskiy marksizm: prodolzhenie diskussiy.* Moscow, Slovo, 2001.

CHAPTER 14

1. Analysing the Soviet-American rivalry, Immanuel Wallerstein in his book *After Liberalism* argues that the USSR remained part of the world system throughout the entire Soviet epoch (see I. Wallerstein, *After Liberalism.* New York, The New Press, 1995, pp. 10–25). Wallerstein maintains that since the system as a whole was capitalist, the Soviet Union, irrespective of its internal system, had to be considered part of the capitalist world. Wallerstein bases his point of view on the argument that the USSR and the US complemented one another in their rivalry, together guaranteeing the equilibrium of the world order that had been established in 1945 and 1946. In paradoxical fashion, the rivalry of the two superpowers effectively ensured a prolonged period of global stability. Here, however, Wallerstein contradicts himself, since he has argued repeatedly and convincingly that the world system is not a political but an economic formation. The unity of the world system is ensured not by

political control, and not even by the trade through which countries exchange their surplus production, but by the participation of countries in the international division of labour. In the same fashion, Wallerstein also writes of the possibility of several world systems or world empires existing simultaneously. The Soviet Union was excluded from the capitalist system of the international division of labour until the early 1970s; moreover, the USSR with its satellite countries tried to establish its own parallel system of the international division of labour under the slogan 'socialist integration'. It was only in the 1970s that the Soviet Union began its economic return to the bourgeois world system, and it is not surprising that at a certain stage the result of this process would also be the transformation of the 'internal organisation' of the former communist countries, as they returned to the zone of peripheral capitalism.

2. *New York Times*, 22 September 1944, quoted in C. Harman, *Class Struggles in Eastern Europe, 1945-83*. London, Chicago and Melbourne, Bookmarks, 1988, p. 24.
3. *Era Nuoa*, 8 November 1946, quoted in ibid., p. 25.
4. *Istoriya diplomatii*, vol. V, book 1. Moscow, Politizdat, 1974, pp. 118–19.
5. A.Kh. Klevansky, V.V. Mar'ina, A.S. Mylnikov and I.I. Pop, *Kratkaya istoriya Chekhoslovakii*. Moscow, Nauka, 1988, p. 414.
6. Such sentiments were typical not just of intellectuals close to the communist movement, but also of many critics of the Soviet system. In particular, Nikolay Berdyaev expressed such views between 1945 and 1947.
7. *Germaniya, iyun' 1953 goda: uroki proshlogo dlya budushchego*. Moscow, Institut Evropy and Ogni, 2003, pp. 13, 15.
8. Ibid., p. 12.
9. *Istoriya diplomatii*, vol. V, book 1, p. 156.
10. It is noteworthy that in Poland during the time of the 'communist regime', the party leadership was three times driven from office by popular uprisings – in 1956, 1970 and during the 1980s. Each new generation of leaders began its rule promising to correct the mistakes of its predecessors, and to a significant degree these promises were fulfilled.
11. *Novyy etap ekonomicheskogo sotrudnichestva SSSR s razvitymi kapitalisticheskimi stranami*. Moscow, Nauka, 1978, p. 5. It should of course be kept in mind that the West at this time was experiencing a bout of inflation, and that part of the 'growth' is to be explained simply by the change in prices. Even in constant prices, however, the increase in trade turnover was impressive.
12. See *SSSR v tsifrakh v 1987*. Moscow, Statistika, 1988, pp. 32–3.
13. See *Ekonomicheskie otnosheniya stran SEV s Zapadom*. Moscow, Nauka, 1983, pp. 128–9.
14. See *Izvestiya*, 18 February 1976.
15. *Novyy etap ekonomicheskogo sotrudnichestva SSSR s razvitymi kapitalisticheskimi stranami*, p. 7.
16. Ibid., p. 29.
17. Ibid., p. 71.
18. Ibid., pp. 7–8.
19. I.S. Bagramyan and A.F. Shakay, *Kontrakt veka*. Moscow, Politizdat, 1984, p. 76.
20. See ibid., p. 21.
21. V.A. Brikin and B.S. Vaganov (eds), *Vneshneekonomicheskie svyazy Sovetskogo Soyuza na novom etape*. Moscow, Mezhdunarodnye Otnosheniya, 1977, p. 125.
22. Bagramyan and Shakay, *Kontrakt veka*, p. 3.
23. Ibid., p. 26.
24. See *Novyy etap ekonomicheskogo sotrudnichestva SSSR s razvitymi kapitalisticheskimi stranami*, p. 72.
25. Bagramyan and Shakay, *Kontrakt veka*, p. 39.
26. W. Reisinger, *Energy and the Soviet Bloc*. Ithaca and London, Cornell University Press, 1992, p. 152.
27. Bagramyan and Shakay, *Kontrakt veka*, p. 41.
28. See *Novyy etap ekonomicheskogo sotrudnichestva SSSR s razvitymi kapitalisticheskimi stranami*, p. 83.

29. Ibid., p. 233.
30. Bagramyan and Shakay, *Kontrakt veka*, pp. 39–40.
31. See *Zycie Gospodarcze*, 9 June 1985.
32. S. Glazyev, *Ekonomika i politika: epizody bor'by.* Moscow, Gnozis, 1994, pp. 207–8.
33. *Razvitie i sovershenstvovanie vneshneekonomicheskikh svyazey.* Moscow, Institut Ekonomiki AN SSSR, 1989, p. 31.
34. Glazyev, *Ekonomika i politika: epizody bor'by*, p. 208.
35. Ibid.
36. O. Davydov (ed.), *Rossiyskaya elita. Psikhologicheskie portrety.* Moscow, Ladomir, 2000, p. 14.
37. T. Kraus, *Kratkiy ocherk istorii Rossii v XX veke.* St Petersburg, Mir i Sem'ya, 2001, p. 240.

CHAPTER 15

1. *Plyusy i minusy*, 2003, no. 12, p. 7.
2. See M. Delyagin, *Ekonomika neplatezhey: kak i pochemu my budem zhit' dal'she.* Moscow, N.E. Chernysheva, 1996; J.E. Stiglitz, *Globalization and its Discontents.* New York and London, W.W. Norton & Co., 2002, p. 143.
3. For a more detailed discussion, see B. Kagarlitsky, *Restavratsiya v Rossii.* Moscow, Editorial URSS, 2003. English translation: Boris Kagarlitsky, *Russia under Yeltsin and Putin.* London, Pluto Press, 2002.
4. L. Nelson and I. Kuzes, *Radical Reform in Yeltsin's Russia: Political, Economic, and Social Dimensions.* Armonk, New York, M.E. Sharpe, 1995, p. 24.
5. P. Reddaway and D. Glinski, *The Tragedy of Russian Reforms: Market Bolshevism against Democracy.* Washington, DC, US Institute of Peace Press, 2001, p. 293.
6. Data on the foreign debts of Russia and of particular corporations are available on the internet at the site of the company Tatneft', at <www.info.debt.ru/newsDetails. phtml?id=220>.
7. See M. Delyagin, *Ideologiya vozrozhdeniya. Kak my uydem iz nishchety i marazma.* Moscow, Forum, 2000, p. 37.
8. *Smysl*, 2 December 2002, p. 49.
9. See Yu.A. Arsky et al. (eds), *Informatsionnoe prostranstvo novykh nezavisimykh gosudarstv.* Moscow, VINITI, 2000, pp. 23–4.
10. *Mir Rossii*, 2003, no. 1, p. 110.
11. See Z.T. Golenkova (ed.), *Sotsial'noe rassloenie i sotsial'naya mobil'nost'.* Moscow, Nauka, 1999, pp. 27, 28.
12. See *Mir Rossii*, 2003, no. 1, p. 110.
13. A. Buzgalin and A. Kolganov (eds), *Kriticheskiy marksizm: prodolzhenie diskussiy.* Moscow, 2001, Editorial URSS, p. 231.
14. See *Byulleten' Inostrannoy Kommercheskoy Informatsii*, 12 August 2000, no. 93. See also a report by the Bureau of Economic Analysis of 1 February 2000, available on the internet at <www.hse.ru/ic/materials/scale.htm>.
15. L. Grigoryev and A. Kosarev, *Masshtaby i kharakter begstva kapitalov.* Report to the 15th international conference 'The Investment Climate and Prospects for Economic Growth in Russia'. The materials of the conference are available on the internet at <www.hse.ru/ic/materials/scale.htm>.
16. Buzgalin and Kolganov, *Kriticheskiy marksizm*, p. 231.
17. An account of the Interior Ministry briefing was placed on the internet at <http://rockefel.hl.ru/del737.html>.
18. Delyagin, *Ideologiya vozrozhdeniya. Kak my uydem iz nishchety i marazma*, p. 39.
19. Ibid., p. 38.
20. See *Smysl*, 19 December 2002, p. 64.
21. Delyagin, *Ideologiya vozrozhdeniya. Kak my uydem iz nishchety i marazma*, p. 48.
22. Stiglitz, *Globalization and its Discontents*, p. 146.
23. Ibid., p. 135.

24. Ibid., p. 145.
25. M. Delyagin (ed.), *Raspad mirovoy dollarovoy sistemy: blizhayshie perspektivy.* Moscow, N.E. Chernysheva, 2001, p. 129.
26. Delyagin, *Ideologiya vozrozhdeniya. Kak my uydem iz nishchety i marazma,* p. 44.
27. See *Russkiy Fokus,* 2003, no. 24, p. 69.
28. *Rodnaya Gazeta,* 2003, no. 6, p. 6.
29. Ibid. Widespread malnutrition has also been reflected in an increase in the death rate; in 2003 average life expectancy in Russia stood at 67 years (*Plyusy i Minusy,* 2003, no. 12, p. 7).
30. *Rodnaya Gazeta,* 2003, no. 14, p. 6.
31. Data of the State Committee of the Russian Federation on Statistics (Goskomstat) are absent from the official site of this state body, but were posted on the internet at <http://news.bbc.co.uk/hi/russian> on 26 June 2003.
32. Delyagin, *Raspad mirovoy dollarovoy sistemy: blizhayshie perspe,* p. 215.
33. *Smysl,* 15 February 2003, p. 59.
34. *Rodnaya Gazeta,* 2003, no. 9, p. 1.
35. *Mir Rossii,* 2003, no. 1, p. 119.
36. *Novaya Gazeta,* 2003, no. 37, p. 1.

Index

www.ingramcontent.com/pod-product-compliance
Lightning Source LLC
Chambersburg PA
CBHW031935090426
42811CB00002B/191